A LISTENER'S
ANTHOLOGY OF MUSIC

Volume II

THE MUSICIAN AS POET, PAINTER, AND DRAMATIST

by

LILLIAN BALDWIN

SILVER BURDETT COMPANY

NEW YORK   CHICAGO   SAN FRANCISCO

PRINTED IN THE UNITED STATES OF AMERICA

Preface

"What's in a name?" Far more than meets the eye, if it be the name of a book. Lettered in gilt Gothic or sober black Roman, the few words on a book's cover hold the reader's hope and the writer's promise for thousands of words to come. One does not choose them lightly. During the years in which this collection of studies of music and musicians has been growing, various titles have been considered and rejected as too prosy, too fanciful, or, perhaps, a bit misleading. But the idea which prompted the work has never varied, and now, by its very persistence, it lays claim to the title under which these volumes go to press — *A Listener's Anthology of Music*.

To the ancient Greeks whose word it was, *anthology* meant a collection of flowers. Because it implied a careful culling of only the choicest blossoms, the word *anthology* was chosen by some imaginative person of the Alexandrine period as the title for a famous collection of choicest Greek poetry. So successful was this borrowing that, within a century or so, the literal meaning of *anthos* — the flower part of the word — was quite forgotten and *anthology*, once a gardener's term, became the property of bookmen.

The literary anthology has long since proved its worth. For the young or inexperienced reader, it serves as a sampler of fine poetry or prose. For the booklover, a good anthology is a pleasant reminder of old favorites and a congenial traveling companion.

The anthology idea has already been extended to music. Many fine collections of songs and instrumental pieces have been gathered together for the convenience of singers and players. Why not, then, an anthology for listeners?

By the very nature of the art it serves, no musical anthology can quite live up to its name. Even those fine collections of songs and instrumental pieces cannot give the music itself. They offer but its symbol, the printed score, which becomes music only when interpreted by a musician. A listener's anthology, limited to mere quotations from score, would seem still further removed from the great art of sound. It is, at best, only a book about music. Yet, in these days of fine phonographs and radio, such a book may be the source of a true anthology — a collection of choice music which the reader may own and enjoy at the turn of a disc or dial.

A Listener's Anthology of Music is contained in two companion volumes. The first, *The Master Builders of Music*, presents the composers who have perfected the larger musical forms, such as the fugue, sonata, opera, oratorio, symphony, art song, and tone poem. It also presents certain fine examples of these forms from the works of the master builders. The second volume, *The Musician as Poet, Painter, and Dramatist*, introduces the outstanding Romantic, Nationalistic, and Twentieth-Century composers, men who have put these traditional forms to new and beautiful use. Together these two volumes offer a fairly comprehensive and, we believe, enjoyable repertory of the world's best music — the music most often heard at concerts and over the radio.

The point of view assumed is that of the average intelligent person, the listener who would like to know more about the music he hears, but has neither time, opportunity, nor training for exploring orchestral scores or the vast domain of music history, biography, and criticism. To add to the listener's enjoyment by revealing glimpses of music's background, and to provide good models upon which he may build his musical taste — this is the purpose of *A Listener's Anthology of Music*.

Foreword

To Those Who Read This Book

In the old days — the days before Beethoven — music was an art of pure sound. It was the expression of purely musical ideas, by which we mean pleasing sequences and combinations of tones moving in interesting rhythms. The composer, seeking to express his ideas, had first to decide what type of music he would write — whether a fugue, an air and variations, a suite of little dance tunes, or a sonata. He then proceeded according to the rules, which were many and definite, particularly if he had chosen music's most ambitious form, the sonata. For to write a sonata meant inventing two well-contrasted main themes and several less important themes for the sake of variety; it meant presenting and developing these themes according to a conventional plan, and at the same time, keeping them fresh and interesting by ingenious changes of rhythm, harmony, and instrumentation. Musical composition was just one long contest between conventionality and originality, and the test of a composer's skill and artistry was the amount of new wine he could pour into the old bottles without bursting them! That it was an amazing amount is proved by the sparkling, potent music of Haydn, Mozart, and Beethoven, though it must be admitted that Beethoven often stretched the old wine-skins precariously.

The earlier masters, following the rules and fashions of their time, created beautiful conventional designs in tone. But because these master designers were also normal human beings, and because tones skillfully composed are inevitably expressive, a great deal of feeling crept into this old-time pattern music. Many a page of it is so charged with feeling that the listener is quite unconscious of the form, which is as it should be. However, this emotion, dominating though it may be, is general and undefined. Listening to Haydn's "Surprise" Symphony, for example, one feels lighthearted and knows that Haydn must have been in a merry mood to write such exuberant music. But just *why* he felt so gay, he did not say, nor can we. The music gives only a general feeling of happiness, very real but nameless. We may, if we like, interpret it in terms of some definite bit of good fortune that has come to the composer, or let it suggest some happy fancy or holiday mood of our own. But this was not Haydn's purpose. He simply meant to write a piece of orchestral music in happy mood and in sonata from. The "Surprise" Symphony, in spite of its title and anecdotal bang, is pure pattern music — in other words, *Classical* music.

And now, a timely pause for definition. The terms *Classical* and *Romantic*, used to designate the two most important and widely contrasted types of music, are as indispensable as they are familiar. Yet unfortunately, they have been responsible for a great deal of confused thinking. As if it were not enough that each of these words has at least two legitimate or dictionary-approved meanings, they seem to have taken on so many misleading shades of meaning that there are actually people who think that *dry, unfeeling,* "*high-brow*" are synonyms for *Classical* and *fantastic, sentimental,* "*slushy*" for *Romantic!* Obviously, then, no writer can feel quite safe in using these terms unless he has first made clear what he means by them.

Coming from the Latin *classicus,* the word *classic* or *classical* originally meant belonging to the first or highest class of society. Our dictionaries still give *first class* as its general meaning. It is quite correct to speak of classical music or a musical classic when we mean simply first-class music, the best of its kind. James Russell Lowell in his "Among My Books" gives this excellent definition: "A classic is properly a book [or piece of music] which maintains itself by that happy coalescence of matter and style, that innate and requisite sympathy between the thought that gives life and the form that consents to every mood of grace and dignity; it is something neither ancient nor modern, always new and incapable of growing old."

But the word *Classical* has also a particular meaning. For many centuries learning and culture as well as social privilege had belonged exclusively to the upper classes. To be sure, the folk had their wealth of tales and legends, their little songs and dances, their handicrafts and homemade pretties. But the arts of literature, music, and painting were devoted to the greater glory of church and court. Composers wrote their music at and for the pleasure of princely patrons. Professional musicians were merely upper servants. This state of affairs reached its heights in the eighteenth century. Never had court life been so elegant, so formal, so polite on the surface — and only the surface mattered. This precious surface calm was not to be disturbed by any squalls of self-expression, certainly not by such low fellows as musicians! Well-bred persons hid their hair beneath heavy powdered wigs, their heart beneath velvet and gold braid, their feelings behind a mask of pretty manners. Music, ever a faithful mirror of life, also tried to hide its feelings behind a mask of form. It too was calm, correct, and politely impersonal. And because it so perfectly expresses those upper-class ideals of formality, the music of the eighteenth century is called the music of the *Classical* Period, and the men who composed it, the *Classicists.*

The calm of that polite world was, as we know, only the calm before a long-threatened storm of revolution which broke near the end of the century. Courtly speeches and pretty, formal tunes were drowned out by rough voices demanding the right to "life, liberty, and the pursuit of happiness" — voices from far across the Atlantic, singing "Yankee Doodle"; voices, all too near, chanting a tragic, triumphant "Marseillaise." Ideas and ideals were changing. It really seemed to be the beginning of a new and better world. For the first time in the history of mankind, the individual became more important than the class!

It is not surprising that poets and artists were carried away by all these fine new ideas of freedom. They too rose in revolt against the formalities of the Classical Period and claimed wider horizons for art. They were particularly intrigued with the idea of freedom for the individual — freedom to cast aside all hampering conventionality and live close to Nature, freedom to question old philosophies and formulate new ones, and above all, freedom to express one's own emotions, to declare one's own personality.

In Germany, Jean Paul Richter, E. T. A. Hoffmann, Heine, Schiller, and the great Goethe; in France, Lamartine and Rousseau; in England, Wordsworth, Coleridge, Byron, and Shelley — they all began to sing the song of the individual. Some of them sang it calmly and nobly. Their songs have lasted. Others sang fantastically and still others with such hysterical abandon that, like most heaven-stormers, they came to grief and kindly oblivion. There was a great deal of dissatisfaction and extravagant pessimism born of this too great optimism, this too passionate self-concern. It was the weakness of unbalanced idealism. Shelley's cry, "I fall upon the thorns of life! I bleed!" is characteristic of the period. To us there seems a better technique for handling thorns than falling upon them. There are even ways of avoiding them. But we must remember that those were heroic times and pardon the artist for the heroic touch of a few drops of blood on the self-portrait!

The poets not only gave expression to this new wave of thought and feeling that swept over early nineteenth-century Europe, but also were responsible for its name. With the greater political freedom brought about by the revolutions came a newly awakened interest in nationalism. Men began to point with pride at the accomplishments of their ancestors. The past became suddenly precious and worth preserving. A little group of German poets started a movement to reclaim their literary heritage. They planned to translate and give back to the people the forgotten tales and legends of the Middle Ages. Because the medieval dialects in which these legends were written stemmed from Latin or Roman roots, they were called the Romance Languages and the legends they recorded were known as *Romances*. These old tales of knighthood, of magic, and of great lovers caught the popular fancy. They were a welcome change from Greek mythology, which had been the main source of subjects for the painters, poets, and opera writers of the Classical Period.

Gradually the meaning of the word *romance* widened to include not only the old romances of the days of chivalry but all fanciful tales of love and adventure. And as for the adjective *romantic*, it seems to have been coined just in time to describe many of the people and events of the period. For example, Napoleon, with his fantastic dream of remaking the map of Europe to his own liking, his incredible conquests, and his spectacular downfall — a romantic figure, if ever there was one! Young Shelley and the picturesque George Gordon, Sixth Lord Byron, dreaming of a beautiful new world, of "poetry in politics," and dying, both of them, far from England, heroes of lost causes, romantic exiles. Romantic — surely no other word so well describes that fusion of imagination, emotionalism, and idealism, of singing optimism and sighing pessimism, that picturesque, self-conscious individualism which is known as the *Romantic Movement*.

Nowhere was the effect of the Romantic Movement more significant or more revolutionary than in music. Up to this time, as we know, music had been an independent art, an island kingdom, as it were, governed by its own exacting laws and quite sufficient unto itself. So self-contained was the Classical ideal that a man might be a great composer and yet know practically nothing of the other arts or of what was going on in the world in which he lived. Even such master musicians as Bach, Haydn, and Mozart, busily creating musical perfection in the form of fugues and sonatas, had little time and less inclination to leave their island to explore the world of outside knowledge. Nor would it have occurred to them that this outside world had any vital relationship to their work.

Then came Beethoven, born an islander but born an adventurer. While still working within the Classical boundaries, he had discovered that certain sequences and combinations of tones, certain compelling rhythms, were more than mere details in a beautiful tonal design. To him they suggested definite feelings and ideas, they were symbols of life in the world outside of music.

Beethoven was intensely interested in the outside world and eager to express it. Nature filled him with religious exaltation which he poured into his music. He wrote a whole symphony expressing the cheerful feelings which came to him in the country. He was caught up by the tide of revolution then sweeping over Europe and America. His passionate admiration for Napoleon, which turned into an equally passionate denunciation, inspired a "Heroic" Symphony inscribed "To celebrate the memory of a great man" — the man Napoleon might have been. Even more keen was Beethoven's interest in current thought. His strong, eager intellect grappled with the problem of the freedom of the will and gave the "Fate" Symphony, the eloquent Fifth, in answer. And in his rare adventures in dramatic music, notably the overtures *Leonore No. 3*, *Coriolanus*, and *Egmont*, he stole much of the thunder from the later Realists.

In spirit, Beethoven was the first, and some say the greatest, Romanticist. Surely he made music speak as it had never before spoken. Yet so perfect is the balance of form and feeling in his music, so sincerely does he express both the Classical and Romantic ideals, that he cannot consistently be listed with either group. Beethoven was — Beethoven.

It was for the composers immediately following Beethoven, for Weber, Schubert, Schumann, Mendelssohn, Chopin, Liszt, and Wagner, that music borrowed from literature the term *Romantic*. In the music of these men we find, not a balance, but a definite shifting of emphasis from form to feeling. The feeling is no longer general but particular, as indicated by suggestive titles. And it is personal feeling, the composer's own emotional or imaginative reaction to something in life or in literature. The Romanticists were great borrowers from literature, but surely they repaid with interest. For, to vitalize the *meaning* of words with the *feeling* of tones is to work a miracle of expression. But how surprised the unlettered Papa Haydn would have been to find these nineteenth-century fellows actually turning to poetry and story books for inspiration and ideas for their music! And, what was even more surprising — downright shocking — they let these poetic ideas set the patterns for their music! Why, that young Schumann actually set his own love affair to music, for all the world to hear! The musician no longer spoke deferentially, as court composer to his prince, but confidentially, as man to man.

Romanticism found expression in many types of music. With Weber and Wagner it took the form of fantastic opera and highly romantic music drama. With Schubert it flowered in the art song; with Schumann, Mendelssohn, and Chopin, in tonal pictures and moods; and with Liszt, in the symphonic poem. Later composers expressed not only their own individuality but that of their countries by introducing folk tunes and idioms into their compositions and by taking their subjects from folklore and legend — this is known as *Nationalism* in music.

In its extreme phase, musical Romanticism passed over into what is known as *Realism* or *Program Music*. The early Romanticist had been content with a single mood or subject, as in Schumann's *Warum* or Mendelssohn's *Fingal's Cave*. But the late Romanticist or Realist presents not one, but a whole series of pictures or events. He becomes a musical storyteller or dramatist, as in Strauss's *Till Eulenspiegel* or Dukas's *Sorcerer's Apprentice*. To understand such compositions, the listener must know their stories in advance. Having chosen to tell a story, the composer of program music must follow the story's outline, which seldom, if ever, fits into any purely musical form. For music is made up on the principle of repetition — a circular pattern — while the story or drama moves forward toward its climax in a straight line. Once in a long while a composer manages to combine the two. Strauss, for example, in *Till Eulenspiegel* achieves a *rondo* by repeating Till's theme at stated intervals — Till was the sort of hero who could pop up almost anywhere without spoiling the story. But for the most part, trying to follow a circle and a straight line at the same time results in a sorry compromise. Even in the great music dramas of Wagner one sometimes feels that the music is holding the story back, just running 'round in circles when the drama should be rushing ahead. Program music is far removed from the purely tonal art of the Classicists, even though it be cast in one of the classical forms. A Haydn sonata or even a Chopin nocturne speaks directly to the listener, a Strauss symphonic poem speaks only through an interpreter. Clever and fascinating though it may be, program music can never be musically independent.

Music paid a price for Romanticism. It sacrificed a certain charm of line to brilliance of color. It lost something of the impersonal power of pure tone while it gained in poetic suggestion. And just as the uninspired followers of Haydn and Mozart bored their listeners with deadly stiff sonatas, so the undisciplined Romanticists disgust theirs with sentimental tone doggerel and cheap descriptive music. But the idea of Romanticism is a fine one — by bringing music into closer touch with life, it made it truly the universal language.

In our discussion of the terms *Classical* and *Romantic* we have associated them with the historical periods in which their ideals were originated and emphasized. But these ideals are by no means confined to those periods or to any definite time or place. From the classic pen of Mozart came the charmingly romantic *Eine Kleine Nachtmusik*. And from our most radical young modern composers comes, every now and then, a charming set of old-fashioned variations or a brilliant Classical symphony. Nor are the terms *Classical* and *Romantic* necessarily exclusive. Both may be applied to many a fine piece of music. It is not a question of form *or* feeling, for without form the most fascinating tone poem simply falls apart in a heap of meaningless phrases, and without feeling, the most exquisitely designed sonata becomes a mere tonal exercise. Every masterpiece is a happy combination of form *and* feeling, and the labels *Classical* and *Romantic* merely indicate where the emphasis seems to fall.

As the horizons of our own artistic experience widen, we become increasingly aware of music's endless variety. But as we follow it through its many fascinating forms and phases, we must take good care not to lose the thread of continuity that has made music a great art. Styles may change with the times, our tastes will change with experience, but the essential qualities of music are as unchangeable as those of life itself. Whether a piece be listed as Classical or Romantic, ancient or modern, all that really matters is that it be sincere, expressive, and beautiful in its own way — then it is great music.

Acknowledgments

"To all those whose music and thoughts about music have touched my life." So should read my grateful acknowledgment, for the information and opinion set down in the following pages are the accumulation of all my years. I am indebted to so many musicians, authors, teachers, and music-loving friends and to so many children for their honest and revealing first impressions of music, that it would be quite impossible to name them all. And if, unwittingly, I should use as my own the very words of one of my creditors, I beg him to accept the unconscious quotation as but proof of the inevitability of his own choice of words.

There are, however, certain groups and individuals who, whether they know it or not, have shared in the making of these books. First of all, to the men, women, and children who have used most of this material in schools, in many informal study groups, and in their home listening to radio and phonograph, goes my gratitude for the encouragement of their expressed interest and enthusiasm; to Russell V. Morgan, Director of Music in the Cleveland Public Schools, my chief, very special thanks for loyal friendship; to the musicians and staff of the Cleveland Orchestra and particularly to its Associate Conductor, Rudolph Ringwall, sincere appreciation of many years of friendly and expert collaboration in the Orchestra's concerts for children and young people. And to the one who has given most, to Adella Prentiss Hughes, whose sustaining faith in me and my work, whose intelligent criticism and unfailing sympathy with the idea of music as a humanity have been fuel to my fire, I might say that these are her books as well as mine.

For the loan of many books and musical scores, I am indebted to the library of the Cleveland Orchestra and to the Fine Arts Division of the Cleveland Public Library; and for permission to quote from these scores and to reproduce portions of other copyrighted material most grateful acknowledgment is due to the following authors and publishers:

To the American Book Company for "Music in History," by McKinney and Anderson . . . to Boosey and Hawkes, Inc. (sole agents for the copyright owner, Edition Gutheil, Paris) for Prokofiev's "The Love for Three Oranges" . . . to Mr. John N. Burk and the Boston Symphony Orchestra Concert Bulletin for quotations from their program notes . . . to Coward-McCann, Inc., for "Revolt in the Arts," by Oliver M. Sayler . . . to Thomas Y. Crowell Company for "Twentieth-Century Composers," by David Ewen . . . to Dodd, Mead & Company, Inc., for "Grieg and His Music," by Henry T. Finck; "Edward MacDowell: A Study," by Lawrence Gilman; "Franz Liszt and His Music," by Arthur Hervey; "Saint-Saëns," by Arthur Hervey; "Musical Studies," by Ernest Newman; "Tchaikovsky, His Life and Works," by Rosa Newmarch;

"Fool of the World," by Arthur Symons; and "Life and Letters of Peter Ilich Tchaikovsky," by Modeste Tchaikovsky (Edited by Rosa Newmarch) . . . to E. P. Dutton & Company, Inc., for "Tchaikovsky," by Edwin Evans (in the Master Musicians Series); "Camille Saint-Saëns," by Watson Lyle; and "Sir Edward Elgar," by J. F. Porte . . . to Mr. Waldo Frank for "America Hispana: A Portrait and a Prospect," published by Charles Scribner's Sons. (The volume was reissued in 1940 by the Garden City Publishing Company under the title, "South of Us.") . . . to the H. W. Gray Company and Professor Daniel Gregory Mason for "Great Modern Composers" . . . to Harper & Brothers for "Robert Schumann, His Life and Work," by Herbert Bedford . . . to International Publishers for "Modern Russian Composers," by Leonid Sabaneiev, translated by Joffe . . . to Alfred A. Knopf, Inc., for "Schumann: A Life of Suffering," by Victor Basch; "The Book of Modern Composers," by David Ewen; "My Musical Life," by Nikolai Rimsky-Korsakov, translated by Joffe; and "In the Garret," by Carl van Vechten . . . to The Macmillan Company for "Chopin," by Basil Maine (in the Great Lives Series) and to The Macmillan Company and Professor Daniel Gregory Mason for "From Grieg to Brahms" . . . to the *New York Herald Tribune* for the May 25, 1939, issue . . . to the *New York Times* and Mr. Olin Downes for articles on Prokofiev and Sibelius by Mr. Downes . . . to Charles Scribner's Sons for the Archer edition of Ibsen's "Peer Gynt" . . . to the Viking Press, Inc., New York, for "Twelve Secrets of the Caucasus," by Essad-Bey . . . Finally, especial thanks to Mr. Leonid S. Rubinchek, of the staff of the Cleveland Public Library, for his invaluable assistance as an authority on the transliteration of Russian.

Contents

➤➤≫≪⬅

CHAPTER I

Four Great Tone Poets

FELIX MENDELSSOHN

Hamburg — 1809
Leipzig   — 1847

"I was born February 3, 1809, at Hamburg; began the study of music in my eighth year, and was taught thorough bass and composition by Professor Zelter, and the piano-forte, first by my mother, and later by Herr Ludwig Berger.   In 1829 I left Berlin, traveled through England and Scotland, Southern Germany, Italy, Switzerland, and France, went to England twice more in the springs of 1832 and '33, and was there voted an Honorary Member of the Philharmonic Society.   Since October, 1833, have been Director of the Association for the Improvement of Music in Düsseldorf."   Such was the autobiography sent by Mendelssohn to the Berlin Academy of Fine Arts on the occasion of his election to its membership in the spring of 1834.   Although a model of modesty and condensation, it is little better than a blank page to those who would know something of the brilliant and picturesque career within its dates.

Felix Mendelssohn's story has a long preface.   Indeed, it is but one bright chapter in the dramatic chronicle of a Jewish family in eighteenth- and nineteenth-century Germany.   This chronicle begins in Dessau in the home of a poor man named Mendel, keeper of a little Hebrew day school and writer of Holy Scrolls.   Here, in 1729, was born Moses, Mendel's famous son.   The child had a frail, twisted body but a fine, straight mind which soon mastered all the teacher-father could give it.   Then the ambitious Mendel, wrapping his little son in a ragged cloak, carried him to the Chief Rabbi for instruction.   When, a few years later, the rabbi was called to Berlin, there seemed no prospect of further schooling for his brilliant pupil, Moses Mendel.   But this shy, misshapen boy was not to be denied.   Bravely he trudged after his teacher, and entering Berlin by the one gate open to Jews, he began his lonely struggle with poverty and privation.   He was to learn many things not found in his precious books.

Although no longer physically persecuted, "for the greater glory of God," the Jews of eighteenth-century Germany were subject to every possible restriction, excluded from schools and from all desirable professions, except medicine, and burdened with insulting taxes.   For example, the Jews of Berlin were at one time obliged to buy the wild boars killed at royal hunting parties.   Doubtless some thick-pated politician

18557

thought this a tremendous joke on a race forbidden to touch swine flesh! Then, too, every Jew at the time of his marriage had to purchase a certain amount of china from the royal china factory, accepting whatever the factory manager chose to unload upon him. Moses Mendelssohn — for so his name had been Germanized — acquired with his bride, twenty life-sized china apes which later became great family keepsakes. Since many of the trades in Germany still belonged to the old, exclusive guilds, there was little a Jew could do to earn a living but shoulder a pedlar's pack or deal in old clothes or money lending.

This oppression and isolation had borne both good and evil fruit in the development of the Jewish character. The concentration of the race had strengthened certain noble qualities such as family love and loyalty, religious earnestness, and indefatigable industry, but it had also had a paralyzing effect. Religion cut off from communion with other intellectual life always stagnates. With the masses forced to live in squalor and ignorance, even their own priests, and particularly those from Poland, grew contentious and domineering. The Jews had ceased to think for themselves, and the fine old faith of their fathers was fast becoming a burden of meaningless forms.

Moses Mendelssohn, pondering all this, resolved, as had the Old-Testament Moses, to lead his people out of bondage. But to no Promised Land marked out on the map did he journey. He stoutly opposed a "Back-to-Palestine" movement then under government consideration. What would be gained by sending these neglected, degraded people into further isolation? Before they could worthily inhabit a country of their own, the Jewish people must first find their way back to the Promised Land of learning and culture.

Mendelssohn was now in a position to help them. He had risen from a starving student to the place of tutor in a rich man's family. Then he began to write one philosophical work after another, until he became known as "The German Plato." He won the respect and friendship of the leading thinkers of the day. For, says Hensel, "He first exhibited in himself the type of an educated Jew, and made this attractive enough to Christians to obtain admission for himself into all circles. He then made the Jews fit to follow his example and enter through the breach he had made . . . and it is not too much for me to say that every German Jew who now distinguishes himself anywhere owes the power of doing so more or less directly to Moses Mendelssohn!"

Of Moses Mendelssohn's six children, Abraham, the second son, now enters our story. Abraham Mendelssohn, having a good head for figures, entered the counting house of Fould in Paris. But in his middle twenties he returned to Berlin to marry Leah Salomon, the gifted daughter of a fine German-Jewish family. With Leah's dowry, he purchased a partnership in his brother's bank, and they opened a branch in Hamburg. It was in that northern city that the young people made their first home, and there the famous Fanny and Felix were born. But thanks to Napoleon's schemes, the thriving city of Hamburg became part of the French Empire about this time, and French soldiers were permitted to prey upon the citizens. The Jews were, of course, considered fair game, and Abraham Mendelssohn, unwilling to submit to such abuse, fled with his young family to Berlin. Here, too, they had to endure French domination until the invaders were driven home in the War of Liberation. It was then that Abraham Mendelssohn, at his own expense, equipped two volunteers for the fight, and for this was given the title of *Stadtrath* or Town Councilor.

Upon arriving in Berlin the Mendelssohns went to live with Madame Salomon, Leah's mother, in a large house on the Neue Promenade — one of those picturesque "foreign" streets with houses on one side and a canal, the Spree, on the other. This canal was a source of endless joy to the children. Its smooth surface was perfect for launching paper fleets, and even on stormy days it offered moving pictures of boats and barges for a child watching at the window. The setting of Felix Mendelssohn's childhood and youth was so unusual, so ideal, that one cannot think of him apart from it. And, after all, why should one? Mendelssohn does not stand out from his background as do Bach and Beethoven. He is peculiarly the product of his environment, material and spiritual, and his music, like a flawless French plate mirror, reflects his life and times.

The Mendelssohns and all of their friends seem to have been zealous diarists and correspondents. Fortunately their letters and journals have been preserved, and present not only a series of charming *genre* pictures of early nineteenth-century Germany, but also intimate glimpses of a rarely beautiful family life. Reading the two fat volumes of letters collected by Sebastian Hensel, Fanny's son, "The Mendelssohn Family" becomes a group of very real people. One feels the warmth of their affection for each other, their enthusiasm for all that is fine, and one is cheered by it!

Surely Abraham and Leah Mendelssohn were model parents. The father was a very busy man, but no day was so full, no business problem so absorbing but that there was time and interest for the children and their important affairs. Even when he was away from home, perhaps arranging a loan with a foreign government, he was writing to little Rebecca: "I am glad you had pity on the poor squirrel and took it into the room. If you are having the same disagreeable weather we are having here, not even an elephant could have stayed out of doors." To Fanny at fourteen, he writes: "Do not be vexed with your stoutness; it is one more resemblance to your mother (and you can never be enough like her)." And to tiny Paul, praise for his letter, "without a single mistake and beautifully short." To the budding genius: "You, my dear Felix, must state exactly what kind of music paper you wish to have, ruled or not ruled, and if the former, you must say distinctly how it is to be ruled. When I went into a shop the other day to buy some, I was embarrassed to find that I did not know what I wanted to have. Read over your letter before you send it off, and find out whether, if addressed to yourself, you could fully understand it and execute the commission contained in it." Abraham Mendelssohn was an exacting but not at all a fearsome father — not when he could end a serious birthday letter with: "But I won't preach, and am not old enough to prate! Accept once more my fatherly wishes and take my well-meant advice to heart." And he so often signed himself, "Your Father and Friend, A. M."

How well he played this double rôle may be judged from the letters of his famous son. Writing to a friend after his father's death, Felix Mendelssohn says, "Not only have I to mourn the loss of a father (a sorrow which of all others from my childhood I have always thought most acute), but also that of my best and most perfect friend of the last few years, and my instructor in art and life." Frequently, to his father he wrote in this wise: "I often cannot understand how it is possible for you to have so acute a judgment with regard to music without being technically musical; and if I could express what I feel with as much clearness and intuitive perception as you do, as soon as you enter upon the subject, I never would make another obscure speech all my life long! I thank you a thousand times for this and also for your opinion of Bach." And again, after much fatherly advice on the subject of the oratorio *St. Paul*, to Abraham, now old and blind, Felix Mendelssohn at the height of his brilliant career, writes: "One word of praise from you is more truly precious to me and makes me happier than all the publics in the world applauding me in concert." How little patience one has with some of the present-day biographers who hint at a Felix suffering and repressed by an austere father!

Leah Mendelssohn, the mother, was unusually gifted. As a girl she had played and sung nicely, made exquisite drawings, and chattered fluently in English, French, and Italian, as was the fashion for a miss of her station. She is also said to have read Homer in the original but secretly, for who would want to marry a female Greek scholar, however lovely her eyes or lively her wit! Felix Mendelssohn inherited those eloquent eyes as well as his mother's gracious ways and her artistic imagination. Leah had great ambition for her children. Almost as soon as she saw Fanny, her first baby, she remarked upon her "Bach fugue fingers." And while Fanny and Felix were still mere infants, she sat at the piano hopefully giving them five-minute lessons. All four of her children were musical, and home concerts were a regular part of the family regime. Rebecca had a pretty voice and Paul played quite respectable 'cello, though, of course, Fanny and Felix, pianists and composers, were always the stars.

As the children grew older, an imposing list of teachers was added to the household staff — teachers of language, literature, mathematics, of dancing, fencing, and swimming, of drawing and painting, and of music in all its branches — the very best that money could command. But Abraham Mendelssohn did not consider his duty done with their hiring, he backed those teachers as no modern P. T. A. ever dreamed of doing. He himself made the rounds at five o'clock each morning, routing out the sleepyheads and presiding at the breakfast table a few minutes later. No pampered rich man's children for him! Only on Sunday could the sleepers lie abed until seven. Often on those winter mornings, those black, bleak Berlin mornings, Felix, who was always drugged with sleep, must have wished with the old hymnist that "Sabbaths had no end."

The days were all carefully planned, even to the play times. Nor were the evenings frittered away. Papa in his Turkish slippers, reading his newspaper before the fire, Mama with her sewing basket, the children at the piano or listening while someone read aloud, presented a picture of family improvement! With true Jewish regard for time and money, the Mendelssohns saw to it that neither was wasted.

The only shadow that fell across this happy life, was that old shadow of the Jewish problem. In spite of their apparent freedom, the Jews still had much to fear, much to endure. Abraham Mendelssohn knew, only too well, the doors that would close to his children. Even his brilliant Felix, no matter how far his talents took him, would still be a "Jewish composer." Many of Abraham's friends had become converts to Christianity; two of his sisters were ardent Roman Catholics. Yet, out of respect for his father's memory, he could not bring himself to take the step, even though his conscience had consented. Then Leah's brother, whom he greatly admired and who had himself accepted Christian baptism, adding *Bartholdy* to his family name, gave this advice: "It is the justest homage you or any of us could pay to the efforts of your father to promote true light and knowledge. . . . You may remain faithful to an oppressed, persecuted religion; you may leave it to your children as a prospect of lifelong martyrdom, *as long as you believe it to be the absolute truth.* But when you have ceased to believe that, it is barbarism. I advise you to adopt the name of Mendelssohn-Bartholdy as a distinction from the other Mendelssohns. At the same time it would please me very much, because it would be the means of preserving my memory in the family. Thus you would gain your point without doing anything unusual, for in France and elsewhere it is quite the custom to add the name of one's wife's relatives."

Still Abraham hesitated until the day when Felix came home from the Singakademie, weeping because some of the others had laughed at "a little Jew-boy" joining so heartily in the singing of his beloved *St. Matthew Passion.* Felix was the first of the family to be baptized into the Lutheran church. The other children followed, then, some time later, the parents. The father's letter to Fanny at the time of her confirmation, several years later, seems a fitting conclusion:

> The outward form of religion your teacher has given you is historical, and changeable like all human ordinances. Some thousands of years ago the Jewish form was the reigning one, then the heathen form, and now it is the Christian. We, your mother and I, were brought up by our parents as Jews, and without being obliged to change the form of our religion have been able to follow the divine instinct in us and in our conscience. We have educated you and your brothers and sister in the Christian faith, because it is the creed of most civilized people, and contains nothing that can lead you away from what is good, and much that guides you to love, obedience, tolerance, and resignation, even if it offered nothing but the example of its Founder, understood by so few, and followed by still fewer.
>
> By pronouncing your confession of faith you fulfilled the claims of *society* on you and obtained the *name* of Christian. Now *be* what your duty as a human being demands of you, *true, faithful, good;* obedient and devoted till death to your mother, and I may also say to your father, unremittingly attentive to the voice of your conscience, which may be suppressed but never silenced, and you will gain the highest happiness that is to be found on earth — harmony and contentedness with yourself.

This from a man who had said of himself, "I am but a dash uniting Moses and Felix Mendelssohn!"

Music was so much a part of a child's day in the Mendelssohn house that it is difficult to say just when it began to be of special interest to Felix. At the age of nine he made his first public appearance as a pianist, "in his child's dress — a tight-fitting jacket, cut very low at the neck, over which the wide trousers were buttoned; into the slanting pockets of these the little fellow liked to thrust his hands, rocking his curly head from side to side and shuffling restlessly from one foot to the other." This was also the time when he began to compose, the time of that first muddled order for music paper for which his father took him to task. Up to the year 1820 — his eleventh year — he is said to have written from fifty to sixty compositions including a trio for piano and strings, a sonata for piano and violin, a sonata for piano, four organ pieces, songs, a little comedy in three scenes, and a cantata. Many of these compositions had been played before admiring guests at the Sunday musicales which had already become an institution at the Mendelssohns. Almost as remarkable as these youthful achievements is the fact that Felix remained quite unspoiled by the constant shower of compliments. His wise parents had made music such a familiar means of expression, and doing one's best such a matter of course, that the child's attention was fixed on the music rather than on himself. He probably thought that most little boys wrote sonatas and played them, when asked, for their mother's guests!

Crusty old Zelter, his instructor in composition, could scarcely conceal his pride in the boy. In 1821 he wrote to his friend Goethe that he was bringing his "best pupil" to call on him. Laden with good counsel to "Keep a strict watch over yourself; sit properly and behave nicely, speak distinctly and suitably, and try as much as possible to speak to the point. Be good and modest and . . ." Felix and his music master set out for Weimar.

It was a happy time from that first glimpse of Goethe — "He was in the garden and just coming around the hedge" — to the reluctant good-bys a fortnight later. The Sage of Weimar — to Felix, "the old gentleman," "not much taller than Father . . ., but the sound of his voice is wonderful, and he can shout like a thousand warriors!" — was delighted with the "little Berliner." Stop at the Elephant Hotel? Nonsense, the boy must be his house guest! "I have heard so little music in the past years," said the old poet, "that I cannot now get my fill of it." Every afternoon he would lift the lid of the piano, saying to his young guest, "I have not heard you today — now make a little noise for me." Felix would then play for hours — Bach, Haydn, Mozart, Beethoven, Cherubini — Mendelssohn — bringing music down the years in a way that amazed and enraptured his hearers. (And almost caused poor Zelter to burst with pride and joy!) Then, jumping up from the piano, he became a boy again, and claiming a kiss from "my friend Goethe," he would run out into the garden to join the young people, Goethe's daughter-in-law, her pretty sister, little Doris Zelter, and Adele Schopenhauer, and plan for some evening festivity. Sometimes they succeeded in luring Goethe to their parties, even into a whist game, though Zelter warned them that "*Whist* means, 'Hold your tongue.' " It was a wonderful experience for a twelve-year-old boy. Later there were other brief visits to Goethe and letters back and forth, and all his life long Felix Mendelssohn was to feel the power of that great personality.

In the summer of 1822 the entire Mendelssohn family made a trip to Switzerland, stopping at various south German cities enroute. It was quite a triumphal tour, for at each stop they found that Felix's fame had run ahead of them, and people were eagerly waiting to hear him play. It was during this summer that Felix met another talented boy, Ferdinand Hiller, who was to be a lifelong friend. On the way home the Mendelssohns paid their respects at Weimar, and Goethe gave warm welcome to the "young David" who had cheered him with sweet music. There was also a holiday excursion to the Baltic — Felix's first sight of the sea — and a trip with his father to Paris to bring Tante Henrietta back to Berlin.

Felix was greatly disappointed with the music he heard in the French capital. He could scarcely believe, he wrote back to Fanny, that, with the published scores of Haydn and Mozart for examples, a gray-haired man could do as poor a job of orchestration as Auber had done in his opera *Léocadie*. "In the whole opera there are perhaps only three numbers in which the piccolo does not play the principal part! The overture begins with a *tremolando* in the strings, and then the piccolo instantly begins on the roof and the bassoon in the cellar and blow away a melody . . ., the little instrument serves to illustrate the fury of the brother, the pain of the lover, the joy of the peasant girl — in short, the whole opera might be transcribed for two flutes and a Jew's harp *ad libitum!*"

Abraham Mendelssohn had had a definite purpose in taking Felix to Paris. It was time now to decide upon the boy's career. Proud as he was of Felix's playing and composition, he was still fearful that this display of talent might be just some infant-prodigy phenomenon which would neither last nor develop. He had no intention of letting his precious son become merely a second-rate professional. Zelter, of course, was sure of his "best pupil's" success. At Felix's fifteenth-birthday dinner a few weeks before, the old music master had toasted him before all the company, saying: "My dear boy, from this day you are no longer an apprentice, but an independent member of the brotherhood of musicians. I proclaim you independent in the name of Mozart, Haydn, and old Father Bach." And Moscheles, the brilliant pianist who had been spending some time in Berlin and had given Felix a few lessons, had also pronounced the boy an artist. After the first lesson he had written in his diary, "I am quite aware that I am sitting next to a master, not a pupil." But still Abraham was not satisfied. Old Zelter would be prejudiced by his love for the boy. And as for Moscheles, he might be "the prince of pianists" but he was also a Beethoven enthusiast; therefore he could not be quite normal. (Abraham Mendelssohn had a queer blind spot, or rather, deaf spot, where Beethoven was concerned. He called his music "meaningless stuff," and was much annoyed that Felix should think it so wonderful.) Abraham wanted expert opinion. Whom should he ask? Why, Cherubini, sweetly tuneful Cherubini, idol of the Paris Opera, there was the man to consult! To be sure, Felix thought little of him, and they argued about it as the coach jolted Parisward. "But," said Abraham, "what Cherubini says of you shall decide the matter."

Felix's future was in a far more precarious position than he realized, for no one could please Cherubini. Cherubini was a little soul whose own hard-won success had come too late to save him from the bitterness of early disappointment. His biting sarcasm was the despair of young artists and composers whom he would tell to take up preaching or woodsawing. Felix, with three assisting artists, played his own Quartet in B Minor for the great man, who set the *tempo* at runaway-horse speed. It was a mad performance, but when it was over, Cherubini astonished everyone by saying, with one of his rare smiles, "*Ce garçon est riche*," and went on to give the anxious Abraham explicit assurance that his son had talent enough and to spare!

To the Mendelssohns the year 1825 was memorable as the time when life began at Leipzigerstrasse No. 3. For them and their friends this handsome estate near the Potsdam Gate was not a mere piece of valuable property — bricks, mortar, grass, and trees — but a living thing, an extension of the family personality. Fronting on the street, it stood, an imposing house of many spacious apartments. Behind it stretched a park of some seven or more acres, once part of Frederick the Great's hunting preserve. At the rear of the house, grouped about a broad courtyard, was a cluster of low buildings, one of which was used for Abraham's banking offices, another housed the Hanoverian Legation and Felix's young friend Klingemann. Still another was the famous Garden House, with its frescoed ballroom which would seat several hundred guests — an ideal place for the Sunday musicales. In summer the Garden House was most delightful, for then the glass wall on the garden side was removed and only Grecian pillars separated it from flowering shrubs and century-old trees. It seemed as peaceful and remote as a deep forest, and, listening to the small sounds of birds and leaves and falling rain, one could scarcely believe that but a few feet away, beyond that sheltering main house, the Leipzigerstrasse was carrying on its noisy business. The Garden House was given over to the young people. Here they played games, made music, and rehearsed their various entertainments. And here, under the joint editorship of Felix and Adolph Marx, flourished that whimsical paper the *Garden Times*, known in winter as the *Snow and Tea Times*. Writing materials and a manuscript box were left in readiness on the garden table, and all guests were invited to contribute. Many a delightful bit of nonsense with a famous signature found its way into that contribution box.

Shortly after the removal to Leipzigerstrasse 3, Felix entered the University of Berlin, where he attended lectures for several years, not, however, taking any degree. Meanwhile, he was increasingly absorbed in his music. This was the time of the writing of the *Midsummer Night's Dream* Overture and the disappointing first opera. It was also the beginning of the Bach revival, which was to be one of Mendelssohn's most important contributions to music.

Bach, most of whose music was unpublished at the time of his death, was still comparatively unknown except to a few musicians. His manuscripts were scattered, and many of them destroyed. One — no less than the manuscript of the *St. Matthew Passion* — had been rescued by Zelter from among the wrapping papers of a cheesemonger! It was his prize possession, and sometimes, as a special treat, he would pass out the precious parts to the chorus at the Singakademie. There nine-year-old Felix Mendelssohn first thrilled to the wonderful music and begged to be allowed to copy it, but Zelter refused. Several years later, however, he permitted Madame Salomon to have a copy made as a Christmas present for her grandson Felix. Bach became a favorite with the Mendelssohns. Fanny, at thirteen, could think of nothing nicer than to memorize twenty-four Bach preludes and play them for her father's birthday. Felix, in Paris, wrote indignantly of the French who "believe Bach to be a mere old-fashioned wig stuffed with learning." And now, in the winter of 1827, to prove to his friend Schubring that Bach's music was anything but a dry mathematical exercise, he got together a chorus of sixteen voices, the original size of Bach's choir, and set to work rehearsing the *St. Matthew Passion*.   Every Saturday night for more than two years the little group met and sang Bach.   The idea spread, and since anything Felix Mendelssohn did was considered worth trying, musicians in other cities began to hunt out the music of the old Leipzig cantor.   Publishers, not to be left behind, resolved to add some Bach to their catalogues, even if they lost money by it.   Meanwhile, Mendelssohn's little group had become so enthusiastic that nothing less than a public performance by the Singakademie would satisfy them.   Zelter protested that the "public" would never stand for an entire concert of Bach.   But Felix and his friend Devrient, an opera singer who had joined the Bach group, persisted until on March 11, 1829, a century after its last performance, the *St. Matthew Passion* was first given in Berlin.   It was such a triumphant success that the Crown Prince ordered a second performance, which was given a fortnight later on Bach's hundred and forty-fourth birthday.   "To think," cried Felix jubilantly, "that it should be an actor and a Jew that give back to the people this greatest of Christian works!"   It was but the first of many such gifts, for, as the most popular pianist, organist, and conductor of his time, Mendelssohn did more than any other one man to reveal to audiences and artists the beauty of Bach's music.

Felix Mendelssohn was now in his twenty-first year.   His university days were over, his musical training finished, as far as teachers and lessons went, and there remained only the graduate school of experience.   In preparation for this, he was to make the "Grand Tour" which was considered part of every young gentleman's education.   "Traveling will do you good," said his father.   "It will be an opportunity to make your talents known in different lands and give you the independence you sadly need."   England seemed a good point of departure, for there two old friends waited to welcome Felix, young Klingemann of the Hanoverian Legation and the pianist Moscheles.   So in early April, 1829, Mendelssohn set out from Hamburg, and after three days of anything but a *Calm Sea and Prosperous Voyage* (of which he had written so poetically) his boat crept up the Thames in a fog to that "single-storied country" inhabited by "a population of black boots, manned by giant, dodging umbrellas."   But when the fog lifted and the wan traveler had been fortified by a good British dinner, his spirits rose.   "London is the grandest, most complicated monster on the face of the earth," he wrote. . . . "Not in the last six months in Berlin have I seen so many contrasts and such variety as in these three days. . . .   Such a whirl, such a roar!"

Young Mendelssohn made a quick and lasting conquest of London.   He was by no means a stranger, the English press having begun to note his achievements at thirteen.   And now, armed with a sheaf of letters of introduction and heralded by the distinguished Moscheles, he found all doors open to him.   Once inside, his romantic appearance, beautiful manners, and yet more beautiful playing took stout British hearts by storm.   His letters were so full of dinners, balls, water-parties, and fêtes of Arabian-Nights magnificence that the unpretentious folk at Leipzigerstrasse 3 were astonished and a trifle anxious.   Abraham wrote a most fatherly letter reminding his son of the purpose of that trip to London.   But with all the gaiety, Felix had not neglected his music, and his first public appearance, in May, showed him quite as successful on the stage as in the drawing room.

He gave a number of concerts, at one of which "to the dismay of all musicians" he played Beethoven's Concerto in E-Flat. He was ever the champion of Bach and Beethoven! His final concert, a benefit for flood sufferers in Silesia, was so well attended that according to his home letters, "ladies peeped out from behind the double basses . . . the Johnston ladies, who had strayed between the bassoons and the French horns, sent to ask me *whether they were likely to hear well!* One lady sat on a kettledrum. Madames Rothschild and K. Antonio accommodated themselves on benches in the anteroom; in short, the affair was extremely brilliant."

After this strenuous season Mendelssohn joined Klingemann on a summer tour to Scotland and Wales. This wild, legend-haunted country affected the young artist strongly. Writing of Holyrood Palace, he says: "Everything around is broken and mouldering, and the bright sky shines in. I believe I found today in that old chapel the beginning of my 'Scotch' Symphony." What he found in that curious pattern of land and sea which Nature has woven in the North Atlantic is, as he himself said, best told in the music of his *Hebrides Overture*.

It had been his plan, after the Highland holiday, to return to London in September, work for a few weeks at his composing and study of English, and then go back to Berlin in time for the wedding of Fanny and her painter lover, Hensel. But he had been scarcely a week in London when a cabriolet in which he was riding overturned, and he was laid up for weeks with a badly injured knee. He missed his dear Fanny's wedding, and came limping back to Leipzigerstrasse 3 in December, barely in time to rehearse the operetta he had written as a surprise for Leah and Abraham on their silver wedding day. The operetta, *Return from Abroad*, was given by a family cast, including even the unmusical Hensel, whose part was confined to one note throughout. Hensel missed his note, "though it was blown and whispered to him from every side," but the piece was a great success, and later became quite famous in England as *Son and Stranger*.

Late in the following spring — 1830 — Mendelssohn resumed his travels, this time southward bound. At Weimar he paused to pay a brief, and last, visit to Goethe, then on to Nuremberg, Munich, Salzburg, Vienna, fêted in each city in princely fashion. Autumn in Italy was a golden time, and his letters were filled with graphic descriptions of scenery, rare old buildings, and rarer paintings. Then, on the first day of November, the traveler reached Rome, rented a luxurious little apartment, and settled down for six months. His adventures were to range from the most magnificently solemn church ceremonies to the gayest folk festivals. He saw the old Pope buried and his successor installed with ancient pomp and circumstance. He thrilled to the beauty of the Roman Easter and flirted and danced through Carnival week. Nor were his musical experiences less varied. A friendship with the elderly Abbot Santini, a collector of old manuscripts, introduced him to the traditional music of the Roman Catholic Church; while an acquaintance with Berlioz, then at the height of his joyous conceit, for he had just won the *Prix de Rome*, gave him a shocking glimpse of revolt against everything traditional. One can scarcely imagine more striking opposites than these two — the elegant, conventional Mendelssohn and the disheveled, intractable Berlioz!

That young Mendelssohn had none too high an opinion of music and musicians in Italy is evident in his letters. Abraham Mendelssohn fretted over this hypercritical attitude. It was one thing to cherish high ideals of humanity and art — he had spent his life fostering them in Felix — but it was quite another and a fatal thing to worship perfection to the point of intolerance. He could not bear to see this son, who was so genial and warmhearted with his family and friends, becoming haughty and *hochnasig* with strangers. "The boy grows more exclusive hourly," he stormed, and wrote a sharp letter on the subject. Felix Mendelssohn would have been a happier man and, perhaps, a greater artist had he been a little less critical and less sensitive to criticism. He was always a trifle *superfine*, and, in consequence, he suffered from "crumpled rose petals."

The Italian sojourn was a happy one of sight-seeing, parties, meetings with interesting people, letter writing, and sketching. Mendelssohn was clever with brush and pencil, which were as much a part of his traveling outfit as is the Kodak of today. But he was by no means an idle pleasure-seeker, and when, in June, 1831, he left Italy, he took with him the *Hebrides Overture*, completed, the "Scotch" and "Italian" Symphonies, well under way, a number of short sacred works, and the *First Walpurgis Night* as proof of a winter's work.

By a roundabout route through Switzerland and the Rhine towns, in which he spent the autumn, he finally arrived in Paris. A live and eager city greeted him. The memory of the terrible "Three Days" of revolution still haunted people's minds; everything seemed to have received fresh impetus, and art, riding this high tide of emotion, felt the stirring of new ideals. Many a young poet and musician had been fired by the St. Simonians, a politico-religious party who preached a universality which should recognize no national boundaries to the life of the mind and heart. "The highest aim of art," they cried, "is to awaken, in its own way, the feeling of the infinite." Another group, fascinated by the *mazurkas*, the *polonaises*, and the warlike *krakowiaks* of the languid young Polish pianist Chopin, were caught up in a frenzy of patriotic feeling which was to mark much of the music of the late nineteenth century as definitely national.

Paris was full of artists, good, bad, and indifferent, all hoping to win the coveted Parisian laurels. Among them were many of Mendelssohn's old friends, including Ferdinand Hiller. No time was lost in introducing the newcomer, who was soon the center of such a whirl of gay excursions, private musicales, and public concerts that little time was left for composition. A characteristic letter from headquarters, Leipzigerstrasse 3, brought a stern reminder that since Paris was now the very hub of the operatic universe, this was the chance to find a French libretto and write the long-dreamed-of opera. The young man's reply is quite significant. He did not approve of French libretti. "One of the distinctive characteristics of them all is precisely of a nature that I should resolutely oppose, although the taste of the present day may demand it. . . . I allude to that of immorality." And, after illustrations of his point from several of the current opera stories, he ends, "All this produces effect, but I have no music for such things. I consider it ignoble, so if the present epoch exacts this style and considers it indispensable, then I will write oratorios!"

Mendelssohn stayed in Paris from December until April, and Hiller's "Memoir" records many an interesting encounter with Chopin, Liszt, Ole Bull, Meyerbeer, old Cherubini, and lesser lights. There were disappointments, too. The Conservatoire Orchestra, which had presented Mendelssohn to the Parisian public in an enthusiastic performance of the *Midsummer Night's Dream* Overture, rejected his "Reformation" Symphony as "too learned, too much *fugato*, too little melody." And there was sad news from Germany — the deaths of Tante Henrietta, his dear friend Rietz, and his hero, Goethe. Nor did a light attack of the cholera, then raging in Paris, improve his spirits. And when the London Philharmonic Society, which had made him an honorary member two years before, wrote asking him to write a new work for it and himself conduct it, he gladly accepted.

How lovely the English countryside looked — green meadows, lilacs, primroses, and little coral oak leaves gleaming in the April sunshine! Even "that smoky nest" in Great Portland Street seemed inviting. And how satisfying the frank and sturdy Klingemann, the calm Moscheles, after the excitable, slightly artificial Parisian musicians! Health and spirits rose, and Mendelssohn plunged into an orgy of concert giving. The manuscript score of the *Hebrides Overture*, now under a new title, *Overture to the Isles of Fingal*, was presented to the Philharmonic Society; the first volume of the *Songs Without Words* was brought out by a London publisher; there were visits with old friends and meetings with new. All too quickly the two months flew by. In July, 1832, after more than two years' absence, Felix Mendelssohn was back again in the Leipzigerstrasse. He was now twenty-three years old, his *Wanderjahre* were over, and the serious business of life lay before him.

Abraham Mendelssohn might easily have settled the question of his son's future. Art had not yet passed the period of patronage, and as a rich man and great music lover, the elder Mendelssohn might consistently have become Felix Mendelssohn's patron. There was the quiet Garden House, a perfect workshop, the circle of stimulating friends, the charming Sunday music — everything a young artist could wish. And there was the devoted family eager to keep him at home, where he could work at his composing with no responsibility beyond an occasional trip abroad or to some German city to play and conduct his music. But it had long ago been decided that Felix must be independent, a musician who lived by his work. The decision held.

Already several things had come his way — a return engagement in London for the following spring, a commission from Frankfort to write an oratorio, and an invitation to conduct the Lower Rhine Festival to be held in Düsseldorf in May, 1833. For a time it also looked as if he might have a chance to stay in Berlin as Conductor at the Singakademie, a position left vacant by the recent death of Zelter. But Mendelssohn's youth, his Jewish background, and a strong rival kept him from being elected to this position.

So in the spring of 1833, after a hurried but successful trip to England, he went to Düsseldorf to rehearse and conduct the festival. It was held in a large whitewashed hall in a restaurant garden and attended by crowds from all the neighboring country. So successful was the affair that Mendelssohn was offered a permanent position as "director of all public and private musical establishments in the town" at a salary of six hundred *thaler* (about $450) and with leave of absence from May to November. His father, who had gone down to the festival, was much pleased, and wrote home, "One thing I especially like about Felix's position here is that, whilst so many others have titles without any office, he will have a real office — without any title." Apart from some disputes with the theater, Mendelssohn was happy at Düsseldorf. He lived pleasantly, composed a great deal, made friends with an interesting group of painters and himself had lessons in water colors; and, most important of all, in the two years of his directorship, he changed the Lower Rhine Festival from a local, rustic celebration to a brilliant music festival that attracted all Europe.

In 1835 Mendelssohn was asked to come to Leipzig as conductor of the Gewandhaus Concerts. The salary offered was the same six hundred *thaler* as at Düsseldorf, but the position was much more important. Leipzig, with its great markets, bookshops, and ancient university, was just the combination of the commercial and the intellectual to appeal to a Mendelssohn. For Felix Mendelssohn, Leipzig was forever hallowed as the place where the beloved *St. Matthew Passion* was written, the place where Bach had lived and worked for twenty-seven years. Moreover, Leipzig was much nearer Berlin than was Düsseldorf, a point not to be overlooked in those days of no railroads and automobiles. And best of all, the Gewandhaus Concerts — so-called because they were given in the Gewandhaus, the Cloth Hall of the old Clothmaker's Guild — were a famous institution dating back to Bach himself. And the Gewandhaus Orchestra was at that time, probably, the finest orchestra in Europe, though not so fine as Mendelssohn was to make it.

The Leipzig years marked a period of almost incredible activity. No laborer in field or factory worked harder than this frail-looking musician. But Felix Mendelssohn worked happily. He had been brought up to believe that the thing he worked for — the serious thing — was the true joy. How strange and how fitting that he should have found that old saying of Seneca, *Res severa est verum gaudium* (The serious thing is the true joy), carved above the platform in the Leipzig Gewandhaus! To him, conducting those celebrated concerts was not just a job, it was a challenge, an opportunity to show what he could do for the art he loved, and he seized it with enthusiasm.

Under his direction the already able orchestra became world-famous. It may be true that instead of delving deep into the underlying meanings of music Mendelssohn played happily on the surface. Nevertheless, he was a fine conductor and one to whom all orchestras are indebted. His personal magnetism drew the players to him, and his gracious manners made even a rehearsal something of a social event. But he was not easy, he brought discipline into the orchestra. There was no talking in his presence, and none of that terrible zooey tuning up which had once caused the choleric Handel to hurl a kettledrum into the midst of his players. And there was a minimum of confusion, thanks to his use of the baton.

It had been, and still was, the custom for a conductor either to sit at a keyboard instrument, nodding his directions to the *Konzertmeister*, who then relayed them to the orchestra, or, standing before them, violin in hand, to signal with the bow and even come to the rescue of a flagging *tempo* by vigorous fiddling. It seems an absurd technique to a generation accustomed to the sight of the eloquent baton. Yet when

Mendelssohn and a few others pioneered with their sticks, they were laughed at and called "the elegant school" of conductors! Mendelssohn's wonderful memory was an asset in conducting, for it enabled him to watch the players rather than the score and to illustrate any point that might come up without having to rummage in the library. He was interested in improving the finances as well as the artistry of the orchestra, and himself went before the City Fathers to get extra pay for his men. Small wonder they were willing to obey his little stick and pour their very hearts out when it beckoned!

In planning his programs Mendelssohn did great service for the appreciation of music. He had two hobbies — the revival of old works and the introduction of new. Bach, Beethoven, Haydn, and Mozart were played by his fine orchestra as they had never been played before. Audiences marveled at what they had missed. And as for the younger composers, they too marveled that their music could sound so good! Leipzig became a Mecca for artists and composers. Chopin, playing his delicate waltzes, Liszt, with his brilliant transcriptions, little Clara Wieck and her sweetheart, Robert Schumann, bashful Niels Gade from the North, even that wild fellow, Berlioz — all of them had a hearing and a cordial welcome at the Gewandhaus.

One of the things Mendelssohn had set his heart upon was the establishing of a "solid academy of music" in Leipzig. It took a number of years and much plotting and planning, but at last, in January, 1843, the first prospectus of the famous Leipzig Conservatory was published with Professors Mendelssohn and Schumann heading the faculty list. Mendelssohn was not much of a teacher, and frankly admitted it. "Whether it is that I take too little pleasure in tuition or have not sufficient patience for it, I cannot tell, but, in short, I do not succeed at it." Yet his interest in the school never failed, and, less than a month before his death, Moscheles's diary records, October 8 — "Examination of pupils for entrance at the Conservatory. Mendelssohn took an active part in the proceedings, tested them in thorough bass, and wrote out examples on the blackboard. Whilst they were at work, he sketched the most delightful landscapes — ever a creative genius!"

During the Leipzig years a perfect stream of compositions flowed from his pen: the *Hymn of Praise*, incidental music for *Antigone*, *The Tempest*, and the remainder of the *Midsummer Night's Dream* music, quartets, concertos, the two great oratorios, *St. Paul* and *Elijah*, and a number of organ works. From the many references to Mendelssohn's organ playing we know that he must have been something of a virtuoso on that instrument, as well as the piano. There is the familiar story of how once when he was playing at St. Paul's, London, the congregation simply remained in their seats after the postlude. Mendelssohn played on and on, and finally they had to send the organ blower away to indicate that there could be no more of this wonderful music, even if the organist were willing, because there was no more wind in the pipes! And he was equally skillful in writing for the organ. His fugues and sonatas have become an important part of the schooling and repertory of modern organists. In addition to his own compositions for the organ, Mendelssohn edited a series of Bach's organ works.

Mendelssohn's activities were not confined to Leipzig. Each year he was asked to conduct the Lower Rhine Festival, an occasion he much enjoyed. Then, Frederick

William IV, newly come to the throne of Prussia, had a scheme for a great academy of the arts at Berlin. There were to be four divisions — painting, sculpture, architecture, and music — each headed by the best man available. Mendelssohn was chosen for the music school, a great honor and all the more attractive since it would mean living at Leipzigerstrasse 3 again. But there were all his plans for Leipzig, his splendid orchestra, his dream of a conservatory! It was a difficult decision, and kept him upset for over a year. Fortunately for Leipzig, the elaborate Berlin scheme fell through, and Mendelssohn got off by promising to become director of a special cathedral choir which, with a small picked orchestra, would be available for occasional church festivals and grand concerts in Berlin. He returned happily to Leipzig but with one more responsibility.

The constant suitor, however, was England. Mendelssohn made, in all, ten trips to England, seven of them during the Leipzig years. Not since the days of Handel had music flourished so in England, and, oddly enough, it was the same type of music, the oratorio, which made these two German composers such outstanding figures in English musical history. Mendelssohn had been the pet of London from his boyhood, but when, in later years, he began to conduct the great festivals at Liverpool and Birmingham, bringing to life the choral works of Bach and Handel and his own beautiful oratorios, British enthusiasm knew no bounds. From Queen Victoria and Prince Albert, who likened him to a "second Elijah," a prophet of true art, to the humblest mill hand taking part in the festival chorus, the English claimed Mendelssohn as a musician after their own singing hearts. An amusing incident occurred after the Birmingham Festival of 1846. The performance had been advertised with big posters, which were afterward covered by other posters announcing a holiday excursion. The second set were not quite long enough to cover, and the astonished public read:

> The Oddfellows of Birmingham will make an extraordinary trip to Worcester, Gloucester, and Bristol, returning next day. Leader — Mr. Willy.
>   Conductor — Dr. Mendelssohn.

Had it been true, what a crowd there would have been!

Mendelssohn's personal life was equally eventful during the Leipzig years. Scarcely had he taken up his duties at the Gewandhaus when news came of his father's sudden death, a heavy blow to the devoted Felix. And when, seven years later, Leah Mendelssohn died, it seemed as if the whole background of his life had dropped away. Fortunately, the foreground was full of happiness. In 1836 Mendelssohn had generously given up his summer holiday and gone to Frankfort to take charge of a choral society, the *Cäcilienverein*, for a sick friend. This good deed was well rewarded, for in Frankfort he met and promptly fell in love with Cécile Jeanrenaud, the daughter of a French Protestant clergyman. Although ten years younger than he, the pretty little Cécile was the one and only girl for Felix, and in the following spring they were married. As the years passed, their home in Leipzig with the five pretty children rivaled the Leipzigerstrasse 3 in charm and contentment.

The last trip to England, when in addition to many symphony concerts he had conducted six performances of the *Elijah* within a fortnight, exhausted Mendelssohn.

His friend, Sir Julius Benedict, watched him anxiously. "It is scarcely possible," he wrote, "to convey an idea of the expenditure of nervous and physical power to which this susceptible and fiery being was subjected hour by hour during this brief passage of his life. Pressed forward by the burning impulses of his nature and the desire of honorable fame, as well as excited by the ardent homage of enthusiastic fellow musicians, he lived years, whilst others would have lived only hours." And when this same friend, bidding him good-by, regretted that he could not stay a little longer in London, Mendelssohn replied, with what seems a strange premonition, "Ah, I only hope that I have not already stayed too long. One more week of this unremitting fatigue and I should be killed outright."

To break the tiresome journey back to Leipzig — and oh, how tiresome nineteenth-century traveling could be — Mendelssohn stopped for a day's rest in Frankfort. There word was brought that his sister Fanny, while rehearsing a little group for one of the Sunday musicales, still held in the Berlin Garden House, had suddenly lost consciousness and died a few hours afterward. It was more than Felix Mendelssohn could bear, for Fanny had been the sharer of all his hopes and dreams, his artistic second self. With a cry of anguish he fell senseless to the ground. A blood vessel in his head had burst, and for days it was feared that he would never recover. Gradually, however, he grew better, and went with his family to Baden-Baden. But it was a dreary summer, for, as he had written to Fanny's husband, it was "a changed world for all of us now."

There was much to be done. Managers and publishers wrote asking his services, sketches for new works lay waiting to be completed, even that long-sought opera libretto, Geibel's *Lorelei*, now fell into his hands — but he could not respond. "I force myself to be busy," he wrote, "in the hope that hereafter I may become so from inclination and that I shall take pleasure in it." But there seemed to be no joy left in the world. The spring was broken, the bright, vivacious Felix had become a melancholy Tristan. He tried desperately to fit into the old life at Leipzig. For a time they thought he was really getting well, and why not? He was a young man, only thirty-eight. But in the autumn he had a series of light paralytic strokes, and on the fourth of November, 1847, Felix Mendelssohn died.

Germany mourned "as if a king had died." After elaborate services in Leipzig, a special train carried the body to Berlin, stopping all through the night at different towns where sad little groups, singing by torch light, bade farewell to a loved musician. And nowhere was the grief more genuine than in England, where, with performers and audience dressed in black, they marveled at the beauty of Mendelssohn's imperishable monument, the *Elijah*.

THE ARTIST

To be born in a gutter, live wretchedly in a garret, die young and unrecognized, lie forgotten — preferably in a pauper's grave — until appreciation has set in, then rise, the wonder and admiration of a later generation — such seems to be the evolution of the creative artist, and woe unto him who reverses the process! Mendelssohn reversed it. He was well-born, lived happily, wore his laurel wreaths, enjoyed his own funeral flowers of popularity, and ended — so say the musical smart set — with his artistic reputation in the gutter.

Every generation seems, for some strange reason, to be a little suspicious and more than a little scornful of the beliefs and enthusiasms of the one that has gone before. Postwar youth laughs at the "gay nineties," who, in turn, laughed at the "mid-Victorians," who in turn — well, it has been one long laugh all the way back to Adam. But when all the ha-has have died away there is usually a re-evaluation. Then, free from prejudice and unjust comparisons, people and things are judged for what they are really worth, and many a temporary discard comes back.

Mendelssohn, being a Victorian, has had to suffer the debunking for which that period has been famous. But now, in the twentieth century, the laugh seems to be moving on. One may admire a Turner, quote a lovely line of Tennyson, enjoy *Fingal's Cave* or even one of the *Songs Without Words* quite openly! It is no longer the fashion either to extol or execrate Mendelssohn. The pendulum of his fame, having swung high, swung low, is coming to rest somewhere near center.

The reasons for the extremes of Mendelssohn's over- and under-rating are not far to seek. At a time when rebellious young Romanticists were shocking their elders by tossing form aside and reveling in feeling; when crazy Richard Wagner was talking — and writing his "endless melody"; when Berlioz was running wild and young Brahms was making people think; that nice, conservative Felix Mendelssohn was soothing and flattering mid-nineteenth-century ears with music they could understand and enjoy. He tried no newfangled tricks, never excited the audience or upset the critics. In other words, he was not disturbingly original, profound, or heroic. And how they loved him! But by the time the excitement of his untimely end had died away, public taste had begun to overtake those forerunners, Wagner, Brahms, and the rest, and this same nice Mr. Mendelssohn was labeled "old-fashioned"; his music, "shallow," "insipid," "hackneyed."

Mendelssohn's music has not changed a note. It is neither better nor worse than it was in those days of overpraise and overblame. But the time has come for a new and fairer trial. To condemn Mendelssohn for not being Beethoven is no way to determine his standing as an artist. The standard of judgment for an artist is, roughly stated, this: We rate highest those men who have not only composed beautiful music, or painted beautiful pictures, but have also added something new and useful to the forms, techniques, or expressiveness of their art. For example, Haydn, Mozart, and Beethoven are considered great composers not only because of the beautiful music they wrote, but also because they did most to organize and perfect music's master pattern, the sonata. Bach was a great contributor, not of new forms, but of marvelously rejuvenated old ones — the dry old fugue was a glorious thing by the time he got through with it! Mendelssohn was content to use the traditional forms as he found them, and although he was full of the new romantic feeling, he was far too cautious to let it run away with him and make him conspicuous. Therefore he made no major contribution to the art and cannot claim quite so high a place as an original artist.

And now for his music. Perhaps, as Daniel Gregory Mason suggests, the fairest test to apply to Mendelssohn's music is Matthew Arnold's test of great poetry — to be truly great it must contain "great thoughts, greatly expressed." To the last part of the test, Mendelssohn's music more than measures up. His expression was faultless. What he had to say, he said beautifully, but he seldom chose to say much of serious importance. He may have had "great thoughts," but, excepting the oratorios, he did not often express them in music. His was delightful "party talk," telling you what he had seen on his travels or in his imagination, rather than what he really felt about life.

Wagner, commenting upon *Fingal's Cave*, called Mendelssohn "the greatest of landscape painters," and no more clever criticism was ever made. Mendelssohn loved to paint landscapes, with brush as well as with tones. He had a painter's imagination — one that waits for the eye to prompt it. And, like most landscape painters, he had little interest in the people in his pictures — they were merely figures whose red caps or black cloaks lent a pleasing touch of color. He wasn't good at drawing them and, in a letter from that Highland holiday, he tells of letting his friend Susan put the figures into his landscape! Fancy a Beethoven or a Richard Strauss letting anybody else do the human part of *Coriolanus* or *Till!* This habit of looking at the world as a fascinating landscape dotted with houses and people is reflected in Mendelssohn's music. It, too, is beautiful, picturesque, and impersonal. There is seldom a real person in it. The landscape painter has gone no further than the door of the cottage, no deeper than the cloak of the solitary figure on the path. But the landscape painter must be judged within his own province. One cannot say that Corot's *Misty Morning* is a poorer picture than Rembrandt's *Portrait of an Old Woman*, with its worn, telltale face. Each artist has accomplished what he set out to do; what more can be asked?

Granted, then, that Mendelssohn expressed the surface rather than the depths of life. The surface has its place — surely we cannot do away with it! Nor can we be forever agonizing and philosophizing. We need, sometimes, to come to the surface and simply enjoy the sunshine unthinkingly. Mendelssohn's music does reflect a consistent and perhaps monotonous sweetness and light. But why should this be considered so much less artistic than the consistent and monotonous gloom for which certain other composers have won approval? And as for Mendelssohn's music being "hackneyed," it must be remembered that only a piece with real and universal appeal ever becomes popular enough to earn the flattering term "hackneyed." Later composers who have so superciliously criticized Mendelssohn's music as hackneyed need have little fear that their own works will ever become worn with too much playing!

So much for the imperfections. Now for the perfections of Mendelssohn's music. Its outstanding characteristic is beauty of form, a clean-cut design, and a balance of phrase and of harmony. But this formal beauty is by no means coldly conventional. Mendelssohn's music is full of life and color, full of fairies — if not Puck and Peaseblossom, then little nameless sprites which seem the very spirit of song and dance. It is fine, almost superfine music. Sometimes, as when we look at ivory carving, we marvel at the exquisite workmanship, then turn with relief to something done in stone — a rugged page of Bach.

Mendelssohn's knowledge of the orchestra was amazing, his use of it highly original. Such innovations as the divided strings in the beginning of the *Midsummer Night's*

Dream Overture, the three trumpets in the Wedding March, and many another masterly touch were afterward effectively used by that prince of borrowers, Richard Wagner.

Compared with the *Lieder* of Schubert, Schumann, Brahms, and Hugo Wolf, Mendelssohn's songs seem somewhat slight. Yet, who knows a more perfect example of smoothly flowing melody than the charming, *On Wings of Song:*

But it is in the part-writing that he shows his gift of pure harmony and the skill gained from long association with the work of that master part-writer, Johann Sebastian Bach. From such simple duets as "Oh, wert thou in the cauld blast" to the great choruses of *Elijah*, Mendelssohn yields place to few as a choral composer.

Mendelssohn was one of the first among modern composers to sense the dramatic possibilities of the Passion-type music. Bach's *St. Matthew Passion* had been the most thrilling musical experience of his boyhood. He was also an admiring student of Handel, and, like him, an adopted son of England, fatherland of oratorio. So it seems quite fitting that he should have carried on for these two older masters and have distinguished himself by writing the first of the great modern oratorios. The modern oratorio, by which we mean that of the nineteenth and twentieth centuries, may be said to be the outgrowth of the old Passion music, the Handelian oratorio, and the Romantic spirit which characterized nineteenth-century music drama.

The old Passion music, having as its subject the trial, suffering, and death of Christ, was a solemn part of the Lutheran service and bound by rigid convention. Handel's *Messiah*, although it celebrated the triumph of Christ and His church, was not sacred music in a liturgical sense; that is, it did not have to follow any order of service. But while it was freer than the Passion music, the very sacredness of the subject and of the hero called for a formal treatment. Even Handel's secular oratorios were formal in the stiff style of old Italian opera — long, florid arias sung by pompous principals, and rather set choruses.

Mendelssohn's oratorios belong to a time when form was yielding to feeling, a time when people were intensely interested in their own and other people's emotions. Heroes, villains, kings, crowds were no longer lay figures in the social drama but individuals, human beings every one of them. Now Mendelssohn's heroes, St. Paul and Elijah, were mere men whose stories could be treated dramatically with no fear of irreverence. His choruses were crowds of real people, not just so many pairs of lungs and vocal cords trained to produce a grand choral effect. His priests of Baal were religious fanatics, and their passionate appeal leads up to a moment of stark tragedy when their god fails them! One suffers with them. And in the episode in the desert when Elijah despairs and is comforted by angels ("It is enough," "Lift thine eyes," and "He, watching over Israel"), the discouraged old prophet comes closer to us than any repentant Tannhäuser or languishing Tristan. Here Mendelssohn ceases to be a landscape painter. One cannot help wondering what he might have done with opera, had he ever found a libretto to his liking. Would he have lived up to the promise of the

Midsummer Night's Dream? Would his wings of song have been equal to the heights of music drama?

For certain fine choral techniques Mendelssohn is indebted to Bach and Handel, but he owes them nothing for the orchestral part of his oratorios. This was his own contribution, and, thinking of the use of the strings in *St. Paul*, of the overture to *Elijah*, and of many another gorgeous effect for organ and full orchestra, what a contribution it was! How Bach would have rejoiced in it after his own frail little string band!

To sum it all up, Mendelssohn's position as an artist is this: He was not a path maker, he opened up no new realms of musical expression. His was the more thankless yet quite important task of uncovering old trails and, perhaps, checking the too impetuous rush down the new. He was a valuable link between the reserve and finish of the Classical School and the exuberant, run-away fancy of the Romantic. He was, as has been cleverly said, "a Romanticist with a Classical equipment." Mendelssohn suffered from a too-great popularity and to such an extent that he was allowed neither personal nor professional privacy. Every letter, every chance remark, every scrap of manuscript was published — an exposure which no reputation can sustain. His popularity also made him the victim of a flock of imitators, and while imitation may be sincerest flattery, it is also one of the quickest, surest ways of surfeiting people with the original. Like all people who are eager to please, Mendelssohn talked too much — chattered out a lot of pretty, shallow little pieces which shallow musicians literally loved to death. But Mendelssohn also wrote the E Major Sonata; the Octet and Quintet in A Minor; the Violin Concerto; the "Scotch" and "Italian" Symphonies; the *Hebrides*, *Meeresstille*, the *Ruy Blas* and *Melusina Overtures;* and the incomparable *Midsummer Night's Dream* music. These lie far above the clouds of passing criticism. They are of those things of beauty which are a joy forever.

Overture, Fingal's Cave

In the summer of 1829, at the end of his first triumphant visit to England, Felix Mendelssohn and his young friend Klingemann went off for a holiday in Scotland. Klingemann, an amateur author, was armed with pads and pencils, while Mendelssohn, who was to be the official illustrator of the expedition, lugged easel and color boxes. A sheaf of delightful diary-letters was the result. In them the travelers complain that "the Highlands and the sea brew nothing but whiskey and bad weather"; and tell of sickening little coastal steamers where passengers lay head to toe — "herrings are lodged in spacious halls, compared to us," and, as the waves twirled them about, "ladies, as a rule, fell down like flies." But they were deeply stirred by the romance of that legend-haunted land and by the wild, lonely beauty of nature. "When God Himself takes to panorama painting," writes Felix, "it turns out strangely beautiful."

Most enchanting of all were the Hebrides, that line of curious islands crumbled from the coast of Scotland by the restless fingers of the North Atlantic. At five o'clock, one misty August morning, the two young men took the little excursion boat to Staffa and Fingal's Cave. Klingemann writes: "Staffa, with its strange basalt pillars and caverns, is in all picture books. We were put in boats and lifted by the hissing sea up the pillar stumps to the celebrated Fingal's Cave. A greener roar of waves surely never rushed into a stranger cavern — its many pillars making it look like the inside of an immense organ, black and resounding, and absolutely without purpose, and quite alone, the wide gray sea within and without." And Felix:

> On one of the Hebrides: August 7, 1829.
> In order to make you understand how extraordinarily the Hebrides affected me, the following came into my mind there.

Here he writes some twenty bars of music which, with little change, were to be the beginning of the beautiful concert overture *The Hebrides*, also called *Fingal's Cave*.

As the music of *Fingal's Cave* begins, those measures taken by Felix Mendelssohn at the sea's dictation:

give a strange sense of the rise and fall of the waves, the endless, purposeless lapping of water. Like a shell held to the ear, the music seems a messenger from the sea. Not only the motion but even the dynamic changes from soft to loud seem to be those of nature, rather than of man's planning. Now and then a long green roller breaks with a boom:

and from far above comes a lonely voice:

To Wagner this woodwind passage suggested wailing winds, but it might also bring the thought of sea gulls, whirling, dipping, uttering their wild, lost cry.

Then, like a sudden burst of sunlight, comes the warm second theme:

which gradually leads up to a stormy climax ending in a clarion call from the brasses:

One cannot resist the fancy of Triton, trumpeter of the seas, who, as the ancients believed, with his conch shell stirred the waves to anger, then blew them back to calm. For those who prefer fact to fancy, this trumpet call marks the end of the Exposition. Not even old Triton himself could blow the sonata pattern awry for Felix Mendelssohn!

The Development now begins with soft fragments of the main theme, repeatedly interrupted by the loud call. The waves have lost their rhythmic rise and fall and are running brokenly. A charming souvenir of the second theme follows:

Then the main theme is heard, at first sedately:

Then in sudden gay *staccato:*

Mendelssohn, always at his best in *scherzo* mood, now sets the whole orchestra sparkling and frolicking as if a crowd of nymphs and dolphins were passing by — Neptune's court, perhaps. Again the horn call sounds, rousing the waters to wild excitement, and the sea god sweeps by, charioted on a roaring wave that breaks into a plume of rainbow spray:

Then, beneath slowly trilling violins, the tranquil lapping of the waves begins again. (It seems almost too prosaic to label such loveliness *Recapitulation!*) One recognizes with pleasure the return of familiar themes, but always freshened by some little change of rhythm, some new harmonic or instrumental tint. It is characteristic of Mendelssohn that while he followed traditional forms as carefully as any of the older Classicists, his gift of melody and his Romantic love of color kept him from repeating any part of a work exactly.

Near the end the music rises to a last brief climax, then dies away with one high flute tone, gleaming like a solitary first star above the quiet water. This beautiful tone picture is like a window inviting escape from a noisy, crowded room. Looking out from *Fingal's Cave* upon the wide and lonely sea with its symphony of wind and wave and wild birds crying, one's thoughts, too, seem to reach out toward far horizons, and one is reminded of the song of another great Victorian, born the same year as Felix Mendelssohn:

> Break, break, break
>> On thy cold gray stones, O Sea!
> And I would that my tongue could utter
>> The thoughts that arise in me.
>
> — ALFRED LORD TENNYSON

A MIDSUMMER NIGHT'S DREAM

In the summer of 1826 the young Mendelssohns discovered Shakespeare. The new translations by Schlegel and Tieck had just made his wonderful plays available in German. Hour after hour Fanny, Felix, Rebecca, and Paul and a group of their friends read aloud together, sometimes acting out the parts with grave faces for the tragedies and shouts of laughter for the comedies. Their favorite was that delicious confusion of lovers, clowns, and fairies, *A Midsummer Night's Dream*. And indeed, its forest magic must have seemed quite possible there in the lovely old garden at Leipziger-strasse 3. Felix was so fascinated by it that he had to try his hand at translating it again, this time into music. The result was the beautiful *Midsummer Night's Dream* Overture. It was not, technically, an overture until twenty years later when the play was given with added incidental music at the King's Theater in Berlin. It is really a symphonic poem picturing the fairy world of the play, a world into which some hapless mortals blundered, and it always seems like a gay fresco or a colorful procession such as sometimes unrolls itself from an old Persian scroll.

A Midsummer Night's Dream is one of those tangled tales which Shakespeare loved to toss together and then smooth out in his inimitable way. It involves four groups of characters — Duke Theseus and his train, two pairs of young lovers, a company of yokels, and the whole court of fairyland. The place — ancient Athens; the time — why, the wedding time of Duke Theseus and Hippolyta, Queen of the Amazons, a time of such festivity that even a group of simple Athenian workmen are inspired to give a play in honor of the great day.

But, on the eve of the royal wedding, one of the Duke's noblemen comes flying to him demanding the law upon his daughter, Hermia. It seems that Hermia, a too attractive young person, has rival suitors, Lysander, whom she loves to distraction, and Demetrius, whom her father favors. Now by the law of Athens, a daughter must marry the man her father chooses or be punished either with death or the cloister.

The Duke, happy in the anticipation of his own wedding, is loath to enforce this law which will bring such unhappiness upon two other lovers, and he gives the young people a month in which to think things over. Hermia and Lysander waste no time in thinking — they promptly plan to meet that night in a wood just outside the city and run away, far away from the peril of Athenian law.

Hermia, all a-flutter, confides their plan to her friend Helena, who unwittingly ruins everything by relaying it to the rival suitor, Demetrius. Before his infatuation for Hermia, Demetrius had been Helena's sweetheart, and now, Helena hopes that the news of the runaway will show him just where he stands with Hermia and send him back to her. But Demetrius, far from angrily giving Hermia up, rushes off to the wood to bring her back. There seems nothing for the miserable Helena to do but go tagging after.

The wood which the lovers have chosen as a trysting place happens to be the favorite haunt of the fairies. It also happens that this is Midsummer Night, the one time of all the year when fairies are supposed to swarm over the earth and cause strange and inexplicable things to occur. But tonight even the fairy world is upset. King Oberon and his pretty Queen Titania have been quarreling about a changeling boy they both want. Oberon in a moment of malicious anger calls Puck, his arch sprite, and bids him fetch a magic flower, the juice of which, dropped in the eyes of the sleeping Titania, will cause her to fall in love with the first creature those eyes happen to see upon awakening.

Oberon has seen the lovers, worn out with wandering and asleep in the wood, and even his hard little fairy heart is touched by the plight of poor Helena. So he tells Puck that, while he has the magic flower, he shall find Demetrius and squeeze some of the juice into his eyes so that he will again love Helena. Puck, coming first upon the sleeping Lysander, mistakes him for Demetrius and drops the juice into his eyes, then later, finding Demetrius, fixes his eyes too. Unfortunately, both young men upon awakening happen to see Helena and, of course, fall madly in love with her. So now Helena, who had no lover, has one too many, and Hermia, who had two, has none at all! Midsummer madness indeed!

While all this has been going on, the Athenian workmen have come into the wood to rehearse their play, and what a rehearsal it is! When it is over, Nick Bottom, the leader, exhausted by his Thespian chores, lies down to nap. Puck discovers him and, mischief-maker that he is, claps a donkey's head upon the unsuspecting fellow. Nick's friends, of course, are frightened out of their wits at sight of him, and run off home, and Nick, looking at his reflection in a pool, is properly horrified. A fellow should know better than to venture out on Midsummer Night!

Meanwhile, Titania, who has been sleeping near by, wakens. The first thing she sees is Nick with his donkey head, but so potent is the juice of the magic flower that she straightway loves him dearly. She calls her fairies, and they wreathe Nick's ridiculous long ears with garlands of flowers and make the greatest fuss over him. And Puck, hidden in a neighboring bush, all but bursts his naughty sides a-laughing.

Things now seem to be at the peak of confusion. The baffled lovers are fighting and spitting at each other like cats, Nick is making a complete donkey of himself —

and so is Titania. Oberon decides to take a hand. He removes the donkey's head and sends Nick trotting off home, restores Titania's sight, and they make up their quarrel. The fairies troop in to celebrate the reunion of their King and Queen, and dance merrily in the moonlit wood.

Early in the morning the lovers, lying on the ground, quite worn out with their night's adventure, are wakened by the sound of hunting horns. A joyous surprise awaits them, for, at Oberon's command, Puck has undone the mischief of the magic flower, so that Demetrius now sees only Helena, and Lysander, only his Hermia. The horns come nearer. It is the Duke and his followers out for an early morning run. The Duke is happy to find the young people so well content, and persuades Hermia's father, who is in the hunting party, to consent to her marriage to Lysander. Demetrius shall have his Helena. The three couples — Theseus and Hippolyta, Hermia and Lysander, and Demetrius and Helena — have a grand triple wedding. Bottom and his troupe crown the festivities with their sidesplitting tragedy, the fairies have their wood to themselves again, and "they all live happily ever afterward."

Overture

A few "wind-blown notes":

and a soft blue light of unreality steals over the picture. There they are, the fairies:

tiny creatures flitting by in a luminous gnat dance. One has a feeling of countless numbers and, at the same time, of incredible lightness. This is not due to any of the familiar tricks of *tempo*, dynamics, *staccato*, or melody line, but to the divided strings — violins in four parts — something then quite new and surprisingly effective.

And there is what the children like to call the "fairy sentinel":

a sort of periscope chord poking up out of the woodwinds and taking a look around. All fancy aside, this chord with its moment of quiet does indeed guard the listener from the hypnotic effect of a too continuous jigging rhythm.

Following the fairies comes a group which, if tunes tell anything, must be the Duke and his retinue:

passing by in pomp and circumstance. As they disappear, a roguish little face peeps out for an instant and is gone:

Puck — surely!

Then come the lovers strolling by with the romantic second theme:

the most beautiful melody of all.

Next, a sudden fanfare suggests King Oberon, but he remains unseen. What does appear (and now we realize that it was their drum, whacking away so inopportunely a moment ago in the lover's melody) is the group of workingmen, an awkward squad with a hobbledehoy tune:

as different as can be from the dignified Duke's march or the smooth song of the lovers
— ridiculously different, since it ends in a blare of heehaws:

suggesting Bottom's asinine adventures.

The cast of characters is now complete. There are no new tunes excepting this
dreamy fragment:

which might be a sleep motif for Titania and the lovers, suggesting that season of
false peace when Puck with his magic flower slipped about strewing confusion.

For all its poetic program, this music is written in sonata form. Up to this point
we have had an effective little Introduction; a conventional Exposition section presenting two main themes, each with several sections; and a Development in the form
of a free fantasia, and it has served as a perfect frame for the picture. But now that
we come to the Recapitulation, the well-disciplined Felix, minding the rule, repeats
the first section exactly, even to those magical opening chords — which now have no
dramatic significance! One wishes that he had let his imagination get the better of
his training! However, the returning fairies and the contented snores of Bottom in
the bassoons quickly charm away this slight disappointment, and the music goes on
with the beautiful lover's tune first in importance.

The coda is like a pleasant memory, returning just as one is falling asleep. There
are the fairies, there, the Duke's party, but all in a delightful, drowsy haze. Then,
with four long, soft "Amens," sometimes interpreted as the elves' blessing on the House
of Theseus, and the mysterious opening chords, now most appropriate to the passing
spell, the Midsummer Night's Dream fades away.

The overture was first played as a piano duet by Fanny and Felix at one of the
Mendelssohn Sunday musicales, but was soon scored for orchestra, for which it was
intended. Appropriately enough, the *Midsummer Night's Dream* Overture made its first
English appearance on Midsummer Night, 1829, with the young composer conducting.
His elderly friend Thomas Attwood, organist at St. Paul's, had felt such anxiety about
the score — it was still in manuscript — that after the concert Mendelssohn gave it to
him for safekeeping. What was the old gentleman's dismay the next morning to find
that the precious manuscript was missing — gone as mysteriously and completely as if
Puck himself had spirited it away. He must have left it in the hackney coach he had
taken from the concert hall! Attwood could scarcely bear to break the bad news to
Mendelssohn. But when he did, instead of blowing up in a rage or falling down in a
faint, the imperturbable Felix replied, "Don't distress yourself, Sir, I'll write another

copy." And from that indelible memory, Mendelssohn rewrote the entire score, so correctly that it matched the orchestra parts note for note. The fact that the missing manuscript turned up almost a hundred years later at the Royal Academy, of which Attwood had been a director, in no way affects the incident.

The *Midsummer Night's Dream* Overture is amazing music, and we add the qualifying phrase "for a seventeen-year-old boy to have written" merely to increase the amazement. The music needs no apology, it is a stroke of pure genius. And it is quite significant that when, twenty years later, the mature Mendelssohn was commissioned to write incidental music for this same play, he not only used this work of his boyhood without altering a note, but strove to create the new *Midsummer Night's Dream* music in the same spirit. Sir George Grove remarked that the *Midsummer Night's Dream* Overture "brings the fairies into the orchestra." We might add that it also brings the fairies into the audience. It seems to create a fresh new world, and, as a small boy told me quite confidentially, "When the orchestra plays this music, there are lights on the horns like the little lights of fairyland."

Scherzo

Twenty years had passed since the *Midsummer Night's Dream* days in the Mendelssohn garden at Leipzigerstrasse 3. Felix was a man of many affairs in Leipzig, Rebecca was living in Italy, Fanny and Paul were middle-aged married folk, yet they were all keenly interested in the presentation of their favorite play in Berlin, and especially in the new music Felix had composed for it at His Majesty's command. In a letter to Rebecca, Felix says: "There are twelve numbers in the *Midsummer Night's Dream*, and the dead march for Thisbe is quite in the style of my mock preludes which used to make you laugh so; it is written for a clarinet, a bassoon, and a drum, but it's no good trying to describe it." (Fanny wrote that she could scarcely believe he would have the impudence to bring it before the public!) He goes on to say, "It is amusing that the public of Berlin should be so surprised and so delighted with our old favorite among the beloved William's plays." And Fanny, writing to this same absent sister, says: "The music is the most enchanting thing you ever heard. . . . The interludes are real masterpieces, and were performed to perfection. Never did I hear an orchestra play so *pianissimo*. The three middle acts are separated by music alone — the curtain not falling at all." She continues with most entertaining descriptions of costumes and acting, including the improvisations of Moonshine's dog, who gave the Lion an untimely bite and had to be replaced next night by a stuffed dog.

Felix Mendelssohn had not lost the fairy touch, judging from the *Scherzo*, to be played before the curtain rises on the second act. The first measure of the music brings them trooping in:

Peaseblossom, Cobweb, Moth, Mustardseed, and all Titania's fairy train.   And this energetic little tune:

with its nose to the ground, must belong to her busy elves.

Playing along the line of these orderly dancers is a little leaping figure:

probably "that merry wanderer of the night" who follows his own Puckish pattern and keeps step with no one.

The middle, or Trio part, of the *Scherzo*, with its threatening, surging *crescendo* and little frightened scurryings down woodwinds and strings, reminds us of Titania's command:

> Then, for the third part of a minute, hence;
> Some to kill cankers in the musk-rose buds;
> Some war with rere-mice for their leathern wings,
> To make my small elves coats; and some keep back
> The clamorous owl, that nightly hoots and wonders
> At our quaint spirits.

The elves' tune sounds reassuringly above the din of battle.   There is fierce drum fire from the valiant toadstool corps.   Puck, the impish onlooker, leaps higher than ever in his excitement:

Then quite suddenly the turmoil ceases.   Up from the strings shoots a chromatic passage, clear and sharp as a shaft of moonlight leading back to the dancing fairies. With a ripple of flutes and some last light skips as if the dancers simply leaped off into space, the *Scherzo* ends.   Up goes the curtain on the Athenian wood at midnight, and the voice of Puck challenges a fairy who is out gathering dewdrops,

> How now, spirit, whither wander you?

Nocturne

The third act of *A Midsummer Night's Dream* ends with Puck, hovering over the tearful exhausted lovers, whispering:

On the ground
Sleep sound:
I'll apply
To your eye,
Gentle lover, remedy.
When thou wakest,
Thou takst
True delight
In the sight
Of thy former lady's eye:

*   *   *

And all shall be well.

Only a curtain of music separates the confusion of Act III from the happy waking of Act IV. The honey-sweet voice of the French horn sings this lovely little night piece:

to an accompaniment of closely companioning bassoons and distant basses.

And once, near the beginning, two high violin tones gleam starlike above it for a moment.

The *Nocturne* is in simple three-part song form, and the second melody introduced by violins and answering oboes:

makes pleasant contrast, with its rising line and gentle agitation. The beautiful horn song returns, sings on to its quiet ending, after which Master Mendelssohn lets flutes and strings, in a gentle coda, cover the sighs of the delighted listeners.

Wedding March

Here come the lovers, full of joy and mirth.

And to music so familiar, so perfectly obvious, as to need no comment. Following the first glorious outburst:

are two lesser tunes in the same exultant mood:

and:

Then comes the quieter section:

and:

and the slightly wistful:

Knowing march form, one of course expects the return of the first part. But somehow, when it does come that first theme seems to be breaking in out of sheer, irrepressible joy, so perfectly has Mendelssohn caught the happy wedding spirit.

Most of us have our own associations with this beautiful, "hackneyed" music — pictures of bridal parties being played triumphantly down the aisle and out into a gay confusion of confetti and congratulations. But the original ending, as described by Fanny Mendelssohn to Rebecca, was this: "The most beautiful part of the whole piece, and the only thing which I never thought much of in reading the play, is the last scene, where the court goes off in procession to the splendid wedding march, and you hear the music gradually dying away in the distance, till suddenly it breaks into the theme of the overture and Puck and the fairies reappear on the empty stage. I assure you it is enough to make one cry!"

And now, in the quiet of midnight, the fairies bless the house of Theseus and the newly wedded pairs. And Puck, broom in hand, having swept the dust of mortals behind the door, recites his little epilogue:

If we shadows have offended,
Think but this, and all is mended,
That you have but slumbered here,
While these visions did appear.

Songs Without Words

We have said that Mendelssohn was not an original artist in the sense of having contributed new forms of musical expression. But while he may have opened no new musical highways, he came, by happy accident, upon a most charming bypath in those intimate little piano pieces which he called *Songs Without Words*. They were something quite new and different from the airs and dances of the old suites or the movements of piano sonatas. They were truly vocal in that the melody was made to speak so plainly that one was reminded of the absent singer. There was the song — only the words were lacking, and somehow that didn't seem to matter!

These little pieces appear to have grown out of that charming Mendelssohn home life, judging from Fanny Mendelssohn's letter to a friend, dated December 8, 1828: "My birthday was celebrated very nicely. . . . Felix has given me three presents, a *Song Without Words* for my album (he has lately written several beautiful ones)," and she goes on to mention two other gift pieces. So they were, at first, album pieces, musical greetings and compliments to friends. Then, as the years passed, the collection grew until the present catalogue of Mendelssohn's works lists eight volumes of six songs each (two of the volumes were collected after his death), in all, some forty-eight *Songs Without Words*.

They reflect many moods, from that of the lilting *Spring Song*:

the busy, contented *Spinning Song*:

to the somber *Funeral March*:

Among these forty-eight wordless songs are several that might well have gone unsung, but not one that is vulgar or shoddy. And of the good ones, it really is a pity that three or four should have been worn threadbare while twice that number remain unknown. For, when all is said and done, Mendelssohn's *Songs Without Words* are one of music's prettiest gifts to the home pianist.

"Know'st thou the land where lemon trees are blooming?" — Mignon's song with its longing refrain, "'Tis there, 'tis there, Beloved, I would go" — has found its echo in German hearts since the days of Frederick Barbarossa and his golden dreams of Italy. German feet have worn a path across the mountains to that mysterious summer land; German poets, painters, and musicians have worshiped at the shrine of Italian beauty. And always these pilgrims have brought back, not photographs of Italy, but idealized paintings, travelers' tales of a land of heart's desire.

It is, then, not surprising to find young Felix Mendelssohn among these enthusiasts. Arriving in Venice in October, 1830, on the best of terms with himself and all the world, he writes home, "Italy at last! And what I have all my life [he was twenty-one] looked forward to as the greatest felicity is now begun, and I am basking in it." He continued to bask for ten happy months, and he always called his Symphony in A Major, sketched during that time, the "Italian" Symphony. Unlike his "Scotch" Symphony, this music was not intended as an impression of a country or its people. There is no attempt at his favorite landscape painting and no suggestion of folk idiom except in the last movement, the *Saltarello*, which really detracts from the dignity of the symphony. For one so devoted to the sonata, it seems a strange inconsistency — Mendelssohn's one wild oat! The "Italian" Symphony is pure German. It is simply a reflection of Mendelssohn's own lighthearted mood, just another of those overflowings of German delight in Italy.

The *Andante*, the second movement, is for many listeners the choice part of the "Italian" Symphony. Like a canticle from some early Italian lady's "Book of Hours" — one of those beautiful medieval handmade books with pages bordered in berries, flowers, and queer little beasts — the music has the plaintive charm of far away and long ago. It scarcely seems to belong to a public concert hall. This exquisite reticence is quite remarkable when one remembers that it is the music of a youth whom genius and adulation might so easily have made a hopeless "show-off." It is written in what might be called ballad style — one stanza, one melody after another, telling its story simply and with no display of rhetoric in the telling.

Two austere measures:

like the fateful first line of some old legend, serve as introduction. Then the song begins:

It is one of those tunes that seem to speak directly to the listener. But while it holds the attention, one is aware of the stately movement of the accompanying low strings, a charm which Bach worked in the softly stepping basses of his "Air for the G String."

The stanza is repeated with violins singing the melody and two flutes humming a soft obbligato:

The second stanza is in somewhat brighter mood:

Yet its brightness seems that of a pressed flower. Oddly enough, this tune has a recognizable likeness to Schubert's "Trock'ne Blumen," the "Dead Flowers" of the "Maid of the Mill."

A third stanza, introduced by solo clarinet:

is rudely interrupted by the stern opening measures, heralding the return of the first melody, now slightly altered:

The other two themes come back for a moment, then once more the legendlike call:

The first melody answers, but now the voice falters, breaks under its burden of feeling, and is silent. An unfinished song, a broken lute, a faded flower — the loveliness of yesterday.

ROBERT SCHUMANN

Zwickau — 1810
Endenich — 1856

Robert Schumann was in truth his father's son.   Possessed of the same poetic in-
stincts, the pluck and moral courage of the father plus the genius of the son produced
Schumann the artist.   August Schumann, the father, was an unique character.   Son
of a poor village clergyman, August was born, not with a silver spoon in his mouth,
but a quill pen, which pricked and tickled him all his days and kept him serving literature, if only in the outer courts.   His brief biography tells a brave tale of the adventures of a boy who had a real love of learning and little besides enthusiasm to keep it
alive.   All his father could do for him by way of education was to teach him his three
R's and then send him, at the age of ten, to stay with his grandfather in a little town
where the school was considered a shade better than that of his own village.   From
the school August received most indifferent training, but from a young uncle, a boy
of about his own age, he caught a lasting fever for poetry and philosophy.   The two
youngsters read it together and tried writing it, and when, at the age of fourteen,
August left school to become apprenticed to a merchant, they kept it up by correspondence.   After a long day as clerk in a cotton warehouse, August would spend his evenings studying.   He taught himself double-entry bookkeeping, French, and enough
English to read and enjoy the poetry of Milton and Young.   He wrote a little play
and two small volumes of essays and poems and began to dream of making his living
as a writer.

About this time, the young uncle fell heir to some money and went off to the University of Jena.   The less fortunate August had to content himself with a position in
a grocery shop at Leipzig.   But the great University of Leipzig offered such irresistible
temptation that at the end of six months August cast caution and groceries to the winds
and enrolled himself as a student.   He had the luck to sell a story, and the small sum
it brought paid his modest expenses for several months.   But, alas, before his next
work, a novel, was finished, the money was more than finished, and the ambitious
author had to go back into business.   This time, however, he went to the near-by
town of Zeitz to work in a bookshop, where at least the wares were more to his taste
than meal and potatoes.

But in Zeitz he fell in love.   His Johanna's father, the town's medical officer, would
consent to a marriage only on condition that August give up the whole precarious
business of books and become a substantial merchant, a grocer, with a shop of his own.
So back to the meal and potatoes went the gallant suitor.   It is rather amusing to
know that in order to make money with which to start his food shop, he set to writing
with such zeal that within eighteen months he had turned out seven novels and the
greater part of a commercial handbook.   Incidentally, the poor fellow ruined his
health.

At the age of twenty-one, Grocer Schumann set up his shop and his home in the
town of Ronneburg.   But it was no time before he had added a little circulating

library to the grocery, using his own collection of books as a beginning, and, with Johanna helping in the shop, was doing some writing on the side. The literary end of the business began to crowd the potatoes, and August Schumann decided, father-in-law or no, to abandon all public relations with food and become a bookseller and publisher. He also became one of his firm's most prolific authors, leaving some sixteen volumes, among which were commercial textbooks, encyclopedias and anthologies, and translations of Byron and Scott. The new venture prospered, particularly the publishing end of it. Soon August asked his brother to join in partnership, and they moved to Zwickau, where the big post roads and a sizable Latin School promised better business.

Zwickau then numbered only some four thousand inhabitants. Lying on the left bank of the broad Mulde, amongst gardens, meadows, and fertile fields, and with the Windberg rising to the West, it made one of those pleasant prospects for which Saxony is famous. Where the medieval walls and moat had been, a girdle of beautiful gardens now enclosed the inner town. But a fine old Gothic church, a many-gabled Cloth Hall, and a number of picturesque private dwellings kept the young Zwickauers mindful of their town's antiquity.

This little city entered music history by way of an item in the birth notices of the *Zwickauer Wochenblatt* early in June, 1810: "On the 8th of June, to Herr August Schumann, notable citizen and bookseller here, a little son." It is highly probable that most of the *Wochenblatt* readers skipped this notice entirely in their eagerness to get to the real news of the day, the movements of Napoleon's troops. For Zwickau, lying on one of the main routes to Russia, saw thousands of confident French soldiers march out, followed by the emperor and empress and their glittering staff; saw the shattered remnants of that army, famished and frozen, straggle back; saw its own food supplies commandeered and its own citizens stricken with an epidemic of fever. It was authentic background for "The Two Grenadiers."

"Little son" — christened Robert Alexander, was the fifth of the Schumann children, his mother's darling *Lichtpunkt* (bright spot) and his father's dream child. Nothing was ever quite good enough for this beautiful baby, and from his godmother, the burgomaster's widow, down to the grubby little "devil" in the printing shop, they loved him and spoiled him so that he never got over it. And perhaps it was just as well, for the music of Schumann is alive with the memories of that happy childhood. As Victor Basch says, "He knows how to speak *of* the very young and *to* the very young as no musician before or after him has spoken."

When Robert was six, he was sent to a private school, and at seven, began to have lessons with the town's best musician, the organist at St. Mary's Church. To the teachers of 1816 he was merely a good little pupil. But from the accounts of those growing years, it is plain that little Robert Schumann was that most precious and interesting phenomenon, a truly creative child. No sooner had he realized what a story, a play, a piece of music was than he wanted to make one, too. No one lured or goaded him into self-expression or made him self-conscious about it. Models were never lacking, especially in the way of stories and poems. Having inherited his father's love for books and with a whole shopful to feed upon, he became a greedy little bookworm. His imagination would go to work upon whatever he read and dramatize it, after which there had to be a performance by a neighborhood cast.

He also experimented with tune-making — dances and songs — played by the composer to an admiring home audience. Because there was so little good music to be heard in Zwickau, the child's father took him to Karlsbad to hear the famous pianist Moscheles — the same Moscheles who inspired young Felix Mendelssohn. It was a thrilling and unforgettable experience for nine-year-old Robert Schumann.

At the age of ten Robert entered the Zwickau Lyceum, where he was to spend eight years preparing for the university. Here, as in his primary-school days, the most significant part of his education seems to have gone on outside the classroom. August Schumann took the keenest interest in the development of all four of his sons, and spent many an hour discussing literature and the importance of the study of foreign languages with them. The older boys were to go into the family book business, and the youngest — ah, who could tell into what far fields his dream child might wander! Robert was fortunate in finding among his school fellows several boys who enjoyed music. He and young Pilzing explored the works of Haydn, Mozart, Beethoven, Weber, Hummel, and Czerny by way of four-hand piano arrangements. And Robert organized an orchestra which he conducted from the piano. The fact that he concocted much of the score library, supplying missing parts, adapting, and composing, only made the activity the more interesting. The father was the orchestra's loyal backer. He provided a good grand piano, music racks, and an enthusiastic audience of one.

Sometimes the players would lay aside their music and beg Robert to put on one of his picture shows. Even as a boy he showed the unusual gift for tone painting and characterization that was later to distinguish his *Carnaval*. His comrades loved to get him started at this game, and would stand around the piano shouting with laughter as they recognized the subjects of the sketches.

Besides the home music, there were delightful evenings at the hospitable Carus home where Robert learned to love chamber music. He also learned to love a lady — the charming young Frau Carus, who sang the Schubert songs so beautifully to his accompaniments. It was his first calf love, but since the lady's husband was included in the romance, it passed into a lasting friendship devoid of melodrama or of anything disagreeable.

Meanwhile the records of the Lyceum mention public entertainments at which Robert Schumann appeared as composer, pianist, and reader. At fifteen he was leader of a German Literary Society made up of Lyceum pupils. Its statutes began with the statement "that it is the duty of every man of culture to know the literature of his country," and went on to lay out the following program for each meeting:

1. Reading of some verse or prose masterpiece.
2. Reading of the biography of a celebrated author, and opinions thereon.
3. Explanation of obscurities.
4. Reading of original poems by members, and criticism by the audience.

Robert's adolescent imagination was simply steeped in poetry. When he was not riding the clouds with Schiller, Goethe, and Byron, he was delving in the classics — Homer, Sophocles, Tacitus, Horace, and Cicero, read in the original Greek and Latin.

But the important literary event was his discovery, at the age of seventeen, of Jean Paul Richter. It is almost unbelievable, to a generation brought up to expect some psychological reality even in its fiction, that anyone should have taken Jean Paul seriously. His novels — a confused mixture of rather pathetic idealism and vague philosophies, thickly frosted with marshmallow sentiment — we tersely catalogue as *gush*. Yet Jean Paul was the idol of young Germany in the early nineteenth century. His languishing moods, his extravagant style and mannerisms were imitated as faithfully as are the hard-boiled Hollywoodisms of today. Robert Schumann was an ardent follower. A sample of his state of mind comes from a Jean Paulish letter written to a friend, telling of a holiday excursion in the course of which he and Liddy — the sweetheart of the moment — had climbed the Rosenburg to see the sunset:

> At last, when the sun had sunk and whole spring-tides of blooming roses glowed dimly from its dying rays, when the mountain tops began to blaze and the forests to burn with fire, and immeasurable creation dissolved into soft rosy masses; and as I gazed into this ocean of crimson and all, all became condensed into a single thought, and while I grasped the great idea of the Godhead [he was seventeen!] and Nature, my Beloved and the Godhead stood in ecstasy before me and smiled kindly upon me — lo! as rapid as a flash, a black cloud arose in the east, and more of them arose and piled themselves upon high, and I seized Liddy's hand and said: "Oh, Liddy, even so is life!" And I pointed to the dark crimson massed on the horizon and she gazed at me mournfully and a tear stole from her eyelid. Then, I believed that I had once more found the ideal, and silently I plucked a rose — but, as I tried to offer it to her, a thunderclap and a lightning flash broke from the east, and I took the rose and scattered its petals — that thunderclap awakened me from a lovely dream — I was back again on earth. . . . When I took leave of her, she again pressed my hand violently, and the dream was gone — the dream is gone! And the lofty image of the ideal fades away, when I think *of how she talks about Jean Paul.* Let us leave the dead to their sleep!

Poor Robert — his ideal shattered because little Liddy was too human to enjoy philosophizing in the midst of a thunder storm! This effusion is not quoted with the shameful purpose of holding a young heart up to ridicule, but because it is a forecast of a life which was to be one long round of rosy dreams and thunderclap awakenings. And much of the ecstatic soaring and melancholy brooding of Schumann's music may best be interpreted as lingering reflections of the romantic Jean Paul days of his youth.

August Schumann died in the summer of 1826, just when his son most needed him. Gifted, painfully sensitive, thoroughly spoiled, Robert at sixteen was difficult. The frank and joyous child had grown into an introspective youth who would sit at his piano in the twilight, improvising and sometimes sobbing at the mystery of life as he dreamed it. A few more months and his days at the Lyceum would be ended — then what? The father, who had been the close companion of his son's artistic life, had realized that it could not be denied. He had intended that Robert should go on to the university for a liberal arts course, but that he should also have every chance to make the most of his music. Frau Schumann, however, could not see that this poetizing and mooning at the piano promised any worthy career for her *Lichtpunkt*. Robert should go to the university and take up something substantial, preferably the Law. Robert's guardian, a practical man of business, agreed with this decision, and in March, 1828, the young dreamer went down to Leipzig and matriculated as *Studiosus Juris*.

As reward for his docility, he was to have a short tour through Bavaria before settling down to his law books. He started off with a friend, young Gisbert Rosen, also a devoted Jean Paulist, and together they explored the quaint old Bavarian towns. Rosen was on his way to Heidelberg to enter the university there. Day and night he sang the praise of this oldest and most picturesque of German universities, and the more he praised, the less Robert thought of Leipzig. By the time they parted, Robert was through with Leipzig and mentally on his way to "Alt Heidelberg."

However, the road to Heidelberg was not yet open — his recent matriculation and his mother's consent to a change of plans were to be reckoned with — so Robert decided to say nothing and endure a year at Leipzig. And, as if in haste to get it over, he threw his things together and without waiting to regale the family with a single traveler's tale went rushing off to Leipzig, barely three hours after returning from his holiday! The letters of the following months are full of complaints and self-pity. Leipzig was "a horrible hole." "Not a hill, not a valley, not a wood where I can indulge in meditation; not a place where I can be alone except this shut-up room with everlasting noise and racket below." With all sympathy for his suffering from city noises, it is only fair to state that the "shut-up room" was really two very handsome rooms, unlike ordinary student quarters and containing a good grand piano.

"Chilly jurisprudence," he says, "with its ice-cold definitions, would crush the life out of me from the start." As for student life, it was "far too low" for this toplofty young gentleman. In a letter to his mother, he writes: "I go regularly to university lectures, play piano two hours every day, read a few hours or go for a walk — my sole recreation. In a neighboring village, Zweynaundorf, in the loveliest part of all the surroundings of Leipzig, I often spend whole days alone studying and writing poetry. So far, I have not cultivated the acquaintance of a single student. I go to fencing school, am friendly to everybody, but am extremely careful about becoming intimate with anyone. I find that without being standoffish one can assume a certain air with these fellows so that they keep their distance and do not treat one as a freshman." What a dunce the fellows must have thought him, with his "air"! After all, he *was* a freshman, a green, eighteen-year-old freshman, not even in good standing. For, while in this letter to his mother, written in June, he speaks of going regularly to lectures, we find him in August, writing to Rosen, "I have not been to a single lecture yet, but have been working at home — that is, have played the piano, written a few letters and *Jean-Pauliads*." Such conflicting statements, whether bits of bravado or plain fibs, are unbecoming, to say the least.

Nor was it quite true that the solitary walks were his "sole recreation." His old friends the Carus family were now living in Leipzig, and he was a constant visitor at their home. Pretty Frau Carus, his first love, had become a successful concert singer, and a most interesting group of artists frequented her music room. It was there that

Robert met the pianist, Frederick Wieck, with whom he began to study. And it was there that he first heard nine-year-old Clara Wieck play, little dreaming that he was listening to the future Frau Clara Schumann!

In his first year away from home, one of Schumann's greatest weaknesses began to show itself — his utter lack of a sense of the value of money. There seems also to have been a corresponding lack of delicacy when it came to asking for it. When he was in funds, he would spend royally upon everything and everybody, and when he had not so much as a penny left, which was often the case, he would beg so ingeniously that his mother, his brothers and sister-in-law, his friends, even his crusty guardian could not resist him. Here are two specimens of his art of begging, one to his mother:

> This contempt for money and squandering of money is pitiful in me. You would hardly believe how careless I am, and often I obviously throw money out of the window. I always reproach myself and make good resolutions, but next moment I have forgotten them and again find myself giving a big tip. Foreign countries and travel have much to do with it, but most of all my confounded recklessness. I am afraid I am incorrigible.

and this masterpiece to his guardian:

> How much you would oblige me, most honored Herr Rüdel, if you were to send me as soon as possible as much as possible! . . . Believe me, a student never spends more than when he has not a penny in his pocket, especially in the small university towns where he may get as much as he likes on credit. During the last seven weeks, there was a fortnight when I had not a farthing, and I can tell you candidly that I have never spent so much as in these seven weeks. The innkeepers write down with double chalk, and one has to pay with double crown pieces.

As Niecks says in his admirable biography of Schumann, "An Anthology of Begging Letters culled from Schumann's early correspondence would supply us with the best possible examples of the kind." He then goes on to say that the young man's extravagant habits and misrepresentations — intentional or otherwise — must have caused anxiety to those who were interested in him. However, says Niecks, "There was no real cause for fear — Schumann was saved by the nobility of his character and by his genius."

In the spring of 1829, just a year after his matriculation at Leipzig, Schumann set out for Heidelberg. He had convinced his mother that the change was important, "for the sake of my profession, because the most famous jurists are at Heidelberg." On the way he struck up an acquaintance with a young novelist, and the two made a leisurely tour of the Rhine country. This new friend was a jolly fellow and quite a revelation to Schumann. To think that a successful writer of romance dared to laugh in public and show honest enthusiasm for beer and sausages! And to think that anyone could enjoy the beauty and grandeur of the Rhine without dropping a single tear! As if by magic, the moody youth who had taken such care to make the Leipzig students "keep their distance" was transformed into a merry Robert Schumann who made friends with everyone — fat, elderly ladies, traveling salesmen, even a pair of old Dutch soldiers going third class and full of tales of Waterloo. And so gay were the sight-seeing trips, so numerous the treats of *Rüdesheim* wine, coffee, and cigars, that by the time he reached Mannheim, Robert's pockets were inside out and he had to walk the rest of the way. He arrived in Heidelberg at nine o'clock on a May night, tired, dusty, but all elated over a gorgeous sunset.

During that first summer term at Heidelberg, Schumann honestly tried to interest himself in his legal studies. He was full of admiration for Thibaut, who was something of a celebrity in music as well as law, and attended his lectures dutifully. Between terms, he took an eight weeks' trip to Italy with the usual results — new friendships, new enthusiasms, but the same old cry of "Please send me as much as possible — as soon as possible." Returning to Heidelberg in October, he moved into new rooms selected for him by his friend Rosen, and began a season of activity in everything but the law. His home letters confess: "Of course, I am not famous for the regularity of my attendance" to lectures. He seems, however, to have been quite famous for the regularity of his attendance upon all festive occasions — balls, parties, sleigh rides, masquerades. And he had found his place in the musical life of Heidelberg where his charming piano playing made him welcome. Even Thibaut contributed to his delinquency by inviting him to the weekly evenings of music at his house. Knowing Schumann's genius and his genuine love of music, it is not at all surprising that the applause and appreciation of these musical people should have completely upset any good intentions he may have had toward the career planned for him by his mother and Herr Rüdel. And, shameful as his neglect and evasions may be, there is something rather pitiful in such a statement as this: "All my musical doings seem to me like a splendid dream that existed once, and of which I can only remember dimly that it did exist. And yet, believe me, if I ever achieved anything in the world, it was in music. I have always felt a powerful impulse towards music, and, without overestimating myself, perhaps also the creative spirit. But — bread-and-butter study! Jurisprudence so ossifies and freezes me that no flower of my imagination will ever again long for the world's spring."

In July, 1830, Robert Schumann wrote what he rightly recognized as "the most important letter I have ever written or am likely to write." It was the letter to his mother, asking to be allowed to give up the pretense of studying law and try for a career in music. "My whole life," he wrote, "has been one long struggle between poetry and prose, or, let us say, between music and law. . . . In Leipzig I lived carelessly and troubled myself little about my career. I dreamed and loafed and accomplished nothing. Here [Heidelberg] I have worked more, but both there and here I have become more and more deeply attached to art. Now I stand at the crossroads anxiously considering the question — which way? If I follow my instinct, it points toward art — I believe the right way. But — do not be angry with me for I say this in all love and tenderness — it has always seemed to me as if you barred the way in that direction. You had, of course, your reasons, good, motherly reasons, which I understood and which we both called 'the precarious future and uncertain bread.' But what is to be done now? There is no more torturing thought for a man than that of an unhappy, empty future which he has prepared for himself." Having tugged at his mother's heartstrings, he then begs her to write to Wieck, his former piano teacher in Leipzig, and ask his honest opinion as to her son's fitness for a musical career.

Frau Schumann wrote to Wieck and received in reply a shrewd estimate of her Robert's musical ability and character. "With Robert's talent and imagination, I undertake, within three years, to make him one of the greatest living pianists" — surely pleasant reading for any mother. But — what followed must have given the good lady a *Schreck* — Wieck said he could not answer for "the abominable tricks which his unbridled fantasy plays on both of us" or for his wavering disposition. Robert will have to be cooler headed, more manly, more willing to hoe the hard rows of technique and theory. The techniques must have been sadly lacking when Robert himself confessed that "although I could play any concerto at sight, I had to go back and learn the scale of C major!" Wieck agreed to teach him, but suggested a six months' trial at serious study before making the final decision on a musical career. To this Frau Schumann and Robert agreed, the latter replying ecstatically, "No criticism shall dishearten me and no praise shall make me lazy. . . . I mean to be worthy of the name of your pupil."

Life began at twenty for the musician Schumann. Having spent several weeks — and all his allowance — coming up from Heidelberg, he arrived in Leipzig deflated in mind, body, and estate. His first letter to his mother, dated October 25, 1830, was indeed *touching*. He has no money for postage, piano tuning, or hair cuts. He has pawned his watch, is sustaining life on boiled potatoes, is down to his last candle, and could not even buy a pistol with which to shoot himself (not that he has the least intention of so doing)! After this sad report, he asks that she send him all of his letters to her — "I should like to see whether I have changed much in these last two and a half years." Not much, Robert!

However, he did work hard, if perhaps spasmodically, at his music. He attacked the piano energetically under Wieck's direction and put in long hours of practice. He also took up the study of theory and composition with Dorn, Director of the Leipzig Opera. The fact that Wieck was so often away on concert tours with Clara, his child prodigy, must have seriously interrupted the piano lessons, but on the whole, Schumann seems to have been quite optimistic about his progress. He was determined to fulfill Wieck's promise that he could become one of the "greatest living pianists." Yet he must have been conscious of that wavering between poetry and music which had beset him from childhood, for he wrote to his mother: "If only my talents for poetry and music were concentrated into one, the light would burn brighter and I might go far," and then adds this ambitious bit: "I can aim at being four things only — conductor, music teacher, virtuoso, and composer." All too soon Fate was to concentrate for him, leaving only the rôle of composer!

At Heidelberg, Schumann had often carried about with him a small dumb keyboard which he used to strengthen his fingers. Now, in his eagerness to progress, he devised a contraption which held up the weak fourth finger while the others were being exercised. Wieck forbade the use of this "finger tormentor," but, he says, "Robert used it behind my back to the righteous dismay of his third and fourth fingers!" As a result, his right hand was lamed and, in spite of months of treatment, never

recovered.   Gone were all those rosy dreams of becoming "the greatest living pianist."
This was real tragedy.   Yet Schumann, who had always whined at trifles, took this
blow gallantly.   "Don't be uneasy about the finger," he wrote his mother, "I can
compose without it"; and later, "I shall take up violoncello, for which I only need
my left-hand fingers.   It is most helpful, too, in symphony-writing."   Time and Schumann's genius proved that this accident which turned him toward composition was
indeed a blessing, though in painful disguise.   For the very qualities that made Schumann successful as a composer — his solitary, introspective nature and his love of
daydreaming — would doubtless have made him an unsuccessful virtuoso.   Moreover,
what would a brilliant pianist Schumann have meant to us?   No more than Moscheles,
Paganini, and many another forgotten virtuoso whose gifts have flashed, cometlike,
across the sky and are now but a legend.

And so, in 1832, when the injury was pronounced permanent, Schumann's artistic
lifeline shows another break.   His piano studies with Wieck had, of course, to be given
up, and about this same time his work with Dorn came to an end.   Schumann acknowl-
edged that these theoretical studies had been of great value and had given him a
"beautiful clearness" which he would not otherwise have had.   But he could not
agree with Dorn that "in fugue lies the whole art of music — Heavens!"   Instinctively,
he seemed to sense that the time had come for him to take his own way, and in a letter
to his first teacher, the old organist at Zwickau, he says: "Bach's *Wohltemperiertes
Clavier* is my grammar, and, moreover, the best.   The fugues in their order I have
analyzed down to the smallest details; this is of great use and, as it were, of morally
strengthening effect on one's whole being, for Bach was a man — out and out; with
him nothing is half done, morbid, everything is written out as if for eternity."   Could
there have been a better antidote for Jean Paulitis than a stiff, self-administered dose
of Bach!   Ah, Robert, now you *are* changing!

Schumann saw a great deal of the Wiecks, even after his piano lessons ceased.   He
had lived for a year in their house, and they had all grown genuinely fond of the gifted,
exasperating fellow.   The Wieck children adored him.   No one else knew so many
nice games and tricks, could think up such amusing riddles and charades, or tell such
amazing stories.   Schumann's ghost and robber tales thrilled and chilled their small
bones to the marrow!   And when he sat at the piano making story music — well, by
comparison, Papa's playing was simply less than nothing!   He was their hero.   The
little boys copied him faithfully, and ten-year-old Alwin pacing up and down with
hands folded behind his back would say, "This is the way Schumann does."

Most charming and most curious was the friendship with Clara.   At one of the
Carus musicales, Robert Schumann had first seen Clara, a little girl of nine who played
remarkably.   Now, in 1832, she was the famous Clara Wieck who had appeared in
many cities, played for Goethe at Weimar, and even made a successful concert tour to
Paris.   Clara at thirteen, old for her years, and Robert, at twenty-two and always
young for his, became quaint companions.   Besides the games, the excursions to the
zoo, and the long walks which they all shared, these two had their music.   Robert was
proud of Clara's playing, and she, as eagerly interested in everything he wrote.   When
she was in Leipzig, they spent hours together at the piano, and when she was away

giving concerts, they kept up a lively correspondence full of musical news and personal nonsense.   To Clara, in Frankfort, he wrote:

.. . . I know you are a wise one and understand your old moonstruck charade maker — so, dear Clara, let me tell you that I often think of you, not as a brother thinks of a sister, or one friend of another, but rather as a pilgrim thinks of the picture above a distant altar.   During your absence, I have been to Arabia to get all sorts of stories that would please you — six new stories of doubles, one hundred and one charades, eight amusing riddles, and some horribly lovely robber stories and some about the white ghost — Whoo-oo-oo, how I shudder!   Alwin has grown into a very nice boy; his new blue coat and leather cap, like mine, suit him uncommonly well.   There is nothing much to say about Gustav, except that he has grown astonishingly — you will be surprised, for he is nearly as tall as I am . . . and Clemens is the drollest, dearest, most head-strong little boy.   He talks like a book and in a booming voice. . . .   Have you been composing? and what?   I often hear music in my dream — then you are composing. I have got to three-part fugues . . . beside this, a sonata in B minor and a book of *Papillons* are finished. . . .   The weather is glorious today.   How do the apples taste in Frankfort?   And how is that high F in Chopin's skipping variation getting on?   My paper is coming to an end — everything comes to an end, except the friendship with which I am Fräulein C. W.'s warmest admirer —

R. Schumann

and again, reporting his progress:

My work will remain, like many others, a ruin, since for a long time it has produced nothing but erasures.

To Robert, visiting in Zwickau, Clara wrote:

. . . Ah, what a lot of news I had to tell you.   But I will not do it or you will just stick at Zwickau — I know you. . . .   Listen: Herr Wagner [Richard] has got ahead of you; a symphony of his was performed, which is said to be as like as two peas to Bee-thoven's symphony in A major.   Father said that Schneider's symphony, which was given at the Gewandhaus, was like the freight wagon which takes two days to get to Wurzen, always keeping in the same track, and a stupid old wagoner with a great peaked cap keeps on growling at the horses: "Ho, ho, ho, hotte, hotte!"   But Wagner drives in a gig over stock and stone, and every minute falls into a ditch by the road, but in spite of this, gets to Wurzen in a day, though he looks black and blue. . . .

Well! you are a pretty fellow to leave your linen behind in the carriage!   Have you got it back from the driver?   I am looking forward to Christmas very much, and the piece of cake that I am going to save for you is already waiting for you, although it is not baked yet.

Give my love to everybody, and write me an answer very soon, only write nice and *clearly*.   Hoping to see you here very soon, I end my letter and remain

Your friend,
Clara Wieck

and later:

I was just winding my way like a worm through your sonata which two gentlemen from Hanover wanted to hear, when a letter came — now from whom? thought I.

Robert's diary is full of Clara — she had played this or that *divinely*, she had grown "taller and prettier," she had been scolded by "the old man." He seems to have been slow to realize that his affection for Clara was outgrowing the big-brother stage. Besides, she was away winning triumphs in Berlin and Paris while he sat at home with a lame hand and a cupboard full of compositions nobody wanted. Looking back upon this time, he sums it up in a letter to Clara, dated 1838:

> . . . My individual life began at the time when I first became certain of myself and my talent, decided on art, and turned my powers into the right direction. That is, from the year 1830 onwards. You were then a funny little girl with a fund of perversity and a pair of beautiful eyes; and cherries were your ideal of happiness. . . . Even then the thought sometimes glimmered in my mind that you might perhaps become my wife; but it all lay too far in the future; however this might be, I had always loved you heartily, as befitted our ages.

Then he tells of the depression he began to feel in 1833 — discouragement about his compositions, the loss of the use of his hand, the death of his favorite brother, followed shortly by the death of that dear sister-in-law, Rosalie Schumann, who, through all his boyish scrapes, "took care of me, always spoke the best of me, cheered me up, in short, thought highly of me." After Rosalie's death, he says:

> . . . during the night of October 17, there came to me all at once the most terrible thought that a man can ever have — the most terrible punishment heaven can send — that of losing reason; it overpowered me with such violence that before it all comfort, prayers were silenced as if they were mere scorn and mockery — my breath stopped at the thought, "Suppose you could no longer think!"

What a strange forecast of that tragic morning, twenty years later, when Robert Schumann went into exile at Endenich because he could "no longer think"!

In this blue mood which not even Clara's merry letters could chase away, he drifted into sentimental affairs with Henrietta and with Ernestine — Clara's friend. He was even secretly engaged to Ernestine for a year, and it was not until 1836 that he woke up and proposed to Clara. And then what a tempest arose! Clara accepted, but Papa did not. It had never occurred to Schumann that his old friend and teacher would not welcome him as a son-in-law. Instead, here he was threatening to shoot him if he set foot in his house! Frederick Wieck certainly played the rôle of obdurate father to perfection, yet there is something to be said on his side of the question. He was a joyless man who had fought his way up from poverty by sheer determination. The best years of his life had been given to Clara's training. To him she meant not only companionship and the gratification of his fatherly and professional pride, but also his main source of income. He wanted no son-in-law, and surely no young man of "wavering disposition" and "uncertain bread." True, Schumann's talents were beginning to be recognized — Wieck himself had been first to admire them — but thus far, they had earned mainly applause. Frederick Wieck knew what poverty meant; also, the bitterness of an unhappy marriage. What an exchange for Clara's brilliant career!

For three miserable years the fight for Clara waged. Friends were enlisted on both sides, and letters, ardent, despairing, bitter, flew back and forth. At one time each of the lovers thought the other faithless. Litzmann's two volumes, "Clara Schumann — An Artist's Life," based on letters and diaries, give a detailed account of these years. It is romantic reading! And all the while Schumann was pouring out his heart in music, and poor Clara, torn between two loyalties, was leading the strenuous life of a celebrated concert pianist. But even in these trying days, the old whimsical note sometimes sounds in their letters: "So the Kaiser has talked to you," writes Robert. "Didn't he ask you: 'Do you know Signor Schumann?' and you answer, 'A little, Your Majesty.' I wish I had been there — Will they make you an Imperial-Royal something or other?"

Time after time the lovers appealed to Frederick Wieck only to find him more violent in his refusals. He behaved like one demented, making scandalous accusations against them and even forbidding Clara the house. Finally the young people went to the law courts, asking permission to marry as soon as Clara came of age, and, on the eve of her twenty-first birthday, in 1840, a rather forlorn little wedding took place, secretly, in a village near Leipzig. "One part of my life is now ended," says Clara's diary; "if I have known much trouble in my youth, I have also known much joy — I will never forget that."

But this sorry lovers' tale was to have an unexpectedly happy ending. When Frederick Wieck made no reply to the announcement of the birth of his first grandchild, Clara and Robert gave up all hope of reconciliation. What, then, was their surprise and delight when, in 1843, this letter from her father came to Clara:

I continue to have a genuine and undisturbed love of art, and it follows that the work of your talented husband cannot remain unconsidered and unrecognized by me. I will prove this to you by asking you to let me know in advance when there is any chance of my hearing in public some of your husband's latest compositions, which are so much praised by connoisseurs. I would come to Leipzig on purpose.

and, later in the same year, a second letter, to Robert:

We were always united where art was concerned. I was even your teacher; my verdict decided your present course for you. There is no need for me to assure you of my sympathy with your talent and with your fine and genuine aspirations.

In Dresden there joyfully awaits you
Your Father
Fr. Wieck.

"It is very characteristic of Wieck," says Hadow, "that, after barring his front gate against the rebels, he should invite them in through the door of the music room." The invitation was cordially accepted by the Schumanns and never regretted by Wieck, who lived to see the marriage he had opposed prove an ideally happy one and Robert Schumann, one of the great composers of his period.

During the years from 1830 to 1840, Schumann's professional life was still following that divided trail of music and literature which had lured him since his boyhood.

Leipzig had become one of the important music centers of Europe. The choirs of the Thomaskirche and the Singakademie, the famous Gewandhaus Orchestra, and the Stadttheater made every type of music available. As Schumann listened to the works of the great masters, he felt an urge, not only to write music, but to write about music, and began to send critical articles to the papers. Then, in 1833, a group of friends, mostly young writers and musicians, fell into the habit of meeting every night for supper and an exchange of ideas at a restaurant called the *Kaffeebaum*. One of their pet topics was the unsatisfactory state of music criticism in Germany. "Then," writes Schumann, "one fine day an idea flashed across the minds of the young hotheads, 'Let us not be mere idle lookers-on; let us set to work to make things better so that the poetry of art shall be restored to its place of honor.'" Their plan was to start a new and better musical paper, one which would be "fresher and more varied in tone than existing papers. . . . The more brains, the more ideas, even though they clash!" And with a brave prospectus, beginning:

> The day of reciprocating compliments in criticism is dead and buried. We shall never disinter it. If we feared to attack that which is bad, we should be but poor supporters of what is good. etc., etc.

the *Neue Zeitschrift für Musik* came into being.

Schumann was editor incognito, but at the end of the first year, he openly announced himself as sole proprietor and editor, a position which he filled for ten years. The list of contributors shows many a distinguished name, including that of Richard Wagner. Editors struggling with procrastinating authors might take this tip from Schumann, who wrote to his Bremen correspondent, "If you keep us any longer in suspense about your article, I shall have to make formal announcement of your death in next week's issue."

The most important contributor to the *Neue Zeitschrift* was the editor himself. Realizing the value of having articles written from many different points of view, and lacking the required assortment of contributors, he proceeded to create them out of his own imagination. There was Florestan, the forthright, outspoken fellow, Eusebius, the dreamer, Master Raro, the conservative, who kept peace between the two; and a few who represented real people, such as Chiarina (Clara Wieck) and Felix Meritis (Mendelssohn). He called them the *Davidsbündler*, the brotherhood of young Davids, out to slay all narrow, intolerant Philistines. These imaginary people became very real to Schumann, and by playing them off against each other, he was able to present and argue every side of a question in lively fashion. Needless to say, the *Neue Zeitschrift* became a popular and important influence in German musical life. As its founders promised, it served "to draw attention to the past and the works it has produced . . . and to prepare the way for a new poetic era." Schumann was generous in appreciation of his contemporaries, and Mendelssohn, Liszt, Chopin, Berlioz, Robert Franz, and many others found recognition in his columns.

Wagner he did not like. Wagner was too excitable, too wordy, too full of himself to please the reticent Schumann. There is an amusing anecdote of a meeting of these two, after which Schumann complained that Wagner talked incessantly, while Wagner complained that Schumann sat there as if he were dumb and left him to do all the talking! When years later, in Dresden, Schumann saw the score of *Tannhäuser*, he wrote to Mendelssohn, "Wagner is a clever fellow, full of ideas and audacious beyond belief, but he really is incapable of conceiving four bars that are beautiful, or even good, and writing them down consecutively. . . ." But after hearing it, he came out with, "I must take back much of what I said about *Tannhäuser* after reading the score. On the stage, the whole impression is quite different. I was powerfully affected by many passages."

Schumann had a great talent for musical criticism. He believed it to be something far above fulsome flattery and petty faultfinding; something more revealing than mere technical analysis or the rating of one composer or composition as better or worse than another. Music may be a language, but to many listeners it is a foreign language. It is the peculiar province of the critic to act as interpreter, translating the composer's strange symbols into familiar words and ideas through which the listener may enter into the experience of the music. And if the critic is artist enough to have caught the spirit of the music, and poet enough to express it in words, then his interpretation also becomes a work of art. As Schumann himself puts it, "The highest criticism is that which itself leaves an impression similar to that aroused by the work which calls it forth. . . . Criticism has to concern itself with three things: the flower, the root, and the fruit; that is to say, poetic content, form, and technique. It has first to distinguish the poetry of the work, that which constitutes its basis and inmost soul. Next, it has to study it from the point of view of technique, analyzing the architecture of the periods and the relations between melody and harmony. Finally, it has to examine how far it is suited to the capacity of the person called upon to execute it — to the singer's voice, or the pianist's or 'cellist's hands." Such are Schumann's ideals of criticism, and he was exactly the combination of musician and poet to achieve them. Indeed, there are those who feel that Schumann, the critic and aesthetician, was a greater artist than Schumann the composer!

And what of the compositions of this eventful decade? The years 1830 to 1839 might be called Schumann's "piano period" since he wrote exclusively for that instrument.   To his early twenties belong the Variations on the Name, Abegg with its theme:

he loved to play with this sort of musical spelling; the light and graceful *Papillons* (Butterflies), Intermezzi, and Impromptus; the *Etudes Symphoniques*, the Sonata in F-Sharp Minor, and the famous *Carnaval*, all overflowing with fresh melody, vigorous rhythms, and daring harmonies — young Schumann at his best. Then followed the *Davidsbündlertänze*, eighteen character sketches of this fantastic society and their doings; the Toccata; the delightful *Fantasiestücke*, Opus 12; the Fantasie Opus 17, dedicated to Liszt and often called Schumann's masterpiece for the piano; the *Kreisleriana*, a set of pieces inspired by the wild, clever Kapellmeister Kreisler of one of Hoffmann's Tales; and the inimitable *Kinderscenen* (Scenes from Childhood). Fresh and spontaneous as ever, these works lack the amateurish touches noticeable in the earlier compositions. The willful young genius was working his way through deeper experience in life and in music to a serious artistry.

A young musician could not have found a better developing ground than Leipzig in 1835. In that year, Felix Mendelssohn had arrived as conductor of the Gewandhaus Concerts, and, like a magnet, had drawn Liszt, Chopin, Berlioz, Moscheles, Ferdinand David, Gade from Norway, young Sterndale Bennett from England, and many others to Leipzig. It was a brilliant circle whose achievements and high standards gave new impetus to the musical life of the city. As editor of the most popular musical paper, as well as being a rising young composer, Schumann became an important member of the group. He had much to give and much to get in the way of encouragement and constructive criticism.

The Schumann-Mendelssohn friendship was an oddly interesting affair. Although only one year older than Schumann, Mendelssohn had already won world recognition as a composer, performer, and conductor. He was, in every way, a finished artist, a musical authority. With his social gifts and musical prestige he seemed, indeed, "a regular God" to Robert Schumann, who in company sat shy and silent as a self-conscious boy, and in his music spoke a strange and suspicious language. From first to last, Schumann admired Mendelssohn without reservation, called him "the first musician of his age" and said that he would "always look up to him as to a lofty mountain peak." Mendelssohn, much as he esteemed Schumann, the man, could not respond with equal enthusiasm for the artist. In the first place, he had no sympathy with writers on music — poetic criticism had not existed in the great days of Bach and Beethoven, so why now? Also, with his own ease and clearness of expression, he found much that was "awkward" in Schumann's half-articulate striving to translate poetry into music. And, no doubt, his sense of propriety may have been shocked at the way in which this queer fellow, who refused to join in the small talk at a party, would publicly expose his most intimate emotions in his compositions! Schumann was a dreamer, Mendelssohn, a "practical" artist who might well have said, with him called the "Faultless Painter,"

> I can do with my pencil what I know,
> What I see, what at bottom of my heart
> I wish for, if I ever wish so deep —
> Do easily, too — when I say, perfectly,
> I do not boast, perhaps . . .
> I do what many dream of, all their lives,
> — Dream? strive to do, and agonize to do,
> And fail in doing.
> — Robert Browning, in "Andrea del Sarto"

Mendelssohn, however, showed Schumann's music generous consideration on the Gewandhaus programs, gave him many helpful suggestions, and later, appointed him professor of music at the new Leipzig Conservatory. Schumann was one of the most sincere mourners of Mendelssohn's death, yet their friendship was never based upon mutual appreciation.

In 1838, Schumann, who had long felt drawn to the city of Haydn, Mozart, Beethoven, and Schubert, ventured to Vienna to establish his *Neue Zeitschrift* in what he thought to be the place most hallowed by musical tradition. He was sadly disillusioned to find both himself and his paper "out of place." The Austrian capital was interesting, the people, genial enough, but musically, light-minded. And as for the honest, open discussion of music and musicians which was the *Zeitschrift's* reason for being, that was simply strangled by the red tape of Austrian censorship. He had, however, one compensating adventure in Vienna, and that was the unearthing of several unpublished manuscripts of his adored Schubert, among them that of the great C Major Symphony. His own composition seems to have flourished there, for, among other things, he brought back the *Blumenstücke* (Flower Pieces), the *Humoresques*, the *Nachtstücke* (Night Pieces) and the familiar *Faschingsschwank aus Wien* (Carnival Jest from Vienna) into which, by way of making a *lange Nase* at the censors, he slipped the forbidden "Marseillaise." He had gone to Vienna in September. He was back again in Leipzig in March, quite content with the musical atmosphere of Bach's city!

And now we come to the year 1840 — the year of the long delayed marriage with Clara, the famous "song year." As a pleasant prelude to this year of happiness, Schumann had received from the University of Jena an honorary doctor's degree with all the attendant compliments and superlatives. More substantial recognition had begun to come in the sale of his music, and, with his wedding only a few months away, his happiness was so great that he literally burst into song. His letters to Clara, then on tour in North Germany, are full of his song writing:

> . . . Since yesterday morning I have written nearly twenty-seven pages of music, (something new) of which I can tell you no more than that I laughed and cried for joy over it. . . . all this music nearly kills me now, it could drown me completely. Oh, Clara, what bliss to write songs! Too long I have been a stranger to it.

and again:

> . . . I have again composed so much that it sometimes seems quite uncanny. Oh, I cannot help it, I should like to sing myself to death like a nightingale. . . .

It was indeed uncanny, for in that one year he wrote more than a hundred and thirty songs — songs that expressed the heights of his heart's desire and, in the opinion of many, the heights of his power as a composer.

Schumann was now thirty years of age, yet the most interesting and significant part of his life lay behind him. The biographer who has savored the romance of that youth and early manhood cannot help wishing that his chronicle might end with that golden 1840. Granting much that is happy and beautiful in the sixteen years that lie ahead, nevertheless, their tragedy, long drawn out, makes the untimely deaths of young Mozart, Schubert, and Mendelssohn seem merely brief, sad endings to inspiring tales.

In 1841, having, as it were, sung himself out, Schumann turned his attention to orchestral music and wrote three symphonies and the Concerto in A Minor for piano and orchestra. 1842 was entirely devoted to chamber music. With characteristic abandon to the interest of the moment, he shut himself up for an intensive study of all of Beethoven's quartets. Emerging, he then wrote three quartets of his own within a month, after which came the beautiful Quintet for Piano and Strings (Opus 44). The following year (1843) was eventful in many ways. His Quintet, with Clara at the piano, was enthusiastically received. Then Berlioz came like a brisk wind blowing through Leipzig, leaving in his wake some delightfully whimsical copy for the *Zeitschrift*. In April the second Schumann baby was born, also the new Leipzig Conservatory of Music. Schumann was engaged as professor of piano and composition, a position which the solitary dreamer held none too happily or successfully. This was also the year of reconciliation with Papa Wieck and of the successful presentation of *Paradise and the Peri*, a secular oratorio "for bright and happy people." For some time, Schumann had been longing to try his skill at opera writing, but, like Mendelssohn and many another, he was hard to please when it came to a libretto. *Paradise and the Peri*, a phantasy from Moore's "Lalla Rookh," pleased him and, while not operatic material, gave a chance for some fine dramatic choral music.

But the strain of all his musical and literary labors was beginning to tell on the high-strung, oversensitive Schumann. Material cares also increased with his growing family. "We are spending more than we earn," he notes anxiously. There is none of the jauntiness of those irresponsible student days when it was rather picturesque to write home that you were down to your last candle and sustaining life on boiled potatoes! Reluctantly he had to consent to Clara's plan for a concert tour in Russia. Proud as he always was of her playing, he found it more than a little difficult to fit himself into what he called "my undignified position" as mere husband of a celebrity. But he made the best of it, and in January, 1844, went with her to Russia and came back refreshed and cheered by Clara's artistic and financial success. By midsummer, however, he was laid low with one of those serious nervous attacks to which he had been subject since boyhood. At times his memory was a blank. He could not sleep and was haunted by a strange terror of death. The doctors ordered a complete change and rest from all creative work. So, in 1845, giving up the *Neue Zeitschrift* and his classes at the Conservatory, Schumann and his family moved to Dresden, hoping that the higher altitude and less strenuous life of the smaller city would benefit the sick man.

The Schumanns spent six years in Dresden. Robert seemed to improve in health and was soon at work again. He reviewed Bach and, as a result, wrote a goodly number of fugues of his own; wrote the Symphony in C Major, which he disliked because he said it had "illness in every bar;" and completed the *Faust* music, which had been interrupted by his illness. His interest in stage music increased, and no wonder, with Kapellmeister Richard Wagner producing his revolutionary *Tannhäuser* at the Dresden Opera and reading from the manuscript of his new *Lohengrin* at the weekly meetings of the musical group. Soon Schumann took up the old search for a libretto, this time choosing one based upon the legend of St. Genevieve. But his *Genoveva*, written with such high hopes, was to prove a disappointment. There were all sorts of irritating delays in its production, and when at last it was given, it survived but three performances. It was, says Hadow, "too serious to be 'pretty,' too heavy to be dramatic." Schumann simply did not have the flair for stage writing.

After the first year or so, life in Dresden became almost as strenuous as it had been in Leipzig. Schumann formed a Choral Union, a group of sixty or more singers who sang once a week under his direction and much to his enjoyment. And, when his friend Hiller left Dresden, he also took over the conductorship of the *Liedertafel*, a men's singing society. There were occasional concert tours to Vienna, Prague, and Berlin, where Clara played and Robert conducted his own works, and the old mad pace of composition seems to have increased.

In a letter of 1848, Schumann wrote, "We are all pretty well; sometimes melancholy bats flutter around me, but music drives them away again. . . . I have been very industrious this year — indeed, it is perhaps the most fruitful year of my whole life." Fruitful it certainly was, for within a few months he had written nearly thirty works of importance, including the *Manfred* music; the Concertstück for four horns and orchestra; the *Spanisches Liederspiel; Waldscenen* (Woodland Scenes) and *Bilder aus Osten* (Pictures from the East) for piano; the *Album für die Jugend* (Album for Young People), begun as a birthday present for his little daughter, and the charming *Lieder für die Jugend* (Songs for Children).

When revolution broke out in Dresden — that same revolution which resulted in exile for the hotheaded Richard Wagner — Schumann simply withdrew to a nearby village and went on composing. Clara's diary gives an exciting account of their escape when the insurgents were going from house to house forcing citizens into their army. She and Robert ran out through a back garden gate, and by one means or another, made their way to shelter with friends who lived outside the city. But — they had left five young children with the servant in Dresden! Robert dared not return, and so, at three o'clock in the morning, the distracted Clara made her way back through barricaded streets, past men armed with scythes, to her house where she found the children calmly sleeping. She "tore them from their beds," dressed them, and, gathering together a few belongings, managed to get back to Robert.

But even after peace was restored, Dresden with its interest centered around the court failed to satisfy Schumann. He missed the artistic and intellectual life, the fine choirs, the orchestra, and the musicianly listeners of Leipzig. And so, when Hiller wrote, suggesting that Schumann succeed him as director of secular and sacred concerts at Düsseldorf, the idea was appealing. Düsseldorf was, to be sure, neither Leipzig nor Vienna. But it was a picturesque old town in the beautiful Rhineland, the people were frank and friendly, and the musical life quite flourishing. Mendelssohn had once spent several happy years there, so why not Schumann?

The early autumn of 1850 found Robert and Clara Schumann and their children settled in Düsseldorf. The settling was something of a trial and it took time and several domestic uprootings before they found a place where street noises, neighborhood pianos, Clara's practicing, and the doings of the lively Schumann youngsters would not interfere with Robert's composing. However, things promised well, the first season's concerts were successful, the orchestra and singers cordial to the new conductor, and the directors more than pleased to think that they had secured the services of the celebrated Dr. Schumann. Then, quite unaccountably, this pleasant atmosphere began to change. Tennyson might have been describing Schumann's career at Düsseldorf when he wrote:

It is the little rift within the lute
That by and by will make the music mute
And ever widening, slowly silence all.

The choir and orchestra at Düsseldorf were made up mostly of amateurs. What they had accomplished in the way of choral and particularly of orchestral music was due mainly to their enthusiasm and to the talent and *personality* of their conductors. They had been fortunate in having a succession of skillful leaders — Mendelssohn, Rietz, and Hiller. But Robert Schumann, like many another creative musician, was not a good conductor. He was never happy or effective in a crowd, and an orchestra is nothing if not a crowd — a vociferous crowd which has to be blended into one-man expressiveness. Schumann was a star-rover, a drifter, not a leader. He had neither the prompt presence of mind, the dash, the precision, nor the physical assertion to hold an orchestra together. He often failed to set the *tempo*, even to give the initial beat, and when some enterprising player set out "on his own," as they really had to do, Schumann did not even notice it! There is a pathetic story of his pleasure when the idea occurred to him of fastening his baton by a cord to his sleeve button — now it would not be forever rattling down on the floor!

Rehearsals became strained — the players held Schumann responsible for their poor performance, and he, in turn, asked what could be expected with such poor performers! The dissatisfaction grew, the assistant conductor was given charge of part of the work, and it all ended in some painful correspondence and interviews with the directors and Schumann's resignation (1853). Meanwhile, he had taken refuge in composition, working with the same old energy. But his Düsseldorf compositions, even the "Rhenish" Symphony, were the work of a broken man.

In the midst of this unpleasantness, a great happiness came to the Schumanns when, on a September morning in 1853, an awkward blond boy of twenty appeared on their doorstep with a letter from the violinist Joachim introducing "Herr Brahms from Hamburg." Not since his separation from Mendelssohn had Schumann met a musical talent so congenial to his own. In that admirable collection of essays, "Music and Musicians," Schumann had written, "It is more difficult for a man to discover his ideal within his own heart than in that of another." And now, as the clear outline of his own ideal was growing blurred, he discovered it — that bright ideal of romantic youth — in this heaven-sent Johannes Brahms. The Schumanns were delighted with the young man's playing, particularly when he played his own compositions. And they loved his happy vitality, his honest, blue-eyed view of life. They took him into their home, advised him about his music and his future, and displayed him to their friends as proudly as if he had been a dear older son. Schumann, after a ten years' silence, wrote an enthusiastic article for the *Neue Zeitschrift* announcing the advent of a genius:

There has come among us a youth who will give expression to the highest ideals of our time. His thought sweeps forward strong and impetuous as a torrent; yet the banks are bright with painted butterflies and melodious with the song of nightingales. . . . We give him greeting on his entry into the strife. If wounds await him, there are also palms and laurels; whatever the issue, he will bear himself as a valiant warrior.

A keen criticism — a true prophecy! The encouragement of Robert and Clara Schumann was a priceless gift to this young and unknown artist. In that happy month of music at Düsseldorf, little did any of them dream how soon and how splendidly Johannes Brahms was to begin to repay his debt to them!

In the winter of 1853 the Schumanns started on what turned out to be a triumphal tour of Holland. Never had Clara's playing or Robert's music been more appreciated. This success and the happy discovery of Brahms seemed to give Schumann a fresh lease on life. He came back with many plans for the new year, for, besides composition, he was again interested in writing articles for the papers and in collecting for his "Dichtergarten für Musik" (The Poet's Garden of Music), an anthology of quotations about music from the great poets and philosophers. "My Garden is getting on splendidly," he wrote to a friend. "I have found some glorious passages in Homer and Plato." But it was the last flare of a dying flame, for this was 1854 — the "terrible year."

It soon became evident that Schumann was a hopelessly sick man. The improvement at Dresden had been but temporary, and every period of apparent vitality was followed by one of deeper depression. He was haunted, first by a single musical tone, then by broken melodies which he tried to take down — wonderful melodies which he said Schubert and Mendelssohn were bringing him from beyond the grave — and he heard warning voices that he could not quite make clear. It was a terrible time. Fearful of what he might do in a moment of confusion, he gathered together his clothes and manuscripts and begged to be taken to an asylum. Then, one rainy February morning, when little Marie was sitting with him — they never left him alone now — he went quietly into his bedroom and did not come back. An hour later, a tragic little procession made its way through excited Carnival crowds to the house in the Bilkerstrasse, bringing home the wreck of Robert Schumann. He had slipped out of the house and thrown himself into the Rhine, from which some fisherman rescued him.

In a private hospital at Endenich he lived for two nightmare years in a haze of half-memory — a gentle, clear-eyed child. Clara, poor thing, bravely carried on, giving concerts in England and elsewhere, for there were seven Schumann children — seven futures in her hands. She never saw Robert again until the very end.

During all that tragic time, it was young Brahms who visited the sick man, cheered the children in their mother's absence, and upheld Clara with the strength of his valiant, loving heart. It was Brahms and Joachim who led the way on that July evening, 1856, when a little group of friends walked with the body of Schumann to the Old Cemetery by the *Sternentor* in Bonn. And it was Brahms who, forty years later, stood with the Schumann children while Clara was laid beside Robert.

Thinking of Schumann's life, with its strangely mingled pattern of strength and weakness, clear sunshine and darkest shadow; and of how his music seems the audible token of his love of friends, of children, of Clara — of all that to him was true and beautiful, one is reminded of those lines from "Locksley Hall":

Love took up the harp of Life, and smote on all the chords with might;
Smote the chord of Self, that, trembling, passed in Music out of sight.

"Your music is so entirely your own," wrote young Clara Wieck to Robert Schumann in 1838, and in these few unstudied words characterized Schumann the Artist. Schumann's music *is* entirely and peculiarly his own. It comes from the very depths of his individuality and expresses not only what he feels but also what he thinks about his feelings. It is very personal music, yet, as you listen, his dreams become your dreams, his music, entirely *your* own!

First and last, Schumann's music impresses you with its meaning. It seems to be something more than music, "a concord of sweet sounds," as the old masters made it. There are the familiar rhythms, melodies, and harmonies woven together into patterns of beautiful sound, but, strangely enough, those patterns have ceased to be conventional designs and have become pictures! What is it that has filled this music with images of sights and sounds and peopled it with figures of the visible world? What has it that the perfect music of Mozart lacked? Why, that touch of *imagination* which is the particular property of the poet.

Schumann was born a poet. His love of music made him a poet-musician. Luckily, he was born in a wonderful time for poets — the early Nineteenth Century. It was a time when the old tales of romance and knightly adventure were being revived in all their glamour; when the new ideals of social and political freedom were still morning-fresh and thrilling with promise; when life itself seemed very full of poetry. Literature and art, faithful reflectors of the times, responded with what is known as the *Romantic Movement*. Composers, too, no longer content to work with impersonal tones and tone patterns, turned to literature and life for their inspiration, and created *Romantic* music. It was a type of music which demanded broad general culture, lively imagination, and quick human sympathy, as well as good musicianship. And because Schumann was better read and more intellectual than the impulsive Schubert, more emotional than the conservative Mendelssohn, more balanced than the erratic Berlioz, more manly and wholesome than the exotic Chopin, and, withal, an excellent, Bach-bred musician, Schumann is the most representative of *Romantic* composers.

Schumann's music, although born of poetic ideas, is never bound by them. He did not mean to tell a definite story, but rather to start his listeners to romancing for themselves. "People err," he said, "if they think that a composer puts pen to paper with the predetermination of expressing or depicting some particular fact. Yet we must not estimate outward influences and impressions too lightly. . . . The more elements congenially related to music which the tone-picture contains, the more poetic and plastic will be the expression of the composition. . . ." There is no denying that Schumann hoped to convey his poetic ideas to his listeners — to show them *Butterflies* and *Woodland Scenes*, to introduce them to the characters of *Carnaval* — and in that hope, he gave his pieces fanciful titles, mottoes, and quotations. (He was the first composer to do this.) But his titles do not limit the freedom either of the music or of the listener's imaginings. One could hardly supply the titles from hearing the pieces, yet, knowing them beforehand, one can better appreciate Schumann's skillful tone picturing. And there is something quite significant in the fact that Schumann chose his titles *after* the pieces were written, as if the music had revealed itself to its creator and told him what it was!

If Schumann's music was "entirely his own," so, too, were his ways of working. He is the only composer on record who has taken up each form of music successively, mastered it, said what he had to say in it, and then passed on to the next. His greatest piano works were written before 1840, then came the wonderful song year, then a year of symphony writing, followed by one of chamber music, then, *Paradise and the Peri*, marking his entrance into the field of dramatic music. Even his convalescence in Dresden was turned into a contrapuntal spree! All of which goes to prove that, dreamer though he was, Schumann was also a logical thinker with unusual gifts of concentration and thoroughness.

His techniques were equally original, for, excepting the comparatively few piano lessons with Wieck and that brief and stormy study of composition with Dorn, Schumann had found his own musical way with the works of Bach and Beethoven as guidebooks. To him, melody and harmony were "the Queen and King of the chessboard." And, he whimsically continues, "The Queen (melody) has the most power, but the King (harmony) turns the scale." Rhythm he fails to include among the important pieces of the Royal game. But judging from his music, which is conspicuous for its syncopations, contrasted accents, and determination to escape being shut in by bar lines, rhythm was the Knight, riding a fresh and frisky horse!

Schumann's melodies are characteristically brief, almost telegraphic. Indeed, it is one of his triumphs that he can say so much in so few tones. His themes do not flow into and out of each other as do those of Beethoven. They march along, one after the other, in a gay procession. But though fragmentary and somewhat disconnected, they have an almost childlike beauty and appeal, and they are unforgettable.

Harmony was Schumann's strong point — the King that "turns the scale." He loved a good earful of sound, and in his hours of improvising at the piano used to keep the pedal down until he had a great clash of antagonistic tones going. In fact, says Sir Hubert Parry, "he had little objection to hearing all the notes of the scale sounding at once!" On these keyboard ramblings he discovered many audacious combinations of tones which he transferred to his pieces with highly original results. Dissonance, cleverly used, is always effective in imaginative music. It marks the height of the storm, the moment of shipwreck, plays the ogre of the fairy tale, and, best of all, the policeman who keeps the listener from snoozing on any park bench of consonance.

Schumann was a great student of counterpoint, as might be expected of one who had chosen Bach as his master. But it is no imitation Bach counterpoint that we find in his music. Here again he shows his originality by using this clever, formal device for purely expressive purposes. His contrapuntal melodies never seem to argue with each other, nor even to discuss serious subjects, but rather to be engaged in intimate, almost affectionate small talk. If one dared speak lightly of so ancient an institution, one might say that Schumann wrote conversational counterpoint!

To musical form, the sonata in particular, Schumann was curiously indifferent. He knew all the rules of theme relationship and key distribution, but he had little need of them in his short lyric pieces. And when he did use them — and correctly — in his symphonies, quartets, and overtures, it was quite evident, as Hadow points out, that "there is much difference between *obeying* rules and *mastering* them." But what he lacked in form, he made up in style. Here his gift of concentration saved him. He tried to make every note say something and to do away with all cluttering *arpeggios* and meaningless scale passages, and thus avoided confusion. He practiced what he once preached to a young musician, "the chief thing is that the composer should *keep clear the ear of his mind!*"

Although Schumann wrote every type of music, he was not equally successful in each. He is least effective in his dramatic music, mainly because his forte was description and not action. Nor is he at his best in writing for the orchestra. Schumann's gift was for brilliant, short flights, and when he undertook that long and devious musical journey, the symphony, he found some parts of it rough going. This is particularly true of his first movements in the Development sections which call for expansion, not concentration. Here he labors, and, by his own statement, only "Talent labors, genius creates." His *Adagio* and *Scherzo* movements, however, are rarely beautiful, for here he is on familiar ground — short lyric forms in song and dance mood.

Added to his difficulties in handling the larger forms was a lack of instinct for instrumentation. His scoring is often thick and heavy, and at times he seems to be orchestrally color blind. The players must have felt his failure to bring out the special beauties of their instruments and shown their dissatisfaction, for, in writing to his publisher about one of his orchestral works, Schumann sarcastically remarks, "I am glad to get it performed by the gentlemen of the orchestra who taste a new composition as if it were a sour apple." But in spite of their flaws, there are so many compensating beauty spots in Schumann's four published symphonies that no less an authority than Dr. Spitta rates them "nearest of all to the 'Immortal Nine' of Beethoven."

It is, however, in the piano pieces and the romantic songs that we find Schumann in all the morning glory of his genius. The piano was his instrument — the friend to whom he had confided the dreams and longings of boyhood, the voice which had spoken for him in all the turbulent emotions of a shy and silent young manhood. It was so much a part of him that it seemed to register naturally his every mood and to reflect for him the whole world. This no doubt accounts for the amazing variety of Schumann's piano music. There is the "child" music, the *Kinderscenen*, about children, the *Album für die Jugend*, for children, music which has never been equaled in its poetic understanding of child nature. There is music for and about young people — *Papillons*, *Carnaval*, the *Davidsbündlertänze*, as gay and carefree as youth itself. And there is music for students, amateurs, and *virtuosi*, although the latter is not of the usual "show off" type. Schumann intensely disliked all forms of display, and once gave a fellow composer this excellent advice: "Every now and again, I find the pianist too much in evidence in your music; if you aim at anything beyond mere ephemeral effect, you must pitch him overboard." The happy freedom which Schumann felt at the piano gave his music not only variety of mood but also the quality of improvisation, as if he had simply poured out his heart with no thought of audience, pen, or paper.

Song writing was a real gift to Schumann. As a boy playing accompaniments for pretty Frau Carus, he had learned to love Schubert's songs, but beyond that, he had never been particularly interested in vocal music or given it any study. Then, in 1840, the year of his long-delayed marriage with Clara, he experienced another of those emotional "overflowings," this time in song. Song writing became his chief delight. "I cannot help it," he wrote to Clara, "and should like to sing myself to death like a nightingale." In that wonderful "song year" he wrote more than a hundred and thirty songs, some of the most beautiful songs in all the literature of music.

Schumann's songs have the same fresh melodies, the same rich harmonies and vigorous rhythms that mark his piano pieces. And they have another even more distinguishing characteristic — an almost perfect blending of music and poetry. Here Schumann, the literary man, had the advantage over the less discriminating Schubert, who simply seized upon the inspiration of a poem and made off with it, unmindful of such minor details as the fitness of single words and phrases. In his wonderful song, "Der Wanderer," for example, Schubert's music reaches its dramatic climax just where the hero's hat blows off! But does he care? Not in the least. He lets it blow, and so effectively that it seems pedantic, ungracious of us to smile at the inconsistency. Schumann, on the other hand, who loved words as only a poet can, savored every shade of a verse's meaning and interpreted it in tone.

Schubert, with his rippling brooks, his galloping horse, and mournful hurdy-gurdy, had led the way in an altogether new type of suggestive accompaniment. Now Schumann, the pianist-composer, goes still further and makes the accompaniments an integral part of the song. Sometimes voice and piano seem to be singing a duet, as in the exquisite little song, "The Nut Tree" (Der Nussbaum) where, above softly rustling *arpeggios*, the voice sings:

and the piano answers:

Schumann also wrote poetic little preludes and postludes as if to hold the song within an atmosphere all its own. One feels this in a song like "Mondnacht" (Moon Night, often translated, Moonlight). At the end of each of the first two stanzas, the voice pauses and the piano dreams on. There is no full cadence until the end where the poet's soul, filled with the magic of moonlight, spread its wings and,

> Flew through the silent country
> As if 'twere flying home.

And then, as if to spare us too rude an awakening, Schumann lets the lovely picture fade as gently as it came.

The use of the half cadence at the end of the earlier stanzas, as in "Moon Night," to give the effect of an unbroken flow of song is one of Schumann's most original touches.

And, in "In Wondrous, Lovely Month of May" (Im wunderschönen Monat Mai), the composer adds to the poet's suggestion of the unsatisfied longing of springtime by ending the song on an imperfect — unfinished — cadence.

With Schumann's songs, as with the piano pieces, it is difficult to make a selection. There is the calm and lovely "Lotus Flower" (Lotusblume), the passionate "Dedication" (Widmung), and "Spring Night" (Frühlingsnacht), the superb "I Chide Thee Not" (Ich grolle nicht), inspired love songs that have never been surpassed. There is "The Two Grenadiers" (Die beiden Grenadiere), a fine rousing song that bursts into the "Marseillaise." Robert Schumann was but a tiny child when Napoleon's armies with flags and music and gay gold braid marched through Zwickau on the way to Russia and then, months later, came straggling back, famished, frozen survivors of defeat. Those dramatic scenes must have made some impression on a sensitive little mind, enough to have given "The Two Grenadiers" convincing reality and to have made the "Marseillaise" the most thrilling tune in the world for Robert Schumann. And one cannot leave Schumann's songs without mentioning "Marienwürmchen," a dear little song about a ladybug, a real song of childhood.

Summing it all up, then, we might say that the distinguishing characteristics of Schumann's music are: Poetic content — that is, the ideas and imagination that lie behind it; variety and intimacy of mood; and a picturesqueness rather than formality of musical expression. In other words, Bach, Haydn, and Mozart were musicians, while Schumann was, in the fullest sense of the term, a tone-poet.

Fantasiestücke

Of Schumann's groups of piano pieces, none is more familiar or more delightfully Schumannesque than the *Fantasiestücke* (Fantasy Pieces), Opus 12. They were written in 1837 at the height of his piano period and, incidentally, of his love affair with Clara. Writing to a friend, he says, "I am often overflowing just now, and do not know where to stop." The eight *Fantasiestücke* are part of the overflowing.

Musically, they are excellent examples of Schumann's style of writing in simple song form, concisely, and with a light lyric melody above a firmly knit foundation. And they are written with such ease and perfection that Schumann always spoke of them with entire satisfaction. Poetically, they are also Schumann at his best — mood pictures, each with a title to start the listener's imagination.

Des Abends

The first piece is *Des Abends* (In the Evening):

in which the softly sinking melody, the hazy effect of a right hand playing triple time against a left hand's duple, seem to weave a spell of twilight about the music and the listener.

Aufschwung

In sharp contrast comes *Aufschwung* (Soaring):

an impetuous up-rushing piece with its melody placed in the very middle of the harmony — a favorite Schumann trick. It emerges for a moment in the contrasting section:

as if a calming hand were trying to stay the flight. But it is only for a moment — then away again, soaring on to a triumphant ending.

Warum?

And now a tiny piece, a scant page, a mere forty-two measures of music, as brief in utterance but as long in import as the challenging word of its title — *Warum?* (Why?). It is the ancient question which Man has asked of life since his beginning. Now Schumann, a true questioning Romanticist, asks it in tones — a questioning phrase over a restless, syncopated bass:

He makes no effort to find an answer — who ever has found an answer? Instead, by clever polyphonic imitation, he makes other voices echo the question. The crowd increases as an alto voice comes in with a minor version:

Then the first voice is heard again. Three times it puts the question, once, as in the beginning, then repeats it against a more doubtful sounding harmony, and then with the first tone lengthened:

an insistent, unsatisfied "Why?"

Rarely does an artist express such intensity of meaning and feeling in so small a space. I know of but one other instance — Albrecht Dürer's *Betende Hände* (Praying Hands), a little detail drawing of two folded, upward-pointing hands which seem to express the very essence of Man's supplication as Schumann's *Warum?* expresses his "everlasting why."

Grillen

With flashing change of mood, *Grillen* (Whims) seems to spring from the keyboard:

It is marked, *Mit Humor* (With Humor) — Schumann, first to title his pieces, was also first to suggest the manner of interpretation. The fun seems to come from the clowning rhythms, particularly in the middle part where the accent falls perversely and persistently on weak beats while the meter plays a dodging game through triple and duple beat, syncopation, and what not — *Whims* indeed!

In der Nacht

Many musicians consider *In der Nacht* (In the Night) the most poetic of all Schumann's short pieces, and the composer himself, in a letter to Clara (1838), admits that it is his favorite, too. In that same letter, he gives this interesting bit of information about *In der Nacht:*

> No sooner had I composed it than I was enchanted to find that my music contained in it the story of Hero and Leander. As I played it, the incidents rose up before my eyes: Leander's plunge into the waters of the Hellespont, Hero's call, his response, he gains the shore, and then the *cantilena* that I have thrown round their embrace. At last the agony of parting, and the darkness of the night that covers everything.

The music is marked *Mit Leidenschaft* (with passion).   Here again, we have the typical fragmentary Schumann melody:

and beneath it that vigorous, running accompaniment.

It is not difficult to follow Schumann's Hero and Leander fancy, now that he has suggested it.   One can hear quite plainly that passionate cry in the night:

the rushing water, the voices calling, "the *cantilena* that I have thrown around their embrace":

and in those last stormy measures moving down, down, down — "the darkness of the night that covers everything."

Schumann was a happy lover when he wrote this music, and perhaps it is a bit morbid to think ahead to those terrible nights that were to come — nights of fearful visions, comforted by angel voices singing melodies which a broken man tried pitifully to record.   And yet this, too, seems to surge and sigh through the music of *In der Nacht*.

Fabel

Fabel (Fable) is well named.   It begins with an obvious "Once upon a time":

Then things begin to happen:

and keep right on happening to the end, where it sounds suspiciously like the pointing of a moral!

Traumes Wirren

Traumes Wirren (Dream Fancies) is a fairy piece, so swift and airy that it is impossible to catch even an idea of it from a quotation:

It is almost impossible to play it unless one has flying fingers like those of young Clara Wieck, who first played and loved it.

Ende vom Lied

Schumann brings the *Fantasiestücke* to a joyous conclusion with a robust piece which he calls *Ende vom Lied* (End of the Song):

It is marked *Mit gutem Humor* and so it is, good humored as a German folk song.

It is interesting to know that Schumann considered some of the *Fantasiestücke* unsuitable for public performance — too long or too intimate. Pianists and audiences have not agreed with him. But one does agree with this shrewd criticism of the work, taken from one of his letters to a friend: "Some music is difficult to read and strange, like many a composer's handwriting; but once you have grasped its meaning, you wonder how any other could have suggested itself."

As he wrote his piano pieces, Schumann spoke of "overflowing" and of not knowing where to stop. So one feels, trying to make a selection from them. How can we pass by the *Carnaval*, the *Kinderscenen*, the *Novelletten*, the *Nachtstücke*, the delightful *Faschingsschwank*, and so many others? And, oh, we really can't pass that weird and wonderful little piece from *Waldscenen, Vogel als Prophet* (Prophet-bird)! In his opera *Siegfried*, Wagner plays with this same intriguing superstition, that many a mysterious secret would be revealed if only Man could learn the language of the birds. Wagner's bird song is beautiful, although it does seem to come from a painted canvas forest. A boy might learn to play it on his reed pipe — might even learn its meaning. But Schumann's music, wild and sweet as the call of a thrush at twilight:

is the song of a spirit world which Man may feel but never know.

Overture — Manfred

One of the oldest legends in the world, based upon one of the oldest situations in the world, is that of the man who tried to "read the riddle of the painful earth." In the Middle Ages, this man who refused to accept the solace of unthinking faith and dared to pry into the forbidden mysteries was represented as having bargained with the Devil, who allowed him to have hidden knowledge, the power of magic, and human love, and then at a stated time claimed him, body and soul.

In 1604, Marlowe put the legend into dramatic form in his *The Tragical History of Doctor Faustus*. Later, in that wave of spiritual change and questioning which swept over Europe — Germany in particular — at the end of the eighteenth century, the old legend was revived. Philosophers, trying to find a clue to the meaning of life, recognized themselves in this medieval hero who had sought knowledge at any price. The likeness intrigued them, and a perfect epidemic of Faust stories, plays, and poems broke out — some thirty different ones in Germany alone. The greatest of these was Goethe's immortal drama. Nor could such a subject fail to attract the tone poets. There is any amount of Faust music. Beethoven at one time considered writing some; Liszt produced a "Faust" Symphony, and young Wagner began one; Berlioz wrote his *Damnation of Faust* and Gounod, his famous opera *Faust;* and in our own day, Busoni took a turn at it in his opera *Doktor Faust*.

It was inevitable that Faust should appeal to the poet-composer, Schumann. One of his finest works is the *Scenes from Goethe's Faust*, and, as if he could not part with the hero, he portrays him again in the *Manfred* music. For Byron's dramatic poem, *Manfred*, is but another version of the old Faust legend, inspired, no doubt, by Goethe's drama. After reading *Manfred*, Goethe remarked, "This singularly intellectual poet has taken my *Faust* and extracted from it the strangest nourishment for his hypochondriac humor." Certain it is that he extracted from it all the despair, for *Manfred* is as somber as a stormy twilight.

Goethe's *Faust* begins grandly in Heaven with a diverting dialogue between The Almighty and Mephistopheles, who claims that Man is so vile and stupid that he has "scarce the heart to plague the wretched creature." The Almighty thinks better of his creation, and the two lay a wager as to whether or not Mephistopheles can get possession of Man's soul. Then the tale comes down to earth, to the man chosen for the test. It is old Doctor Faust who bargains shrewdly with the Devil, has his youth restored, enjoys a very earthly love affair with a charming young girl, and, in the very nick of time, redeems his soul from the Devil by love and good works. While it is full of serious significance and noble lines, Goethe's *Faust* has its lighter, brighter moments. The love scenes with the fair Marguerite are humanly appealing, and the Devil himself is most beguiling.

In "Manfred," however, there is not one bright moment, not one human touch. The lovely heroine is replaced by a pale phantom of Astarte, the ancient Phoenician Goddess of Love; and the bright Mephistopheles, with his scarlet cloak and feathered cap, gives way to a "dusk and awful figure . . . his face wrapt in a mantle." The scene is laid in the high Alps, isolated between heaven and earth. It is midnight, and, beside a guttering lamp, Manfred sits alone with his remorse and bitter thoughts. He has learned that:

> Sorrow is knowledge: they who know the most
> Must mourn the deepest o'er the fatal truth,
> The Tree of Knowledge is not that of Life.

In his anguish, he uses the magic power that has been given him to summon the spirits. They appear — Spirits of Air, Earth, Water, Fire, Storm, Darkness, and Manfred's guiding star, a wild comet — awaiting his command. He then bids them bring the one thing he desires, forgetfulness, but that is the one gift beyond their power.

Despairing, Manfred wanders out upon the Jungfrau, and as he watches the day break over the mountain peaks, he exclaims:

> How beautiful is all this visible world!
> How glorious in its action and itself!
> But we, who name ourselves its sovereigns, we,
> Half dust, half deity, alike unfit
> To sink or soar, with our mixed essence make
> A conflict of its elements, and breathe
> The breath of degradation and of pride,
> Contending with low wants and lofty will,
> Till our mortality predominates,
> And men are — what they name not to themselves,
> And trust not to each other.

He determines to spring from the cliff and find forgetfulness in the abyss below. But, as he is about to act, a passing chamois hunter seizes him, draws him to safety, and takes him to his cottage. As they talk together, the hunter cannot understand this strange man who mourns that he has lived so long and must continue to live:

> . . . ages — ages —
> Space and eternity — and consciousness,
> With the fierce thirst of death — and still unslaked!

Manfred leaves the hunter's cottage and passes on into a valley with a tumbling waterfall. Taking some of the water in his hand, he tosses it into the air and calls up the Witch of the Alps. He tells her how all his life he has been lonely and thirsting for knowledge and how, when knowledge was given to him and human love, he sinned and destroyed it. He begs again for forgetfulness, but in vain. As the Witch vanishes, Manfred begins his famous soliloquy.

> We are the fools of time and terror: Days
> Steal on us, and steal from us; yet we live,
> Loathing our life, and dreading still to die.

Goethe said of these lines, "Hamlet's soliloquy appears improved upon here" — praise indeed!

In his wandering, Manfred enters the cavernous hall of Arimanes, Prince of Earth and Air. The Spirits, Destinies, and Fate surround his throne, which is a globe of fire. Manfred is commanded to bow down, but, rash mortal that he is, he refuses to bow before any but the "overruling Infinite." His very boldness convinces the Spirits that he is no ordinary mortal, and when he asks a boon, it is granted. He asks them to summon Astarte, Goddess of that love which he has betrayed, that she may forgive or condemn him. The spirit of Astarte appears and tells him that tomorrow will end his earthly ills. But when he pleads that she will speak the one word, *forgiven*, the phantom only says, "Farewell," and fades away.

The last act takes place in the castle where, with his anxious serving man, Manfred awaits the morrow that shall end his ills. An old abbot comes to plead that this son of a noble house give up the "converse with the things which are forbidden to the search of man" and make his peace. Manfred replies that it is now too late. The abbot goes sadly away, but returns to fight for the soul of this doomed man. He finds, to his horror, that "dusk and awful figure" which has come to summon Manfred to his reckoning. But, with a last burst of courage, Manfred defies the summoning spirit, crying:

> . . . I know my hour has come but not
> To render up my soul to such as thee;
> Away! I'll die as I have lived — alone!

The spirit reminds him of his many sins which cannot go unpunished, to which Manfred answers:

> What I have done is done; I bear within
> A torture which could nothing gain from thine:
> The mind which is immortal makes itself
> Requital for its good or evil thoughts.

And, as the world dims before his dying eyes, he seizes the abbot's hand, saying:

> Old Man! 'tis not so difficult to die.

and the poem ends with the abbot's speech:

> He's gone — his soul hath ta'en its earthless flight.
> Whither? I dread to think — but he is gone.

It is interesting to know that while Byron wrote *Manfred* as a dramatic poem, not a play, he, nevertheless, wanted music for it. Both Schumann and Tchaikovsky fulfilled his wish. Schumann arranged the poem for stage presentation and wrote sixteen pieces of incidental music for it — the overture, some solos and choruses, and an *entr'acte*. But *Manfred*, from the very mystical treatment of the subject, was not altogether successful on the stage and has rarely been given as a play. The Overture, however, which is considered Schumann's finest orchestral work, has become a favorite concert piece.

Three swift chords (syncopated against the conductor's baton, since there has been no audible beat to give the feeling of syncopation), then a long, slow introduction which seems to grope its way through mournful chromatics, now and then breaking into sudden, sharp cries in the violins. The stage is set for tragedy and conflict, not of armies with banners flying and bugles blowing, but the deadly silent struggle of a man fighting for his own soul. A trumpet call heralds the hero:

the stormy Manfred. Everything about this theme — the somber minor tonality, the constant, struggling syncopation, the restless accompaniment — suggests the agitation, the desperation of this man whose

> . . . solitude is solitude no more,
> But peopled with the furies.

In contrast to the trumpet heralding of the Manfred theme, flutes and violins announce the second, the Astarte theme, with an anguished cry:

This second theme seems to have three quite definite parts which Walter Spalding interestingly interprets as first, the haunting vision of Astarte, symbol of Manfred's lost love:

then "a note of impassioned protest":

perhaps his cry of, "Astarte! My beloved! Speak to me!" and last, "a love message of tender consolation":

Schumann's two themes are as dramatic as Beethoven's *Coriolanus* themes and as cleverly contrasted — which brings us to a word from the workshop. *Manfred* is not only Schumann's finest orchestral work, but one of his finest examples of structure. It is cast in sonata, or first-movement, form which calls for key contrast, usually major against relative minor, in the two main themes. But here, both of Schumann's characters, the tragic Manfred and the haunting Astarte, demand minor coloring. So he gets around the difficulty by contrasting minor against minor, and still keeps a proper relationship by putting the second theme in the key of F-sharp minor which, while not harmonically related to the E-flat minor of the first theme, is a very near neighbor through the common tone G♭-F♯. Beethoven himself could not have done better!

But Beethoven might have done better with the Development section which follows, for here Schumann seems to have difficulty in making his musical and dramatic ends meet. It really takes a Richard Strauss to tell a story vividly and yet not drop a single stitch in the musical pattern. However, slightly labored and less inspired though this middle section may seem, as it sweeps into the Recapitulation, bringing back the Manfred and Astarte themes, who would quibble? It is grand music!

The Coda is fifty-one measures of sheer inspiration. Woodwinds and brasses play a funeral dirge for a hero:

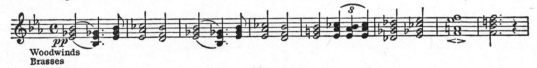

a gorgeously solemn tune worthy of one who has fought a good fight. Then comes the strangest dialogue between trumpets, playing the dirge, and woodwinds and violins, singing fragments of the Astarte theme:

as if the lovely vision were still visible to his dimming eyes.

Weaker:

and more broken:

grows the music.   Then a last flare of that impetuous spirit: "Old man! 'tis not so difficult to die."

and — "He's gone. . . .   Whither?"

As with *Coriolanus*, *Till Eulenspiegel*, and all such works, knowing the poem gives meaning to the music.   And, we might add, knowing Schumann gives double meaning to the *Manfred* Overture.   It is almost a self-portrait, for Schumann, too, saw visions and dreamed dreams, and through bitter years fought back the shadow that in the end was to turn his light into darkness.   He might well have said with Manfred:

> . . . in my heart
> There is a vigil, and these eyes but close
> To look within . . .

FRÉDÉRIC CHOPIN

Zelazowa Wola — 1810
Paris   — 1849

The end of the eighteenth century marked one of the many tragic periods in the history of Poland.   Since 1795 that unhappy country had been dismembered by her powerful neighbors, Austria, Germany, and Russia.   Then, in 1807, Napoleon, reconstructing the map of Europe, had created the Duchy of Warsaw.   Again there was a Poland!   It was to last only until his fall, eight years later, but long enough to fan the flame of Polish patriotism to a white heat and to create a lasting hero worship for France.

During these troubled times, a young Frenchman, Nicolas Chopin, had come up from Nancy in Lorraine to seek his fortune in Warsaw.   He found mostly misfortune, for war and political turmoil drove him from business to soldiering and finally landed him in the little village of Zelazowa Wola as tutor in the household of a Polish nobleman.   There he met and married a Polish girl of "poor but noble family," and there, on the twenty-second of February, 1810, his famous son and third child, Frédéric, was born.   It is said that Chopin made his entrance into the world to music, for at the very moment of his birth, a party of village musicians, on their way to a wedding, had stopped in front of the house to play a serenade for his mother.

Later in that same year, the father was made professor of French at the High School in Warsaw, and the Chopins moved to the city. As the family increased, there were three little daughters, Nicolas Chopin found it necessary to increase his income and so turned his home into a small boarding school for the sons of rich men. This, then, was Chopin's background — a refined and sheltered home in a city animated by a passionate patriotism and an almost hysterical hope for the future of Poland.

Frédéric was a gentle child, delicate as a little girl and devoted to his mother and to his music. He was by no means a prodigy, or treated as one, but just a simple, modest child with a fine natural talent. He began to play the piano at a very early age and made his first public appearance on his eighth birthday, playing at a benefit concert for an aged poet. Frédéric was thrilled at the thought of going out in the evening, staying up so late, and wearing his new velvet coat and broad English turn-over collar! When he came home that night and his mother, who had been unable to attend the concert, asked what the audience had liked best, the small artist replied proudly, "Oh, Mama, my collar!"

During his boyhood, Chopin had several music teachers whose chief virtue seems to have been that they let him alone, giving him the fundamentals of music and then letting him use them in his own way. He went to school and to college, where he worked well but not brilliantly. And, strangely enough, both at home and at school, Frédéric Chopin was known and loved for his good humor and clever mimicry. The rôle of clown seems curiously inconsistent with the melancholy Chopin the world was to know. What a thousand pities that ill health and the morbid sentimentality of Paris in the eighteen thirties should have smothered this gift of gaiety!

The year 1825 was the real starting point of Chopin's musical career, for it was then that he first won public recognition by his playing — not his collar — and composed his first music. These first compositions were a rondo, the work of a conscientious pupil, a polonaise, and two mazurkas, first of the long line that was to make him Poland's greatest composer. At seventeen, he was allowed to leave school and give all his time to his music. With a table and an old piano, he fitted up a studio in a little room under the roof and went seriously to work.

At nineteen, Chopin was famous in Warsaw, where he had taken part in many concerts, now playing his own works. He had made a brief trip to Berlin, where the opera and the musical life had greatly impressed him. And he had been much petted and entertained by Polish aristocracy, in whose palaces and country estates the fastidious young man formed a lasting taste for luxurious living. But local fame was no longer enough for him. He felt, and rightly, that he should have the judgment of a larger city. So in the summer of 1829, with three young friends, some letters of introduction, and the small sum of money his father could spare, Chopin set out hopefully for Vienna. He gave several concerts in Vienna and was received with enthusiasm, if with the slight reservation that his playing, though quite delightful and original, was a trifle light and lacking in volume. Writing to the family in Warsaw, Chopin says that the public, accustomed to the "big drums" of the virtuosi and to the "pigeon catching" of certain gesticulating pianists, finds his playing scarcely showy enough. "But," he says, "I should rather that they would say that I played too softly than too brutally"; and adds, "It is my way of playing. I know that it greatly pleases the artists and the ladies." [1] Pleasing the ladies was always one of the things Chopin did best! From Vienna, he went to Prague, then to Dresden, returning to Warsaw in the early autumn.

But happy as he was to be at home again, the praise of Vienna had given him an appetite for travel. Besides, he was restlessly in love with a young singer, still in training at the Conservatory. In a letter to his friend and confidant, Titus, he says, "I have, perhaps to my sorrow, found my ideal." In those two words, *sorrow* and *ideal*, taken with their romantic nineteenth-century meaning, Chopin gives the key to his whole emotional life. He was fated to be forever pursuing an ideal which brought him only sorrow! What is so characteristic of both Chopin and his period and so utterly incomprehensible to a later "go-getting" generation is the fact that he languished in secret. For, as he goes on to tell Titus, "For six months now I have dreamed of her each night, and I have never spoken to her." And although Frédéric and his Constance finally did meet, they seem to have seen very little of each other except at public concerts, and she may not even have known what devastation her blue eyes had wrought!

Chopin wanted to go to Italy, stopping at Vienna on the way. But he was so full of sighs and indecisions that it was a whole year before he could tear himself away from Warsaw. "I haven't courage enough to name a day for leaving," he wrote his friend; "I have a presentiment that if I leave Warsaw, I shall never see my home again" — and a true presentiment it proved. Then, coming out of church one day, he saw Constance. "My eyes caught her glance. I tore off into the street, and it took a quarter of an hour to pull myself together. Sometimes I am so mad it is terrifying. But a week from Saturday I shall leave, come what may. I shall stuff my music into my valise, her ribbon into my soul, my soul under my arm, and, *en avant*, to the *diligence!*" On the eleventh of October he gave a last concert at which Constance sang, dressed in white, with roses in her hair. And on the first of November he left Warsaw. His friends gave a farewell banquet at which a cantata, written in his honor, was sung. Then they presented the traveler with a silver cup filled with the earth of Poland and sent him, sobbing, on his way.

At Kalisz he was joined by his friend Titus, and the two young men arrived in Vienna in the best of spirits. But how different it all was from the Vienna of the first visit! Some of Chopin's friends had left the city; no one seemed particularly eager to arrange concerts for him; and, as a last touch, came the news that an uprising against Russia had broken out in Poland. Titus straightway outfitted himself and rushed off to join in the fighting. Chopin hesitated, then hired a chaise and galloped after his friend, only to turn back when he realized that his frail body would be useless except as a target for Russian bullets. His father wrote begging him not to give up his career for nothing. So, reluctantly, he stayed on in Vienna, pouring out his patri-

---

[1] We are indebted to Henry Holt and Company, Inc., publishers, for this quotation from "Polonaise; The Life of Chopin," by Guy de Pourtalès, translated by Charles Bayly, Jr. (Copyright, 1927.), and for excerpts on pages 72–79.

otism in fiery polonaises. It was a lonely, dreary winter. Mail from Poland was slow and irregular, and Chopin fretted himself sick imagining his family and friends dying horrible deaths in Warsaw. Then, too, he was keenly sensitive to the Austrian hatred of his country, sometimes expressed in such remarks as this, overheard in a restaurant, "God surely made one mistake when he created Poles!" But, in spite of it all, Chopin had his music, he was young and a very agreeable fellow, and, as spring opened, he went to more and more concerts and parties, made new friends, and had a much better time than he liked to admit. He realized, however, that professionally there was little for him in Vienna, and when summer came, decided to leave — not for Italy, as he had first planned, for war had broken out there — but for London. His passport read, "by way of Paris," yet in France he was destined to live and die.

He traveled slowly, stopping in several German cities, and at Stuttgart heard of the tragic capture of Warsaw by the Russians. It was the end of Poland's hopes. As usual, in moments of extreme emotion, Chopin turned to his piano and poured out his heartbreak in an improvisation which later became the "Revolutionary" Etude, Opus 10, No. 12. How truly Chopin was to be his country's spokesman was shown in a dramatic incident of more than a century later. In the autumn of 1939, when the German army was about to march into Warsaw, the mayor of the city ordered this same "Revolutionary" Etude played on the air as the last message from free Poland to a sorrowing world. To return to young Chopin and his travels, it was now more than ever necessary for him to go on to Paris and make a success for his own and his family's sake. But, as Pourtalès says, "The young exile little suspected that he was to be, according to Paderewski's beautiful metaphor, the ingenious smuggler who would allow the prohibited Polonism to escape across the frontier in his portfolios of music, the priest who would carry to the scattered Poles the sacrament of nationalism."

Chopin was twenty-two years old when he arrived in Paris. As the stagecoach passed the city walls, he climbed up beside the driver to get his first view of the Paris streets. And what a sight it was! Political groups and bands of students and artists, each in its own uniform, even a group of marchers crying, "Poland! Poland!"; hawkers bawling the shameful titles of such scandal sheets as *The Loves of the Priests;* idlers, children, dogs, milling about in the crowd while sober citizens and patient horses won thoroughfare as best they could. He had seen nothing like this in Warsaw or Vienna or in orderly Berlin! The noise and vulgarity offended him, but the activity, the surging life was stimulating. And the thought that out of that crowd might step Chateaubriand, Hugo, Lamartine, Gautier, Balzac, Dumas, Merimée, Heine, Ary Scheffer, Delacroix, Cherubini, Rossini, Meyerbeer, Berlioz, Liszt, or a dozen others who were making the literature, art, and music of Paris in 1831 — that thought was thrilling beyond words!

Shortly after his arrival, Chopin went to call on the leading pianist of Paris — Kalkbrenner, a pompous man who played in the grand manner and gave himself every air of authority. Kalkbrenner complimented Chopin's playing, but suggested that he study with him for three years. What a storm this suggestion caused both with Chopin's Paris friends and at home in Warsaw! Three years indeed! Mendelssohn, who was spending a season in Paris, considered it a piece of impertinence. Father

Chopin saw neither the need nor the wherewithal for such a session. And good old Elsner, Chopin's boyhood teacher, sent sound advice by way of sister Ludwika's letters. Elsner had always had faith in Chopin's originality, and now saw danger of the young man's becoming an imitator of a showy, fashionable pianist. "As soon as you begin imitating, you cease to create," he warned, and went on to say that he did not want to see Frédéric become a flashy concert pianist but "to attain the goal toward which nature is urging you and for which she designed you." That goal, in Elsner's opinion, was composition, and right he was, excepting that he visioned Chopin as a successful writer of opera — Polish opera.

But Chopin was too conscious of his shortcomings to have any great notions of his powers as a composer. He wrote back, "To be a great composer one must have enormous knowledge" . . . and then painted a doleful picture of the many young composers in Paris who sat waiting — and starving — in the hope of having their works performed. No, he would try his luck as a pianist, at least for a while. He began to study with Kalkbrenner, but it took only a few lessons to convince him that his friends had been right. However, he managed to part with Kalkbrenner on such good terms that that great man helped arrange Chopin's first Paris concert.

The concert was a financial failure, but otherwise a brilliant success. Added to the charm of Chopin's playing was the fact that he was Polish, violently Polish. The fall of Warsaw had brought many Polish refugees to Paris and made anything Polish the fashion! The audience was pleased with him, the critics amiable, and Chopin became a lion. But alas, a lion must have food — this one also had to have kid gloves and his mane curled, and playing for charity paid no bills! Then one day, so the story goes, when money matters were reaching an acute stage, Chopin, crossing the boulevard, had the luck to meet a compatriot, Prince Radziwill. The Prince was a clever amateur musician, and was interested in Chopin. He persuaded him to play at a musicale at the Rothschild house. That contact was the Midas touch, for after that evening Chopin was showered with invitations and requests for lessons — lessons to young aristocrats at twenty *francs* an hour!

As the *francs* came in, Chopin's latent love of luxury came out. He took the greatest pains and pleasure in choosing rugs, silver, crystal lustre, and effective flower arrangements for his rooms. Roses and orchids were his favorites — one can scarcely imagine Chopin with a ginger-jar full of field daisies! He wore beautifully tailored clothes and white gloves, rode about in a smart cabriolet of his own, and gave expensive suppers. Yet it was not altogether affectation. These elegancies were an extension of his fastidious personality, a background for his peculiar genius. As Pourtalès cleverly puts it, "For Chopin, as later for Wagner, the superfluous was the only necessity." And Chopin worked hard in the midst of his orchids and crystal. During those early Paris years he composed a large part of his best music.

To all appearances Chopin was successful, financially, socially, and artistically. How his struggling brother musicians, looking down from their garrets, must have envied him riding by in style to the house of one of his many friends or to some concert where his music was to be played by such artists as Liszt and Moscheles! Yet Chopin was not happy, he never could be really happy. He was by nature melancholy and oversensitive, and even in these years of apparent health carried death beneath his dandy's coat — the fatal tuberculosis which was to take his father, his sister, and himself. And always he was consumed by longing for home. There is a story that once when a pupil was playing his third Etude in E major, one of his loveliest melodies, he suddenly clasped his hands and cried, "Oh, my country." For Chopin love of Poland was not a pose but a passion. Writing to a friend he says, "On the surface I am gay, but within I am consumed. Dark forebodings, restlessness, insomnia, homesickness, indifference to everything. Pleasure in life, then immediately afterward, longing for death." And once he aptly said that he was in this world like the E string of a violin on a contrabass.

In 1832 and '33, Chopin played frequently in concert with Hiller, Liszt, and other artists, but publicity became more and more hateful to him. "I am not at all the person to give concerts," he confided to Liszt. "The crowd intimidates me; I feel asphyxiated by their breaths, paralyzed by their curious stares, mute before these strange faces. But you, you are destined for it, because when you don't win your public, you know how to knock them dead."

A respite of real happiness did come to Chopin in the summer of 1835. His parents had written that they were going to Karlsbad to take the cure. Imagine their surprise when, on the morning after their arrival, a messenger wakened them at four o'clock with the news that Frédéric was there waiting to see them! They had not been together for five years, and their joy must have been touching. Frédéric became a happy child again, and wrote to his sisters, "We walk together, holding the arm of our sweet little mother. . . . We drink the water and eat together; we tease and abuse each other; talk about you and imitate naughty nephews. . . . And here it has come true, this happiness, this happiness!"

But not even this happiness could last. Parting from his parents, Chopin went on to Dresden to visit his friends the Wodzinskis — he had seen them the year before in Switzerland. Since his childhood he had been friends with the three Wodzinski sons, former pupils of his father's boarding school, and with their younger sister Marja. But Marja at nineteen, mistress of many minor talents in music, painting, and embroidery, and of a major talent for charming young men, was quite another person. Chopin, always versatile in falling in and out of love, was soon lost to the world. He asked her to marry him, she consented, and the morning of their parting became one of Chopin's tenderest memories. Marja gave him a rose, he gave her a little waltz, which she called *La Valse de l'Adieu!* Chopin never would publish it during his lifetime, and it seems rather too bad that after his death greedy hands should have tossed his little keepsake to the world as Opus 69, No. 1, *Waltz in A-Flat Major*.

Chopin returned to Paris with his heart full of Marja and the sweet sorrow of their parting. He shut himself up and began to compose, and in the following year published the Concerto in F Minor, the *Grande polonaise* for piano and orchestra, and the Ballade in G Minor, said to be the monument of his love. At first Marja wrote, affectionately, telling him how much they missed dear Fritz. Then the letters became fewer, sometimes merely postscripts to her mother's letters, and such prosy postscripts about woolen stockings and mama's tooth which had to be pulled. Finally Marja has nothing to tell him but that it is thawing, and when the last letter ended, "Believe in the lifelong attachment of our whole family for you and particularly of your naughtiest pupil and childhood friend.

> Good-by, think of us,
> Marja"

Chopin knew that another dream was ended. He gathered Marja's dull little notes together and placed them with the rose she had given him at parting in an envelope on which he wrote the two Polish words, *Moia Bieda*, "my pain." This poor little packet, tied with a ribbon, was found among his things after his death.

Although he had accepted the breaking of his engagement in silence, Chopin was so bitterly hurt that his disease, now ominously apparent, grew worse. His friends were alarmed, and one of them, Pleyel, hoping to divert him, took him for a short visit to England. Mendelssohn, who was then in London, wrote to Hiller, "It is said that Chopin came here suddenly but paid no visits. One day he played magnificently at Broadwoods, then fled. It seems that he is very ill." It was at this time that Chopin's life took its strange last turning.

The affair of Chopin and George Sand is a story in itself, too long and too subtle for hasty telling. It has already been told many times and seen on stage and screen as a typical "French novel" scandal, as a highly idealized love affair, or as an interesting and unique psychological situation. Whatever may be the truth or the teller's point of view, it is unquestionably the story of two individualists, too extreme to be measured by conventional standards. George Sand, whose real name was Aurore Dudevant, was one of the "emancipated" women of the Romantic Period. She affected a man's name and dress, smoked cigars, went to bed at six in the morning and rose at noon, divorced her husband, adored and spoiled her two children, and reveled in the expression of eccentricities which she mistook for manly freedom. She was absurd, but she was generous, loyal, and decent in her own odd way. George Sand was a deep thinker, and played her part in the intellectual struggle of the age, the Romantic "search for truth," and "love, free and divine." And she contributed a number of problem novels to the wordy literature of the period. Balzac, who admired everything about George Sand except that she dressed her little girl in boy's clothes, said, "Without knowing the French language, she has *style*." It is evident even in the translations of her writings.

Chopin met George Sand at a musicale in 1837, met and disliked her. "How repellent that woman, Sand, is!" he remarked to a friend. "Is she really a woman? I could almost doubt it. . . ." It is not surprising that her looks failed to appeal to a man of Chopin's taste, for she was a dumpy little person with a double chin and a swarthy skin — and six years Chopin's senior. Her one good feature was the "beautiful big eyes of a heifer." But George Sand found this pale, aristocratic looking young pianist very attractive — most women did. As an artist she responded to his music, and as a kind, motherly soul she was touched by his unhappiness and ill health. They were to meet frequently at the houses of mutual friends, particularly with Liszt and his Countess, who really brought them together. Little by little Chopin ceased to find her "repellent."

George Sand's son, Maurice, was a delicate child, and in the winter of 1838 she planned to take him to the island of Majorca, just off the Mediterranean coast of Spain. In her "L'Histoire de ma vie," which, incidentally, is her best book, she tells how, while she was making her preparations to go south, Chopin said to her that if he were only in Maurice's place, he believed that he would soon be well. The thought came to her, Why not take him along? What did this searcher for truth and for "love, free and divine," care for the Mrs. Grundys of Paris! Chopin's friends had been urging him to go to a warmer climate. His physician, who was also attending Maurice, had said to George Sand, "You will indeed save Chopin if you give him air, exercise, and rest." It took no little arguing, for Chopin was a creature of habit, every change, however small, was a terrible event in his life, and now, although he wanted to go, he discovered a dozen reasons for staying! But finally her stronger will prevailed, and off they went to Majorca — George Sand, her son and daughter, Maurice and Solange, and Chopin, whom she also called "the child."

At first they could find no place to live, since to their dismay there was no hotel on the island. But eventually they found a house in the valley outside the town of Palma. It was called the *House of the Wind*, and so it was; there was not so much as a stool or a soup pot in it, and they had to buy furnishings at great trouble and expense! But for a time all went well. "The sky is turquoise," wrote Chopin, "the sea, lapis lazuli, the mountains, emerald. The air? The air is like heaven. It is sunny during the day, the world is in summer dress, and it is warm; at night, songs and guitars for hours on end. Enormous balconies hung with vines, walls dating from the Moors. . . . The town, like everything here, resembles Africa. In short, life is delicious." But they had not reckoned with the rainy season at Majorca. After the first downpour, the damp walls began to swell. There was not so much as a fireplace in this "warm" country, only little braziers which choked them with smoke. Chopin caught cold and began an incessant coughing which frightened the natives. Terrified that they might be infected with tuberculosis, the servants left, and poor George Sand had to do the cooking, care for the invalid, trudge into town for supplies, and try to keep her children's lessons going.

The place became uninhabitable, and they moved into an abandoned monastery which Chopin describes in a letter:

Can you imagine me thus: between the sea and the mountains in a great abandoned Carthusian monastery, in a cell with doors higher than the *porte-cochères* in Paris, my hair uncurled, no white gloves . . . ? The room is shaped like a coffin; it is high with a cobwebbed ceiling. The windows are small. . . . My bed faces them, under an Arabic rose window. Beside the bed is a square thing resembling a bureau, but whose use is problematic. Above, a heavy chandelier (this is a great luxury) with one tiny candle. The works of Bach, my own scrawls, and some manuscripts that are not mine — there is my entire furniture. You can shout as loud as you like, and no one will hear; in short, it is a strange place. . . . The moon is marvelous this evening. . . . Nature here is kind, but the men are pirates. They never see strangers, which is the reason they do not know what to charge. So they will give an orange for nothing and ask a fortune for a trouser button. Under this sky one feels permeated with a poetic sentiment that seems to emanate from all the surrounding objects. Eagles soar over our heads every day, and no one bothers them.

But as the winter wore on, it was useless trying to persuade himself that he liked life at Majorca. The old monastery became a place of horror, particularly on the days when George Sand and the children went off for long excursions over the island and left him to its haunted solitude. Yet out of this very nervous fear came some of Chopin's loveliest fantasies. George Sand tells of the time when she and Maurice, on their way back from town, were caught in a heavy rain and did not get back to the monastery until late at night. They found Chopin in a state of such feverish excitement that he did not at first recognize them. He told of having seen them dead and himself drowned in the lake, with icy water pounding on his breast. "That evening's composition was full of the raindrops sounding on the resonant roof of the monastery, but they were transposed in his imagination and in his music into tears falling from heaven on his heart." There is no record of just which of the preludes this is — he was at work on them at this time — but it is commonly supposed to be the sixth, in B minor.

Chopin grew more and more ill, and they determined to leave the island. It took them three days to reach Palma, for they had to transport the invalid in a sort of wheelbarrow, and the jolting and anxiety brought on an appalling hemorrhage. They found the island's only boat, loaded with pigs, setting out for the mainland, and on this the forlorn little party embarked. Poor Chopin lay on a wretched pallet; the thrifty captain would not give him a decent bed because, he said, it would have to be burned to prevent infection. At Barcelona, he probably would have died had it not been for the ship's doctor on a French sloop of war which chanced to be in port. By slow stages they made their way to Marseilles, and there waited for summer and the sick man's improvement. Both came, and one May morning they set out for George Sand's little country place at Nohant. Never were travelers more grateful for home!

By the end of the summer they were ready to return to Paris, and wrote to obliging friends to find two apartments, "windows facing south, decent stairways . . . no hammering blacksmiths in the neighborhood . . . no young ladies, no smoke or unpleasant odors." Chopin, having stipulated "dovelike" walls — "I like pearl gray because it is neither striking nor vulgar" — went so far as to sketch a floor plan of his dream apartment. One does not envy the task of their house-hunting friends! At last they were settled in a house in the Rue Pigalle, George Sand in an upper apartment, Chopin on the ground floor. In her apartment, the mornings were given over to the children's lessons, with tutors coming and going. Chopin's part of the house saw a procession of pupils. It is rather surprising that this most frail and temperamental artist should have enjoyed teaching. But he seems to have given lessons with both pleasure and success, which was fortunate, since it was his chief source of income. In the afternoons, both artists were busy with their creative work, she at her novels and Chopin, his composing. But at dinner they all met, and afterward friends came in for those famous evenings of music, poetry, and conversation. Between them, Chopin and George Sand knew everyone worth knowing, which was saying a great deal, since this was the Paris of the eighteen forties!

The summer holidays were spent at Nohant in much the same way, even to the guests, although Chopin did less teaching and more composing in the country. But Chopin preferred Paris. "I am not made for the country," he said, "although I do rejoice in the fresh air." George Sand, however, was happiest at Nohant, and often spent much of the winter there. But even when they were apart, she was always anxious about her invalid and writing to one person and another to please see that he did not forget to drink his breakfast chocolate and his ten o'clock bouillon, and, above all, that he did not go out without his muffler! It was doubtless as good a life as Chopin could have led. He had someone to look after him — he surely needed it; he found Solange and Maurice, "the terrible children," amusing, and the brilliant, strong-willed George Sand a complement to his own pearl-gray personality.

But it was the children, at first such merry little comrades, who brought about the final break between Chopin and George Sand. Maurice was his mother's spoiled darling, and to his credit he loved her devotedly. As he grew older he began to notice his mother's frequent unhappy moods and to blame them on the petulant, exacting invalid who shared their home. The fact that Chopin was a famous artist counted for nothing whatever to this undisciplined boy. Then one day at Nohant, when Chopin made the mistake of meddling with Maurice's love affair, there was a scene. Maurice threatened to leave the house, but Chopin insisted that he was the one to go — after all, it was George Sand's house. So back to Paris he went, distraught, as he always was at any emotional upset. A short time later Solange married a violent fellow who literally came to blows with her mother. George Sand forbade the young couple her house, but Chopin, who had always loved Solange, received them cordially at his apartment in Paris. This led to the two last letters — a dignified one from Chopin, a scornful reply from the lady, mocking his paternal attitude — then a long silence. The ties of those eight years were broken. The two saw each other just once again, and quite by accident, on the steps of a friend's house in Paris.

After that "bad year," as Chopin called 1847, he composed nothing more. He was too lonely and brokenhearted, too mortally ill. He now had to be carried up and down stairs and lifted into his carriage and bed like a little child. Everything was too great an effort. Yet he summoned strength for a last Paris concert in February, 1848. The house was crowded, for a Chopin concert was a rare event. The stage and even the stairs were banked with flowers. Chopin played exquisitely, his famous *pianissimo* now seemed a sort of spirit touch. When it was over, he fainted. A week later came the February Revolution and abdication of Louis Philippe. It was the end of an elegant epoch of crystal lustre and the perfume of the lilies of France.

For Chopin, life in Paris was now but a procession of days filled with painful memories. Indeed, to him life anywhere seemed of little importance. And when a former favorite pupil, Jane Stirling, a Scotch woman, urged him to come to London, he agreed. From April, 1848, to January, 1849, this phantom man dragged himself about England and Scotland, giving concerts and lessons. His audiences were enthusiastic; his pupils, devoted. He made friends and money, both of which he sadly needed. But it was an alien world, and he was, as he said, "ridiculously homesick" for the Paris which was no longer home. In his letters to his family and friends, he still shows flashes of that boyish humor. "The London Philharmonic Orchestra," he writes, "is like their roast beef or their turtle soup — energetic, serious, but nothing more." And, "I have not yet played to any Englishwoman without her saying to me, 'like water,' meaning that my music flows like water!" And as for the ladies who played for him, and there were many, "They all look at their hands and play wrong notes with much feeling!" But Chopin sincerely appreciated these good people. At Calder House Manor the Stirlings almost killed him with kindness. "There is nothing I can desire that I do not immediately receive," he said. "They even bring me the Paris papers every day." One of them was greatly concerned about his soul. "She is always telling me that the other world is better than this one; and I know all that by heart!" Chopin was soon to have a chance to find out for himself.

After his return to Paris, early in 1849, he had to give up his lessons and with them a good part of his income. His friends were put to it to invent plausible stories for certain expenditures they made for him, including the low rent of the very pleasant apartment they had engaged! For Chopin's Polish pride would never have let him accept outright the help they deceived him into taking. Good Jane Stirling sent twenty-five thousand *francs* which smoothed the course of the last weeks.

More than anything Chopin now wanted to see his own people. At his request, his sister Ludwika brought her "thimbles and needles" and stayed with him through the summer. A friend of his childhood, now the Abbé Jelowicki, came also, and at the end persuaded Chopin, who had neglected his religious duties, to receive the Sacrament. "Thank you, friend," said the sick man, after it was over. "Thanks to you, I shall not die like a pig." His pupils ran in and out constantly, and his friend, the beautiful Countess Delphine Potocka, came all the way from Nice and sang for him. So many friends, but not the one he loved most — not George Sand! "And she said to me that I would die in no other arms but hers!" he whispered.

Chopin knew that he was dying, and expressed his last wishes, his farewells to his friends quite calmly and clearly. He asked his sister to burn all his inferior compositions. "I owe it to the public," he said, "and to myself to publish only good things. I kept this resolution all my life. I wish to keep it now." Unfortunately and unfairly this wish was not respected. To two dear friends he said, "You will play Mozart together for me, and I shall hear you."

The sad vigil ended early on an October morning, 1849. It took Paris thirteen days to prepare a fitting funeral service for its Chopin, for the curé at the Madeleine had to obtain special permission to have women sing in that famous old church. Without them it would have been impossible to give Mozart's *Requiem*, which Chopin so loved. During the offertory they played two of the preludes; one, the "Raindrop" Prelude written at Majorca that stormy night when Chopin had seen death. Then to the sound of his own famous Funeral March, for the first time played by an orchestra (it had been orchestrated for the occasion by Reber), the long procession started for Père-Lachaise. There they left the poor body of Chopin, but not the heart — that was taken back to Warsaw to rest in the Church of the Holy Cross. There was no eulogy spoken at the grave, as was then the custom. But just as the body was being lowered, "a friendly hand" scattered on the coffin earth from a silver cup. It was the cup which, nearly twenty years before, had been given to a sobbing boy as he left his home, the earth of a Poland which no longer existed except in the pages of that boy's music and in the hearts of his countrymen.

THE ARTIST

Chopin is unique in that he is the only one of the great composers to confine himself to one instrument. Aside from a handful of Polish songs, a trio for piano and strings, one or two works for 'cello and piano, and, of course, the orchestral parts of his two piano concertos, he wrote only piano music. But his exclusive world was by no means a narrow one. So completely did he explore and possess it that, with the exception of a few touches of Impressionistic color, little has been added to piano style or pianistic effects since Chopin's time.

In the music of Chopin the listener is perhaps most deeply impressed by the beautiful lyric melody and the play of harmonic color. Although an instrumental composer, Chopin was at heart a singer. His is one-voice music, one voice of lovely melody floating above a richly colored background. The secret of this gorgeous background lies not only in Chopin's choice of just the right tones but also in his skillful blending of them with the damper pedal. In the days of Haydn and Mozart, before the advent of the damper, the pianist had to be content with only those notes the left hand was actually playing, and did the best he could to make the accompaniment sound full by spreading the chords. The result was those stiff little *arpeggio* accompaniments known as the Alberti basses. With the damper pedal, which came into use about 1780, the left hand could strike, let us say, certain quite low notes, leave the tones sustained by the pedal, and be free to play chords or *arpeggios* up nearer the right-hand positions, which, of course, made possible a much more richly shaded accompaniment. Chopin was past master of this type of accompaniment, and in the left-hand parts of his music wrote many notes which are simply touches of color. This was one of his special contributions to piano playing and piano composition. Of the *tempo rubato*, with which he achieved certain individual rhythmic effects, we shall speak later.

Chopin's music bears unmistakable traces of his illness. Its touching languor and weariness are often but the reflection of his own breathlessness. But the delicacy, the dreaminess of his music are the reflection of his own poetic personality. However, this fragile Chopin is not the complete artist. It is unfortunate that so often the strong Chopin of the manly ballades and the splendid polonaises is forgotten.

It was characteristic of Chopin that he left behind him so little for the discoverers. There were a few unpublished manuscripts which, unfortunately, were not burned as he had requested. But there were no unfinished ones. Chopin not only completed every composition he set out to write but also polished every note with painstaking care. There are no loose ends, no rough edges. And there was something about both his playing and his composition that could not be imitated by his pupils and admirers. When he died it was the utter end — he was, indeed, an unique artist.

To make a selection from Chopin's works is a thankless task which leaves one with the feeling of having taken so little and left so much! In the following selection offered for special consideration we seem to have left out the more pretentious compositions

— the Etudes, those wonderful studies, each based upon some technical problem which Chopin illustrates so beautifully that it becomes a little tone poem, the sonatas, the Scherzi, and the Fantasies. We have chosen instead the familiar Chopin, the music loved by amateur pianists and understood by everybody. After all, this may well be the greater Chopin!

The Polonaises and Mazurkas

Love of Poland was the ruling passion, the constant element in Chopin's life. As a little boy in Warsaw he had thrilled to the tales of Polish heroes; as a young music student he had collected and experimented with Polish folk tunes; and as an exile in Paris, a man literally without a country, he had created for himself a spiritual Poland in music.

Although Nationalism had not yet become a definite phase in music's development, Chopin was its real pioneer. For centuries composers had been using folk tunes, but using them merely to enrich their own music, often translating them out of the folk idiom. Chopin, with exactly the opposite purpose, used his own music to glorify the folk music of Poland, to bring out all its latent beauty and poetry and make it express the spirit of the nation. Even before the fall of Warsaw and while the young Chopin was still in Vienna, a family friend, the author Witwicki, had written to him encouraging this ideal: "I am deeply convinced that you could become a national composer and discover an extremely rich vein of expression which would bring you no ordinary fame. But always keep nationality in view — nationality and once again nationality. . . . Just as there is a native climate, so is there a native melody. The mountains, forests, streams, and plains all have a native, inward voice." Chopin not only heard that voice but also broadcast it for all the world to hear. And by the middle of the nineteenth century, composers in Hungary, Norway, Bohemia, and all over Europe were listening attentively to their own national voices.

Speaking of Chopin's mazurkas, Liszt said, "Preserving their rhythms he ennobled their melody, enlarged their proportions, and wrought into their tissue harmonic lights and shadows as new in themselves as were the subjects to which he adapted them." The same is true of Chopin's treatment of the polonaise, and it was in these two forms that he reached the heights of nationalism.

Polonaise in A Major, Op. 40

Originating at the court of Henry of Anjou in 1574, after he had come to the throne of Poland, the polonaise reflects the martial splendor of the days of knighthood. It was the processional music to which the Polish nobles and their ladies entered the great hall of state. Because of the excessive gallantry of the knights and the equally excessive coquetry of the ladies, the stern outlines of the march were softened, and the polonaise became more of a processional dance. Later it was used less formally as the dance or grand march by which the master of the house opened every ball, not with the youngest or most beautiful, but with the most honored — often the oldest — of the ladies present. Liszt, in his description of the polonaise, says, "The polonaise is the true and purest expression of Polish national character, as in the course of centuries it was developed." In it Chopin saw a symbol of war and love, of the strength and tenderness of his people.

The polonaise is always in triple meter, with the accent on the second beat of the measure, and written in simple song form. But there is nothing simple about it, at least for the foreigner. One has only to try to clap the tune pattern while the Polonaise in A Major, Op. 40 is being played to discover both its tricks and the truth of the saying that only a born Pole can do justice to the polonaise.

Chopin wrote fifteen polonaises. They seem of two distinct types, one, martial and triumphant, symbolizing the days of Poland's greatness, the other, gloomy and dejected, the expression of Poland's downfall. The celebrated A Major Polonaise, called the "Military," is one of the triumphant ones. It was written in the abandoned monastery at Majorca during that awful winter when Chopin, ill and depressed, lived in a fever dream. In the night after he had composed it, so the story goes, he was terrified to see the door of his cell open and a long procession of knights and ladies in ancient Polish costume file slowly and silently by — ghosts summoned by his music!

The polonaise begins with a majestic theme in which one hears rolling drums and clanking armor:

sees the sweeping plumes and velvets, and all the vivid pageantry of ancient ceremony. The music has a Winged Victory stride!

The second theme suggests a voice in fervid speech, accompanied by gallant gestures:

to which a gentler voice replies. Here we sense that contrast of strength and tenderness of which the polonaise is the symbol. The dialogue is interrupted by a rumbling trill and fierce commanding chords, but only for a moment. The voices are heard again, and when they have said their say, the processional moves onward to the martial music.

Surely this polonaise is an illustration of the "cannon buried in the flowers" with which Schumann described some of Chopin's music. Surely this is no "hospital talent," and the fact that it is the work of a man mortally ill only makes it the more splendid and courageous!

Mazurka in B-Flat, Op. 7, No. 1

If the polonaise reflects the heroic spirit of Poland, the mazurka is an even truer reflection of that mingling of high spirits and low, of wild merriment and morbid melancholy which marks the Slavic temperament. Again we quote Liszt, who, speaking of the mazurka, says, "Coquetries, vanities, fantasies . . . vague emotions, passions, conquests, struggles upon which the safety or favors of others depend, all, all meet in this dance."

The mazurka is in three-four or three-eight time, and usually the first part of the measure contains the quicker notes:

although there are a number of variants of the pattern. Chopin loved the mazurka, and nowhere does he show his nationalism to more artistic advantage. The mazurka's major-minor mood seemed made to express what some one said of him, "His heart is sad, but his mind is gay." And its whimsical, changeable nature gave him opportunity to indulge in the *tempo rubato*, for which he is famous, although he was by no means its inventor!

Tempo rubato is simply the adjustment of time values to the player's emotional impulses. It is not *robbed* time, as the word *rubato* would indicate, but *borrowed* time. And whatever the player borrows from one note or phrase he must pay in full to some other, or the rhythmic framework will fall to pieces. Chopin, although he "leans freely within his bars," pausing here for effect, adding a whole shower of extra notes there in a cadenza, paid back scrupulously. No matter how freely his right hand seemed to wander through the melody, the left policed the rhythm on strict beat, and at the end of the measure or phrase the two always came out together. Liszt once remarked, "A wind plays in the leaves, life unfolds and develops beneath them, but the tree remains the same — this is the Chopin *rubato*." *Rubato* is a delicate trick, and in the hands of an artist (the only hands that should ever touch it) is scarcely perceptible. The listener is not aware either of borrowing or robbery, merely of a delightful freedom of motion as when a flower sways lightly on its stalk but neither bends nor breaks.

During his lifetime Chopin published forty-one mazurkas, of which the one in B-flat, Op. 7, No. 1, is perhaps best known. It starts off in a gay mood:

almost flirtatious, if we are to believe the manly *fortes* and coquettish *pianos*.

Then a second theme enters, *legato*, at first, but soon growing wayward:

The tune of its first phrase is repeated, but with what teasing little changes of time values, accent, and phrasing, as one glance at the score shows!

In the third section the Slav speaks:

The first phrase is the same old Slavic chant used by Tchaikovsky as the main theme of his *March Slav*. And now, in this the most emotional of the three melodies, the *tempo rubato* flourishes!

One could easily weave a story around this music, which is not so strange when we find one authority describing the mazurka thus: "At its best it is a dancing anecdote, a story told in a charming variety of steps and gestures."

THE VALSES

The waltz, taking its name from the German *walzen*, to turn, was the overwhelmingly popular dance of Germany, France, and England a century ago. It was beloved by young people, but suspected by their elders of being a "twosing" dance of doubtful propriety. Lesser composers enriched themselves by turning out a quantity of *tum-tee-tee*, *tum-tee-tee* tunes, and greater composers enriched music with brilliant concert waltzes.

As a dance the waltz was simply one good turn after another. Likewise, the music was just one little eight-measure tune after another. There was no limit, save the composer's ingenuity, to the number of these melodies, and no relationship between them. All that was asked was that the composer keep to triple meter, accent on the first beat, and join the tunes without the loss of a step. Schubert, Strauss, Brahms all wrote waltzes after this pattern.

Chopin, as might be expected, made the waltz an aristocrat. His music bears no trace of the folk *Ländler*, the humble ancestor of the waltz. It does not suggest, as does Schubert's, a party of merry boys and girls dancing at a village inn with Franz at the battered piano making up waltzes. Nor does it picture the fashionable dance pavilions of Vienna during the reign of the Strauss Waltz Kings. As Schumann declared, "The dancers of Chopin's valses should be at least countesses!" They should also be skillful dancers, for Chopin's valses are not only elegant but temperamental. He admitted that he could not even play a waltz in the Vienna fashion, that is, liltingly but in even, swinging *tempo* (one really cannot speak of a Viennese waltz as *strict!*). But in spite of the fact that the dancer must be prepared for surprising *accelerandos* and languishing *ritardandos*, a number of Chopin's valses can be danced.

But those which the musical world designates as the *Chopin Valses* are not really dance tunes but little tone poems in waltz time. Someone has happily described them as "dances of the soul and not of the body." Chopin is making music for listeners, not dancers. Instead of the eight-measure tunes, barely large enough to turn around in, Chopin wrote spacious sixteen-measure melodies. These he arranged in a definite design with careful thought as to key relationship and mood contrast. Sometimes he even added an introduction and coda. The effect is not one of a number of tunes strung together haphazardly to keep a dance going, but of a well-planned musical composition. We might say that Chopin raised the status of the waltz from foot to head music. Nor was the heart forgotten, for within the measures of this most popular of dances Chopin caught and held the tender smiles and sighs, the ribbons and the rosebuds of nineteenth-century romance.

Valse in C-Sharp Minor

Of the many Chopin Valses, none is more poetic or more characteristic than the familiar one in C-sharp minor. It is made up of three melodies, first:

one of the loveliest expressions of Chopin's wistful, twilight mood.

The second is full of gentle animation:

and the third a smiling major melody:

[85]

Indicating the three melodies as A, B, and C, the Valse in C-Sharp Minor follows this design: A–B–C–B–A–B. The joinings are smooth, as of course they would be, since Chopin is playing back and forth between the keys of C-sharp minor and A-flat major. But the contrast between melodies of long-held notes and rippling *arpeggios*, of drooping line and upward sweep, and between major and minor mood gives delightful variety to the music.

The waltz has had its turn. Young people of today think of it as just an old-fashioned dance that grandmother loved. Chopin, too, may be a bit old-fashioned, but one cannot imagine a time when the Valse in C-Sharp Minor would fail to give pleasure.

The Preludes

In the days of Bach a prelude, literally, was a little piece for the musician to *prae ludere*, to play before, a larger work. It was really a necessity to the fugue, for the fugue invariably begins with a single voice announcing a theme, or subject, which is its key. If the listener misses a single note of this subject he is lost. So to focus attention and prepare an entrance for that all important first note, the prelude was devised. Because of the close attention to be demanded by the fugue, the prelude was purposely short and simple — just an informal little tune, as if the player were improvising for a moment before beginning his serious business of fuguing. The same type of prelude served the classic suite, not that the gigues and gavottes required either preparation or mental effort, but because their active dancing rhythms seemed all the gayer in contrast to a songlike air or prelude.

Bach was too original and frugal an artist to waste the opportunity of a prelude by making it a mere call to attention. He felt that while it was gathering and holding the listener's ear, the prelude might just as well be saying something interesting for itself. So while his preludes are always written in the same key as the succeeding fugue or suite, they seem to have a mood and a message of their own. Often a delicate prelude precedes a vigorous fugue, or a rollicking prelude is followed by music of austere dignity. The surprise is delightful!

Chopin was a devoted student of Bach, and it may have been this detached quality of the older master's preludes that suggested to him the writing of preludes complete in themselves. At any rate, Chopin wrote a series of these tiny tone poems, some of them no more than couplets or quatrains, and called them preludes. They prelude nothing, unless it be the dream into which the susceptible listener can so easily drift!

The Chopin preludes are associated with his winter in Majorca. Musicologists argue hotly as to whether any or all of them were actually composed there. Be that as it may, we know from his letters and from the writings of George Sand that Chopin was at work on them during that winter, and that an advance payment on them from his publisher financed his share of the Majorcan adventure. He probably had the sketches for most of them in his portfolio before he left Paris, finished them at Majorca, wrote a few additional ones, and from them all then selected the twenty-four which were to make the set known as Preludes, Op. 28.

Two of the most beautiful and justly celebrated of these Preludes are the D-Flat, No. 15 and the B Minor, No. 6, both said to have been written while he and George

Sand and her children were living in the abandoned monastery on the island of Majorca. Both have been called the "Raindrop" Prelude after George Sand's famous story of the night when she and the children, delayed by a tropical storm, returned to the monastery to find Chopin almost delirious. In a waking dream he had seen them drowned and himself lying at the bottom of the lake, and when he really saw them he thought they were ghosts! When they had calmed him with the assurance that, although wet and weary, they were quite alive, Chopin played for them the music born of his dream of death, music with a background of raindrops beating rhythmically on the roof of an old monastery, and of tears falling in a lonely heart.

Prelude in D-Flat, No. 15

No less an authority than Paderewski calls the Prelude in D-Flat, No. 15, the "Raindrop." Even in its peaceful beginning one hears the continual patter of the rain in the bass:

accompanying a wistful melody. Then, passing into the key of C-sharp minor, the mood changes. The rain now beats ominously in the treble:

and the melody grows menacing with a crouching, creeping terror which gradually rises to a positive exaltation:

One feels something of the grandeur that is always a part of Nature's tragic moods, the grandeur of a thunder storm and of the sea in tempest. The persistent, monotonous pounding of the rain is almost intolerable, like a bad dream from which there is no escape. The awakening comes with the re-entrance of the D-flat theme:

How serene and fresh it seems, a world of sunshine after storm, of the return of loved ones after aching absence.

Prelude in B Minor, No. 6

Although less dramatic, less programmatic than the one in D-flat, the Prelude in B Minor, No. 6 is more intense in mood. Here, too, one hears the ceaseless fall of rain above a melody full of tears:

This is hopeless music:

sinking at the end into despairing silence.

Who but Chopin, a "violin string" tensed to breaking on the contrabass of a hard world, could have compressed so much anguish into one little page of music! Surely it lends itself to George Sand's picture of the half-delirious Chopin who, when he saw his friends appearing out of the storm and coming toward him in the flickering candle-light, startled them with a great cry, rose, and in a strange voice said, "Ah, I knew you were dead!" The Prelude in B Minor is a threnody, a death lament, which, suitably enough, was played on the organ at Chopin's funeral at the Church of the Madeleine.

From the old serenades for strings and wind instruments, the *Nachtmusik* of Haydn's and Mozart's time, comes the nocturne of the Romanticists. The piano, to be sure, is not an out-of-door instrument, and the pianist cannot go a-serenading with his fiddling brothers. But John Field, the Irish pianist-composer, saw no reason why he might not make a little *Nachtmusik*. So he wrote a number of charming small pieces in serenade mood and called them nocturnes.

Chopin admired John Field and, as a young man, imitated the delicately shaded expression that distinguished Field's playing. He was also fascinated with Field's idea of the nocturne, for Chopin was a lover of wistful, graying twilight and the hush and mystery of night. Field's nocturnes are as naïve and unpretentious as moonflowers; Chopin's are painted lilies, tuberoses, and sometimes, passion flowers. The nocturnes often betrayed Chopin into an expression of too-sweet sentiment and a morbid melancholy which made the sturdy Field exclaim, "He has a talent of the hospital!"

But in spite of this weakness, Chopin's nocturnes seem to have been the most admired of all his compositions, with the exception of the valses. Played by a sympathetic and nonlanguishing pianist and in their rightful setting, which is the small concert hall or, better still, one's own music room, their muted mood becomes sincere and appealing.

Nocturne in G Minor, Op. 37, No. 1
Nocturne in G, Op. 37, No. 2

The pair of nocturnes known as Opus 37, written in the spring of 1840, are, if not the most masterly, at least quite typical of Chopin's night pieces. The first, in G minor:

with the middle part, said to have been suggested by the chanting of monks:

is very popular. It has a certain Chopinesque charm, but its complaining theme does grow tiresome, and its commonplace chorale neither refreshes nor inspires the listener. There is something stagey and a trifle self-conscious about it.

But the second, Nocturne in G, is Chopin in his most delightful twilight mood. Arthur Symons, writing his poem "The Chopin Player," might have been thinking of

[89]

its first theme:

when he wrote:

> Like butterflies upon the garden beds,
> Nets of bright sound.   I follow them: in vain.
> I must not brush the least dust from their wings:
> They die of a touch; but I must capture them,
> Or they will turn to a caressing flame,
> And lick my soul up with their flutterings.

And the second theme in gentle barcarolle rhythm, with harmonies shifting like sunset tints on the water, is one of the most beautiful melodies Chopin ever wrote:

Through quite magical modulations it comes swaying back to the fluttering first theme, then a pause and the drowsy ending:

Chopin's music often makes one think of Shelley's poetry, and this little nocturne seems spirit twin to Shelley's Fragment, "To Music."

> Silver key of the fountain of tears,
>   Where the spirit drinks till the brain is wild;
> Softest grave of a thousand fears,
>   Where their mother, Care, like a drowsy child
>   Is laid asleep in flowers.

In the winter of 1835 Chopin returned to Paris refreshed by a long and stimulating holiday in Germany. He had enjoyed a reunion with his parents at Karlsbad, become engaged to Marja Wodzinska in Dresden, and parted from her with tenderest regrets. He had stopped in Leipzig, enroute to Paris, and visited with Mendelssohn, Schumann, and the Wiecks. He had become greatly excited over the poetry of his countryman, Mickiewicz, who had retold the old legends of Lithuania in ballade form. Brimming with all these emotions, Chopin felt an urge to create. And so dynamic was this urge that it carried him away from the traditional forms which he had been content to use — the prelude, sonata, and etude, the national dance forms, and the nocturne — and inspired him to create a form of his own, the ballade.

Up to this time the ballade had been a form of literature, an epic narrative said or sung by a solo voice. Now Chopin made the piano play the rôle of the solo voice of the narrator and gave to his wordless music the unity and the feeling of the old ballade of poetry. The ballade was his only contribution to musical form, but a highly artistic one. Niecks says, "None of Chopin's compositions surpass his ballades in masterliness of form and beauty and poetry of content. In them he attains the height of his power as an artist." Chopin wrote four ballades, each entirely different from the other, but all with the same ballade feeling, the same logical, well-knit plan.

Ballade in G Minor

The G Minor Ballade is the first of the four. The music obviously tells a story which must have been in Chopin's mind, but just what story we do not know. Some interpreters like to think it the story of Chopin's love for Marja, which was certainly uppermost in his mind at the time. Others insist that the G Minor Ballade is based upon Mickiewicz's poem, *Konrad Wallenrod*, which is the more likely since there is not only a close parallel between the themes and events of the music and those of the story, but Chopin is also said to have told Schumann that he had been "incited to the creation of the ballades by the poetry."

The story of Konrad Wallenrod is laid in the late fourteenth century when the Knights of the Red Cross, a Teutonic Order, were waging war against the pagan Lithuanians in the name of Christianity. In one of their innumerable battles the Knights slew the Lithuanian leader, took his seven-year-old son, Konrad, prisoner, and made him a page in the household of the grand master of their Order. Young Konrad became a great favorite, and the old knight adopted him and raised him as his own son. The boy was often in the company of an aged minstrel. Nobody knew who the old man was, but because of his sweet music and because Konrad loved him, he was allowed to stay at the grand master's castle. This old minstrel was, in reality, a Lithuanian nobleman, a friend of Konrad's dead father, sent by the Lithuanian people to keep their young prince mindful of his duty to his own country. And so all through his youth the boy was planning vengeance upon the Christians who had caused the death of his father. As a young soldier he pretended to be captured in a skirmish with the Lithuanians and returned to his own country, where he married a lovely pagan lady and began his work of building up his father's kingdom. But this work was interrupted by ten years' absence while fighting in the wars against the Moors. Returning at last, famous for his brave deeds, Konrad feigned Christianity so zealously that he was made commander of the Knights of the Red Cross in the place of his dead foster father. Then his work of vengeance began. He stirred up strife in the Order, wasted its resources, and finally led the Knights into a losing battle against the Lithuanians. But Konrad was not to enjoy his revenge. He was recognized by some of his old comrades, and met a traitor's death. It was said that he had never smiled from the time he had first heeded the fateful voice of the old minstrel!

The ballade begins with a brief but portentous introduction, ending with a sighing, legendlike phrase.

In the last chord the bass E-flat has been the cause of much controversy. Some editors have seen fit to replace it with a smooth sounding D natural. But most Chopin students insist that the dissonant E-flat was no slip of the pen. Niecks says, "This dissonant E-flat may be said to be the emotional keynote of the whole poem. It is a questioning thought that, like a sudden pain, shoots through mind and body."

Then comes the main theme:

Call it, if you choose, the voice of the old minstrel telling the young prince of the wrongs suffered by his people and urging redress; or call it simply the theme of sorrow and tragedy which plays the leading rôle in this and many another story. However it may be interpreted, it remains the musical foundation upon which the ballade is built. Our fancies, our interest, and our enjoyment must follow its fate.

The second theme in E-flat:

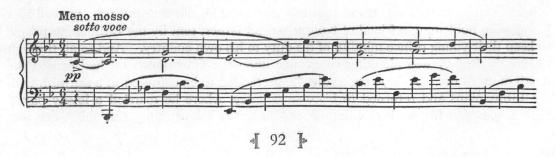

might be called the theme of happiness, the bright thread in this somber web. Beautiful in line, color, and sentiment, it does all that a second theme should do by way of contrast. And it satisfies the poetic idea of the story, suggesting the brighter hours of Konrad's boyhood when, forgetting the dark sayings of the old minstrel, he was loved and petted by the knights and by his foster father. It also suggests the happiness of his love and marriage, and the satisfaction he might have felt in honor and fame. But always that fateful first theme recurs, bringing thoughts of ancient wrongs and of vengeance.

The two themes alternate in fascinating fashion and variation, and there are other little motifs. At one place after a delicate cadenza, a playful valse is heard for a moment, but disappears before the happiness theme. Then the questioning main theme returns and leads *presto con fuoco* into a perfect whirlwind of emotion. The passionate close of the ballade suggests the complete abandonment to the conflict. Then funereal chords, soft but threatening, answered by a defiant statement of the heroic ideal:

and a wild triple *forte* in descending chromatics brings the swift and tragic end.

Who could call the art that produced the G Minor Ballade "feminine"? Chopin's body was frail, his manners fastidious to the point of effeminacy, but his brain was masculine and his heart courageous!

MARCHE FUNÈBRE

The two most famous funeral marches in the world are those by Beethoven and Chopin. Oddly enough both are movements from classical sonatas — Beethoven's, the second movement of his "Eroica" Symphony, Chopin's, the third movement of his B-Flat Minor Sonata for piano. Beethoven's march takes its logical place among the other movements of the symphony, but Chopin's seems to bear so little relation to the rest of the sonata that we suspect it of having been written as a separate piece, as it is always played.

Two rhythmic introductory measures set the lagging pace and the mournful march begins:

One can scarcely imagine more deathly music than this. The notes seem weighted and the reluctant rhythm drags the muscles and the spirit into the very depths of depression.

At first the line is always downward, then comes an upward sweep, like the cry of a pleading voice:

but always it is answered by the hopeless marching tune.

The trio section in bright major key, upward line, and easy, graceful rhythm:

is so exactly what we would expect in the way of relief and contrast from an artist of Chopin's unerring musical judgment that the familiar interpretation — "a rapturous gaze into the beatific region of a beyond" — seems almost beside the point. It is heaven enough to escape for a moment from the gloom of the march! But it is only for a moment — the march returns and is repeated, note for note, as it was in the beginning.

The *Marche Funèbre* is perhaps the one example of a Chopin composition which really needs the orchestra. It may be the memory of Beethoven's Funeral March, so effectively orchestrated, which in comparison makes the piano sound strained and inadequate in the Chopin march. It is often played by bands at state funerals. But the band arrangement with the predominant brass necessary for a marching procession seems to give the music a theatrical taint. One does not trumpet real grief! The Chopin *Marche Funèbre* needs strings, for only strings can cry out like human voices, only strings can pulse and vibrate like human hearts. The *Marche Funèbre*, as we know, was orchestrated for Chopin's funeral, but here again, since it was used to accompany the cortège to Père-Lachaise, the orchestration was mostly for wind instruments. If there is any other orchestration, it is little known, but there should be one which would adequately interpret Chopin's idea of the dignity of sorrow.

OTTORINO RESPIGHI

Bologna — 1879
Rome   — 1936

In April, 1936, Italy lost one of the most important figures of her twentieth-century musical renaissance, Ottorino Respighi. Since its beginnings, about the year 1600, opera had been the center of Italy's musical interest and activity, while symphonic music, although it, too, was of Italian origin, was but a neglected Cinderella. With the turn of the twentieth century a number of Italy's young composers began to realize that the long and exclusive devotion to opera had weakened Italian music. Throwing the weight of their talents upon the side of instrumental music, they set about restoring the balance. One of the first and the most widely successful of these wise young men was Ottorino Respighi.

Respighi began life with an artistic heritage. His grandfather was master of the chapel in one of Bologna's large churches, his father, a successful teacher of piano, and his mother, one of a family of sculptors.   Music was an everyday matter in the Respighi household, and little Ottorino was soon set to work at the piano under his father's direction. Because he showed unusual promise, he was later sent to the Bologna Liceo Musicale to study violin and composition. The boy was equally interested and gifted in both these branches of music study, and when at nineteen he left the Liceo with diplomas in both, he could not decide whether to try for a career as a concert violinist or as a composer.

In his early twenties Respighi was still undecided and playing a double rôle. In public he was a successful young violinist, in private an eager experimenter in musical composition. In 1902, Martucci, his teacher in composition, left Bologna, and about the same time Respighi made up his mind to give up the concert stage and devote himself to writing music. Once the decision was made, he burned his bridges by selling his violin. There were never any half measures for Respighi!

Wishing to broaden his outlook by seeing something of the world and the ways of musicians outside Italy, he began what was to be a long musical pilgrimage. His first important stop was at St. Petersburg where lived the musician he most admired, Rimsky-Korsakov. Here he stayed for some time, working with the Russian master, who taught him the secrets of picturesque and colorful orchestration as only he could teach them. From St. Petersburg Respighi went to Berlin, where he studied with Max Bruch, and finally, in 1913, returned to Italy and went to Rome, where he was shortly afterward appointed professor at the Liceo Reale de Santa Cecilia. In 1924, as recognition of eleven years of outstanding success as a teacher, he was elected by unanimous vote to succeed Enrico Bossi as Director of the Liceo Reale de Santa Cecilia, a position he occupied until his death.

Respighi was a master teacher. His active, inquiring mind never lost its zest for learning. It did not blight his creative life or cramp his style to spend part of his time with less mature students. Their reactions to the techniques and aesthetics of music interested him. Indeed one of his students, a young enthusiast for Gregorian chant, interested the Maestro in her subject and in herself to such a degree that she afterward became Madame Respighi. It goes without saying that the students found Respighi inspiring and delightful. He was a small man, calm and simple in his manner and fluent in speech. He could be fluent in eight or nine languages, which, remarkable as it may seem to us one-language Americans, was nothing at all in the Respighi family, which could boast a Cardinal Mazzofanti, master of forty-eight! With his mane of hair, massive brow, deep, smoldering eyes, and stormy chin, Respighi is said to have looked so like Beethoven that his students, meeting him in the corridor of the Liceo where the Canova bust of Beethoven stood, loved to edge him over to it and compare the two. The familiar death mask of Beethoven always hung above Respighi's piano, and a visitor who found Respighi sitting at the keyboard in the twilight tells of the reflection he saw in the ebony lid of the piano — two pale faces, startlingly alike!

Respighi loved the country quiet of his villa, *I Pini* (The Pines), on the outskirts of Rome. But, believing that a composer should keep in touch with the busy currents of life, he also spent much of his time in the city. His studio, high above the Via Nazionale, with its windows overlooking Rome, its red Roman tiling, its priceless old furniture, tapestries, books, and music seemed a suitable setting for this scholarly artist. Respighi was something of an antiquarian and as keenly interested in his country's past as in her future. His studies of old Italian music had convinced him that the sources of modern Italian music lay not in the folk songs, which opera had worn threadbare, but in the severely graceful melodies of the seventeenth- and eighteenth-century suites and *canzoni*. He was a generous helper in the preparation of a national edition of these early Italian classics.

Of Respighi's own works the early compositions were more or less imitative and undistinguished. But with the trilogy of symphonic poems, *The Fountains*, *The Pines*, and *The Festivals of Rome*, and *Church Windows*, his individuality emerged. Respighi's music shows two distinctly Latin traits; first, a feeling for construction, for proportion and balance — the Latins have always been fine builders; second, a serenity, rare in modern times. Perhaps the most interesting characteristic of Respighi's style is that it seems to be a fusion of the old and the new, of the national and the international. We feel something of all times and of all countries in his music. His intention was never to astonish the world, but merely to go on record with a calm and sincere expression of his own thoughts and feelings.

Although Respighi loved the orchestra best and was one of the pioneers in Italy's return to symphonic music, he was also to be known as a composer of opera. As he once whimsically remarked, "Every Italian writes an opera if he is given half a chance and some paper." In his operas *The Sunken Bell* and *The Egyptian Mary*, however, he breaks with the Italian tradition by making the orchestra more important than the voices. But his last opera, *La Fiamma* (The Flame), is, in his own words, "a return to the people. It represents my need to sing simply and sincerely for the great mass of the people."

Four American visits as guest conductor of his own works and the memories of his devoted American pupils have made Respighi rather well known in this country.

While he was with us he was, of course, beset by interviewers eager for his American impressions. He was enthusiastic in his praise of American orchestras which, he said, were the finest in the world. But when asked what he thought of so-called American jazz, he cautiously replied that it was "interesting."

Three operas, several charming orchestral suites, chamber music including the beautiful Doric Quartet for strings, a violin sonata and a concerto, and a handful of lovely songs make up the list of Respighi's compositions — not a long list, yet a fair output for one who spent many years in preparation, who served music in so many ways and died at the age of fifty-seven.

THE FOUNTAINS OF ROME

Few composers have aspired, much less succeeded, in setting a city to music. But Respighi in his orchestral trilogy *The Fountains*, *The Pines*, and *The Festivals of Rome*, tonal impressions of nature, of historic memories, and of the moods of the people, has caught the very spirit of the Eternal City.

No people have ever loved the lilt and sparkle of playing water as have the Romans. Long ago the poet Horace said, "I am the friend of fountains," and no true Roman, ancient or modern, is without some sentiment for the fountains which are "the joyful voice" of Rome.

In the old Imperial days Agrippa first dreamed of making Rome a city of running water, and built at his own expense two hundred aqueducts, one hundred and thirty reservoirs, several baths and fish-pools, and more than two hundred fountains. Later emperors, not to be outdone, built new aqueducts, bringing vast streams of water down from the hills, until in Trajan's time Rome had some thirteen hundred fountains.

The splendor of Imperial Rome passed. Her mighty armies, her pageants, and festivals faded into world memories, and her beautiful buildings crumbled to historic ruins. But the fountains of Rome played on, the only happy things in a fallen city. And today, as in ancient times, they flash in the sun in busy market places, play among the statues in cool marble basins, and send up sparkling jets between the cypress trees in dim old gardens. They are still the joy and pride of the people.

Small wonder then that these fountains should have been the inspiration of the first and finest of Respighi's series of Roman sketches. Prefacing the score of *The Fountains of Rome* is this note: "In this symphonic poem the composer has endeavored to give expression to the sentiments and visions suggested to him by four of Rome's fountains, contemplated at the hour in which their character is most in harmony with the surrounding landscape, or in which their beauty appears most impressive." Respighi himself is said to have written the brief description which prefaces each of the fountains.

The Fountain of Valle Giulia at Dawn

The first part of the poem, inspired by the fountain of Valle Giulia, depicts a pastoral landscape; droves of cattle pass and disappear in the fresh, damp mists of the Roman dawn.

In the sixteenth century Pope Julius owned a vast estate extending from the river Tiber eastward up the valley which has since borne his name. Here on a little road leading toward the northern spur of Mount Parioli, he built a great villa. Because the highway was dusty and steep at this point and because, as some say, Julius wanted to ease a conscience which pricked him for having tapped one of the great aqueducts for his own use, he decided to make a resting place for the country folk who toiled up and down from the little farms on the Campagna, taking their flocks, their fruits, flowers, and vegetables to the markets in the city below. So he built two public fountains, on the right, one for animals, and on the left against the wall of the villa, a very beautiful one for human travelers. Today the windows of the villa are walled up, and the stately columns and capitals, the tablets with their Latin inscriptions, and the carven coats of arms are gray with lichen. But the fountain still stands, a jocund old head said to be a likeness of merry *Papa* Guilio himself, with a dolphin on either side, and all three of them sending quiet little streams through their water-worn teeth.

"Those who visit Villa Giulia in the early morning," writes a traveler, "may see the country carts drawn up before the fountain of Pope Julius, sleepy drivers, tired horses, and responsible little dogs refreshing themselves with water."

The music begins with the murmuring figure which throughout the piece is to suggest the fountain:

Copyright, 1918, by G. Ricordi & Co.

Clearly and cleverly has the composer assigned the orchestral parts. Harp and strings play the water motif; brasses with gentle, harmonious lowings, suggest the flocks and herds; while the woodwinds appropriately become shepherd pipes. Yet it is done without the slightest taint of imitation. So delicate is the suggestion of men, animals, and fountain that they blend into the idea of a pastoral landscape, just as their little motifs blend into music which would charm us even if we had no hint of the picture in Respighi's mind.

After a brief, bubbling introduction, an oboe gives out the main theme:

Copyright, 1918, by G. Ricordi & Co.

which has that feeling of all the time and space in the world, so characteristic of a pastoral tune.

Then a clarinet is heard:

a second shepherd, perhaps, coming up on the other side. A bassoon joins them and presently another oboe.

Then the mood changes. Oboes and a solo 'cello join in a lovely song in bright major tonality:

The water motif begins to glisten with chromatics. There is an expectant pause. A solo oboe pipes the first theme again, but now a sense of warmth and light steals through the music and a momentary lifting up of eyes and hearts. Surely this is the sunrise!

The picture then fades until only the echo of a shepherd's call floats back as he disappears down the misty valley.

The Fountain of Triton in the Morning

A sudden loud and insistent blast of horns above the trills of the whole orchestra introduces the second part, "The Triton Fountain." It is like a joyous call, summoning troops of Naiads and Tritons, who come running up, pursuing each other and mingling in a frenzied dance between the jets of water.

The Fountain of Triton dominates an open square in front of the Barberini Palace and the shops which have gradually crept up beside it. Dolphins uphold a huge shell upon which stands a Triton, trumpeter of the seas. In his hand he holds a conch shell upon which he blows such a mighty blast that the obedient streams of water leap out and break over his shining body. Although roughened by centuries of weather and water, he looks very much alive. And he seems to breathe all his splendid energy into his call, a call which surely every passer-by must hear!

We hear it in the introduction to Respighi's music, loud and clear in the horns:

followed by a leaping and trilling of strings and woodwinds and by a shower of chromatic scale passages.

Then flutes, clarinets, and harps begin the scherzo:

a tune in morning mood, as whimsical as the playing water and as impossible to quote.

A second motif follows:

for woodwinds and celesta, against trilling violins and upward running harps.

The music frolics on, leaping:

and tossing, then grows quiet. The sound of Triton's horn, now muted and far away, becomes a bridge leading into the next movement.

The Fountain of Trevi at Midday

Next there appears a solemn theme, borne on the undulations of the orchestra. It is the fountain of Trevi at Midday. The solemn theme, passing from the wood to the brass instruments, assumes a triumphal character. Trumpets peal; across the radiant surface of the water there passes Neptune's chariot, drawn by sea horses and followed by a train of sirens and tritons. The procession then vanishes, while faint trumpet blasts resound in the distance.

This most pretentious of the four movements pictures the most pretentious of the fountains, Trevi, in the brazen light of noon. Built against the wall of the Palazzo Poli, the Fountain of Trevi has three heroic figures, Health and Fertility standing at the sides, while down from the center colonnade rides Neptune behind his plunging horses. From beneath each of these figures (Trevi means *three way*) dashes a stream of water in joyous freedom after the long imprisonment of its journey from the hills. Down the terraces of rustic rock it foams and shouts its way and swirls into the mossy pools below. Here, often as not, may be seen the latest model of Roman street urchin companioning the ancient sea gods. For Trevi is a small boy's dream come true — a fountain of pennies! He who tosses a coin into the waters of Trevi, so the legend goes, will surely return to Rome some happy day, and rare is the traveler who can resist the idea!

Like the fountain, Respighi's music is all exuberant energy. Because Trevi is the fountain over which the sea god himself presides, its music is dominated by the majesty of the brasses. A solemn theme for bassoons:

Copyright, 1918, by G. Ricordi & Co.

passed on to the horns and borne upon choppy little waves in the strings, serves as the introduction.

Then the trombones announce a theme:

Copyright, 1918, by G. Ricordi & Co.

which might well be the voice of Neptune shouting above the triple *forte* confusion of the plunging, tossing strings and woodwinds.

Later, to an accompaniment of descending chromatics, a horn theme:

Copyright, 1918, by G. Ricordi & Co.

and near the end a triumphant call from trumpets and trombones:

Copyright, 1918, by G. Ricordi & Co.

emerge. However, this music is less concerned with tunefulness than with giving the impression of unbounded vitality.

In the calm that follows, one feels that it is not the fountain which has spent itself, but the less enduring onlooker.   The waters of Trevi and the immortal Neptune plunge on, though we have walked away.   We hear now only the quiet voice of a clarinet above the gently rippling water:

And the last faraway note of the trumpet call:

mingles with the first soft tones of the next movement.

The Fountain of the Villa Medici at Sunset

The fourth part, "The Villa Medici Fountain," is announced by a sad theme, which rises above a subdued warbling.   It is the nostalgic hour of sunset.   The air is full of the sound of tolling bells, birds twittering, leaves rustling.   Then all dies peacefully into the silence of the night.

From misty dawn in the Valle Giulia, through lighthearted morning and noisy noon, moves this Roman day to an end in the twilight on the Pincian Hill.   Here, in its beautiful old gardens, stands the famous Villa Medici, built by a sixteenth-century cardinal and now for many years the home of the French Académie des Beaux-Arts.

Directly before the door of the Villa and set in an opening in the thick ilex trees is the fountain of the Medici, a shallow marble urn with a single column of water quietly rising, falling, and overflowing into the little pool at its base.   For centuries this plain little fountain has looked out over the panorama of the Seven Hills: on the patterned squares of the city, the bright domes of S. Carlo al Corso and St. Peter's, and beyond to the Campagna stretching away to the sea.   And because the Pincio with its wonderful view is the most popular promenade in Rome, the fountain has watched generations of young seminarists with their color-splashed cassocks, officers in bright uniforms, lovers upon whom the sunsets are wasted, singing students, beggars, flower girls, nursemaids and babies — all the picturesque processional of Roman life passing to and fro in the summer twilight.

"Often," says a Roman visitor, "very early in those spring mornings which are so fair in Rome, or maybe on an autumn evening under a moon great and golden as the sun, I have wandered through the city of fountains for the sake of their song.   And as I turned toward the Pincio, presently, still far off, I hear the most beautiful voice in Rome, the single melody, languid and full of mystery and all enchantment, of the fountain before the Villa Medici, where, under the primeval ilex, a single jet of water towers like some exquisite lily to droop and fall in unimagined loveliness into its brimming vase of marble."

To an accompaniment of softly wimpling harps and celesta and the sound of distant bells, the flutes and English horn give out that "single melody, languid and full of mystery and all enchantment":

As the music dreams on, the air seems filled with the rustling of leaves and the subdued vesper song of the birds. From the strings comes a haunting call:

thrice repeated and ever more poignant — the wistful voice of twilight.

Then the strings bring back the enchanting melody, the song of the fountain, which is echoed by a solo flute. Below in the city the evening bells begin to ring; from the strings comes a sudden flush of color, like the rose-gold afterglow of sunset, and a suggestion of organ tones. "Then all dies peacefully into the silence of the night."

➤➤✂︎◀︎◀︎

CHAPTER II

Voices of the North

Mirrors, from the first woodland pool that puzzled primitive man to the French plate confection on Beauty's dressing table, have always been mysterious things, breeding strange legends and superstitions. In olden times, people gifted with second sight were supposed to see in mirrors, crystals, and basins of clear water, glimpses of life's hidden mysteries. All of which seems but an absurd fancy to our science-spectacled eyes.

But fact and fancy are not nearly so far apart as most of us think. We live quite intimately, every day, with the most magic of mirrors, the most flawless of crystals — music. Those who have the gift of musical second sight — and you need not be the seventh son of a seventh son to have it — may see life strangely and beautifully reflected in patterned tone.

Beethoven's Fifth Symphony holds no image of the untidy, eccentric man his neighbors knew, but rather that of Man the Struggler, the master of his fate. And as we gaze, the image gradually blurs, takes on familiar outlines and expressions, and to our surprise becomes our own; we see *our* struggles and triumphs reflected there!

Not only Beethoven, but you or I also are to be found in music's mirror. It reflects whole races and nations of men. Like the shadowy third rainbow we sometimes see after a shower, it even reflects the background of nature and events against which those nations have played their parts.

Folk music is the natural mirror, the little pool which catches flickering bits of color and motion; composed music, the French glass with its steadier, more studied image. And when composed music makes conscious use of folk themes and folk spirit, why then it becomes a triple mirror reflecting a nation from every angle, past, present, and future.

There is no more faithful reflection of national life than the music of the North, those winter nations, Norway, Sweden, Denmark, and Finland. Nature has made this a land of striking contrasts: somber forests and smiling meadows, towering peaks and deep-sea valleys, brief colorful summer days and dark months when the sun hides below the horizon and when, in the old days, winter was "a long and fearsome night when God knew what was abroad, and the peasants huddling together about their fires fiddled and sang and retold old tales to forget the evil things that screamed in the wind."

Life has never been easy in the North, yet out of the long dramatic strife with the elements came not only the vigor and independence which marks the Scandinavian people but also a love of nature such as is not to be found in the easygoing South. One could scarcely be indifferent to as much wild beauty as the North affords. Only five per cent of the huge country of Norway is inhabited, seventy per cent being peaks and glaciers, with the remaining twenty-five dense forest. The little farms and villages lie far apart, completely cut off in winter. Neighbors are more often blessings than bores, which may account for the warm hospitality and the hilarious merrymaking of the Scandinavian peasants when they do get together. Isolation has given the Northmen one of their finest traits, the habit of reflection, which makes them poets and idealists.

The northern peoples are deeply religious. They served their old Norse gods in fear and trembling, and although they were among the earliest Christian converts, a faint shadow of their pagan days still lingers in remote places.

An old Icelandic wonder tale tells of a hero, Olafur, who, riding far into the mountains, came upon an elf maiden who said:

"Come, you, and live with us."

"Not will I with fairies live," said Olafur stoutly, "rather will I believe in God." To which the elf maiden replied:

"Even though you live with elves you can fully believe in God." Which naïve statement expresses something characteristically Scandinavian. They just can't quite give up their fairies, and fortunate it is for literature and music!

The music of the North, like the life it expresses, is dramatic and reflective. In it we hear a mountain ruggedness, a Viking strength, and a tenderness as delicate as the pale birch trees of the northern spring. We hear sadness, too, not so much the sort caused by human emotions as the mystic, awesome feeling that comes of being much alone with wild nature.

Northern music has a strange sweetness. It is never the heavy mimosa and jasmine of the southern folk song, but a fragrance like wild grape bloom, a haunting sweetness that stirs old memories. And there is a gentle blurring of major and minor which must have come from the ever-changing northern sky.

Love of country and love of music are dominant themes in the life of the North, and it is not at all surprising that the two have mingled and given us, in the music of Grieg and Sibelius, reflected images more true and more beautiful than reality itself.

EDWARD HAGERUP GRIEG

Bergen — 1843
Bergen — 1907

After that brief, black hour when Bonnie Prince Charlie and his ragged band of dreamers were driven from the field of Culloden, bringing to an end one of the most romantic of history's true stories, many discouraged Scotchmen left their native land to seek homes elsewhere. Among them was a young man named Greigh. He had loved the rugged beauty of the Highlands and the breath of the North Sea, and he hoped to find their like again. So turning his back on the easygoing South, he pushed on to the Norseman's country and settled in the quaint old city of Bergen. Here he translated his name to the Norwegian "Grieg," and married a Norwegian girl; and here, a century later, his great-grandson, Edward Grieg, tone poet of the North, was born.

One can scarcely imagine a happier setting for childhood than that pleasant Grieg home. How different it was from the disorder and desolation that shadowed poor little Ludwig van Beethoven or the bleak poverty that was forever pinching valiant little Franz Schubert! The father was an amiable, cultured man and an enthusiastic amateur pianist, although later he confessed that he never could care for the curious music his famous son wrote. Madame Grieg, the boy's mother, was a pianist. As a young girl she had studied in London and Hamburg and had appeared as piano soloist in many formal concerts. After her marriage she opened her home on one evening of each week to the music lovers of Bergen, and delightful times they had, playing and singing the old favorites, trying new compositions, and discussing music and music makers. Tucked away in one corner of the room a happy little boy sat listening. He did not always understand the music or the talk, but he felt the joy and the enthusiasm of those evenings and knew that this music which sounded so pretty must be something important to cause such a stir in the world of grownups. This same clever mother wrote poems and little plays, and could tell the most enchanting stories of the Vikings and the legendary kings, queens, and warriors of old Norway whose daughter she was.

Years afterward when someone asked Grieg, then a famous composer, what was the first great success of his life, he replied that it was an early experiment on his mother's piano, "that wonderful mysterious satisfaction as I stretched out my arms over the piano, to discover — not melody, that was still far off, no — that there was such a thing as harmony. First a third, then a chord of three notes, then a full chord with four, ending at last with both hands. O joy! a combination of five, a ninth chord! When I discovered that, my happiness knew no bounds. That was indeed a success! No later success ever excited me as that one did. I was then about five years old." Four-year-old Franz Schubert had a like thrilling adventure with chords, and it is rather significant that these two little twigs, bent toward discovering pleasing combinations of tones, should have grown into masters of the most charming and unusual harmonies.

When Edward Grieg was six, his mother began to give him lessons on the piano.

Little did I then suspect that disappointments awaited me. But only too soon was it clear to me that I would have to practice, and that did not suit me at all. And my mother was strict, inexorably strict. Her mother heart must surely have found joy in the fact that many things came quickly to me — evidence of the artistic nature — but she never showed the least sign of any satisfaction. On the contrary, there was no joking with her if she found me dreaming at the keyboard instead of diligently practicing my lesson. And even if I summoned all my strength to practice my finger exercises and scales and all the other devilish technical stunts that seemed to my childish mind stones instead of bread, she still kept the reins in her hands, even if she were not in the room. One day her threatening voice came from the kitchen where she was preparing the midday meal: "Shame, Edward; F-sharp, F-sharp, not F!" I was overpowered by her masterfulness.

At about this same time the child started to school. Compared with the many interests at home, school seemed a dull place. Grieg admits that he was a lazy little thing with a head full of excuses for getting out of lessons, even to the extent of standing under dripping eaves until he was so wet that the teacher would have to send him home. "Often," he says, "I made the intimate acquaintance of a stick."

Once in a boresome arithmetic class, a brilliant idea struck him. "In order to finish as soon as possible, I left out all the ciphers, since, as I understood it, they meant nothing." It does not tax the imagination to guess what followed! "But," says Grieg, "I profited through experience, and since then have learned to reckon with ciphers."

One day when asked to bring a composition to school, young Edward brought Variations on a German Melody, for Piano, by Edward Grieg, Opus I. "The teacher, for reasons I have already indicated, was not very fond of me; he arose, came to me, looked at the music book, and said, in an especially ironic voice, 'Is that so? The boy is musical — the boy is a composer — really now!' Then he opened the door into the next classroom, called the teacher, and said to him, 'Here is something worth while. The little rascal here is a composer!' Both teachers turned over the pages of my book with apparent interest. All the children in both classes stood up. It was a great moment, I was anticipating a great triumph — but it was one of those times when it is not wise to be too hasty. For hardly had the other teacher turned to his own class, when my teacher suddenly changed his tactics, seized me by the hair till I saw stars, and said roughly: 'The next time you will bring your dictionary — do you hear? — and leave this stupid stuff at home!' Ah, so near the heights of joy, and then suddenly to be plunged to depths of woe! How often that has happened to me in later life! And it always reminds of that first time." Opus I was tossed into the fire! From such a picture of school life one is not surprised that gentle little Edward Grieg hated it and was tempted to extremes of naughtiness to get away from it, even for a little while.

But in spite of all the music which the boy constantly heard and made, his first ambition was to be a preacher, and curiously enough his idea of preaching was mixed up with a passion for poetry. He would memorize all the poems in his school readers and then declaim them, in season and out — mostly out, it seemed to his long-suffering family. "When my father, after dinner, would settle himself for a nap in his armchair, I could not leave him in peace, but would take my place behind a chair which represented my pulpit and preach away, with no regard for his feelings whatever!"

Like all Scandinavians, the Griegs were great lovers of nature. They lived in a beautiful country place, and the children — there were five of them — had a happy out-of-door life. Sometimes the father took the two little boys on excursions into the mountains where Edward was overwhelmed with delight at the wild and lovely scenery. The old folk tales his mother had told him would then come alive, and he could see the trolls in their little pointed caps creeping in and out of the crevices of those towering rocks and the nixies peering through the sparkling veil of the waterfalls.

He loved to lie on his back in the tall meadow grass and watch the lazy summer clouds sailing like fairy fleets across the sky. The world seemed a giant picture book which by some magic had caught sounds and scents as well as color, and as he turned the pages, Edward decided that the very nicest thing a man could do would be to paint these pictures for himself. Yes — he would be an artist!

Then one summer day, a rider came galloping up the road and right into Edward Grieg's life, bringing new dreams for old. It was Ole Bull, the world-famous violinist, come back to his home town, Bergen, for a visit. The boy had often heard of this master fiddler whom his mother and father knew well. It seemed too wonderful that his idol should be there talking and laughing as if he were just an ordinary person! "Speechless with astonishment we listened to the marvelous tales of his journeys to America. That was indeed something for my childish fancy! When he was told that I had composed some music, I was obliged to sit at the piano; all my entreaties were of no avail. Today I am unable to understand what Ole Bull could find in my childish musical efforts. But he was quite serious, and spoke earnestly with my parents. Suddenly Ole Bull came over to me, shook me by the shoulders in a way that was peculiar to him, and said, 'You must go to Leipzig and become a musician.' All looked lovingly at me, and I had a feeling as if a good fairy was stroking my cheek."

And so to Leipzig went Edward Grieg in his sixteenth year, feeling as he said, "like a parcel stuffed with dreams." He was admitted at once to the great conservatory, quite a triumph for one so young. At first he was mortally homesick. The "dark, tall, uncanny houses and narrow streets" of old Leipzig seemed to take his breath away. He clung to his short belted blouse as the one reminder of the boys at home, and went about so disconsolately that the husband of his landlady took him to task with, "Now see here, my dear Grieg, we have the same sun, the same moon, and the same God that you have in Norway!" Gradually, through his music, he recovered, and became a part of the interesting new life about him.

The Conservatory of Leipzig, although famous as the school founded by Mendelssohn and fostered by Schumann, was at that time sadly lacking in system. Each professor went his own way, and young Grieg shifted about for some time before he found teachers who understood his needs and appreciated his peculiar gifts. His harmony classes were conspicuously unharmonious as to relations between teacher and pupil. The boy insisted upon his own combinations rather than those of the book, and upset the teacher whom he in turn accused of teaching "the solution of musical riddles" rather than the writing of music. He was still given to daydreaming over the keyboard when he should have been doing diligent scales, and there was no watchful mother to cry from the kitchen, "Shame, Edward!"

When he was eighteen he suddenly awoke to the fact that the other "foreigners," especially the English boys, among whom was the brilliant young Arthur Sullivan of *Mikado* fame, were leaving him far behind. He realized that if he would progress, he must do the drudgery faithfully as they did. So in an acute attack of conscience our dreamy Norwegian boy began to work night and day, scarcely allowing himself proper time to eat and sleep, and the result was not the merry triumphs of those red-cheeked Britishers, but a serious illness which left Grieg a frail fellow with only one lung. His mother came and took him back to Bergen to recover, but as soon as the summer was over he insisted upon returning to Leipzig, where he completed the two remaining school years, winning honors both as composer and performer.

So Edward Grieg, not yet twenty, came home with a German conservatory diploma in his pocket, German musical models in his head, but the spirit of Norway singing in his heart. Naturally his parents and musical friends, among them the composer Gade, expected Edward to settle down with his nice new education and play a musical version of the old game of "follow the leader." Had he not a variety of styles from Mozart to Mendelssohn to pattern after? And while they applauded the original compositions he played at his first formal concerts, they shook their heads and warned him that his music sounded a little too Norwegian.

While the young composer stood hesitating at the crossroads, Ole Bull came along and a second time pointed out the way. The violinist had a country home near Bergen where he spent most of his summers. He welcomed this interesting son of his old friends, and Grieg was only too happy to be with the great man. They played Mozart together in Ole Bull's studio, sometimes joined by Edward's brother John, who was an excellent 'cellist. But more often the two would tramp the mountains rejoicing in the silvery peaks, the lakes and fjords, and the little valleys gay with wild flowers. And best of all were those wild-flower tunes — the old folk songs and dances which the peasants in remote hamlets would play for them. Ole Bull would gather these tunes and take them away to delight his audiences in Europe and America.

He little suspected what influence they were having on young Grieg. To love the old tunes and play them was one thing, but to think of using them as the germ of serious composition was quite another, and he actually advised Grieg to stick to Mozart and not do anything rash and "modern"! It was rather like feeding a fire with one hand and pouring on water with the other!

Then Richard Nordraak appeared, twenty-one, full of musical ideas, and enthusiastically Norwegian, and the two young fellows were friends at once. Nordraak lacked training, but he had an artist's soul and a splendid purpose which Grieg was technically equipped to carry out. Together they planned to write and encourage music which should be as distinctly Scandinavian as their mother tongue. They would do this by glorifying Scandinavian folk music.

Every country has its folk music which is the expression of national traits rather than the emotions of any one composer. A typical Scotch, Negro, or Oriental folk song has certain features which are as racially identifying as any peculiarity of stature, coloring, slant of eye, or prominent cheek bone. But beautiful and vital as folk music may be, it is too casual, too simple in form to do more than glimpse a single mood, and when played on an instrument without the help of words or dance steps to give it variety, it soon becomes monotonous in its repetition. A composer does not simply transplant a folk song into the midst of a symphony, where it would be as out of place as a jack-in-the-pulpit in a bed of Darwin tulips. Instead he studies it, looking for any odd scale steps, noticing every rhythmic quirk and dislocated accent, and then with these characteristics in mind fashions a suitable setting for his folk theme. The theme itself may undergo many changes, turning upside down and inside out and appearing clothed in various colored harmonies. Sometimes the folk tune never really appears but simply furnishes a model for original themes from which the musician composes his piece.

In such ways Grieg and Nordraak hoped to give a Norwegian flavor to their music. They also founded a society, the object of which was to bring forward the works of young northern composers, and musical Copenhagen began to "go Scandinavian" in earnest. Then Nordraak died, and Grieg and the others had to carry on alone.

It was at about this time that Grieg first met his cousin Nina, the daughter of a famous Danish actress. The girl had a charming voice, and Grieg fell so in love with the singing and the singer that he was inspired to write that most popular of songs, "I Love You" (Jeg elsker Dig). They became engaged; Nina's mother objected, not that she disliked Edward, but simply because, as she said, "He is nothing, he has nothing, and he makes music to which no one listens." Nevertheless, they were married, and like lovers in a fairy tale, they lived happily ever afterward. Grieg wrote most of his songs to and for his wife. Nina Grieg was not a great artist, but she seemed so much a part of those lovely lyrics of the North and sang them with such sincerity and charm that her English and European audiences, accustomed to their conventional opera singers, felt a delightful sense of refreshment at her concerts. And it was not long before she might have said to her mother, "He *is* something, he *has* something, and he makes music to which *everyone* listens!"

Only two real shadows fell across the lives of these good companions — the constant anxiety over Grieg's frail health and the death of their only child, a little girl of thirteen months. The child's death was a great sorrow, for Grieg loved children dearly, and to the end of his life he would speak wistfully and tenderly of some cunning little trick of this long-lost baby.

On the whole, Grieg's life was a pleasant one. Twice he visited Italy, seeing much of Liszt, who was then in Rome. The older master was quick to see the unusual beauty of Grieg's music and generously praised it. On one occasion, after he had played Grieg's piano concerto at sight in brilliant fashion, Liszt cried, "Go on, I tell you, you have the right stuff in you! And don't let them scare you." Words which heartened Grieg many times when little critics wrote that he had "stuck in a fjord and couldn't get out," and similar nonsense.

Grieg enjoyed a popularity and an enthusiastic appreciation such as few composers have known during their lifetimes. He went back to Leipzig and received a perfect ovation. London lost its head over his music, and he went there repeatedly to conduct his orchestral works and give piano and song recitals with his wife's assistance. In Paris Grieg experienced one of the most dramatic moments of his life. He had received an invitation to give a concert there just at the time when the notorious Dreyfus case was being settled. Grieg, like thousands of people the world over, was shocked at the apparent lack of justice in that famous trial, and replied that he could not accept an invitation to play in a country where such an outrageous thing could happen. The papers made much of his reply, and said that he had insulted France. Four years later he was again asked to give a concert in Paris. This time he accepted, but for a while it seemed that the evening was to be a failure. A group of rowdies hissed, stamped, whistled, and cried, "Show the insulter of France the door!" Grieg calmly waited until those who wanted to hear his music had demanded quiet. Then the program began, and the listeners were so carried away by its beauty that even one of the enemies, who probably found himself joining in the wild applause, jumped and shouted, "we applaud only the artist and great musician." Grieg was not seriously troubled by this unusual demonstration. He wrote to a friend, "Well, I have, in my old age, at last succeeded in getting hissed! But who can tell, if I had not been hissed, I would perhaps not have had such an enormous success!"

Aside from these concert tours, Grieg lived quietly in his beloved Northland. For a time he stayed in Christiana, where he busied himself with teaching, composing, and giving concerts with the Musical Society of which he and Svendsen were founders and conductors. Then the government, in recognition of the splendid service which the Griegs had given to the music of Norway, granted them an annuity which made it possible for Grieg to give up teaching and conducting and devote all his time to composing.

Characteristically, they left the city to seek the quiet and beauty of nature and the peasant music they so loved. For a time they lived at Lofthus, a picturesque spot on a branch of the Hardänger Fjord. There, in what he thought to be an inaccessible spot, Grieg had a tiny studio built, just big enough for a piano, a fireplace, and himself, for he never could bear having anyone listen, not even his wife, while he was composing. But the sound of his piano was like the music of the Pied Piper in its drawing power, and often he would find quite an audience of curious people gathered outside. There seemed nothing to do but have a "moving bee," so Grieg's peasant friends came and rolled the little "tune house" down to a place quite near the water where it stood amid lonely pines and boulders, far from any road. But it wasn't long before people were coming in row boats to listen! So Grieg gave up Lofthus, and taking his "tune house" with him, went to an isolated spot in the heart of the mountains about four miles from his birthplace, Bergen. There on a hill overlooking a lake, he built a pleasant house with a terrace from which he could view the country for miles around and study the stars of the lovely northern sky. He called the place Troldhaugen (Troll's Hill), which seems appropriate for the dwelling of one who had always felt more at home in the wood with the elves and fairies than in the crowded cities. At the entrance of Troldhaugen stood a post with this inscription: "Edward Grieg does not desire to receive callers earlier than four o'clock in the afternoon."

But for all this solitude seeking, Edward and Nina Grieg were friendly folk and delightful hosts to many a musical pilgrim. Grieg was a lively companion, loved a good story, and his own conversation sparkled with a Puckish humor. When one thinks of his poor body, how for more than forty years he literally fought for breath much of the time, the wonder is that he could ever be merry, much less write music as rollicking as his Norwegian Dances, or as heroically strong as the *Sigurd Jorsalfar* march! Like Robert Louis Stevenson, he proved that genius may ignore even a broken body.

Grieg had a slight figure, quick, nervous movements, a rather large head covered with long, light hair, usually tousled, and eyes, "superb green-grey, in which one seems to catch a glimpse of Norway, its melancholy fjords, and its luminous mists." Tchaikovsky says, "He had an uncommon charm, and blue eyes, not very large, but irresistibly fascinating, recalling the glance of a charming and candid child . . . it is not surprising that everyone should delight in Grieg and that he should be popular everywhere — in Paris, London, Moscow."

All sorts of honors were heaped upon Grieg. He was elected to the Swedish Academy of Music, the Musical Academy at Leyden, the French Academy of Fine Arts, given honorary degrees of Doctor of Music at Cambridge and at Oxford, but none of it turned his head. When a friend wrote, congratulating him on being elected member of the French Legion of Honor, Grieg wittily replied: "I thank you for your congratulations. My election as member of the French Legion is, however, an 'honor' I share with 'legions,' so let us waste no more words about it." He valued these expressions of esteem, but he was too modest to display the imposing titles and decorations. Once when on a concert tour the reigning duke of a German state presented him with a badge of one of the orders — a very particular compliment — Grieg simply said, "Thank you," and put the decoration in one of the rear pockets of his dress coat. But the duchess saved him from committing a serious social blunder. "My dear Mr. Grieg," she said, "let me show you how such a badge should be worn," and fastened the decoration with her own hands on the lapel of his coat.

Although often invited, Grieg never came to America. He dreaded the long sea voyage, and once told some American friends that he would consider crossing only in case they could give him a written guarantee that the Atlantic ocean would behave itself!

He lived quietly at Troldhaugen until the summer of 1907, when an urgent invitation came to conduct a Grieg program at the Leeds Festival in England. He yielded to the temptation and got as far as Bergen, where he was to take the boat, when he became so ill that he was taken to a hospital instead, and there early one September morning he died in his sleep, as gently as he had lived.

All the world grieved at his passing, but the Norwegians, from king to shepherd boy, felt a sharp personal loss, for no composer was ever dearer to his countrymen than Grieg. Over forty thousand people came to the Bergen Museum of Art, where Grieg's funeral was held, and heard as a last message from the master a short program of his music, ending with the beautiful Funeral March in A Minor which he had written as a tribute to his dear Nordraak.

Grieg's body was cremated, and his friend and neighbor, Frants Beyer, tells the last of the story: "On Troldhaugen is a mountain wall facing westwards toward the fjord. Its summit is crowned with small birches and spruces. At the bottom the rocks are covered with a dense growth of ferns, bird cherries, mountain ash, and birches enwreathing the place. Grieg had repeatedly spoken to me of this spot as his last resting place, the last time only a few weeks before his death. In accordance with the wishes of Mrs. Grieg, who was at that time in Denmark, one evening in April, 1908, while the setting sun sent its rays into the simple grotto and a blackbird sobbed its soft tunes in the spruces above, I, in presence of my wife and Mr. Bull, put the urn containing Grieg's ashes into the cave, and a stone was placed in front." It reminds one of the lines from Stevenson's beautiful "Requiem,"

This be the verse you grave for me:
"Here he lies where he longed to be."

All the world loves a label and few writers can resist the temptation to fashion one. Such intriguing titles as "Father of His Country," "Sunshine City," "Flowery Kingdom" are bits of poetry which never fail to catch the popular fancy. Yet taken too literally, clever labels become almost libels, for like the few lines of a caricature they so overemphasize certain peculiarities that we remember them only and fail to look for anything further.

In the indefinite world of art, labels are often sadly misleading. The critic who first called Grieg a "miniature painter" unwittingly did him an injustice. True, Grieg wrote mostly little pieces and never a symphony, oratorio, or opera — the murals of music. And he did create a fragile beauty which might well be compared to the delicate translucence of painting on porcelain or ivory. But Grieg's spirit was far from miniature. Even in his shorter works there is no suggestion of microscopic detail or the "reduced image." Who could call the Triumphal March from *Sigurd Jorsalfar* or the "Shipwreck" from *Peer Gynt*, No. 2 fragile? Or who, hearing the beautiful "Autumn Storm" or "Eros" flinging their lusty challenge to the northern winter, could think of porcelain? Grieg could, when he chose, put as much virility into a single page as many another composer has expressed in a ponderous sonata. After all, one need not be colossal to be heroic!

Like Schubert, Schumann, Chopin, and Mendelssohn, Grieg sought to enchant the senses of his listeners until they could hear the voices, see the pictures, and dream the dreams his music conjured. The large, intricate patterns were not suited to his purpose, for who ever heard of a dream's being logical! Grieg's music is intimate, suggestive, intangible, and like the other Romanticists he cast it in smaller molds. His choice of the shorter forms was further influenced by the folk songs which were his inspiration.

From these same Norwegian songs and dances come many of the peculiarities which hallmark Grieg's music: the open fifths which strum along in the bass suggesting the peasant bagpipes:

the downward curve of the melody, so typical of all Norwegian music:

and, most characteristic of all, the short phrases, often only two or three measures in length, yet each phrase an entire musical thought, repeated, almost literally, in one key after another.

then, a moment later:

Daniel Gregory Mason has cleverly said, "Grieg never weaves a tapestry, he assembles a mosaic." It is true that the threads of his melody do not mingle to form new designs, as Beethoven's do, but lie side by side, each little motif complete in itself and easily recognized even when it appears in a different colored harmony. This so-called "wallpaper pattern" method of composition, charming as it is in many of his works, was Grieg's greatest weakness.

But interesting as a composer's mannerisms may be, they are not the music lover's chief concern. It is the spirit of the music that touches us down where we live. In Grieg's music we hear the voice of the North as he heard it in the music of the people. He once said, "The fundamental trait of Norwegian folk song as contrasted with the German is a deep melancholy which may suddenly change to unrestrained gaiety, mysterious gloom, and indomitable wildness."

The mingling of major and minor modes in Grieg's music is like the ever-changing light in the mountains where sun and shadow play at hide-and-seek with cloud and crag. And there is a fawnlike beauty in many of his pieces, as if a half-wild creature gazed at us for a breathless second out of gentle, melancholy eyes, then went crashing away into the bushes in exuberant leaps and bounds. And always there is the feeling that fairies and trolls are not far away — at any moment we might glimpse a gnomish face!

Grieg expressed the Norwegian spirit so perfectly that people often mistake what is entirely original for local color. His harmonies were his own, as were most of his melodies. In fact, he rarely if ever used a folk tune outright. He simply borrowed the idiom and the atmosphere, and it is hardly fair to say that he borrowed these. As a son of the North, they were rather his inheritance — the idiom, his mother tongue, and the atmosphere — the air which he had breathed from babyhood. So, while Grieg's music is unmistakably Norwegian, it is just as unmistakably "Griegian." It is the expression of an individual as well as a country, otherwise it could not be called art, for art can never be merely a page from a geography.

People everywhere love Grieg's music, as they love Schubert's, because it is not only beautiful, but also warmly human in its various moods, and unpretentious enough to make friends with even the amateur. Only a great chorus can give us oratorio, a great orchestra, the symphony, but a little group or a single performer can wake Grieg's music to life. And the very briefness of his exquisite songs and tone poems lends them a peculiar personal appeal. Grieg himself might have written this little quatrain:

> I would be the lyric
> Ever on the lip
> Rather than the epic
> Memory lets slip.

For his celebrated dramatic poem, *Peer Gynt*, Ibsen borrowed the name, the setting, and many of the incidents from the fantastic folk lore of the Scandinavian peasants. In the character of Peer he is said to have purposed to show his countrymen a not very flattering portrait of themselves, forever boasting of the past glories of Norway while neglecting their present duty toward her and indulging in idle dreams for her future.

However, the satire and "local hits" of a generation ago are of little concern today. For us Peer Gynt is simply a fascinating wonder tale, its hero, the literary brother of Sinbad, Tom Jones, Br'er Rabbit, and the host of other merry rascals whose adventures tickle the fancy of law-abiding folk.

Peer Gynt was the village n'er-do-well, a great hulking fellow of twenty who lived with his widowed mother Ase in the tumble-down ruin of what had once been a proud and prosperous homestead. Peer would not work, but spent his days roaming the mountains with his gun. He seldom brought home anything but a wild story of some marvelous escapade of which he was always the hero. Poor Ase was almost distracted. To live in poverty was bad enough, but to have her only son laughed at by the neighbors and despised for his boastful, lying tales was more than her pride could bear.

As the play opens, Peer is telling his mother another of his impossible stories. She knows it is not true and reproaches him bitterly, reminding him that at that very moment, while he stands there tattered and unkempt, boasting of how he will some day be a prince, the village is gathered to see the girl he might have married, "Ingrid, a golden girl, land entailed on her," marry another man!

Peer replies that it is not yet too late for him to go a-wooing, and seizing his little mother in his arms, starts off to the wedding! Ase, horrified at this last mad notion, threatens to tell the wedding guests just how worthless Peer is, unless he puts her down and turns back home. Instead, Peer perches her safely out of the way on the roof of the millhouse and goes on to the wedding alone!

Arrived at the scene of festivities, Peer as usual tries to attract attention by telling how he once conjured the devil through a wormhole into a nutshell and then shut him in! The wedding guests are disgusted, all but Solveig, a lovely girl who for some strange reason seems to care for Peer in spite of his untidy looks and his crazy talk. She even offers to dance with him.

But Peer Gynt cannot be satisfied with any ordinary merrymaking. An imp of mischief seems to possess him, and the next thing they know, he has stolen the bride and is off up the mountainside with the terrified girl slung over his shoulder! Soon the whole parish is after him with sticks and stones and angry threats. This is just too outrageous a prank, even for Peer Gynt! They'll teach that young good-for-nothing a lesson he'll not soon forget! But although the poor bride, Ingrid, whom Peer had abandoned in the forest, is found and brought safely back, Peer Gynt escapes.

He is now a real outlaw and wanders about the mountains, where he encounters saeter girls, voices in the dark, and even the troll people, into whose kingdom he stumbles. After a while he builds himself a little hut far up among the peaks, and here, one evening, Solveig comes to him. She has always loved him and had faith in him, and now that he is an outcast she can no longer be happy in the village and has given up her home and her family to share his lonely life.   She says:

> I ran upon show-shoes; I asked my way on;
> They said, "Whither go you?"   I answered, "I go home."
>
>   *   *   *
>
> Down below it was airless, one felt as though choked;
>
>   *   *   *
>
> But here, with the fir-branches soughing o'erhead, —
> What a stillness and song! — I am here in my home.
>
>   *   *   *
>
> The path I have trodden leads back nevermore.

Peer welcomes Solveig to his hut.   He is touched by her devotion and her beauty. But even these cannot still the restlessness within him.   Strange dreams beckon him on, and bidding Solveig wait for him, he starts off again, first paying a farewell visit to his mother, whom he finds on her deathbed.

The rest of the story tells of Peer's adventures in foreign lands.   But whether in America, Egypt, or Morocco, and whether in fortune or out, he is always the same boastful fellow, absolutely blinded by delusions of his own grandeur.

At last, a grizzled old man, Peer wearies of wandering and returns through storm and shipwreck to his homeland.   It is a desolate homecoming, for no living creature waits to welcome him.   There are only legends of a young scapegrace named Peer Gynt, who never did a good deed nor made a friend while he lived among them, and who finally drifted off to foreign lands where he has probably been hanged long since.

The last scenes are a curious mingling of the real and the unreal, of fantasy and of the allegory of a misspent life.   In them Ibsen follows the old Scandinavian folk instinct to dramatize everything.   As Peer wanders on the heath thinking over his past life, thread balls roll along at his feet, murmuring:

> We are thoughts:
> Thou shouldst have thought us!

A sighing in the air whispers:

> We are songs:
> Thou shouldst have sung us!

And broken straws cry:

> We are deeds:
> Thou shouldst have achieved us!

Then Peer meets the Button Moulder, who tells him that he was meant for a shining button on the vest of the world, but that somehow his loop must have given way so that he was no good as a button, and therefore he must be melted and recast.   Peer protests that he is not such a bad fellow; he has been something of a bungler he admits, but not a real sinner, and at least he has always been himself.   But the Button Moulder says that for all his selfish, lawless ways he has never been himself, not the self he was meant to be. That is exactly the point! And moreover, he has been too idle to be either a good man or even "a sinner of really grandiose style."

Peer begs to be allowed to prove that he has a list of real sins to his credit and that he has been himself. But wherever he goes for proof, he is either laughed at for his make-believe sins or greeted as one of the many characters he has pretended to be! The Button Moulder grows impatient, and is on the point of throwing Peer in the casting ladle when they see a tiny light gleaming through the trees. It is the light from Solveig's hut, and as they approach they hear her singing. She appears in the doorway, dressed for church, with a psalmbook wrapped in a kerchief and a staff in her hand, a gentle, sweet-faced old woman. Peer flings himself at her feet. Surely she whom he has really wronged, whose life he has wasted in lonely waiting, surely she can cry out the list of his sins! But Solveig says that in her heart he has always been the man God meant him to be, his own true self. And the story ends on that theme, dear alike to medieval moralists and romantic poets — man's redemption through the love of a good woman.

A stage version of *Peer Gynt* was made, and for it Grieg wrote his famous incidental music, twenty-two pieces in all. Unlike its hero, Peer, who went gadding about the wide world, this folk play is rarely ever given outside of Norway, where it is generally considered Ibsen's most important work. So Grieg very wisely combined four of the best pieces of his incidental music into a suite for orchestra. This *Peer Gynt* Suite made such a sensation among concert audiences that later four more numbers were chosen, and we have *Peer Gynt* Suites, No. 1 and No. 2.

In arranging the suites, Grieg thought only of pleasing musical contrast, and for that reason the pieces do not appear in the same order as the incidents which they illustrate in the drama. Suite No. 1 includes "Morning," "The Death of Ase," "Anitra's Dance," and "In the Hall of the Mountain King," while Suite No. 2 gives "The Abduction of the Bride," "Ingrid's Lament," "Arabian Dance," "Peer Gynt's Return (The Storm)," and "Solveig's Song."

Peer Gynt Suite, No. 1

Morning

In his wanderings Peer Gynt met with many misfortunes and discouragements. Once when his schemes had failed and he was tired and disheartened, he decided that the present was "not worth so much as a shoe sole" and that he would turn his attention to the past. So at daybreak we find him in the desert before one of the colossal monuments which were the glory of ancient Egypt, the statue of Memnon, son of Aurora, Goddess of Dawn. This statue was said to make a peculiar singing sound at sunrise. The Greeks said it was the voice of Memnon hailing his mother as she rode across the sky. Science explains the sound as the effect of the dawn wind and the first sunrays striking the porous Nile sandstone which had cooled during the night. The Singing Memnon was one of the wonders of the ancient world, and even today, though it is mute since its restoration after an earthquake shock, it is still fascinating to travelers.

Peer sits there in the dark waiting to hear this voice of the past, and as the sky begins to brighten and the breeze to stir, he says:

> How strange now, — I really fancied there came
> From the statue a sound.   Music, this, of the Past.
> I heard the stone-accents now rising, now sinking.

But for all its Egyptian setting, this morning song is purely Norwegian! Its very marking, *Allegretto pastorale*, suggests a simple country scene.   There is a mystery and magic about the sunrise which does strange things to us, and it may be that Peer Gynt, watching for the day to break, saw instead of African desert, the mountains of his homeland, with the early light flushing the snowy peaks, flashing in the fjord below, and glinting from the sleek coats of cattle grazing in the upland pastures.

Grieg paints this simple pastoral picture by using a single theme in evenly flowing rhythm.   The flute begins softly:

then the oboe reflects the theme and in the last measure lifts it to a higher level:

Again and again this little melody appears, each time in a new and fresher key, giving us the feeling of a brightening sky.   A beautiful shimmering passage in the strings:

broken by a brief figure in the bass:

gives a misty touch to the steadily increasing light, a light film of cloud, perhaps, floating for a moment against the rosy sky.   Then the dawn theme again, the last time cleverly divided between violins and woodwinds.   Clarinets and flutes, trilling on the restless seventh scale-step like birds not quite awake, delay the ending and again suggest the shy Aurora of the north countries rather than the sudden bolder dawn of the tropics.   Then three lovely last chords gently push the fiery ball above the horizon and proclaim the triumph of light over darkness.

The Death of Ase

Scapegrace that he was, Peer Gynt loved his mother, and although he had broken her heart with his foolish ways, he could not start off for foreign lands without bidding her good-by. So at the risk of being caught by the villagers, who had not forgiven him for stealing the bride, he slipped back one evening to his old home and peeped in at his mother's window. He was shocked at what he saw. The room was almost bare, for the furnishings had been taken for debt, but on a little old bed in one corner lay his mother, alone and dying, his name still on her lips.

How happy she was to see him, and how bitterly shamed he felt at his neglect! He wanted to cheer her, so he began to talk of the only happiness he could remember in his mother's life, the days of his childhood.

It is one of Ibsen's master touches, as well as one of the supreme achievements of modern drama, this death scene which becomes a strange game of make-believe between a remorseful man and a delirious old woman, to whose dimming senses nothing is real but the joy of having her little boy again.

PEER

Nay, now we will chat together,
  But only of this and that, —
Forget what's awry and crooked,
  And all that is sharp and sore.
Are you thirsty? I'll fetch you water.
  Can you stretch you? The bed is short.
Let me see; — if I don't believe, now,
  It's the bed that I had when a boy!
Do you mind, dear, how oft in the evenings
  You sat at my bedside here,
And spread the fur coverlet o'er me,
  And sang many a lilt and lay?

ASE

Ay, mind you? And then we played sledges
  When your father was far abroad.
The coverlet served for sledge-apron,
  And the floor for an ice-bound fjord.

PEER

Ah, but the best of all, though, —
  Mother, you mind that too? —
The best was the fleet-foot horses —

ASE

Ay, think you that I've forgot? —
  It was Kari's cat that we borrowed;
It sat on the log-scooped chair —

PEER

To the castle west of the moon, and
  The castle east of the sun,
To Soria-Moria Castle
  The road ran both high and low.
A stick that we found in the closet,
  For a whip-shaft you made it serve.

ASE

Right proudly I perked on the box-seat —

PEER

Ay, Ay; you threw loose the reins,
  And kept turning round as we travelled,
And asked me if I was cold.

*　*　*

ASE

Best bring from the closet the prayer-book;
  I feel so uneasy of soul.

PEER

In Soria-Moria Castle
  The King and the Prince give a feast.
On the sledge-cushions lie and rest you;
  I'll drive you there over the heath —

ASE

But, Peer dear, am I invited?

PEER

Ay, that we are, both of us.
  (*He throws a string round the back of the chair on
which the cat is lying, takes up a stick, and seats him-
self at the foot of the bed.*)
Gee-up! Will you stir yourself, Black-boy?
  Mother, you're not a-cold?
Ay, Ay; by the pace one knows it,
  When Grane begins to go!

ASE

Why, Peer, what is it that's ringing?

PEER

The glittering sledge-bells, dear!

ASE

Oh, mercy, how hollow it's rumbling!

PEER

We're just driving over a fjord.

ASE

I'm afraid! What is that I hear rushing
  And sighing so strange and wild?

PEER

It's the sough of the pine-trees, Mother,
  On the heath. Do you but sit still.

ASE

There's a sparkling and gleaming afar now;
  Whence comes all that blaze of light?

PEER

From the castle's windows and doorways.
  Don't you hear, they are dancing?

ASE

Yes!

PEER

Outside the door stands St. Peter,
  And prays you to enter in.

ASE

Does he greet us?

PEER

He does, with honour,
  And pours out the sweetest wine.

ASE

Wine! Has he cakes as well, Peer?

PEER

Cakes? Ay, a heaped-up dish,
  And the dean's wife is getting ready
Your coffee and your dessert.

ASE

Lord, Lord! Shall we two come together?

PEER

As freely as ever you will!

ASE

Oh, deary, Peer, what a frolic
  You're driving me to, poor soul!

PEER

(*Cracking his whip*)
Gee-up; will you stir yourself, Black-boy!

ASE

Peer, dear, you're driving right?

PEER

Ay, broad is the way.

ASE

            This journey,
It makes me so weak and tired.

PEER

There's the castle rising before us;
  The drive will be over soon.

ASE

I will lie back and close my eyes then,
  And trust me to you, my boy!

PEER

Come up with you, Grane, my trotter!
  In the castle the throng is great;
They bustle and swarm to the gateway.
  Peer Gynt and his mother are here!
What say you, Master Saint Peter?
  Shall mother not enter in?
You may search a long time, I tell you,
Ere you find such an honest old soul.

       *   *   *

       (*Turns toward his mother*)
Why, what makes your eyes so glassy?
  Mother! Have you gone out of your wits —?

      (*Goes to the head of the bed*)
You mustn't lie there and stare so!
  Speak, Mother; it's I, your boy!
(*Feels her forehead and hands cautiously; then
throws the string on the chair, and says softly:*)
Ay, Ay! You can rest yourself, Grane;
  For e'en now the journey's done.
      (*Closes her eyes, and bends over her*)
For all of your days I thank you,
  For beatings and lullabys!
But see, you must thank me back, now —
     (*Presses his cheek against her mouth*)
There; that was the driver's fare.

The musical score of "The Death of Ase" covers but two printed pages, yet that brief space seems to hold all the despair and longing the world has ever known. The music makes not the slightest attempt to suggest the scene as Ibsen describes it. How tawdry it would be to have sledge bells and galloping horses trying to picture that fantastic drive to Heaven's gate!

Grieg knew what every true musician knows, that music's first duty is the expression of human emotion. Therein lies its power and its supremacy even over words, lines, and colors. He knew, as Ibsen knew, that Peer's childish make-believe was just a screen to hide the despair in his heart — words so often float lightly on the surface while life's deepest joy or bitterest sorrow surges down underneath where few can see. So while the drama shows us the death scene as it might have appeared to some scandalized neighbor, the music plays the real tragedy.

It is simple music, based on two short themes as stark and elemental as the feelings they express. As we listen to the violins, muted with emotion, their message seems as strangely real as if a human voice had spoken directly to us. And the measured rhythm which never falters from beginning to end gives the impression of a slow but very sure passing — a solemn recessional — it might be of life, of hope, or of leaves and flowers at the fall of the year.

There is no introduction, sorrow doesn't seem to need one. We hear Peer's heart crying out in its remorse and longing:

This theme always reminds one of Diderot's contention that in certain musical passages we "overhear the human voice." And, unpardonable as it is to impose one's own interpretation upon other listeners, I always seem to hear that voice saying, "Mother, dear!"

Three times this first melody is repeated, and each time the voice rises and grows more intense, even as the speaking voice is apt to do under stress of emotion.

Then the answer comes — a plaintive, sinking theme which might suggest resignation or the futility of anyone's crying out against death, or the sick woman's ebbing strength:

To me it seems again the human voice, the voice of the mother whose faint, last whisper proclaims the love and loyalty of her life in the words, "Oh, my son!"

While in this second theme, four times repeated, the music definitely descends, both in its gradually lowering pitch and in the downward line of the melody itself, Grieg is too much the artist to let it degenerate into monotony, a chute down which we slide to utter dejection. He keeps it interesting and alive by a little countermelody in which the violas push softly upward against the drooping violins:

The little coda, or formal closing, is merely a reiteration of the last notes of the second theme, three notes, three times repeated:

as if Peer, now that all the passion is spent, had to convince himself by whispering again and again the incredible news that his mother is really gone.

"The Death of Ase" is great music, and not because it so admirably fits the scene for which it was written. The whole Peer Gynt story might be forgotten and the name of this music changed to simply "A Lament," or even "Andante Doloroso," and still we could not resist its appealing beauty. It is music for all time and for all people because it expresses feelings which we have all experienced whether in the poignant sorrow of death or merely the wistful twilight sentiment:

> I have so loved thee but cannot, cannot hold thee.
> Fading like a dream, the shadows fold thee.
> Ah, couldst thou but a little longer stay!
> Goodbye, sweet Day,
> Goodbye, sweet Day!

Anitra's Dance

While wandering along the west coast of Morocco, Peer Gynt happened upon a cavern where thieves, frightened by their pursuers, had hidden rich booty — the Emperor's robes and his milk-white charger. Now, as we know, nothing pleased Peer so much as a disguise, and since he was also sorely in need of some transportation other than his own tired legs, he promptly decked himself in the royal robes, mounted the horse, and galloped gaily out across the desert. After a time he came to an oasis on which stood the tents of an Arab chief. When the chief and his people saw Peer in his imposing outfit they were filled with awe and hailed him as a prophet sent from Allah. Peer was not one to refuse such a grand chance to pretend, and we find him, this Norwegian peasant, all but smothered in silks and jewels, resting on cushions, drinking coffee, and smoking a long Turkish pipe, while an adoring bevy of girls, including even the chieftain's daughter, Anitra, dance and sing before him.

> The Prophet is come!
> Wake the flute and the drum!
> The Prophet, the Prophet is come!

After the tranquil "Morning" and the somber "Death of Ase," "Anitra's Dance," like the third movement of a symphony, brings to the suite the welcome contrast of the dance. The story background of this number is Oriental, and a less artistic composer might have tried to imitate, movie-fashion, the monotonous, droning music of the Eastern bazaars. Not so Grieg. He makes a fascinating little tune after the rhythmic pattern of the Polish mazurka, graceful, dainty, and quite cosmopolitan in its charm. Then by his clever orchestration he suggests the scene in the Moroccan desert and the Bedouin dancing girls.

Only strings are used in the scoring — for the accompaniment, plucked strings which remind us of the many lutelike instruments of the Orient, and for the melody, muted strings. But how different the effect of these muted strings from those which sang the dirge of Ase! The *staccato* notes that trip so lightly up and down certainly give no impression of mourning. They are dancers, joyous, abandoned, but decently veiled as becomes ladies East of Suez.

After a short, strumming introduction, the dancing girls appear:

It is easy to picture them moving with light running steps on the *staccato* notes, then whirling in characteristic oriental fashion, tambourines fluttering above their heads on the trills. The musical phrases are short, so, doubtless, are the dancing phrases, for these girls know but the tiny stage of a Turkish rug! And the tinkle of the triangle, marking the accent, suggests the armlets and anklets of the dancers.

The second theme with its languorous gestures, might be the beguiling Anitra, herself:

Then follows a delightful bit of imitation — a musical device which may be defined as the more or less exact repetition by one instrument of a tune portion played by another instrument:

Suddenly the first theme reappears in a bright major key as if the dancers had boldly peeped from behind their veils:

but it is only for a moment — soon they are as decorous and mysterious as before.

In the repetition of the first part Grieg enriches the effect by bringing in the lower strings to imitate the melody and also to play little counterthemes of their own. There is just a touch of yearning in the voice of the 'cello:

which might be a shadow of homesickness flitting across Peer Gynt's mind, even in the midst of all of this elaborate entertainment given in his honor.

One expects the music to end with the two sharply plucked bass notes — they certainly sound final enough. But these are not common dancing girls, amusing a bazaar crowd. A Bedouin princess and her maidens are offering entertainment and hospitality to a prophet. A surprising last chord:

matching a like one heard at the very beginning:

adds a touch of courtesy and ceremony.

Harmonically, it is interesting to find "Anitra's Dance" bounded on the top, or north, by a major chord — its dominant — and on the south by its tonic minor chord!

In the Hall of the Mountain King

In Peer Gynt's fantastic adventures with the troll people, Ibsen's play becomes a true folk piece. For the Old Man of the Mountains and his legions of gnome subjects were a very real and fearsome power in the old days. Even today, with Christian church spires pricking the sky of every valley and prayer books carefully kerchiefed in every cottage chest, the Scandinavian peasant can still see plenty of signs of troll mischief, and therefore steps carefully through the woods. One never can tell about fairies!

After stealing Ingrid, the bride, and abandoning her in the forest, Peer fled high up into the mountains to escape the angry wedding guests. As he roamed about among the beautiful shining peaks, he was seized by a fit of disgust at his own crazy ways. Gazing upward he cried:

> Yonder sail two brown eagles.
> Southward the wild geese fly.
> And here I must splash and stumble
> In quagmire and filth knee-deep!
> > *(Springs up)*
> I'll fly too! I will wash myself clean in
> The bath of the keenest winds!
> I'll fly high! I will plunge myself fair in
> The glorious christening font!
> I will soar far over the saeter;
> I will ride myself pure of soul!
>
> *   *   *
>
> Peer Gynt, thou art come of great things,
> And great things shall come of thee!

He leaps forward but runs his head against a rock, falls, and remains stretched senseless on the ground. As he regains consciousness, the Green-clad One appears, and, alas, for his recent good resolutions, Peer cannot resist trying to make an impression on her. He tells her that he is a king's son, and when she replies that she is the Mountain King's daughter and seems quite pleased with his attention, he goes with her to her father's palace. This may be his chance to become an emperor, if only of a troll kingdom!

In the great hall Peer is led before the throne on which sits the Old Man of the Mountains, crowned and sceptered and surrounded by a great assembly of troll-courtiers, gnomes, and brownies. The crowd examines Peer with curious, hostile eyes, but the King seems much taken with the idea of having a mortal for a son-in-law. He agrees to give Peer his daughter and the realm to her dowry if Peer will promise to stay with them always, and to shun day and deeds and every sunlit spot.

To which Peer replies: "Only call me king, and that's easy to keep."

But there are other conditions to be met. If Peer is to be a troll prince, he must eat troll food, and he is straightway served with a sample by troll waiters with pigs' heads and white night-caps.   It is a nasty mess.   Peer makes a dreadful face, but thinks he may get accustomed to it in time.

Next he is told that he must throw off his Christian man's garb and dress like a troll even to the silk bow at the end of his tail.   Peer protests that he has no tail and what's more wants none.   It is a bit too much like making a beast of a man!   But the Old Man roars,

None comes courting my child with no tail at his rear!

so Peer allows a tail with a bright orange bow to be fastened on by the troll chamberlain, who says:

Just try with what grace you can waggle and whisk it.

Then the Old Man says that he must have his eyes slit so that he may see as a troll sees, which is exactly the opposite to mortal sight.   He gets out his sharp tools to do the slitting, and promises Peer that soon black will seem white, ugly seem fair, big seem little, and dirty seem clean.   But this is too much, too big a price to pay even for the honor of being called King Peer!   Peer says he will take his leave, but the Old Man warns him that the Mountain King's gate opens not outward.   The Green-clad One, overcome with shame at being deserted, falls in a faint, and confusion follows.

THE OLD MAN

Dash him to shards on the rock-walls, children!

THE TROLL-IMPS

Oh, dad, mayn't we play owl-and-eagle first.
The wolf-game!   Grey-mouse and glow-eyed
    cat!

THE OLD MAN

Yes, but quick.   I am worried and sleepy.
Goodnight!   (*He goes*)

PEER
(*Hunted by the Troll-imps*)
Let me be, devil's imps!
                (*Tries to escape up the chimney*)

THE IMPS

Come brownies!   Come nixies!
Bite him behind!

PEER

Ow!   (*Tries to slip down the cellar trap-door*)

THE IMPS

Shut up all the crannies!

THE TROLL COURTIER

Now the small-fry are happy!

PEER

(*Struggling with a little Imp that has bit himself fast
to his ear*)
                Let go will you, beast!

THE COURTIER

(*Hitting Peer across the fingers*)
Gently, you scamp, with a scion of royalty!

PEER

A rat-hole —!   (*Runs to it*)

. . . .

THE IMPS

Slash him!

PEER

Oh, would I were small as a mouse!
                                    (*Rushing around*)

THE IMPS

(Swarming round him)

Close the ring!   Close the ring!

PEER

(Weeping)

Were I only a louse!
(He falls)

THE IMPS

Now into his eyes!

PEER

(Buried in a heap of Imps)

Mother, help me, I die!
(Church bells sound far away.)

THE IMPS

Bells in the mountains! The Black-Frock's
   cows!
(The trolls take flight, amid a confused uproar of yells and shrieks. The palace collapses; everything disappears.)

Only a born Norseman, one who from childhood had known the Little People of the Mountains intimately, could have written "In the Hall of the Mountain King." In this music Grieg is not concerned with universal emotions — although the piece might easily be named "Tantrum" and fit most of us at times — he is painting a picture instead, a picture of Peer Gynt harassed by the furious troll pack.

A prolonged note on muted French horns suggests that moment of suspense when the trolls, their vicious little eyes glittering in the weird underworld twilight, crouch ready to spring upon this rash mortal who has dared to reject a troll princess.   Then out they come, old ones first, bent and knobby with centuries of dampness.   The 'celli and basses, playing *pizzicato*, show them circling around, animal fashion, to get a good look at their prey:

while the other trolls mark time with grotesque elbowy movements:

There is only one theme, repeated again and again as the trolls swarm out of the crevices of the rocks — old trolls, young trolls, big trolls, little trolls, as the various instruments show us.   They circle around Peer, grunting, snarling, and hunching their shoulders in a bizarre dance of hate.   Faster and faster move the twisted legs, louder and shriller grow the spiteful voices, until with shrieks of fury:

they fall upon him, scratching and pinching until the poor fellow is quite frantic with pain and terror.

Then a muffled sound is heard, distant church bells, "the Black-Frock's cows," a sound no evil spirit can endure. With a final crash the troll palace disappears, and a stiff, sore-headed Peer finds himself lying quite alone on the mountainside!

What an amazing effect Grieg has achieved with one monotonous little rhythmic theme! He dares to repeat this theme eighteen times, and "gets by" with it through the fantastic variety of his harmonies and instruments. But the real secret of the piece lies in that avalanche of *tempo* that obliterates every hint of monotony as it goes sweeping by. It is one of the cleverest *accelerandos* in all musical literature, and if we really give ourselves up to the music — and how could any normal set of muscles resist it? — we arrive at that final crash almost as excited and breathless as if we, too, had been chased by trolls! There is a wildness about it that we do not have even in our liveliest dances. An old Norwegian superstition holds that the fiddler who learned his tune from a fairy — and such a thing was known to have happened — would be unable to stop playing it until rescued by having his fiddle strings cut! Grieg must have learned this tune from a nix, for it almost runs away with both player and listener!

Peer Gynt Suite, No. 2

Ingrid's Lament

Alone in the high mountains, Ingrid sits weeping. It is early morning, the morning of her wedding day. She should be safe in her own chamber at Hegstad Farm, surrounded by laughing, chattering bridesmaids and without a care beyond the straightening of a ribbon and the settling of the tall bride's crown! Was it only last night that the friends and neighbors trooped in to sing and dance and drink the health of bride and groom? And then came that horrid Peer Gynt, pushing in where he wasn't wanted. He had found her alone for a moment in the storeroom, seized her, flung her over his shoulder, and before anyone knew what was happening, had gone scrambling up the mountain like a goat! Never can she forget that wild flight, with the whole parish in a pack at their heels:

And now the heartless fellow has run off and left her, weary and all forlorn, and heaven knows how far from home! Her wedding finery is ruined, torn and lost in the bushes — everything is ruined! Was ever a poor girl so unhappy!

The melody mourns in short downward phrases — a hopeless voice. The rhythmic pattern varies slightly, and there is even a touch of brighter major, but not for a moment do we lose the mood of lamentation, of one devastating idea constantly reiterated. And the whole tune seems to be threaded on a single tone, a D which the violas play in a persistent syncopation:

There is a repetition of the melody in which the grief seems to grow more intense. The violins lift their voices, the violas quicken the pace. There are more instruments and more notes adding new tints to the somber coloring. The lament reaches its climax in a sharp cry of pain. Then come a few sobbing measures:

down which it seems to descend into the very depths of despair.

But a sudden fury of tympani:

brings a reminder of the cause of all this woe, Peer Gynt, and that mad dash up the mountainside:

Twice it is played, then four empty closing measures.

It is all simple enough, musically. But many of our young moderns who say nothing so complexly would do well to consider such simplicity. And in reply to those oversophisticated critics who smile indulgently at Grieg's music and murmur, "pink bonbon," there is more than a possibility that the world's taste for honest sweets will outlast its curiosity about bird's-nest soup!

Solveig's Song

Peer Gynt's Arabian adventures end in his galloping off across the desert with Princess Anitra, an unwilling captive, on his saddlebow. But the wily Anitra wastes no time lamenting. She flatters and coaxes until Peer hands over his jewels, his purse, and even his embroidered girdle and stockings — Peer was gorgeously gotten up in stolen finery. Then, when he has dismounted for a moment, Anitra gives him a smart cut with the riding whip, the great white horse another, and dashes back across the desert.

Peer stands thunderstruck. Then, as is his habit when beaten, he begins to rationalize. It is time to try something new, anyway. It might be interesting to delve in antiquity. Surely he is bored with the doings of living men, and as for women — "Ah, they are a worthless crew!"

Then, like one of those mental pictures which the cinema manages so effectively, scene ten holds the stage for the brief moment of a song. It is a summer day in the far North. In a little clearing in the forest stands a rude settler's cabin with reindeer horns over the door and a flock of goats by the wall. Near the open door a middle-aged woman, fair haired and comely, sits spinning in the sunshine. It is Solveig, in whose heart Peer Gynt has always been the man God meant him to be, and not the worthless fellow the world knew. As a young girl she had given up everything and followed Peer, the outlaw, to this forest hut, bringing peace and happiness for a time. Then, one evening, Peer had gone out, saying mysteriously, "Be my way long or short — you must wait!" Years have passed with no word of the wanderer, but Solveig, symbol of faithful womanhood, sits waiting.

Now she glances down the forest path, and sings softly, to herself:

> The winter may go, and the springtime, too, pass by,
> The summer flowers may droop, and the weary year may die,
> But you will come again, that I know, that I know,
> And you will find me waiting, I promised long ago!
>
> — *Trans. by* L. L. B.

In the orchestral arrangement the violins, accompanied by harp and lower strings, takes the voice part:

It is a lonesome tune, but Solveig is not sad. She smiles and calls to her little flock, and then to the whir of the spinning wheel, she hums a lilting refrain:

There is a moment's pause, then she sings again:

> God keep you, where'er in this world you may be,
> God bless you if no longer His sunshine you see!
> For you I'll be waiting until life ends, my Love,
> And if you've gone before me, we two will meet above!
>
> — *Trans. by* L. L. B.

and again, the haunting refrain.

"Solveig's Song," whether sung or played, with its typical Norse contrast of *L'Allegro* and *Il Penseroso*, is one of Grieg's loveliest lyrics.

Arabian Dance

The "Arabian Dance" from *Peer Gynt* Suite, No. 2, belongs to the same part of the play as the better known "Anitra's Dance." Peer Gynt, masquerading as the Prophet, is being entertained in the tent of an Arab chief. Princess Anitra and her maidens dance for him. This is the dance of the maidens.

To an accompaniment of drums, triangle, and cymbals, the piccolo gives out the tune:

which with its characteristic little three-tone figure:

suggests the whining skirl of an Oriental flute.

But when the flutes take up the theme, and the strings add an accompaniment of those telltale open fifths, then for all its piccolo skirling this tune might have come piping down any Norwegian valley!

There is a tuneful middle section, equally un-Arabian:

after which the first part of the dance returns.

As pseudo-oriental music, the "Arabian Dance" is unconvincing, and certainly it is "sub-Grieg." However, in the play, where the attention was centered on the dancers, it probably passed as an agreeable jingle.

Peer Gynt's Return — The Storm

After years of wandering, Peer Gynt, still unsatisfied, takes ship for Norway. An old man now, with grizzled hair, we see him leaning on the ship's rail, looking off toward the land. In the glow of a stormy sunset he recognizes the familiar mountain peaks — "Hallingskarv in his winter furs" and "Jokel, his brother, with his ice-green mantle still on his back" and "Folgefann, like a maiden in spotless white" — old friends, all of them!

Sadness steals over him as he realizes that there will be no human friends to welcome him. A few old people may, perhaps, remember that a Peer Gynt once lived in the village, but they will also remember what a good-for-nothing he was! Why, the poorest sailor on the ship will have someone to welcome him, someone who will make a special treat for supper and light an extra candle to celebrate his home-coming. "There is nobody waiting for old Peer Gynt."

These bitter thoughts are interrupted by a sudden lurch of the ship. A weird light fills the sky as the sun sinks behind a fog veil. The wind is up, clouds are scudding past, the sea is "running high as houses." The sailors spring to their places as the captain calls, "Here comes the storm!"

A smashing, trembling chord:

a cry, sharp and bright as forked lightning:

and the low roar of the waves:

Over and over we hear them, the shivering chords, the wild sea-cry, and the roar of the breakers. Nearer and nearer they come, and with them a feeling of excitement as if the listener were watching there beside Peer Gynt, with the spray flying in his face and the deck pitching beneath his feet.

There is no melody here, no nice little Grieg tune, only sounding fury. Just once there is a sad little scrap of song:

as if a human voice had managed to make itself heard above the tempest.

But it is soon drowned by the voice of the storm. How the wind screams in the rigging:

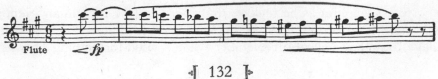

And always this high wailing is echoed far below in the basses, as if the very depths of the sea were torn by the gale.

Then, gradually, the storm dies away. The little sea-cry sounds as if blown back from a distance, the wind no longer screams, nothing is heard but low muttering thunder, then silence. It is the silence that seems to speak. We do not need to be told, in words, that the ship went down, and with it, those men for whom the children wait and the extra candles burn.

Grieg, the Norseman, knew his sea and the terrible stillness that can follow its raging. Grieg, the artist, knew the value of silence, of the quiet ending which gives the listener a chance to come to his own conclusions and fixes the picture forever in his memory. And the listener who has once heard Grieg's storm music adequately done, places it with Mendelssohn's *Hebrides Overture* and Wagner's Overture to *The Flying Dutchman* in his gallery of musical marine paintings.

MARCH OF ALLEGIANCE — SIGURD JORSALFAR

Less well known than the *Peer Gynt* music, but quite as effective, is the music Grieg wrote for Björnson's drama *Sigurd Jorsalfar*. Björnson's hero was the young Prince Sigurd, called Sigurd Jorsalfar — Sigurd the Crusader. Fired with the prevailing zeal to rescue the Holy Land from the Mohammedans, Prince Sigurd, a romantic youth of barely seventeen, gathered a band of knights and, in the year 1103

> Magnificent and gay,
> In sixty long ships, sailed away.

From Norway down to England, on to France and Portugal, through the Mediterranean Sea to Sicily they went, putting in at many ports and meeting with amazing adventures until at last they came to Constantinople.

Sigurd loved a princely show. His ships had costly figureheads, elaborately carved and gilded. His tall blond warriors in their shining coats of mail looked like the pictures of the old Norse gods. His horse is said to have worn golden shoes, and it pleased him to use walnuts for firewood. So rich were all his appointments that even the bejeweled kings of the Orient had never seen the like.

After three years of crusading, Sigurd decided to return home over land, and gave all his ships to the Emperor at Constantinople. The Emperor returned the courtesy with a gift of fine Arabian horses, and Sigurd and his knights started for Norway. All along the way, hospitable princes welcomed them with feasts and celebrations, and as they neared their own country, crowds of loyal people went out to meet their prince.

But at court there was a less happy state of affairs. A jealous older brother, joint ruler of the kingdom, had, during Sigurd's absence, tried to seize the throne for himself alone. The dramatic episode of Sigurd's home-coming is the theme of Björnson's play.

The second act of the play takes place in the kings' hall, a vast, galleried room. At one end rises the dais with the long tables and high-backed chairs of the two kings and the noblemen; at the other end, wide doors. Banners bearing the emblems of

Norway and pieces of bright weaving hang from the galleries, while rich carving and gay colors decorate the great crossbeams overhead, the doorposts, and the furniture. Swinging fish-oil lamps, pine torches stuck in sconces, and cavelike fireplaces fill the hall with flickering light.

The galleries are crowded with spectators. Excitement tingles in the air, for this is the day when the kings hold court and the knights and noblemen renew their oath of allegiance. Will they be loyal to Sigurd the Crusader or will they give the crown of Norway to the greedy, scheming Eystejn? To this tense scene belongs the March of Allegiance (sometimes called the Triumphal March).

Knowing the story, it would be a blind listener who could not see the picture! The great doors are flung open, the heralds enter:

blowing all the bustle and chatter into silence. Then the 'celli begin to play the stately melody of the march:

Violins take it up, and the music swells as the procession moves down the hall. A horn speaks:

and the oboe answers:

Other voices join with shouts of enthusiasm:

and then the whole orchestra crashes into the march.

In the trio, or more quiet middle section of the march, one is reminded less of the story of Sigurd than of a characteristic feature of Norway. This little interlude of tender, wistful melody with its shifting harmonic lights and shadows:

suggests the bright and fragile beauty of the North, so striking in contrast with its dark forests and rugged mountains. In both trio and march we recognize that characteristic of Grieg's music — the short phrase continually repeated at different levels and with different harmonic and instrumental colorings.

After the trio, a rolling of drums and blare of trumpets takes us back to the kings' hall. There is never a doubt as to what is happening there, for only courage and loyalty could inspire such steadfast music. And in the brief coda one can almost hear the clash of sword on shield and the lusty voices of Sigurd's men, shouting their allegiance.

JOHAN HALVORSEN

Drammen — 1864
Oslo — 1935

For many years the people of Christiania, now Oslo, saw the same familiar figure at the conductor's desk in their National Theater. An imposing figure it was, with a Viking physique, tawny mane, and rugged face from which deep brown eyes surveyed the world with a fine dignity. This simple, earnest man was Johan Halvorsen, an artist little known abroad, but one of the pillars of Scandinavian music.

As a boy, Halvorsen served for ten years as flutist in the military band of his home town, becoming acquainted with the other instruments at the same time. Then he went off to Stockholm and later to Leipzig and Liége to study the violin, and for a number of years figured as a concert violinist and teacher of his chosen instrument.

During all this time he was making experiments in composition, and nearly always it was theater music that he wrote. This keen interest in the theater led him to accept the position of conductor of the theater orchestra of Bergen, where he lived for seven years. The isolation of this Norwegian city developed close association among its musicians and music lovers. Halvorsen learned to know Edward Grieg intimately, and became his devoted admirer. Later he married Grieg's niece, and it was most fitting that it should have been Halvorsen, who, at the time of Grieg's death, came back to Bergen to conduct the music at the memorial service given in the master's honor.

In 1899 Halvorsen went to Christiania as conductor of the National Theater Orchestra. His intimate knowledge of many instruments, his sensitive and discriminating musical taste, and his splendid mental and physical poise made him a very skillful conductor. He was always a great worker, and frankly Norwegian in his spirit.

Halvorsen did much to further the growth of music in Norway. He gave many programs made up entirely of the unpublished works of young Norwegian composers. "Even if they are not so masterly," he said, "it means more than mere encouragement to these young writers, for in getting an opportunity to hear their faults they may get a grasp of how to better them." One wishes that poor young Schubert, and many another nameless one, might have known a Halvorsen. Think of having written an "Unfinished" Symphony and never having heard it!

Norwegian listeners are also indebted to Halvorsen for his indefatigable drilling of local orchestras and choruses so that they could give symphonies and operas which otherwise might not have reached that far corner of the musical world. People from all the country 'round flocked to Christiania to hear these programs. It was a big thing for Norway, and a big thing for any artist to have cheerfully given his best to his own community when world renown was all the fashion!

Triumphal Entrance of the Boyars

Halvorsen wrote the "Triumphal Entrance of the Boyars" half a century ago. Since that time these swaggering chiefs have cantered 'round and 'round the world, attracting the attention of everyone who loves a bit of barbaric color and a stirring rhythm — and who does not!

This march is part of a suite called "Dance Scenes from Queen Tamara," and has for its literary background Lermontov's poem, "The Boyar Orcha." Its historic, or we might better say, its geographic setting goes back to the old days when Russia was more Oriental than European, with its society centering around the feudal leader or boyar, who had much the same status as the ancient Scottish chief.

Gogol's story, "Taras Bulba," gives a vivid picture of that half-nomadic corner of Europe where the hamlets were little more than military camps. In case of war or uprising, and such was the case most of the time, the boyars simply rode through the villages shouting, "Hey, ye beer-sellers and brewers, ye blacksmiths and sowers of buckwheat, cease to waste your knightly strength; 'tis time to win Kazak glory!" And in an incredibly short time, every man would appear on horseback, fully armed — a company such as a recruiting officer would dream about mustering!

In times of peace these same boyars would ride grandly into the villages to execute justice, and usually the offenders as well, for there was much blood mingled with this justice. Three cases there were for the sword: lack of proper respect for superior officers; making light of the orthodox faith or the customs of ancestors; and the heinous crime of being a Turk, for the Kazaks were heathenishly zealous in drawing the sword for the glory of Christianity!

They slept on the ground, and rode like centaurs. Their life was a wild, free manifestation of a certain side of Russian nature. Yet for all their hardihood, they were great dandies. Gogol describes the sons of old chief Taras Bulba setting forth in search of glorious trouble clad in "red Morocco boots with silver heels; trousers wide as the Black Sea, with thousands of folds and plaits and supported by golden girdles; from the girdles hung long slender thongs, with tassels and other jingling things for pipes; the Kazak coat, of brilliant scarlet cloth, was confined by a flowered belt; embossed Turkish pistols were thrust into the belt; swords clanged at their heels. Very handsome indeed were their sunburned faces, set off with little black moustaches beneath their black sheepskin caps with golden crowns."

Doubtless the boyars whose entrance this music pictures were just such a grand-opera group! We hear them coming, swinging along at an easy, rocking pace: [1]

with the oboe suggesting the skirl of some little oriental pipe. This theme, first given by clarinets, is repeated, and works up to a grand climax with shrill, fifelike flutes leading, cymbals crashing, drums rolling, sharp *sforzandos* in the brasses like clanking swords, and an undertone of bagpipes droning down among the 'celli and bassoons. A brave company, these chieftains and their retinue!

The entrance theme then shifts to a major key:

with violins leading, and followed by a charming flute passage against dainty plucked strings. This quieter mood is suddenly broken by the drums rousing the brasses to a pompous performance which would seem to accompany the passing of the boyars themselves:

The captains and lesser folk come trotting after them in a repetition of the first two sections, and the cavalcade disappears in the briefest of codas, a whirl of drums, and one crashing chord.

Throughout this music we hear soft, incessant hoofbeats, and feel ourselves gently rising and falling with the riders in the saddle. We are not allowed to forget for one moment that these are mounted men, not foot marchers. And although the music is written in march form, it would be difficult to step to it without pacing!

Halvorsen has scored it with a clever eye to color, and managed to contrast a strength and grace quite in keeping with the picture of these half-savage plainsmen and their thoroughbred horses.

[1] Copyright, by Carl Fischer, Inc.; quotations used by permission of the publisher.

ARMAS JÄRNEFELT

Viipuri — 1869

Armas Järnefelt, born in Viipuri in 1869, is a Finnish musician better known for his musical activities in his own country than for his compositions. He had the usual conservatory training at home, followed by study in Berlin and Paris, and for several years held minor positions as conductor of theater orchestras in various German cities. He then returned to Finland as director of opera in Helsinki, and later held a similar position in Stockholm. Järnefelt returned to Helsinki as director of the National Conservatory, but later accepted the directorship of the opera at Helsinki.

He has written a number of songs and choruses and several works for orchestra. Compared with the serious music of his countryman, Sibelius, Järnefelt's compositions seem slight, both in form and content, but his music is pleasing, sincere, and nicely made. It is well worth the occasional notice of players and listeners.

BERCEUSE

Simple and exquisite as a wild anemone swaying in the wind is this charming Finnish cradle song. It has the characteristic Scandinavian touch of sadness, just enough to suggest the gathering darkness, the mists, and the chill breath of the mountain night that make the firelight seem so cosy and the mother's song so comforting:

As befits a true lullaby, there is but one theme, crooned again and again — first by the solo violin, then by the 'cello, and finally by all the strings in unison. Järnefelt has given a perfect setting to his lovely melody. Muted strings accompany the solo instruments; then, as all the strings join in the song, two clarinets, two horns, and a bassoon make the background. All through the piece, beneath the smooth, clear song, there is a ceaseless rocking motion, not with the melody, but against it in the gentlest of syncopations:

which suggests the picture of a peasant mother beside a homemade cradle whose rockers have worn a little flat with the lullabies of several generations of babies. It is just such trifles that make perfection!

This cheerful little Praeludium, or prelude, scored, like the Berceuse, for a small orchestra, is just a Finnish country dance dressed up for a formal concert. To a mechanical little figure on plucked strings:

which reminds us of the monotonous sawing of a peasant bass-viol player, or even of the more rustic accompaniment of clapping hands, the quaint dance tune appears with the oboe, flute, and clarinet sounding very much like country pipes.

When we have heard quite enough of the dance, Järnefelt introduces this little song theme as a bit of contrast:

Then the merry jigging tune is heard again, completing the familiar musical pattern — A–B–A; the dancers take themselves off, one at a time, the musicians give a final scrape, and the performance is ended.

JAN SIBELIUS

Tavastehus — 1865

From the northernmost of all civilized countries, the winter land of screaming winds, drifting snows, and scant, pale sunshine, comes the voice of the primeval North in the music of Jan Sibelius. To the world, Sibelius is known as Finland's greatest composer and one of the most outstanding musical figures of the twentieth century. But to Finland, Jan Sibelius is a national hero, beloved by every school child and toasted from roadside tavern to royal banquet hall — Jan Sibelius, Finland's most eloquent ambassador to the outside world! A century ago the Hungarians honored Liszt in much the same way. It is significant that the Finns and the Magyars, the two vital branches of the ancient Ugrian family tree, should both regard their creative artists, the men who interpret the spirit of a nation, as worthy of as much or more honor than the heroes of the battlefields!

However, these two national heroes have little in common when it comes to their acceptance of this honor and publicity. The brilliant court life, the adulation, and incense which Liszt loved would have choked the man of the north woods, who dreads even a business trip to Helsinki because of all the festivity and loving fuss made over him. Not that Sibelius is a melancholy Jacques, as is sometimes mistakenly inferred from his somber music and from his photograph which shows a massive head, high-browed and square-jawed, with piercing, deep-set eyes. He looks, indeed, more like a man of action, a builder of towers and bridges, or the master of some great industry, than a sensitive artist. But those burning eyes are often filled with surprising tenderness, and those firm lips can break into the most jovial of smiles. As one biographer puts it, Sibelius's "disposition is as ruddy as his health."

For many years Sibelius has lived in a little kingdom of his own, in the country, thirty miles north of Helsinki. His huge log house, the Villa Ainola, named for his wife, stands on a dirt road just out of Järvenpää, a village so tiny that the trains do not regularly stop there. But one has only to tell the conductor on any northbound express that one is going to see Sibelius, and *presto*, Järvenpää becomes the most important point on the line!

Sibelius, christened Jan Julius Christian, was born December 8, 1865, in the inland town of Tavastehus, where his father was stationed as regimental doctor. Like Grieg, he had the good fortune to spend his childhood in the pleasant, peaceful atmosphere of a cultured home. Nature and music became his first and lasting loves, and both were encouraged by his wise parents. Before he was old enough to go to school, little Jan had already explored the keyboard of the family piano. From the days of his first childish music lessons, he showed an annoying preference for making his own tunes instead of practicing those of other people. At ten he was the proud composer of a little piece for violin and 'cello (entirely *pizzicato!*) called *Drops of Water*.

The boyhood years from eleven to twenty were devoted to regular school work at the Finnish Model Lyceum. Jan was never a distinguished pupil. His wandering wits often caused his teacher to remark with a sigh, "There now, Sibelius is off in another world again!" But he was a lovable boy, and always the leader in games and pantomimes. He was happiest when conducting the small boys' orchestra of the school. At fifteen he turned seriously to music and began to study the violin. He was fascinated by it, and is said to have wandered, fiddle in hand, through the woods near Tavastehus, playing snatches of tunes that seemed to come from the trees and streams. Then more than ever he wanted to be a composer, and pored over books of harmony, theory, and composition, borrowed from the library.

At his graduation from the Lyceum, Sibelius entered the University of Helsinki as a student of law. It was the wish of his mother that he prepare himself for some government post. His music had always been a matter of family pride, but the uncertain position of a professional musician in an isolated Finnish city was not considered good enough for Jan. However, the young man himself soon settled the matter by taking up the study of violin and composition at the Musical Academy of Helsinki. The more he accomplished in music, the less he did with law, until at the end of the first year he was permitted to give up the neglected university classes and spend his whole time in the work he loved.

Sibelius was fortunate in having teachers who could appreciate and stimulate his peculiar genius. He worked with all his might and went about with his head in the clouds. So original was his imagination and so fantastic its expression that, in the words of one of his fellow students, he behaved normally "like the rest of us when drunk!" At the Academy Sibelius won a scholarship which, with a small government grant, made it possible for him to go to Berlin to study. Here he perfected his knowledge of form and technique, and in the brilliant concert life of the German city realized for the first time the thrilling possibilities of symphonic music. After a year in Berlin and a brief holiday in Finland, which he celebrated by becoming engaged to General Järnefelt's pretty daughter, Sibelius went to Vienna. The *vivace* tempo of Viennese life was something quite new to the slow, serious Northerner. He studied with Fuchs and Goldmark, heard a great deal of music, and met many notable musicians who gave him advice and encouragement.

The summer of 1891 found Sibelius again in his own country, where a few months later he married Aino Järnefelt, accepted a professorship at his alma mater, the Musical Academy, and made Helsinki his home. Finland was at this time undergoing an acute attack of nationalism, brought on by some high-handed suppression of Finnish privileges by the Russian government. Feeling ran high, and the impulsive Sibelius joined several patriotic groups. He also became convinced that it was his duty to express his love for Finland in his music. The result was a five-part symphonic poem for large orchestra, chorus, and soloists, *Kullervo*, based upon an old national hero tale. This music, which seemed to voice just what the Finnish patriots were feeling, aroused the greatest enthusiasm and made its composer famous. After *Kullervo* followed *En Saga*, the *Karelia Suite*, and, in 1894, that supreme expression of national feeling, *Finlandia*. With the appearance of one more major work, the *Lemminkäinen Suite*, Sibelius's position as the musical spokesman of Finland was so definitely recognized that the government voted an annual grant of money which would free him from the necessity of teaching for a living and permit him to devote himself to composition.

From this time on, Sibelius became not only Finland's spokesman but also her ambassador, traveling on concert tours to all the leading countries of Europe. In 1914 he came to the United States to take part in the Norfolk Festival of Music. He was bewildered and deeply moved by the warmth of his welcome, for he had no idea that his music was well known and loved so far from its native Finland. He promised to return to America the following year, but that, like many another happy promise, was broken by the first World War.

The war years brought suffering to this sensitive artist. The greater part of his income was cut off. After Finland's declaration of independence of Russia, the civil war between the Red and White Guards spread even to quiet Järvenpää, and brutal searching parties went storming through the composer's home. Through these dark days Sibelius worked on at his music, creating a surprising number of things, among them several of his great symphonies.

It was Sibelius's fate to see a second and more terrible World War, and with his beloved Finland on what he must have sadly felt to be the wrong side. Many of his precious original manuscripts, left with his Leipzig publishers, were among the air-raid casualties of that city. The war cut off British and American royalties on his music, and inflation reduced the worth of his state pension as Professor Emeritus of Music at the University of Helsinki to a mere pittance. American friends felt great concern lest Sibelius be in actual want, and some of them approached him with the idea of a benefit concert. To this the staunch old man replied, "I am in the same boat as the rest of my fellow Finns and have no complaints. . . . I am grateful for the thoughtful idea . . . but I don't want any favors. I am just an ordinary Finn, and I don't want to be treated differently than my fellow countrymen." However, in April, 1945, the Philharmonic Symphony Society of New York sent Sibelius a thousand dollars tactfully labeled as "an additional royalty payment." They made it clear that this was no gift but a token of gratitude from those whose constant enjoyment of his music was something money could not buy.

In 1935 the whole world of music joined in celebration of his seventieth birthday. Finland declared a national holiday, and in Paris, London, Berlin, Rome, New York, Boston, and Philadelphia, orchestras played Sibelius programs. Perhaps the greatest tribute came from America, where a poll among radio listeners for favorite symphonic music revealed the name of Jan Sibelius first choice among all living composers!

The eight symphonies, Sibelius's masterpieces, were all written in the twentieth century. Yet they bear practically none of the marks of "twentieth-century" music as we know it in the later works of Stravinsky, Schönberg, or Ravel. It is as if the infection of fearsome tonal experimentation had passed little Järvenpää by. As we listen to Sibelius's music, written in the symphonic form as Brahms left it more than a century ago, there is no feeling of cramped style. We recognize the accepted conventions of harmony, melody, and rhythm, with here and there a Finnish touch of three-halves or seven-quarter meter. Sibelius has felt no urge to go tradition-smashing or to try any spectacular tricks. He really is quite old-fashioned. Yet the twentieth century has seen no more profoundly original artist than Jan Sibelius, because in his music it is always Jan Sibelius speaking directly, sincerely, and often sublimely. David Ewen, in his admirable sketch of Sibelius, says: "If he has succeeded in proving nothing else, he has convinced us that no form of music is ever out-moded for the composer who has sufficient imagination and talent to pour into it new ideas and sentiments."

The outstanding characteristic of Sibelius's music is its intense nationalism. It is a broader and a deeper nationalism than that of the Norwegian or the Russian composers, for it does not rely upon national subjects — the symphonies are just as Finnish as *Finlandia* — and it does not depend upon the conscious and constant use of folk tunes and idioms. Sibelius never borrows directly from folk music, nor does he try to imitate it. He does something much finer — he breathes the folk spirit into the body of art music. Just as an educated man, through his greater command of language, can give a better description of his country than a stammering peasant, so Sibelius, with all the tools of composition at his command, gives a more convincing picture of Finland than is found in the artless, fragmentary music of the people.

The story of the Finns is one of ceaseless conflict with man and nature. They are said to have belonged to one of the numerous Asiatic tribes that scattered over Europe some three thousand years ago. Pursued by misfortune, these people wandered for centuries until at last they came to the strip of land, a veritable jumping-off-place —

now known as Finland — and settled there.   But their struggles had only begun.   The mountains and forests were forbidding and the climate so inhospitable that they had to fight for every yard of cultivated soil.   What was even harder, they found themselves wedged between two powerful nations, Russia and Sweden, who turned their poor country into a perennial battleground.   But regardless of which greedy neighbor was taking his turn on their throne, the Finns remained through the centuries a proud and unconquerable people, jealously guarding their own traditions and ideals, and philosophically biding their time.

The music of Sibelius speaks of Finland's past; of those forgotten generations that once roamed the mysterious black forests and cowered through the long Arctic night. It is melancholy music, but how could it be otherwise when, according to *The Kalevala*, the harp or *Kantele* given to all Finnish singers, had this origin:

> The *Kantele* of care is carved.
> Formed of saddening sorrows only;
> Of hard times its arch is fashioned
> And its wood of evil chances.
> All the strings of sorrow twisted,
> All the screws of adverse fortunes;
> Therefore *Kantele* can never
> Ring with gay and giddy music,
> Hence this harp lacks happy ditties,
> Cannot sound in cheerful measures
> As it is of care constructed,
> Formed of saddening sorrows only!
> — *From* JOHN MARTIN CRAWFORD'S *translation*

Though melancholy may be its keynote, the music of Sibelius is full of the spirit of the old Scandinavian heroes, full of the strength and courage which are the roots of Finnish nationalism.   And even more clearly than it pictures the people, this music seems to reflect the North Country.   Its subdued harmonies, bare melodic lines, and rugged rhythms paint a wintry landscape — snowfields edged with shadowy firs, gaunt gray rocks, ice-gray water, and cold sky faintly touched with gold at sunset.   Like his ancestors of the days of the sagas, Sibelius, too, is a nature worshiper.   From what other source could he have drawn the notes of grandeur and of hushed reverence that sound so persistently in his music?   In his own words, given in an interview while on his American tour, Sibelius states his credo: "It pleases me greatly to be called an artist of nature, for nature has truly been the book of books for me.   The voices of nature are the voices of God, and if an artist can give a mere echo of them in his creations he is fully rewarded for his efforts."

It is unlikely that Sibelius, now past eighty and worn with age and anxiety, will ever again compose a significant work.   But even so, he has made his contribution to the expression of the spirit of World War II.   Olin Downes, writing in the *New York Times* in 1940, puts it thus:

It seemed in the earlier years of the century that Sibelius was the one composer in the whole modern field whose scores did not speak the language of the escapist, but plainly of things to be faced. There were the reverberations of what was gathering under civilization's surface. There were to be heard deathless defiance and the proclamation of the invincible spirit of man. The cry moved us strangely then, we hardly knew why. Now we understand. And so it is that Sibelius appears today — the one hero and prophet whose music is singularly abreast of the times, the world and its needs.

SYMPHONY No. 2 IN D MAJOR

Proudest of the honors conferred upon the venerable Jan Sibelius is the title "the greatest Finnish Symphonist." Despite the charm and the popular appeal of the tone poems, *Finlandia* and *The Kalevala*, pieces inspired by Finnish nationalism and Finnish folklore, Sibelius knows that the symphony still stands as the supreme test of a composer's art.

Sibelius has eight symphonies to his credit, works which in originality of idea and excellence of craftsmanship may be placed beside the great symphonies of Beethoven and Brahms. Like those of Beethoven and Brahms, the Sibelius symphonies are based upon musical rather than poetic ideas. Yet, like Beethoven and Brahms, Sibelius, master of classical form, is a poet and a romanticist at heart. He loves color and knows how to use it; he loves life and knows how to express it. Not one of his symphonies bears a descriptive title. Yet in every one there is a sense of time and place and human emotion. The voices of Nature and of his beloved Finland speak in every line of his music.

It is not surprising then to find that while Sibelius gave his second symphony the formal title, Symphony No. 2 in D Major, he nevertheless had a definite poetic idea in mind when he wrote it. He is said to have told an intimate friend that his intention was "to depict in the first movement the quiet pastoral life of the Finns undisturbed by thoughts of oppression. The second movement is charged with patriotic feeling, but the thought of a brutal rule over the people brings with it timidity of soul. The third movement portrays the awakening of national feeling, the desire to organize in defense of their rights, while in the *Finale*, hope enters their breasts and there is comfort in the anticipated coming of a deliverer."

To musicians this second symphony of Sibelius is most interesting because, particularly in the first movement, it introduces an entirely new principle into symphonic form. Up to this point it had been the custom in the Exposition section of the first movement to present two or more themes, definite melodic personalities; to take them apart in the Development section, often making new themes of the fragments; and then to put them back together in their original form in the Recapitulation section. Sibelius simply reverses this process. In the Exposition section of his second symphony he presents mere fragments of themes, lets them grow into definite melodies in the Development section, and reduces them again to their original fragmentary form in the Recapitulation.

This topsy-turvy thematic procedure is at first puzzling to ears accustomed to conventional first movement form. But after several hearings the effect is one of peculiar strength and beauty, for as Cecil Gray points out, "this is the method of Nature and of life itself: Sibelius's most characteristic movements are born, develop, and die like all living things."

Allegretto — Poco allegro

A simple rising figure for strings introduces a snatch of country dance tune for oboes and clarinets: [1]

echoed by the horns at the end of each phrase.

This gay pastoral mood gives way to a more serious statement for violins alone:

followed, almost immediately, by this thematic fragment:

which is later to become an important part of the movement.

An agitated passage for strings, *pizzicato*, then leads to this vehement announcement by the woodwinds:

At first this seems to be merely another of those melodic bits of which the movement has consisted thus far. But on a second hearing this fragment begins to hold the attention, and when the solo oboe gives it out for the third time, slightly altered in minor key, one realizes that something significant is happening. And so it is, for this solo oboe is announcing the opening of the Development section, a Development in which this particular scrap of melody is to grow until it seems to take possession of the whole movement.

"From a purely technical point of view," says Cecil Gray, "nothing is more remarkable in the entire range of symphonic literature than the way in which the composer, having presented in the Exposition a handful of seemingly disconnected and mean-

[1] Themes reprinted by permission of Associated Music Publishers, Inc., New York City.

ingless scraps of melody, proceeds in the Development section to breathe life into them and bring them into relation with one another."

The Recapitulation begins with the return of the country dance motif, its horn echoes interestingly varied. Then, having reached its emotional climax in the Development section, the movement gradually breaks up into the thematic fragments from which it grew and ends, as it began, with the simple figure for strings alone.

Tempo andante, ma Rubato

The conventional second movement of the classical symphony is usually built upon the principle of contrast between a songlike first theme and a more vigorous second theme. Sibelius amplifies this by contrasting several groups of themes. The effect is dramatic, and suggests a conflict of moods quite in keeping with the composer's intention to write a movement "charged with patriotic feeling, but the thought of a brutal rule over the people brings with it timidity of soul."

The *Andante* begins with a roll on the kettledrums and a rather mysterious *pizzicato* passage for low strings over which the bassoons give out this mournful tune:

It is immediately followed by a restless episode which rises to a climax in this despairing cry:

A pause — then from divided strings comes a quiet, hymnlike second theme:

with oboes and clarinets singing this lovely sequel:

Throughout the rest of the movement these familiar themes seem to engage in the struggle between moods of light and darkness, ending in empty fifths, a mournful cry:

Darkness prevails.

Vivacissimo

The third movement, *Vivacissimo* — in reality, the *scherzo* of the symphony — starts off with a lively theme in 6/8 rhythm for strings:

This theme reminds one of the famous Beethoven *scherzo* themes, not only in its bold outline but also in its mood, which is one of tumult rather than gaiety.

A second theme follows shortly, given out by flute and bassoon, three octaves apart:

These two subjects, playing back and forth with ever-increasing animation, make up the whole first section of the movement, which is cast in the traditional *scherzo-trio-scherzo* form.

Then soft drum taps put an end to this bustling activity and make way for the trio in which the oboe sings a melody as beautiful as it is simple:

This tender interlude lasts for but thirteen measures. Then, with interesting changes of orchestration, the lively *scherzo* returns, followed, rather oddly, by a repeat of the trio, which leads without pause into the last movement.

Finale — Allegro moderato

So adroitly has Sibelius led us by way of the repeated trio that the *Finale* bursts upon us as a revelation. We feel the mingled wonder and exaltation which always comes with the discovery that, all unsuspecting, we have been prepared for a breath-taking event!

The first phrase of the solemn chant is given out by the strings:

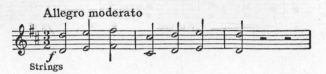

which seem to pause, awaiting the affirmation of the horns, then end triumphantly:

In effective contrast the woodwinds introduce the singing second theme, in wistful mood:

Following the composer's thought, one remembers that in 1902 the freedom of Finland was yet but a hope in the hearts of the people and that back of its brightness lingers the shadow of suffering and doubt suggested by the murmuring low strings.

The plaintive melody might be that of a Finnish folk song, for Sibelius is so filled with the spirit of his country that his melodies are inevitably national in character.

Yet this singing theme, like the chorale in *Finlandia*, is not a folk tune but an original Sibelius invention.

After the Statement of the two main themes comes the conventional Development and Recapitulation sections of the sonata form in which Sibelius has chosen to write his *Finale*. But there is nothing stilted or academic about this conventionality. The music grows and glows as it sweeps along until by the time it reaches the coda:

every instrument in the orchestra is shouting the hope of Finland's triumph.

Surely the Sibelius symphonies — and none more than this delightful No. 2 in D Major — are a living refutation of any notion that the symphony is an outmoded form, an absurd musical vehicle belonging to a bygone generation. Listening to this music one must admit that in the hands of a master, the symphony — the orchestral sonata — is still the best, the streamlined model for swift, sure transportation of musical thought and feeling!

VALSE TRISTE

The well-worn *Valse triste* is part of the music for the drama *Kuolema* (Death), written by Sibelius's brother-in-law, Arvid Järnefelt. This accounts for its program.

It is midnight. In a room dimly lighted, a sick woman lies sleeping, and at the bedside her son, worn out with watching, has also fallen asleep. Gradually, a rosy light steals through the room, and with it the sound of distant music, a weird waltz tune:

The sleeping woman wakens, and, as if hypnotized by the music, rises from her bed and begins to sway to and fro with its rhythm. In the half light, her long white nightgown looks strangely like a ball dress. She waves her arms and beckons as if inviting a crowd of unseen guests to join in the dance. The music brightens:

But no matter what new melodies the ghostly orchestra may start — and there are several — the 'celli always bring them back to the same hopeless ending:

As the dancers glide about the room, the sick woman mingles with them and tries to make them look into her eyes, but they avoid her glance.   In the midst of the third waltz, a charming duet for flute and clarinet:

the music breaks off.   The sick woman seems to sink exhausted on her bed.   But presently she gathers her strength, and the dance goes on with even greater energy:

At the height of the delirious gaiety, there comes a knocking at the door, a low, steady rapping of drums.   Instantly all is confusion with strings, in a *stretto*, literally crowding like panic-stricken guests trying to escape.   A moment's silence, then that despairing cry:

The shadowy guests vanish; the music dies away on a long-drawn sigh:

Death stands at the door!

Slightly mawkish as this little piece may be, its shuddering sadness has an appeal which cannot be wholly discounted by intellectual musicians.   It has what most sentimental music lacks, the ring of sincerity.   This could scarcely have been inspired by the fantastic death scene in Järnefelt's play.   It is better explained as the expression of a shuddering fear which haunted the composer's own life.   For *Valse triste* was written in 1903 when Sibelius, threatened with deafness, lived in the shadow of perpetual silence. Fortunately, Sibelius recovered the health and spirit to write those great, rugged symphonies which make his poor little *Valse triste* seem trivial!

THE SWAN OF TUONELA

The Swan of Tuonela is the third of four symphonic poems, the *Lemminkäinen Suite*, based upon episodes in the great Finnish epic, *The Kalevala*. The word *Kalevala*, like the Norse *Valhalla*, means the dwelling place of heroes, and *The Kalevala* is a wonderful collection of runes which sing the amazing adventures of the legendary heroes of Finland.

One of the favorite characters of *The Kalevala* was Lemminkäinen, a jolly, reckless fellow who was always getting into scrapes and out of them by his skill in magic. In the course of his wanderings, Lemminkäinen came to the North Country. There the first sight that met his dazzled eyes was Pohjola, the lovely Maiden of the North, seated on a rainbow, spinning. It was love at first sight for Lemminkäinen, and he straightway went to Pohja, mother of the lovely one, asking to marry her daughter. But the wily Old Woman of the North, determined to test his valor, replied:

> I will give my only daughter,
> Give the youthful bride you ask for,
> If the river swan you shoot me;
> Shoot the great bird of the river,
> There on Tuoni's murky water,
> In the sacred river's whirlpool,
> Only at a single trial
> Having but a single arrow.

It was a task requiring superhuman courage, for the "great bird of the river" was the Swan of Tuonela, that mysterious creature that floated, singing, on the black and awful river which separated the Land of the Living from the Land of the Dead (known in Finnish mythology as Tuonela). Boldly Lemminkäinen set out on his quest. But as he approached the death-stream, a serpent, hurled by a hidden enemy, pierced his heart, and he fell lifeless in the coal-black water.

It is not, however, the adventure of Lemminkäinen, but the Swan of Tuonela,

> The longnecked, graceful swimmer,
> Floating on the black death-river
> In the sacred stream and whirlpool

that Sibelius pictures in the music.

Against a dim background of muted strings and softly rolling drums, a solitary horn sings the swan song:

The weird, unearthly call is answered from time to time by viola and 'cello:

passing travelers, perhaps, crossing over to Tuonela, Land of the Dead.   And reaching after them, the voices of violins rise in poignant lamentation:

But there is little suggestion of human sorrow in this music.   The melancholy swan song, flowing on as endlessly and aimlessly as the mysterious river, seems to hold the listener in a strange No-Man's-Land of the emotions, where joy and sorrow are but passing shadows, devoid of all reality of feeling.

Once during the song the accompanying violins, in a curious *pizzicato* figure, suggest the flapping of wings:

and the harp ripples as if the water stirred with the great bird's movement.

Almost imperceptibly the music works up to its climax, where for a brief moment the strings in unison break into a dirge:

to the beat of funeral drums.   Then again the plaintive swan song floats out above the muffled drums and quivering strings, played *pianissimo* with the back of the bow, and with the sighing of a 'cello:

the legend ends.

For almost half a century *The Swan of Tuonela* has been a favorite of concert audiences everywhere.   The quiet intensity of the music, its mood of mystery and unearthly melancholy cannot fail to impress even those who do not know its story.   But to those familiar with the page from *The Kalevala* which inspired it, *The Swan of Tuonela* is one of music's most beautiful tone paintings.

FINLANDIA

Finlandia is a true song without words.   Its message is direct and unmistakable. In every corner of the civilized world this music, with its contrasting motifs of strength and tenderness, means but one thing — love of country.   In Finland the sound of *Finlandia*, like the sight of the flag, arouses such enthusiasm among the people that at one time, during the Russian domination, its performance was forbidden.   And it is said that at a concert in Riga, 1904, Sibelius was permitted to conduct the work only under the title, *Impromptu.*

In the brief, concise pages of this tone poem, the composer has made a thumbnail sketch of a nation.   With a harsh chord, a stern and solemn statement from the brass, and a blare of trumpets, Sibelius suggests the background — Finland, scene of agelong conflict between hostile men and nature.

Then, ushered in by spirited strings, comes the bold theme:

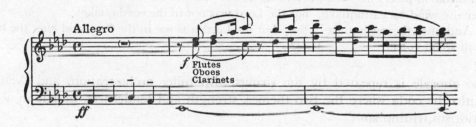

that pictures a people marching confidently and courageously through centuries of adversity.   So full of life and vigor is this music that it seems as if it might go on and on, endlessly.

But, as if to remind us that a nation cannot survive by physical force alone, the militant theme is interrupted by the beautiful, quiet chorale:

The sharp contrast of *Finlandia*'s themes with the implied contrast between physical and spiritual power, brings to mind those Old Testament verses recounting the adventures of Elijah:

> And behold, the Lord passed by, and a great and strong wind rent the mountains, and brake in pieces the rocks, before the Lord; but the Lord was not in the wind: and after the wind an earthquake; but the Lord was not in the earthquake:
>
> And after the earthquake a fire; but the Lord was not in the fire: and after the fire a still small voice.

The chorale is repeated by the strings with fuller orchestration, and eventually leads into the coda where the two themes, strength and tenderness, mingle in a hymn of patriotism triumphant.

So genuine is the national feeling in this music that even Sibelius's statement, "the thematic material of *Finlandia* is entirely my own," could hardly convince people that *Finlandia* was not a fantasia composed upon folk tunes. It seems rather to have been just the other way about, for in the chorale Sibelius has given his country a national hymn! And what a gift it is! No wonder this man who can set a nation's love and loyalty to music is honored as a hero!

➤➤⧼⧼⧼

CHAPTER III

Russia Speaks

In Russia an artist is first a patriot. — HUNEKER

Russian art is the perfect illustration of the familiar saying that art is but the reflection of life. Reading Russian literature, looking at Russian paintings, or listening to Russian music, one is conscious of a common spirit of nationalism which seems to breathe the breath of life into every masterpiece. This nationalism is something far broader and deeper than any flag-waving allegiance to man-made boundaries or governments. The Russians are patriots in the old Greek sense of the word — *patriotes*, loving, living, and dying for the things "of one's fathers." In our own time Russian patriotism, tried by the fire of Nazi invasion, has shown itself a heroic example to all the world.

No one can hope to understand or enjoy Russian art without a glimpse of the life behind it. The key to that life and to the history and character of the people lies in the usual place — under the mat, as it were, of the natural features of the country.

Russia — and we are thinking now of pre-World War I Russia, from which has come the great Russian art — was an immense country, covering a sixth of the whole land surface of the earth. In the north were black forests, in the south the Steppes or plains, fertile to the west but burning out to arid desert in the east. Whether forest or prairie, this great level mass of land was continental, having very little coast line. Even the rivers, rising in marshes and lakes and making their leisurely winding way to unimportant seas, were of little use for travel. Seas and rivers were the ancient highways of commerce and culture, and Russia, depending upon caravans traveling overland, was more or less isolated.

Monotony characterizes the Russian landscape. In a country so vast, so level, and so slowly varying in its belts of vegetation, the traveler must expect to see, day after day, the same plants and animals, the same houses, the same manners and customs. In the old days the Russian knew no challenge to find new ways of living. If for any reason he moved to another place, it was but to live the same old life in similar surroundings. And so it happened that Russian culture was extended rather than increased.

Sharply contrasted with this monotony of landscape is the variation of climate which might also be expected in so immense a land untempered by the sea. Some parts of Russia know fierce extremes — hot, dry summers, long, bitter winters, brief, stormy autumns, and still briefer springs. These variations of climate and seasons give Russia a variety of nature pictures: There are the Steppes, in spring, a sea of waving grain, grass, and flowers, changing in summer to the gold of ripening harvests and burnt pampas grass, and then to boundless snow fields; and there is the magical white winter of northern Russia where the snowy landscape, seen through the sparkling air and against the peculiar blue sky, takes on an unreal beauty.

These natural features, the uniformity of the land surface and the intensity of the climate, are reflected in the temperament of the people. The Russian bears the hall-mark of all Slavic peoples — the capacity for lightning change from resignation to revolt. And having lived for centuries in a country where life was a constant struggle with hostile nature, with invasions from without and oppression from within, he has developed a curious blend of energy, persistence, and patience with a happy-go-lucky *Nichevo!* — "we should worry!"

This temperament is in turn reflected in two strangely antithetic ideas of beauty — the love of monotony, endless repetition, and contemplation of nature's somber moods on the one hand and, on the other, a love of the most vivid and violent contrasts of color.

Russian history also plays an important part in the development of Russian art. The early period was one filled with adventure, romance, and warlike deeds. The eleventh and twelfth centuries found Russia carrying on a thriving trade by caravan and not lacking in culture. Then, at the beginning of the thirteenth century, just when Europe was about to blossom forth in the art and scholarship of the Middle Ages, Genghis Khan, the Scourge of God, swept down from Chinese Tartary with his Mongol hordes, took possession of the Steppes, and cut Russia off from the western world.

For more than two hundred miserable years Russia wore the Tartar yoke. Racial pride and public spirit all but perished, and the people substituted religion for the patriotism they could not express, becoming almost fanatical in their devotion to the Greek church. Then from all the petty principalities, Moscow emerged, added to itself other principalities and powers, drove out the Tartars, and by the middle of the fifteenth century Russia became a nation. But the first century of her nationality was a time of trouble. No sooner were her princes freed from foreign enemies than they began to fight among themselves.

Then Peter, third Tsar of the Romanov line and descendant of a Boyar, one of the hereditary chieftains of Russia, came to the throne. The world was to know him as Peter the Great. He found Russia three hundred years behind the rest of Europe in commerce, culture, and learning, and wearing "a hampering garment of Orientalism." Burning with zeal for his country, Peter began his reforms by tearing the garment to shreds. He replaced the loose army of paid mercenaries with young Russians drafted from every walk of life and trained to military service. He built a navy, serving first as shipbuilder's apprentice to learn how a boat should be made. He made the legis-lature more democratic, replacing the old Boyar idea of hereditary power with the modern idea that service alone counts. He encouraged agriculture and industry, and threw open every possible "window to the west," bringing to backward Russia Euro-pean education and culture.

The years that followed brought a mixture of good and evil. As Russia grew in power among the nations, she became conspicuous alike for the brilliance and culture of her upper classes and for the desolation of her peasants and serfs. The melancholy note of oppressed humanity as well as the monotony and somberness of nature became characteristic of Russian life and art. Social unrest seethed and fermented, giving rise to Nihilism, Bolshevism, and many another strange "-ism" which has found expression in the Russia of our day.

The culture which Peter and, later, Catherine the Great sponsored was imported. Literature, music, musicians, and even the language of the court were brought from France, Italy, and Germany. It was not until the early years of the nineteenth century that Russia found her musical tongue in the person of Mikhail Glinka (1804–1857), the first composer to use Russian folk themes and Russian subjects for his music. Other Russian composers lost no time in building upon Glinka's good foundation. They are still at work, and Russian art music, though little more than a century old, occupies a significant niche in the Hall of Fame.

Although Russian art music was late in flowering, its sources, Russian folk and sacred music, were vital and flourishing from ancient times in every part of this vast country. The folk songs are of endless variety, due not only to the fact that the Great Russians and the Little Russians show the usual differences of northern and southern peoples, but also to the fact that singing has always been an integral part of Russian life.

In remote farms and villages hundreds of simple souls have a song for almost every moment of their lives. The peasant baby falls asleep to a monotonous, mournful lullaby, perhaps such as this masterpiece of repetition:

As a child he sings at play, for most of the children's games have some funny little chant; as a lad he joins the carolers at Christmas and Easter, sings and dances in the streets on feast and fair days, and pours out his heart in serenades and love songs; as he becomes a man, the stream of folk song broadens to take in still more phases of his life. He sings in the fields, the plowing, seed-sifting, and harvest songs, and at the canal as he helps to haul the barges on the sluggish rivers. He sings at village gatherings where the old hero songs are going round, at church, and at weddings. And at last, when all is over, he sleeps his last sleep to the old funeral songs sung by his neighbors.

While many Russian folk songs are sad, many others, particularly the dancing songs, are extravagantly merry. But even though their rhythms be lively and their words cheerful enough, the tunes are apt to sound a bit doleful to western ears. This plaintiveness is due to certain peculiar traits which distinguish both Russian folk and art music.

To begin with, the Russian uses other scale forms than ours, old modes which have come down from the ancient, beautiful music of the Greek church. The intervals and cadences of these old modes give a sense of loneliness as of vast open spaces and far horizons. Most typical is the fall from the fourth scale step to the keynote:

heard in so many Russian folk songs. Like all Slavic peoples the Russians prefer the minor modes, though they do not hesitate to mingle major and minor more freely than we would dare.

The themes of Russian folk songs are usually short. Indeed, the songs themselves are short, some of them having but three measures. These short themes are very limited in range, rarely moving beyond the fifth or sixth scale step. The older the song, the narrower the range. This narrowness and the fact that the themes are constantly repeated give that monotony which is so characteristically Russian. Daniel Gregory Mason describes it as suggesting that the singer, "under some baleful spell, wandered helplessly in the circle of four notes."

The Russian feels none of the German's or Englishman's obligation to end his song properly on the keynote. Just as often as not he brings up in a dominant harmony on the fifth scale step, as in the lovely "Through the Meadow":

or on the second, as in "In the Shade of the Garden Strolling":

leaving us with an unfinished feeling. This lack of finality is but music's way of expressing the basic Russian trait of indecision which Turgenev and Gogol bring out in their novels.

Russian rhythms are even more casual and wandering than the melodies. As one writer says, "They reflect the Russian with his free and easy ways, clear, sober mind, and his need of elbow room." Here we find no neat little song patterns phrased in multiples of four measures. A Russian folk song may stop with seven, nine, or whatever number of measures it takes to tell the singer's musical tale. Frequently it is metered in foreign sounding groups of five or seven beats, and the accent shifts from one syllable to another in the same word or from one word to another in the same verse, to the despair of the conventional musician. As for the meter signature, it may change at every bar line. Mussorgsky was running true to folk form when he let a child's song ramble from seven-four to three-four, five-four, six-four, and so on, twenty-seven changes in fifty-three measures!

The *tempo* of the song and the tone in which it is sung depend upon the situation. Mme. Eugenie Linev in her scholarly book, "Peasant Songs of Great Russia," tells of asking some peasant women to sing a certain song for her. The women inquired whether she wished it sung as in the fields or as in the spinning room. The field fashion, it seemed, was in a loud, slow voice as befitted the immensity of the out-of-doors, while that of the spinning room was lighter, quicker, and in an intimate, subdued tone.

A Russian folk song generally begins with the principal melody sung in a low key by one voice or in unison, then passes into several parts, returning periodically to the unison, usually at the begining of each new stanza. The secondary parts, the *podgoloski*, are not accompaniments to the melody as are our familiar alto, tenor, and bass. They are really imitations or variations of the melody — little tunes which each singer improvises according to his own imagination, as the Negro does, putting in an "Oh!" or an "Ah!" whenever he feels like it. The richness of the harmonic effect depends upon the number of original singers in the group. The untalented ones merely "move their voices about," as the village critics put it, or "yawn" through the song.

This old song, "Oh, Ye Hills," built on the typically Russian scale:

with the flattened seventh step, is an excellent example of the low, unison beginning, the voices joining in an imitation, the plaintive four-one cadence, and the meter change with the second stanza.

Stanza 2

But anyone who has heard Russian peasant singers knows that it is not so much the songs as the singing that matters. Caught in cold print, these songs seem as pathetic as wild flowers pressed between the pages of a book. It is not that the Russians have any special beauty of voice, although there are lovely voices in the Ukraine, from which the best singers come, and there are, to be sure, those human double basses trained to descend to incredible depths:

It is, rather, their ideal of singing that lends such peculiar charm to the singing of the peasant chorus.

The ideal of the trained western choir is to "sing as one man," that man being the director who uses the several voices as so many keys of an instrument upon which he interprets the song. But the Russian folk chorus sings not as one man, but as many men, each one pouring his own feelings into the mold of the song but instinctively careful not to mar the beauty of the mold.

The peasant does not learn his song — he lives it. Often, as in the picturesque singing games, he acts it out. The chorus, like that of the ancient drama, serves as narrator and commentator, forming a circle within which the singers who take the parts of the characters of the song — the lovers, husband and wife, cruel stepmother, and abused maiden — dance or act as they sing their scraps of dialogue. Sometimes there is a leader who sings the tale while the chorus merely exclaim or repeat at the end of each stanza.

And just as the child recreates a pet nursery tale again and again with fresh enthusiasm, so the Russian makes his song anew each time he sings it. The little singsong tune, continually repeated, does not seem boresome to him, only comfortable and familiar. And besides, he knows his song so well that he misses no chance for effect and can add many an intriguing extra touch if it suits his fancy. How frivolous and superficial any acquired "style" in singing seems, compared with this basic appreciation of the possibilities of a song!

Through many dark centuries Russian folk music, like the pool of a magic spring, held the reflection of the collective life of the people against the time when men of learning should seek the source and by their art and craft give this reflection to the world through Russian art music. Music is still reflecting life in Russia, life that has known the turbulence of social revolution, devastating war, and the countless perplexities of reconstruction. But there are many who have faith enough in beauty to believe that when the clamor dies away, Russian music will be even greater than of old, greater because it will belong, not to the leisure class alone, but to the folk from which it sprang. In art as in government, "Sovereignty rests with the people."

ALEXANDER BORODIN

St. Petersburg — 1834
St. Petersburg — 1887

In that variously named city best known as St. Petersburg (but after 1914 called Petrograd and since 1924 called Leningrad), Alexander Porphyrievich Borodin was born, lived for fifty-three useful years, died, and is buried. Unlike his musical colleagues, Balakirev, Rimsky-Korsakov, and Mussorgsky, Borodin did not spend his boyhood in the country, storing up impressions of folk life, folklore, and folk music which would later find expression in his own work. Yet in many ways he was the most Russian of the Russians, the one of whom a French critic remarked, "There is a man who does not strive to make Russian music; it exudes from every pore."

The nationalism of Borodin was something far deeper than any surface contacts or conscious loyalties. It was a matter of long inheritance, for in his veins ran the blood of the last kings of Imeritia, that most beautiful of ancient Caucasian kingdoms. This royal line claimed descent from King David, and bore on its coat of arms quarterings of harp and sling — appropriate emblems for one who was to be champion of the new Russian School of music.

Alexander Borodin was brought up by a wise mother who gave careful attention to his education and humored his early enthusiasm for science and music. Alexander was lucky in having for a playmate a youngster named Shchiglev, already a little prodigy in chemistry and an ardent music lover. The boys had a grand time with their team of hobbies. They would play piano duets — Haydn, Mozart, Beethoven — in the intervals between chemistry lessons. They were to be seen perched side by side in the balcony at nearly every concert, and lost their heads completely over chamber music. In order to understand it more fully they took lessons, Borodin on 'cello and flute, Shchiglev, on the violin. And of course they tried their hands at composition.

When Borodin was sixteen, it was decided that he should become a physician. He entered the St. Petersburg Academy of Medicine where he did six years' excellent work. The only blot on his college record was an examination in which he failed because he cited a passage of Scripture in language which was considered entirely too free and easy!

But the mere business of becoming a doctor was not allowed to interfere with the hobbies. No matter what the weather, Borodin and Shchiglev still went to concerts or trudged miles, the one carrying his fiddle, the other, his flute or 'cello, to take part in some musical gathering. Sometimes these gatherings were of incredible duration — Shchiglev in his reminiscences mentions one that began at seven in the evening and lasted until the same hour the next day!

From these same reminiscences comes this amusing anecdote: One night the two friends were making their way home along a footpath, a few yards apart; it was pitch-dark, and the street lamps gave an uncertain light. Suddenly Shchiglev heard a loud noise, followed by complete silence. As he hastened to his friend's assistance, he heard a little tune issuing from underground — Borodin had fallen into a cellar, and his first thought was to try his precious flute to see that it was none the worse for the mishap!

All during the years at the Academy of Medicine the experiments in composition were going on. Borodin wrote little pieces which were called "Romances," but he was careful not to show them to anyone.

Nor was the chemistry neglected. Against the advice of his professors, Borodin spent long hours in the laboratory. His teacher, the great chemist, Zinine, recognized the boy's talent for science and was jealous of all rival interests. One day, before the whole class, he said, "Monsieur Borodin, you would do well to occupy yourself less with 'Romances.' You know that I rely upon you as my successor; but you think of nothing but music; you make a mistake in hunting two hares at once."

However, Borodin continued to hunt both hares, and with surprising success. No sooner had he finished at the Academy than he received an appointment as surgeon in a military hospital. Two years later he was given the degree of Doctor of Medicine and sent to Germany at government expense to complete his scientific training. Yet another two years found him back in St. Petersburg as assistant lecturer in chemistry at the Academy of Medicine. Such rapid advancement in his profession could scarcely be the reward of wild rabbit-chasing!

Borodin was always a serious scientist. He devoted himself to research in chemistry, and his writings were published in technical magazines both in Russia and abroad. Besides these he left twenty treatises on chemistry and valuable manuals which were used in the Academy laboratories for many years.

But it was his teaching that filled his life most completely. "I love my profession and my science," he said. "I love the Academy and my pupils. My teaching is of a practical character, and for that reason takes up much of my time. I have to be constantly in touch with my pupils, because to direct the work of young people one must be always close to them."

He lived in an apartment on the same floor as his laboratory. When he was not actually in the midst of his students, they could hear him playing his piano next door. They could always count on an invitation to supper when they worked overtime in the laboratory; and whether they lingered to talk over their studies, finances, or love affairs, or to dream through an evening of his music, they were sure of the sympathy of this clever, gentle man.

Rimsky-Korsakov in his "My Musical Life" gives an interesting glimpse of Borodin.

Anybody could enter his house at any time whatsoever and take him away from his dinner or his tea. Dear old Borodin would get up with his meal or his drink half tasted, would listen to all kinds of requests and complaints, and promise to "look into it." People would hang on him with unintelligible explanations of their business, gabble and chatter by the hour, while he himself wore a hurried look, having this or that still to do. My heart broke at seeing his life completely filled with self-denial owing to his own inertia. . . . Leaving out of account the girls, their protégées, of whom there was never any lack, their apartment was often used as a shelter or a night's lodging by various poor or visiting relations who picked that place to fall ill or even to lose their minds! Borodin had his hands full with them, doctored them, took them to hospitals, and then visited them there. . . . Several tomcats also found a home in Borodin's apartment. . . . You might be sitting at the tea table and behold! Tommy marches along the board and makes for your plate; you shoo him off, but Yekatyerina Sergeyevna [Madame Borodin] invariably takes his part and tells some incident from his biography. Meantime, zip! another cat has bounded on Alexander Porphyrievich's shoulder and twining itself about, has fallen to warming his neck without pity. "Listen, Dear Sir, this is really too much of a good thing!" says Borodin, but without stirring; and the cat lolls blissfully on.

Rimsky goes on to tell of the irregular hours, meals at any and all times, and night turned into day; for Madame Borodin suffered from asthma, could not sleep, and usually got up at midnight.

In spite of the fact that their home life was "one unending disorder," the Borodins were happy. They had no children of their own, but they were devoted to each other and to their music. They had little money, but they were content to live simply, finding happiness in the things money cannot buy and sharing that happiness with their adopted daughters and with a host of friends. It seems fitting that death should have come to Borodin when he was surrounded by friends at a masked ball at which he was host. In the midst of an animated conversation he suddenly fell forward, and his guests discovered to their consternation that the kindly heart had simply ceased to beat.

Along with his other activities Borodin was an enthusiastic champion of higher education for women and one of three founders of the School of Medicine for Women at St. Petersburg. At his death his old pupils decorated his coffin with a silver crown bearing this inscription, "To the founder, protector, and defender of the School of Medicine for Women, to the supporter and friend of the students. From the women doctors qualified between 1872 and 1887."

Music, as we know, had always been a joy to Borodin. From his boyhood he had been a delightful pianist, a creative listener, and a shy but eager dabbler at composition. It was not, however, until he was twenty-eight and settled as a professor at the Academy that he gave any serious thought to composing. Then he met Balakirev, the man with a genius for inspiring other men to musical feats beyond their fondest imaginations. Balakirev convinced Borodin that he could and should make a contribution to the new Russian music. He persuaded him to join the famous "Five" — Balakirev, Cui, Rimsky-Korsakov, Mussorgsky, and Borodin. These men met together regularly to examine and criticize each other's writings. This "clinic," presided over by Balakirev, the only trained musician in the group, took the place of the usual academic training in composition. Indeed, Balakirev, with his criticism and suggestion, was the only teacher Borodin the composer ever had.

Borodin lacked neither talent nor inclination, but only time for composition. And, as he wrote to a friend, "Even if actual time were not wanting, I have absolutely no mental leisure; tranquillity is indispensable to this work, and my thoughts are always elsewhere," — probably with some little chemist in need of a job or with some girl determined to be a doctor even at the risk of wrecking her matrimonial chances!

The poor man had to steal time for his writing, much of which was done when he was too ill for his other work. "And so," he says, "my musical friends, reversing the usual custom, never say to me, 'I hope you are well,' but 'I hope you are ill.'" He was so modest about his music and so afraid of throwing his scientific work into the shade that he tried to be an anonymous composer. His work, however, was too brilliant to hide its light under a bushel, and we find him whimsically lamenting: "My two symphonies will both be performed in the same week. Never before has a professor at the College of Medicine and Surgery found himself in such a position!"

Out of this crowded and all too short life came two excellent symphonies, two string quartets, a piano suite, an opera, and a small but unusual group of songs. And while it is not an important work, one cannot resist mentioning the "Paraphrases," of which Borodin speaks in one of his last letters.

I take the liberty of sending you, for your little girls, my — or rather *our* — "Paraphrases," twenty-four variations and fourteen little pieces for the piano on the favorite theme of the "Coteletten Polka":

which is so popular with the little ones in Russia. [American children know it as "Chopsticks."] It is played with the first finger of each hand. The origin of this humorous work is amusing. One day Gania (one of my adopted daughters) asked me to play a duet with her.

"Well, but you do not know how to play, my child."

"Yes, indeed," said Gania, "I can play this":

I had to yield to the child's request, and so I improvised the polka which you will find in the collection.

In this unique duet one player keeps "Chopsticks" going while the other plays the piece Borodin wrote and which needs more than one finger on each hand, to say the least. The "Coteletten Polka" caused much laughter among Borodin's friends. Cui, Rimsky-Korsakov, and Liadov each wanted to try his hand at a similar piece, and before they got through with it they had twenty-four variations and fourteen little pieces on this nursery theme. They amused themselves by performing it with people who could not play the piano. Liszt heard of it, and was so pleased that he wrote an introduction, and the "Paraphrases" were published, dedicated "To little pianists who can play the theme with one finger of each hand."

Although his music was acclaimed at home and abroad, particularly in Belguim, to which he made two triumphal visits, Borodin always thought of himself as a musical amateur. He was an amateur in the literal sense of the word, for he wrote for sheer love of it. Music was his hobby, and he never knew the humiliation of writing potboilers. But his music, written only when he had something to express in this much-loved medium, is not at all amateurish in the sense of being musically or technically deficient. Borodin had the Russian flair for suave melody, bold rhythms, and gorgeous color, and his orderly, scientific mind and well-tempered emotions were quick to sense the beauty of balance and form in music.

Borodin the scientist is almost forgotten after a century of progress. Other schools, other treatises, other manuals and methods have replaced those upon which he spent himself. But the comparative handful of musical compositions wrested from a busy life have not been replaced. Every year they become better known and more appreciated the musical world over. Through his music, Borodin, prince of amateurs, has achieved immortality.

Prince Igor, Borodin's only complete opera, was more than sixteen years in the making. This long delay was not due to any lack of interest on Borodin's part, quite the contrary. The subject of *Prince Igor*, taken from legends of the long struggle between the Russian Princes and the Polovtsi, a nomadic people of eastern origin who harried Little Russia in the twelfth century, had a peculiar attraction for this man of Caucasian blood.

With a scientist's passion for research, Borodin set to work to prepare himself for the writing of his opera. He searched the libraries for stories and songs of the Tartars who had roamed the lower Steppes. He studied books of travel, collections of native melodies, and even delved into the language of these picturesque people in his eagerness to saturate himself with the atmosphere of twelfth-century Russia. It is no wonder that historians consider *Prince Igor* an almost perfect picture of its period.

But his devotion to *Prince Igor* proved its undoing! After all this research, Borodin could not bear to trust the libretto to someone who might be less accurate, less sympathetic, and therefore decided to write it himself. He was no dramatist. He could create striking scenes, but he did not know how to connect them. He knew so little of how to weave a plot that he let his villain disappear altogether at the end of the first act! This lack of dramatic interest is doubtless the reason why the opera is so seldom given. But faulty as the libretto may be, there is no contesting the beauty and magnificence of *Prince Igor* as a series of vivid musical stage pictures.

When he finally began to compose the music, Borodin found himself confronted with fresh difficulties. Here is his own account, taken from a letter to a friend:

In the midst of my academical and scientific work, commissions, committees, and various meetings, I have very little time left to devote to music. . . . Meanwhile, I am like a consumptive who, scarcely able to breathe, still dreams of a goat's-milk cure, of a journey to the south, of rambles through meadows carpeted with flowers. I, too, dream of writing an opera.

But what a difference between the consumptive patient and myself! He might carry out his aspirations if health were restored to him, while I can hope for nothing better than to fall ill. In fact, when I am tied to the house with some indisposition, unable to devote myself to my ordinary work, when my head is splitting, my eyes running, and I have to blow my nose every minute, then I give myself up to composing.

I have been thus indisposed twice this winter, and each time I have raised a new stone in my edifice. This edifice is *Prince Igor*.

I have already written a grand Polovtsian march, an air for Yaroslavna, the complaint of Yaroslavna in the last act, a short chorus for women in the camp of the Polovsti, and Oriental dances, for the Polovtsi were an eastern people. I have collected quantities of materials, and completed several numbers. But when shall I have finished?

How grieved he would have been had he known that the answer to his question was — never! For Borodin was never to see *Prince Igor* come to life upon the stage. The opera was not published until three years after his death, and then only through the efforts of his friends, particularly Rimsky-Korsakov and Glazunov, who completed and orchestrated the unfinished portions.

The Polovtsian Dances, the most popular and most truly representative pages of the opera, occur at the end of the second act. Prince Igor and his son, who have led an expedition against the ancient enemy, are prisoners in the Polovtsian camp. But Khan Khonchak, the Tartar chieftain, who can be as gracious as he is terrible, has ordered a festival in honor of his royal prisoners.

Slave girls with tambourines, slave boys bearing drums and other primitive instruments, warriors, priests, all the motley retinue of a Tartar chieftain come trooping in, and the magnificent entertainment begins. There are a number of dances, some of them mingled with singing, and in the opera the curtain falls upon a wild shout of "Our Khan, Khonchak!"

There are several Polovtsian Dances in *Prince Igor*, but those most familiar to concert audiences are the Young Men's Dance and the Girls' Dance. A throbbing rhythm in percussion and strings:[1]

and a compelling figure in bassoons and 'celli:

create a mood of savage joy which increases as the men join in, stamping fiercely in the brasses:

while the woodwinds and violins shriek and whirl in a barbaric motif:

This wild dance gives way to a lovely Girls' Dance, oboe and violas playing the languorous melody:

[1] Quotations from *Prince Igor*, by Alexander Borodin, used by permission of the publisher, G. Schirmer, Inc.

as the voices of the slave girls sing of the distant summerland of their birth:

> Fly, my song, across the mountains,
> O fly, my little song, on swift winds winging!
> Fly to that lovely land of golden sunshine,
> O land of home and love and sweet birds singing!

'Celli and English horn take up the tune a bit wistfully:

> There the sea is gently murmuring and sighing
> 'Neath the moonlight's silver gleaming.
> And there the fragrant breath of opening roses
> Fills all the silent night with sweetest dreaming.

The higher voices repeat the first version of the theme ending with:

> O fly, my song of home, fly far away!

through which sounds a phrase like a sigh born of memories unbearably sweet:

While we have been under the spell of this dream tune, the Young Men's Dance has slipped back through a subtle shifting from 2/2 to 12/8 meter, a soft but persistent drumbeat and the ghost of the whirling dance figure. It has actually been going on all through the repetition of the song theme, and now breaks out again in all its wild energy!

It is followed by a final section which begins with the theme of one of the earlier dances in the set, The Dance of the Savage Men:

and ends in a riot of sound and color.

Much of the brilliancy of the Polovtsian Dances is due to the orchestration, which in certain spots shows the touch of Rimsky-Korsakov's master hand. How surprising it is to hear, in the Young Men's Dance, the crude native pipes and drums, in the Girls' Dance, the strumming of the ancient *guzla*, then to lift the eyes to the stage and see a modern orchestra playing on the last word in percussion instruments, woodwinds, harps, and violins!

And it is even more astonishing that such stark, naked savagery could be let loose and yet give no impression of the music's running wild. For this admirable restraint that prevents even these savage dances from becoming mere orgies of sound, we may thank the orderly mind of the scientist which always served to balance the heart of Borodin the artist.

A third and last astonishment comes with the realization that the Polovtsian Dances are as much in the modern manner, as fresh and as vital as if they had been written only yesterday!

IN THE STEPPES OF CENTRAL ASIA

In the year 1880 Russia celebrated the twenty-fifth anniversary of the reign of Tsar Alexander II. The jubilee program included a series of elaborate historical pageants, or *tableaux vivants*, and for one of these, *The Success of Russian Arms in Asia*, Borodin wrote the music, *In the Steppes of Central Asia*.

Prefacing the score is this description of the picture from which the composer worked:

Amid the silence of the sandy steppes of Central Asia are heard for the first time the strains of a peaceful Russian song. From the distance come the sounds of horses and camels approaching nearer, and also the strange, melancholy strains of an Eastern melody. A caravan escorted by Russian soldiers is crossing the vast desert. Confident and fearless the travelers continue their long journey safeguarded by Russian arms. The caravan recedes farther and farther into the distance. The song of the Russians mingles with that of the Orientals in a common harmony, until both are gradually lost upon the plain.

The scheme of the piece is simple and effective. Since the music is to accompany a caravan crossing the desert, Borodin uses the old "approaching-and-passing" idea with not only the usual increase and decrease in loudness to suggest here and there, but also a moving from near and far keys. The human figures are represented by two themes, one Russian and one Eastern.

A soft high E in the violins, sustained for more than fifty measures, suggests the monotonous background of the steppes. A wearisome thing it is to cross those endless miles of sand and feather grass, pricked here and there by a stunted thorn bush. Never a house, a tree, a hill, or a stream breaks the dreary landscape; only a desert eagle drifting in the empty sky or swooping down to fight with the caravan dogs over the carcass of a horse — grim reminder that others have passed this way. Small wonder that the traveler's eyes and hopes are always fixed upon the horizon over which some sign of life may appear!

And now over the horizon of Borodin's tone picture appears a solo clarinet singing "a peaceful Russian song":

which is taken up by a horn. As the procession comes nearer, the dull padding of horses and camels is heard in softly plucked bass strings.

Soon an English horn enters with an oriental melody:

not unlike the song of the slave girls in the Polovtsian Dances. Indeed, it is thought to be another of the old Tartar tunes discovered by Borodin in the extensive research made for *Prince Igor*.

On comes the caravan with the two themes alternating to the accompaniment of muffled hoofbeats. It passes directly before us, the Russian theme loud and near in the key of C major and the camels tramping heavily in octaves. Then the English horn, repeating the oriental melody, leads out of the prevailing A minor tonality into the sunshine of A major. And now the song of the Russians mingles with that of the Orientals in a common harmony:

As the caravan disappears fragments of the two tunes overlap as if blurred by the distance. The Russian air floats faintly back from a high flute, then nothing remains but the muted violins with their high E — the vast emptiness of the steppes of Central Asia.

An amusing incident connected with this music is found in one of Borodin's letters to his wife. Borodin and Liszt had formed quite a friendship, based on mutual admiration of each other's work. In 1881, shortly after *In the Steppes* was written, Borodin went to Weimar to visit Liszt, taking along a number of his scores. Liszt took a fancy to *In the Steppes* and insisted that Borodin arrange it for four hands so that they might play it on the piano. Borodin set to work, but before he had gone very far, in rushed the impulsive Liszt with another bright idea. They would play it that very night at a party at Prince Wittgenstein's!

Poor Borodin was dismayed. He had not brought along proper evening clothes and did not want to go to Prince Wittgenstein's party, much less appear as one of the performers of a half-finished piano duet. He protested, but (quoting from the letter) Liszt replied: "Do not vex me! You shall thump the bass and I will bang the treble, and it will go splendidly! The latter part [which was unfinished] you must thump by yourself."

"And," writes Borodin, "the obstinate old gentleman actually did as he threatened. At the Wittgensteins' we played the first portion as a duet, and I had to finish it alone. . . . I dedicated *In the Steppes* to Liszt. He embraced me and thanked me warmly." It seems most appropriate that Borodin's only piece of program music should have been dedicated to the man who, as the originator of the symphonic poem, was program music's chief exponent at that time.

In the Steppes is not to be compared musically with Borodin's symphonies or his *Prince Igor*. Yet it is unquestionably an effective piece, unpretentious, well made, and with two beautiful, singable melodies. Borodin was surprised that this "occasional piece" should have pleased people outside of Russia. "Why," he exclaimed, "my *Steppes* has gone the round of Europe from Christiania to Monaco!" And today, more than half a century after his death, *In the Steppes* is still going!

MODESTE PETROVITCH MUSSORGSKY

Karevo   — 1839
St. Petersburg — 1881

The life story of Modeste Mussorgsky offers little opportunity to the ambitious biographer. It is a rather dull story, unenlivened by dramatic episodes and ending pathetically in delirium tremens on Mussorgsky's forty-second birthday.

There was, however, a charming childhood spent in the picturesque countryside some two hundred miles south of St. Petersburg. The Mussorgskys were typical small landowners, living comfortably in their pleasant village and enjoying what they could transplant of books and music from the larger world outside. There was the father, a man of considerable education, the mother, a very fair pianist, a brother, Filaret, and little Modeste. Most important among the lesser members of the household was the children's nurse, for it was she who sowed the seeds of that passion for folk life and folklore which was to flower so magnificently in the composer's music. "My nurse," says Mussorgsky, "taught me nearly the whole of the Russian folklore." Her vivid tales of the terrible Kastchei, the witch, Baba-Yaga, the heroic Ivan Tsarevich, and the fatally beautiful Tsarevna caused the sensitive little boy many a sleepless night.

As soon as Modeste realized what the piano could do in the way of storytelling, he began trying to make it tell of these fascinating characters. The child's evident musical talent delighted his parents. He began to have lessons, and between his mother and a German governess received a fairly good start in his musical education.

When he was ten, he and his brother were sent to a boarding school in St. Petersburg. Later Modeste passed into a Military Cadet's School and on into a school for ensigns, for he was to make the army his life calling. But all through his school days he had kept up the study of music, and we find him, at seventeen, a smart young officer who could "play snatches of *Trovatore* and *Traviata* to the delight of the ladies."

It was at this time that he met, in the common room of the military hospital, the young army surgeon, Borodin. Both young men were more or less bored with their military duties and delighted to discover a common interest in music. That same winter Mussorgsky made the acquaintance of some of the other talented amateurs who later were known as the famous "Five." Eagerly he accepted their ideas and became the most zealous of them all in the cause of Russian music.

Although he had made a brilliant record at school, particularly in history and philosophy, and had passed all his government examinations creditably, Mussorgsky had no real interest in a military career and, as his interest in music grew, he began to grudge the time spent at the garrison. He decided to resign his commission and devote himself to music. His friends, realizing the advantage of a dependable income, urged him to stick to soldiering, but the young hothead would not listen. He was only twenty when he burned his economic bridges. Twenty-two years lay before him, years in which poverty, nagging potboiler jobs, repeated nervous breakdowns, and intemperance were to play havoc with a life so auspiciously begun!

Yet in spite of the retrogression of the man, Mussorgsky the artist forced his way steadily forward and upward. The scattered musical harvest of his short life was of a quality that marked him the one real genius in that brilliant Russian band, the "Five."

Mussorgsky lacked almost everything a composer should have in the way of techniques. As a student he had spent all his time learning to play the piano, and later, when he turned to composing, he was too eager to express himself and too afraid of being hampered by rules to settle down to any serious study of musical composition. Because he belonged to the period in which all Russian artists were crying, "Away with all social and artistic conventions." "Go to the people for inspiration!" Mussorgsky felt no regrets for his professional shortcomings. Fine as it may have sounded to shout this battle cry of freedom and renounce all rules and techniques, the fact nevertheless remains that, had it not been for the technical knowledge of his friend

Rimsky-Korsakov, and the latter's years of patient editing and revising, much of Mussorgsky's music would have remained unintelligible and unknown.

Fortunately, genius always transcends knowledge, and Mussorgsky, for all his technical slips and his fatal habit of leaving his work unfinished, is generally acclaimed as the greatest of Russian composers because he was the most successful in his efforts "to put the actual living man into music" — his own words.

He believed that art is an expression of human life, a means of communication, and that art, like life itself, is subject to constant change; and he believed that the artist entrusted with this expression of life should be, above all else, sincere. This passion for sincerity made Mussorgsky, at times, an uncompromising realist, and explains certain unpleasantly dissonant passages in his music. If music were to express life, he reasoned, then music must follow life even into ugliness — a rather dangerous philosophy!

Mussorgsky devoted his art to the expression of the life of the Russian people, the people he had known and loved from childhood. And so steeped was he in Russian folk music that he used its idiom unconsciously. As with Grieg, the music of his country was his mother tongue; he could not speak any other. It is said that his great opera, *Boris Godunov*, an historic opera generally supposed to be just a glorified collection of folk songs and dances, contains, in reality, not one real folk tune! The tunes are all of Mussorgsky's own making, but so perfectly in the folk spirit and idiom that they seem more Russian than the Russians!

Mussorgsky's music is peculiar in that it never follows musical forms, that is, the development of themes or patterns of sound such as we find in the works of Mozart, Beethoven, Brahms, or even of his own countryman, Tchaikovsky. It follows, instead, the feelings and the rhythms of spoken language and of bodily movements. In fact, it follows life so faithfully that it might be called mimetic music. Mussorgsky knew no formulas. He never wrote a phrase or a cadence from habit. Each piece might have been his first, for, as someone has cleverly put it, "Mussorgsky is never like himself."

Among Mussorgsky's masterpieces are the well-known *Pictures at an Exhibition*, originally piano sketches; the orchestral work, *A Night on Bald Mountain;* two operas, *Boris Godunov* and *Khovanshchina*, both magnificent pictures from Russian history. But greatest of all his works are the songs which mirror the very heart and soul of the Russian people.

To Mussorgsky a song was not a vocal solo with an instrumental accompaniment. A song was a miniature music drama in which the voice was responsible for the narration and description while the instrument provided the background and all the gesture and byplay. A song melody was never merely a tune which fits the mood and meter of the text; it had to fit every word. The tune itself had to sound like talking, and like Russian talking. Is it any wonder, then, that these songs defy translation and will always be exiles in French, German, or English, no matter how charmingly they are sung?

Three song cycles stand out as characteristic: "Without Sunlight," six songs for low voice which are poignant reveries on happiness forever past; the wonderful "Songs and Dances of Death," in which Death plays the rôle of friend, comforting the peasant lost in the forest on a winter's night, soothing the sick child with a lullaby, and serenading the dying girl as an ardent lover; and a third cycle, the matchless "In the Nursery."

"In the Nursery" is Mussorgsky at his best. Each song is a scene from the drama of childhood in which comedy and pathos mingle enchantingly. In the first song, "Nurse, Tell Me a Tale," we hear the child, who might well be tiny Modeste himself, begging Nanny for a story of the bogeyman, or the lame prince whose every step brings a mushroom popping from the ground, or of the queen whose sneeze was so loud that it broke all the windows! This remarkable little song changes meter from 7/4 to 3/4, 5/4, 6/4, and so on, twenty-seven times in fifty-three measures to accommodate all these fascinating characters!

Then comes "Stand in the Corner!" a saga of the crime and punishment of an upset workbasket and inkstand. Next, "The Beetle," a breath-taking encounter with a buccaneer insect who finally lies upside down, waving his feelers and begging for his life. The fourth song is a naïve "Cradle Song for the Doll," in which Dolly is entreated to remember her dreams so that she may tell them when she wakens. The "Child's Prayer" follows, a precious song in which the small suppliant remembers such a long string of people that he forgets "what comes next" and has to be sternly reminded by nurse that next is, "God bless *me*, and make *me* a good boy."

There is a shocking episode of the wicked cat at the robin's cage, and last, "The Hobby Horse," with its delightful ending where the attention of the horseman, who has taken a tumble, is tactfully diverted from his bumps.

"In the Nursery" is loved wherever it is known. It would be a callous listener, indeed, who could resist the eager little voice of Mishenka! Liszt wrote a letter of warm appreciation which brought the following comment from Mussorgsky, "Liszt amazes me! If I *am* a musical simpleton (as some of the critics had said), it seems that I was not one when I wrote 'In the Nursery.' For to understand children, to look upon them as human beings with minds of their own and not as so many amusing dolls, is not the privilege of simpletons."

Like Robert Louis Stevenson, Mussorgsky did not picture the child world as an onlooker, gazing fondly and indulgently from grown-up heights. He re-entered that world, became a child again, thrilling and sulking with Mishenka, then revealed it all to us with the subtle simplicity of the truly great artist.

Mussorgsky is an unique figure in the annals of music. Chaotic in his methods of living and working, eccentric in his philosophy of art, almost too fantastically free and too narrowly national even for his own countrymen, his works find increasing favor in the musical world of today because they are so alive and because Mussorgsky went so deep into nationalism that he actually came out on the other side — internationalism. His little Mishenka answers just as readily to the name of John, Hans, Giuseppe, or Chang!

INTRODUCTION TO KHOVANSHCHINA

The opera *Khovanshchina* has for its setting one of the most dramatic and one of the most gloomy periods in Russian history. Tsar Peter, afterward Peter the Great, was a child of ten; his sister Sophia was regent, but the government was really in the hands of two rival princes, Khovansky, representing the old, traditional, sleeping Russia, and Galitsin, the New Russia then awakening to the ideas of the western world. The Boyars, old feudal lords of Russia, had been deprived of much of their power, and the people were bewildered and oppressed. Against this background of social and political unrest stands out the calm figure of the priest, Dositheus, leader of a fanatical group known as the Old Believers. By his iron will and a strange hypnotic power he controls even the two princes. Years afterward, Peter the Great called the long series of struggles and intrigues, in which Prince Khovansky and his party played such an important rôle, "Khovanshchina," and Mussorgsky has given the same title to his opera.

There is a slight love story in *Khovanshchina*, but it is shadowed, as is the music itself, by the religious element which was the dominating force in Old Russia.

The music of the Entr'acte recalls the incident, early in the story, where Prince Galitsin, in spite of his western education, summons a young woman, said to be clairvoyant, to foretell his future. The young woman is Martha, one of the Old Believers. She takes a basin of clear water and, gazing into it, calls upon the spirits of the underworld to show her Galitsin's future. Then, trembling, she tells him that she sees the proud Prince Galitsin, bereft of power and riches, ragged, hungry, and desolate, wandering in exile. No more horrible fate could overtake him, for exile, to a prince of Old Russia, did not mean idle days of pleasuring along the Riviera, but the living death of Siberia.

While the rival princes are occupied with their petty intrigues, the Boyar Shaklovitsy has been working to rid the country of all this corrupt government and save the throne for young Peter, who is the hope of the landowning lords and of the people. The storm bursts in the fourth act, where, in the first scene, we see Prince Khovansky stabbed at his banquet table and, in the second, Prince Galitsin led away into exile just as Martha had prophesied. While the frightened crowd fills the public square murmuring over the tragic fate of the two powerful princes, word comes that the whole sect of Old Believers is condemned to death. Dositheus calmly commands that they take their own lives rather than die at the hands of heretics. Obeying their old priest, these simple, innocent people build a huge funeral pyre upon which they stand, singing their hymns until the flames silence them forever. The curtain falls upon this terrible picture, to the sound of the trumpets of Tsar Peter's victorious army, symbolizing the rising of the New Russia from the ashes of the Old.

Five variations on a lovely clear-cut theme form the Introduction to *Khovanshchina*. It is a tone picture which Mussorgsky himself called "Dawn over Moscow."

Soft *arpeggios*, rising from violas to flutes, prelude the quiet melody which is given out by oboes and second violins:

It is a true *aubade*, announcing the dawn with bird calls and the winding of a far-off hunter's horn.

Again the rising *arpeggios* are heard, this time leading into a minor variation, characteristically and drearily Russian:

Above softly rustling scale passages in the violins, the solo oboe now takes up the song:

which sinks to an end in a long downward melody line.

A quicker section follows, in which clarinets, bassoons, and 'celli have the melody:

accompanied by somber chords on the harp and a fateful drumming by the contrabass. Softer grows the mood as flutes and clarinets repeat the theme in tonalities of F-sharp major. The solo clarinet sings it for the last time in a placid D-flat:

against lightly shimmering strings and fluting bird calls.

There is none of the splendor of sunrise, none of the brassy brilliance of Rimsky's *Coq d'Or* — nothing but the mild blue sky and the quiet of early morning. This peaceful music, in striking contrast to the barricaded street which the slowly rising curtain now discloses, is a dramatic introduction to the tragic story of spiritual conflict between the old and the new Russia.

Entr'acte

The Entr'acte, somber and fateful, occurs between the scenes of Khovansky's death and Galitsin's exile. It is really an orchestral version of Martha's wonderful song, "The Divination by Water."

A tolling bell introduces the theme of the song:

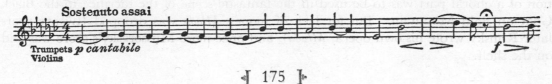

It flows on, smooth but relentless, over a restless little figure:

which suggests dark water and which never stops throughout the piece.

As the melody goes on:

ending with the heartbroken phrase:

it seems to express an exile's passionate longing for home.

The deadly monotony of the music is broken by a glimmer of something new in the oboe solo:

But it is only for a moment. The insistent water motif, like a spirit of the underworld, draws us back into the presence of a fate that cannot be averted, and the music ends, as it began, with a tolling bell.

The orchestration of *Khovanshchina* is an amazing example of true appreciation and unselfishness. Here we have one artist not only completing but enhancing the work of another, yet keeping himself entirely out of the picture! The orchestration of *Khovanshchina* is Rimsky-Korsakov's, but the music — the spirit — is pure Mussorgsky.

A Night on Bald Mountain

A Night on Bald Mountain, one of Mussorgsky's few orchestral works, had a checkered career. Written in 1860 for piano and orchestra, it was originally intended for the drama, *The Witch*, but after a long disagreement between composer and dramatist, it was laid aside. Mussorgsky then rewrote it as a symphonic poem, but was never quite satisfied with it. Ten years later, Borodin, Rimsky-Korsakov, and Mussorgsky were commissioned to write an opera, *Mlada*, based on scenes from pre-Christian Russia. Once more Mussorgsky's *Witches*, as he called the piece, came out, and with the addition of a choral part was to be used in the fantastic scene of the sacrifice to the Black Goat on Bald Mountain. But for lack of money *Mlada* was dropped (twenty years later Rimsky wrote his own opera, *Mlada*), and once more Mussorgsky's score was laid on the shelf.

The Witches next appeared as an interlude in Mussorgsky's opera, *The Fair at Soro-chinsk*, but the composer died before the opera was finished.   As his musical executor, Rimsky-Korsakov revised and reorchestrated *A Night on Bald Mountain*.   While it is probably true that the fastidious Rimsky did tame the Devil by putting him to school, without this discipline Mussorgsky's wild, crude score might never have come to per-formance.

A Night on Bald Mountain is a musical description of an unholy ceremony said to have been held on St. John's Eve on the Bald Mountain near Kiev.   Here crowds of witches and sorcerers met to worship Satan, who appeared among them in the form of a great black goat or as the Black God, Chernobog.   All night long these creatures of darkness celebrated, shrieking and dancing, muttering their Black Mass, and prac-ticing their Black Magic.   This horrid revelry had a fearful fascination for the ancients and for later poets and musicians, too, judging from the fact that Goethe in his *Wal-purgis Night* and Berlioz, Boito, Gounod, Liszt, and Mussorgsky have all pictured the Witches' Sabbath.

Mussorgsky attached this program to his score:

> Subterranean noises and unearthly voices.   Appearance of the Spirits of Darkness and of the Black God (Chernobog).   His glorification and the Black Mass.   Witches' Revel.   At the maddest moment the bell of the little village church sounds in the dis-tance, scattering the Spirits of Darkness.   Daybreak.

A long *Allegro feroce* with bustling strings, heavy-treading basses, and a sound as of rushing wings in the woodwinds pictures the gathering of the Spirits of Darkness, climaxed by the apparition of the Black God in a sinister theme for bassoons and brasses and low strings:

Presently the oboes and clarinets introduce a theme which is to become most familiar:

Chanted over and over and always followed by a sort of inverted genuflection:

it suggests the celebration of the Black Mass.   The music, through a little phrase theme, growing ever faster and more furious, works itself up to a pitch of excitement which ends in an exultant fling in the brasses:

A whirring of strings and a wailing little woodwind motif:

provide a moment's lull, but it is soon over. After a brief transition passage for full orchestra, the whole mad business repeats itself until, at the height of the revelry, a sudden downward rush of strings and woodwinds suggests the flight of the evil Spirits.

The church bell sounds, and serene violins announce the break of day:

This melody leaves us in no doubt but that it is a Russian dawn! And to those who have heard Mussorgsky's lovely aria, "The Divination by Water," from the opera *Khovanshchina*, it is hauntingly familiar.

Rising *arpeggios* in the harp suggest the mounting light and color of the sky, and the peaceful sunrise picture is completed by a snatch of pastoral melody for the clarinet:

answered by the flute:

It is a shepherd's song, and, by its ending, again unmistakably Russian.

Beautiful as these final themes may be, the chief interest in this music lies not in melody, but in tonal atmosphere and vigorous, picturesque rhythms.   To fully appreciate Mussorgsky's achievement, we of a generation accustomed to picturesque music must remember that there was comparatively little of it in the Russia of 1860.

PICTURES AT AN EXHIBITION

In the middle of the nineteenth century, Victor Hartmann, a young Russian artist and architect, died, and his sorrowing friends arranged a memorial exhibition of his pictures.   One of these friends, the composer Mussorgsky, was so moved and inspired by this showing of Hartmann's drawings and watercolors that he re-expressed them in a series of brilliant little piano pieces which he called *Pictures at an Exhibition*.   Preluding and connecting these tonal pictures are variations of a theme which Mussorgsky named "Promenade" and in which he represents himself walking about the gallery from one picture to another.

Mussorgsky was an impetuous, poorly trained artist.   His unfamiliarity with instruments often caused him to write for piano music which called for the sweep and color of a large orchestra.   Had it not been for the labor of his friends, particularly Rimsky-Korsakov, who completed his unfinished works and reorchestrated others, many of Mussorgsky's grandest ideas would have been lost.   One day not long after Rimsky's death, Maurice Ravel and Serge Koussevitzky were talking about Mussorgsky's music, and Ravel, praising the piano pieces, *Pictures at an Exhibition*, no doubt spoke of how effective they would be for orchestra.   Whereupon Dr. Koussevitzky asked Ravel to orchestrate the *Pictures* for his use.   And that is how it came about that this delightful music, now played by orchestras everywhere, was arranged by Ravel and presented for the first time by Koussevitzky in Paris in the spring of 1923.   The first American performance was given three years later in Boston.

Promenade

The music begins with the "Promenade" theme:[1]

Allegro giusto, nel modo russico

Trumpet

announced by a trumpet.   Soon the horns, trombones, and tuba join in, and later, strings and woodwinds, until at the close of this short prelude the whole orchestra is promenading around the gallery.

"Promenade" is a typical Russian melody with its downward fourth step and alternating 5/4, 6/4 measures.   This purposeful yet rather wandering rhythm cleverly suggests the visitor at an art gallery, intent upon seeing the pictures, yet a bit uncertain as to where to begin.

Gnome

The visitor pauses before Hartmann's drawing of the gnome. In clever lines the artist has caught the quick, furtive movement of the grotesque little figure. The music *is* that movement; first, the sudden starts and wary pauses:

then a curious, bandy-legged capering in the woodwinds:

Weirdest of all is the lurching, prowling theme for muted brass and low woodwinds:

There is a sense of heaviness, perhaps the weight of fear, the weight of rocks which overhang this strange underground creature.

After all the jerky posturing and some very queer swishing sounds in the low strings and woodwinds, there is a wild up-rushing passage, and the gnome vanishes.

The Old Castle

With slightly slower step the visitor approaches the next picture. It is a castle of the Middle Ages, unreal in its atmosphere of far away and long ago:

Beneath its darkened walls a troubadour sings in the wistful voice of the alto saxophone:

All quotations from score by permission of Russischer Musikverlag G.m.b.H., Berlin, Copyright, 1929.

It is a mournful song with a burden of wandering which Mussorgsky catches in the keyless tonality of medieval music. On and on it goes, over a droning 'cello tone. There is little change of mood until the very last measures where the troubadour, with a final twang on his lute, cries a strange, "Ho, la!"

Alto Saxophone

Tuileries

The trumpet recalls the visitor from the dreaming mood of the "Old Castle." He is striding purposefully along:

Moderato

Strings

when suddenly his attention is arrested:

Ritardando

Violas pizz. *mf*
'Celli

by a gay little picture of everyday life, children and their nurses taking the air in the Tuileries Gardens in Paris.

There seems to be an amiable playground bantering going on, which Ravel, with his flair for orchestral color, has given to the woodwinds.

With the picture setting one easily imagines a naughty little-boy oboe in the teasing theme:

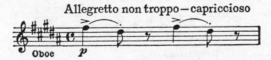

Allegretto non troppo — capriccioso

Oboe *p*

which sounds suspiciously like the classic "Smarty, smarty!"

This is answered by a chattering little-girl flute:

Flute *p*

Back and forth fly the taunt:

Oboe

and the saucy answer:

rising in pitch with the excitement.

Then the soothing voice of the violins:

suggests the nurse trying to make peace. Twice she has to speak to them. It doesn't seem to have much effect, for the teasing goes on:

But there is such merry laughter in the clarinets as the children scamper off that the picture is an altogether bright and happy one.

Bydlo

There is no "Promenade" between the "Tuileries" and the next picture, "Bydlo." Perhaps they hung side by side! "Bydlo" pictures an old Polish peasant cart called *bydlo*. It has enormous wooden wheels, and is drawn by oxen.

String and woodwind basses lumber along in a steady oxlike rhythm:

which keeps up throughout the piece.

Above the rumbling of the big wheels is heard a monotonous song:

Since it is a Russian folk tune, one can fancy the driver singing to pass the time on the laborious ride.

At one point the tune sounds more cheerful:

Both the song and the rumble of the wheels grow very loud as the cart passes us. Then the sound fades and dies away as the old *bydlo* passes out of sight.

Ballet of the Little Chickens in Their Shells

As the visitor turns away from the "Bydlo," the "Promenade" is heard in a minor key:

Something about the picture of the old oxcart has started a sober train of thought, which is suddenly interrupted as a curious drawing catches his eye. It is almost as if the drawing called out to him, for right in the midst of the serious "Promenade" there is a distinct and irrelevant chirp:

"What in the world?" one can imagine him saying. He pauses before the picture which he was about to pass by, and reads, "Ballet of the Little Chickens in Their Shells." "Why, this must be one of the drawings Hartmann made for the stage scene of that French ballet *Trilby*. Well, upon my word!"

And that is exactly the way one feels, listening to the music of the little chickens dancing in their shells:

Such a fluttering and twirling of oboes and clarinets! And such a chirping of flutes, with now and then a long, high-pitched "Peep"!

Then a slower, heavier theme enters:

There is a clumsy likeness to parts of the first theme. (One can't resist the suggestion of the hen!) All around this second theme the little chicks keep up their shrill chorus. Then the dancing theme returns and the whimsy ends with a droll tailpiece:

As contrast to the "Bydlo," this "Ballet of the Little Chickens in Their Shells" is perfect!

Samuel Goldenberg and Schmuyle

Whatever may have been the Hartmann picture which inspired it, this Mussorgsky music is as clever a tonal caricature as was ever written. Hartmann had chosen as his subjects two Polish Jews, Samuel Goldenberg and Schmuyle, the latter of so little consequence that he does not even rate a first name in the title! Mussorgsky, who had made a study of ancient Hebrew melodies, carried out the Jewish idea to the extent of using two old Hebrew tunes to represent his characters. But Mussorgsky's heroes belong to no special race, creed, or time. They are universal types, the boaster and the whiner — we all know them.

First Samuel Goldenberg speaks in a pompous unison of low woodwinds and strings:

He is fat. He is prosperous. He struts, and boasts of his business, his family, and of the importance of Samuel Goldenberg. He probably wears a heavy watch chain spanning his spherical vest. He loves the sound of his own voice.

But alas, poor Schmuyle! He is as thin and seedy as the muted trumpet which presents him:

He makes nervous little movements with his hands, and he whines. He tells Goldenberg a hard luck tale that ends in a perfect wail:

They both talk at the same time.   Goldenberg's voice sounds all the more unctuous rolling along under Schmuyle's anxious, trembling tones.   Finally Schmuyle begs:

But Goldenberg, disgusted with such a miserable, sniveling creature, snarls a "get out!" and in two fierce triplets:

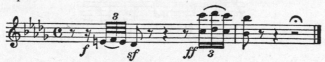

wipes Schmuyle right out of the picture.

The Market Place in Limoges

A persistent sixteenth-note rhythm and a little sharp-tongued theme:

pictures two market women wrangling over their wares in the old market place in Limoges.   They keep it up until the whole market place is in an uproar.   There is no other theme — how could there be!   The composer does not even try to write any formal ending to such a hullabaloo.   Right in the midst of a furious tirade the trombones announce the solemn *Largo:*

Catacombs

Hartmann's picture shows a visit to the catacombs of Paris by lantern light.   Mussorgsky writes his music in two sections, calling the first *Sepulchrum Romanum.*   Through somber chords, now loud, now soft, comes a pale lantern gleam of melody:

and a sense of the echoing emptiness of this timeless, motionless city of the dead.

Then oboes and English horn in a ghostly version of the "Promenade" theme:

introduce the section marked *Cum mortuis in lingua mortua,* "with the dead in the language of the dead." The music, soft and fragmentary, gives an impression of mystery and yet of tranquillity. There is a haunting sadness in the oboes' question:

and the clarinet's answer:

and a sense of the futility of man's wondering about death in the curious last chord in B major. This music arrives at no conclusion understandable in the language of the living.

The Hut on Fowl's Legs

This Hartmann drawing was a design for a clock in the shape of a hut on fowl's legs. Fantastic as this may seem, every Russian child would recognize the hut as the home of the fearful witch Baba-Yaga. Baba-Yaga had a horrible fondness for human bones, which she pounded to a fine meal in a great iron mortar. When she wanted to travel, so the legend goes, Baba-Yaga rode through the air in this glowing iron mortar, oaring it along with a pestle and sweeping out its track with a fiery broom.

In his music Mussorgsky has pictured not so much the hut on fowl's legs as its fearsome owner and her dark doings. In the first sinister notes one imagines the old witch stirring about:

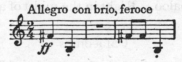

perhaps climbing aboard her red-hot mortar:

It rises up:

and as it swoops and darts through the air, Baba-Yaga chants in malicious glee:

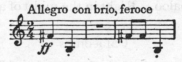

There is a mysterious middle section in which, under quivering flutes, the bassoon and contrabass make a sort of witches' brew:

Then the first part returns, and up and off she goes in a hair-raising flight through the entire orchestra!

The Great Gate at Kiev

Victor Hartmann was an architect, and among his drawings was a plan for a great entrance gate at Kiev. Since Kiev was no longer a walled city, the great gate was to be an ornamental and symbolic arch through which the pageant of the old city's life would come and go. Hartmann designed it in the massive style of old Russia, and in that style Mussorgsky has built his music.

Trumpets announce a processional theme, strangely like the "Promenade" theme:

Brasses, drums, and cymbals escort it in its stately progress.

Following this national hymn comes a churchly theme:

as dimly beautiful as an old icon painting. Both of these themes are repeated with elaboration.

There is an impressive choralelike section in which rhythms of three against two surge with mighty force. The music grows in volume, chimes ring out, and great bells clang as it sweeps to the gorgeous climax. This is ancient Muscovy, majestic, mysterious, beautiful, a fitting finale to a work dedicated to a Russian artist and to Russian art.

PETER ILITCH TCHAIKOVSKY

Votkinsk — 1840
St. Petersburg — 1893

Peter Ilitch Tchaikovsky was born in eastern Russia in the little village of Votkinsk. His father held the important position of inspector of government mines, and the family lived luxuriously in a fine house with a staff of servants and even a little army of a hundred Cossacks for protection. The elder Tchaikovsky was an affable man, his wife, a charming hostess, and they made their home a social center for the few cultured families of the neighborhood and the young government employees exiled in this out-of-the-way corner of the world.

When Peter was four years old, a governess was brought from St. Petersburg to take charge of the education of an older brother and a cousin who made her home with them. Peter was not considered old enough to share these lessons, but, when he saw the other children marching off to the schoolroom, he set up such a howl that he was permitted to join them. The valiant four-year-old attacked the problems of learning with such vigor that he soon caught up with his elders, and by the time he was six he could read both French and German fluently. Although he was an absent-minded youngster, usually guilty of missing buttons and of hair only half brushed, he had such a charming little mind and such beguiling ways that he was easily the favorite pupil.

He was a very sensitive child, always the merriest, maddest, or mournfulest of the group. "Brittle as porcelain," Fanny the governess used to say, and the reproofs that passed so lightly over the other children would upset him alarmingly.

Peter was a passionate little patriot with a love for everything Russian which lasted his whole lifetime. One day Fanny found him looking through an atlas and, when he came to the map of Europe, fervently kissing Russia and as fervently spitting upon all the rest of the world. "When I told him he ought to be ashamed of such behavior," writes Fanny, "and that it was wicked to hate his fellow men who said the same 'Our Father' as himself, and reminded him that he was spitting upon his own Fanny who was a Frenchwoman, he replied, 'Oh, you need not scold me. Didn't you see me cover France with my hand first?'"

There were no musicians and no concerts in Votkinsk. Unfortunately, even Fanny had nothing to offer in this line, so our future composer's early musical experiences had to come from a music box which his father had brought from the city. Peter adored the magic box and would sit by the hour listening to its tinkling tunes. There were two Mozart tunes which were his favorites and may have been the beginning of his lifelong enthusiasm for Mozart. The child teased some sketchy music lessons from his mother, who could play simple things on the piano, and as soon as his tiny hands could manage the keys, astonished the family by playing the music-box tunes. He took such delight in his playing that they had to drag him away from the instrument, and even then he would drum his tunes on the window pane. When, on rare occasions, guests who really could play or sing came to the house, Peter was almost beside himself with joy.

In the autumn of 1868 the Tchaikovskys left Votkinsk for St. Petersburg. The happy days in the schoolroom with Fanny were over. Peter and his brother were sent to school, where the long hours, longer assignments, and the thumps and whacks of boisterous school boys wore the delicate child to a shadow. Fortunately, at the end of a year, the father again took a position as inspector of mines, and the family returned to country life.

In his tenth year Peter made a second trip to St. Petersburg, this time to go to preparatory school, and after two bitterly homesick years entered law school. Meanwhile the family fortunes had sadly changed. The mother, whom Peter all but worshiped, had died, and the father, retiring from active service, had brought the younger children to St. Petersburg and joined the household of his brother. Shortly afterward he lost his fortune.

Peter was now nineteen, had just finished law school and, since it was necessary for him to earn his living, had entered the Ministry of Justice as a law clerk. Here he spent four negative years, careful not to do anything wrong but wholly uninterested in the law and all its works. That he was the same absent-minded Peter of the half-brushed hair is shown by the following incident. One day he had been sent to another department of the Ministry with an important document bearing the signature of his chief. On the way he stopped to talk with someone. As he talked he kept tearing off bits of the paper he held and chewing them — an absent-minded trick he had with programs, newspapers, and the like — until, to his horror, he discovered that he had consumed most of the document! There was nothing to do but recopy it and brave his chief for a second signature.

But this bored young official had a gay enough life when off duty. His uncle's home was full of young people who with their friends kept up a continual round of parties. Peter was much in demand on account of his music. During his school days he had kept up his piano study and played all the popular parlor pieces delightfully. His friends marveled at his gift of improvisation, and declared that no one could reel off the waltzes and polkas for the dancing as entrancingly as Peter Ilitch.

One evening he and a cousin, a young army officer who was also a clever pianist, began talking about music. "Among other things," says Tchaikovsky, "my cousin said that it was possible to modulate from one key to another without using more than three chords. This excited my curiosity, and to my astonishment I found that he could improvise whatever modulations I suggested, even from quite distant keys. I asked him where he had picked this up and discovered that there were classes in connection with the Musical Society where one might learn all this wisdom."

Piqued by his cousin's superior knowledge, Tchaikovsky lost no time in joining these classes. But he was still the dilettante, "getting by" with flashes of native ability rather than by any serious work. Music intrigued him so that he played with the idea of a musical career, but he always lacked confidence in himself. In a letter to his sister he says, "You know I have power and capacity, but I am ailing with your malady, which is called 'Fragmentariness,' and if I do not become enthusiastic over a thing, I am easily done for."

Then one day the great Anton Rubinstein, idol of the conservatory students, visited the harmony class in which Tchaikovsky was dallying. The master was struck by the cleverness and the carelessness of the young law clerk's exercises. After class he called him aside and spoke with him so severely, yet with such keen appreciation of his gifts, that from that moment Tchaikovsky the amateur was never heard of again.

The next letter to his sister reveals an altogether different person. "My musical talent — you cannot deny it — is my only one. This being so, it stands to reason that I ought not to leave this God-sent gift undeveloped. . . . So, after long consideration, I have decided to sacrifice the salary and resign from my position. But it does not mean that I intend to get into debt, or ask for money from father, whose circumstances are not very flourishing just now. First I hope to get a small post at the conservatory next season (as assistant professor); secondly, I have a few private lessons in view; thirdly, and what is most important of all, I have entirely given up all amusements and luxuries so that my expenses have very much decreased." He goes on to say that he may never be a great composer, but "one thing I know for certain. I shall be a good musician and shall be able to earn my daily bread."

And so Peter Ilitch gave up the fashionable drawing rooms of St. Petersburg for a bare little room only big enough for a bed and writing table, where he often worked all night long on some score he wished to lay before his teacher the next day. Like the hero of one of the old Russian folk tales who sat out the first thirty years of his life in idleness, then rose up with the strength of ten and did wonders, Tchaikovsky now astonished his friends and teachers.

He had anything but an easy time financially. His father, though he had always been interested in Peter's music, could give him little besides encouragement. In the blackest moments his friends advised him to try to get back into government service. Modeste Tchaikovsky, in his biography of the composer, says, "One friend seriously proposed that he accept the fairly good paying position of an inspector of meat. To the great advantage of all meat consumers and to the glory of Russian music this proposal came to nothing."

Then a deliverer appeared in the person of Nikolai Rubinstein. He had founded a conservatory of music in Moscow, and, needing a teacher of harmony and theory, asked his brother Anton to send one from St. Petersburg. Anton recommended Tchaikovsky and Tchaikovsky accepted. The work was hard, the hours long, and the salary — well, it amounted to about twenty-five dollars a month. But the honor was worth much to an unknown young man, and the life was congenial. Nikolai Rubinstein took Tchaikovsky into his own house and treated him as a dear younger brother. There were several promising young men connected with the conservatory: one became a noted violinist; two, famous critics; and a fourth, Tchaikovsky's future publisher. This little group gave Tchaikovsky sympathy and confidence at the time when he most needed them, helped to make his works known, and were staunch friends to the end of his life.

Tchaikovsky spent eleven years in the Moscow Conservatory. He never considered himself a good teacher — probably because his heart was in his composing. But his scrupulous accuracy, orderly habits, and wonderful memory for musical examples made him a better teacher than he himself realized. These teaching years were surprisingly rich in composition, for Tchaikovsky worked day and night. But all the while he dreamed of an ideal life in some quiet country place far from the sight of student notebooks and the sound of student scales, where he might give his whole life to musical impression and expression.

The way in which his dream finally came true reads like a fairy tale. Once upon a time, the time when Tchaikovsky was struggling for an artistic existence, there lived in Moscow a quiet, middle-aged woman named Nadezhda Filaretovna von Meck. She had led a busy life as the mother of eleven children and the wife of a man who, largely through her courage and good business sense, had risen from a petty government official to a wealthy railroad engineer. Now, widowed and living in retirement, Madame von Meck was able to gratify the one great desire of her life, the desire for music.

At the Moscow concerts she had become interested in the music of the young conservatory professor, Tchaikovsky. Through one of his pupils she chanced to learn of the composer's financial struggle and of his longing for freedom. Wishing to help him, she sent Tchaikovsky a commission for a violin and piano arrangement of one of his works. She paid him lavishly, and ended her formal note acknowledging the work with this gracious sentence, "Your music makes life easier and pleasanter to live." It was the *Leitmotiv* of a rare and beautiful relation.

More commissions followed and an exchange of friendly letters which gradually became confessionals of the writers' thoughts not only on music but also on philosophy, religion, and life itself. Apart from his professional friends, Tchaikovsky was a lonely man, and these companionable letters from an understanding woman, who had seen much more of life than he had, became dearer to him than the commissions which were their excuse. He was proud, and he suspected that Madame von Meck might not really want all these arrangements for which she insisted upon overpaying him. He finally wrote and told her so. She replied, "I want to keep you for the service of the art I adore. . . . So, you see, my thought for your welfare is purely egotistical, and so long as I can satisfy this wish I am happy and grateful to you for accepting my help."

Later, at a crisis in Tchaikovsky's life when he felt that he could not accept her proposal of a yearly allowance which would enable him to give up teaching and be free for his composition, Madame von Meck asserted her right to use her own money as she pleased, writing frankly: "In my opinion, it is not the tie of sex or kindred which gives these rights but the sense of mental and spiritual communion. You know how many happy moments you have given me, how grateful I am, how indispensable you are to me, and how necessary it is that you should remain just as you were created; consequently what I do is not done for your sake but for my own. . . . You hurt me. If I wanted something from you, of course you would give it to me, is it not so? Very well, then we cry quits. Do not interfere with my management of your domestic economy, Peter Ilitch."

So for thirteen years, until he no longer needed help, Nadezhda Filaretovna managed Tchaikovsky's "domestic economy." He, in return, wrote charming diarylike letters sharing with her his travels, his thoughts, his work, and giving her the joy of feeling that she, who could not create a single musical phrase, had nevertheless helped to give the world a legacy of beautiful music.

Madame von Meck and Tchaikovsky never met. They were artists enough to realize that a nervous, grateful man and a generous, elderly woman might intrude upon this "fellowship of kindred minds." It was too precious to be risked.

The same year that brought this perfect friendship into Tchaikovsky's life brought a strange and tragic relationship. Tchaikovsky had once had a brief love affair with an opera singer who came to Moscow. It was a sort of spring idyl, the passing of which he had accepted quite philosophically. As the years passed, his friends would sometimes suggest that he ought to marry and have a home, and Tchaikovsky himself considered it in a vague, impersonal way. He even went so far as to write to his brother, "I have been thinking about myself and my future. My reflections have resulted in the firm determination to marry some one or other." A week later, to the same brother, "What comfort it is to return to my pleasant rooms and sit down with a book! . . . I shudder when I think that I must give it all up."

But no amount of "firm determination" could make Tchaikovsky a marrying man. Much as he loved people and craved companionship, he was by nature a solitary person and shrank from the everlasting intimacy of domestic life.

Then one day in his thirty-seventh year a young woman, whom he scarcely knew, wrote him a letter confessing that she had loved him for a long time. Tchaikovsky, rather touched by the letter, made the mistake of replying. Several other letters followed, and he finally went to see the girl. What happened is best told in one of his own letters to Madame von Meck.

I found myself confronted by a painful dilemma; either I must keep my freedom at the expense of this woman's tragedy (this is no empty word, for she loved me intensely) or I must marry. I could but choose the latter course. Therefore I went one evening to my future wife and told her frankly that I could not love her, but that I would be a devoted and grateful friend. I described to her in detail my character, my irritability, my nervous temperament, finally my financial situation. Then I asked her if she would care to be my wife. Her answer was, of course, in the affirmative. The agonies I have endured since that evening defy description.

To the dismay of his friends, Tchaikovsky married the girl. Their little home seemed ideally pleasant and peaceful, but to Tchaikovsky it was a place of torture. He did not love his wife and he could not bear her devotion to him. Pity for her fought constantly with his sense of truth and sincerity. He blamed only himself — and Fate — for this unhappy situation. Naturally, he could do no work. In a few months it was all over, the home broken up, and Tchaikovsky seriously ill with a nervous breakdown that brought him to the verge of insanity.

As soon as he was able to travel, his brother took him abroad where a Swiss autumn and an Italian winter restored his poise. Gradually he took up his work again, and returned to Russia in the spring, a sound, sane man full of plans for the future.

Thanks to Madame von Meck, whose offer of the annuity had come during his illness, he did not have to return to the old drudgery of teaching, and, after a few years of what he called "the nomadic life," he finally found the little country place of his dreams. Compared with the luxurious houses of other men of his position, Tchaikovsky's little home in Maidanovo, a village near Klin, was modest indeed. But he was happy as a child in it, and impractical as a child in buying things for it. After furnishing his library with books and music, to him the most important household necessities, he proceeded to buy two horses, of which he had no earthly need, and an old English clock which would not run! Luckily he had a faithful servant, Alexis, who looked out for such trifles as beds, chairs, tables, and cook-pots.

Life at Maidanovo moved with clockwork regularity. At eight Tchaikovsky took his morning tea, usually without anything to eat; then read his Bible and a chapter or two from whatever philosophy or English book he happened to be studying; went for a short, brisk walk; and by nine-thirty was ready for the morning's work of composing, orchestrating, correcting manuscripts, or writing letters. Punctually at one, he dined; then, whatever the weather, went out for a long country tramp. He usually went alone, for this was the time of real creation, the time when he thought through the ideas for his music. He would jot these ideas down as they came to him, then work them out at the piano the next morning. At four o'clock he would come home to tea, read the papers if he were alone, or chat with visitors. At five he again retired to his study to work until seven. Then another walk, this time with company, into the fields to watch the sunset; dinner at eight; an evening of piano music, books, conversation, or cards, including endless games of patience; and then, to bed.

Invited guests were most welcome at Maidanovo, though they saw little of their host, and must often have been somewhat dismayed at the unorthodox housekeeping and meal planning of Alexis and Peter Ilitch. As for uninvited guests, they just didn't come a second time! The most serious disturbers of the peace were the peasant children, whom Tchaikovsky had spoiled by giving them coppers. When he went to walk they followed him in flocks, and it may have been in self-defense that the composer gave the local priest money to found a school for them.

But dearly as he loved his country home, "the Hermit of Klin," as his friends called him, was forever wandering away from it. Tchaikovsky was cursed with restlessness which made him feel that "every place is better than the one in which we are." Consequently, Switzerland, Rome, Paris, the Caucasian Mountains were all, in turn, promised lands to which he fled with eager expectations, only to suffer agonies of homesickness for Russia and then depart with equal enthusiasm.

In the later years many of Tchaikovsky's journeys were undertaken for the purpose of conducting his own works abroad. He certainly had no gift for conducting. His first experience, during the Moscow teaching days, was a sad fiasco. Tchaikovsky declared that he could not remember a note of the music, couldn't see the score, and felt as if his head would surely roll right off his shoulders unless he put down the baton and held it on! Fortunately, the orchestra did not lose its head and knew the piece well enough to play fairly decently in spite of wrong cues. But it was ten years before Tchaikovsky could be persuaded to mount the conductor's stand again. Unlike Wagner, who was sure of himself when all the world was against him, Tchaikovsky seemed to wait for the world to convince him that he was a person of artistic importance. As confidence came to him, he lost much of his stage fright and became a fair conductor, as he had every right to be with his splendid musical equipment and his charming personality.

The diaries of his concert tours are most entertaining and interesting, not only for their glimpses of famous people, but also for their revelation of Tchaikovsky's broad-mindedness and artistic generosity. From the "Diary of My Tour in 1888," a German tour, comes this about Brahms:

Going to Brodsky's for one o'clock dinner . . . I saw the famous German musician for the first time. Brahms is rather a short man, suggests a sort of amplitude, and possesses a very sympathetic appearance. His fine head, almost that of an old man, recalls the type of a handsome, benign, elderly Russian priest. . . . Brahms's manner is very simple, free from vanity, his humor jovial, and the few hours spent in his society left me with a very agreeable recollection . . . but in spite of all efforts to the contrary, I never could, and never can admire his music. . . . There is something dry, cold, vague, and nebulous in the music of this master which is repellent to Russian hearts. From our Russian point of view Brahms does not possess melodic invention. . . . Yet it is impossible in listening to Brahms's music to say that it is weak or unremarkable. It is all very serious, very distinguished, apparently even original, but in spite of all this the chief thing is lacking — beauty!

Tchaikovsky's opinion of Brahms changed somewhat as the years passed, though these two masters had entirely opposite ideas as to musical beauty. Tchaikovsky always respected Brahms highly. Once when Madame von Meck accused the Russian composer of spending too much time on opera, which they both agreed was the least satisfactory of all musical forms, he replied, "You are quite right to regard this insincere form of art with suspicion. . . . Let me only add that to refrain from writing operas is the work of a hero, and we have only one such hero in our time — Brahms. . . . This heroism does not exist in me, for the stage with all its glitter attracts me irresistibly."

At the same dinner at which Tchaikovsky met Brahms, the diary tells of another meeting.

There entered the room a very short, middle-aged man, exceedingly fragile in appearance, with shoulders of unequal height, fair hair brushed back from his forehead, and a very slight, almost boyish beard and moustache. There was nothing very striking about the features of this man . . . but he had an uncommon charm and blue eyes, not very large, but irresistibly fascinating, recalling the glance of a charming and candid child. . . . He proved to be the Norwegian composer, Edward Grieg. . . . I think I am right in saying that just as Brahms was undeservedly disliked by the Russian musicians and general public, so Grieg had known how to win over Russian hearts once and for all. In his music there prevails that fascinating melancholy which seems to reflect in itself all the beauty of Norwegian scenery, now grandiose and sublime in its vast expanse, now grey and dull, but always full of charm to the hearts of Northmen, and having something akin to ourselves, quickly finds its way to our hearts.

Grieg is probably not by any means so great a master as Brahms; his range is not so extensive, his aims and tendencies are not so wide, and apparently in Grieg the inclination toward obscurity is entirely absent; nevertheless, he stands nearer to us, he seems more approachable and intelligible because of his deep humanity.

Tchaikovsky, intensely Russian, felt akin to Grieg, who was as intensely Norwegian. He simply mistook nationality for humanity, not being able to see the woods for the trees. Brahms's humanity had nothing to do with maps; it touched every living thing from philosopher and sage down to the least toddling peasant baby or the stray kitten that crossed his path.

Tchaikovsky came to New York in 1891 as guest conductor at the opening of Carnegie Hall. He gave six concerts in America, four in New York, one in Philadelphia, and one in Baltimore. The diary is amusing in its American impressions. The composer, barring his usual nostalgia for Russia, had a gay good time in this strange country and found it most interesting. "The houses downtown," he writes, "are simply colossal; I cannot understand how anyone can live on the thirteenth floor!" He was delighted with his American audiences, but disgusted with the following notice in the *New York Herald:* "Tchaikovsky is a man of ample proportions, with rather grey hair, well built, of pleasing appearance, and about sixty years of age. He seemed rather nervous and answered the applause with a number of stiff little bows. But as soon as he had taken up the baton he was quite master of himself." "It annoys me," writes Tchaikovsky, "that, not content with writing about my music, they must also write about my personal appearance. I cannot bear to think that my shyness is noticeable or that my 'stiff little bows' fill them with astonishment!"

The last years of Tchaikovsky's life were full of travel. He was now famous both at home and abroad, an honorary member of the French Academy, and Doctor of Music, *honoris causa*, at Cambridge University. Warsaw, Vienna, Hamburg, Brussels, Paris, London, New York, were all clamoring for his presence. Meanwhile, on his desk in the pleasant house at Klin, lay a mountain of manuscript awaiting correction. "Even in my dreams," he wrote, "I see corrections and flats and sharps that refuse to do what they are ordered." And singing and surging in his brain was his new symphony, the sixth, which he called *Pathétique* and of which he said, "I certainly regard it as quite the best and most sincere of all my works. I love it as I have never loved any one of my musical offspring before."

In October, 1893, Tchaikovsky went up to St. Petersburg to conduct the first performance of this new symphony. Shortly after the concert, while lunching in a restaurant with his brother and favorite nephew, he drank a glass of unfiltered water. Three days later the St. Petersburg papers shocked the world with the news that Peter Ilitch Tchaikovsky, aged fifty-three, Russia's best known and best loved composer, was dead of cholera.

THE ARTIST

One can scarcely consider Tchaikovsky the artist and not contrast him with his Russian contemporaries, the famous "Five." The "Five" — Balakirev, Borodin, Cui, Rimsky-Korsakov, and Mussorgsky — were extreme nationalists. They were possessed by one idea, the development of a school or style of music founded on the national traits of Russian folk melody, rhythm, and color, and having as its background Russian legend and literature. Some of them considered the study of the great masters of music not only unnecessary but actually dangerous, since it might corrupt their precious Russian style.

Tchaikovsky, on the other hand, was a cosmopolitan, a man of the musical world. He loved Russia as deeply and truly as any of the "Five," but he wanted more than just a close-up of his country. He wanted a far view through the perspective of Western culture. Early in his career, Fanny Dürbach had taught him not to spit on the rest of the world!

Before he had ever traveled beyond the Russian frontier, Tchaikovsky knew and loved the works of Mozart, to him always "the culminating point of all beauty in the sphere of music"; and Beethoven, of whom he said, "My relationship to him reminds me of that which I felt in my childhood to the God Jehovah. I bow down before the grandeur of some of his creations, but I do not love Beethoven!" Later in life he greatly admired Schumann, Chopin, and Berlioz, and open-mindedly studied the to-him-unsympathetic music of Brahms and Wagner.

As for the "Five" he heartily disapproved of most of their music, but was on friendliest terms with the individual members of the group. His diary contains many bits like this, "Read through Rimsky's *Snegurochka* and was astonished at his mastery. I envy him, and I ought to be ashamed of it!" These nationalists, in turn, thought Tchaikovsky "old-fashioned." So, for a long time he was, as some one has cleverly said, "too German for the Russians and too Russian for the Germans."

Tchaikovsky was a cosmopolitan in literature as well as music. Shakespeare, Byron, Dickens, George Eliot, Dante, and Goethe were all favorite authors, and one has only to look at the texts of his songs and the subjects of his tone poems to see that he touched the master minds of many lands.

Careless critics have labeled Tchaikovsky a master of melancholy. It is true that nowhere in music may be found such an expression of overpowering grief as in the last movement of his *Pathétique* Symphony. It is true that his music reflects his life, the life of a nervous, highly sensitive man with a double heritage, that of the temperamental Slav and of the Russian upon whom the oppression of centuries had left its mark. Tchaikovsky was a thinker, and if his thoughts on the mysteries of life cast a shadow over his work, why, he was not alone in his gloom. David, Jeremiah, Sophocles, William Shakespeare, and many another great artist have borne him company. And as Walter Raymond Spalding wisely observes, "until the millennium arrives, a sincere and artistic expression of the sorrows of humanity will always strike a note in oppressed souls." [1]

Tchaikovsky poured out his emotions in an astounding number and variety of works: ten operas, six symphonies, six symphonic poems, three ballets, three overtures, four orchestral suites, chamber music, concertos, a large number of piano pieces, and a hundred or more songs. His music is not flawless in form like that of Beethoven, nor is it serene and thoughtful like that of Brahms. Sometimes it is true that his "manner is better than his matter," but it is beautiful music, unrivaled for lovely melody and exquisite coloring. Melody and color, these were Tchaikovsky's great gifts.

[1] From "Music, an Art and a Language," by Walter R. Spalding. Copyright, by The Arthur P. Schmidt Co.

Once in the early Moscow days, Tchaikovsky unknowingly gave what is probably the fairest estimate of his artistic status. A gushing lady had asked the young composer what were his ideals. Amused, and doubtless a bit disgusted, Tchaikovsky replied in his simple, charming way, "My ideal is to become *a good composer*."

ANDANTE CANTABILE, STRING QUARTET NO. 1 IN D, OPUS 11

Professor Peter Tchaikovsky of the Conservatory of Moscow was very anxious to spend the summer of 1871 abroad. His monthly salary of some thirty dollars refused, however, to stretch that far, and he was, accordingly, low in mind. Then Nikolai Rubinstein suggested that ever-present help of musicians in time of trouble, a benefit concert of the young composer's own works. It was a bright idea but somewhat dimmed by the fact that there were, at that time, so few works — only an opera, which, of course could not be given, some piano pieces, and a handful of songs. Obviously something would have to be written for the occasion, and, since Tchaikovsky had no funds with which to hire a large hall or the services of an orchestra, it was decided that the new work should be a string quartet. Quartet No. 1 in D, Opus 11, was the result. Although it is one of his earlier and less pretentious works, this quartet is quite characteristic of Tchaikovsky.

The beautiful second movement, a true singing *Andante*, has an interesting story. It is said that one day while Tchaikovsky was busy in his study the persistent whistling of a plasterer at work beneath his window annoyed him so that he had to lay aside what he was doing. Later the workman's tune kept singing in his ears and would give him no peace until he had hunted up the fellow and asked about it.

It proved to be just an old Russian folk song, something about

> Johnny on his sofa sitting
> Fills his glass and gaily drinks,
> And when he's no longer thirsty,
> Of his pretty sweetheart thinks.

As is so often the case with folk songs, the foolish words seem strangely inadequate for such a lovely tune:

It is a typically Russian tune with its mixed measures of four and five beats, its vague ending on the dominant, and the telltale IV–I cadence.

Tchaikovsky was charmed with the tune and uses it, with slight meter change, as the main theme of the *Andante cantabile*:

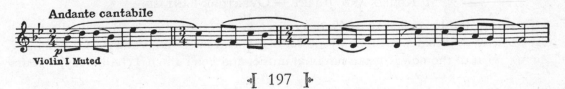

Then he plays with the theme, adding a melody in imitation of the folk song:

varied by a little rhythmic figure:

as the viola echoes the violin.

The second theme is a characteristic Tchaikovsky melody, gracious and appealing:

At first it is accompanied by descending chromatics plucked by the 'cello. Near the end it is heard again, an octave lower and accompanied by softly strummed chords.

Then comes a little phrase poignant as a cry of longing:

The melody falters:

until the folk theme returning, fragmentary but reassuring, carries it on to a quiet ending.

Years after that benefit concert, which it is gratifying to know did finance the trip abroad, a musical evening was given in Moscow honoring Count Leo Tolstoy. Tchaikovsky's *Andante cantabile* was played. "Never in the whole course of my life," writes the composer in his diary, "did I feel so flattered, never so proud of my creative power, as when Leo Tolstoy, sitting by my side, listened to my *Andante* while the tears streamed down his face."

Surely not one of the famous "Five" has succeeded better in glorifying the Russian folk song!

Romeo and Juliet — Overture-Fantasie

One day in the spring of 1869 three friends were walking together in the woods near Moscow — Nikolai Kashkin, professor of piano at the Conservatory, Mili Balakirev, moving spirit of the new Russian national music, and Peter Ilitch Tchaikovsky, a young composer in whose work the two older men were keenly interested. Balakirev was explaining to his companions an idea for some music based on the story of Romeo and Juliet. He visualized, or shall we say *auralized* it in detail, with its contrasting motifs representing Friar Laurence, the hostile houses of Montague and Capulet, and the "star-crossed" lovers. He even suggested the tonalities which he thought would be effective for these motifs and the form, that of the *overture-fantasie*, a clumsy name for program music, soon to be replaced by the more appropriate *symphonic poem*. As Balakirev talked, Tchaikovsky, who was a great Shakespeare enthusiast, was so taken with the idea that he agreed to write the music, which was exactly what the wily Balakirev had intended. Such was the beginning of the *Romeo and Juliet Overture*, which, writes Kashkin, "always brings to my mind the memory of a lovely day in May, with green forests and tall fir trees among which we three were taking a walk."

After a summer holiday companioned by the gentle ghosts of Shakespeare's immortal lovers, Tchaikovsky returned to Moscow and began to write the overture. All the while, Balakirev had kept up a running fire of questions, criticisms, and suggestions, extending even to the composer's way of working. Balakirev certainly knew his Tchaikovsky when, in a letter of October 4, 1869, he advised him to put on his rubber shoes, take his stick, and go for a walk on the boulevards, starting from the Nikitsky. "Let yourself become permeated with the subject," he writes, "and by the time you reach Sretensky, I am sure you will have found some theme or episode." Then he tells him to carry that first germ about in his head and keep thinking about it until something vital springs from it. That Tchaikovsky was permeated — possessed by the subject — and that something intensely vital sprang from this possession is proved by the beautiful *Romeo and Juliet* music.

The composer has not attempted to follow the action of the play, but to present its moods and characters. Friar Laurence appears first, clad in churchly harmonies for clarinets and bassoons:

This sober, slow-paced music seems an almost prophetic prologue to the tragedy of passionate love and hatred.

In striking contrast comes the *Allegro giusto*, bursting in with impetuous flutes and violins:

suggesting the feud between the two great households of the Montagues and Capulets. With dashing scale passages and woodwind cries, keen-edged with piccolo, the music works itself up to a climax. Harsh chords in a startling, realistic rhythmic pattern:

suggest the clashing of blades while an excited running figure in the strings might well be the desperate footwork of the swordsmen.

As the encounter ends, a little mourning figure is heard in the woodwinds. Alas for this ancient enmity which is to bear such bitter fruit! On this sighing note, the love theme enters:

> How silver-sweet sound lovers' tongues at night,
> Like softest music to attending ears!

After Tchaikovsky's death this melody was found among his papers, with words, to be sung by Romeo:

> O night of ecstasy, but linger with us!
> O night of love, spread thy dark veil above us!

indicating that the composer had once thought of writing an opera *Romeo and Juliet*.

Immediately after the love song comes an exquisite sequence of chords for muted strings:

at which the delighted Balakirev exclaimed, "It has the sweetness of love, its tenderness, its longing." In the notes for the opera, which was never written, this music was played during the touching farewell scene in Juliet's chamber, when Romeo, a Montague, banished from Verona for having slain one of Juliet's Capulet kinsmen, takes leave of his bride of a few hours. Then the love song is heard again, high and heartbreaking in the woodwinds, above sadly murmuring strings.

Following the love music, which ends the Exposition of themes, comes a Development section in which the feud theme and that of Friar Laurence are heard in various forms.   Then, in the Recapitulation, the conflict is resumed, and mingled with it the sound of the love song and Friar Laurence's solemn warning.   Suddenly the tumult is interrupted by an ominous message from the bassoons and basses.   The lovers are dead.   For a moment all is silent.   Then to dolorous funeral drums, the dirge begins:

a woeful reminder of Romeo's ecstatic song.   Gray and empty woodwind harmonies:

suggest,

> A glooming peace this morning with it brings,
> The sun for sorrow will not show his head.

and broken fragments of the love music drift up and away in the strings.

The overture has what seems to be a strangely inappropriate ending of several loud, accented measures.   Tchaikovsky's friends protested, and Mme. Rimsky-Korsakov, who made the piano arrangement, was finally given permission to let the music die away with those last drifting violin tones.

Although an early work, the *Romeo and Juliet Overture-Fantasie* is one of Tchaikovsky's most charming compositions.   All the passion and tenderness of his own young heart seems to have found expression in this beautiful music of love and death, and there is Shakespeare in it, too!

March Slav

During the Turko-Serbian War, in 1876, a great wave of Slavonic patriotism swept over Russia.   The Serbs, like the Russians, are a Slavonic people, and their wholesale massacre at the hands of the Turks could hardly fail to arouse the sympathy and bitter resentment of their northern kinsmen.   At last, Tsar Alexander II came out as champion of the Balkan Christians and declared war on Turkey.   Feeling ran high in Russia as the troops marched off to defend the faith and the weaker southern Slavs.   Nikolai Rubinstein, head of the Moscow Conservatory, organized a grand concert for the benefit of wounded soldiers, and for this concert Tchaikovsky, an ardent patriot, composed the march, first called the *Russo-Serbian*, but afterward the *March Slav*.

Introduced by muffled drums and the tramp of heavy feet, the bassoons and violas give out the dirgelike theme:

said to be an old Slavonic folk tune.   Surely no succession of tones could more clearly portray an oppressed people than this tune with its hopeless, downward line.   As it is taken up by the different voices of the orchestra, it becomes a despairing cry.

The answer rings out full of promise:

It is followed by a running to and fro which suggests the bustle of preparation.   Again the mournful theme, the cry for help, sounds more urgently than ever in triple *forte* for full orchestra.   This time a bugle answers, and in quickstep, the Russian troops march off to a spirited little folk tune:

(This is the trio section of the march.)

As the ordered activity of the music grows, one pictures company after company falling in, the color of bright uniforms, the cheerful, tearful excitement of the crowd. Then, above all this lively fifing and drumming of marching men, which is the visible evidence of power, sounds the voice of a great nation:

the majestic hymn of old Russia.   One has only to compare its first four measures with those of the hopeless Serbian tune, to realize music's amazing powers of expression, for here are the heights and depths, courage and despair.

After the trio section, the two first themes return, leading this time into a brilliant coda. Another little quickstep march enters:

Più mosso. Allegro

mf

Clarinet

and with it plays the national anthem, ending the march on what the Russians regarded as a prophetic note of victory.

The tremendous success of the *March Slav* in Russia, 1876, can, of course, be explained as an imposing example of the workings of wartime psychology. But there was something more than mere timeliness in the appeal of *March Slav*, for it still continues to interest the rest of the world by the sheer dramatic power and intensity of its emotions.

OVERTURE, THE YEAR 1812

Four years after the composition of the *March Slav*, Tchaikovsky was again commissioned to write an occasional piece, this time, the occasion being the consecration of the Cathedral of the Redeemer, in the Kremlin, Moscow. The celebration was also to include a commemoration of the events to which the building owed its origin, namely, the tragedy and triumph of the year 1812. For it was then that Napoleon, abandoning the Russian campaign which had opened with his Pyrrhic victory at Borodino, began that terrible winter retreat from Moscow. What suffering might have been spared had Hitler, before entering upon his Russian campaign, remembered Napoleon's fate or heeded Tchaikovsky's prophetic music rather than those siren "voices" which led him and his people to ruin!

With these events in mind, Tchaikovsky wrote the *Solemn Overture, The Year 1812*. In the introduction and the closing he uses an appropriate Russian hymn, "God Preserve Thy People." The body of the work is built upon two original themes and the familiar "Marseillaise" and Russian National Anthem, whose tonal conflict is supposed to represent the battle between the French and Russians. Like all of Tchaikovsky's works, this overture is a good piece of musical construction. The orchestration is clever, particularly the pealing bells which at the end suggest the sounds heard in the Kremlin on a Russian feast day.

It was a huge success at the celebration for which it was written, and is still a favorite in Russia and with listeners elsewhere. But for all its popularity, *The Year 1812* is not nearly as fine a piece of music as the *March Slav*. It is not even altogether authentic, since in 1812 "The Marseillaise" was probably no longer in use in the French army and the old Russian National Anthem had not yet been written. Tchaikovsky himself never liked the work, and protested when he was asked to conduct it on his Berlin tour in 1888, saying, "I considered and still consider my *Overture 1812* quite mediocre, having a particular and local significance which makes it unsuitable for any but a Russian concert room."

The composer's own criticism of *The Year 1812* as "mediocre" reminds us of two important facts, never to be lost sight of in the evaluation of music — first, that the popularity of a piece cannot be considered a valid test of its worth. It is true that most really great music is popular in the fine literal sense of "loved by the people." The "Londonderry Air," Bach's "Air for the G String," the Beethoven Fifth Symphony, Strauss's "The Blue Danube Waltz" are loved by people everywhere because they are beautiful and expressive tonal patterns; in other words, the secret of their popularity lies in the music itself. Much of the popularity of such compositions as *The Year 1812* lies outside the music, in events associated with certain times and places and in sensational effects such as full orchestra, crashing ahead at top speed and quadruple *forte*, suggesting a tone fight. And even when history, repeating itself, as in the Russian triumphs of World War II, revives the interest in *The Year 1812*, its popularity is still due to timeliness rather than to musical beauty *per se*. A second point to remember is that the signature of a great composer does not necessarily insure a piece of great music. Even genius has its dull moments, too many of which have been perpetuated by those who put their faith in a name. Compared with his symphonies, discriminating critics will agree with the composer himself that *The Year 1812* is sub-Tchaikovsky.

Symphony No. 4 in F Minor

Tchaikovsky wrote six symphonies. The first three are interesting, but, as someone has said, they scarcely pass beyond the frontiers of his own country. The last three, however, are world travelers. They speak a universal language. Of these three remarkable symphonies, No. 4 in F Minor, composed in 1877, is most characteristically Russian and most striking in its directness of expression.

Tchaikovsky, if one may presume to label genius, was an emotional rather than an intellectual composer. Hypersensitive, passionately Russian, and of uncertain balance, his heart often betrayed his head. He lacked the restraint, the comforting support of an accepted philosophy of life. Unlike the music of the great German masters, Bach, Beethoven, and Brahms, which, rising from deep springs of feeling, flows in well-marked channels, Tchaikovsky's music is a mountain stream, storm-fed, which spends itself in a splendid devastating flood. Even when he writes a symphony, that most restrained of musical forms and one which he knew well, Tchaikovsky pours out his feelings so impulsively, so dramatically, that the listener suspects a story, a program back of the music.

In the Symphony No. 4 in F Minor, this feeling of a program is particularly noticeable, so noticeable that Tchaikovsky's friends wrote asking him about it. Two priceless letters in reply give Tchaikovsky's own interpretation of the symphony as well as his ideas on program music. To Taneiev, who had remarked that the first movement of the Fourth Symphony made the impression of a symphonic poem with a definite program, Tchaikovsky replied:

> As to your remark that my symphony sounds like program music, I agree with you. Only I do not see why that should be a fault. On the contrary, I should be sorry if symphonic works were to flow from my pen which express nothing, but consist merely of chords and a play of rhythms and modulations. Of course my symphony is program music, only it is quite impossible to formulate its program in words; it would have a ludicrous effect and give rise to ridicule. But should not this be the case with a symphony, the most lyrical of all forms? Should it not express all that cannot be expressed

in words, but which fills the soul to overflowing and calls for expression? . . . I did not in the least endeavor to express new ideas. At bottom my symphony is an imitation of Beethoven's Fifth Symphony; that is to say, I imitated not its musical content but its fundamental idea. What do you think — has the Fifth Symphony a program? Not only has it a program, but there cannot even be the slightest difference of opinion as to what the symphony purports to express. Almost the same underlies my symphony; and if you have not understood me, it follows that I am no Beethoven, about which I have never had any doubt! I will add that there is in this symphony of mine not a single bar which I have not felt and which is not an echo of my innermost soul-life.

Andante sostenuto; moderato con anima

Although Tchaikovsky says to Taneiev that it is impossible to put the program of the Fourth Symphony into words, he does a rather complete job of it in the letter to *ma meilleure amie*. Because the first movement is long, and because, in Tchaikovsky's works, formal analysis is apt to get lost in admiration of charming melodies and superb orchestration, we may safely take the composer's own words — and music — for it.

"The introduction is the kernel of the whole symphony, the main thought:

This is Fate, that momentous power which hinders the desire for happiness from attaining its aim; which sees to it that well-being and contentment do not get the upper hand, that the sky is not cloudless — a power which, like the sword of Damocles, hangs always over our heads; a power which poisons the soul. This power is inevitable and unconquerable. There is nothing one can do but submit and lament in vain:

"The feeling of depression and hopelessness becomes stronger and stronger, more and more burning. Is it not better to turn from reality and lose oneself in dreams?

"O joy! What a tender, what a sweet dream is this! A beaming human being, promising happiness, beckons to me:

How beautiful! The importunate first motif of the *Allegro* now seems far, far away. Gradually the whole soul becomes wrapped in a dream-web. All that is dark, all that is joyless is forgotten.

"Happiness! Happiness! Happiness!"

This dream happiness finds expression in a ghostly little waltz for first and second violins to a throbbing drum accompaniment:

But at the end of each phrase, like an impossible echo, we hear the woodwinds sighing the lament of the first motif:

an episode of haunting beauty.

"No," continues Tchaikovsky, "these are only dreams. Fate drives them away:

"So it is with life, only an endless round of somber realities and fleeting dreams of happiness. There is no haven; you are driven hither and yon by the waves until the sea at last swallows you. This is, roughly, the program of the first movement."

In spite of its program character, this movement is based solidly on traditional first-movement form, with but one structural exception — in the Recapitulation, the main theme returns, not in the expected tonic key of F minor, but in D minor and in unusually shortened form.

Andantino in modo di canzona

"The second movement," writes Tchaikovsky, "shows sorrow in a different state. It is that melancholy feeling that encompasses us when we sit at home alone in the evening, wearied by our work; the book which we have been reading has slipped from the hand; a whole swarm of memories rises up. How sad that so much is already past and gone! Yet it is pleasant to recall those early years. We regret the past and have not the courage to begin a new life. We are rather weary of existence. We should like to refresh ourselves and look back, revive many a memory. We think of joyous hours when the young blood was still foaming and seething and found satisfaction in life. We think also of sad moments, of irretrievable losses. All this lies already so far, so far behind us. It is sad, and yet sweet to brood over the past."

"Sad and yet sweet" is the music, the lovely *Canzona* based upon two Russian folk songs. The first is a wistful little tune given out by solo oboe above *pizzicato* strings:

It is immediately repeated by the 'celli against a rising countertheme in the clarinets.

Then, to a curious accordionlike accompaniment in woodwinds and brass, the strings announce the second melody, in old Greek mode:

Later a third theme enters:

which, even to the ominous brasses, reminds us of the original lament of this symphony.

These themes are used, rondo-fashion, with the first melody, richly varied, prevailing.

There are strange contradictions in this music. It is so naïve, yet so sophisticated; so full of feeling, yet, at times, so coolly impassive — all of which may be summed up by saying that it is so very Russian, so very Tchaikovsky!

Scherzo — Pizzicato ostinato

"In the third movement no definite feeling is expressed. Here are capricious arabesques, intangible forms which whisk through the imagination when one has been drinking wine and is a little excited. The mood is neither gay nor sad. One thinks of nothing in particular; lets the imagination take its own course, and it delights in drawing the most wonderful lines. Suddenly there emerges from memory the picture of a tipsy peasant and of a street song. . . . In the distance one hears military music passing by. Such are the disconnected images which come and go in our brain when we are falling to sleep. They have nothing to do with reality; they are unintelligible, bizarre, fragmentary."

The moods and images of this third movement may, as Tchaikovsky says, "have nothing to do with reality," but not so the music. This *Scherzo* which, with the exception of a brief middle section for woodwinds and brasses, is played entirely by *pizzicato* strings, is a *tour de force* which only one having much to do with the realities of orchestration could have accomplished!

Impish plucked strings start off with a tune:

which might have been inspired by a shimmer of dancing gnats!

Suddenly the oboe holds up the dance with a long note and then, with the bassoon, plays an irresponsible little tune:

which surely must picture the "tipsy peasant" of Tchaikovsky's letter.

Then "in the distance one hears military music passing by":

This is a clever touch of true *scherzo* — the joke being on the strings, for the brasses make their military music by playing the first theme with absurd halts, in just half its original pace. There is all sorts of clever fooling — the piccolo impertinently turns the second theme upside down; strings and woodwinds argue over the main theme, each trying to start it in a different key, and at one time they share it between them, each taking two notes at a time!

Utterly fantastic, delicate, and delightful, this *Scherzo* is as masterly a bit of humor as was ever caught on the lines and spaces of a musical score.

Finale — Allegro con fuoco

"Fourth movement. When you find no joy within you, look around. Go among the people. See, they know how to enjoy themselves, they give themselves up fully and wholly to their joyous feelings. The picture of a popular festivity. Scarcely have you forgotten yourself, scarcely have you lost yourself in the contemplation of the joy of others, when the indefatigable Fate again announces its presence. But the other mortals do not concern themselves about you; they do not even see you; they do not notice at all that you are lonely and sad. O how they enjoy themselves; how happy they are! And you say that everything in this world is somber and sad? After all, there is still joy, simple, primitive joy. Enjoy the joy of others, and — you can still live.

"This is all I can tell you about my symphony, my dear friend. Of course, my words are not clear and not sufficiently exhaustive. But therein lies the peculiarity of instrumental music that it cannot be analyzed."

The tumultuous *Finale* begins with a fanfare for full orchestra:

Before this first theme has been fully stated, the woodwinds hint at the Russian folk song which oboes and bassoons are later to announce as the second theme:

This theme is put to various and impressive use. First of all, it suggests the folk in this picture of a popular festivity. Then, in an harmonically varied version for strings:

it grows wistful enough to reflect Tchaikovsky's mood when he says, "they do not notice at all that you are lonely and sad." And when, at the climax of the movement, it bursts out in triumphant fugal form in the basses, it reminds us that in this Fate symphony, the song of victory is as Slavic:

as Beethoven's was Teutonic:

(It is interesting to note that most of the main themes of this symphony begin with a descending scale-line of four or five tones — the characteristic downward melody line of peoples who have lived under climatic or political oppression!)

The triumphant fugue is dramatically interrupted by woodwinds and trumpets announcing the Fate motif which is the motto of the entire symphony:

Then, little by little, the *Finale* pulls itself together again and ends with a boisterous triple *forte* for full orchestra — "After all, there is still joy, simple, primitive joy!"

Such is the Tchaikovsky Fourth — sensational, even trivial in spots, but making up for its lack of restraint in an amazing spontaneity; making up for its lack of profundity in a wealth of imagination and glowing color which, unless the world goes black and white, will always charm us.

Symphony No. 6 in B Minor — Pathétique

Tchaikovsky was an intensely sensitive person. Life with its intricate pattern of bright and dark moods — his own, those of nature and of other people, even of the characters in history and literature — touched him so deeply that he could not express himself without betraying the feeling that was the undercurrent of his thought. It is this emotional quality in his music that awakens such immediate echo in the hearts of his listeners. But far too much has been said about Tchaikovsky's emotionalism, his nervous instability, and morbid melancholy. These qualities did color his work, but they did not motivate it. Tchaikovsky was too reserved a man to indulge in a public display of self-pity; and he was too fine an artist to descend to writing "sob stuff" — a mere bid for sympathy. His music, no less than Beethoven's, is a sincere expression of life as he felt it. But, being a Slav, a Romanticist, and a nervous, over-sensitive man, Tchaikovsky lacked the Teutonic calm, the Classical restraint, the physical poise of Beethoven, and, as a result, his music sometimes suffers a touch of hysteria.

Of all Tchaikovsky's works the most dramatic and emotional is the sixth and last symphony. There is no clue to its meaning beyond the title, suggested by his brother Modeste, who writes:

> The morning after the concert [at which the symphony was first played] I found my brother sitting at the breakfast table with the score of the symphony before him. He had agreed to send it to Jurgenson, the publisher, that very day, and could not decide upon a title. He did not wish to designate it merely by a number, and had given up his original intention of calling it "A Program Symphony." "Why program," said he, "since I do not intend to expound any meaning?" I suggested "Tragic Symphony" as an appropriate title. But this did not please him either. . . . Suddenly the word *pathétique* occurred to me, and I returned to suggest it. I remember as though it were yesterday, how my brother exclaimed, "Bravo, Modeste, splendid! *Pathétique!*" Then and there, in my presence, he added to the score the title by which the symphony has always been known.

And the title *Pathétique* — in English, *pathetic* — means, says the dictionary, "affecting the emotions, especially pity or grief; moving, stirring." One scarcely needs to be told that this is "moving, stirring" music! And surely the title leaves the listener free to interpret the pity or grief according to his own fancy, which was the composer's purpose.

There is absolutely no foundation for the sensational story that Tchaikovsky wrote the *Pathétique* as a lament for his own approaching death. On the contrary, he had felt particularly well and happy during the spring and summer of its composition. And he was pleased with the work itself, writing to the favorite nephew to whom he dedicated it: "I certainly regard it as quite the best, and especially the most sincere, of all my works. I love it as I have never loved any one of my offspring before." And to his publisher he wrote: "On my word of honor, I have never felt such satisfaction, such pride and happiness, as in the consciousness that I am really the creator of this beautiful work." The *Symphonie pathétique* was Tchaikovsky's swan song, but he had no such thought when he wrote it. It was merely a strange and tragic coincidence that within a few days after the first performance of this music, Tchaikovsky should have died suddenly of cholera.

Although this symphony has the usual four movements, their distribution is quite unusual. Instead of the thoughtful first movement, the singing second, the whimsical third, and the vigorous, optimistic *finale*, Tchaikovsky sings his song in the second theme of the first movement; grows whimsical in the second, voices all his optimism and energy in the third, and ends with a veritable *De Profundis*. But Tchaikovsky never was a formalist. He was master of all of the traditional forms and valued them, but never hesitated to alter them for his own purposes.

Adagio: Allegro non troppo

From the shadows of an outlying tonality (E minor, the subdominant), comes the introduction to this Symphony in B Minor. The bassoon speaks:

a melancholy prophet, forecasting the sadness from which neither man nor this music can escape; forecasting also the main theme:

The sadness now takes on a restlessness:

Little melodic figures flit by in strings and woodwinds, at first running lightly, but later breaking into noisy, headlong flight. Excited voices call back and forth. Gradually the restless striving yields to the quiet second theme:

a song of unsatisfied longing as only Tchaikovsky could sing it. After the lovely song theme, a flute and bassoon begin an expressive dialogue:

Other voices join in, commenting, perhaps, upon the song, which now returns in full harmony, suggesting a great organ. The song ends with what in olden times would have been called an *envoy* — the poet's parting words — and on a "dying fall":

the theme sinks into silence.

The Development section opens with a crash, out of which rushes an angry version of the opening motif:

accompanied by fierce violas. Tempestuous violins and woodwinds and loud brasses carry the music to a climax. In a sudden hush, the trumpet, trombones, and tuba intone a fragment of the Russian *Requiem:*

which is followed by a fresh outburst.

Then comes one of the finest pieces of Tchaikovsky's workmanship — the return of the main theme. Beginning in the faraway key of B-flat minor:

the little despair motif works up, through a slow *crescendo*, rising step by step, until at last it breaks into the tonic key of B minor:

played by violins, echoed by woodwinds and horns. But soon the wildness of grief seems to pass, and the whole orchestra, triple *forte*, but in solemn measure, joins in dignified lament. Quietly, the beautiful second theme returns, leading this time into a coda:

After all the emotional conflict of the movement, these closing measures seem strikingly simple — as simple as the acceptance which ends most of man's struggles with destiny, and as pathetic.

Allegro con grazia

The second movement is an escape from striving and longing into a mood of gentle gaiety. It is also a famous example of the effective use of 5/4 rhythm. The familiar meter patterns of two and three beats and their multiples are merely adaptations of Nature's rhythms — the heartbeat, breathing, walking steps which go in slightly accented pairs, the cantering of four-footed creatures, and Nature's innumerable rockings and swayings. We Anglo-Saxons are apt to think of all rhythms as falling into these simple patterns of twos and threes. Any other grouping disturbs us. Indeed, someone, speaking of this movement of the *Pathétique*, has said that it sounds "like a perverted waltz which could not be danced unless one owned three legs."

However, there are races, notably the more emotional and impulsive Slavs, who feel a pulse of five and seven as well as of two and three beats. The 5/4, so often found in the folk tunes of the Hungarians and Russians, is a very flexible and light-footed rhythm. Since it will not march or settle into a steady swing or jog-trot, it seems best suited to wandering or fanciful moods. It has been much used by modern composers, seeking to get away from the restrictions of "the old order." All of which is rather amusing to those who remember the antiquity of the 5/4 rhythm, which, according to some writers, is an inheritance from the ancient Greeks passed on to the Russian Slavs by the Greek Church.

This supposedly irregular 5/4 rhythm has a very definite pattern. It is merely a steady alternation of two and three beats — a measure of three added to a measure of two, or vice versa. While our Anglo-Saxon muscles may never respond quite naturally to the 5/4 rhythm, our minds can accept it as logical and enjoyable.

'Celli lead off in the dancelike theme of the *Allegro con grazia:*

It is interesting to notice that for all its wayward shifting from two to three beats, the melody keeps within conventional eight-measure phrases.

In the middle section of this simple three-part piece, the shadow of the *Pathétique* falls, ever so lightly, on the music. Flutes and violins take on a tearful note above an insistent, hypnotic drumming of bassoons, basses, and tympanum:

Then the graceful dance theme returns, goes through its paces exactly as in the beginning, and ends with a brief coda in which many voices seem to be calling their farewells.

Allegro molto vivace

The gigantic march-scherzo, which makes this third movement anything but the light part of the symphony, begins with a busy theme in triplets:

which claims the attention not by its melody but by its bustling motion. Then, out of the confusion of running strings and woodwinds, sounds a fragment of melody:

a distant bugle call ending unexpectedly on a defiant note. At first soft and incomplete, this motif gradually grows louder and fuller, until the whole orchestra bursts out with the splendid march:

The construction of this movement is simple. In due time the first theme returns and works itself up to a furious climax. Then, with a wild lashing of strings and woodwinds, the second theme comes back, now in the key of G major and scored for full orchestra, and marches in barbaric splendor to its noisy finish.

There has been no little wonder and questioning as to why Tchaikovsky did not let the symphony end with this burst of overwhelming energy. Surely it would have fulfilled all the requirements of the traditional *Finale* — vigorous, optimistic mood, rapid *tempo*, and conclusive themes. Indeed, it compares well with the famous *Finales* of Beethoven's Fifth and Ninth Symphonies. But, compare Tchaikovsky and Beethoven in their attitude toward life — there is the answer to the question. The sturdy Beethoven believed that Man, through sheer power of will, could conquer Fate — he himself had done it. And in his two great symphonies on the subject of human conflict, he leaves Man triumphant. Tchaikovsky, with the melancholy fatalism of his race, leaves Man spiritually defeated and lamenting.

Mr. Philip Hale, long dean of American music commentators, insists that the taste of triumph in the third movement is the reason for the final and hopeless lamentation. "The man triumphs," he writes, "and knows all that there is in earthly fame. Success is hideous, as Victor Hugo said. The blare of trumpets, the shouts of the mob may drown the sneers of envy; but at Pompey passing through Roman streets, at Tasso with the laurel wreath, at coronation of Tsar or inauguration of President, Death grins, for he knows the emptiness, the vulgarity, of what the world calls success."

"This battle-drunk, delirious movement must, perforce, precede the mighty wail —

> The glories of our blood and state
> Are shadows, not substantial things;
> There is no armour against fate,
> Death lays his icy hand on Kings.

Adagio lamentoso

From the depths, the strings like lost souls cry out:

(By a curious crossing of parts in these first measures, the individual violin parts are quite meaningless, but their combination gives this clearly defined melody:

As if in answer, the violins and violas, closely echoed by the 'celli and basses, sing a song of consolation:

But there is no comfort, no healing for this *Weltschmerz*, this mortal pain of longing. With a little uprush of strings, sounding strangely like a stifled moan, the bittersweet lament returns, growing more poignant with each refrain. Finally it dies down, and the ominous sound of a distant bell brings back the second theme.   But it is no longer a song of consolation.   It, too, is overcome with sadness:

And so, into the shadows from whence it came, this grief-stricken music dies away.

There is the touch of tears in Tchaikovsky's music, a touch unfortunately lost to many of the composers of our day, who tickle the intellect but seldom reach the heart. Tchaikovsky's sadness passes the bounds of the purely personal or conscious.   He laments not any known sorrow, but rather, the ancient *lacrimae rerum* of which poets have always sung.   And there is dignity in his lamentation, for:

> Nobility and sorrow somehow find
> A kinship.   In the exalted courts of mind
> Our laugh is jester and our grief is king.
> Tho' happiness be found the fairest goal,
> Man in his pleasure seems a trivial thing,
> And tears the coronation of the soul.
>
> — *Author Unknown*

MIKHAIL IPPOLITOV–IVANOV

Gatchina — 1859
Moscow — 1935

"Venerable Russian Composer Appears with Bolshoi Theater Orchestra" — this apparently commonplace headline in the *Moscow News* of February, 1934, was copied by newspapers all over the world and read with interest and surprise, for it brought vividly to life one who had seemingly dropped below the horizon.   In many music histories Ippolitov-Ivanov had been listed "disappeared during the revolution following the World War."   The fact that he had been prominent in the musical life of the old regime and had composed the special music for the coronation of the last Tsar had doubtless made that disappearance advisable.

"Half a century has passed into history since Ippolitov-Ivanov raised a baton before what was then a St. Petersburg symphony orchestra and drew from it the beautiful strains of an overture he had composed from Russian folk melodies," said the *Moscow News*.   Then followed an account of the 1934 celebration at which the Soviet Government presented Ippolitov-Ivanov with the Order of the Red Banner before an enthusiastic audience "thickly sprinkled with government leaders and artists at the peak of their careers, who applauded until the tears came to this white-bearded Russian of seventy-four whose fifty years of musical life mark a whole epoch in the music of his country."

Mikhail Mikhailovich Ippolitov-Ivanov was the son of a former mechanic at the old Imperial Palace at St. Petersburg. At the age of eight the child went to live with an older sister whose home was in a village some distance from St. Petersburg. Here young Mikhail began his musical career as the only soprano in the choir of the village church. He also had violin lessons with the priest, probably in exchange for his choir service. Two years later, during a musical evening in the village, the boy offered to substitute for an absent singer and take the fourth part in a quartet. The older musicians, to humor the child, let him try, but before the evening was over, were so impressed with his performance that they arranged to send him to the conservatory at St. Petersburg. This plan was a disappointment to Mikhail's father, who had hoped to make an expert mechanic of his son. Nevertheless, to the conservatory Mikhail went, remained for six years, a favorite pupil of Rimsky-Korsakov, and came out well grounded in the musical classics of Russia and Europe.

When he was twenty-two, Ippolitov-Ivanov received his first important post as director of the Music School and conductor of the symphony concerts of the Imperial Musical Society in the Georgian city of Tiflis, then capital of the General Government of the Caucasus. He had already become interested in this fascinating country through a friendship with two Caucasian musicians. Arriving in Tiflis, he lost no time in familiarizing himself with the music of these mountain peoples and made a valuable collection of the songs of Georgia. He was the first to make use of the melodies of Russia's Eastern nationalities, those melodies so highly prized by Soviet composers of today. It was while living in Tiflis that Ippolitov-Ivanov wrote the well-known *Caucasian Sketches*.

Returning to Russia in 1893, Ippolitov-Ivanov was made professor of composition and later director of the Conservatory of Moscow. He was also in charge of the State Theater of that city. Meanwhile he was composing — orchestral works, including a symphony, several concert overtures, his Armenian Rhapsody, five operas, cantatas, and chamber music, none of it great music but all of it acceptable. Sabaneiev makes a fair appraisal of Ippolitov-Ivanov as a composer when he says, "He was the possessor of a very simple and in the highest degree a naïve talent, clear and childishly pure."

Then came the blank years of war and revolution and the amazing return of this son of Old Russia as a Soviet composer. During his Soviet period this valiant old man produced his symphonic poem, *Mtsiri*, the famous *Voroshilov March*, and an opera, *The Last Barricade*. The opera, based on the Paris Commune which had filled the newspapers and caught the fancy of the composer when he was but a boy of twelve, was actually produced in Paris.

Moscow made a great pet of Ippolitov-Ivanov, and when, one morning in the spring of 1935, he was found dead in his bed, mourned him with sincerity and ceremony. Comparatively little has been written about this man who linked the Old Russia with the New, but if Ippolitov-Ivanov had taken time from his musical activities to write his memoirs, what a tale he might have told!

CAUCASIAN SKETCHES

In all the world there is no more fabulous spot than the Caucasus, that giant wall which divides Asia from Europe. The ancients called it "the ring of mountains which encircles the earth as a ring encircles the finger." In these mountains the old gods were said to have taken refuge when Christianity drove them from their Greek and Roman temples. Here, close to the stars, the Titans lived and fought, hurling whole mountaintops in their rage; here Jason searched for the golden fleece; and here Prometheus stole the sacred fire and gave it to man.

Old geographers called the Caucasus "The Land of Tongues." The name is still appropriate, for innumerable as the mountains themselves are the peoples living among them — Christians, Mohammedans, Pagans, Jews, and strange men who in stranger dialect boast their origin in the old proud phrase, *Civis Romanus sum*, "I am a Roman citizen."

The mountains shelter both peoples of ancient and magnificent culture, like the Georgians and Armenians, and wild fragments of forgotten races for whom science has never been able to account. The wise men of the mountains say that, when God was planning the flood, He first decided to save two of every kind of animal in Noah's ark, as every child knows. But when the devastating waters began to rise, He felt such pity for man that He decided to save two from every humankind as well. These racial specimens were hidden on the peaks of the Caucasus, which are higher than Mount Ararat, and it is from them that the myriad and mysterious mountain tribes are descended. And, believe it or not, the fact remains that "the mountain folk are not Europeans, and they are not Asiatic; they are Caucasians — that is to say, a special race of men that will endure."

It is said that in the clear mountain air one may, from a high peak, see across the whole of the Caucasus, from the shores of the Black Sea to the gorges of Daghestan. Yet today, within that comparatively small area, probably as many as three hundred unrelated languages are spoken. Only rarely does one group understand its neighbor's speech. And still more rarely has one of these languages a written form. Prayers and preaching are set down in Arabic, the scribes look after that, and in every village there is sure to be someone who can interpret. Otherwise, what is there that the hill people would need to write down? News flies through the mountains as if on magic wings, and as for the old legends, why, they are the heritage of the storytellers. What a heritage it is — tales of saints and jinn, of the mad heroism and crafty tricks of robber knights, of lovely ladies, of buried treasure, and of the days when the Roman Emperors and the Crusaders passed that way.

To young Ippolitov-Ivanov, who was for twelve years Director of the Tiflis Music School, this remote corner of the world was a never-failing source of interest and the inspiration of his best-known work, *Caucasian Sketches*, a four-part suite for orchestra.

In the Mountain Pass

The opening sketch, "In the Mountain Pass," shows this wild country in a peaceful, pastoral mood. Far off among the peaks a horn calls:

and is softly echoed, a pleasant sound of shepherds calling their flocks or signaling to each other across the valley. A rippling figure for muted violins suggests the little streams that sparkle down the face of the rocks, while in the woodwinds a murmuring theme:

makes its leisurely way.

The music grows louder, the picture clearer, as if a morning mist had lifted. The tinkle of a sheep bell is heard, and again the horn call, soft but insistent, leads into the second section.

The second theme, unmistakably a song, introduces the human element into the picture. Someone is coming through the pass, singing happily on his way:

He disappears, leaving the pass to its little pastoral symphony of rippling water and distant, echoing horn calls.

In the Village

During the hours of daylight the narrow passes between the mountains become the gateways of adventure. In and out go travelers, traders, huntsmen, shepherds, friends from distant villages, and now and then a black-browed chieftain and his tribe, bound on heaven knows what savage errand.

As evening falls the life of the *aul*, or mountain village, concentrates in the court-yard of the mosque and on the doorsteps of dwellings. Here the latest raid is reported and here the ancient epics are recalled "so that the young men may learn something useful and the old men may die in peace, knowing that they leave worthy successors behind them."

"In the Village" from *Caucasian Sketches* suggests just such a scene. The sun has dropped behind the gray peaks of Daghestan; the cattle are safely folded for the night; prayers at the mosque are over; and down the narrow, ledgelike street the villagers straggle home to little houses which burrow into the cliff at the back and from the front look rather like spice boxes on a giant's shelf. Here and there the faint glimmer of a pipe or a murmured greeting invites sociability. It is the old men's hour, the time for treasured tales of long ago.

The tale begins:

another voice takes it up:

then both voices together:

The first voice continues:

to an accompaniment of several voices as if the listeners, knowing every word of it by heart, could not refrain from commenting. The second voice, however, gathering up the threads of the story, brings them back to the original theme.

But the mood of far-away and long-ago is interrupted by something definitely here-and-now, as an Oriental drum taps out the lively rhythm of a native dance:

and the oboe, sounding like one of the wailing eastern pipes, takes up the tune:

It might be a spirited incident in the old men's story or it might be a group of young people passing along the street. Whatever it is, the venerable storytellers have no intention of giving way to it, and as the dancers disappear, we hear the two voices taking up their tale of bygone days.

This little sketch is an exquisite study in instrumental tone coloring. The dialogue of the English horn and the viola perfectly illustrates the likeness and difference of the two instruments, while the oboe shows at its plaintive best. The combination of instruments, the delicacy of the orchestration, together with the characteristic rhythms and harmonies, give an atmosphere as different from the theatrical effects of most pseudo-Oriental music as is the street of a Caucasian mountain village from the over-incensed alleys of a western Chinatown.

In the Mosque

From the minaret the muezzin calls the hour of prayer:

There is a moment's hush, and then from within the mosque comes the sound of chanting:

The ears of the Western World would never recognize this as sacred music. Yet it has a reverence, a quiet self-abasement which makes some of our shouting *Te Deums* seem almost arrogant. There is something about the rise and fall of the little rhythmic figure that suggests the movements of the Mohammedan at his prayers. Surely there is no mistaking the voice of the priest, alternating with the responses, or the music's mood of supplication. "In the Mosque" is but a fragment of a piece, yet curiously appealing.

The March of the Sardar

The rest of the world may split itself up into nations, but for the average Caucasian the idea of nationality is incomprehensible. For him the family or tribe remains, as it was in the beginning, the unit of society. The members of a family are bound to each other by blood ties which lead, if need be, to blood vengeance. Degrees of relationship have nothing to do with it, the claims of distant cousins being just as binding as those of brothers. Only a large family can hope to survive, and neither wealth, wisdom, nor princely rank can compare in value with a host of male relations. Hence the prayer of the mountain folk, "God grant, above all, that the numbers of my relatives may increase and that those of my enemies may diminish."

As with all tribal peoples, the Caucasian chieftain or *Sardar* is the man of importance. He is the owner and protector of the village. When he rides forth at the head of a knightly expedition to plunder the Russian mails, levy tribute on passing caravans, or empty the pockets of unfortunate travelers, the pride, envy, or terror his appearance may create depends entirely upon the number of his followers.

In "The March of the Sardar" we see the Caucasian chief in all his glory. The composer has called the sketch a march, but the captivating rhythm:

which precedes the melody and never falters throughout the piece belongs to no biped but to prancing Arabian horses.

The piccolo, in martial mood, introduces the chief:

A fine figure he is with his flashing dark eyes, menacing black mustaches, his sheepskin cap, and voluminous cloak. The light flashes from his golden dagger and from the long sword that hangs at his side. He rides like a centaur.

In the middle section of the march the pace slackens to an easy canter:

A conversation begins among the woodwinds, the clarinet remarking:

and the oboe answering:

Surely there is no suggestion of the ferocious brigand in this gracious music. It sounds much more like a polite conversation about the beauties of the mountain landscape or some tale of love and romance. Such a conversation is by no means improbable, for the Caucasian, we are told, has a surprising vein of poetry and chivalry in his make-up. Essad Bey, in his "Twelve Secrets of the Caucasus," describing the famous brigand, Kerim, says, "He was what is called a noble character; he only plundered the wealthy, and even then, only men. Toward women he was a gallant cavalier and, when he attacked a railroad train, he would rob the men down to their very shirts but merely kiss the ladies' hands. He never touched them, even if they had sacks full of gold with them."

As the conversation goes on, hoarse voices from the brass section add their comment, and finally the whole company joins in. Then, gradually we become aware of something the trombones are trying to say, although at first they don't get very far with it:

But they keep repeating it in different keys until even the most casual listener must recognize it as the beginning of the original theme. Yes, the trombones are very evidently trying to change the subject, and at last they succeed in leading the whole orchestra back to the adventure of the day, and with clanking swords, flying hoofs, and a flutter of gay colored cloaks, the Sardar and his picturesque retinue disappear around the corner of the mountain wall.

SERGE PROKOFIEV

Sontsovka, Ekaterinoslav — 1891

Serge Prokofiev, born on the Sontsovka estate in the Ukraine, was another of those brilliant little Russian boys destined to add to the musical name and fame of his country. His mother, an excellent pianist, noticed the child's unusual interest in her playing, and began to give him music lessons when he was little more than a baby. The urge to create showed itself at an equally early age, as so often happens with musical children. One day the five-year-old Serge overheard his parents discussing the terrible famine then raging in India. Much impressed, he proceeded to compose a *Galop Hindou*, in which he, seated at the piano, galloped off to India on horseback, carrying food to the starving people. Although his piece was in the key of F major, the small composer had left out the B-flat. It was probably just a childish mistake, but a rather amusing early edition of a Prokofiev who never hesitated later to leave out the keynote of a piece if it pleased him to do so. At seven, after a trip with his father to Moscow, where he was taken to hear *Faust* and *Prince Igor*, Serge wrote his first opera, libretto and all. He called it *The Giant*, and he and his cousins performed it at his uncle's house. A second and more ambitious opera *Desert Island* soon followed, with some orchestral instrument parts added to the score.

When the boy was ten years old, his parents wanted expert opinion of his talent and took him and his manuscripts to Taneiev, the well-known teacher and composer. Taneiev recognized unusual ability in the childish pieces, but told Composer Serge that his harmonies were commonplace — too much I–V–I. Eleven years later this same Taneiev was shocked at the daring of Prokofiev's dissonances. When he protested, Prokofiev replied with a malicious grin, "But I have only followed your advice, Sir. When I was a child, you told me to develop a more interesting harmony, which I at once proceeded to do."

At that first interview Taneiev recommended that the boy be sent to study with Glière. Young Prokofiev must have been a devastating pupil. His cleverness and energy knew no bounds, but he was a born rebel, possessed to have his own way, his own ideas, his own tunes. Time and again he tore up his exercises and compositions because he thought they sounded like those of other composers.

Glière introduced his talented pupil to Glazunov, who was convinced that the boy should go to St. Petersburg for thorough musical training. The parents agreed, and at thirteen young Serge entered the Conservatory of St. Petersburg, where he remained for ten years. During that time he interested and exasperated many masters, among them Rimsky-Korsakov. He composed a symphony, two operas, six sonatas, and a hundred or more piano pieces, all of defiant originality.

While this early work distressed the musical authorities, it intrigued a group of modernists, who used to invite Prokofiev to play his works at their concerts. Some of his pieces even found their way into print. Although he had broken every rule and tradition for which the Conservatory stood, in 1914 this amazing young man graduated with three diplomas (in piano, composition, and conducting) and, in addition, the Rubinstein prize for piano-playing!

Soon after his graduation Prokofiev made a holiday trip to London. There he met a famous countryman, Serge de Diagilev, the great impresario of the ballet. Diagilev, who had an uncanny faculty for sensing latent talent, became interested in Prokofiev and commissioned him to write a ballet for the Ballet Russe. Prokofiev was delighted, as well he might have been. As soon as he got back to Russia he began the work, choosing for his subject a tale of the Scythians, fierce nomads who had once roamed the Ukrainian steppes. When the ballet was completed, Diagilev liked the music but considered the subject unsuitable for dancing. Prokofiev revised his score for orchestra alone, and the *Scythian Suite* made its bow on the concert stage.

Meanwhile, World War I was changing the course of life and thought in Russia and everywhere else. The fortunes of war were kind to Prokofiev. As the only son of a widowed mother he was excused from service. While other young men were killing each other, Prokofiev, safe in his studio, carried on his own little musical revolution. A second ballet, *Chout;* an opera, *The Gambler;* the First Violin Concerto; two piano sonatas; a strange incantation for choir and orchestra, *Sept, ils sont sept;* and the "Classical" Symphony all bear the dates 1915–1917.

In the fall of 1917 Prokofiev decided to come to America. When he applied to the Russian government for permission to leave the country he was told, "You are a revolutionary in art just as we are revolutionaries in politics. We need you here with us." However, they did not compel him to remain in Russia. After a perilous twenty-six days' journey across Siberia, Prokofiev reached Japan. Then by way of Honolulu and the Golden Gate, he entered the United States and arrived in New York in the summer of 1918.

America gave Prokofiev a hospitable welcome with many engagements and commissions, even though it often held its ears after listening to his music. He stayed here until early in 1921, then completed his circuit of the earth by going on to Paris, where Diagilev was to produce his ballet *Chout.* But the end of that same year (1921) found him once more on this side of the Atlantic for the world première of two of his works. Both of these events took place in Chicago. The Chicago Symphony Orchestra programmed his Third Piano Concerto with Prokofiev himself as soloist, and the Chicago Opera produced his opera *The Love for Three Oranges.*

Prokofiev then returned to Europe, and for several years Paris was the center of his busy life. Although he traveled here, there, and everywhere on concert tours, he continued to turn out a surprising number of compositions, including three more symphonies. But, as was the case with his compatriot, Stravinsky, an exile in Paris, Prokofiev's chief interest at this time was in the ballet. One of his most ambitious works was the ballet *Le Pas d'acier* (The Age of Steel), intended as a tribute to Soviet Russia.

In 1934, Prokofiev returned to Russia and has become one of the leading figures in his country's musical life.

History has proved that predictions as to the future of contemporary music can be surprisingly wrong and are at best rather futile. The startling style of Prokofiev's music has provoked a great deal of criticism. There are those who see in it merely the tonal echo of a revolutionary, machine-mad age. Others feel that Prokofiev has made a real contribution in his use of dissonance as an element of music. Unlike his predecessors, who used dissonance as a savage supplement to sonority in their battle scenes and thunderstorms, Prokofiev uses it sparingly, even delicately, to give an acid tang to his impudent wit. And even Prokofiev, a more mature Prokofiev, has this to say:

I strive for greater simplicity and more melody. Of course I have used dissonance in my time, but there has been too much dissonance. Bach used dissonance as good salt for his music. Others applied pepper, seasoned the dishes more and more highly, till all healthy appetites were sick and until the music was nothing but pepper. I think society has had enough of that. We want a simpler and more melodic style for music, a simpler, less complicated state, and dissonance once again relegated to its proper place as one element in music, contingent principally upon the meeting of melodic lines.

Prokofiev's music with its vigorous rhythms, sparkling harmonies, and clear-cut outlines is unquestionably clever music. What it lacks is heart. Prokofiev stimulates and amuses but seldom if ever inspires. Thus far he seems to have looked at life with his tongue in his check. Perhaps he has been just a little too clever, too fortunate.

But Prokofiev is still growing. In the same interview with Olin Downes in the *New York Times*, which gives us Prokofiev's own thoughts on dissonance, is this on melody:

> What people usually accept as melody is that musical phrase which, above all, is not new in intervals, rhythm, or style. Thus Puccini is a composer considered especially melodic — that is, his themes fall into the category of intervals and chords to which the human ear has long been accustomed, and which it is in the habit of accepting. But it is obvious that with the passage of years the recipe for melody changes.
>
> However these questions are considered, it is obvious that there is an immense desire to win back to simplicity, to reach again, as it were, a clear spot in the forest and chart the course of music anew. And here is a striking thing, though significant of just what, if anything, each must judge for himself; there is a return to classic forms which I feel very much myself. As regards opera, I sense the need for some refreshing of ideas and alterations of form. . . . But in the field of instrumental or symphonic music I do not feel the same need. In that field I am well content with the forms already perfected. I want nothing better, nothing more flexible or more complete than the sonata form, which contains everything necessary to my structural purpose.

The appreciation of melody, which is the emotional element in music, and the "immense desire to win back to simplicity" may yet produce great music from the brilliant pen of Prokofiev.

"CLASSICAL" SYMPHONY

The New York audience of 1918 which assembled to hear the American première of this first symphony by one of the most radical of modern composers received something of a shock, pleasant or otherwise. The stage was sparsely populated. No proud array of brasses, no chimes or xylophone, not even a gourd or a piece of bamboo fishing pole met the eye. Instead of the gadget-laden modern orchestra, there sat the small orchestra of the eighteenth century — two flutes, two oboes, two clarinets, two bassoons, two horns, two trumpets, kettledrums, and strings. When the first theme rippled from the violins, the name *Mozart* flashed before them as on a screen. That theme might well have come from the overture to *The Marriage of Figaro* or from any of the gayer Mozart symphonies.

Pausing in the midst of his revolutionary and, to some, offensive dissonance, Prokofiev tried to imagine what Mozart would put into a symphony if he were living now. The result was the "Classical" Symphony, as delightful a surprise as a violet in October. Although written in Petrograd during the Revolution of 1917, this fresh and joyous music is not the product of Soviet Russia. It is the direct expression of Prokofiev's adoration of the music of Mozart, the music of a period when art mirrored the serene and ordered beauty of life, not, perhaps, as it is, but as it ought to be.

Allegro

With a brisk old-fashioned chord and flourish, the first movement begins, its lively main theme announced by violins: [1]

Soon the flute introduces a transitional passage:

which, after playing about a bit, leads into the second theme:

The *Allegro* is cast in the classical first-movement form. There is the regulation Development section with attractive variations of harmonic and instrumental color and an interesting syncopated version of the second theme. The Recapitulation opens with the return of the main theme, now in the contrasting key, C major, of the second theme. But the transitional passage, bringing the second theme to the tonic D major, establishes the expected unity of key, and with a short coda the movement closes.

Larghetto

Four measures for strings serve as introduction. Then the first violins give out the theme:

Several little episodes follow, and there is a great deal of running about, scale passages, in the lower strings. But there is no other melody well enough defined to be called another theme. The theme, in slightly varied instrumentation, appears again near the end, and the dainty *Larghetto* closes with the same four measures in the strings with which it opened.

---

[1] Russischer Musikverlag G.m.b.H., Berlin. All quotations from score, reprinted by permission.

Gavotta

Gaily the little *Gavotta* leaps in after the close of the *Larghetto:*

The first section contains but twelve measures. Then follows a trio section, with a theme for flutes and clarinets:

above an organ point in the strings, sounding like the old droning *vielle*, or hurdy-gurdy, which played the early peasant gavottes.

The first theme is then repeated in exactly the same way, and the dance ends with a little upward skip.

Molto vivace

Without introduction the strings give out the vigorous main theme of the *Finale:*

After a brief but animated working over, it is followed by the second theme, beginning with an insistently repeated note in the woodwinds over a broken chord accompaniment in strings:

As in the early classical symphonies, the Exposition section is repeated.

The Development concerns itself mainly with the second subject. Then the first theme returns, given out this time by flutes instead of the strings, which play a counterpoint against it. The second theme reappears, now in the key of D major, and the "Classical" Symphony comes to a convincing close.

In the long drought of groping modern music, what could be more refreshing than this respite of clear outlines, significant themes, and charmingly simple orchestration?

Russischer Musikverlag G.m.b.H., Berlin.

Perhaps the most delightful thing about the "Classical" Symphony is that, while it is so unmistakably Mozartian, it is by no means imitation Mozart. The "Classical" Symphony is an appreciation of Mozart in the truest sense of the term. And it is living proof of the sincerity of Prokofiev's own statement, "I want a simpler and more melodic style for music."

Marche and Scherzo from The Love for Three Oranges

From an eighteenth-century Venetian comedy by Carlo Gozzi came the idea for Prokofiev's *opéra bouffe*, *The Love for Three Oranges*. The composer himself wrote the libretto.

Gozzi's comedy was based upon the old Italian fairy tale of the man who would not laugh. This unfortunate fellow is the son of the King of Trifles, whose picture may be seen in any deck of playing cards. Court physicians tell the anxious father that the only cure for his melancholy son is a hearty laugh. But how are they to bring about this cure, when the Prince is known to have no sense of humor? At the King's command the court magician arranges a gay festival at which all sorts of merry little devils dance and play their most amusing tricks. But the dreary Prince will not laugh!

The festival is a failure, and, to add to the gloom, it is discovered that the evil witch Fata Morgana has come, all uninvited, and is mingling with the merrymakers. The guards seize her and attempt to put her out. In the struggle the old witch loses her footing and turns an awkward somersault. The sight is so ridiculous that even the gloomy Prince bursts into uncontrollable laughter. The cure! The cure has been effected! Everyone rejoices, but the joy is short-lived. Fata Morgana, furious with the Prince for having laughed at her, calls down a terrible curse upon him. He will never be happy until he has fallen in love with three oranges and has had his love returned!

It seems a ridiculous and hopeless condition to impose upon anyone. But the Prince and a companion set out in search of oranges. At last, after many adventures, they come to a weird castle, where some oranges of unusual size are kept by a comic old cook. The Prince, overcome with thirst, opens one of these monstrous fruits, and to his amazement out steps a beautiful Princess who has been kept prisoner there by the wicked Fata Morgana. But since, according to the spell, the oranges are to be opened only at the water's edge, the Princess drops dead. The Princess in the second orange shares the same fate. The third, most beautiful of all, begins to droop as soon as she is released from her orange skin. But the Jesters, *Les Ridicules*, conventional Italian comedy characters, who have been watching the whole play from towers at the side of the stage, rush to the rescue with buckets of water. The Princess is revived, and she and the Prince live happily ever afterward.

It is a fantastic tale, and Prokofiev turns it into an amusing burlesque of grand opera. His clumsy characters parody the too-tragic operatic heroes and heroines, and his take-off of operatic ensembles is clever clowning. The music is light and mocking, as befits the tale.

Several years after the appearance of the opera, Prokofiev arranged from it a symphonic suite of six movements: **I.** *Les Ridicules* (The Ridiculous Ones); **II.** *Scène Infernale* [*Le Magicien Tchélio et Fata Morgana jouent aux cartes*] (Scene Infernal [The Magician Tchélio and Fata Morgana play at cards]); **III.** *Marche;* **IV.** *Scherzo;* **V.** *Le Prince et la Princesse* (The Prince and the Princess); **VI.** *La Fuite* (The Flight).

Marche

The little march, which is heard several times, serves as a sort of *Leitmotiv* for the opera. It is most effective just before the scene in which the witch takes the fatal tumble. There is something grotesquely fateful in the theme:

with its blatant outburst:

its heavy, clambering basses, and growling brasses.

Scherzo

The *Scherzo* also belongs to the scene of the witch's fall, which causes even the gloomy Prince to laugh, but results in the curse which sends him searching for love in the form of three oranges. The music begins with a light humming in the violins above an excited *pizzicato* in the lower strings:

which might well suggest the agitation at the discovery of Fata Morgana among the guests and the attempt to put her out. After some moments of this humming, buzzing introduction, the *scherzo* theme is heard:

and a ridiculous, tumbling theme it is. In a moment it is followed by peals of shrill laughter. The music works itself up to a frenzy, then suddenly sinks into the original mood of suppressed excitement.

This little piece is the true *scherzo* of old Italian comedy, in which the jest always had a point that pricked the victim sharply. The malicious, bittersweet harmonies, and the whimsical quick changes of *tempo* and dynamics mark the music as typical Prokofiev.

DMITRI SHOSTAKOVICH

St. Petersburg — 1906

Old Russia speaks in the legend-haunted music of the famous "Five"; cosmopolitan Russia, in the works of Tchaikovsky, Rachmaninoff, Stravinsky, and Prokofiev, men of the musical world rather than conscious nationalists; and now, in the middle of the twentieth century, Soviet Russia speaks in the strange, ideological music of Dmitri Shostakovich.

Shostakovich is peculiarly the product of his time. Born in St. Petersburg in the autumn of 1906, the child must have had many a glimpse of the pomp and circumstance of that ancient city of the Tsars. The eleven-year-old Dmitri saw the Bolshevik Revolution change not only the life of his city, but, in the end, its very name to Leningrad. The stirring years that followed bound the eager, responsive youth heart and hand to Soviet ideas and Soviet culture. He knew no other.

For *La Revue Musicale* (December, 1936), Shostakovich wrote this brief sketch of his musical life:

> I was born in 1906 at Leningrad. My musical leanings became manifest in 1915, and I began to study music at that time. In 1919 I entered the Conservatory at Leningrad, completing my course in 1925. I worked there under the direction of L. Nikolaiev (piano and theory of composition), of Professor M. Sokolov (counterpoint and fugue), and of Professor M. Steinberg (harmony, fugue, orchestration, and practical composition). My studies at the Conservatory complete, I continued to attend the class in composition directed by Professor Steinberg. I began to compose at that time. My symphony [first], which has made the round of almost all of the world's orchestras, was the product of my culminating studies at the Conservatory.
>
> I was then absorbing with enthusiasm, and quite uncritically, all the knowledge and fine points which were being taught me. But once my studies were finished, there came the necessity of assorting a large part of the musical baggage which I had acquired. I grasped that music is not merely a combination of sounds, arranged in a certain order, but an art capable of expressing by its own means the most diverse ideas or sentiments. This conviction I did not acquire without travail. Let it suffice that during the whole year of 1926, I did not write a single note, but from 1927 I have never stopped composing.
>
> In this interval of time, my technique has become more finished and secure. Working ceaselessly to master my art, I am endeavoring to create my own musical style, which I am seeking to make simple and expressive. I cannot think of my further progress apart from our socialist structure, and the end which I set to my work is to contribute at every point toward the growth of our remarkable country. There can be no greater joy for a composer than the inner assurance of having assisted by his works in the elevation of Soviet musical culture, of having been called upon to play a leading rôle in the recasting of human perception.

In a statement published in the *New York Times* (December, 1931), he gave his reasons for composing music with a political program:

> I am a Soviet composer, and I see our epoch as something heroic, spirited, and joyous. . . . Music cannot help having a political basis — an idea that the bourgeoisie

are slow to comprehend.   There can be no music without ideology.   The old composers, whether they knew it or not, were upholding a political theory.   Most of them, of course, were bolstering the rule of the upper classes.

We as revolutionists have a different conception of music.   Lenin himself said that "music is a means of unifying broad masses of people."   Not a leader of masses, perhaps, but certainly an organizing force!   For music has the power of stirring specific emotions in those who listen to it.   Good music lifts and heartens, and lightens people for work and effort.   It may be tragic, but it must be strong.   It is no longer an end in itself, but a vital weapon in the struggle.

Convinced that his music was Soviet music, the young composer set to work "with sharpened creative pen" to make his contribution to the fatherland.   He had made a brilliant beginning.   His First Symphony was, and still is, immensely popular.   His talent for musical satire, a talent he himself valued highly, blossomed in a fantastic opera, *The Nose,* and in three successful ballets, from one of which, *The Golden Age,* comes the famous discordant polka, "Once in Geneva," satirizing the Geneva Disarmament Conference.

Reprinted here by permission of Leeds Music Corporation, Am-Rus Edition, New York, New York.

The next opera, *Lady Macbeth of Mzensk,* was enthusiastically received by Soviet musicians, and enjoyed a run of two years in Russian theaters.   Then, like a bolt from the blue, came an article in *Pravda,* entitled "Confusion instead of Music," denouncing *Lady Macbeth* as vulgar, a "leftist monstrosity," and an "un-Soviet perversion of taste." It seemed that Shostakovich's satirical talent had overplayed itself.

For a time it looked as though this career, so brilliantly begun, had come to an untimely end.   But, encouraged by his friends, Shostakovich kept on composing, and on November 22, 1937, the *New York Times* carried a wireless dispatch with these headlines, "Composer Regains His Place in Soviet.   Dmitri Shostakovich, Who Fell from Grace Two Years Ago, on Way to Rehabilitation.   His New Symphony Hailed. Audience Cheers as Leningrad Philharmonic Presents Work."   The "Work" was the Shostakovich Fifth Symphony with no satire, no political program as had his "October" Symphony, No. 2, and the "May First" Symphony, No. 3.   This is a mature and cautious Shostakovich who, no doubt, had the immortal Fifth Symphony in mind, for, as one writer says, the Shostakovich Fifth "comes nearest to being a translation of Beethoven into the language of present-day Russia." [1]

It has been whimsically remarked that Shostakovich was lucky with his odd-numbered symphonies but unlucky with the even-numbered.   The First, Third, and Fifth were successful.   The Second, which includes a factory whistle in the score,

[1] Quotations from "Dmitri Dmitrievitch Shostakovich," by Nicolas Slonimsky, reprinted by permission from *The Musical Quarterly,* October, 1942. Copyright, 1942, by G. Schirmer, Inc.

might be called Shostakovich's contribution to the passing fashion of industrial music. The Fourth Symphony aroused so little interest at its rehearsals that Shostakovich withdrew it, and it has never been publicly performed. The Sixth, a programless symphony, was eclipsed by three politically important cantatas which appeared at the same time.

Then came the Seventh. Shostakovich had sketched the plans for this symphony before the outbreak of Russo-German hostilities, announcing, "In 1941 I hope to complete my Seventh Symphony which I shall dedicate to the great genius of Mankind — Vladimir Ilitch Lenin." But the summer of 1941 found Leningrad under siege and Shostakovich serving as a fire-fighter at the Conservatory of Music, where he was head of the piano department. "Meanwhile," he says, "in the first hot July days I started on my Seventh Symphony, conceived as a musical embodiment of the supreme ideal of patriotic war. The work engrossed me completely. Neither the savage air raids nor the grim atmosphere of a beleaguered city could hinder the flow of my musical ideas. . . . I worked with an inhuman intensity. I continued to compose marches, songs, and film music, and attended to my organizational duties as chairman of the Leningrad Composers' Union, and then would return to my Symphony as though I had never left it." Surely no symphony was ever written under more dramatic circumstances. The subject was changed from, "the great genius of mankind — Vladimir Ilitch Lenin" to "the ordinary Soviet citizens who have become heroes of this patriotic war." The dedication reads, "It is to our struggle against Fascism, to our future victory, to my native city, Leningrad, that I dedicate my Seventh Symphony."

The first playing of this work was less a concert than a patriotic celebration, with diplomats, officials of the Red Army, and many notables present. In a special program note written for the occasion, Shostakovich quoted the proverb, "When guns speak, the muses keep silent," then added, "Here the muses speak together with the guns." Later, Shostakovich wrote in *Izvestia*, "Music does not cease in besieged Leningrad. Art, which in any other country would be relegated to the background at such a time, has in our land become a weapon against the enemy. From the inspirational sound of symphonies, songs, oratorios, and marches, the Soviet people draw their strength for the battle."

And the music? It is characteristic of Shostakovich's style and technique to which his intense earnestness and sincere emotion have given unusual appeal. Too many outside influences entered into both the composition and the hearing of this music to make fair judgment of it possible by contemporary critics. It is doubtful that the Seventh Symphony contains enough purely musical beauty to warrant its hour and twenty-six minutes' playing time, but that, too, must be left to the decision of listeners of the future.

In 1944, an eager and curious public awaited the Shostakovich Eighth Symphony. It is perhaps enough to say that this work ran true to the tradition of the unlucky even-number symphonies. Of the Shostakovich Ninth Symphony, which had its American premiere at Tanglewood in the summer of 1946, the eminent critic, Olin Downes, remarks that it is a work "of very modest proportions [which] implies an important change in Shostakovich's creative procedure." One cannot help wondering if the "change" is for the better. Or is Shostakovich to be another whose genius, flowering early, cannot quite keep its promise?

Shostakovich has a very definite style and technique which he consciously cultivated. All of his nine symphonies and his chamber music have these hallmarks. A very rhythmic opening theme, bristling with chromatics and usually given out by a solo instrument; as in his first symphony:

Reprinted here by permission of Leeds Music Corporation, Am-Rus Edition, New York, New York.

Individualized instrumentation and special effects, such as violin *glissandi;* extremely wide range, from the lowest depths of the brass to the highest tones of the strings; prominent percussion — even to kettledrum solo; insistence of one note, particularly for *tremolo* strings, as in the second movement of the First Symphony where the second violins are condemned to some 576 repetitions of a high E, lasting one minute and thirty-eight seconds; sudden modulations into the tonic; long scale runs; and the inclusion of the piano as an orchestral instrument.

Shostakovich is a brilliant pianist — he is cleverly caricatured playing with eight nimble fingers on each hand! He has contributed charmingly to the literature of his instrument in the twenty-four Preludes, written in the twenty-four major and minor keys, and, it is said, all written in one day. His chamber music shows his happy talent at its best, and the Piano Quintet, which won the Stalin prize of 100,000 rubles, is considered by some critics to be his finest work.

Dmitri Shostakovich is one of the most interesting musicians of his period. He has lived and labored intensely and with the courage of his convictions. For all his aggressive originality, his art has a substantial and varied background extending from Beethoven to Prokofiev. When the hysteria and impact of war and social experimentation are over, there will still be good years in which a mature and mellow Shostakovich may create great and timeless music.

CHAPTER IV

The Heart of Hungary

In the southeastern corner of Europe lies a little country, Hungary, home of the Magyars. For centuries this country struggled to keep its face to the west, but always with an anxious glance over its shoulder eastward. For Hungary is one of the points where Occident and Orient meet and the ancient battleground of the Cross and the Crescent. The western world owes a great debt to the brave Hungarians who once formed a living wall between its civilization and the fanatic Moslem hordes that sought to destroy it.

In happier times of peace the Hungarians have made rich gifts to the arts. They have always loved music enthusiastically and sincerely. Even before they had homes these people had music. We are told that back in the dim year 451, when the fierce Attila withdrew his wagons, the dirges of the Huns echoed over the battlefield and that strange musical instruments were found among grimmer trophies.

To many people Hungarian music means gypsy music. This, however, is only a half-truth, for there is much more to the music of Hungary than its wild gypsy beauty. It has ancient roots sunk deep in folk art and in the chants of the early church, and it has a modern flowering in intellectually disciplined composition.

The Magyars, originally a nomadic tribe of eastern origin, settled on the green aprons of the Carpathians in about the ninth century and became a peaceful pastoral people. A few centuries later other strangers from the East appeared, a curious horde of ragged, sun-browned men and women who said they came from Egypt. They swooped down on the towns and villages of Europe like flocks of gay colored birds, begging, bartering, stealing, and telling fortunes. Soon every country knew these "gyptians" or "gypsies," feared them, and persecuted them.

But the Hungarians, perhaps because of their eastern blood and the faint race memories of their own wanderings, were kind to the gypsies and allowed them to pitch their tents in peace.

The gypsy did not ask a foot of ground or a stick of timber of his own. To him, in the words of an old gypsy song:

Worldly goods which you possess
Own you and destroy you.
Love must be like the blowing wind!
Capture the wind within your walls
And it grows stale and poison.
Open tents, open hearts,
Let the wind blow!

As a matter of fact, the verbs "to have" and "to owe" do not exist in the Calo or gypsy language. All the gypsy wanted was variety and freedom. In Hungary he found both: heat and cold, mountain and plain to satisfy his fierce, changeable nature, and a friendly people who let him wander as he willed.

The gypsies had something to give in return for Hungarian hospitality. They were marvelous workers in metal. To work with fire out in the sun or under the stars was exciting; to hear the noise of the bellows and the clang of the anvil was amusing; and to watch the sparks fly up and disappear all in an instant was poetry the gypsy understood.

Homer mentions the gypsies as the people "beloved of Vulcan," god of the forge, whose secrets they keep. And there is an ancient Macedonian legend that says it was a gypsy who forged the nails for the crucifixion of our Lord, and that is why all his kinsman have been condemned to wander from one place to another ever since.

The people of Hungary were glad to have such skillful workmen in their midst, and to this day there is not a village but has its gypsy blacksmith.

Even in our country we know the gypsy as a clever tinker. It is said, for instance, that one of the big hotels in Philadelphia always has a gypsy tinker to mend its copper kettles and boilers. And does the gypsy do his mending in the hotel? Ah no, he carries the kettles off to his camp at the edge of town. He is still keeping the secrets of Vulcan!

But the gypsy's greatest gift to Hungary was his music. In addition to the tribal tunes which he brought with him, he quickly appropriated those of his adopted country, warming them with a fire and color all his own. With the music-loving Hungarians, these wild gypsy fiddlers who could make them laugh or cry at will soon took the place of the stolid peasant players. The people preferred the gypsy version of their folk songs and dances. And so it happened that the gypsies became the music makers of Hungary, and even the Hungarians have forgotten which tunes were originally theirs and which were gypsy — and what does it matter?

The gypsy cares so little for facts that he has no recorded history, only a few old fireside tales, and he is so skeptical of the power of words that he has no epic poetry and comparatively few songs. Gypsy voices, victims of constant exposure to the violence of the elements and the emotions, are too poor even to please their owners.

The gypsy's tale is one of feeling. How better can he tell it than in the one pure language of feeling, instrumental music? His fiddle is his best friend and interpreter.

> I've known no father since my birth,
> I have no friend alive on earth;
> My mother's dead this many a day,
> The girl I loved has gone away;
> Thou, violin, with music free
> Alone art ever true to me.
> — *Old Gypsy Song*

Next to his violin the gypsy loves his cimbalom, a curious instrument whose ancestry may be traced back to Nineveh and the psaltery and tinkling cymbal of the Bible.

In appearance the cimbalom in use today resembles the spinet of our great, great grandmothers. The steel wires are spread out on a horizontal board like the strings of a piano and struck with two cloth-tipped wooden sticks. The thin bell-like tone of the cimbalom lends itself both to the wistful mood of Hungarian music and to the trills and frills that ornament it. Originally cimbaloms were used only by the gypsies, but now it is said that in Hungary there are over ten thousand of them in use by individuals and in orchestras.

Every gypsy is by birthright a musician. He plays literally "by heart." Why learn to read notes, he asks, when you can play anything you wish by ear or by inspiration? The leader of the gypsy band will fiddle a tune, and his men will follow him, building up an elaborate accompaniment right out of the blue. Johann Strauss used to tell of how one morning, when he was rehearsing a new and unpublished piece with his orchestra, he noticed a gypsy lingering just outside the door. That same evening Strauss went to a restaurant where a gypsy band was playing, and to his utter amazement heard his own new waltz played almost perfectly! The gypsy band leader had caught the theme, his men had done the rest.

Although gypsy players have such remarkable rhythms of their own, they find it almost impossible to play accurately those of other composers. Dohnányi tells of trying to help a gypsy classmate at the conservatory with the "Pilgrim's Chorus" from *Tannhäuser*. This is the way Wagner wrote it:

This is the way the gypsy played it:

and it was useless to try to help him!

Gypsy rhythms are invariably in groups of two or four beats. The triple measure seems as foreign to the Hungarian or gypsy genius as the rather artificial sentiments of the polonaise, minuet, or waltz. There is an interesting theory that the syncopation — the dislocated accent we sometimes call "ragtime" and "jazz" — so characteristic a feature of Hungarian music, is due in great part to the peculiarities of the language.

The gypsy uses certain intervals, not common to European harmony, which have given rise to what is known as the Hungarian scale:

One has only to hum these notes from the fifth downward to discover the secret of the heartbroken wail of gypsy music. The Hungarians find this peculiarity satisfying. One of them once said, "We like sad music so much that I think we would even listen to a funeral march at a picnic."

Everyone knows the gypsy's fondness for decking himself with beads and earrings. His music is full of trinkets, too. He festoons his melodies with trills and turns, decorating each note as the old Moors did each brick of the Alhambra.

But for all his cleverness, the gypsy is too fond of freedom to work steadily at his music or to bother his brains with any knowledge of it. His lovely tunes, like the sparks from his forge, would have glittered and gone out had it not been for scholarly musicians like Liszt and Brahms who caught and held them in the permanent molds of ordered music.

FRANZ LISZT

Raiding — 1811
Bayreuth — 1886

The story of Franz Liszt offers a wonderful opportunity for the writing of a theme and variations. Indeed, it would require one of those monumental sets of variations beloved of the seventeenth century to do him justice. For, in his three quarters of a century, Liszt was a child prodigy, a dazzling virtuoso, a highly original composer, a successful Hofkapellmeister, an idolized teacher, and a musical philanthropist; and he was a most romantic Don Juan, an anxious father, an ecclesiastic, and a pathetic old man — in short, one of the most violently acclaimed and accused of men. Obviously the complete Liszt is quite outside the province of a brief sketch, and we shall merely state the theme and mention the variations, developing but one — Liszt the composer.

Franz Liszt was born in the year of the Great Comet, surely an appropriate omen for one whose genius was to flash across the musical firmament leaving a fiery trail behind it! His father was Hungarian, a land agent for the ancient family of Esterhazy, Haydn's patrons. His mother was a woman of lower Austria. Franz was their only child. Raiding, the estate village where Franz was born, was a mere cluster of wooden buildings set down in a monotonous, marshy landscape. Life there would have been dull enough had it not been for occasional gossip and glimpses of glittering Eisenstadt and Esterhazy, the two country estates where the Prince lived in fairy-tale splendor. The only other bits of color came from oddly different sources — the church, with its mysterious, candlelit pageantry; the peasantry in holiday blue and scarlet; and the gypsies who roamed the countryside. And through it all, like a bright connecting thread, ran the sound of music — organ tones mingling with boys' voices in the old Gregorian service, hearty country voices singing the folk songs of Hungary, wailing, unearthly voices of the gypsy fiddles, and the distant sound of Haydn's little string band making its chaste pattern-music in the palace garden on a summer night. There was something unreal about it, just as there was something unreal in that blending of religious mystery, gypsy wildness, and true nobility of heart and manner which made up the personality of Franz Liszt.

Adam Liszt, the father, was a musical enthusiast whose chief delight was playing the violin, guitar, and piano. He must often have been at least on the fringes of the palace musicales, for he remembered Haydn, and had seen and heard Hummel and

Cherubini. Naturally he wanted to pass on this greatest joy to his little son, and, as soon as possible, began to give him piano lessons. Franz showed such surprising ability that, at nine, he was invited to play at a public concert given by a blind pianist. Shortly afterward the proud father took him to the palace to play for his Prince. The Prince and his friends were delighted with the boy and made up a fund to finance six years of expert training. The Liszt family left Raiding and, at the age of ten, Franz entered Vienna, the city of Haydn and Mozart, of Beethoven and Schubert.

For two years the boy studied with Czerny, that famous fabricator of finger exercises, and so sensational was his progress that those who heard him play said here was a second Mozart. Adam Liszt was also intrigued with the Mozart idea, and, when Franz was twelve, planned a long concert tour, first through the German cities, then to Paris, where they would pause for lessons at the Conservatoire, and then on to London. They started off, and the German cities welcomed and exclaimed as they had exclaimed sixty years earlier over young Mozart. But disappointment awaited them in Paris. Cherubini, the old dragon of the Conservatoire, refused to take Franz as a pupil. It was against the rule to admit foreigners, and Herr Liszt would have to content himself with other teachers. But they had letters of introduction from Hungarian and Austrian nobles, and with these and the boy's really great gift, it was not long before *le petit Liszt* was the pet of Paris. Newspapers called him a second Mozart, the ninth wonder of the world; print shops sold his picture; and he was loved and lionized by all the fine ladies of the capital. Soon the thrifty Adam was able to send back a tidy sum, earned at concerts, for Prince Esterhazy to invest for the boy. But it was not all joy for Franz. Even as a child, he had a serious side which rebelled at empty flattery. He hated being advertised as younger than he was, and it hurt his pride to be carried onto the stage in his manager's arms and kissed by flocks of gushing, sentimental women. "I would rather be anything in the world," he cried, "than a musician in the pay of great folk, patronized and paid by them like a conjurer or the clever dog, Munito!" In after years he did a great deal toward raising the status of musicians and demanding the recognition of their professional dignity.

In the spring following their arrival in Paris (1824), they went to London, where Franz was equally well received, and for the next three years, traveled back and forth between Paris and the French provinces and England, giving concerts. But in the summer of 1827 came a disaster like that which had overtaken young Mozart, who had lost his mother in France. Adam Liszt died suddenly of typhoid fever, and young Franz was left alone in a strange land, to bear his grief, pay the bills, and make all the sad arrangements as best he could. He sent for his mother to join him in Paris, and they established a little home. The pampered boy was now the responsible head of a house, with a living to earn for two and his own future to plan. He was just sixteen.

The next six years were uneventful but deeply significant for Liszt. He gave up the concert tours as too uncertain and made his living by giving piano lessons. But withdrawal from public life meant anything but stagnation for this impressionable young artist. He was living in what was then the most excited and exciting city in the world — the Paris of 1830. The combined stimuli of the Romantic Movement, then at its height, and the July Revolution had resulted in a perfect seething of emotion and new ideas in society, philosophy, religion, and art. Liszt was so thrilled by them all that he scarcely knew which way to turn, as this quotation from a letter shows: "Homer, the Bible, Plato, Locke, Byron, Hugo, Lamartine, Chateaubriand, Beethoven, Bach, Mozart, and Weber are all around me. I study them, meditate over them, devour them with avidity." About this time he also had one of his recurrent religious attacks, and could hardly resist the temptation to go into the Church. And, added to all this, came his first and devastatingly unsuccessful love affair. No wonder that the historian Mignet, whom Liszt had startled by asking him to teach him the entire literature of France, should have remarked, "In the brain of this young man reigns great confusion."

Nor were the scales and *études* of aristocratic *demoiselles*, his pupils, Liszt's only musical fare. Paris in 1830 was the center of the World of Art. Opera had deserted Italy, and Rossini, Bellini, and Meyerbeer were holding forth in the French capital. A great pedagogue, Cherubini, ruled at the Conservatoire, and a group of young unknowns whose names were to be the ornaments of the century were airing their outrageous views and playing their wild music from garret to salon.

Three of these musicians had a great deal to do with pointing Liszt's future career. First, there was Paganini, that mysterious Italian, who looked like a specter and fiddled — well, there were sensible people who really believed that he had been taught a magic by the Devil himself! Paganini simply fascinated young Liszt, and made him aware of the emotional values of a supertechnique. There was Berlioz, in all the mad grandeur of his imagination, making a veritable three-ring circus of the orchestra and himself the ringmaster. And there was Chopin, just a year older than Liszt, and like him, a South European, a pianist, and a very picturesque, self-conscious young man. The two were devoted friends. No doubt Chopin's contentment with the small world of piano music acted as a valuable antidote for the extravagant ambitions inspired by Paganini and Berlioz. And, unquestionably, Chopin's poetic use of the native Polish dance forms awakened Liszt to the possibilities of his own Hungarian heritage.

During these Paris years of varied and exciting influences, Liszt himself was practicing, often ten hours a day, developing that dexterity which was to make him the "Paganini of the piano." And he was trying out all sorts of new pianistic effects. He had transcribed the nine symphonies of Beethoven for piano and even attempted to reproduce the colossal orchestra of Berlioz's *Symphonie fantastique* with his two hands — those long fingers are said to have looked as if they had twice as many joints as other people's. He also played the new piano music of Schumann and of his friend Chopin so understandingly that the latter said: "I should like to steal from him the way to play my own études." But for all this, he had done nothing of importance in the way of original composition. He was literally struck dumb with admiration for other men's music.

And now, at twenty-two, with tastes and talents fully matured, he runs away with another man's wife, or, to be exact, she runs away with him. Here we might as well take time out for that pet variation of the Liszt theme, Liszt and the Ladies. Since whole volumes have been written on the subject for those who demand exposure of every intimacy of an artist's life, we need only consider it briefly and in relationship to his career as an artist. Tall, slender, with Dantesque profile, long hair, and courtly manners, Liszt, like Byron, was fated to be a sentimental hero in a sentimental age. And when, in his pleasant baritone, he quoted poetry and spouted philosophy; when, at the piano, he lost himself and his listeners in a passionate flood of emotion, why, he seemed the very embodiment of the romantic ideal. Naturally, he was the prey of any strong-minded woman, who, having married early a man of Mama's choice, later fancied herself cheated out of her share of this fine new freedom and began to dabble in literature, philosophy, and self-expression *ad libitum*. Such a one was Marie, Countess d'Agoult. She was six years older than Liszt, had a husband who "did not understand her," and three children, the death of one of whom was the occasion for exaggerated sympathy and "understanding" on the part of young Liszt. The Countess was rich, handsome, serious minded, and utterly without sense of humor. Although she had no love for music, she unfortunately had great love for Liszt, and their affair ended in an elopement.

They lived first in Switzerland, later in Italy. Liszt was again playing concerts, earning a tidy sum, which he needed in his establishment, and a growing reputation as a pianist. What is still more important, for the first time in his life he began to write his own music. Whether he would ever have done it had he remained in Paris, no one can say, but his isolation with the Countess certainly turned his attention to composition, which was, at least, one good result of that affair.

Ten years passed between the elopement and the final parting of Liszt and his Countess, but it took less than half that time to bring disillusionment to both of them. She had neither interest in nor sympathy with the world of music, which laid increasing claims on Liszt. He, in turn, had had more than enough of her temper. Moreover, how could a man lead the strenuous life of a concert pianist, travel from city to city, keep up his strength and his repertory with a fretful woman and five young children as retinue? For, in addition to the two surviving d'Agoults, there were now three little Liszts — Blandine, Cosima, and Daniel. Liszt loved his children and always provided for them, and the death of Blandine, shortly after her marriage, and of his son, Daniel, at the age of twenty, were among the real sorrows of his life. Cosima, who deserted her husband, Liszt's friend von Bülow, for his other friend and protégé, Richard Wagner, brought even greater sorrow and anxiety to her father, perhaps because he recognized his own weakness in her. Unfortunately, Cosima did not inherit her father's splendid generosity.

In 1839, the Countess took the children back to Paris where, for a time, she shared a house with Liszt's mother, a lady who, for all his fondness for her, seems to have counted for little in her son's life. After that the Countess and Liszt spent several summer holidays together, then gradually drifted apart, she to her literary labors — as Daniel Stern, she wrote a number of dull books containing spiteful allusions to Liszt — and he to the most brilliant part of his career as a virtuoso.

The virtuoso years, 1839 to 1847, are known as Liszt's *Glanzperiode*, the period of splendor. Splendor was indeed the word for everything connected with it from the dazzle of the playing, the audiences, the unprecedented box-office receipts, down to the specially designed traveling coach used as bedroom and drawing room, and the three hundred and sixty odd cravats, one for each day in the year. No sooner had Liszt arrived in Vienna than he offered to take over the whole responsibility for financing the proposed Beethoven Memorial in Bonn. This spectacular generosity and the series of Beethoven Memorial concerts that followed made him the lion of Vienna.

A further dramatic touch came with his visit to Hungary — a deputation had come all the way to Vienna to invite him. The prevailing excitement over nationalism was stirring Hungary just then, and the people were eager for a hero. Besides, the Hungarians loved music, and the idea of this young musician who had honored his country in all the leading cities of Europe appealed to them. So Liszt, who had left his native land, a little boy of ten, came back, eighteen years later, as the most famous living Hungarian. His concerts were turned into festivals of patriotism as well as of music. He was fêted with banquets, balls, and serenades, escorted from place to place by torchlight processions and military bands thundering out Hungarian airs. He was presented with the jeweled sword of honor and with a patent of nobility, and the people of Budapest even stayed up after ten o'clock at night in hysterical celebration! But most interesting was his visit to the gypsy camp on the outskirts of Raiding, the town where he was born. Liszt himself gives a fascinating account of this visit in his book, "The Gypsies and Their Music." The gypsies played for him, and the impressions of their delirious *friskas* and mournful *lassans* were later to be immortalized in his own famous Hungarian Rhapsodies.

It is impossible to follow Liszt through the seven years of his concertizing, for he played in almost every country in Europe. But it is interesting and important to consider the reason for his phenomenal success. To begin with, Liszt was a master showman. He was, to be sure, rather absurd in his dress — the stagy Hungarian clothes, the many cravats, the green gloves, and the array of medals and orders dangling from his coat lapels. And his mane of shoulder-length hair seems to have been responsible for the disparaging term, "long-haired musician." He also had many theatrical gestures. Sometimes he would even leave the platform between numbers, and laugh and talk with his friends in the audience.

But not even Liszt could have held musical Europe spellbound for years by mere mannerisms, however picturesque or amusing. It was the matter and the manner of his playing that was vital. In his repertory, Liszt had the advantage over all his predecessors, for he had at his command not only the music of Bach, Scarlatti, Mozart, Beethoven, and other old masters, but also all the "new" music of Weber, Schumann, Chopin, as well as his own "parade pieces," his transcriptions of operas and symphonies and of Schubert's songs, and the Hungarian melodies which were later to take the form of his rhapsodies. It was a huge and varied list, and, oddly enough, with a few exceptions and timely additions, it is still the standard repertory for concert pianists.

Liszt established not only the repertory but also many of the conventions of modern piano playing. He was the first to play with profile — that famous *profil d'ivoire* — turned toward his hearers. Other pianists had either faced the audience or turned their backs upon it. He was the first to dare a whole program of piano music and to play it without notes. He was the first to call such a performance a *recital* in spite of protesting critics who said, "What does he mean by it?" "How can anyone *recite* at the piano?" That *how* was the secret of Liszt's playing. He did speak through the piano. To him it was no mere contrivance of keys, hammers, and strings for the display of finger magic and intricate, beautiful tone patterns, but a means of communication from one heart to another. With his peculiarly sensitive touch and marvelous dexterity, he could make it sing like a voice or sound like a whole orchestra. And by demonstrating that this percussion instrument can respond to every shade of feeling, he struck the death blow to unemotional piano playing. Intelligent audiences no longer expect or want a vaudeville performance at a piano recital, but they do demand, and always will, that composer and performer speak to them through the music.

Schumann, who hated display as much as he valued free expression of feeling, made in a letter to Clara Wieck what was no doubt a very fair criticism of Liszt the pianist: "How extraordinary his playing is, so bold and daring and then again so tender and delicate. . . . But there is a good deal of tinsel about it, too." Liszt himself tired of the tinsel. Again, as in his boyhood, he rebelled against the unreality, the falseness of his rôle as a celebrity. The serious side of him longed for quiet in which to contemplate life and art and, above all, a chance to write his own music, which had thus far given place to mere transcriptions of other men's music and to flashy improvisations. And so, just when his splendor was shining brightest, at the end of a triumphal tour of Russia, Liszt shocked the world with the announcement that his career as a virtuoso was over. He was then thirty-six years old. He never again played in public for money. Many years later, writing to his friend and biographer, La Mara, he said, "Since the end of '47, I have not earned a single farthing by piano playing, teaching, or conducting."

The Grand Duchess Marie Paulowna had, for some time, wanted him to come to Weimar as musical director of the Grand Ducal court. For three months during the winter season he would have complete control of the musical life of the city, and the remaining nine months would be free for his own composing. It seemed an ideal arrangement, even to the three months of active directorship, for Liszt's long interest in the "new" music of Schumann, Chopin, Berlioz, and others had become a zealous championship. Now, as court music director, with an opera and concert hall and a staff of trained musicians, he would be able to produce any work he chose. In the days of Goethe and Schiller, Weimar had been famous as the center of German literary culture. Why might it not become in the days of Liszt an equally important musical center? Lured by hopes and dreams of the "music of the future," of which his own should be a part, this man who had been earning thousands of pounds a year and whose financial prospects seemed unlimited went to the small city of Weimar to give all that he had for a paltry two hundred pounds (less than a thousand dollars) a year.

Liszt spent twelve years at Weimar, twelve of the busiest, happiest years of his life. His prestige and magnetic personality drew musicians and music lovers from all over the world, and little Weimar became a veritable Court of Music. Everyone came to see and hear what the great Liszt was doing, and few were disappointed. The whole literature of music seemed to come to life at his command. At the opera, old works were revived, new ones introduced, all lavishly mounted, rehearsed, and supervised in every detail by Liszt himself. At the concert hall, the programs ranged from the oratorios of Handel, through the nine symphonies of Beethoven, to an entire week of Berlioz! Nor was variety of repertory the only outstanding feature. Liszt himself conducted these programs, and his genius for interpretation, his bold individuality of expression set an altogether new standard of orchestral playing. Berlioz had already done much to make the orchestra more expressive, and would have done more had he only had an orchestra of his own to work with. But it remained for Liszt, the first of the piano virtuosi, to become the first of a long line of highly individualistic, "prima donna" conductors, extending down to the Toscaninis and Stokowskis of our own day.

It was in Weimar that the famous Liszt-Wagner collaboration began. Here, one day in May, 1849, the stormy Richard appeared, carrying a forged passport, the manuscript of his *Lohengrin*, and the clothes in which he stood. The Dresden police were on his trail because he had taken part in the recent revolution in that city. Then, in his own words,

> The very day when my personal danger became a certainty, I saw Liszt conducting a rehearsal of my *Tannhäuser*, and was astonished at recognizing my second self in his achievement. What I felt in composing the music, he felt in performing it; what I wanted to express in writing it down, he proclaimed in making it sound. Strange to say, through the love of this rarest friend, I gained, at the moment of becoming homeless, a real home for my art, which I had longed and sought for always in the wrong place.

And from Liszt comes this reference to their relationship:

> Wagner, having made such brave innovations and accomplished such admirable masterpieces, my first care must be to conquer a foundation, a root, for his works in German soil at a time when he was an exile from his country, and all the little theaters in Germany were afraid to risk his name on their programs.

The two thick volumes of their letters, covering a period of more than thirty years, from Wagner's exile in Switzerland to the consummation of his career at Bayreuth, show that Wagner gained far more from Liszt than a home for his art. Everything from money to musical ideas passed between them, and always in a one-way traffic. Liszt was always the giver, happy to be of service to this artist he so wholeheartedly admired. Wagner, in the arrogance of his triumphant genius, never seemed to question his right to ask Liszt for money or to appropriate his themes or his daughter without even asking! And when Liszt died, at the home of the widowed Cosima, it was hoped that the death of "Wagner's father-in-law" would not interfere with the current Bayreuth festival! It did not, for he was buried hastily, not in Weimar, where his poor old bones would have felt at home, but in Bayreuth, which he loathed, and there he lies to this day under an ugly monument designed by his grandson Siegfried.

And now, having followed Liszt's own precedent of giving other people's affairs first consideration, we come at last to a brief mention of Liszt's own compositions. They are far from last in importance, for the Weimar years were the years of the symphonic poems and the Hungarian Rhapsodies, which we shall discuss later; of the brilliant B Minor Sonata, the *Dante* and *Faust* Symphonies, examples of Liszt's original and disputed use of these formal musical terms; of the songs and the piano concertos — in fact, the years of his power as a composer.

But in the midst of his success at Weimar, a new pattern of life was already shaping itself. His patroness, the Grand Duchess, had died. The young Grand Duke, Charles Alexander, admired Liszt so much that many years later he was to remark, "Liszt *was* what a Prince *ought to be!*" But he was more interested in the theater than in music, and grudged the expense of some of his Kapellmeister's elaborate productions, particularly a proposed mounting of Wagner's *Ring*. The Grand Duke was probably one of the many who did not care for Wagner or his music. Then, too, there was the little matter of Liszt's Princess, a matter of scandalized nose-lifting among honest burgher wives, even after ten years.

Liszt's Lady of Weimar was Carolyn, Princess of Sayn-Wittgenstein — another runaway wife. She was Polish, married at seventeen to an uncongenial Russian Prince of her father's choosing. After several unhappy years together, they had separated, and with her little girl, the Princess had gone to live on her own estates near Kiev. Here Liszt had met her on his last concert tour. The Princess Carolyn was not a beautiful woman, but her Polish enthusiasm for music and literature, her scholarly though rather narrow mind, and, above all, her religious bent gave her much in common with Liszt. Even her friend the Grand Duchess agreed that she seemed an ideal companion for the quiet life of study and composition Liszt was planning to live in Weimar. And so she proved to be, for, in the twelve years in which they shared the Villa Altenburg, her orderly ways of living and her sympathy with his ideas were responsible for much of the success of Liszt's many and varied plans. In his will, drawn up just before he left Weimar, Liszt says, "All that I have done and thought in the last twelve years I owe to her whom I have so ardently desired to call by the dear name of wife . . . to Jeanne Elizabeth Carolyn, Princess Wittgenstein."

Meanwhile, the question of Princess Carolyn's divorce had been constantly before the Russian ecclesiastical courts. The Prince, her husband, was adjutant to the Tsar, and neither he nor the government meant to risk the loss of her estates by freeing her. In fact, as a runaway, a great deal of her property had already been confiscated. The affair lagged despairingly, but at last in 1860 came word that the Russian authorities had granted the decree, and it only remained for the Roman Church to give consent to their marriage. The Princess hastened to Rome to lay her case before the Pope. His Holiness, feeling sorry for the lady and greatly admiring Liszt, was kindly disposed. Liszt, who, with true dramatic instinct for an exit, had resigned his position at Weimar, was to join the Princess in Rome as soon as the Weimar Festival ended. They were to be married on his fiftieth birthday. On the evening before the wedding day, the church of San Carlo al Corso was hung with flowers, the many candles set. Liszt sat with the Princess in her apartment. It was late, almost midnight. Just as he was on the point of leaving, a messenger from the Vatican came with a letter for the Princess. Her husband's family had demanded a fresh inquiry into the case. The Pope had no choice but to grant it. She could not marry her lover, Franz Liszt.

Rumor ran high as this strange romance took on the sober background of Papal Rome. The lovers decided to devote their talents to the Church — not a new idea for either of them. The Princess buried herself in the writing of a twenty-four volume work on theology, mysticism, and church history. Liszt lived more or less in seclusion with his sacred books and music, and every evening he went to see the Princess. After three years of this quiet life, Liszt gave a concert in the Palazzo Barberini, at which he played two old favorites, Weber's *Invitation to the Dance* and his own transcription of the "Erl King." It was his farewell to the world. The *Abbé's* stocking already lay hidden in his pocket, and a few days later he received four of the seven degrees of priesthood. He could not celebrate Mass or hear confession, but he was doorkeeper, reader, acolyte, and exorcist. Later he was made honorary canon of Albano. Shortly afterward he went to live in the cloister of Santa Francesca Romana. In Rome and in a suite of rooms at the beautiful Villa d'Este at Tivoli he was to spend at least part of each year for the rest of his life.

Although the *Abbé* Liszt was no longer *of* the world, he was decidedly *in* it and by no means resigned to a life of inactivity. Writing to someone, just after his ordination, he says, "Yes, Sir, it is true that I have joined the ecclesiastical profession, but not a bit through disgust of the world and even less through lassitude for my art." The creative flame burned as brightly as ever, and the motto of his youth, *Genie oblige*, "Genius carries responsibility," was still his watchword. During the first years of his priesthood he secretly hoped to be made director of the Lateran and Sistine choirs. Since, for some good reason, this never came about, he turned to the writing of sacred music, of which the most outstanding was the fugue on the name B A C H and the two monumental oratorios, *Christus* and the *Legend of St. Elizabeth*. It may have been the spell of those dim old churches — St. Peter's, St. Mark's, the shrine of his own gentle St. Francis at Assisi; it may have been the blessing of Italian sunshine falling in a little village on the Adriatic where he used to walk along the sandy shore with his friend the *Abbé* Solfanelli, sometimes stopping to rest and read vespers and compline in a beached fishing boat; something gradually lessened the fierce drive of Liszt's ambition and gave him what he called *santa indifferenza*, a blessed indifference. Music became more a recreation, a matter of personal pleasure, and his purpose was no longer to attain perfection of performance or composition, but to put his knowledge and experience at the disposal of others — to pass on his torch to young, unwearied runners. It was a perfect state of mind for the beginning of his *vie trifurquée*, the three-fold life, which was to be the last phase of his career.

Grand Duke Charles Alexander, who had never ceased to regret the loss of Liszt, had at last, in 1869, persuaded him to return to Weimar for a part of each year. Liszt was given a truly royal welcome, for the Princesses themselves had furnished the little house in the *Hofgärtnerei* which was to be his home. It was a pleasant place, and the music room with its many windows, its pale gray walls, its crimson furniture, and gay Algerian hangings became a place of hallowed memories for most of the famous musicians of the next half century. Here for seventeen years, in April, May, and June, the lovely Weimar springtime, Liszt received his pupils. One of them describes him:

Liszt is the most interesting and striking-looking man imaginable. Tall and slight, with deepset eyes, shaggy eyebrows, and long iron-grey hair, which he wears parted in the middle. His mouth turns up at the corners, which gives him a most crafty and Mephistophelian expression when he smiles, and his whole appearance and manner have a sort of Jesuitical elegance and ease. . . . But the most extraordinary thing about Liszt is his wonderful variety of expression and play of feature. One moment his face will look dreamy, shadowy, tragic. The next, he will be insinuating, amiable, ironic, sardonic; but always the same captivating grace of manner . . . he is all spirit, but half the time, at least, a mocking spirit, I should say. . . . He wears a long *Abbé's* coat reaching nearly down to his feet. He made me think of an old-time magician more than anything, and I felt that with a touch of his wand he could transform us all.

And so he could. His quick sympathy and generous attention put them at their ease as they played for this greatest of all pianists. And many a budding young composer, fearfully submitting his *magnum opus* for Liszt's criticism, was overcome with surprise at his own music as the master brought it to life. Then, said one of them, "he would make a criticism or play a passage, and with a few words, give you enough to think about all the rest of your life!" With the exception of rare performances for charity, Liszt played only for his pupils. And what an experience that was, for his hands, those hands, "so flexible and supple that it makes you nervous to look at them," had not lost their cunning. "I can scarcely bear it when he plays!" cried little Amy Fay in adoration.

Liszt was always happiest with his pupils. Perhaps their eager youth and ambition brought back his own. Much of the best of him lived on in them, for Liszt's influence can only be compared to that of the master painters of the Renaissance who, gathering their disciples about them, unwittingly established traditions which came to be known as definite schools of art. Liszt would accept no money for his inspired teaching. His was a priceless gift and he, a godly giver.

But Weimar was only one part of the *vie trifurquée*. Hungary now claimed her famous son, founded a Royal Academy of Music, and persuaded Liszt to serve as its honorary president. He spent the first three months of every year in Budapest, teaching, advising, and planning for the new institution. Not so much is known about this side of his life, chiefly because the correspondence relating to it is in Hungarian and little of it has been translated. But we do know from the Hungarian Rhapsodies and Marches, the *Hungarian Coronation Mass*, and from various transcriptions of Hungarian operas that Liszt did his share in building up the literature of national music. From his constant reference to the noble families of Hungary, he was evidently made much of by the aristocracy. There seems to have been enough of the old Liszt left in the *Abbé* to inspire noble ladies to embroider curtains and cushions for his apartment in the Academy and to enjoy entertainment in princely castles where "five cooks worked night and day" and lackeys ran to and fro like ants in a hill, serving the hundreds of guests. Liszt could still grace such a life, and, after all, as someone has suggested, his exquisite manners would have been wasted in exclusively professional circles.

January, February, March in Budapest; April, May, and June in Weimar, and the rest of the year in Italy or traveling. In his later years Liszt became almost as much of a vagabond as the gypsies who roamed the *puztas* of his native Hungary. Wherever one of his own works was to be produced, wherever one of his pupils might need him or some charity profit by his presence, in Vienna, Strasbourg, Berlin, even as far as Paris, Antwerp, or Holland, there he would appear.

Occasionally he would spend a short time with Richard and Cosima Wagner, either at their holiday home in Italy or at Bayreuth. His interest and enthusiasm for Wagner's music had never flagged. *Parsifal* he considered the miracle of the age. The fact that so many of his own themes were presented in dramatic style at Bayreuth in no wise marred his pleasure. Once or twice Richard paid public tribute to the genius and noble friendship of Liszt, but privately the Wagners neglected him. Liszt had never been happy over Cosima's affair with Wagner, for von Bülow, her mistreated husband, was his dear friend and pupil. Cosima, in turn, resented the Princess Wittgenstein, and, besides, she was her hardhearted mother's own daughter. As for Richard, his egotism was as colossal as his ambition and genius. He was quite incapable of taking the smallest interest in anything or anybody not immediately useful to him. At the height of his Bayreuth fame and elegance, Wagner no longer needed Liszt, and automatically forgot his former "second self."

It is, however, the Italian summers and autumns that give the pleasantest pictures of the later Liszt. Some of the time he spent in Rome, where a few of the Weimar disciples usually followed him, and where one of his granddaughters, Blandine's child, kept him company. With his music, his devotions, and his many friends, the days were crowded, but there was always time for the visit with Princess Carolyn and their favorite dinner of baked ham and red Hungarian wine.

But his real haven was the beautiful Villa d'Este. Its fountains and ancient cypress trees by sunlight and moonlight held him in admiration for whole days at a time. And the music they inspired, *Les Jeux d'eaux à la Villa d'Este* and *Les Cypres de la Villa d'Este* seem to strangely prevision the colorful impressions of Debussy and Ravel. Sacheverell Sitwell, in his very readable book, "Liszt," gives this charming glimpse of the *Abbé* at Villa d'Este:

> Here dwelt the old magician, the black-gowned Merlin, who began his day at four o'clock in the morning, going, lantern in hand, to early mass. He lived in utter simplicity, taking his meals on that incomparable terrace, until the early evening drove him indoors to the candlelight. When, perhaps, he would play and the long, empty corridors would fill with sound; but most evenings, he was weary, and weary not least with his own skill. And there were letters to write; last of all, before he went to sleep, his letter to the Princess.

Few of the great musicians have had more fortunate lives than Liszt with his hosts of devoted admirers and his unusual faculties and talents unimpaired to the end. Yet it is only fair to certain fine qualities in his character to admit that he, too, had many real griefs. He was always a hero, but toward the end, a rather desolate hero. As he journeyed from Rome to Budapest to Weimar there must have been many times when he felt himself to be what he really was, a homeless old man unable to afford even the comforts of first-class travel. For Liszt, who had given away fortunes to charity, had to think twice before spending a few pennies for cab fare. His salary during the years of his directorship at Weimar was, as we know, less than one thousand dollars a year, and after that for forty years his total income rarely amounted to as much as two thousand dollars annually. Most of this came from his publishers for the sale of his transcriptions — not his own compositions. This was Liszt's real sorrow. His own music, that which is most intimately dear to every musician, was curiously neglected. Some of the piano pieces, it is true, were too difficult for the average player, but this does not explain the neglect of his other works. It may have been partly due to a sort of jealous reaction to his great fame, for a man of Liszt's striking individuality is bound to provoke prejudice. Then, too, there was much that was new and strange in his music. He was too modest to push his own claims. He even urged his friends and pupils not to risk the popularity of their programs by including his works. He had no generous, fearless champion such as Franz Liszt had been to Wagner, Berlioz, Schumann, and many another unknown composer. There is both irony and pathos in his half-humorous remark, "But who will now help Liszt?" It has been rather the fashion to smile at the *Abbé* Liszt, as if his black soutane were a clever masquerade costume. But those who know him cannot fail to realize that the priestly virtues of humility and voluntary poverty were fundamentals of his character long before he took the vows of Rome. Liszt had need of a *santa indifferenza* to soften the sharp edges of ingratitude. His magnificent generosity deserved it.

Ever a great actor, Liszt himself set the stage for the last act in his dramatic career. He had always loved an anniversary, and now in celebration of his seventy-fifth year, he planned a program which might well have been named Defiance of Age or Threescore and Ten Triumphant. Early in the year 1886 he had sent his last manuscripts to the publishers. They were two elaborate transcriptions of works by new Russian composers. It is typical of Liszt that he never yielded to the old man's temptation to live in the past. When Wagner had died and he realized that that chapter in the history of the "music of the future" was ended, he simply looked a little farther ahead, saw the Russian Nationalists appearing over the horizon, and went out to welcome them with encouragement and appreciation. Having delivered his manuscripts and said what he must have sensed was a last farewell to Rome and Budapest, he set out, via Paris, for England, after an absence of forty-five years.

His two weeks in London were one long festival of concerts, dinners, and receptions attended by nearly every celebrity of the time. People, realizing the importance of these gatherings, brought their children to see and hear this grand old man of music. And Liszt, ever the gracious guest, broke his long silence and played again and again, played as only Liszt could play, to the delight and amazement of his hearers. Somewhat to their surprise, he usually played Chopin, very little Liszt. He was received at Windsor by Queen Victoria and was guest of honor at a gala performance of *Faust*, and afterward at a dinner at the Beefsteak Club given by the leading man — Henry Irving, an actor of Liszt's own stripe.

Leaving London, he crossed to Antwerp for Holy Week, then back to Paris, where his *Legend of St. Elizabeth* was to be given. Then to the wedding of his granddaughter, Daniela; to Weimar for a few weeks in his little house in the *Hofgärtnerei*, and on to

Bayreuth to attend the August Festival. But on the last lap of his journey he caught cold. It is said that a pair of young honeymooners opened the window in the second-class compartment in which he was sitting out the night, and Liszt, unwilling to spoil their evident pleasure in the black forests flying by, sat for hours in the cold night air. Incurably romantic, the poor old man was incurably chilled, and died of pneumonia a few days after reaching Bayreuth. It had been a wonderful year, a true Liszt year, but it fell short of reaching that seventy-fifth birthday. By the twenty-second of October the ivy was growing green upon the grave of Liszt at Wahnfried.

The Artist

Liszt, the brilliant pianist and conductor, the picturesque hero of a romantic age, has been a legend for more than a century. Eclipsed by that brilliant figure, Liszt the composer, the contributor to his art, has stood half-hidden in the shadow of obscurity. It is not difficult to see how this could happen. With an artist seated at the piano or waving a magic wand over an orchestra, seeing and hearing is believing. Thrills may be had for little or no effort. But a composer's score, its music hidden in a maze of little black notes, as gold is hidden in the earth, takes hard digging on the part of someone before it will come to light and shine. Liszt lacked diggers. Even if his music had been much played in his own day, it would have seemed pale beside the music of Wagner which, incidentally, presented so many of Liszt's themes in such large and glowing style! And so, as Huneker says, "The true history of Liszt as a composer has yet to be written!" It may be long in the writing for the veins of his golden genius are many and deeply buried in biased criticism and in other men's music. But once excavated, great will be the surprise and delight.

Liszt was an extreme Romanticist in his devotion to color and poetic content in music. He was less a builder than a painter — a painter out for effects. If, upon close scrutiny, you discover that what you thought a fishing boat is merely a blob of paint smudged in with the thumb, why, do not cry "Imposter!" Just keep your distance and you will still see a fishing boat!

As for the literary background of Liszt's music, it is safe to say that no musician ever had wider contacts with the other arts. Homer, the Bible, Dante, Goethe, Shakespeare, Schiller, Lamartine, Victor Hugo, Byron, Raphael — he knew them all. He spoke eight languages, read all the principal reviews, especially the scientific ones, and once, when asked what he would have been had he not been a musician, replied jestingly, "The first diplomat in Europe." He is well described by the old-fashioned phrase, "a man of many parts." Although a patriot at heart, Liszt was not a nationalist in his music. Life and circumstances had made him an internationalist — a fact which seems to have been overlooked by the critics who in Germany abused him for being a Magyar, in Hungary, for having German tendencies, in France, for not being French born! It should be remembered that among musicians Liszt was the first and perhaps the greatest cosmopolitan.

And now for his purely musical equipment. Liszt had a fluent gift of melody. In fact, his pieces sometimes seem almost too full of pretty tunes, like cake so full of raisins that it is a bit too sweet and apt to fall apart. In the variety and virility of his rhythms he ranks with the highest. It is, perhaps, enough to say that he was a Magyar. We have already spoken of his skill with color, which of course means effective choice of keys and harmonic combinations as well as of instruments. His music is distinctly homophonic — one voice sings a clearly outlined tune, supported by an elaborate accompaniment. This characteristic, combined with his feeling for poetry, made Liszt a really fine song writer. It seems strange that, outside of "Mignon's Lied," "Die Lorelei," "Du bist wie eine Blume," and "Es muss ein Wunderbares sein," so few of his beautiful songs are known or sung!

In his sacred music, the *Abbé* Liszt was no doubt just as sincere and devout as Bach or César Franck. But, born actor that he was, he could not help sensing the dramatic in religion, in the Roman service, and even in the relation of God and man. For that reason his Masses and oratorios, compared to the *St. Matthew Passion* or *The Beatitudes*, seem a shade too operatic. Edward Dannreuther, writing for the Oxford History of Music, puts it picturesquely when he says of Liszt's *Hungarian Coronation Mass*, "The style of the entire Mass is as incongruous as a gypsy musician in a church vestment."

Liszt's piano music falls naturally into two general divisions — the song and symphony transcriptions and fantasias on themes from famous operas, and his original piano compositions. Of the transcriptions it might be said that they were a successful pioneering in music appreciation. Although a transcription is, at best, but a second-hand affair, yet in Liszt's hands the Schubert songs and the Beethoven symphonies became known and loved by hundreds who might otherwise never have heard them. The original piano compositions were typical virtuoso pieces. After all, one could hardly expect a man who could make the piano sound like a whole orchestra to write a simple, Haydnish piece. His own mastery of the instrument gave him the right to compose showy pieces, and such of them as lacked musical merit have been justly punished by going out of fashion. But the orchestral effects for which Liszt was unjustly criticised were a perfectly legitimate widening of the piano's powers of expression. No one questions them today. Such compositions as the Etudes, the *Waldesrauschen*, the Ballades, and the beautiful Sonata in B Minor, to mention a few, are important and permanent additions to the literature of the piano.

Strangely enough, this man who had spent half a lifetime at the keyboard of a piano was to make his unique contribution to his art in the field of orchestral music. The Romantic composers, when they attempted to pour their new story music into the old sonata form, found themselves faced with the ancient problem of the square peg and the round hole. It just would not work. Schumann, in his large orchestral works, tried to modify the sonata, got tangled in the Development section, and sacrificed the dramatic action of the story. Berlioz, casting the old forms aside, sacrificed coherence. But Liszt, with his keen analytic mind, realized that a new form would have to be devised for this new type of instrumental music — one which would hold the music together and at the same time not hold back the action of the story.

His scheme was to divide the music into sections corresponding to the different phases of the story; then bind them into a clear and unified whole by using related keys for the various sections (an idea borrowed from the sonata); and by using little motifs suggesting the characters and events of the story.   Instead of the two conventionally related and presented main themes of the sonata, there may be any number of these little motifs, and they may be modified in all sorts of ways to suit the story-teller's purpose.   As long as they are recognizable, the listener has the comforting assurance that it is still the same piece — an assurance he often lacks in the wandering music of Berlioz.

Liszt, who was always clever at naming things, called his new form the *symphonic poem*.   It was a good name, for the music is literally *sym-phonic* in that the voices are "sounding together" in an organic unity;   and it is poetic in that it presents, not the abstract beauty of a tonal design, but a definite idea inspired by the world outside of music.   The distinguishing feature of the symphonic poem is its *unbroken continuity*. One is conscious of the beginning and ending of the different sections or moods of the poem, but there are no rigid stops as between the movements of the sonata.

Other composers had perhaps forecast this principle of program music, but it was Liszt who organized and developed it into a workable form.   And so important and useful a form has it proved that, as Daniel Gregory Mason says, "Our century might almost be called the century of the symphonic poem, just as the nineteenth century was the century of the symphony, and the eighteenth, the century of the suite."

Forgetting then the legendary Liszt, no one can deny that music today is richer for the real Liszt.   To him we owe not only that most useful form, the symphonic poem, but also new ideals of expressive performing and conducting.   His complete abandonment to mood, safeguarded by perfect technique — a bright flag flying free from a pole deeply grounded — is largely responsible for the live, extempore element in modern music.   He was an artist of generous ambition, tireless energy, and unrivaled experience and culture — a truly great artist.

LES PRÉLUDES

Liszt not only invented the form and the name *symphonic poem*, but in his own twelve poems:

What One Hears on the Mountain — after Victor Hugo	*Festival Sounds*
The Lament and Triumph of Tasso	*Funeral of a Hero*
Les Préludes — after Lamartine	*Hungaria*
Orpheus	*Hamlet*
Prometheus	*The Battle of the Huns* — after Kaulbach's painting
Mazeppa	*The Ideals* — after Schiller

also showed the wide range of its possibilities in both subject and treatment.

He prefaced his score of *Les Préludes* with these lines from Lamartine's "Meditations poétiques" which had inspired it.

What then is life but a series of preludes to that unknown song of which death sounds the first solemn note?   Love is the morning glow of every life;   yet where is the heart upon whose first blissful happiness some storm does not break, blowing away its young illusions and consuming its very altar with a bolt of fatal lightning?   And where the soul, thus cruelly bruised, that does not, when the tempest rolls away, seek rest and healing memories in the calm of country life? But not for long will man linger in the kindly quiet of nature. When the trumpet sounds the alarm, away he hastens to the post of danger, whatever be the cause that calls him into war, knowing that in combat he will find again full consciousness of all his powers.

With this as guide the meaning of the music is clear and our enjoyment complete, which is all the composer hoped for. Yet *Les Préludes* is such a perfect example of the symphonic poem, as Liszt conceived it, that for the musicianly listener a closer examination brings added pleasure.

The music falls logically into six sections — an Introduction and Conclusion, and sections corresponding to the four moods of the poem, "Love," "The Storm," "Country Quiet," and "War." To give it unity, Liszt builds the entire musical structure upon two brief, contrasting motifs. The first is a dreamy, idealistic theme:

Here we find but another version of that famous three-note motto:

beloved of Bach, Beethoven, Weber, Franck, and who can say how many others! Some psychologist should make a study of the perennial fascination of this particular tone sequence! The second motif:

is stronger, more intense in its feeling.

To fully appreciate the cleverness with which Liszt colors and changes these two little scraps of tune and makes them serve his poetic purpose, one really should see the orchestra score of *Les Préludes*. It is like watching a magician working his wonders!

Beginning with the little three-note motto:

Liszt develops it into a long, meditative introduction. It is fateful, questioning music quite in keeping with that first line, "What then is life but a series of preludes to that unknown song of which death sounds the first solemn note?" For a moment the music grows bold, suggesting, perhaps, the hero in all his defiant strength before he has experienced either love or the blast of disillusionment. Then violins and 'celli begin to sing the beautiful first theme:

cantando
Violins II
'Celli

echoed by a solo horn. And then, with the well-known horn melody:

espress. ma tranquillo
Horns
(Violas)

the love section begins. Woodwinds take up the melody, and presently the solo horn is heard again in the dreamy first motif, which the flutes echo wistfully, brokenly. This is Liszt, the great lover, speaking.

A muttering in the low strings:

'Celli   p

gives the first sign of the storm. Then suddenly it breaks in a short, violent version of the first motif:

Allegro tempestoso
f

It rages and roars with shrill chromatic winds and murky diminished-seventh harmonies — all the familiar storm properties of the movies. But theatrical and hackneyed as it may seem today, it was not so when Liszt wrote it almost a century ago. How he must have reveled in all this orchestral *Molto agitato!*

"The tempest rolls away," and a peaceful oboe begins to sing the joys of country life:

Moderato
p dolce espressivo
Oboe
rit.   a tempo

Musically this *Allegretto pastorale* is the most charming part of the whole poem. A happy solo horn:

Allegretto pastorale
Solo Horn
p dolcissimo

and woodwinds call back and forth.   A gay flute pipes:

It is not Beethoven's country — real country of wild nature and simple peasants.   It is a Watteau landscape with decorative shepherds and shepherdesses dancing and singing their *bergerettes*.   But it is delightful and in faultless taste.

Above the light pastoral theme, the strings begin to sing the second theme, and now for the first time we have the full song, the song of love refreshed by "country quiet," restored by "healing memories."

But the hero is roused from his dream of love by the alarm of the brass:

How simple, that transformation of the dreamy first motif into a war march, but how magic!   Racing strings suggest the excitement of combat.   And all the drums, which until now have been silent, are let loose and join the fray.   Even the love theme becomes a martial song:

Then in the coda, Liszt recalls the vigorous theme of the introduction:

as if to show us the hero whose life he has preluded, restored to the "full consciousness of his powers."

There is, to be sure, a certain theatrical taint in this music, a bit of tinsel and here and there the flash of a paste jewel.   But there is also lovely melody, luscious harmony, superb orchestration, and the mark of the master craftsman.   The music of *Les Préludes* is a perfect reflection of the poem that inspired it.   It is typical Liszt, typical Romantic music.

HUNGARIAN RHAPSODY, No. 2

When, in 1839, Liszt returned to Hungary as a famous pianist and national hero, he found that he had forgotten almost every word of his native tongue.   It was a strange experience, this mingling of vague childish memories (he had gone away at the age of ten) with a mature artist's impressions of a vivid country like Hungary. Naturally what most appealed to Liszt was the music of Hungary, the old folk tunes, not as stolid peasants sang them, but as the gypsies played them. He spent many hours in the gypsy encampments listening to their music and observing the fascinating pattern of gypsy life. The result was his picturesque book, "The Gypsies and Their Music," and the twenty Hungarian Rhapsodies.

The idea of collecting and using gypsy tunes was not a new one. Haydn, in his long years at Esterház, had transplanted many a one into his string quartets. And later Schubert, who for two summers was music teacher to the young Countess Caroline Esterhazy, had used them in his Hungarian marches and melodies. But Liszt had a far more ambitious plan. As he sat by the campfires listening to the gypsy fiddlers, he realized that they were not just playing tunes, they were telling the story of an ancient people. "This *is* music," he exclaimed. "It can speak, it can narrate, it can even sing!" He would use these old airs, not as mere folk tune arrangements or to give a dash of gypsy flavor to a classical sonata, but as national ballades.

He carried out the idea even to the happy choice of the name, *rhapsody*, used with much of its original meaning. *Rhapsody* is a Greek word, going far back to the days when books were few and reading a rare accomplishment. For their tales of heroes and of high adventure on the "wine-dark sea," the ancient Greeks depended upon professional storytellers who went from town to town. Often in a moment of deep feeling or of dramatic climax their tales would soar above the ruts of common speech into a metrical chant. These wandering poets were called *rhapsodists*, and their epics, or at least such portions of them as could be chanted in one recitation, were called *rhapsodies*. To Liszt the old Magyar tunes as the gypsies played them, going from one mood, one incident to another, were real rhapsodies. He said of them, "These pieces do not recount facts, it is true. But those who know how to listen will easily catch from them the expression of states of soul, forming a compendium of the nation's ideal."

In his Hungarian Rhapsodies he purposed not only to picture the emotional life of the people but also to reproduce on the piano the effect of the gypsy band even to the tapping, rattling cimbalom and the solo flights of the leader! Thanks to his genius for technical effects and to the wild spirit of his playing, Liszt's Rhapsodies were a brilliant success, such a success that they unfortunately helped to narrow the meaning of the word. No doubt many people will always think of rhapsody or the adjective *rhapsodical* as something wild, abandoned, and quite lawless.

Liszt's Rhapsodies are by no means lawless. They follow the definite if somewhat vagrant form of the *czardas*, a dance of the wayside inns on the *Puszta*. It is characterized by the alternation, at well-proportioned intervals, of the melancholy *lassan* and the boisterous *friska*. Its meter is always duple and is saved from monotony by many changes of *tempo*, rich ornamentation, and an almost constant syncopation. This syncopation is one of the conclusive proofs that Hungarian music began, not with the song, but with the dance. It was evidently a teasing, unconventional kind of dance in which the dancer, instead of taking the step on the beat, as expected, avoids it.

The gypsy — and Liszt — usually begins his music with a *lassan*. It is of that particular kind of slowness suggesting the dignity of sorrow, the solemnity of a mourning procession.   Any number of these heartbroken tunes are to be heard from one end of Hungary to the other.   Then, having exhausted his store of tears and sighs, the gypsy bursts into the delirious jubilation of the *friska*.   As might be expected, the *lassan* is usually in a minor key, the *friska*, in major, and the *friska* is heavily accented, with constantly increasing *tempo* working up to a mad climax.   Sometimes, in order to lengthen the piece, several *lassans* are strung together, followed by several *friskas*.

The Hungarian Rhapsodies were originally written for piano and played by Liszt himself.   Many years later, with the assistance of one of his pupils, he arranged a number of them for orchestra.   There were fifteen in the first series, afterward extended by five more, the last one still unpublished.   With so many to choose from, one can understand the lament of Liszt enthusiasts at the neglect of the eighteen in favor of the "eternal" Second.   Yet we, too, have chosen the Second because it is so constantly heard that it is an embarrassment not to recognize it;   because it is effectively recorded;   and, most of all, because it is thrilling and beautiful music.   And we have chosen the orchestral version, which, with its appealing strings, plaintive woodwinds, and defiant brass, seems a definite improvement upon the piano in any other hands than those of Liszt.

The Second Rhapsody begins with a statement as portentous as those first lines of the Book of Genesis:

In the beginning
God created the heavens and the earth.

Then the low strings take up the tale of ancient grief and longing:

Now and then flutes or clarinets break suddenly into a profusion of notes that have nothing to do with the tale — just the gypsy shaking his bangles.

As the music goes on, the dignity of the beginning gives way to a restlessness expressed in the typical ragged gypsy rhythms:

and:

and:

There is an interesting similarity in these three motifs, as if three people were saying the same thing in slightly different words. There always seems to be the suggestion of a group in gypsy music.

The mournful theme is heard again, ending this time in an awe-inspiring repetition of that fateful first line, chanted by the bass strings.

Then the restless motifs reappear, brightening into a higher key and quickening in *tempo.* A gathering excitement runs through all the instruments. An instant's pause, and they fairly fling themselves into the furious gaiety of the *friska:*

In the impetuous melodies that follow:

and:

and:

one can imagine the different incidents in the story or picture different couples rushing into the firelit circle to add their variations to the wild dance. All the colors of the orchestra, from triangle to trumpet, flash in this music. The chromatics of woodwinds and strings suggest wild winds or shrill voices.   Then, just as the revelry reaches its height, comes the sudden memory of the old sorrow!

But, why grieve?   Tomorrow the sun will shine again, so

> Open tents, open hearts,
> Let the wind blow!
> — *Old Gypsy Song*

KARL GOLDMARK

Keszthely — 1830
Vienna   — 1915

To be writing music or playing the piano in the days when Liszt, Wagner, and Brahms were taking the musical world by storm was for any lesser artist to play a rather thankless second fiddle.   Although somewhat overshadowed by the genius of his great contemporaries, Karl Goldmark became one of the popular composers of his time, especially in his native Hungary and in Germany and Austria.   And the pleasure which his music gave to audiences of 1930, at the celebration of his centennial, proved that Goldmark's was more than a passing popularity.

Karl Goldmark was the son of a Jewish cantor whose slender purse held no money for a child's music lessons.   But young Karl was as ambitious as he was talented.   He worked away at his music with the help of a generous schoolmaster, and by the time he was twelve, was playing his violin acceptably enough to earn a little money with a theater orchestra.   Then an older brother managed to send the boy to Vienna to study at the Conservatory, and for a short time all went well.   But those were years of constant political unrest, of plots and cruel suspicion.   The benevolent older brother was accused of having been mixed up in one of the many minor revolutions and had to flee to America.   As for young Karl, he not only lost his financial backing but almost his own head.   For he, too, was arrested one day and clapped into prison with the cheering prospect of being shot at sunrise for being untrue to his country!   Fortunately for him and for the many who have enjoyed his music, Karl's innocence was proved.

But no amount of hardship or misfortune could shake young Goldmark's determination to become a first-rate musician.   He contrived somehow to live while he taught himself piano and singing.   His little lamp burned far into the night as he studied the scores of master composers, discovering the endless ways in which they had made melody, rhythm, and harmony serve their purpose.   He also read everything he could in other fields and taught himself several modern languages.   Surely this boy deserved the modest success that came to him!

Goldmark spent the greater part of his long life in Vienna, a celebrated teacher of piano and a popular composer. He wrote concertos, chamber music, and symphonies, but is best known for his operas, overtures, and tone poems. He had a real flair for the stage, and if only the libretto of his *Queen of Sheba* had been worthy of Goldmark's music it would never have been laid upon the shelf of seldom-heard operas. The overture *In Springtime* and the tone poem *Sakuntala* have the same pleasing tunefulness and color as the "Country Wedding" Symphony.

As an artist Karl Goldmark is one of the many good musicians to whom, in all appreciation, is given secondary rank — men of fine talent but not genius. He gave to his art no new forms or techniques. Neither did he write profoundly nor with startling originality in the existing forms. Nevertheless he served it well. His music is sincere, beautifully made, and enjoyable. The world needs its Goldmarks as well as its Beethovens. No one can, or should, live on the heights all the time, and not to be able to see and honestly enjoy the beauty of the lower levels seems as great a misfortune as never to have known the peaks!

"Country Wedding" Symphony

The "Country Wedding" Symphony was first played in Vienna in 1876, the year in which it was written. According to the definition of the classical symphony — a sonata for orchestra — the "Country Wedding" is not a symphony at all, for not one of its movements is written in the first-movement form which characterizes the sonata, nor are the relations of its themes or sections conventional. The "Country Wedding" is really a modern suite in five parts: 1. Wedding March (Variations); 2. Bridal Song (Intermezzo); 3. Serenade (Scherzo); 4. In the Garden (Andante); 5. Dance (Finale) — all bound together by the poetic idea of a country wedding rather than by the purely musical relationships of a symphony's movements.

In translating the title *Ländliche Hochzeit* from the original German into English, it must be remembered that *ländlich* means *country* and not *peasant*. If the composer had meant to picture a peasant wedding, he would have called it *Bauernhochzeit* and suggested the gay costumes, the rustic jokes, and peasant dances, for in Goldmark's time a peasant wedding was a real folk festival. This is a village wedding, perhaps of the burgomaster's Elsa and the doctor's tall Anton. It is evidently a summer wedding when the simple country setting is most charming. The wedding party walks to church, as was the custom, and afterward gathers at the home of the bride to celebrate the happy event. The music is gay but never boisterous, and there is a certain dignity, a touch of reverence and pure sentiment that seems to refine its merriment.

Wedding March

The first and longest movement is called Wedding March, but it is far more than a march both in the character of the music and the situations it suggests. The theme, played through to the end by low strings in unison, is a simple march tune:

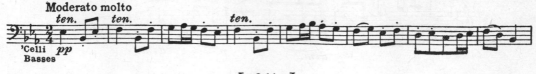

Then follows a set of thirteen variations expressing the many moods of a wedding day. The fourth is a gently sighing *Andante con moto:*

But its wistfulness is quickly forgotten in the gay *Allegretto* and laughing *Allegro vivace* of the fifth and sixth variations.

The eighth, *Allegro scherzando,* is full of bells. The twelfth, a chorale in solemn organ tones, suggests the service in the church. Then number thirteen plays the bridal pair down the aisle in a triumphant version of the march for full orchestra. Gradually one instrument after another drops out, the march sounds fainter and farther away as the wedding procession passes from sight.

Bridal Song

The Bridal Song is a lyric in mood and form. One can imagine it sung by the friends of the bride, following a pretty, old-world custom. The clarinets lead off in the main theme:

Oboes, clarinets, and strings then join in a little duet:

which is taken up by the whole chorus of instruments.

The second stanza might be the good wishes of the bridesmaids:

and just as it begins to be almost tearfully tender, the clarinets change the subject to the happy first theme.

Then it seems as if one of the bridesmaids, perhaps the dearest friend, steps forward to offer a loving greeting:

which is repeated by the violins, while the basses play a soft accompaniment cleverly contrived from the theme of the Wedding March.

The first stanza comes back, and the song ends with the gracious phrase:

and a wave of the hand:

Hail and farewell.

Serenade

The Serenade reminds one of an old-time madrigal, one of those dainty love songs of Queen Elizabeth's day in which each singer seems to be taking his own way and time with the tune, and yet the voices weave a lovely web of tone. And so clear and free are these particular voices that it might be a serenade of wood thrushes!

As in the Bridal Song, the clarinet leads off in a bubbling phrase:

which immediately effervesces through the whole orchestra, even down to the sober basses.

Two oboes then begin to sing:

a tune that might easily drift into pathos were it not for the humorous sound of bagpipes:

Bassoons
Low Strings

and energetic fiddles:

Violins *mf*

The two main themes play in and out among the instruments and at different key
levels — higher levels, as if the voices rose in excitement. For a moment the song
seems lost. The serenaders are all chattering at once, each trying to be heard. It
makes one think of the many-voiced — polyphonic — music of Bach.

Then out of the joyous tangle of sound the first theme emerges, and its little up-
flung phrase is caught up by the various voices. The oboe duet is heard again, the
bagpipes wheeze cheerfully, and with soaring strings and woodwinds the charming
Scherzo ends.

In the Garden

True to symphonic tradition, the *Andante*, always the most emotional movement, is
the heart of the "Country Wedding." The lovers have stolen away from the merrymakers and in the quiet of the garden exchange their vows of love and constancy. The
composer tells us that they are alone. There is an intimate sense of two, a shy little
bride:

Clarinet *p sehr zart und träumerisch*   *p*

and an ardent lover:

'Celli *p cantabile*

Slowly, through many beautiful variations of melody and harmony, the music rises to
a passionate climax. Every voice in the orchestra speaks, but there is no suggestion of
a crowd of people, as in the Serenade. There is only a crowd of emotions which, in
the end, subside into that timid, almost reluctant first theme:

Oboe *pp*

Clarinets *pp äusserst zart*

For all the passionate promises made by moonlight, tomorrow's sun of reality will shine in the garden!

Dance

After a brief fanfare, the second violins lead off in a whirling figure:

which quickly becomes a four-voice fugue. As the woodwinds take up the theme, bassoon and violas enter in a countersubject of more jogging pace:

and they all dance together. Surely this is no dry fugue but as jolly a bustle as anyone could wish!

After a queer chromatic slide in flutes and violins and some squeezy accordion sounds in the basses, the violins give out the second theme:

not a fugue this time but a comfortable, straightaway jig broken by the most oddly discordant lulls followed by earsplitting outbursts. Someone seems to be getting funny!

The original round dance then returns in all its fugal vigor. In the midst of the merriment a memory of the tender scene, In the Garden, comes back for a moment:

a delightfully poetic touch and surely a grateful rest for ears and muscles tense with whirling and jigging. Then on with the dance which serves as a happy ending and an effective *finale* to the "Country Wedding."

ERNO VON DOHNÁNYI

Pressburg — 1877

A musician of many gifts is Erno von Dohnányi. Concert audiences all over the world know him as one of the important Hungarian composers of his day and as a brilliant pianist and conductor. A smaller but no less admiring group knows him as a master teacher.

Dohnányi grew up in a musical atmosphere. His father, a professor of science and mathematics, was also a skillful amateur 'cellist, and from him the boy had his first music lessons. Young Erno's favorite play was "giving concerts." Standing on a stool, stick in hand, he would conduct an orchestra of one obliging little sister before an audience of empty chairs.

At the age of seventeen, Dohnányi graduated from high school and entered the Royal Hungarian Academy of Music at Budapest. Here his interest was divided between piano playing, at which he excelled, and composition, which had a great fascination for him. Even as a child, Dohnányi had taken pleasure in thinking out and writing down his own musical ideas, and as a mature composer he has often made use of themes from his boyish notebooks. It is not surprising, then, that after three years of intensive study he should have won, at the age of twenty, the King's Prize for his Symphony in F.

But this interest in composition did not interfere with Dohnányi's career as a concert pianist, and for years he was hailed, both in Europe and America, as one of the world's great pianists. At the age of forty-five he had given more than a thousand concerts.

For a time Dohnányi taught piano in the famous Hochschule für Musik in Berlin. Then he returned to Budapest, where he served for a number of years as Director of the Royal Hungarian Academy of Music, his own alma mater, now known as the Royal Hungarian Franz Liszt College of Music. He has also made a distinguished contribution as conductor of the Budapest Philharmonic Orchestra.

Dohnányi is a man of average height and blond coloring. He is quiet and reserved in manner and has always been seriously interested in philosophy. In 1923 he was given the degree of Doctor of Philosophy by the University of Szeged. He has many interests and, as one who knows him well remarked, "One can easily speak to him about subjects other than Dohnányi and get a response!"

As a composer Dohnányi is a happy combination of Classicist and Romanticist. His music shows respect for all the niceties of musical form and techniques. He is ever a careful workman. While he seldom indicates any particular poetic content by even so much as a suggestive title, his music glows with color and with the warmth of human emotion. Dohnányi heartily approves of experimentation and the search for new ways and new forms. But he feels that much of the ultramodern music is nothing but a search, a search for the sensational rather than the beautiful, and therefore a worthless search. He is convinced that music is made by musicians, not by adventurers, however clever.

Perhaps the most surprising and delightful characteristic of this serious man and artist is his rare sense of humor. One commentator says of him, "He has written the only music I know that recaptures the spirit of laughter which seems to have disappeared from music since the eighteenth century." The charm of Dohnányi's laughing music is that it laughs for the pure love of laughter, never for the love of vulgar suggestion. His musical jokes are always in good taste, his bassoons are merry clowns, not drunken rowdies. One of the happiest examples of Dohnányi's gift of gaiety is the Variations on a Nursery Tune for piano and orchestra. Here every musical device of canon, fugue, and counterpoint is used with schoolmasterly precision, yet the piece is inscribed, "For the joy of the friends of humor and the vexation of all others!" And what joy it has given. How many friends it has made for this creator of sincere and beautiful music!

SUITE FOR ORCHESTRA, OPUS 19

The suite is one of the oldest of musical forms and one of the most perennially satisfying. Within its easy boundaries the composer finds freedom, and the listener, the greatest returns for the least outlay of attention and understanding. The suite, as the name implies, is based on a sequence which gives it balance and continuity. The original Classical suite was a set of little dance tunes chosen and arranged to give an effect of pleasantly contrasted rhythms. Then, with the Romantic shifting of emphasis from form to poetic content in music, came the idea of basing the sequence of the suite on the moods or incidents of a single story. The result was such modern suites as the familiar *Nutcracker*, *Scheherazade*, Ravel's *Mother Goose*, and many others.

Dohnányi's Orchestral Suite, Opus 19, published in 1911, is still another variation of the suite. It follows the classical tradition in having no poetic title or program, yet it is unmistakably Romantic in its moods and quite modern in its harmonic and instrumental coloring. It is, moreover, a shining example of *popular music* in the highest sense of the term. Popular, because it makes immediate appeal to all sorts of people. Yet this appeal is made without resort to any cheap tricks, without even the suggestion of a picturesque title. Dohnányi's suite appeals because of the irresistible charm of the music itself.

Andante with Variations

The first movement of the suite might be called a "color card" of the orchestra, so clearly does it present and contrast the different choirs. In form, it is a set of short variations on a simple theme which is given out by the woodwinds: [1]

and taken up at once by the strings. The reedy sweetness of the woodwinds and the suave tone of the violins are at first contrasted, then blended delightfully as the two choirs join in repeating the theme.

[1] Excerpts printed by permission of Associated Music Publishers, Inc., New York, owners of the copyright.

Variation I. Strings and woodwinds outline the theme in a curious flickering rhythm above which the flutes and clarinets, in bubbling ornamental passages, sound with startling clearness. Later the strings sing a *legato* version of the theme:

Variation II. Ushered in by the horns, the theme is then taken up by brisk woodwinds:

accompanied by *pizzicato* strings and is energetically dealt with.

Variation III. Here, by way of contrast, we have a tranquil *andante* with 'celli singing the theme in Brahmslike contentment:

while oboe, horn, and viola decorate it with delicate countermelodies.

Variation IV. The fourth variation is a lively *allegro* with the English horn stepping off the theme in seven-league-boot skips:

to an accompaniment of *arpeggios* in flutes and clarinets and a humming figure in the divided strings.

Variation V. To a brisk beating of kettledrums, the bassoons make a clownish presentation of the theme:

which is greeted by what might easily be fancied as rippling laughter from the clarinets. There is a great deal of hopping and skipping in the accompaniment, and the variation works itself up to a merry climax.

Variation VI. The last variation, less rhythmic in its interest, begins with the brasses singing a choralelike version of the theme:

It is taken up by the woodwinds and harps while the violins hold a persistent high F. Then gently the strings lead back to the lyric mood of the first statement of the theme, and a long *diminuendo* brings the movement to a quiet close.

Scherzo

To a steady tapping of A in the kettledrums, the flutes and clarinets give out the whimsical little theme:

which is answered by *staccato* strings. Urged on by the tapping drums, it passes through several phases, always in the lightest and brightest of harmonic colors, and makes up the main part of the *Scherzo*.

Then the clarinet introduces the lilting theme of the trio section:

and now the low strings replace the drums in tapping out the urgent A.

The first section returns in slightly modified form and with a souvenir of the trio theme in the horns. Then the clarinets give out the first phrase of the main theme, and the harps in a rushing *glissando* sweep up to a thin high tone, the point of the joke, as it were, where the woodwinds join them. But the kettles have the last word:

Romanza

The *Romanza*, as the name implies, is a rather vague romancing on three themes. The first, a sentimental melody for the oboe:

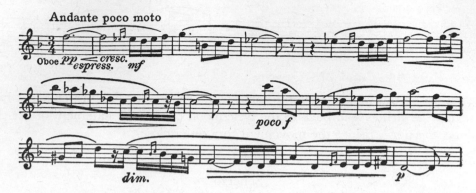

to an accompaniment of plucked strings.   It is later repeated by solo 'cello.

The second theme is a plaintive little tune for English horn:

which is rather rudely interrupted by the third, a florid melody introduced by solo violin:

and taken up, canon-fashion, by the solo viola and 'cello.

Fragments of all three themes in curious faded harmonies make up the last part of the *Romanza*, which seems to wander off into a dream.

Rondo

The last movement of the suite is a rondo with a vivacious little march as its basic theme:

A *forte* chord for full orchestra precedes the second subject:

Then, after a swift descent in the woodwinds, the first theme comes 'round again in proper rondo-fashion.

Here the flute interrupts with an impish, Till Eulenspiegelish figure:

snatched from the second measure of the main theme. Various instruments take it up and play with it until the strings, as if to put an end to such nonsense, lead into a swinging melody for bassoons, violins, and violas:

And now, instead of returning to the main theme, the composer merely suggests it before passing on to a brilliant new tune in which the whole orchestra joins. There is something about this melody:

and about the arrogant rhythm:

even if one did not hear the click of castanets, that suggests Spain. It is as if a Spanish gypsy had wandered over the border and mingled his tunes with those of his Hungarian brothers.

As the movement continues, phrases of familiar melodies are heard, and then a last appearance of the main theme, the little march tune, fulfilling the classical rondo requirement of a basic theme repeated at least three times. It works up to what promises to be a vigorous and consistent ending. There is a crash of cymbals, a moment of suspense, and then instead of the expected coda, comes a surprising and effective curtain call of the plaintive theme with which the suite opened:

As it dies away, the deferred coda takes its place and brings the suite to a swift and brilliant ending.

VARIATIONS ON A NURSERY TUNE — FOR ORCHESTRA AND PIANO, OPUS 25

An old French nursery song, "Ah! vous dirai-je, maman," gave Dohnányi the theme for this clever set of variations. It is as simple a theme as one could imagine and for that reason simply perfect for variation. Mozart, in 1778, wrote variations on it for piano and to this day is sometimes honored as the originator of the tune! It is also one of those tunes which the whole world knows. French *enfants* sing it as, "I will tell you, Mama dear"; German *Kinder* call it "The Question"; English and American children know it as the "Alphabet Song," and no doubt it has made its guileless way into many other countries. It is probably this sense of familiarity, of having come across a forgotten childish possession — a surviving tin soldier or treasured picture card — that amuses and touches an audience on hearing Dohnányi's "Variations on a Nursery Tune."

It begins with fifty sonorous measures *maestoso* for orchestra, with no hint of the theme. The meaning of this stern and oppressive introduction seems to be interpreted by the words of the little song:

Ah! vous dirai-je, maman, I will tell you, Mama dear,
 Ce qui cause mon tourment!   Why I sit a-crying here,
Papa veut que je raisonne Papa seems to think I can
 Comme une grande personne;   Reason like a grown-up man,
Moi, je dis que les bonbons But good candy, any day,
 Valent mieux que la raison.   Is worth more than sums, I say!
         — *Trans. by* L. L. B.

There it all is — the tyranny of *Papa*, who expects little son to reason like a grown-up man; the despair of the small reasoner, who thinks that bonbons are worth far more than reasoning; and the appeal to *Maman*, who might be moved to offer just such sweet consolation!

In admirably absurd contrast to this top-heavy introduction comes the tinkling theme, given out by the solo piano:[1]

[1] Excerpts printed by permission of Associated Music Publishers, Inc., New York, owners of the copyright.

But even in this bare statement, one has a suspicion in the second phrase that things may not remain as simple as they seem:

and with the first variation, one is sure of it!

Variation I.   Here the theme is carried on by *pizzicato* strings while the solo piano, in broken triplet figures, weaves a sparkling net around it.

Variation II.   In resolute 4/4 time, the horns give out the motif:

to which a jaunty — almost impudent — answer is made by the piano, flutes, and clarinets.   The whole variation is a dialogue with a suggestion of argument between the moods of work and play.

Variation III.   The theme is here transformed into lovely flowing phrases for unison strings:

to which the piano replies antiphonally:

Variation IV.   This variation is really a brisk dialogue between the highest and lowest woodwinds, with the piano supplying an accompaniment of *staccato* chords.

Variation V.   Reminiscent of another childish treasure, the music box, is this whimsical little variation in which the glockenspiel plays the nursery tune, first in major and then in minor, with harp and piano suggesting the rhythmical, murmuring mechanism.

Variation VI.   The same lightness characterizes this variation in which piano, woodwinds, and brasses weave in and out against a background of plucked strings, like children in a game of tag.

Variation VII.   Here the little theme undergoes a Johann Strauss transformation and becomes for a moment a Viennese waltz.   The piano leads off, followed by violins.   It is a lovely waltz but — and just as we are about to say that it bears no relationship to "Ah! vous dirai-je, maman," the strings are heard picking out the little tune in 2/4 time as accompaniment to the waltz!

Variation VIII. Before the waltz ends we hear the drums which lead into the next variation, a sturdy march. The horns bring in the second phrase of the song where Papa unjustly demands grown-up reasoning. They bring it in in doleful minor, and, well, one could scarcely call this a cheerful tune!

Variation IX. Variation IX is a boisterous *scherzo* in which a mocking derivation of the theme:

given out by the bassoon, becomes the jest of the xylophone, glockenspiel, and piccolo.

Variation X. After an eight-measure interlude in which the music seems to compose itself into a more decorous mien, the low brasses and reeds announce the theme in the slow and stately form of a *passacaglia:*

Nowhere does Dohnányi display the adaptability of the theme or his own cleverness to better advantage than when he turns the naïve nursery tune into one of the most dignified and sophisticated of early Italian dances. The strings lighten the gravity with a gracious phrase:

which is taken up and answered by the piano. But all the while, the basic theme goes quietly forward in the low strings. Near the end the *tempo* quickens and an *accelerando* and *crescendo* lead into:

Variation XI, a chorale with solemn theme given out by the brasses and an impressive churchly ending.

Finale fugato. Piano and woodwinds in curiously disjointed scale passages play an introduction, then the violas present the theme which takes its final turn as a lively little fugue, elaborately ornamented by running sixteenth figures in the piano. Suddenly it breaks off, and the nursery theme in its simplest form reappears. But a growl from the contrabassoon recalls the composer to the serious business of proper *finale* for a concert piece, and the end comes with a dash and a flashing *glissando* in the piano.

This delightful set of variations was published in 1922 and was introduced to American audiences in 1924 by the Chicago Symphony Orchestra with Dohnányi himself at the piano.

RURALIA HUNGARICA

Hungarian folk tunes have always attracted composers. Liszt's masterly use of them made him a national hero, and composers from other countries, notably Brahms and Berlioz, have been equally enthusiastic borrowers of these bright, colorful themes. With the growing interest in nationalism which has characterized the music of the twentieth century, we find Hungarian composers, such as Kodály and Bartók, making folk themes and idioms the basis of their work. Dohnányi, however, loyal Hungarian that he is, made in his earlier work no deliberate attempt at musical nationalism.

But with *Ruralia Hungarica*, a set of five pieces for orchestra published in 1925, he joined his countrymen in exploiting the zestful songs and dances of Hungary. *Ruralia Hungarica*, as the name implies, voices the spirit of the Hungarian countryside. One of the most beautiful moments in the suite is the slow movement.

Andante poco moto, rubato

Like the voice of an ancient minstrel, the oboe begins this musical tale of rural Hungary:[1]

and in winding triplets accompanies the solo viola in the opening theme:

This songlike theme is carried on by the 'celli:

while woodwinds and horns continue the triplet figures. The suggestion of a leisurely and rather aimless old ballad is heightened by the rhythm which wanders between 4/4, 3/4, and 5/4.

[1] Excerpts printed by permission of Associated Music Publishers, Inc., New York, owners of the copyright.

The mood of the music brightens as the clarinet introduces a major theme:

which is taken up and amplified by the horns and other woodwinds.

Then comes a section marked *rubato*, in which the first song theme is treated in true Hungarian gypsy style. Here the singer abandons all musical patterns and precedent and follows only his own vagrant fancy. After this brief outburst the oboes bring the theme back to the mood of the beginning, and the movement ends in a dreamy quiet.

CHAPTER V

Bohemia Greets You

"Great Sir, Bohemia greets you." — *A Winter's Tale*

"The only way to draw a map of Europe from memory is to begin with a lozenge in the middle and label it Bohemia." True enough, but although it has been lying right there in the middle since ever maps began, for many people Bohemia has remained almost as mythical a country as she was in the days when Shakespeare, by a generous stretch of poetic license, spoke of the "coast of Bohemia," giving this inland country the one thing she never can have! Today we must look for this old country under a new name, for, after World War I, Bohemia, Moravia, part of Silesia, Slovakia, and some of Ruthenia — all except the last a part of the ancient Czech kingdom — became the Republic of Czechoslovakia.

In the Middle Ages, Bohemia, because of her central position, was very well known. Until the fifteenth century all the main trade routes passed through Prague, making it a great and busy city. Then the Bohemians, ever in advance of the times, demanded certain reforms in the church and began a search for truth and freedom of conscience which ended in their being the first nation to embrace Protestantism.

Bohemia, however, continued her pioneering not only in modern ideas of freedom of conscience, but also in democracy and education. In an age when the world was trusting might to make right, Bohemia was discovering that "knowledge is power." The University of Prague, founded in 1348, was the first of the universities of central Europe. The great Komensky, known to us as Comenius, was the first since Plato to stress the spiritual values of education and to declare that the schools should be "the workshops of humanity." Incidentally, his "Orbis Pictus" (1658) was the first picture book ever made for a child.

There would doubtless have been equally splendid beginnings in art, literature, and music. But the early seventeenth century, the period when other nations were laying the foundations of their art life, found Bohemia in the thick of a fanatical religious war. The flower of her young manhood was sacrificed, thousands of her best families were sent into exile, her treasuries were drained, and her independence lost. For more than three hundred years Bohemia was a subject state, a part of the Austrian Empire. The Hapsburgs, who were nothing if not thorough, saw to it that this subjection was social and cultural as well as political. German language, German education, German art and music ruled Bohemia with a heavy hand. Not until 1861 when Austria, alarmed by the breaking away of the Italian provinces, decided to give her other subject states more liberty, did Bohemia begin to have an art life of her own. And not until the autumn of 1918, when the ancient empire of the Hapsburgs was dismembered, did Bohemia gain her freedom.

But all through the dark years the spirit of Bohemia burned with a clear and steady flame, sustained by the knowledge that, although a stronger army might confiscate property and take away political freedom, no outside power could destroy the national independence and the spiritual heritage of a people. The love and loyalty which they were forbidden to show grew into an idealistic patriotism, far stronger and finer than any flag-waving, speech-making brand. And when at last the spirit of Bohemia found musical expression, there was no bitterness, no lamentation, but the most joyous music in the world.

It is typical of the fine tolerance of the Bohemians and worthy of notice that, after three centuries of longing for freedom, when Czechoslovakian independence was proclaimed, no acts of violence or revenge were committed against the Germans; and that a Bohemian scholar and patriot could say, "The German influence had many advantages for our development. It taught us to be thrifty and industrious and made us efficient in science and organization; it made us less emotional and more rational than the other Slavs."

The Czechs are Slavs, and, like the Russians, energetic, courageous, sensitive, and artistic, and here the likeness ends. They have none of the Russian melancholy, born of life under merciless conditions in a vast and wintry land. Bohemia's subjection, stifling as it was to national expression and marked with tragic incidents, was a civilized affair compared with the corruption and cruelty that shadowed the Russian people under the Tsars. And whatever the man-made hardships, there was that never-failing source of Czech joyousness, a beautiful, fertile country where Nature, at least, was kind.

But the outstanding difference between the Czechs and their Russian brothers is the difference between East and West. Centuries of intimate contact have tinged Russian life and art with the mystery, the fatalism, the barbaric splendor, and the too heavy perfumes of the Orient. Of all this the Czechs show not a trace. They are Westerners, and though more impulsive and emotional, they share with their Teutonic neighbors a sound philosophical outlook on life and with the English a belief in justice, peace, and fair play. The colors they love are Nature's own, sunflowers, geraniums, blue cornflowers, and daisies, all in a merry, garish bunch. The perfumes they love are those of hayfields and pine forests.

The Bohemians have always been a music-loving people. Early medieval chronicles describe them as "much given to singing and dancing." Although denounced by the stricter religious sects and discouraged by the Hapsburg rulers, this singing and dancing persisted, and even as late as the last century, Dvořák found over forty different kinds of folk dances, the most popular of which, the *polka*, *furiant*, and *dumka*, he raised to symphonic rank. The old saying, "You cannot separate a Slovak from his songs," is equally true of all the Czechs. There are dance songs, festival songs, work songs, songs for weddings and funerals; there are epic songs dealing with heroes of history and legend and lyric songs ringing every change on the love theme — a rich and beautiful musical inheritance.

Generally speaking, the folk songs of Bohemia are the most simple, those of Slovakia, the most ancient and complex, while those of Moravia stand between the two, but all share certain distinguishing Czech characteristics. Many of them are written in major mode. When they do drop into the minor, they are only mildly melancholy, seldom wailing or sentimental. Words seem to be of secondary importance in the Czech songs, which are much more instrumental in character than the folk songs of Italy, Germany, or France. The vigorous rhythms are those of the dance, rather than of poetry, and the interesting harmonies show the influence of fiddle, clarinet, and bagpipe, which have always played an important part in Czech life.

But the unique characteristic of Czech folk music is the reflection of the Czech spirit of joyousness. It is something quite different from the rather naïve merriment of the German, the temperamental gaiety of the Italian, or the reckless mirth of the Russian folk. Czech joyousness seems to well up from some underlying faith in life itself. It was this spirit, singing and dancing in her folk tunes, that gave continuity to the history of Bohemian music through the long wait for the chapter headed "Art Music"; this spirit, that inspired and vitalized the work of Smetana and Dvořák during the years of Bohemia's renaissance; and it is this spirit which, like a lodestar above uncharted seas, gives shining promise of Bohemia's musical future.

FREDERICK SMETANA

Leitomischl — 1824
Prague   — 1884

Bedrich (Frederick) Smetana, called by his countrymen, the father of Bohemian music, came of a sturdy line of industrious, music-loving tradesmen. His father must have been an unusual fellow, for at nineteen he decided to have an education, went back to school, and not only retrieved his neglected three R's, but also learned to play the violin fairly well. Then he took a wife and decided to earn his living by brewing the ales for which Bohemia is famous. For several years he followed his trade from one village to another, sharing the up-and-down fortunes of a country harassed by Napoleon's armies.

One of Brewer Smetana's fondest ambitions was to have a son. He had, instead, an unbroken procession of little daughters, six of them. Then, one day in the spring of 1824, a servant girl ran to him with the good news that his seventh child was a boy. He seized her 'round the waist, and they went whirling about the brewery yard in a galloping dance of celebration, and thus began the story of a sunny childhood.

Little Bedrich soon began to show that he, too, shared the family love of music. When he was barely five, his father placed a small fiddle in his hands. The instrument so fascinated him that he would not put it down and clung to the bow for hours. At first he did not like the piano. "My father pulled my ears and let me do penance on my knees," he says, "and then I went to my first music lesson." But when the precocious five-year-old began to make pieces of his own, he found the piano a most convenient instrument upon which to try them and liked it well enough. His teacher wrote down some of these early compositions, and two of them are still preserved.

Bedrich made his first public appearance at the age of six and a half, playing a piano solo at a celebration in honor of the Emperor's name day. From the beginning Smetana lived his music heart and soul. The audience was delighted with the clever, smiling child who played with such real feeling. He soon became a famous little figure in the castle concert rooms where everyone petted him and predicted a great future.

When the boy was seven years old the family moved to southern Bohemia. Here Bedrich completed grammar school and entered the *Gymnasium* or high school. Then, because it was necessary for a Bohemian boy to speak German, Bohemia being under Austrian rule, Bedrich and his brother were sent across the border to a German town to learn the language. "We wept for three days and nights," writes Smetana, and after a few months the father transferred them to another town and school. But young Bedrich yearned for bigger things, and at the end of three years persuaded his father to let him go to Prague.

It had been decided that he was to become a lawyer, and he dutifully began his preparation. But the musical fare of Prague was too tempting, and young Smetana was music hungry, for, although he had kept up his study and been fortunate in having good teachers of violin, organ, and singing, he had never had a chance to hear much music. Now, in spite of the handicap of little time and less money, he managed to satisfy his hunger at the opera and in concert halls. He was particularly fond of chamber music and, with some of his fellow students, organized a string quartet. Since none of the young players had money, score buying was a problem. This was solved by Smetana's marvelous music memory. He could carry away whole compositions almost note for note after a single hearing. So the boys would pool their pennies and send him to the Zofin Island military band concerts where, for a very little, one might hear Beethoven symphonies, Mendelssohn overtures, and, now and then, some of the new music, such as a piece by Berlioz. Smetana would listen intently, then hurry home and jot down what he had heard, and the next evening the quartet, well pleased with its investment, would be trying out a new score! What made this feat all the more remarkable was the fact that Smetana had as yet no systematic musical education, no knowledge of harmony or composition to help him grasp the design and the meaning of large works. This was pure talent gleaming like a vein of gold uncovered by nature itself. Smetana further augmented the quartet's library with scores of his own, for he had never given up his early habit of tune making.

But, alas, the brighter shone the music, the deeper fell the shadow on his school work. Then one day a rude professor mimicked Smetana's broad German accent, and the laughter of the class so hurt the boy that he would have nothing more to do with the school. Shortly afterward, Smetana senior came up to Prague to see how son was getting on, was properly shocked at what he found, and promptly took the young man home, saying that, if he would not be a lawyer, he could now turn farmer! It was a sadly chastened composer who tossed hay in his father's fields that summer.

But in the early autumn a visiting cousin who was a professor in the *Gymnasium* at Pilsen talked the father into letting him take Bedrich back with him. He found the boy a room in a cloister where several of the professors lived. Here for three years young Smetana led a most exemplary life attending classes, then hastening back to his room before six in the evening when the cloister gates closed. His one diversion was his music. Smetana was always a delightful pianist. His housemates loved to hear him play, and often the professors would take him with them when they were visiting in the town.

Smetana finished school to his father's satisfaction, but he wanted more than ever to make music his profession. The father would not hear of it. He was proud of the boy's playing and had always encouraged it, but he considered music an amusement and no sort of career for his precious son. The Smetana determination met in what seemed to be a hopeless deadlock. But again the professor cousin came to the rescue. He recognized the boy's unusual gift and the seriousness of his devotion to music, and finally won the father's consent to let him try a year or so in Prague.

So with high heart and about eight dollars in his pocket Bedrich Smetana, aged nineteen, returned to Prague. This time his father's consent had no financial accompaniment. Young Smetana was to support himself, and this he set about doing by giving piano lessons. Too many other students seemed to be doing the same thing, and Smetana succeeded in earning barely enough for one meal a day. There were months of hunger and loneliness, but never a complaint nor the bitterness of self-pity. Hardship always seemed to make Smetana just a little more gentle, more sympathetic with struggling men and women about him. Fortunately he had a few faithful friends who helped him gain admission to a good music school where he began his first study of the science of music. Another friend introduced him to the Society of Artists, and here he met the president of the Conservatory. This man became interested in Smetana and recommended him for the position of music teacher in a nobleman's family. During the winter he taught the count's children at their town house and kept up his own study at the school. In the summer he would go with the family into the country and there work out the problems set by his professors. Four years of this saw him through music school.

At twenty-three Smetana stepped out into the world with very definite plans. He would go abroad on a concert tour, then return to Prague, start a music school of his own, organize an orchestra, and get married. The concert tour, made in troubled revolutionary times, was none too successful, but the marriage was a triumph. From his boyhood Smetana had loved a brown-eyed Katharina who lived next door. The two had kept up their friendship, meeting at holidays, and when later he went to Prague to study and found her a student in the same music school, it seemed as if the Fates were indeed taking a hand in their affairs. Katharina was a clever and ambitious musician, and during their student days she held Smetana to her ideals as well as his own. She was tremendously interested in him, but for a long time all the love-making was on his side. When he finally did win her, it was as if he had won another professional honor, a degree of music *cum amore*.

As for his music school and orchestra, they were slow growing, thanks to the political conditions of the country. For more than three hundred years Bohemia had been subject to Austria not only politically but also culturally. The Austrians, knowing that nothing vitalizes a people more than the expression of their national spirit in music, painting, and literature, had carefully suppressed all such expression. The Bohemians, forbidden an art life of their own, became so resentful toward all things Austrian that they could scarcely enjoy even the beauty of music created under Hapsburg rule, and fell into a state of hopeless indifference. With the revolution of 1848 came an intoxicating breath of freedom, but it was followed by a period of reaction which was even gloomier than before. Smetana resisted with all his might, and through his music school, his concerts, and his own compositions tried to keep alive the interest in music and lay foundations for the truly Bohemian art of which he dreamed. It was during this heavy-hearted time that he composed those first polkas, so full of joy and freshness.

For all the discouragement at home, Smetana was not without inspiration from abroad. As a student he had set up three musical heroes: Beethoven, whose joyousness and challenge to life he worshipped; Schumann, who as the poet of youth seemed intimately near to him; and Chopin, with whom he shared not only Slavic blood and a passionate patriotism, but also a tender and refined spirit. Chopin, Smetana loved!

But these three who influenced Smetana so deeply were known to him only through their music. Two living heroes were to appear, and just when he needed them most. In 1846, Berlioz came to Prague on a concert tour and presented, among other things, his *Symphonie fantastique*. To Smetana this bold, fiery music seemed an expression of the awakening life of the European nations. It was like a powerful pick-me-up to an exhausted traveler.

That same year brought an even more famous visitor, Franz Liszt, the moving spirit of the later Romanticists. Smetana was fascinated by Liszt's playing and learned a great deal from it. He dedicated his Opus I, Six Dances for Piano, to the master pianist, and Liszt, with his characteristic generosity, asked to hear the young composer's works and gave him criticism and encouragement as no one else had done.

From the early days of this friendship comes an amusing story. Liszt asked Smetana just how his name should be pronounced. Calling Beethoven to his aid, Smetana replied:

My name is always:

but never:

In 1856, Smetana was offered the position of director of the Philharmonic Society of Gothenburg, Sweden, and accepted it, hoping for a respite from the depressing life in Prague. Mere freedom, however, was not enough for this ardent Bohemian, and pleasant as the four Swedish years were, they provided little inspiration. But during this time Smetana was invited to spend a summer with Liszt. Weimar was then the Mecca of musicians, and eager young artists from all over Europe were flocking there to study with Liszt and to join in the fight for a new and freer art. All this enthusiasm and freshness of view went to Smetana's head. It was as if his most extravagant dreams had suddenly become a reality.

Two of the Weimar ideas particularly intrigued him. First, that of the symphonic poem in which the music takes both its ideas and form from some episode in life or literature. To Smetana this seemed the answer to the haunting question, "How can we bring music in closer touch with life and with the thought currents of the age?"

He was also moved by Liszt's plea for modern comic opera. By *modern* comic opera, Liszt had in mind something quite different from the old *opera-buffa*, which simply burlesqued and ridiculed. He wanted a true picture of the sunny side of life, not a caricature. He pointed out to his pupils the fact that life is just as full of comic situations as of tragic ones, and that this happy humor is also worthy of the artist's talents. He urged the young artists to try to solve the problem of musical comedy as artistically as Wagner had solved that of musical tragedy. This idea of opera based on the warm, humorous side of life took root in Smetana's mind and later bore delicious fruit.

Full of enthusiasm, Smetana went back to Gothenburg and wrote three splendid symphonic poems of his own. Then came the real turning point in his career. Italy, which had also worn the Austrian yoke, rose in revolt and became a free nation. Stunned by the loss of the rich Italian provinces, Austria decided to avert further disasters by establishing some sort of representative government in the rest of her variegated empire. Although real independence did not come to the Czech peoples until after World War I, the blight of Hapsburg absolutism was lessened, and with the other subject nations the Czechs enjoyed a freedom they had not known for centuries. A great stirring began in the political, social, and artistic life of Bohemia, and Smetana hastened back to Prague to take part in it.

He was full of plans for creating a new musical life in Bohemia. It was no little task, for while the government at Vienna had lifted the ban on Bohemian art, it would provide no funds for any nationalistic projects. Nearly all the art institutions, the schools, theaters, opera, etc., were still in German hands. But Smetana was dauntless in his efforts, and within a surprisingly short time there rose a temporary theater, tiny, but all Czech. A Czech song festival was organized from the two hundred and more Czech choral societies which had mushroomed up overnight; there were the beginnings of Czech opera and of the now famous Czech Philharmonic Society; and best of all, there was the first flowering of original Czech art music.

It was in this field of original Bohemian music that Smetana made his most unique and permanent contribution. He had very definite and different ideas about nationalism in music. He was not at all satisfied with mere local color. "By the imitation of the melodies and rhythms of our folk songs no national style will be formed, but at most, a weak imitation of the folk songs themselves," he said. He felt that Bohemian art music should be something far greater than "forgery," as he used to call it, of Bohemian folk music. In their tone poems, operas, symphonies, chamber music, Bohemian composers should seek, first of all, to express the *spirit* of Bohemia, the special characteristics of the Czech people.

Chief among these characteristics is a joyousness which even centuries of oppression could not destroy. Nineteenth-century music had not been conspicuously joyful. The Romantic composers were much more given to sighs than smiles; and the nationalists, the wistful Scandinavians and the somber Russians, had sung in a persistent minor, enlivened by occasional outbursts of rather violent peasant merriment. In contrast, the sunny Czech humor seemed almost an affront to Romantic tradition!

And how strange a phenomenon is the public's taste for melancholy music! The lamentation of the despairing lover, the musings of the pessimist, or even the hysteria of the hypochondriac seldom fails to find an answering echo in the heart of an audience. And although a stirring rhythm or a bit of clowning is relished now and then, sheer joyousness, such as Smetana's, which should be accepted as a precious gift, is apt to be regarded as trivial by the high-brow and tame by the low!

Though Smetana determined not to limit his music by a narrow use of folk themes and idiom, he was a thorough nationalist in his choice of subjects. His operas take their stories from Bohemian legends and from village life; his tone poems are pictures of Bohemia's beautiful rivers, fields, and forests, its ancient castles and folk festivals; and his piano pieces glorify the characteristic Bohemian dances, the *polka* and the *furiant*.

As the years passed the number and variety of Smetana's activities became almost incredible. He took over the conductorship of the Czech opera and made it a first-class training school for orchestra and singing students. He organized the first Czech subscription concerts, became choirmaster of the largest choral group, and helped found a society in which workers in all the arts might come together. He even served as critic, hoping through his writing about music to educate both artists and public.

Czech music could not have had a better leader. Smetana's contagious enthusiasm soon set other and younger men to work. His musical knowledge and sound judgment held all their projects level, and his charming personality kept everybody reasonably happy through the difficult days of pioneering. From all accounts he must have been a delightful person, for he combined the mind of a scholar, the heart of a poet, the buoyant, out-of-doors joyousness of a Czech peasant with the less conspicuous virtues of a thoroughly fine man.

But Smetana's season of happy activity was to be all too short. Early in the year 1874, his fiftieth year, he began to hear tones differently in each ear, then a persistent high tone, and then suddenly, one night in October, he heard nothing at all. It was the bitterest misfortune that could have overtaken a musician. Yet not even total deafness could kill Smetana's joy in life and work. In those first tragically silent days he set to work on his great cycle, "My Country," and within a month had finished the score of *Vysehrad* — The Castle, and *Vltava* — The River.

Smetana's music now became more personal. In this strange new world his thoughts seemed to turn inward. He liked to recall the past, his childhood, pictures of home and of the happy days with Katharina and the little daughter, both long dead. His beautiful string quartets, "From My Life" and "From Home" are expressions of these memories.

But the strain of making music in a soundless world was too great even for Smetana's shining spirit. Shortly after his sixtieth birthday his mind became so disturbed that he was taken to an institution for the insane, and in that gloomiest of places this joyous musician died.

To his countrymen Smetana gave music so alive with Czech spirit that even hearing it was for them self-expression. He was their spokesman to such a degree that at times Austrian authorities suspected Smetana's music of "high treason" — but fortunately could do nothing about it, since even the most vigilant censor is helpless before mere tones!

To the musical world Smetana gave a broader idea of nationalism. His compositions are not puppets dressed in picturesque folk costumes. They are real and they live by reason of their sincerity and their purely musical beauty. And to listeners everywhere this warmhearted Czech gives a joyous zest for life.

Nejedly, his compatriot, speaking of Smetana's art says, "Nothing weakens the life-vigor of a man so much as sadness, and nothing strengthens him so much as joy. Hence, being the most immediate product of this attitude toward life, art can never live merely by pessimism, skepticism, and sadness. This is why mankind has always considered its special benefactors to be the artists who have been able to infuse gladness into human souls, and therefore, joy in life for its own sake."

OVERTURE TO THE BARTERED BRIDE

The Bartered Bride is the second of Smetana's eight operas. Written during those first years of awakening nationalism, it fairly glows with youthful enthusiasm, and is the gayest as well as the most Bohemian of all his works. True to his conviction that a composer should seek first of all to express the spirit of his country, Smetana based his opera on the characteristic joyousness of the Czech people. For this joyousness he did not look to the cities, which for centuries had borne the brunt of Austrian oppression, but to the country where, in spite of everything, life had remained entirely Czech.

True to the Liszt idea of modern musical comedy, Smetana determined to make *The Bartered Bride* a serious work of art and at the same time gay and amusing. He meant to present a true picture of rural Bohemia and not a caricature. In the folk opera of other countries, the countryman is usually shown as a stupid bumpkin and a laughingstock for the audience. But in Czech art, quite to the contrary, the country people are looked upon as the very backbone of the nation. It is more often the peasant who makes fun of the townsman for having become a fop and a *poseur*. Only too often, when translated and transplanted to the stage of other countries, *The Bartered Bride* is made slapstick comedy and its characters mere rustic clowns. Such misinterpretation is really tragic, for it completely destroys the rare quality of Smetana's humor, in which humanity and heartiness mingle with refinement.

The Bartered Bride is a slight opera, planned on a simple scale, but it is perfect in its proportions and in the way in which the music fits the story, the characters, and the stage doings. There is little action, the characters tell the story, and the humor, centering around the old Czech custom of employing a professional matchmaker, is in the situation rather than in dialogue or pantomime.

The opera begins with a Bohemian village festival. Marenka, a pretty peasant girl, is upset because the marriage broker is arranging a match between herself and Vasek, son of the rich peasant Micha. Vasek is anything but a promising bridegroom. He is stupid, shy, and stammering. This last defect Smetana treats comically by making Vasek stammer always a beat behind in the measure whenever he sings. And beside the fact that Marenka thinks Vasek next door to a fool, she already has a lover, Jenik, whom she dares not openly acknowledge because he appears to be just a wandering fellow with neither trade nor family to recommend him, and she knows what her parents would say to such a match.

The wily marriage broker, suspecting the state of affairs and eager to get Jenik out of the running, tries to persuade him to sell his "claim" on Marenka's affections. When Jenik learns to whom he is to sell his claim, he agrees and signs the document giving Marenka "to the son of Micha." Marenka, properly furious at having been bartered in such fashion, gives Jenik a piece of her mind and threatens to marry Vasek out of pique.

Jenik then tells her that she is more his than ever, by law and a signed document, for he, too, is "the son of Micha," the *eldest* son, who having left home years before had been lost to his family. Meanwhile Vasek, who was really afraid of Marenka and never had wanted to marry her, has fallen in love with a gypsy dancer from a troupe of strolling players. And so the story ends happily for the lovers, if not so successfully for the marriage broker!

The overture to *The Bartered Bride* is of the old-fashioned type which not only forecasts the mood but does it by using the chief themes of the opera. After a vivacious introduction, a sort of "Hear ye!" from the whole orchestra:

the violins announce an energetic theme:

which is taken up by violas, 'celli, and basses in fugal fashion until the whole string section is humming and buzzing with an activity which suggests the merry crowds milling about at the village festival.

This theme leads into one associated with the marriage contract:

a hearty theme as full of satisfaction as if the marriage were already an accomplished fact.

But soon through the noise of the crowd the woodwinds introduce Marenka, in whose theme there is a plaintive suggestion that this marriage business is not so smooth as it seems:

She is interrupted by a joyous melody:

accompanied by a woodwind version of the marriage contract theme, and then the overture turns back to the beginning. Nothing particularly new in the way of themes follows, but the clever orchestration, the colorful harmonies, and the ever-increasing liveliness keep the music interesting. At the last note there is almost a feeling of disappointment that we are not to see the curtain rise, as it does in the performance, upon that Czech fair with its intriguing booths and kaleidoscopic crowds and hear the wholesome folk philosophy of that rousing opening chorus, "Why should we not rejoice when God gives us good health?"

VLTAVA — THE RIVER

In his magnificent work, "My Country," Smetana has shown us nationalism at its best. The proud patriot speaks even in the title, and the music itself is one long celebration of the beauty and glory of Bohemia. But Smetana was too ambitious for Bohemian music to be content with mere musical Bohemianism. He dreamed of a Czech music which would be valued not for its picturesque charm but for those enduring and purely musical beauties which have nothing to do with either time or place. And so, with no fear of losing his Czech inheritance, he studied the works of the great masters and made himself a man of the musical world. For Smetana, nationalism was always a starting point, not a stopping place. He set out to create the best possible music, and because he was both a sincere artist and an ardent patriot, that music became, inevitably, the best possible Bohemian music.

"My Country" is a cycle of six symphonic poems beginning with *Vysehrad*, picturing that ancient citadel at Prague which seems to symbolize the glorious Czech past. Then comes *Vltava* (The Moldau), in which the poet follows the course of the river from its source in the Sumava forest to Prague, where it widens into a majestic stream. *Sarka*, the third poem, recalls the legend of Sarka, the wildest and loveliest of the Bohemian Amazons. *From Bohemian Fields and Groves* is a joyous pastoral inspired by the beautiful Czech countryside. Quite different in mood are the last two poems. *Tabor* honors those famous Hussite fighters who in the dark days of Bohemia's religious wars drove the crusading armies far beyond the frontiers. The Taborites were Smetana's ideal of Czech courage, and he expresses this ideal in valiant music. *Blanik*, which ends the cycle, takes its name from the mountain within whose rocky fastness there sleeps an army of Bohemia's glorious dead, and, says the legend, on the Day of Judgment that shining company will sally forth and lead the Czechs to final victory. At the end of *Blanik*, Smetana brings back the motif of *Vysehrad*, thus linking Bohemia's past and future glory.

"My Country" is a patriot's creed more convincingly stated than if Smetana had said, "I love my country for her natural beauties and the spirit of her people. I glory in her past, dedicate heart and hand to her present, and declare my faith in her future!" For these are but words, while the music gives the *feeling* of tenderness, courage, and triumph.

These tone poems do more than satisfy the listener's love of the picturesque and the artist's demand for musical values. They convince. Their almost compelling sincerity is doubtless due to the fact that Smetana does not depend upon some other man's poems for the background of his music. "My Country" pictures scenes and events which belong to Smetana as a Czech. He creates his own poems, using tones instead of words, and this is perhaps why they are among the most musical as well as the most convincing of all program works.

On the cover page of each score, the composer gives a brief program, doubtless in deference to us "outlanders," since surely no Czech would need one! This is his preface to *Vltava:*

> In the shadows of the Bohemian forests two springs arise, the one, warm and bubbling, the other, cool and quiet. Trickling down the rocks they unite and chatter gaily together in the morning sunlight. Soon this hurrying brook becomes a little river which, flowing farther and farther through the land of the Czechs, swells to a mighty stream, the Vltava. It passes through deep forests where the sound of the chase and the huntsman's horn rings clear; it glides through rich meadows and lowlands where with noisy song and dance a peasant wedding is being celebrated. At night, nymphs and naiads play in its moonlit waters. Its gleaming surface mirrors many a grim old castle, mute witness of the days of knighthood and the glorious deeds of vanished warriors. At St. John's Rapids the stream bursts through rocky walls in a wild cataract and goes foaming on its way. Then, broadening out, it flows past Prague where it is welcomed by the ancient fortress, Vysehrad, and then sweeps splendidly into the far distance beyond the poet's eye.
>
> *Translation* — L. L. B.

A single flute accompanied by scattered, spray-like notes from the harp and violins, introduces the first, the bubbling spring:

The second spring, the cool, quiet one, joins it:

and flute and clarinet ripple along together in delightful fashion.   Smetana loved the clarinet, "the national instrument of Bohemia," and used it effectively and constantly.

Soon the hurrying brooklet broadens with a wavelike figure in the strings and deepens with a long soft horn tone until it becomes the river Vltava.   And now above the rippling water we hear the song of the river:

a simple, happy song voicing the beauty and contentment of the land of the Czechs.

It passes through the deep forest, where a clear call:

the rhythm of galloping hoofs:

and the winding horn:

suggest the hunt.

Then, leaving the huntsmen far behind, it glides into rich farmlands and we hear the merry sounds of a village wedding.   It is a gay dance tune they are playing:

with clever orchestral suggestions of a country fiddler, energetically scraping, and of wheezing bagpipes and the clump, clump of heavy peasant boots.

The scene changes. Twilight falls in dim woodwind harmonies. The river sparkles in the moonlight, and a high, sweet song floats through the night:

as nymphs and naiads trip their wreathing dance.

Then, mingling with the murmur of the stream and the song of the nymphs comes the ghost of martial music:

as some grim old castle with its memories of the days of knighthood is reflected in the water. But this, too, passes, and only the sound of the water breaks the stillness of the night.

On flows the river, singing its happy song, until it reaches the Rapids of St. John. Here, with a wild pounding of brass and woodwinds and eddying, foaming strings, the stream battles with the rocks that would hold it back. Then having forced its way through, the Vltava sings again. It is the old song, heard in the beginning but now transformed by major harmonies and lilting rhythm into a hymn of victory.

Now at its widest part it flows past the ancient fortress and we hear the motif of the *Vysehrad*, symbol of Bohemia's glorious past:

With increasing strength the great river sweeps jubilantly on and vanishes in the distance "beyond the poet's vision."

What valiant, joyous music it is! And when we remember that it was written in those first tragically silent months of sudden, total deafness, then, indeed, "My Country" becomes not only a magnificent cycle of symphonic poems but an even more magnificent monument of human courage worthy of a place beside the Milton sonnet "On His Blindness" and the Beethoven Ninth Symphony.

ANTONIN DVOŘÁK

Nelahozevec — 1841
Prague   — 1904

In a dip of low hills sloping down to the river Vltava (the Moldau) lies a tiny village guarded by an old square castle. But this guardian sleeps as it has slept for centuries with only dim memories of wars and alarms, for Nelahozevec is the most peaceful place imaginable. A single street makes its leisurely way between low white cottages and, as it nears the river, puts out a lane toward the church. This same lane passes an arched gateway opening on a narrow courtyard over which presides an old two-story inn, surrounded by its satellite storehouses and stables, all of them white walled and red roofed in tidy Bohemian fashion.

Although no one ever heard of any great rush of travelers to sleepy little Nelahozevec, the inn was in the old days the liveliest spot in the village. Here, in the morning, flocked the housewives to bargain for the dinner roast, joint, or soupbone, for the inn-keeper was also the local butcher. Here, in the late afternoon and evening, crowds gathered to exchange the ever intriguing bits of village gossip with an occasional item from Vienna or even that far-off America whither so many of their young Linkas and Karels had gone adventuring. Here, under the great walnut tree in summer, or before a roaring taproom fire in winter, a welcome band of strolling musicians would sometimes ply their trade; or the innkeeper himself, young Frantisek Dvořák, would fetch his zither and set his guests to singing the rollicking old folk songs or one of the new national hymns. And here, more than a century ago, was born Frantisek's eldest son and Bohemia's greatest composer, Antonin Dvořák.

For sturdy little Antonin there were the upland woods and pastures where the village children played, the river where the long timber rafts went floating past, and there was always home, the inn, where just anything might happen — it was a spicy life for a small boy. Best of all Antonin liked the music, the times when his father played or when the strangers with the pipes and fiddles came. And how he loved the holiday times when the street was gay with booths and everybody put on his brightest and best and danced the *polka* and *furiant* far into the night. Oh, those were the times when a boy was lucky to be living in Nelahozevec, instead of some outlandish place like London, where folk were said to live soberly inside their houses and where a street was just a perilous stream of ugly black and gray traffic!

To Antonin's great delight there was music at school. The schoolmaster was one of the old-fashioned Czech cantors who also served as organist and choirmaster at the church and could play, after a fashion, on almost every instrument. It is an interesting fact that although Bohemia's art music bears so recent a date, her school music seems to rival her folk music as an ancient institution. Long before the teaching of music was even considered in English and American schools, the old Czech cantors were at work in the most out-of-the-way corners of Bohemia. A famous English traveler of long ago records his astonishment at the singing and playing of Bohemian school children. It is not surprising, then, that music-loving Antonin soon read "parts" well enough to be admitted to the church choir. He also learned enough about fiddling to be able to take a proud place beside his father in the little village band.

By the time the boy was twelve years old there was such a bevy of children at the inn that when a childless uncle living in Zlonice, four hours away, wanted to borrow Antonin, his parents let him go. Zlonice was a larger town with better schools and wider opportunities. The headmaster at the school was a more finished musician than Cantor Spitz of Nelahozevec, and with his help Antonin not only advanced in his singing and violin playing but also added organ and the viola, which became his favorite instrument.

It was not long before Antonin's family followed him to Zlonice, the father hoping to better his inn and butcher business. It was a forlorn hope, and in little more than a year Frantisek Dvořák was bankrupt. But he was determined that Antonin should have that finishing touch to a Bohemian boy's education, a year in Germany to learn the language. So he traded sons with a German miller who wanted his boy to learn Bohemian, and over to Kamnitz went Antonin. Here he kept up his music study, and was seized with an ambition to go to Prague and become a professional musician.

But at this his father called a halt. In the first place, as he pointed out, a man had to have real talent to succeed in a musical career, and maybe these schoolmasters had overrated Antonin's gifts. And suppose he had sufficient talent, what chance was there with all the good positions held by Germans? A Bohemian musician either had to go to some other country or content himself with a village cantorship. Besides, he had no money for his son's music study in Prague, and he needed help in the butcher shop. Antonin was strong and willing and would no doubt succeed in the family calling and had better set about it.

Reluctantly young Dvořák returned to Zlonice. But he determined to make one last desperate stand before giving up his dreams. Perhaps if he were to write some music, his father would believe that he really was a genius. So many people could sing and play fairly well, but to compose, to actually conjure up a piece of music out of your own head, surely that was something extraordinary! He therefore concocted an original *polka*, copied the parts, distributed them secretly among the members of the village band, and gave his father a surprise serenade. The effect was overwhelming, and no one was more surprised than young Antonin. He had not known about the transposing instruments, that trumpets, for example, never sound the tones actually written on the score! His band burst forth with hearty good will, woodwinds, strings, and brasses contending furiously in different keys. Needless to say, after a few minutes of excruciating discord in *polka* rhythm, the would-be composer was consigned to the butcher's block! There is something particularly ironical about this, since today the whole world regards Dvořák as one of the supreme masters of instrumentation! Perhaps the shock of this first disaster helped to awaken that wonderful instinct for orchestration which was to make him famous!

For a year Antonin served the housewives of Zlonice, but all the while he clung doggedly to his ambition to go to Prague. He had a powerful ally in schoolmaster Liehmann who grieved to see the best pupil he had ever had consigned to meat cutting. Liehmann persuaded the uncle to help with a little money, convinced the father that

Antonin really had talent, and, since there were now four younger brothers ready for the business, at last gained his consent. So one day in the October of Antonin's sixteenth year, father and son put on their Sunday best and set out for Prague. A neighbor gave them a lift in his hay cart, and eventually they brought up at "The Bee Inn" in Hus Street, where they stopped until Antonin was safely quartered in a cousin's house and entered in the Organ School.

The Organ School was a poor choice as training school for a future orchestral composer, for it naturally concentrated its teaching upon organ playing. Dvořák knew next to nothing of theory and composition and was a complete stranger to the music of the great masters. He had no money for books or for concert tickets. When the little fund his father and uncle had given him was spent, he had no money for food and lodging. It was all pretty dismal, but Dvořák wasted no time in self-pity. Tucking his precious violin under his arm, he went out and joined a band. It was a modest little band playing only popular music in restaurants, but at least it taught him that trumpets are transposing instruments. His fiddling, together with a church job on Sundays, netted him about nine dollars a month!

As a concertgoer, Antonin had to turn tramp and stowaway. He would linger about the stage door until some good-natured player, coming out for a breath or a smoke, would motion to him to slip back stage. Sometimes the kettledrummer would invite him to crouch behind his portly instruments, and from such sorry listening posts Bohemia's future master received his first impressions of the world's great music.

Unsuitable as was the training at the Organ School, Antonin made the most of it, and at the end of three years came out second prizeman with a certificate stating that he was "admirably fitted to fulfill the duties of organist and choirmaster." But the organ had lost all appeal, now that he knew that great living instrument, the orchestra. What could compare with the color of reeds, strings, brass, and — yes — kettledrums! To listen to an orchestra, to play in one, and, better still, to write orchestral music, this was now his heart's desire, and nothing else mattered.

Fortunately for Dvořák and for the world, he arrived at the parting of the ways just as an alluring new road was being opened. Little could František Dvořák have dreamed, when four years earlier he was objecting to a musical career for his son, that by the time Antonin left the Organ School Bohemia's whole artistic outlook would have changed. Yet so it was, for with the gift of liberty, granted in October, 1860, the long-suppressed social and artistic forces of Bohemia sprang to life. The first national newspaper appeared; leaders arose in literature and painting; and Smetana, hurrying home from Sweden, marshaled the forces of Bohemian music for a vigorous and victorious campaign.

Dvořák found a place as viola player in the orchestra of the newly organized Czech National Theater. But it was to be a long time before he made any real contribution to this new national music. He was a silent, reserved fellow with a good deal of the peasant's suspicion of new things and strange people, and he kept within a narrow circle. But the same appealing eagerness which had opened stage doors to the music-hungry country boy in the old days now made valuable friendships for the young artist. Smetana, conducting the theater orchestra, quickly recognized something very worth while in the dark-eyed viola player; Bendl, leader of the chief choral society in Prague, loaned him valuable scores, and a fellow orchestra player, knowing that Dvořák had no piano, invited him to share his rooms and use his instrument. Dvořák accepted the invitation but found, on his arrival, that the instrument was a miserable old spinet standing in a bedroom already occupied by five other persons — his too hospitable host, a medical student, a professional guide, and two other students — Dvořák made the sixth. In this weird barracks poor Dvořák tried to study his precious borrowed scores and produce some of his own. His Symphony in B-Flat is said to have been composed at this time. But the motley company was too much even for his stoic endurance, and he went back to his former lodging place, boldly putting aside two of his eighteen monthly florins for the rental of a tailor's piano.

To those who think that musical genius is a free gift imposing no real labor upon the fortunate possessor, the story of Dvořák's long apprenticeship would be a revelation. For almost twelve years he lived under the most rigid self-discipline. He knew none of the merry times which Schubert, poor as he was, enjoyed with his friends; none of the affection and encouragement which young Brahms received from the Schumanns; none of the romantic adventures or the wild oats of the youthful Wagner — nothing but patient, lonely plodding. Day after day this young man sat contentedly in his meager little room poring over Beethoven, determined to discover the secrets of that matchless style. Every spare penny went for music paper and every spare hour for study or composition. And with a self-control rarely found in a young artist, Dvořák seems to have made no attempt at performance or publication of his early works. Wagner would never have ceased pestering such influential friends as Bendl and Smetana with his raw first fruits. But Dvořák had ideals which made him tear up and burn as diligently as he composed. Having hitched his wagon to a star, no mere spotlight could dazzle him.

At last, in his thirtieth year, Dvořák was commissioned to write an opera for the Czech National Theater. This was the perfect opportunity for an unknown composer to make his bow. Prague was opera crazy — for Smetana, knowing that the theater will attract even a musically illiterate public, had wisely concentrated upon opera as the best means of arousing enthusiasm for the new Bohemian music. And such brilliant leaders as his *Brandenburgers in Bohemia* and *The Bartered Bride* had established not only opera's popularity but also its tradition. Bohemian audiences expected Bohemian opera to be of the tuneful, folk-song type and distinctly national in spirit.

Unfortunately, Dvořák was then passing through the worst stages of Wagner worship. Wagner had just visited Prague, and Dvořák had followed him through the streets to catch a glimpse of "that great little man's face." He marveled at Wagner's scores — what was *The Bartered Bride* with its simple joyousness compared with this Bayreuth magnificence! Thus possessed, he brainlessly wrote his opera, a peasant comedy entitled *King and Collier*, in elaborate Wagnerian style and went confidently down to pass out the parts for rehearsal. Smetana could scarcely believe his eyes as he looked at this imitation *Meistersinger* score. And the orchestra and singers, accustomed to melodies of the tuneful Mozartian type, could scarcely believe their ears as the heavy *recitative* rolled forth. *King and Collier* got no further than that first reading, and its composer remained but an obscure viola played in the orchestra pit.

This disaster, however, brought Dvořák to his artistic senses. He realized that a Slav masquerading as a Teuton only makes himself ridiculous in both countries. Then, as if to atone for his unfaithfulness to the Slavonic muse, he set to music the fine patriotic hymn, *The Heirs of The White Mountain*, a poem already familiar in every Bohemian household. This simple hymn, sincere and splendid, placed Dvořák's name on the list of Bohemian composers.

Some two years later Dvořák was again commissioned to write an opera for the National Theater. The average man, given this second chance, would have shunned like the plague anything connected with that first failure. Dvořák was far from the average man. He took the libretto of the unlucky *King and Collier* and reset it, preserving, it is said, not so much as one bar of the original score! This time the music was good, but, said the critics, "What a pity that the composer should have spent his genius on such a poorly written libretto!" Dvořák, not to be beaten, hunted up a poet, had the libretto rewritten, revised his music to fit it, and at last presented Prague with an acceptable opera. As Hadow puts it, "The Irishman's knife which had a new blade and a new handle does not offer a more bewildering problem in identity." Surely it was one of the most remarkable feats in the history of opera that a composer could be inspired three times by the same story and each time produce different and better music! But the incident of *King and Collier* is most significant as an illustration of the indomitable pluck with which Dvořák was accustomed to meet the tyranny of circumstance.

Life now began to be, if not easier, at least more settled for Dvořák. He was happily married, recognized in artistic circles, and working successfully in all forms of composition. He resigned his position as viola player in the orchestra and accepted another as organist in a Prague church. But music being ever "a splendid art but a sad trade," neither Dvořák's constant activity nor his wife's good management could quite make financial ends meet. So he applied to the Ministry of Education at Vienna for the pension granted to artists whose work was approved, and to his delight received it. It amounted only to about a hundred and fifty dollars, but it was the equivalent of his year's salary as organist, and, moreover, in winning it Dvořák had taken his first step across the border.

The following year, in order to have more time for his writing, he resigned the position as organist. He again applied for the pension, offering for the committee's approval the beautiful *Stabat Mater*, born of his sorrow at the death of his little daughter. By some incredible stupidity this masterpiece was rejected and the pension withheld. But Dvořák, the dauntless, managed to live and tried again the next year, sending his Moravian Duets and some chamber music. Luckily a new member had just been appointed to the awarding committee — one Johannes Brahms. He at once recognized the genius of this unknown Bohemian and not only saw to it that the pension, substantially increased, was granted but also sent Dvořák's manuscripts to a well-known Berlin publisher with a recommendation which set letters flying to Prague. The duets would be published without delay; would Herr Dvořák send other manuscripts for consideration, and would he accept a commission to write a set of characteristic Slavonic dances? Would he! And so it came about that Dvořák followed that first timid step across the border by a triumphant invasion of foreign territory.

Musical England, attracted by the Slavonic Dances, welcomed each new work by the Bohemian composer, and in 1883 invited him to conduct his *Stabat Mater* at the Albert Hall. This was the first of a number of visits to England, where no composer since the days of Handel and Haydn, except perhaps Mendelssohn, had been so enthusiastically received.

Honors now began pouring in from all sides. The Austrian court decorated Dvořák, Cambridge University gave him an honorary doctorate, Prague elected him Doctor of Philosophy and appointed him professor of composition at the Conservatorium. And in the New World, on an October evening in 1892, an orchestra of eighty, a chorus of three hundred, and an audience of thousands of enthusiastic New Yorkers welcomed with music, speeches, and a huge silver wreath the new director of the National Conservatory of Music of America, Dr. Antonin Dvořák!

How infinitely far away was the little butcher's boy running through the lanes of Nelahozevec with the old priest's lamb chops; the fifteen-year-old viola player earning his nine dollars a month in the cafés of Prague; the young composer supporting a family on a hundred and fifty dollars a year! Here he was in New York, standing in reception lines, encased in unfamiliar stiff shirt and tail coat, director of a big music school at a salary of fifteen thousand dollars a year! He must often have felt with the old woman of the Mother Goose rhyme, "Lauk a mercy on me, this is none of I!" It is interesting to know that when the directors of the new National Conservatory in New York were seeking a director for that institution, two candidates were considered, Antonin Dvořák and a young Finn named Jan Sibelius. The lady who was to interview these candidates was summering in Vienna, and decided that the long trip to Finland was too great an effort; Prague was nearer, and so Dvořák was interviewed and chosen. One cannot help wondering what kind of symphony "From the New World" might have been written had Sibelius come to America in 1892!

The amazing diversity of Dvořák's career might easily have been his undoing had it not been for the unity of his character. Daniel Gregory Mason sums it up in a single sentence, "From first to last, whether in Nelahozevec, Prague, London, or New York, Dvořák was essentially a peasant." For him life was far less complex than for the sophisticated man who considers the motives underlying his own and other people's actions. Dvořák was not acutely concerned with either past or future. He took each day at its face value, living it faithfully, unself-consciously, and with that dogged persistence which was his strongest moral trait. His music is an honest expression of his inner nature. Even in its odd moments, its whimsicality, its occasional wrongheadedness, we feel that Dvořák is not trying to startle his audience or attract attention by being queer. Not at all. He is merely being himself — that odd, whimsical, wrongheaded self. This is why Dvořák's music, like that of Bach and of Beethoven, has such convincing sincerity.

But neither Dvořák's peasant virtues nor his musical genius could ever have been fitted into the niche America had prepared for him. American money had simply bought a lion, a rather sad-eyed captive. No amount of good will on his part or hospitality and appreciation on ours could make him feel at home. He took a small boy's delight in our bustling cities. Trains and boats fascinated him, and he spent a great deal of time down on the Battery in New York watching the ocean liners come and go. Our vast, silent prairies thrilled him. But he was really happy only during the summer holidays which he spent in a tiny Iowa town, Spillville, where friends from home had settled. The brilliant String Quartet in F, the Quintet in E-Flat with two violas, and the lighthearted, tiresomely familiar Humoresque for piano are all reflections of the genial Czech atmosphere of Spillville.

Dvořák had none of the makings of an executive. Self-assertion and practical common sense were his weakest points. His wife had always been the business manager of the family. The rôle of conservatory director must have been uncongenial to him, but he played it earnestly. He was, in his way, an excellent teacher, and many of our best-known musicians were students of "Old Borax," as they affectionately called him. Among other things he gave them much valuable advice on the subject of seeking American themes for American music, and in his own beautiful Symphony in E Minor gave a shining example. America would gladly have kept Dvořák, but he belonged in Bohemia and longed unceasingly for it, and after two and a half years went back to his homeland.

In Prague, he again took up his old life, teaching, composing, and taking part in music festivals. June always found him hurrying to his country place a few miles up the river. Here among his pigeons he found far better company than in any admiring society flock. And watching the sun come up over the hills or wandering barefoot among his vines in the fragrant twilight, Dvořák drew power and serenity from that good earth whence he had sprung.

In the spring of his sixty-fourth year, this man who had never known illness was stricken and died suddenly at the dinner table. A sorrowing crowd followed his body to the churchyard of the Vysehrad, and there every year his countrymen hold a little special service of remembrance for this musician who, with Smetana, is nearest and dearest to the hearts of the Czech people.

THE ARTIST

Of all the great composers Dvořák was probably the least scholarly. He had a peasant background and a peasant type of mind, and while his schooling may have been unusually good for a butcher's boy and his organ training the best that could then be had, it was wholly inadequate for one who was to enter the largest field of musical composition.

But Dvořák had great and compensating gifts. He had spontaneity, imagination, and Czech joyousness, and a rare talent for self-discipline, self-criticism, and instinctive good taste. So with the orchestra in which he played as a laboratory and his borrowed scores as models, he gave himself such training as no conservatory could have afforded and few students would have endured — the training that made Antonin Dvořák, the artist.

Beethoven was his model, Brahms his staunch friend and adviser. From these two master builders Dvořák gained his knowledge of musical form and workmanship. And although his imagination sometimes runs away with him and he falls short of the perfect symmetry of his great models, Dvořák's music always gives the impression of thoughtful planning.

In rhythm, melody, and harmony he needed neither master nor model — he had but to draw upon his intuition and his national musical inheritance. Here it might be interesting to compare Dvořák with some of the other great nationalists, Grieg, for example. Grieg, born a gentleman and formally educated at Leipzig, had to go out and cultivate the folk idioms he so admired. He used Norwegian rhythms and harmonies, but he used them consciously, so consciously and constantly that they became an idiosyncrasy. It was as if a gentleman affected peasant costume. Dvořák, on the other hand, was a peasant, a peasant striving to wear with dignity the dress suit of a man of the world. Even if he had wished, he could not have removed the traces of his folk music background. He uses Bohemian folk rhythms, melodies, and harmonies but quite unconsciously, always fitting them to the artistic molds he has chosen, with the result that he is more deeply national though less "folksy" than Grieg.

The vigor of Dvořák's rhythms and their unevenness — the five- and seven-measure phrases — are a direct reflection of Czech folk music. But there is another rhythmic peculiarity about his music, a little trick that is pure Dvořák. Composers usually make the fabric of their music by weaving together individual *melodies* for the different voices or instruments. Dvořák had neither training nor special aptitude for this time-honored polyphonic style of writing, and wove his firm texture by writing little individual *rhythms* for the different parts. So his music moves not only by the big general swing of it but also by all these little bubbling, dancing, inner rhythms which Daniel Gregory Mason calls a sort of "metrical yeast" working to lighten the mass.

In his tunefulness Dvořák may well be compared with Schubert, for he, too, seemed to pour out a steady stream of charming melody. This comparison, so often made, is all the more interesting when we remember that Schubert had a Czech mother. Taken by themselves, Dvořák's melodies are as fresh and artless as folk songs. Some of them may indeed be folk songs, but whatever their source he makes them his own by his transforming rhythms and harmonies.

Even more characteristic than his rhythms and melodies are Dvořák's harmonies, his treatment of the scale. We know that the growth of European music closely parallels the development of the diatonic — our familiar seven-tone scale. Whatever their differences of style and temperament, the composers of Italy, France, and Germany united in accepting this scale as their unit. Using its intervals, they made their melodies, and upon the relationship of its tones they based their chord progressions and modulations. We also know that some of the tones of the diatonic scale are more closely related than others. Therefore some modulations seem easier, smoother, than others. These easier modulations were accepted as quite right and natural, and any others were frowned upon as remote and unreasonable. And so the diatonic scale with its systems and traditions became dictator to the ears of the Western World.

Bohemia, in political eclipse at the time when this scale system was being evolved, was left comparatively untouched by its traditions, and when several centuries later she came to the making of her own music, it was with unprejudiced ears. Dvořák, accustomed to the lovely wayward harmonies of Czech folk music, and loving color, chose the chromatic — the colored scale — rather than the diatonic, as the basis of his harmonies. Up to this time composers had used this chromatic scale, built in half steps, with all tones equally related, merely for a decoration — a patch of bright color or a bit of embroidery on their diatonic fabric. Dvořák boldly uses chromatic passages as the warp and woof of his fabric. No modulation seems too far away, no chord too distantly related if he happens to fancy its particular color. As Mason again says, "Dvořák loves to descend unexpectedly upon the most remote keys, never knows where he will turn up next, and when he gets too far from home, returns over fences and through 'no-thoroughfares.' " This riotous modulation takes away something of the strength and serenity of Dvořák's music but makes it glow with vivid and surprising color.

More gorgeous even than this harmonic color is the tonal or orchestral color of which Dvořák was one of the great masters. He had a player's practical knowledge of instruments and their registers which enabled him to use them to advantage. His rich, satisfying chords are not happy accidents but carefully planned so that each player is sounding a tone particularly becoming to his instrument, and each choir, if heard separately, would be playing an effective chord. Nor is this marvelous instrumentation a matter of single chords or occasional effects. It runs through Dvořák's music from the first measure to the last, a continuous blending and contrasting of tonal color with here and there the gleam of a single instrument. There are no thin, faded spots in Dvořák's scoring!

It is not surprising that a born colorist like Dvořák should be at his best in orchestral and chamber music. It is true that he wrote a great deal of beautiful vocal music — operas, oratorios, cantatas, and songs inspired by his love of folk poetry and by his deep religious feeling. But Dvořák's chromatic style was better suited to strings and wind than to that more limited instrument, the human voice. And his energetic, uneven rhythms found the slower articulation of words a burden.

As an artist Dvořák stands rather strangely alone. He lived at a time when Romanticism had reached the extreme phases of nationalism and program music; when composers were seeking poetical backgrounds for their music in nature, legend, and literature. Feeling rather than form was their goal, and color rather than line, their tool. Dvořák certainly had the romantic equipment. He was nothing if not national in background and feeling. He was imaginative, impulsive, and the greatest colorist of them all. Yet in spirit Dvořák was a Classicist. Like the great German masters, he was content to express general types of feeling rather than particular emotions. He was more concerned with producing the highest possible beauty of sound than with trying to reproduce the moods of a poem.

One of the chief charms of Dvořák's music is its directness, a sort of unpremeditated quality as if he had just that moment thought of it and not thought too hard! He always spoke of his gift as "God's voice," and listening for that voice he needed no poet's piping. His one concern was to catch the message and write it down in worthy form. And so Dvořák, for all his Slavonic feeling and lavish coloring, is essentially what the Germans would call an "absolute musician" — one whose purpose is to create purely musical beauty.

Smetana also created musical beauty, not for its own sake but as the expression of the soul of the Czech people. He listened to the voice of Bohemia and became her prophet. Pictures of Bohemian life were always clear in his mind, guiding him as he wrote, and it was this poetic meaning rather than a musical one that chiefly concerned him. Dvořák, less the conscious patriot, was the greater artist. He had a wider outlook, a style more generally Slavonic than exclusively Czech, and, thanks to his long apprenticeship to the classical masters, he was the better workman. It is remarkable that Bohemia, after so many silent centuries, should have produced within the same generation Smetana, master of operatic and program music — her dramatic composer — and Dvořák, master of symphonic and chamber music — her epic and lyric poet.

Dvořák wrote the greatest quantity and variety of music, and like all prolific writers, he was not always equally inspired. He wrote rapidly and had a curious habit of refreshing himself after a large work by writing a small one. Many of his most delightful songs and piano pieces belong to these holiday periods.

But whether large or small, inspired or just *Spielmusik*, Dvořák's music is always warmly human. Its beauty is the beauty of this world, for Dvořák never even dreamed of the infinite heights toward which Beethoven and Franck reached out. And it is joyous music. Much of it rings with hearty laughter, and there are smiles — bits of vigorous rhythm and cheerful color — even in the famous slow movements and in the sacred music. To enjoy Dvořák one must take him simply for what he was — a naïve, pious, merry-hearted man, an artist gifted with intuition rather than intellect and with a marvelous instinct for beautiful combinations of tone and tonal color.

OVERTURE — CARNIVAL

Dvořák is always classed among the composers of "absolute music" — those who are content to create purely musical beauty and to express general emotions rather than the moods of a particular story or situation. Yet in his later years Dvořák did write music which, if not exactly program music, is at least romantic in its expression of definite moods and pictures.

Most successful of these later works is the Triple Overture, *Nature, Life, Love*. This was intended as a single work, a triptych picturing childhood, youth, and manhood, and it was meant to be performed as a whole, though the composer was later persuaded to let it be published as three separate numbers.

Nature, Life, Love is not the musical reflection of some poet or painter's feeling, but Dvořák's own emotional impression of these great life forces. He did not supply his score with a word key, as did Smetana, but he spoke freely of what had been in his mind as he wrote these dramatic overtures. When they were first performed in the United States, he approved the program notes that accompanied them so that we have, from these notes, Dvořák's own interpretation.

The first overture is an expression of joy in Nature — such joy as a child might experience in a long day out-of-doors. There is the gaiety of a sunshiny morning, the warm contentment of noon, and the thoughtful mood of twilight. The second overture expresses the joy of youth with its merrymaking and lighthearted love affairs. The third pictures love grown up, and, since Dvořák later renamed it *Othello*, we know that he had in mind all the gentleness, the passion, and the tragedy of love.

Carnival seems a more happily chosen title for the second overture than the original *Life*. Without so much as a note of introduction, the orchestra whirls us into the midst of a Bohemian carnival:

There is no question as to nationality. The vigorous rhythm, the vivacious melody, the clang of triangles, tambourines, and cymbals are unmistakably Slavonic.

After a little this reckless gaiety dies down, and the violins are heard in a beautiful singing melody, as if a pair of lovers had slipped away from the noisy crowd and were lost in their own sweet thoughts:

The woodwinds take up the second part of this melody:

and while this is probably just one of Dvořák's beautiful bits of color contrast, it is quite in keeping with the idea of a conversation *à deux*. But the lovers are soon overtaken by the sounds of revelry which return with even more furious stamping and whirling.

Then, quite unexpectedly, a number of broken chords on the harp and a chromatic cascading of violins introduce the *Andantino con moto* section. Above a persistent little figure begun by the English horn:

a solo flute pipes a quiet pastoral theme:

Just what it is doing in the carnival one cannot quite imagine. It may be only a memory of some lovely country scene, such as often floated through the composer's mind. And it is quite consistent with our idea of Dvořák as a composer of "absolute music," that he is more interested in a theme for its own sweet sake and for its orchestral possibilities than for any special relation it may or may not bear to a poetic idea. Surely this theme which with its accompanying figure is passed around among the instruments justifies its use as a "quiet zone" in the midst of the brilliant, rhythmically compelling carnival music.

Rudely the *Allegro* breaks in again, carrying along all three themes, the merrymakers, the lovers, and the dreamer in its mad progress. Swarms of double *forte*, *sforzando*, and *crescendo* marks seem to sting the notes into a frenzy. Every voice in the orchestra is shouting, the speed grows breathless, as rushing into a showy coda, the carnival comes to an end.

SYMPHONY NO. 5 IN E MINOR, "FROM THE NEW WORLD"

The beautiful Symphony No. 5 in E Minor was written during Dvořák's sojourn in the United States, and because it expresses what America meant to him, he gave it the subtitle, "From the New World." Dvořák is called a classicist because his purpose is to express purely musical beauty rather than poetic ideas taken from life or literature. But no matter how zealously he poured his feelings into the molds of the great classic masters, those feelings remained folk feelings, and Dvořák, first and last, a folk musician. His instinct for the music of the people was the very foundation of his art, and it is not at all surprising that as soon as he set foot in the New World he began to listen for its folk music.

To anyone less trusting than Dvořák the search for truly American music would have seemed all but hopeless. Americans are not a singing people — at least, Americans of the Mayflower brand. Never would they be caught making songs of their joys and sorrows or dancing dull care away on a New England village green. Our man in the street, in the field, or factory, whistles a "hit" tune made for the trade and labeled, *popular*. And even this poor, unconvincing tune is drowned out by the din of traffic and machines. Plenty of good tunes have reached our shores, via steerage, but we cannot claim them. Even the southern mountain songs are mostly transplanted English folk songs. With the exception of the tribal melodies of the Red Man, a few pioneer songs and dances, and the cowboy ballads of the western plains, there is really no folk music which may be called one hundred per cent American. Dvořák collected and studied the tribal melodies of the Red Man, intending to write an American Indian opera with a libretto from Longfellow's poem, "Hiawatha." Unfortunately, that opera never materialized.

In his quest for American folk tunes, Dvořák became intensely interested in Negro music and ran a special notice in the New York papers welcoming Negro students to his classes. He loved to hear these young people sing their spirituals, particularly one boy who sang to him evening after evening, a boy with a golden voice and a fine intelligence, Harry Burleigh.

In an article on "Music in America," written for *Century Magazine* in 1895, Dvořák says:

> All races have their distinctive songs which they at once recognize as their own, even if they have never heard them before. . . . It is therefore a proper question to ask,

"What songs belong to the American and appeal more strikingly to him than any others? What melody would stop him on the street if he were in a strange land and make the home-feeling well up within him?"

Dvořák felt that for many Americans the answer to this question would be the so-called plantation melodies which he said were equaled only by the fine folk tunes of Ireland and Scotland.

The appearance of the New World Symphony started hot discussion as to what extent its themes had been borrowed and as to whether Negro music could be considered pure American folk music. It is true that the Negro, being musically sensitive and a born imitator, probably picked up most of his tunes from his white neighbors. But it is equally true that the sad fate of slavery transformed those borrowed tunes. The white man had had a chance to express himself in many ways, particularly in realizing his material ambitions. His emotions had long been tempered by his intellectual development, and he sang more as a pleasant pastime. But the Negro, having nothing in this world, lived on hopes of the next. Song was his refuge, his compensation, his only real freedom. And as he poured out his heart, the intensity of his emotion re-formed even the rhythm and the melody, to say nothing of the harmony, of those "white" tunes and gave them a folk feeling found nowhere else in American music.

Whether or not they may be called pure American folk tunes, the fact remains that the Negro spirituals were created in this country. They are a product of life in this country and they are an accomplished fact. They will not be added to for the happy reason that their creators no longer live under the conditions which alone made them possible. The Negro spirituals are, psychologically and musically, a great wonder. For, as the poet says:

> What merely living clod, what captive thing,
> Could up toward God through all its darkness grope,
> And find within its deadened heart to sing
> These songs of sorrow, love and faith and hope?
> How did it catch that subtle undertone,
> That note in music heard not with the ears?
> How sound the elusive reed so seldom blown,
> Which stirs the soul or melts the heart to tears? [1]
>
> — James Weldon Johnson

The secret of the spirituals is the spirit that inspired them. Only those, black or white, who share this communion of spirit can ever know this "note in music heard not with the ears." Long years of subjection had given something of the same emotion to Czech song, and it may have been a dim, unrecognized kinship that drew Dvořák to Negro music. He felt its spirit and it moved him to write spirituals of his own.

The charge that Dvořák transplanted Negro melodies bodily into the "New World" Symphony has long been disproved. There may be a fragment of "Swing Low, Sweet

[1] From "O Black and Unknown Bards," by James Weldon Johnson (from *The Century Magazine*, copyright, 1908, 1935, by D. Appleton-Century Company, Inc.) Reprinted by permission of the publisher.

Chariot" used consciously or otherwise in the first movement, but all the other themes are Dvořák's own.   He had no need to borrow melodies, and he was not that kind of a nationalist.   He assimilated the characteristics and the feeling of folk tunes, then created his own melodies.   And it is amusing to know that, when the "New World" Symphony was first being played and while American critics were arguing as to whether it was pure Negro or impure American, Prague was enthusiastically welcoming it as pure Bohemian! Most musicians consider it quite pure Dvořák!

What really distinguishes this great symphony is not its nationality but its internationality of musical beauty and genuine appeal.

Adagio, Allegro molto

In the brief *Adagio* which serves as an introduction, Dvořák seems to forecast the two dominant moods of the symphony.   The opening phrase, sighing through the lower strings:

and echoed in the woodwinds, might well express his longing for cozy Bohemia, a longing intensified by the vast open spaces of the New World.   But it was not all loneliness in this strange land.   There was a vigorous life, there was freedom and challenge that stirred Dvořák's valiant Czech heart.   Surging up from low strings and horns comes a typical Dvořák theme of furious energy:

The *Adagio* shows no trace of the folk type melodies which characterize the symphony itself.   It is quite detached, simply an intimation of Dvořák's state of mind before he began to tell his story.

A sharp stroke of the strings cuts off the *Adagio*, and the horns announce the main theme of the *Allegro*.   It is an interesting theme with its first phrase a steeply up-and-down melody in snapping "ragtime" rhythm:

balanced by a level, answering phrase for woodwinds:

Soon the strings take it up and with a few apparently simple rhythmic and harmonic shifts bring us to the remote key of G minor and an appealing little subsidiary theme:

The lowered seventh step — the F-natural — gives this melody a distinct folk flavor. Some critics recognize it as an Indian touch; others call it typically Negro and point to such songs as "Didn't My Lord Deliver Daniel?" as proof; still others say that it is plainly Czech, even to the bagpipe accompaniment. But whatever its origin, this little tune becomes pure Dvořák in the symphony. No one else could have brought it from its G minor beginning through a brilliant E major to G major with so little fuss and with quite such delicate shadings and then could have ended with the simple phrase:

which leads to the second theme:

This theme has the same syncopated rhythm as the first theme, and bears unmistakable resemblance to the famous spiritual, "Swing Low, Sweet Chariot." The themes being stated, the composer now passes to the second part of the conventional sonata or first-movement pattern — Exposition — Development — Recapitulation.

This Development section betrays Dvořák as the naïve rather than the scholarly musician. Instead of the thoughtful discussion of Beethoven or Brahms in which new musical ideas seem to grow out of the ones already stated, there is a rather fragmentary repetition of the two main themes. The first phrase of the second theme is now answered by the second phrase of the first theme, and there is almost more than enough of that "aspiring *arpeggio*":

The orchestration is, as usual, interesting. Dvořák depends upon change of color rather than of idea for his variety, not the best method, to be sure, but one which he uses with incomparable skill.

The Recapitulation brings back, in order, the three themes of the Exposition. Here again it is the surprising key changes, the delightful blending and contrasting of instruments that charms the listener. A brilliant coda, based upon the main theme, brings this vigorous first movement to a close.

Largo

The *Largo* of the "New World" Symphony shares with that other famous slow movement, the *Andante* of Beethoven's Fifth Symphony, the distinction of being one of the best-loved pieces of music ever written.   The *Largo* is *popular* music in the true sense of the word, "liked by people generally," and the secret of its popularity lies not in its musical beauty, great as that is, but in its heart appeal.   Its quiet measures express so much more than Dvořák's own nostalgia for Bohemia.   It speaks for everyone who has ever known homesickness — Adam, perhaps, yearning for Eden; David, remembering Zion; the wayfarer, haunted by lighted windows; the child away from home at bedtime; and for all who dream of "dear, dead days beyond recall."   The *Largo* is the whole world's song, a song in which homesickness, freed from dross of tears and bitter words, becomes a precious thing of shining beauty.

The magic of the *Largo* is not its melody, but the isolation of those seven opening chords:

Musically those chords bridge the distance between the E minor tonality of the first movement and the D-flat major of the second:

A long harmonic way!   But for Dvořák these seven chords measured all the miles of empty ocean that rolled between the New World and the Old, and for music lovers everywhere they span the distance to some far-off Land of Heart's Desire.

A simple tonic-dominant in the strings:

settles us comfortably in the key.   Then the English horn, lonesomest voice in the orchestra, sings the well-known melody to an accompaniment of muted strings:

One of the finest tributes to the perfection with which Dvořák has accomplished his artistic purpose is the fact that this simple melody is so persistently mistaken for a Negro folk song.   And, what is even more significant, the words of this mythical folk song are "Goin' Home"!

As the song goes on, soft alto voices join in, and at the end the clarinet repeats the cadence twice, the second time in lengthened rhythm:

The effect of this repeated cadence, used throughout the movement, is of indescribable wistfulness, suggesting a lingering farewell too hard to say!   It is all so final, so irrevocable.   And as if to intimate that there is no answer, nothing but emptiness, distance, the high woodwinds repeat those mysterious opening chords.   The strings echo a measure of the melody which fades into a soft murmur as the English horn begins to sing again.   This time the violins repeat the cadence, and muted horns seem about to take up the song.   But they hesitate and as they pause on a long A-flat, the flutes and oboes give out a second melody:

In Dvořák's dream opera, *Hiawatha*, this melody, played by the flute, which is the instrument of Indian lovers, was to have been Hiawatha's lament at the death of Minnehaha.

A haunting melody for clarinets follows:

The coloring here is particularly lovely.   Against the clear tone of the clarinets, somber oboe shades fill in the harmonies, while for background there is a shimmering of violins and a steady treading up and down of plucked double basses.   And all the while the sunshine and shadow of major and minor play back and forth in typical Dvořák style.

Then, on a surprising major chord, the mood changes completely.   The oboe pipes a happy little country tune:

Trilling flutes and rippling clarinets reply and soon the strings join in.   The merriment grows and at its height sharp ears may detect fragments of three familiar themes — the *Largo* song, the "Swing Low, Sweet Chariot," and that "aspiring *arpeggio*" from the first movement, all going at the same time.

But the excitement is brief, and as it dies away the plaintive English horn sings again. Violins take up the second phrase of the song, singing it with little heartbroken pauses, almost as of a voice choked with tears. And at that closing cadence which, all along, has been so expressive, Dvořák gives the master touch. The first time we heard that cadence the chord on the bar beat was a fairly simple one. The next time that chord was fuller by a tone or two, and now, this third and last time, the chord contains that B double-flat which Dvořák has been saving for the final appeal. He uses this rich chord but once, returning to the earlier, simpler harmony in the repeated cadence. This is the restraint of a great artist.

As the familiar melody dies away, a solo violin is heard singing a quiet little after-song, but this, too, loses itself in those isolating chords which mark the boundaries of the *Largo*. An upward flight of violin tones, an echoing chord far below in the basses, and Dvořák's matchless song is done.

Scherzo

The *Scherzo* is a typical third movement, purposely contrasting its merry, dancing mood with the emotional song of the *Largo*. Dvořák has used the Beethoven third movement pattern — *Scherzo-Trio-Scherzo* — and has given the music a particularly boisterous feeling by dividing the heavy beat into several notes.

After a brisk introduction, in which the strings mark the characteristic rhythm, the fun begins. While the woodwinds caper through their dance:

tossing the theme back and forth, the violins are sawing steadily away on one note as if they knew no other. It is the same note they were playing in the introduction, and it happens to be D-natural which, in this case, is that lowered leading tone so typical of folk music. For this *Scherzo* is not only a dance, it is a folk dance. Some authorities claim that this main melody was to have been an Indian dance in the opera *Hiawatha*.

After a repetition of this hopping dance, flute and oboe swing into a smoother melody in a bright major key:

with a seasaw accompaniment in the strings which suggests an accordian or some other wheezy rustic instrument. But the violins will not let this tune alone. They come hopping in and lift the *Scherzo* right back to its minor key and the first theme.

Then follows a curious interlude in which the 'celli seem to be trying to remember that main theme of the first movement. It sounds queer:

and before they can get it straightened out, the woodwinds, impatient to begin the *Trio*, interrupt with a gay tune which sounds like a child's singing game:

Woodwinds

There is a charming second part, even more lilting:

mf
Violins I & II

and full of trills — whole groups of instruments trilling together in chords so that for a moment the orchestra sounds like a bird choir.

This *Trio* is followed by the return of the *Scherzo*, repeated note for note but ending in a clever coda in which the horns, more successful than the basses, recall that vigorous first movement theme and even a bit of "Swing Low." But the violins insist upon the hopping rhythm, and the movement ends, as it began, in *Scherzo* mood.

Allegro con fuoco

It is often claimed that the last movement of a symphony is apt to be its weakest part, as if the composer's inspiration had burned low. Dvořák's fiery *Finale* is certainly an emphatic denial of this claim. Its fresh, vital themes, firm design, and gorgeous coloring make one suspect him of having held his best in reserve.

After nine commanding bars of introduction the theme comes marching in:

Allegro con fuoco

ff
Horns
Trumpets

a veritable conquering hero of a theme which might easily symbolize the power and the promise of the New World. It is a brass theme, if ever there was one, and true to his color sense, Dvořák lets the horns and trumpets have it while the other instruments mark time. Later, violins and woodwinds are allowed to play with it, and by a simple device known to musicians as "rhythmic diminution" applied to the first measure:

and the third measure of the theme:

they turn it into a jigging tune:

surprisingly suggestive of the Emerald Isle.

This lighter mood is excellent preparation for the second theme, a lovely memory of Bohemia, played by solo clarinet:

But one cannot expect a singing theme to last long in an *Allegro con fuoco*. Soon the clarinet's song is caught up by the strings and carried into what Philip Goepp calls a regular "hoe-down." And when in the *mêlée* of merry tunes, "Three Blind Mice"

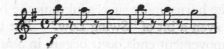

begin to frisk among the instruments, there seems little doubt that this is indeed a folk festival.

Having stated his themes, Dvořák now begins to develop them, making a much better job of it than in the first movement. This time the Development is not just a recoloring of themes but a discussion from which new ideas spring, and it includes not only the themes of the *Finale* but also those of other movements — the main first movement theme, the song from the *Largo*, and the *Scherzo* theme. The familiar melodies come back with most tantalizing changes — here a new harmony, there a different rhythm, and everywhere an amazing variegation of instrument color.

Presently the Recapitulation begins. The main *Finale* theme returns, followed by the second theme, this time in the tonic key of E, for the movement is written in strict sonata form. Then comes the coda and Dvořák makes it a grand summary of the whole symphony. All the important melodies come back for their curtain calls with the two most aggressive ones, the very first theme:

and the marching theme of the *Finale:*

contending for the last bow.

Dvořák's Symphony No. 5 in E Minor is one of those rare works which offers something to every listener. Its sensuous beauty — the rhythm, the melody, and the color

— and its warm humanness make instant appeal to the first-time listener, even though he may know nothing about symphonic music; while for the music lover, the one who listens again and again, it always seems to yield something new, some delightful detail hitherto unnoticed. And even for the students who analyze it and appreciate all its rich complexity, this symphony still leaves an impression of simplicity. Only great art can thus eclipse artifice.

A great many symphonies have been written, but the popular ones can be counted on the fingers of one hand. Dvořák's Symphony in E Minor is one of them. People everywhere love it, and it will live no matter whether it belongs to the New World or the Old — a better title might have been "From Two Worlds." It will live because it is good music, sincerely conceived and beautifully expressed.

JAROMIR WEINBERGER

Prague — 1896

Jaromir Weinberger is one of the outstanding musical Bohemians of today. Because much of his life is yet to be lived, biographers have thus far paid him scant attention. His friends say that he was an unusually gifted child, a clever pianist at seven, and a composer, with something in print, at eleven. He has always had a flair for counterpoint and instrumentation and remarkable skill at improvising. It is said that when tramping through the country with his friends, young Jaromir would sit down at the piano in a village inn and improvise tricky and amusing fugues as easily as most boys rattle off popular dance tunes. He studied piano and composition with the best teachers in Prague and later became a pupil of Max Reger in Leipzig.

In 1922 young Weinberger came to this country to teach composition at the Conservatory of Music at Ithaca, New York. But, like his famous countryman, Antonin Dvořák, he found the New World a bewildering and lonesome place. After a brief struggle with life in the small university town, he gave up and went in search of companionship. Fortunately he did not have to journey all the way to Spillville, Iowa. He came to Cleveland to the home of a boyhood friend, the artist Richard Rychtarik.

Before returning to Prague, Weinberger spent several months with the Rychtariks in Cleveland, and during that time wrote a series of preludes and fugues for piano. Strangely enough, one of these Cleveland fugues, dedicated to Mrs. Rychtarik, reappeared later as the famous fugue in the opera *Schwanda*.

While sojourning in America, Weinberger, again like Dvořák, became interested in our folk melodies and in the then-ubiquitous "jazz." His *Nellie Gray, Cowboy's Christmas*, and *Banjos*, for violin and piano, are based on American folk tunes, and one of his later operas was suggested by a Bret Harte story.

But sooner or later the Bohemian artist answers the call to the colors, and Weinberger, after several years of wandering interests and modernistic experimenting, returned to the musical traditions of his own country. His opera *Schwanda*, gay, tuneful, and thoroughly Bohemian, is a direct descendant of Smetana's *Bartered Bride*. First produced in Prague in 1927, *Schwanda* came to America in 1931 after more than two thousand European performances had proved it to be one of the most popular operas of modern times.

SCHWANDA, THE BAGPIPE PLAYER

Polka, Furiant, and Fugue

The story begins in the farmyard of Schwanda, the Bagpiper of Strakonitz. On week days Schwanda is just a hard-working peasant, but on Sundays and holidays he becomes a famous fellow, for then his polkas fill the air and keep every foot in the village stirring. He has a pretty young wife, Dorota, who, quite unconsciously on her part, has attracted the attention of a genial robber chief, Babinsky. Babinsky lays plans for the stealing of Dorota's heart, but first he must get Schwanda out of the way. So he tells the bagpiper that it is a pity that such talent as his should be hidden away in this little corner of the woods. He, Babinsky, has traveled, and he knows that musicians are loved everywhere. Why, out in the great world there are hundreds of bored, unhappy people just sitting waiting to be amused by such polkas as Schwanda's, and willing to pay for them, too. For example, there is Ice Heart, Queen of a near-by kingdom, who lives under the spell of a wicked sorcerer and is never happy. A few merry tunes and the queen would doubtless be free and Schwanda rich and famous. Why not try his luck? Of course Dorota will cry and make a fuss at his going, so they had best slip away while she is inside filling up the soup bowls! Schwanda is persuaded.

The second picture shows the palace of Queen Ice Heart. In vain her courtiers try to amuse her. Dancers drop exhausted before her, but she only mourns and begs the sorcerer to give back her living heart instead of this heart of ice she now has. Suddenly into the gloomy throne room bursts the master of ceremonies and keeper of the keys, dancing fantastically! Behind him comes a crowd of servants, guards, and villagers all hopping and skipping for dear life, and in their midst, the cause of this amazing spectacle, Schwanda, piping one of his roistering polkas: [1]

What a tune!

Then the piper begins to play pranks in a tipsy half-step version of his polka. Queen Ice Heart smiles — as who doesn't!

[1] Excerpts from *Schwanda* printed by permission of Associated Music Publishers, Inc., New York, owners of the copyright.

A gentler melody follows:

The Queen begins to sway, and by the time the first theme comes back, she is nodding and patting as happily as any peasant. Truly, as Schwanda says, "Where a Bohemian plays, it is always merry!"

The Queen will not let Schwanda go, and as a reward for this gay music which has warmed her cold heart, she says she will marry him. Schwanda replies that his head is in a whirl. Then, as the fact that he is about to become a king penetrates his thick and whirling pate, he exclaims, "To think that I have won a kingdom without arms, only with music!"

In the midst of all this wonder, Dorota, who has been pursuing her runaway husband, rushes in, and a great commotion begins. "This woman Schwanda's wife?" cries Ice Heart. "And does he still love her?" "Why, to be sure," answers the simple Schwanda, whereupon the angry queen orders the pipes taken away and the luckless piper put on trial for his life.

In the third picture we are taken outside the city walls to the place of execution where a crowd has gathered to see the end of Schwanda. The judge tells the condemned man that by the law of the land he is entitled to one last favor. "Then bring my pipes," says Schwanda, "and let me play once more." While they go in search of the pipes, the executioner lays his axe on the block behind him. No one seems to notice a hand moving about the block. The pipes cannot be found, and the judge orders the executioner to do his duty. Schwanda lays his head upon the block, Dorota weeps bitterly, the crowd shudders, the blow falls, and no harm is done! Clever Babinsky has substituted a broom for the headsman's axe! As the people cheer, Babinsky places the pipes in Schwanda's hands and tells him to show what he can do and quickly! Schwanda blows as never before, and the whole crowd, executioner and all, go dancing and prancing back into the city.

But Schwanda's troubles are not over. No sooner is he free from the executioner than Dorota proceeds to take his head off for running away from her and for agreeing to all that nonsense about marrying Queen Ice Heart. She scolds, Schwanda pleads and protests, and Babinsky joins in, apparently as peacemaker but slyly encouraging Dorota whose anger pleases him immensely. This stormy little scene is effectively set in the form of the *furiant*, a Bohemian folk dance of rapid *tempo*, sharp accent, and meter alternating excitedly between two and three beats. In the opera the *Furiant* is, of course, a vocal trio, but even in the orchestral version we can distinguish the three speakers.

First, Dorota rebukes Schwanda in sharp accents:

These emphatic two-beat measures lend themselves well to her accusation, "Faithless one!"

In vain Schwanda calls her by her pet name.   She only makes fun of him whose words are "sweet as marzipan":

Thus far Schwanda has only seemed to echo Dorota, but now he begins to feel abused and protests that she is not fair to him:

Then the hearty voice of Babinsky joins in:

These themes, with slight variations and interesting changes of instrument color, bring the *Furiant* and the quarrel to a happy ending.

Schwanda, however, growing a bit self-righteous now that he is about to be forgiven, adds, "And anyway, Dorota, I don't see why you should have scolded me so when I never even kissed the Queen.   Why, if I gave her so much as the least little part of a kiss, may the Devil take me" — which the Devil promptly does!

The next picture shows Schwanda's adventures in Hell.   He is again rescued by Babinsky, who plays at cards with the Devil, betting Schwanda's freedom against half the Devil's kingdom, and wins.   During his sojourn in the underworld, it seems that Schwanda's pipes have greatly intrigued the Devil who tries to play on them, producing a discordant and truly devilish version of the polka.   The Devil begs Schwanda to play for him, but Schwanda refuses until just as he is leaving, then, seizing his pipes, he plays, as a farewell to Hell, this pert little tune:

Weinberger, in turn, seizes the Bach-burlesque theme in polka rhythm and uses it as the subject of an amusing fugue. The subject is introduced by second violins and taken up, successively, by violas, first violins, 'celli, and basses, with woodwinds capering alongside in little chromatic figures. The brasses are added gradually, and as the horns give out the fugue theme, the violins bring in the polka tune:

in dancing counterpoint.

There are several brief interludes, and then comes the *stretto*, the closing part of a fugue where the different instruments or voices carrying the subject crowd and overlap each other. There is a long *crescendo*, throughout which the trumpets constantly intensify the main subject, until finally all themes are united in a broad and impressive conclusion.

In spite of the theory that set pieces disturb the action of an opera, *Schwanda* survives even a fugue. And who, hearing this rollicking piece, could call the fugue a dry musical form? Bach himself would have enjoyed it and doubtless would have taken off his hat to the brilliant counterpoint of this modern melodist.

Under the Spreading Chestnut Tree

Under the Spreading Chestnut Tree, composed in the early spring of 1939, was dedicated to the New York Philharmonic Symphony Society and its conductor, John Barbirolli, who gave it the first performance in the autumn of that same year. For the program notes of that first concert Mr. Weinberger sent this pleasant little story.

A newsreel was my inspiration. The summer of 1938 I spent at Juan les Pins, on the French Riviera, the Côte d'Azur. One evening I went to a movie in the open air. In the news reels nowadays you usually see dictators and a very few honest people, so I was surprised to see something agreeable. I saw a Boys' Camp in England, many young people, and among them, in democratic simplicity, His Majesty the King. He was dressed in the same sweater as his young subjects, and he joined them in singing and laughing. They sang a wonderful old folk tune. The song had not only very thrilling words, but an amazing, wonderful tune; it is a so-called Gesture Song.

At several points the music suddenly stopped, and His British Majesty with his loyal subjects started to clap their hands, jump to their feet, and start a pantomime, finally joining again in singing the tune to its end. I liked the whole scene very much and I said to myself: "This is the theme for which you, Jaromir, shall write variations and a fugue."

These are the words of the song:

> Under the spreading chestnut tree
> When I held you on my knee,
> Oh, how happy we could be,
> Under the spreading chestnut tree!

The composer goes on to say that he would like the following analysis of the music to be printed in the program book of concerts at which his composition is performed. It is also printed on the flyleaf of the score. To Mr. Weinberger's analysis we add quotation of the theme:

Theme: "Under the Spreading Chestnut Tree": [1]

The period is in eight bars. The third and fourth are a transposition of the first and second — the seventh and eighth are a repetition of the first and second. The melody itself is very well constructed, leading to a climax in the middle of the tune. The intervals of the first and second (and therefore of the seventh and eighth) bars are the same as if read from right to left in a mirror.

Following the theme, the piano has a transitional passage of several bars to the first variation. During the entire work the piano keeps the connecting function and is never used as an orchestral instrument.

Variation I: "Her Majesty's Virginal." This Variation is built in the form of a canon with its model as follows:

       1. bar   2. bar   etc.

Oboe: theme from right to left (as in a looking glass)
      French horn: theme same as oboe
        'Celli: theme in the original version
   Violas: theme in the original version

The second part of this Variation develops the looking-glass canon on the sext [the interval of the sixth].

       1. bar   2. bar   etc.

  First violins: theme in its original version
      Second violin: theme as looking glass in the sext.

In the score I marked these inversions with the Latin designation: *More Hebraeorum* (In the Hebrew Manner). The end of the looking-glass phrase is marked like this:

TFEL EHT OT THGIR EHT MORF DAER ESAELP

Variation II: "The Madrigalists." The madrigal was one of the favorite forms during the 15th and 16th centuries. This Variation pays homage to the composers of that early form of music.

Variation III: "The Black Lady." Heroine of Shakespeare's sonnets.

Variation IV: "Scottish Highlanders." Some years ago, while spending some time in London, a strange music awakened me. This was the first time I had ever heard the music of bagpipes, en masse. To transfer these striking sounds to a symphonic orchestra, I wrote the following key for the woodwinds: B♭ C D E F G♭ A♭ B♭. Two small flutes play the same bagpipe figuration in aliquot [so many] tones. [These small flutes are

[1] Reprinted by permission of Associated Music Publishers, Inc., New York City.

over-blown to produce tones of higher pitch than the fingering would normally give and suggest the bagpipe's thin shrillness.]

Variation V: "Pastorale." It has never been my good fortune to see the English landscape. An old classic painting in the British Exhibition in the Louvre in Paris provided the imagination for this Variation.

Variation VI: "Mr. Weller, Senior, discusses widows with his son Samuel Weller, Esq." The 23rd chapter of Charles Dickens' "Pickwick Papers" establishes this classical example for a stubborn generalization. In this Variation the solo bassoon answers to everything in the same stubborn manner as his pattern, the coachman Weller, in his imperturbable opinion of widows.

Variation VII: "Sarabande for Princess Elizabeth, Electress Palatine and Queen of Bohemia." Elizabeth Stuart (1596–1662), daughter of James I, was a lady of unusual beauty and education. She was the unhappy winter queen of my unhappy native country. This Variation is written in the Dorian mode on C♯.

Fugue: The subject of the Fugue has eight bars.

The first statement of the subject is given out by the trumpets in the inversion. Bassoons make the second statement, *More Hebraeorum* [that is, from right to left], and in the same manner, the trombones give the third statement of the subject. The work closes with a double fugue giving the fourth and last statement of the subject, combined with the original theme, *Under the Spreading Chestnut Tree*, a fair sample of the brilliant cleverness which characterizes Weinberger's music.

CHAPTER VI

Sketches from Spain

The artist's and the poet's theme,
The young man's vision and the old man's dream.

Castles in Spain! To those who have traveled there, even by proxy of books and music, it is not at all surprising that Spain should have become the symbolic land of daydreams. Where else, they say, would one find so strange a mingling of the real and the unreal, such fantastic contrast? Temperatures and temperaments ranging from the polar glacial to the African jungle; starkest poverty playing proudly against a sumptuous backdrop; Sunday and Monday blending in churches hallowed by so many centuries of human emotion that the peasant, saying her prayers with her basket of live fowls beside her, seems a perfectly harmonious detail of the picture; antiquity, in the person of the small donkey with his festoon of colored worsted balls, bobbing along side by side with that pinnacle of modernity, the Hispano-Suiza automobile; and over it all the spell of Spanish sunshine, Spanish rhythms, and the alluring *mañana* which cheerfully consigns to a remote tomorrow anything that might mar the enjoyment of today.

Spanish life has always been set to music. Yet, strangely enough, music was for centuries the Sleeping Beauty of the arts in Spain. To the cultured Spaniard it was inconceivable that music could be an art of reason. He regarded it as merely fit to "distract the frivolity of women and the dissipation of men," and tolerated it only as folk song or as part of the service of the church.

Sacred music, however, had its great day in Spain. There was a time, early in the sixteenth century, when nearly all of the best composers for the great Roman choirs came from Spain, the popes recognizing the Spanish mind as more serious than the Italian and therefore better suited to the making of serious music. And it was these Spanish composers who had most to do with the founding of the school of church music of which Palestrina is the crown. Indeed, one of the brightest names in the Palestrina group is that of a Spaniard, Victoria, or Vittoria, as the Italians called him.

After this brilliant period Spanish music took a siesta of almost four centuries during which there were no outstanding Spanish composers, and such music as was to be heard in Spanish cities was but the lighter offerings of France and Italy.

Then, in the later eighteen hundreds, the Sleeping Beauty began to stir. Spain had learned from harsh Master Mars the lesson that a nation can be great, not by clinging to the medieval ideal of an empire on which "the sun never sets," but only by its moral and intellectual distinction. Spaniards began to ask themselves, "What is the real spirit of Spain? What are her great traditions?" And Spanish composers, quickened by the spirit which had already been at work in the art of other countries, the spirit of nationalism, began to long for an art music which should consciously express the soul of Spain as folk music had been unconsciously expressing it for centuries. They set to work seriously, with the result that some of the most interesting and promising music of our time is coming from Spain.

True to tradition, modern Spanish music is a mingling of the very old with the very new. Its heritage had lain undisturbed for centuries, but accumulating interest all the while. And when the heirs, these modern Spanish composers, finally got around to spending it, what a fortune they had! There was no excuse for their compositions to sound strained, self-conscious, and slightly hysterical, as did those of many of their contemporaries. There was no need for them to exert themselves to be original, to glean where older composers had already reaped. The field was all their own, rich, ripe, and untouched. Is it any wonder, then, that their music, so fresh and real and intensely Spanish, should be so convincing? It reminds one of the first few but startling blossoms that put out from a well-rooted shrub.

To appreciate this Spanish music, also the amazing amount of beautiful pseudo-Spanish music which has been written by composers of other countries, one must know something of this heritage, this national background from which it takes its color.

Spain, known to the ancient world as the Iberian Peninsula, is one of the great continental bridges of the eastern hemisphere. For as Russia, on the north, connects Europe with Asia, so Spain, on the south, connects Europe with Africa. This Iberian Peninsula is also a bridge between two great and historic seas, the Mediterranean and the North Atlantic. Across this bridge from the earliest times has moved a slow procession, a pageant of races — Phoenicians, Greeks, Carthaginians, Romans, Vandals, Visigoths, Moors, gypsies, men from France and even far-off Flanders, each group leaving its mark on the life and art which we call Spanish. The clearest imprints, those of which we are most conscious especially in Spanish music, are those of Africa and Arabia.

The music of Spain is so pre-eminently rhythmic that the word *dance* follows the word *Spanish* almost automatically. "Dancing," says Havelock Ellis, "is more than an amusement in Spain. It is part of that ritual which enters into the whole life of the people. It expresses their very spirit." So much a part of their ritual has it been that we find Priscillian, one of the early heretics, declaring that priests were unnecessary, since any one of the faithful — that is, anyone who could sing and dance — could celebrate the offices of the Christian religion! And to this day, at certain seasons, choir boys in the cathedral of Seville and elsewhere may be seen stepping the stately altar dances of eight hundred years ago!

Spanish rhythms are of endless variety, and to really analyze them would be a task as lengthy as it is fascinating. They have, however, certain earmarks by which any listener may learn to know them — crisp accents marked by castanets, tambourines, and other percussion instruments; omnipresent syncopation; and rapid, violent changes of mood and *tempo*.

It is not difficult to recognize the African heritage in this love of beating drums and of shifting accents and in these outbursts of violence. What most of us fail to sense, especially when we try to sing or play Spanish music, is the exaggerated softness and slowness which is just as African as the violence and its necessary complement. Love of idleness, physical inertia, is the natural background for savage, purposeless energy.

Strange as it may seem, the music of Andalusia, most southern and most typically Spanish, is, for all its violence, the emotional expression of a lazy people. Distilled like wine by the burning African sun, it is mellow but heady. It is the music of a proud people. More than three centuries ago, Francis Bacon, reporting on the notorious delays of the Spaniards in their political negotiations, attributed them to "the nature of the people and nation which is proud and therefore dilatory, for all proud men are full of delays and must be waited on. All which have made the delays of Spain to come into a byword throughout the world." And he goes on to say, "Wherein I think his Lordship might allude to the proverb of Italy, *mi venga la morte di Spagna*, 'let my death come from Spain,' for then it is sure to be long a-coming."

But while it is true that all the world dances in Spain, dancing is not the only Spanish institution, nor rhythm the only characteristic of Spanish music worthy of attention. Only recently a cultured Spaniard took exception to the title of a book, "Spain, the Land of the Castanet," though its author had nothing but praise for his country. "Such a title," said the Spaniard, "is no more suitable than if one were to write a book on the United States and call it 'The Land of Breakfast Bacon.' "

Spanish music, while built for rhythm, has beautiful melody, and Spanish dances are very often accompanied by singing even though the tune may be drowned out by the stamping, clapping, and cries of "*Ole! Ole!*" Spanish audiences are notoriously noisy, not through lack of appreciation of the music, but through an excess of appreciation. To them music is a stimulant, noise, an intoxicant, with the result that they often ruin the very thing they love so well.

Typical Spanish melody is as refined as the rhythm is savage. It bears the mark of the Moors who came into Spain in 711, bringing with them *al'ud* — the lute — that companion of song, and leaving behind them, after their nine hundred years' sojourn, buildings, gardens, traditions which still reflect one of the most exquisite civilizations the world has yet known. Unlike the Christian Spaniards who sought the vast and majestic, the Moors loved small and delicate things. And yet, like their Alhambra, which, though one of the most fragile examples of architecture, has withstood time and all the revolutions that have overtaken Spain, the delicate imprints of the Moors have lasted. Theirs is the beautiful *cante hondo* or "deep song," of which the *malagueña* is a type. It is the song of the tragic sense of life so common to folk music, for, says Chateaubriand, "The natural song of man is sad, even when expressing happiness." It begins, more often than not, in true Arabian fashion with a long vocalise on one syllable, then proceeds on its wailing, wavering way. There is an old saying that the *malagueña* is wept and not sung. The melody line is long and unbroken, with few wide skips and with single tones often repeated to the point of obsession, but ornamented with grace notes as elaborately as a Moorish screen is ornamented with arabesques. The intervals are strange to western ears and often unwritable in western symbols.

As for harmony, that most modern of the elements of music, Spanish composers found almost none of it in their heritage. For the music of all ancient and primitive peoples is characteristically that of rhythm and melody, and even today the music of the East is a music of one voice. The Arabs did not put two tunes together for variety's sake as did early western experimenters. They did what to us seems a much more intricate thing — they put two or more rhythms together, singing one and beating another. This counterpoint of rhythm, a trick still used by their Spanish heirs, is often the despair of occidental performers. In addition to this rhythmic accompaniment, the Arabs used a drone bass, which, as some one has cleverly expressed it, is "harmony reduced to its lowest terms."

Just here it might be interesting to mention one of the first and most famous singing schools of which we have record. It was the school of Ziryáb, court musician to the Caliph of Arabian Nights fame and composer of "Ten Thousand Songs," which a *jinni* was supposed to have whispered into his ear as he lay sleeping. In the early years of the ninth century Ziryáb left Bagdad and came to Córdoba, Spain, where he became the idol of the people.

As a teacher of singing he divided his instruction into three courses, Rhythm, Melody, and Ornamentation. The pupil first had to pass a test in singing prolonged "ahs" on every degree of the scale; then he learned the words, marking the strong and the weak beats and the pace on a tambourine; then he was taught the melody; and when that was mastered he was allowed to add the shakes and appoggiaturas and scale passages of ornamentation. Ziryáb's, method might still be used with profit. Certainly it was the key to the music of his time, for before all else was rhythm, the rhythm made by the flow of words and the duration of syllables.

In 1447 a ship sailed into the harbor at Barcelona bringing the first of those wandering "Egyptians" known as gypsies, and with them the beginning of a new era in Spanish folk music. As one follows the gypsy trail in music one is impressed by the powerful influence which these strange people have had on the music of every country in which they have lived. It is a quite unconscious influence, for the gypsy sings and dances to relieve his own feelings, with little regard for his audience and still less for music as an art. The gypsy is never an original creator; he is merely an adapter and an exaggerator.

True to this trait, the gypsies, attracted by the color and motion of Spanish folk music, eagerly seized it for their own, singing, playing, and dancing with an abandon and elaboration which astonished but delighted the natives. Theirs was a gift of style rather than of content — a wanton gypsy gift. Yet it marked Spanish music with the Romany *patrin* and caused the Carmen type of song and dance to be accepted by the uninitiated the world over as "Spanish style."

Much that is delightful and interesting has been written about the music of Spain, but one need never hope to know it by way of books, for words are weak where feeling is so strong. Even the music itself when written down is a barren recollection of the real thing. The Moor and the gypsy alike defy our conventional symbols. It is the way they are done, to the last lifted eyebrow, that gives to these old songs and dances that peculiar fascination which has set generations of artists to building Castles in Spain.

ISAAC ALBÉNIZ

Camprodon   — 1860
Cambo-les-Bains — 1909

The life story of Albéniz reads, in its opening chapters, like an old Spanish rogue tale. Cervantes himself could scarcely have fabricated adventures more fantastic than those which befell this young hero. Isaac Albéniz, born in the spring of 1860 in Camprodon, Catalonia, was one of the five children of a minor government official. The baby's evident delight at the sound of the bugles of a neighboring military post attracted the attention of the family, and his eager listening to the piano playing of an older sister so amused her that she began to give him piano lessons when he was but one year old. At the age of four this amazing baby gave a public performance in Barcelona. He played so well that the audience suspected a trick and had to be shown that there was no older person producing the music behind a curtain.

In after years, Albéniz, speaking of these infant triumphs, said that his father went "a little mad" over the idea of having a child prodigy in the family. At six, Isaac was taken to Paris to enter a competition for piano playing at the Conservatoire. He gave an astonishing performance of Dussek's sonata, *Les Adieux*, and of the last movement of Weber's Concertstück in F Minor. The judges nodded approval, the prize was virtually in his hand. But as he rose from the piano, the young virtuoso, in a fit of typical Albéniz exuberance of spirits, drew from his pocket a rubber ball and threw it against one of the large wall mirrors. Down shattered the glass and with it the prospects of the little Spanish prodigy! No such mad pranks would be countenanced in the sacred precincts of the Paris Conservatoire!

Returning in disgrace to Madrid, where the family was then living, Isaac was entered at the Conservatory. There he pursued his wayward career, practicing what and when he pleased, appearing occasionally in public, dressed in an absurd little musketeer's suit, and at other times, stuffing his young mind with the romantic tales of Jules Verne. At the end of a year, life in Madrid had become far too tame for this nine-year-old. Dressed in his musketeer's suit, with trusty tin rapier at his side, Isaac secretly boarded a train, intending to leave Spain forever behind him. Naturally, the queer little figure aroused the curiosity of his fellow travelers, one of whom chanced to be the Alcalde or Mayor of the Escorial. This gentleman, after questioning the runaway, took him in charge and arranged for him to give a concert at the Escorial Casino. After the concert, which was both a professional and financial success, the good Alcalde put Isaac on the train for Madrid, convinced that he had handled the matter neatly, restored a prodigal son, safe and with a pocketful of money. But it was this pocketful of money, his very own money, that doubtless incited Isaac to further adventure. Why not go on a concert tour, earn a lot more money, and, incidentally, see the world? So he got off the train at Villalba, took one going in the opposite direction, and actually did make a tour, playing in Avila, Zamora, and Salamanca. Bursting with childish pride in his earnings, he started back to Madrid to show them to the family, but the mail coach in which he was traveling was held up by bandits, and the poor little fellow robbed of his treasure.   Since he would not go home empty-handed, there was nothing to do but give more concerts.   So *el niño Albéniz*, as he was called, began those incredible wanderings through Spain, playing wherever he could find an audience.   The child played well enough to attract the attention of musical people.   But the thing that drew the crowds was a vaudeville trick of playing on a covered keyboard, back to the piano, which meant playing with the hands in diametrically opposite position — a quite unusual trick!

After three vagabond years — and what anxious years they must have been for his parents — Isaac, now eleven, came home, only to run away again a few months later. This time, to avoid being caught by the police, with whom he had no doubt been threatened, he went to Cadiz and hid on a ship bound for Puerto Rico.   When the ship was well out at sea, the stowaway came out of hiding and began to ply his trade. The passengers were greatly entertained by his playing, and the young rascal went ashore with full pockets and a sheaf of letters of introduction to influential people in South and Central America.

Albéniz spent several months playing in the cafés and concert halls of Buenos Aires, then came to the United States where, particularly in San Francisco, he had some success.   But, like all who live by their wits, he also had plenty of hardships.   He was often hungry and cold, and always desolately lonely.   The wonder is that the boy survived.   When he had saved about two thousand dollars, he decided to return to Europe.   On the way, he stopped at Havana and gave a concert.   What was his surprise and dismay to see in the audience his father, of all people!   The elder Albéniz had also stopped in Havana, en route to South America on a business trip.   Isaac, being only thirteen, was still subject to parental authority, and had good reason to fear lest his father's displeasure land him in the arms of the police!   But the meeting was peaceful and ended with the sensible decision that Isaac should go on to Europe and spend his time and money in the serious study of music.

He went to Leipzig, where he studied piano and composition until his funds gave out.   Then once more he took to the road, this time in the direction of his own country. He had the good fortune to meet and interest Count Morphy, a patron of the arts. The count brought the young musician to the notice of the King, Alphonso XII, who granted a small pension for the purpose of study.   Brussels at that time boasted a number of excellent teachers, among them the popular Gevaërt, and to him Albéniz went.   In Brussels, he met another Spanish boy, also a music student, who was to become a lifelong friend, Enrique Arbós.   Unfortunately, he also met and joined a set of young good-for-nothings who wasted their time and money in the cafés.   Arbós tells of how sadly Albéniz neglected his music, and of how he, Arbós, used to go to his friend's room, and, finding him nearly always out, would write his name in the thick dust which told plainly that the piano had not been touched for days.   Finally Albéniz and one of his worthless friends made a pact to enjoy life as long as their money lasted, and then make a quick exit.   The friend, evidently first to reach the gruesome goal, hanged himself.   The shock of this tragedy brought young Albéniz to his senses.   He set to work with all his splendid energy and talent, gave a concert in Brussels, and with the money it brought, went to Weimar to study with Liszt.   Little is known of the next two years beyond the fact that master and pupil became close friends; that Albéniz followed Liszt to Rome and then to Budapest; and that because of the brilliance of his playing and the generosity of his nature, so like that of the great Hungarian, Albéniz was called "the Spanish Liszt."

Someone has said that the Spanish artist never stays at home. Surely Albéniz was the typical Spanish rover, for, after his wandering youth and student days, he spent the years from 1880 to 1894 going up and down the world, to Cuba, Mexico, Argentina, to England, Scotland, Berlin, Paris, winning fame as a concert pianist. Yet all the while there was a longing for the home and family which his happy marriage had given him. Successful as he was as a concert artist, Albéniz seems always to have been in need of money. He was forced to turn his talent of composing to account, and at one time is said to have carried a piece of music daily to a Madrid publisher in order to meet his current expenses. "Most of these minor pieces, I think," says Ernest Newman, "were the potboilers of a man who, even when he was writing potboilers, could not forget that he was an artist."

Nor could Albéniz forget the ideals and enthusiasms which had been inspired in him by Felipe Pedrell, composer, teacher, and student of Spanish folk music. Pedrell insists that the lessons he had given Albéniz were merely "half-humorous discussions between two friends. We talked about music, good and bad taste, etc. There was not a hint of pedagogy." Nevertheless, Pedrell's dream of a Spanish art music founded on Spanish folk music made a deep impression on Albéniz and influenced everything he wrote, even the potboilers.

In 1894, Albéniz decided to abandon the rôle of wandering virtuoso for that of composer, a truly Spanish composer dedicated to the expression of Spanish life in music. Unfortunately he spent the precious first years of his serious composing in writing operas which have long been forgotten. In 1899, his first and most important orchestral work appeared, *Catalonia*, a rhapsody celebrating the country of his birth. Two years later came his masterpiece, *Iberia*, originally written for piano and later orchestrated by Arbós.

Albéniz was now living in Paris, the brilliant, stimulating Paris of the nineties. The future looked bright for him and for the new Spanish art music because of him. But his day of physical reckoning was at hand, and old scores of overwork and the neglect and exposure of his vagabond childhood had to be paid. Bravely he fought against ill health, only to lose in May, 1909, when, at Cambo-les-Bains in the Pyrenees, he died at the age of forty-nine.

Jean-Aubry, who knew Albéniz well, pays him this friend's tribute:

He who met Albéniz, were it but once, would remember him to his dying day. At first his effusiveness could surprise, yes, even displease, but soon one felt that a living fire inspired all his gestures, and that the great soul of the man dominated his outward frame; and after one's astonishment would come an affection which nothing could alter. . . . The kindness and the generosity of the man were unsurpassable. He was sensitive without wishing to appear so, and the goodness of his heart was a thing of much charm. He was unstinting in his praise of others; his talk was always of friendship, affection, and joy. I never saw him otherwise. He steeped himself in music as the source of all strength, but nothing in life itself escaped him, and behind his joyous exterior vibrated a heart responsive to the least modulation of the soul. We find it in all his work. . . . He enjoyed himself with juvenile gaiety, and the victims of his jests only loved him the more for them. One would have forgiven him anything, for one was always his debtor.

As an artist, Albéniz was a nationalist in the best sense of the word. He used the rhythms and harmonies peculiar to Spanish folk music — that is to say, being a Spaniard, he spoke his native language. But he rarely borrowed a melody. He was no mere synthesist trying to catch the popular ear with a medley of folk tunes. What he had to say was his own, and he said it fluently and beautifully. The source and the subject of his art was Spain. He saw her face in every country landscape, every crowded city street; he heard her voice in the night winds that swept across the plains of Granada, in the clang of ancient church bells, and in the songs and cries of the people. And with that rare power of suggestion which marks him as a poet-composer, he set the body and soul of Spain to music.

Albéniz gave but ten years to serious composition and died lamenting the fact that the first and best of those years had been wasted in operas and operettas. Yet the belated *Catalonia, Iberia, Azulejos,* and *Navarra* not only place the name of Albéniz among the creators of deathless beauty, but place it first in that significant group known as the Modern Spanish School. Marliave, the French critic, makes what is perhaps the most discriminating estimate of Albéniz's work when he says: "In him the sensuous and melancholy, the joyous and passionate, the wild and chivalrous, the soul of Spain finds itself summarized. And if a Spanish school exists today, conscious of itself, truly national, overflowing with the sap and vitality of youth, it owes itself to the delightful genius of Isaac Albéniz."

FÊTE-DIEU À SEVILLE

Albéniz was more than a nationalist. He was a lover to whom each glimpse of his beloved Spain brought new delight. Her gold-brown landscapes, picturesque villages, and old cathedral cities, her mingled moods of dignity and wild abandon, of fierce activity and dreamy languor never failed to inspire him. His music is but the record of these inspirations. More than half of his pieces bear the names of the places where they were born. "These pieces," says a well-known writer, "are the songs and dances, the sights and sounds of the peninsula, translated with peculiar felicity into the language of the piano, a language which Albéniz has ever successfully extended for his purpose."

The suite *Iberia* is an album of twelve Spanish sketches. Beginning with *Evocación,* which as the name implies evokes the spirit or mood of Spain, the composer then portrays *El Puerto* (The Harbor); *El Corpus en Sevilla,* better known as *Fête-Dieu à Seville* (Corpus Christi Day in Seville); *Rondeña* (a dance); *Almeria* (a port town); *Triana* (a suburb of Seville); *El Albaicin* (the gypsy quarter of Seville); *El Polo* (an Andalusian dance); *Lavapies* (a sort of Lower East Side in Madrid); *Málaga, Jeréz* (home of sherry), and *Eritaña* (a tavern on the outskirts of Seville). *Iberia* is not only an amazing collection of tone pictures and Albéniz's masterpiece but also the cornerstone of modern Spanish music. For Albéniz's work has been the foundation upon which all the later Spanish composers, Arbós, De Falla, Granados, Turina, and others have built.

Fête-Dieu à Seville pictures one of the most characteristic moods of old Spain, the religious fête day. While less important in the church calendar than the great festivals of Christmas and Easter, the early summer festival of Corpus Christi is one dear to Spanish hearts. In many cities, and particularly in Toledo and Seville, Corpus Christi Day has been celebrated for centuries with medieval pomp and circumstance.

Before daylight Seville is astir. Balconies must be hung with colored draperies; flowers and fruits brought fresh from market gardens; festive cakes and wine made ready in family cupboards and vendors' booths and baskets; holiday finery shaken out — and all before eight in the morning, for at eight Seville goes to church. Crowds of men, women, and children pour into the great cathedral, which for five hundred years has been the heart of Seville. It is the largest and, some say, the most beautiful of all Gothic churches.

There, at the high altar, the Cardinal, in eighteenth-century vestments, intones the sacred office. Shafts of colored light from the high windows and the flames of hundreds of candles pierce the scented twilight. Voices blended in the old Gregorian chants accompanied by organ and orchestra ebb and flow in waves of solemn sound. And beneath it all is an undertone of suppressed excitement and expectation as the members of the various *Confradias* — brotherhoods of laymen from every rank and class — make their way through the worshipers to get their tapers and insignia for the procession.

At last the mass is ended, the Cardinal and his attendants come down from the altar, the procession forms, passes once around the cathedral and, to the pealing of bells, out through the great doorway and into the street. Civil guards with bugles, drums, and military band clear the way. Then come the standard-bearers carrying silken banners embroidered with various emblems, crosses of gold and silver, great wreaths of flowers, and often sacred images. After them follows the long line of the *Confradias*, eighty-seven brotherhoods, with lighted tapers; then the canons of the cathedral in white broidered copes and the minor clergy; then the altar boys in their quaint seventeenth-century pages' costumes of crimson velvet with slashed sleeves and plumed hats. These are the famous *Seises*, the boys who every year at the feast of Corpus Christi dance before the altar in the cathedral of Seville, reverently tracing the figures of the sacred double S — *Sanctus, Sanctissimus*. This strange ceremony dates back to the year 1264 when the Church dramatized the Bible stories for the masses who could not read, and showed David and the Israelites dancing before the Ark of the Testament. After the altar boys comes the great crucifix and the incense bearers, and behind them ten prominent citizens carrying a silken canopy beneath which walks the Cardinal bearing the historic monstrance of Seville. Made of gold and set with thirteen thousand pearls and diamonds, gifts of the faithful for five centuries, it contains the yet more priceless treasure of the Church, the Blessed Sacrament.

Past the Town Hall, where seats have been erected for the notables, and on through the crowded streets the slow procession makes its way, unwinding, as it were, the scroll of a nation's emotions. For the procession of Corpus Christi Day is a pageant of the many moods of Spain. Here a group of urchins dance and caper to the music of the band, there the street is bordered with kneeling figures lost in prayer as the Host goes by. And at any moment the solemn hush may be broken by a single voice raised in a *saeta*, a devout little song inspired by just such occasions and as brief and spontaneous as a pious ejaculation, the *saeta*, from which it gets its name. And high above in the Giralda tower clamor the great bronze bells, the age-old voice of the Roman Church which has ordered Spanish life for so many centuries. These were the sights, the sounds, the ever-changing moods which Albéniz translated into the music of *Fête-Dieu à Seville*.

The piece begins with the distant roll of drums, announcing the approach of the procession. Soon we hear the military band playing a gay popular air, *La Tarara*. Beginning in the flutes:[1]

it is passed on to other voices, each adding its own little variation, until the piercing nearness of the piccolos brings the vanguard of the procession upon us. There is the suggestion of marching feet, also of less dignified caperings on the side. All is soon fused with the clanging of the bells and the brasses voicing the power and glory of the Church:

The sound fades as the procession moves on. Then cleverly Albéniz suggests the voices of the people in pious acclaim, a brief *saeta* intoned by solo English horn:

above the murmur of strings.

[1] Excerpts from *Iberia* printed by permission of Associated Music Publishers, Inc., New York, owners of the copyright, and by authorization of the Sociedad General de Autores de España.

The gay marching theme returns, only to be again submerged by the bells and by a remarkable passage in which the brasses and lower woodwinds give the effect of the great cathedral organ. One feels the mounting excitement of the crowd in a riotous version of the first theme from which emerges an irrepressible variation:

in which the whole orchestra joins with noisy enthusiasm.

Then, in a sudden quiet, flute and bassoon begin to chant this plaintive air:

Albéniz liked to call himself a Moor, and surely this melody with its Far-East flavor proves his claim to oriental ancestry.

Gently now the picture fades. A solo bassoon, like a voice of contentment:

makes a final comment as distant evening bells mark the peaceful ending of Corpus Christi Day in Seville.

TRIANA

One of the most interesting of the sketches from the suite *Iberia* is of Triana, that ancient quarter of Seville which lies just across the river. Despite its imperial name — Triana was named for the Roman Emperor Trajan whose birthplace is near by — it has been for many years the gathering place of gypsies, bullfighters, pedlars, strolling players, and other picturesque rascals who live by their wits. The people of Triana are as gregarious as sparrows and seem to spend their lives laughing, gossiping, bargaining, and quarreling in the streets. It is this colorful, irresponsible life that Albéniz pictures in his music.

A rhythmic introduction suggests the purposeless milling of the crowd from which a bold voice detaches itself:

Another, seemingly an old voice, tinged with fatalism, answers:

Their dialogue is cut short by a fragment of modal melody, perhaps of a chant floating out from some chapel window:

It is caught up in rhythmic strumming which ushers in a grotesque little theme:

a veritable street gamin of a tune, featured first by the solo trumpet and then by the solo English horn.

Presently a song, *très doux et nonchalant:*

claims the attention of the crowd. It is taken up by one singer after another, each adding his own little touches to the melody and harmony but keeping the same well-marked rhythm.

Two curious sustained chords interrupt the singing, and then on lightly running *arpeggios* the gamin tune darts in, but is swept aside by the song in which the whole crowd now seems to join. The music swells to a climax, then dies down to a soft *staccato*, a sort of contented tapping of the rhythm.   There is a pause, then out pipes the irrepressible gamin tune.   This time it runs into impudent, mocking chords which, as if they were naughty urchins, are soon put to flight by the authority of the first theme, which loudly claims the last word.

ENRIQUE GRANADOS

Lérida — 1867
At Sea — 1916

"*¡Ay! ¡Pobre Granados, qué gracia tenía!*" — Ah, poor Granados, what gifts he had! This sighing tribute, which almost invariably springs to the lips of his countrymen at the mention of his name, is a faithful commentary on the life and works of Enrique Granados.

Poor Granados, indeed, since his life, a shameful sacrifice to war, came to a tragic close on the torpedoed *Sussex* just at the zenith of his powers and hopes.   But it is unfair to him to think of him as he is so often catalogued in barren biographical dictionaries — "Spanish composer, died at sea in World War I."   For Granados also lived.   And "what gifts he had!" — *gracia* in the ancient, beautiful sense of graces bestowed by the gods who preside over the music and poetry of life.

Granados was the son of an officer in the Spanish army.   He was a gifted child, and his parents were proud to foster his music.   But music, as an art, was a very casual affair in the Barcelona of Granados's childhood.   Teachers were satisfied if a pupil played or sang prettily.   Enrique was clever and charming and easily susceptible to praise.   As a result, he grew up with little practical training and with the dangerous philosophy of "why work when everyone, including myself, is so pleased with me?"

But in spite of his indifferent instruction, the boy acquired a background which was to determine the whole design of his later work.   Spain is a land of singing mothers. And with the native songs in which linger almost-forgotten fragments of old tales of history and romance, of Moorish and early Christian legend, Señora Granados gave her child his real start as an artist.

At twenty Enrique was sent to Paris to study.   Unfortunately, he at once contracted typhoid fever and was kept from entering the regular courses at the conservatory.   He seemed fated to miss the rigorous drills and the tonic of competition which he so sadly needed.   Although his piano playing improved and his musical taste grew with all the concerts he heard, he nevertheless went back to Spain still an undisciplined young rhapsodist with a technical equipment wholly unworthy of his talents.

He had not been long at home before he began to be troubled about the musical taste of his countrymen. Public favor seemed to be divided between sentimental music of the Tosti type and degraded music hall ballads. Why, he asked himself, could Spain not have a popular music which would be truly music of the people, music based on good old Spanish themes? The Scandinavian countries had one, thanks to Grieg and his followers; Russia had one founded by the famous "Five." So the twenty-three-year-old Granados set himself the task of writing music which should glorify the style and rhythms of those old songs of his childhood. The *Tonadillas*, twelve attractive Spanish dances for piano, were the result.

Then he had an ambition to interpret in music some of the paintings of Goya, the great Goya of the later years after he had given up imitating French artists and had become the recorder of Spanish life. Granados, no mean sketcher himself, admired Goya profoundly, and his *Goyescas*, two books of piano sketches, was a brilliant tribute to the older master. Later these sketches were developed into the opera *Goyescas*.

Although Granados wrote two operas, several books of Spanish dances, some chamber music, songs, and a symphonic poem, his own country knew him as a master pianist. He gave piano lessons, and was known for his generosity to poor pupils though he could ill afford it, having very little money and a sizable family to support.

Granados was a lovable fellow, irresponsible as a child and given to the maddest, merriest pranks. His musician friends laughed long afterward over the wild orchestra he formed, in which each of them was to play an instrument he knew nothing about. Granados himself led, performing on a paper-covered comb. Rehearsals were held in an open patio behind a music shop. The strange orchestra became famous — also infamous. One day as they were loudly maltreating a well-known symphony, a shower of rotten eggs, fruit, and vegetable peelings rained down upon them, accompanied by a thunder of banging pots and pans. The neighbors had revolted! But Granados calmly finished the symphony, bowing ceremoniously in his spattered clothes.

Another time he gave the composer Albéniz a horn to try, bidding him make the heavens ring. Albéniz blew, and the heavens rang, but not with clarion tones — the horn had been filled with soapsuds! And they tell of one occasion when Granados, almost late for a train which was to take him to an important engagement, jumped on a passing milk wagon, shouting to the astonished driver, "To the station! To the station! Tell your master Granados commanded you!" And as they rattled through the streets, Granados, from his perch on the milk cans, raised his hat to passing friends as unconcernedly as if he had been riding in a carriage of state.

With his own children he was an incorrigibly fantastic playfellow. He seemed to have none of the characteristic Spanish dignity with its fear of appearing ridiculous. But in society, Granados was anything but *gauche*. "Like Chopin," says Collet, "Granados left the memory of a Prince Charming of music."

In 1916, Granados was invited to come to New York to direct the production of his opera *Goyescas*, the first Spanish opera ever to be given at the Metropolitan. He was very happy over it. He had not had much of what the world calls success, and this seemed to be the turning point in his career. As he confided to a friend on the eve of his departure, he was happy — not so much for what he had already done but because at last he knew what he was capable of doing, what dreams he would realize on his return to Spain.

Goyescas was a success, and as they sailed homeward the composer and his wife were gay with plans for the future. Then suddenly, cruelly, came an end to all the plans and dreams. The captain of the *Sussex* said that at the moment when it seemed that they might save him, Granados saw his wife struggling in the water. Throwing off his life belt he managed to reach her, and with his arms about her they vanished into the sea.

"*¡Ay! ¡Pobre Granados, qué gracia tenía!*"

INTERMEZZO, GOYESCAS

In his first *Goyescas*, which were piano sketches, Granados sought to evoke in music the spirit of the Madrid which Goya knew and painted. It was the Madrid of the early eighteen hundreds with its picturesque *majas* and *majos* (coquettes and mashers), a Madrid of romantic patios, grilled windows, and gardens sweet with scent and nightingale song.

The opera *Goyescas*, which was made from these Spanish sketches, has the slightest of plots — a mere framework for the music and pictures. It is the story of two pairs of rival lovers, a toreador and his *maja*, and a captain of the guards and his lady, who flirt in the first act, fall out in the second, and duel to the death in the third.

It is the music, the lovely Spanish dances, and the scenes with Goya characters and settings which make the opera. The first act, which takes place on the outskirts of Madrid, where a holiday crowd is making merry, is a sort of coming to life of one of Goya's famous tapestry cartoons in which a group of laughing girls are seen tossing a *pelele*, or straw man, in a blanket. Tossing the *pelele*, a stuffed figure of a man which usually represents some tiresome lover, is an ancient popular sport in Spain. The second tableau is after Goya's *El Baile de Candil* — The Lantern-lighted Ball — and the third shows Rosario's garden, where the final love and death scenes take place.

The characters are the types of Goya's brush, and the theme is the sentiment of Goya's time, perhaps of all time, that "in a woman's hands man is ever a *pelele*."

Between the second and third acts and foreshadowing the melancholy ending comes the charming Intermezzo. Granados wrote it in New York, a few days before *Goyescas* was to be produced and, they say, in less than an hour's time.

There is a brief but dramatic introduction in which strings and trombone in bold unison suggest heralds demanding attention for the song that is to follow. The singer strums a handful of rather casual chords and the song begins: [1]

[1] Quotations from the Intermezzo from *Goyescas*, by Enrique Granados, used by kind permission of the publisher, G. Schirmer, Inc.

a lovely sighing melody with a surprising major ending which leads into a vigorous theme for violins:

Again we hear the sighing voice of the 'cello, brightened this time by a little dancing violin obbligato. Near the end the composer adds the soft color of woodwinds and harp, suggesting the delicate sounds and motions of the moonlit garden.

No one could call this Intermezzo great music, but it is good music, simple, sincere, and pleasing. Granados has not overdone the slight themes and gentle rhythms, and, listening, we understand the appraisal once made of him, "Granados had a small voice, but a clear one."

THREE SPANISH DANCES

Oriental

Slight but charming is this group known as *Tres Danzas Españolas*. Like most of Granados's works these little dances were originally written for his special instrument, the piano, but were afterward orchestrated by J. Lamote de Grignon, director of the Symphony Orchestra of Barcelona.

The first of these dances, called *Oriental*, is full of the delicate melancholy of the Moors. The music begins with a little figure:[1]

soft and swaying as a wind in the olive trees. Above it two flutes give out a melody:

of monotonous horizontal line, characteristically oriental.

A solo viola sings the second theme:

[1] Quotations from *Three Spanish Dances*, Copyright, 1946, printed with the kind permission of the copyright owner, the Union Musical Espanola.

a plaintive song in syncopated rhythm, ending with a wail:

Then the first melody returns, and, growing softer and softer, flows along to its quiet end.

Andaluza

From sunny Andalusia comes the music which, at least to the outside world, seems most typically Spanish. It is music with vigorous, changing rhythms, sudden outbursts, and languid melodies, the emotional expression of a southern people in whom violence and indolence are strangely mingled.

To the strumming of guitars, suggested by *pizzicato* strings, the English horn and 'celli announce the theme:

which is caught up by the flutes in a curious, murmuring afterphrase with a sudden glow of major tonality at the end:

Eagerly the strings try to follow this bright lead, but the melancholy English horn will not be diverted.

In the middle section, however, a solo violin succeeds in having its own way with the tune:

and, for a time, transforms it. But again the woodwinds catch it up, and this time their insistent refrain:

brings back the minor mood and the original version of the theme.

For all its characteristic color and rhythm there is a gentleness about this music, a mellowness as surprising as it is grateful. It sets one thinking. Can it be that the

French and Russian composers have given us an exaggerated idea of "Spanish style" as a blare and bang, a glare of crude red and yellow? And were their *Españas* and *Capriccio Espagnols* but tourists' impressions? Surely this less sensational music of Granados seems a more convincing expression of Spain.

Rondalla

In his title, *Rondalla*, we are told that Granados merely meant to present a *jota* with no suggestion of a fable, which is the usual definition of the word. The *jota* is a favorite dance in the province of Aragon, and is said to date from the twelfth century. It is a dance in triple meter, somewhat like the waltz but much freer in form, sometimes, as in this case, swinging into a moment of duple meter or even breaking into song.

The first theme, lightly stepped by the clarinets, is a little rustic dance:

which, as the other instruments join in, changes to a more vigorous duple meter:

and works up to a wild pitch of excitement.

A single oboe repeats the theme to murmured harmonies in clarinets and bassoons:

The mood is changing, and presently we hear the muted solo trumpet singing:

a quaint old *copla*, a bit of "deep song" with its half-sad, half-glad burden.

> I love and no one knows.
> I love so well.
> The deepest loves are those
> One does not tell.

Then the song becomes a duet with an accordionlike accompaniment marked by the whir of castanets.

But even shadows dance in Spain, and moods of longing endure but for a moment. The little song is interrupted by the returning dance theme which brings the *Rondalla* to a whirling, stamping close.

JOAQUIN TURINA

Seville — 1882

As so often happens with interesting persons who have not yet lived their biographies through to a tidy end, it is difficult at this distance to learn much about Joaquin Turina the man. All the more difficult, since he is a busy, modest man who stays in his own country and out of the news columns. Only music critics write about him, and they seem to forget the man in their enthusiasm for the artist — for Turina shares with De Falla the distinction of being one of the two foremost contemporary Spanish composers.

Both are Andalusian to the core, which may account for the statement that "in Andalusia has been created the great music of modern Spain." But they are not alike. De Falla is more the man of the world. His style, while sincerely Spanish in its feeling, is tempered in form by the music of other times and other countries. Turina, however, is so purely Sevillian that, were he a less great artist, he might also be called provincial.

Turina grew up in Seville with the two finest traditions of Spanish music constantly ringing in his young ears. At home, in the streets, market places, and inns, he heard the songs and dances of Andalusia, while in the great cathedral he came to love the church music of Spain, so little known and so rarely beautiful. Indeed, his first music teacher was the choirmaster of the cathedral. Doubtless the religious theme in *La Procesión del rocío* owes its spiritual quality to cathedral impressions made in the sensitive heart of a little boy.

After a period of study in Madrid, Turina went to Paris, where he spent fourteen years and where, from such teachers as d'Indy, he must have learned many of the refinements of composition for which the French masters are famous. His instrument is the piano, which he plays with great artistry.

Today Turina lives and teaches in Madrid. He has a proud list of compositions to his credit — stage works, symphonic poems, a number of charming songs, and chamber music, which is his chief delight. He is also interested in research and has written a brief encyclopedia of music.

Turina's music is picturesque, it reflects the life of Spain as he sees it. But his musical pictures are never done in those crude lines and colorings, the almost "poster" style, so often mistaken for the Spanish idiom. There is about them a touch of deftness and delicacy, a tenderness of feeling which one associates with tempera painting or with the softened tones of old tapestries.

LA PROCESIÓN DEL ROCÍO

"A luminous fresco!" exclaimed Debussy, expressing in two winged words the peculiar charm of this music in which a composer has used tone and tune as a painter would use color and line to make us see. *La Procesión del rocío*, "The Procession of the Dew," is music for "that inward eye" which is the bliss of concerts as well as of solitude. And if as we listen we fail to see the picture, we may know that we have also failed to hear the music.

It is a picture of one of the many religious processions, the *pasos*, which for centuries have illumined the calendar of the Spanish year. For Spain has never lost her love for religious symbols, the relics, the ritual, and the sacred images so dear to the heart of the medieval churchman. And when during Holy Week or on other feast days the great wooden figures, some of them masterpieces of ancient Spanish sculpture, are taken from their niches, dressed in their costliest robes, and borne through the streets, the people feel their faith renewed. It is as if the suffering Christ and the gracious Virgin whom they adore had mingled with them for a passing moment, touching their lives and making their religion an intimate thing of the narrow streets as well as of the great cathedrals. The feeling of caste is lost in the crowd of barefoot penitents that follow the *pasos*. In their masks and ghostly habits they march side by side, white feet of *hidalgos* and gnarled peasant feet that have never known shoes, led by an emotion as ancient and as universal as humanity itself.

Seville is famous for its *pasos*, but it is not one of these gorgeous cathedral processions which Turina has chosen for his picture. He has crossed the river to Triana, the gypsy quarter. Here during the festival seasons or in times of such distress as a plague of cholera, the Virgin of the ancient church of Santa Ana is taken through the streets to share the joys and sorrows of her people.

Midsummer Day, marking the summer solstice and the feast of St. John, is a time of merrymaking in Spain. On Midsummer Eve great bonfires are lit and kept burning all night long. Then it is that water has magic power, and many a maid, on the stroke of twelve, breaks an egg into a basin of water on her window sill and sees, in the swirl of the egg white, the face of her future bridegroom. People with diseased skins roll in the dewy meadows, and no ambitious girl would miss the chance to bathe her face in the dew of Midsummer Morning for beauty's sake. Such a holiday without a *pasos* would be sadly lacking, and it is this procession of the festival of the dew which Turina has painted in luminous fresco.

The long twilight of Midsummer Eve is falling. Shops are closed, homes are deserted, the dim old church is empty, for even the Virgin has left her altar. But the streets are gay with life. Shrill voices fill the air with vendors' cries of balloons, peanuts, fruits, and what not; greetings and quarrelings are heard; and a snatch of song, the click of castanets, or the twang of a guitar tell of little groups of singers and dancers. Triana is *en fête!*

A note on the score says, "*soleares* succeed *seguidillas*, and then a drunken man starts singing a *garrotin*." There is no introduction — with a shout from the wind instruments and a *glissando* of harps and strings the music plunges into the midst of the festivities in a joyous theme, out of which grows a singing melody for flutes, clarinets, and bassoons, followed by a little country tune for the oboes — all in the mood of the Sevillian *seguidilla*, that most lighthearted of gypsy songs.

A noisy crowd breaks in for a moment in loud chords, after which we overhear a fragment of conversation between oboe and clarinet. Then from the viola comes a suggestion of the *soleares* with its mood of sadness.

It is a bit of the "deep song" of which Irving Brown in his charming book of that title says, "It is Andalusia itself. It is like the bare Sierras on which the sun beats implacably without altering the rock while the green grass of northern meadows would be withered by its sharp rays."

The violins catch up the wistful melody, which soon, however, gives way to the dancing first theme and to a vigorous scrap of duple rhythm which might be the drunken man starting to sing his rowdy *garrotin*.

The music grows steadily louder and more festive, with the whole orchestra repeating the lively opening theme. Then a sudden hush falls on the waiting crowd, a muffled drum is heard, and above its persistent beat a piping folk theme heralds the approach of the *pasos*.

Slowly, on a silver car drawn by oxen, *La Virgen Aparecida* — Our Lady of the Vision — passes to age-old music as dimly sweet as her faded face, music which lifts the heart and at the same time clutches at the throat.

Like a grain field bent by the wind, the crowd of merrymakers is bowed by the reverence and adoration which this ancient symbol unfailingly invokes. For a moment the whole atmosphere is changed, as so often and so easily happens with the mercurial temperament of the Latin races. Tapers glow, and the odor of incense mingles with the perfume of the Midsummer Night.

Again the herald's tune is heard, followed by the Virgin's theme now loud and triumphant, through which the trumpets blare the March Royal. The bells peal with all their might — bells that may have pealed on that Palm Sunday in 1492 when Seville welcomed Christopher Columbus back from a New World, for Triana is old, her church of Santa Ana bears the date of 1276.

The holiday theme bursts out again as the procession disappears. Near the end a calm seems to settle over the music, a sort of benediction or afterglow, which, on the very last note, is startled by a triple *forte* chord from every instrument in the orchestra flashing out like a Bengal light in the wanton mood of Midsummer Eve!

CHAPTER VII

Four from France

HECTOR BERLIOZ

La Côte-St.-André — 1803
Paris   — 1869

In all the history of music there is no stranger figure, no more original or picturesque artist than Hector Berlioz. His vivid personality scintillated from so many facets that it is difficult to determine whether he was more poet than musician or more dramatist than poet.

Not the least of his artistic contributions was an autobiography. For, like Benvenuto Cellini, who held that "All men, of whatsoever quality they be, who have done anything of excellence, ought, if they are persons of truth and honesty, to describe their life with their own hands," Berlioz felt that "I myself should record those portions of my agitated and laborious career which may be interesting to the lovers of art." And so Berlioz wrote his autobiography, two volumes of Memoirs supplemented by two volumes of letters, which, with the attention of an artist translator like Symonds, might easily become as popular as the autobiography of the famous Benvenuto.

Into these old-fashioned volumes Berlioz has crowded not only the story of his own life, but also his thoughts on art, music, and life in general. And from their finely printed, yellowing pages, we shall take the material for this brief biography.

Hector Berlioz was born at the beginning of the nineteenth century in a tiny town called La Côte-St.-André situated between Grenoble and Lyons. The Memoirs give a charming picture of his childhood in this pleasant country, of the hillside on which the little town was built, the fruitful valley below, and the snow-capped Alps marching like giants along the far horizon.

Another vivid picture is of a first communion. Six o'clock on a bright spring morning with the wind whispering in the poplars; the child Hector, holding his sister's hand, joins a flock of important little girls in white frocks and veils; inside the church the solemn silence is shattered by a burst of music — the eucharistic hymn; for the small boy "a new world of love and feeling was revealed, more glorious by far than the heaven of which I had heard so much."

"This was my first musical experience, and in this manner I became religious, so religious that I attended mass every day and communion every Sunday. My weekly confession to the director of my conscience was, 'My Father, I have done nothing,' to which the worthy man always replied, 'Go on, my child, as you have begun.'" Berlioz, remembering his youthful idleness, whimsically remarks, "And so I did for several years."

In these days of frenzied family life when too many small boys think of father as a hurried, worried source of nickels or possible punishment, Berlioz's memories of his father are most appealing. Louis Berlioz was a doctor, a quiet, scholarly man, devoted to "the dangerous and difficult art of medicine" and content to practice it obscurely in a tiny village. But he was not content with the kind of schooling the village offered his only son, so he himself took up the task of teaching the ten-year-old Hector. "What a patient, careful, clever teacher of languages, literature, history, and geography he was," writes Berlioz. "He even taught me music. . . . What love is necessary to carry out such a task, and how few fathers there are who could and would do it."

At first the boy's interest was all for maps and faraway places. He knew the names of every one of the Sandwich Islands and much about life in Borneo, but he could not begin to name the departments (corresponding to our states) in France! And so great was his fascination for ships that he says, "Had I chanced to live in a seaport town, I should certainly have run away to sea." Then he encountered La Fontaine and Virgil, and his sea dreams paled before the beauties of poetry.

Hector's first music lessons were given by the good doctor in self-defense. It seems that the boy had found an old flageolet hidden away in a drawer and tried to pick out the tune, Malbrouk — known to us as "The Bear Went over the Mountain," "We Won't Go Home until Morning," etc. "My father," says Berlioz, "annoyed with this tiresome tootling, begged me to lay aside the instrument until he could find time to teach me how to play less discordantly the heroic strain I had selected. He did so, and in two days I was able to perform my Malbrouk tune to the assembled family." Before long Hector had progressed from flageolet to flute, and his father joined with some other families in importing a music master from Lyons to teach the village children.

The boy's twelfth year was marked by two overwhelming discoveries. On a holiday visit to his grandfather he met a tall girl of eighteen who was spending the summer at a neighboring house. To Hector she was a heavenly vision of "brilliant eyes and equally brilliant pink shoes" — the first pink shoes the village boy had ever seen. He fell wildly and absurdly in love. The bewitching Estelle considered herself very much of a young lady and Hector an impossible kid. He mooned about to the amusement of his elders, who, unfortunately, made cruel fun of him. It was just a bit of midsummer madness, but Berlioz never forgot the rapture and the despair of those weeks. "Time itself is powerless . . .," he writes; "no afterloves can quite blot out the first." This little prelude was also to be the coda to his love life, some half a century later.

Hector's second discovery, fortunately less emotionally upsetting, was an old harmony book from which he got the idea of writing music of his own — a far more exciting adventure than merely tootling some other fellow's tunes on a flute. The would-be composer set to work with all the devotion of his fiery little heart. He produced pieces with "impossible basses and more impossible chords" and all tinged with the melancholy of his hopeless love. "My thoughts," he writes, "seemed to be veiled in crêpe." One of these early efforts, a love song with sickly sentimental words, turned up later as the main theme of the *Symphonie fantastique*. "It came back to me," writes

Berlioz, "and it seemed to express the overwhelming grief of a young heart in the pangs of hopeless love. . . . I put it in just as it was."

Dr. Berlioz did not share Hector's enthusiasm for composing. It was all very well for the boy to practice the flute and spend his evenings harmlessly playing trios and quartets with his young friends, but there were to be no foolish notions of a musical career. The time was at hand when Hector should give up his "childish aversion" to sick people and prepare to study medicine.

"But about this time," writes Berlioz, "an apparently trifling incident strengthened my musical bent. . . . I had never seen a full score. One day, however, I found a sheet of paper with twenty-five staves upon it. I realized in a moment the wondrous instrumental and vocal combination to which they might give rise, and I cried out, 'What an orchestral work one might write on that!' From this moment the musical fermentation in my head went on increasing and my distaste for medicine redoubled."

Then Dr. Berlioz played a trump. He presented his son with a huge treatise on anatomy with gruesome life-size illustrations, saying, "This is the book you are to study . . . and if you will promise to work earnestly at anatomy, I will get you a beautiful flute with all the new keys from Lyons." Poor Hector was trapped. He had long wanted just such a flute, and besides, he hadn't the heart to disappoint his father. So, reluctantly, he accepted the terms and began to study the fearful and wonderful makings of man.

At nineteen Hector and a young cousin who had also been studying with Dr. Berlioz set out for Paris to enter medical school. The Memoirs give a horribly graphic account of his first impressions of the dissecting room where greedy rats and sparrows fought for revolting tidbits of human flesh. Hector hated it with all his heart, but for a time kept stoically on.

To him the one redeeming feature of Paris was its music. He heard his first opera, his first orchestra, and it simply turned his head. Then he learned that the Conservatoire library was open to outsiders, and there, reveling in the scores of Gluck, he lost his head completely and resolved to be a composer "in spite of father, mother, uncles, aunts, grandparents, and friends."

Medical books gave place to texts on harmony and composition. The ambitious boy wrote several "wishy-washy" pieces which ended in the scrap basket, then a mass for Innocent's Day, the feast of the choir children. Berlioz tried everywhere to get his mass performed and finally borrowed twelve thousand *francs* and himself paid the chorus and orchestra to give it. The audience approved and the newspapers praised it, but five years later Berlioz threw the mass in the fire along with his other first efforts.

Bold with the success of his mass, the young composer wrote his parents that he had decided to give up medicine and enter the Conservatoire as a regular student. His father made the classic reply of withdrawing his allowance. Hector then went home to plead his cause. He pled in vain. Dr. Berlioz insisted upon his son's choosing what he considered a more manly profession, and Mme. Berlioz, who was very religious and who, like many of her countrymen, associated music with the theater, warned Hector that a musical career was nothing but "a path which leads to discredit in this world and damnation in the next."

Just as prospects seemed hopeless, Dr. Berlioz relented. Hector should go back to Paris and have a trial at music, but if, within a certain time, he had done nothing unusual, he was then to choose another profession. "You know what I think of second-rate poets," said the good man. "Second-rate artists are no better, and it would be a deep humiliation to me to see you numbered among the useless members of society."

"My father," writes Berlioz, "was far less intolerant of second-rate doctors, who are not only more numerous than bad poets and artists but are also actively instead of passively dangerous."

Back to Paris young Berlioz went on an allowance of about twenty-five dollars a month. He might have managed to live and study on this amount, but he could not save enough from it to pay back the twelve thousand *francs* he had borrowed for his mass. He could never bear a debt or obligation of any kind, so he managed to find a few pupils at twenty-five cents a lesson, and began to save every *sou*. He took a cheap little attic room, and instead of taking his meals at a restaurant, bought dry bread, raisins, and prunes, which he ate, seasoned with a beautiful view from one of the Seine bridges. It worked very well for a while, and by the end of summer he had paid half his debt. But as the frosty days began to come, thoughts of firewood, warmer clothes, and hot soup interrupted his dreams by the river. He tried for more work and at last succeeded in getting a place as a chorus singer in a comic opera company.

About this time he met a young chemistry student who was also trying to live on next to nothing, and the two decided to join forces. "We took two little rooms in the Rue de la Harpe," says Berlioz. "Antoine, who was accustomed to furnaces and retorts, undertook the duties of head cook and used me as a mere scullion."

During the next few years Berlioz took life both *presto* and *fortissimo*. He lived mainly on nervous energy, sometimes going for days without food or sleep just to prove, as he said, "what genius can endure." He became infected with the extravagant notions of the young Romanticists and continually saw himself as an actor in a play. He was consumed with a desire to compose something that would astound the music world, and studied furiously.

The Conservatoire teachers, who liked "soothing music" and rule-abiding pupils, were no match for this romantic young rebel and could give him little. Most of Berlioz's knowledge and inspiration came from score-reading and from evenings at the opera for which he was lucky enough to get free tickets. Gluck was his idol. With a little group of fellow enthusiasts he would make serious preparation for every Gluck opera. Then, score in hand, they would follow the performance with jealous care. If the slightest liberty were taken with their precious score, the astonished orchestra and audience would see a gaunt young fellow with an "umbrella" of wild red hair, piercing eyes, and severe mouth rise in the pit and shout, "There are no cymbals there; who has dared to tamper with Gluck?" or, "Not a sign of a trombone, this is intolerable!"

It happened that about this time a company of London players came over to introduce Shakespearean drama in Paris. Berlioz went to see *Hamlet*. He did not then know a word of English, but he promptly fell in love with Ophelia — in person, Henrietta Smithson. For days and nights he wandered about Paris like a madman, eating nothing and sleeping only when and where utter exhaustion laid him low — in the fields, on the snowy bank of the Seine, or on a café table where the frightened waiters thought him dead!

He went to the English theater again and found his lovely Ophelia changed to an even lovelier Juliet. "Ah, I am lost!" he cried. What was to be done? She was a famous actress, he a penniless nobody! For weeks he moped in despair. Then, he writes, "All at once I rose up determined that the light of my obscure name should flash up even to her, where she stood. . . . 'I will show her,' I said, 'that *I also* am an artist!'" His plan was to give a concert of his own compositions, of which he already had quite a collection. To do this he must have a hall, an orchestra and chorus, and copies of his manuscripts. The hall he managed to beg from the Conservatoire; the performers came, some out of friendship, others for the little he could pay; the copies he had to make with his own hand, working sixteen hours a day to do it.

At last, after several near-fatalities, the concert came off, was well received, and Berlioz hailed as a promising young composer. "Would the tidings of my success reach Miss Smithson in the whirl of her own triumph?" he writes. "Alas, I learned afterward that, absorbed in her own brilliant career, she never even heard of my name, my struggles, my concert, or my success!"

Berlioz then wrote to his Ophelia begging to see her, but his letters only annoyed and frightened her, and she sent him word that "nothing could be more impossible." The rejected lover now indulged in a perfect orgy of self-pity and bitterness and, with questionable chivalry, he immortalized the whole sorry episode in a *Symphonie fantastique*.

Through these stormy years Berlioz held fast to one steadying idea — winning the *Prix de Rome*, which meant a five-year student pension and was his only hope for advancement. At first he was simply ruled out as ineligible for competition. Several years later he was allowed to submit a composition, but the judges pronounced it unplayable. The following year he won a second prize, and everyone thought he would surely win first in the next competition. But in this next competition Berlioz did such complete dramatic justice to the subject, which was the death of Cleopatra, that the jury decided not to award any first prize that year rather than encourage a composer who showed "such tendencies." These "tendencies" meant that Berlioz had pictured a remorseful queen, dying by her own hand, and praying to be admitted to the tombs of the Pharaohs. The judges preferred a more ladylike death with soothing boudoir music.

In the midst of the Revolution of 1830 Berlioz made his fifth trial for the *Prix de Rome*. "To the tune of the dry thud of bullets as they struck close to my windows or on the walls of my room," he writes, "I hurriedly dashed off the last pages of my cantata." This time he wrote down to the level of his judges and won. And although he felt little pride in his success and afterward burned his prize piece, it did, as he said, "set on my powers the official seal which would gratify my parents. . . . It was a diploma, a certificate of my ability, and it meant independence, nay, wealth, for five years to come."

Berlioz's account of the hazardous voyage from Marseilles to Leghorn, running full sail in a hurricane, of life at the Academy, of his explorations in old Italian cities and in the mountains is delightful reading. He found the routine of life at the Villa Medici tiresome, possibly because he was older than most of his fellow students. "I was as fierce as a chained dog," he says, "and the attempts of my comrades to induce me to share in their amusements only increased my irritation."

The "chained dog" was friendly at times, it seems, for Berlioz tells of evenings when, sitting around the "little fountain which splashed and flashed in the moonlight," the students sang to the accompaniment of his guitar. Sometimes they gave what they called "the English concert." Then each man sang a different song in a different key. "At a given signal, the performers started off one after the other, and this grand ensemble for twenty-four performers was shouted at a continuous *crescendo* to the accompaniment of the dismal howling of all the dogs on the Pincian, while the barbers, standing at their shop doors in the Piazza below, remarked to each other with a contemptuous smile and shrug, '*Musica francese*' [French music]."

Berlioz had little better opinion of Italian music than the barbers had of this French music. "The words *symphony* and *overture*," he writes, "are used in Rome to designate a certain noise which the orchestra makes before the curtain rises and to which no one ever listens." He was bitterly disappointed in the music at St. Peter's, where he had expected an organ and choir in keeping with the size and beauty of the building. He was homesick for the music of Paris, the concerts, the opera, and the music of the churches, and he felt little urge to compose.

The real joy and inspiration of those Italian years came from the excursions into the country. In a letter to a friend, Berlioz writes, "I am going to try climbing rocks and crossing torrents to get rid of that leprosy of triviality which covers me from head to foot in our infernal barrack. The atmosphere which I share with my fellow manu-facturers of the Academy does not suit my lungs; I am going to breathe a purer air. I am taking with me a bad guitar, a gun, some music paper, a few books, and the germ of a grand work which I shall try to hatch in the woods."

He would wander over the *campagna* or through the Abruzzi mountains, shouting and singing, reciting Virgil, careless of what he ate or where he slept, visiting old monasteries and making friends with everyone he met — bandits, soldiers, and peasants who loved to dance to his guitar.

On one of these excursions his unconventional habits got him into trouble with the police at Nice. "It is quite clear," they reasoned, "that the young musician has not come here to see the opera because he never goes near the theater. He spends his days on the Villefranche rocks . . . evidently waiting for a signal from some revolu-tionary ship. . . . He does not dine *table d'hôte* . . . that is to avoid being drawn into conversation by the secret agents. Now he is gradually making the acquaintance of our officers . . . in order to open up negotiations with which Young Italy has entrusted him. The conspiracy is as clear as daylight!"

Berlioz was summoned to the police station and questioned:

"What are you doing here?"

"Recovering from an illness. I compose and dream and thank God for the sun-shine, the beautiful sea, and the green hills."

"You are not a painter?"

"No."

"Yet you are always drawing something in an album. Is it plans?"

"Yes; plans for an overture for *King Lear*. The designs and the instrumentation are ready, and I think the beginning will be somewhat formidable."

"Whom do you mean by King Lear?"

"He is a poor old English king."

"English!"

"Yes. Shakespeare says he lived about eighteen hundred years ago and he foolishly divided his kingdom between his two wicked elder daughters, who turned him out of doors when he had nothing more to give them. You see there are few kings . . ."

"Never mind the king . . . what do you mean by instrumentation?"

"It is a musical term."

"Always the same excuse! Now, sir, we are well aware that it is impossible to write music walking silently about the seashore, with nothing but an album and a pencil and no piano. So be good enough to tell us where you want to go, and you shall have your passport. You cannot stay here any longer."

" 'Then I will return to Rome and compose there without a piano, if you have no objection.' So the following day I left Nice, reluctant, but full of life and happiness."

Years later in the whirlpool of his Paris life, Berlioz recalls these Italian days "when heart, mind, and soul, all were free; when I could idle, not even thinking unless I chose; free to ignore the flight of time, to despise ambition and laugh at glory; to discredit love, to wander north, south, east, or west; to sleep out of doors, to live naturally, to dream whole days in the soft, hot, murmuring sirocco wind! Perfectly, utterly free! Oh, great, strong Italy! Wild Italy, unheeding of thy sister, Artistic Italy!"

But Berlioz's dynamic personality could not long endure even such delightful vagabondage as this. He longed for Paris, for the old active, anxious life, the sound of an orchestra, and the chance of getting his works performed. He asked and received permission to return to France. "I made a final excursion to Tivoli, Albano, and Palestrina," he says, "sold my gun and destroyed my guitar; wrote in several souvenir albums, treated my comrades to a large bowl of punch; lavished caresses on M. Vernet's two dogs who had been my sporting companions, and had a moment's unutterable sadness at the thought that I was leaving this poetical country, perhaps forever. My friends accompanied me as far as Ponte Molle; then I got into a horrible vehicle and set off" — and so the Italian chapter ends.

By a strange coincidence, Henrietta Smithson, the lost Ophelia of whom he had heard nothing for two years, was also returning to Paris at this time, to direct an English theater. To Berlioz this seemed a clear lead from the hand of Fate. He renewed his attentions and at last succeeded in getting an introduction to the lady. Then misfortune began to rain down upon the poor Ophelia. The English theater failed, sweeping away her fortune and leaving her heavily in debt, and, as a finishing touch, she slipped while alighting from her carriage and broke her leg. Berlioz, now no longer intimidated by her glory, rushed in with offers of love and protection, and, says the Memoirs, "At length, in the summer of 1833, though ruined financially and an invalid, I married her in spite of the violent opposition of her family. . . . On the day of our marriage she had nothing in the world but debts and the fear of never again being able to appear on the stage. My property consisted of three hundred *francs* borrowed from my friend

Gounet, and a fresh quarrel with my parents. . . . But she was mine and I defied the world!"

Poor Berlioz! Defying the world sounds so grand, but was, in reality, such a dreary grind! To pay his wife's debts and take care of his family he worked like a galley slave. He served as assistant librarian at the Conservatoire, corrected proof for publishers, and wrote weekly articles on music for *des Débats*. This journalistic work, which he kept up for thirty years, was a great trial to Berlioz because he dared not speak his mind freely. "This never-ending, still-beginning task poisons my life," he writes. "It is sweet to praise an enemy when that enemy has merit, indeed it is the proud duty of an honest man; while every untrue word written in favor of an undeserving friend causes me heartbreaking anguish." And again he calls it "the lowest depth of degradation to speak one day of a great master and the next day of an idiot, with the same gravity, in the same language. To write nothing about nothing!"

But hateful as this writing was, Berlioz did it well. Even translation, which, as he once said, "withers the flower of expression," does not destroy the charm of his literary style. His writings are full of such whimsical bits of philosophy as, "I am compelled to recognize the fact that absurdities are indispensable to the human mind and spring from it like insects from a marsh. Let us leave them to their buzzing." And, speaking of surly critics, "A naturalist has said that certain dogs aspire to be men; I think far more men aspire to be dogs." And again, "I am not quite sure but that the Englishman, who in one of our restaurants asked for a "melon" or a "tenor" for dessert, was not right in leaving the choice to the waiter. I myself should always prefer the melon; there is less chance of colic with it, the vegetable being far less offensive than the animal."

In spite of his efforts to bridle his tongue, Berlioz was often violent in his criticism. Speaking of "the stolid, bewigged countenance of that barrel of pork and beer called Handel," or referring to the enmity of Handel and Rossini for the less successful Gluck and Weber, "It is impossible for two men of stomach to understand two men of heart" — such comments could scarcely be called tactful! And it was not without reason that one of his friends remarked that Berlioz wrote with a dagger, not a pen. Naturally he made scores of enemies who had only to point from his daring articles to his still more daring music to prove their contention that Hector Berlioz was a madman.

But, says Berlioz, "This life of combat is not without certain charm. . . . It is often pleasanter to smash through a gate than to jump it!"

In the midst of this "life of combat" and haunted by thoughts of rent and doctor's bills, Berlioz wrote his music. But the real tragedy of this life was not the sacrifice of the man for his music, but the sacrifice of music which might have been for the sake of what the man felt to be his duty. A pathetic page from the Memoirs tells a tale of heroic self-denial.

> At the time when my wife's health had become hopeless and was causing me great expense, I dreamed that I was composing a symphony. On awakening the next morning I recollected nearly the whole of the first movement. . . . I had gone to my table to write it down when the thought came to me: "If I write this part I shall let myself be carried on to write the whole symphony. It will be long and perhaps I may spend three or four months on it. That will mean practically no newspaper articles and no money.

And when it is finished I shall be weak enough to have it copied (which will mean an expense of a thousand *francs* or more), and then I will be tempted to give a concert and the receipts will not cover half the cost; my poor invalid will lack necessities and I shall have no money either for my own expenses or my son's fees on board ship. . . ." I threw down my pen, saying, "Bah! tomorrow I shall have forgotten the symphony!"

But the next night he dreamed the music again. "I clung to the thought of forgetting," he says, and waking on the third morning, "all remembrance of it had gone forever."

"Coward!" some young enthusiast will say, "you should have written it, you should have been bold!" Ah, young man . . . if you had looked upon what I did . . . my wife there half dead, only able to moan; she had to have three nurses and a doctor to visit her every day. . . . No, I was not a coward; I was only human. I like to think that I honored art by proving that it had left me enough reason to distinguish between courage and cruelty!

Not many artists would have thus betrayed genius to duty! Wagner in such a situation would undoubtedly have written that dream symphony and let the landlord and the doctor whistle for their money — and who shall say which was the right choice?

Berlioz's only hope of realizing either fame or fortune from the compositions he did write lay in getting them performed. This, as we have seen, meant money for copying manuscript, for rentals of halls, and for orchestra and singers — much money, since Berlioz's works were planned on such large scale that they demanded hundreds of performers. Again and again he organized concerts and festivals that left him penniless and disenchanted.

Toward the end of his life his fortunes began to mend. He made several successful concert tours to Germany, where his music was so warmly received that even his own countrymen began to take notice of it. He also went to Russia and to England, and rejected a flattering offer to go to "the Dis-United States" [an apt description of our country in the year of 1861]. "My musical career," he writes, "will become all that I could wish by the time I am one hundred and forty!"

But Berlioz seemed destined to unhappiness. Those later years in which he had some recognition and enough to live upon were shadowed by an incurable illness which tortured him day and night. And, what was worse, this strange man, who for all his fiery nature was as dependent on affection as a little child, was left quite alone. One by one he saw all those he loved die, his parents, his sisters, Henrietta Smithson, and later, a second wife. Only his son Louis, who was captain of a merchant vessel, was left. Berlioz fairly worshiped this son, his only child. "What should I do without you?" he wrote in one of the many letters to "my dear big boy." A few months later news came that Louis had died of fever and was buried in a faraway port.

"The Last Chapter of All," as Berlioz calls it, might have been taken from one of Daudet's gentle romances. It tells of Berlioz's pilgrimage to the lovely country of his childhood and of the meeting with Estelle of the pink shoes. He was sixty-one, she, nearly seventy. With sweet old-fashioned formality they talked of the years that had passed since that summer when twelve-year-old Hector had loved and lost his *stella montis*. The Memoirs record the conversation:

"May I hope," said I after a long silence, "that you will sometimes allow me to write to you, and occasionally to visit you?"

"Certainly."

Not daring to prolong my visit further, I arose. She went with me to the door, where she said once more, "Farewell, M. Berlioz, farewell. I am deeply grateful for the feelings you have preserved toward me."

And bowing to her, I took her hand, laid it for a moment against my forehead, and then left her.

Back in Paris again the lonely man writes, "I can live more peacefully now. . . . My sky is not without its star. True, she does not love me; why, indeed, should she? But now she knows that I love her. . . . I must try to console myself for not having known her sooner, as I console myself for not having known Virgil, whom I should have loved so well, or Gluck or Beethoven . . . or Shakespeare, who, perhaps, might have loved me!"

"Which of the two powers, Love or Music, can elevate man to the sublimest heights? It is a great question, and yet it seems to me that this is the answer: love can give no idea of music; music *can* give an idea of love . . . why separate them? They are the two wings of the soul."

The Memoirs end, as they began, with lines from Shakespeare, gloomy lines which Berlioz whispered as he lay dying:

> Life's but a walking shadow, a poor player
> That struts and frets his hour upon the stage
> And then is heard no more; it is a tale
> Told by an idiot, full of sound and fury,
> Signifying nothing.

THE ARTIST

"The object of fair-minded appreciation is to understand clearly just what each composer set out to do, i.e., what was the natural tendency of his individual genius; then the only question is: did he or did he not do this well?"[1] This significant sentence, hidden in a footnote to one of Walter Spalding's pages, serves as an excellent starting point for the study of any artist and is peculiarly appropriate to an appreciation of Berlioz. Critics have not always been fair-minded to this great Frenchman. Too often they have simply wasted their wits blaming Berlioz for not being Bach or Mozart, for not achieving what he never set out to do, and missed the fine points of what he really did do!

What was "the natural tendency" of Berlioz's genius? To answer this question we must ask another — what was the intellectual tendency of Berlioz's time? The answer, which is also the explanation of Berlioz's attitude, is the Romantic Movement — that great wave of thought and feeling which swept over Europe, washing away many of the old ideas of truth and beauty.

[1] From "Music, an Art and a Language," by Walter R. Spalding. Copyright, by The Arthur P. Schmidt Co.

The eighteenth century marked the peak of what is known as the *Classical Age*, an age famous for the graciousness and formality of life at court and among the upper classes. Music, excepting that of the folk and the church, belonged exclusively to the privileged people and, naturally, reflected their life. It was serene and impersonal and it followed patterns as conventional as those of the old formal gardens.

Life was real enough for the lower classes and bitterly earnest, as it always has been, for individuals. But no matter what hunger, anguish, or wild joy a composer might feel or see among his neighbors, his music must express only the calm, formal beauty then accepted as art. To have bared his body in public would have been scarcely less shocking than to have shown his naked heart at a concert.

Then, at the close of the eighteenth century the storm which had long threatened this polite world broke. Forgotten men everywhere began to demand their right to "life, liberty, and the pursuit of happiness." For the first time in the world's history individuals became more important than classes, and revolution spread and triumphed.

Art, mirroring life as it always must, had its revolution too. Poets, painters, and musicians broke out of the formal gardens of eighteenth-century conventions and sought their inspiration in highways and hedges. Real life, they claimed, is not necessarily vulgar, and truth and beauty may be found anywhere. And even if truth be sometimes ugly, it is still art's province to express it. As for the old patterns, if they did not fit the new ideas, let them be altered or cast aside for new ones. It was not the way the thing was said, but what one had to say, that mattered. This shifting of emphasis from form to feeling, from cool reason to warm sentiment, from sobriety to enthusiasm — in other words, this *personalizing* of life and thought — is known as the Romantic Movement.

Romanticism flourished in France, where it had vigorous social and political roots. France had not only endured the most thorough and terrible of revolutions at home, but, in the Napoleonic Wars that followed, had wrestled with every nation in Europe. Surely the French had touched life on every possible side! These highly exciting years of Revolution and Empire left a generation physically exhausted and emotionally over-stimulated. All the pageantry and heroics were over, and there remained only the desolate aftermath of war. There was no outlet for the intense nervous energy of the younger generation, and it was seized with an exaggerated melancholy and dissatisfaction. Young men took themselves overseriously and were convinced that their fathers and grandfathers knew nothing of the mysteries of life and death. And young poets and painters, determined to express what they called "truth," no matter how repellent or extravagant, pushed Romanticism to its extreme phase — Realism.

Eighteen-year-old Hector Berlioz, high-strung, rebellious at having to study medicine instead of music, a country boy dazzled by the wonders of Paris, was just the fellow to be carried away by these romantic notions. And he was just the fellow to try to set them to music, to be the musical pioneer of ultra-Romanticism or Realism.

Berlioz was a true pioneer, for he not only opened up a road into a new musical country, but also contrived the tools with which to do it. His early training on the flute and guitar with some scraps of harmony gleaned from an old book left him blissfully free from any hampering knowledge of musical traditions. When he came up to

Paris, he had never heard an orchestra or an opera. Even after he became a student at the Conservatoire, he was largely self-taught. He discovered his own orchestration "by an impartial examination of the regular forms of instrumentation, and of unusual combinations; partly by listening to artists and getting them to make experiments for me on their instruments, and partly by instinct, I acquired the knowledge I possess."

There was never a more original composer, never one who owed less to other people's music. As Ernest Newman says, "There is no one whose speech he tried to copy in his early years, and there is no one since who speaks with his voice. . . . His melody, his harmony, his rhythm are absolutely his own."

Berlioz's point of view was as original as his technique. Where the German Romanticists, Schubert, Schumann, and Mendelssohn, tried to express emotions, Berlioz tried to tell a story, incident by incident. Music, to him, was a dramatization of life, and nothing was too trivial or too personal to be included. He never wrote anything without a title and a definite story background. The story might be taken from history or literature as in his *Trojans*, "Romeo and Juliet," and *The Damnation of Faust*, or it might be an episode in his own life such as the *Symphonie fantastique*.

He called his works *symphonies*, yet there are many sound musicians who protest that they are not symphonies but operas minus scenery and actors. These critics claim, and rightly, that the only legitimate heroes and heroines of a symphony are the themes, the musical ideas; and the only legitimate dramatic action, the development of these themes by purely musical means. A symphony, they say, is already a drama of tones which does not need and should not be burdened by another set of characters, another plot.

Granted that Berlioz did misuse the term *symphony* (which in the beginning meant merely instruments "sounding together"), it is scarcely sufficient excuse for ignoring genius! His music is romantic to the point of being theatrical; it is too colossal in plan to be practical for performance for surely Berlioz was, as Heine said, "a lark the size of an eagle." He is extravagant in his instrumentation — who but Berlioz would have thought of scoring a Requiem for sixteen trombones, sixteen trumpets, five ophicleides (a sort of alto key bugle), twelve horns, eight pairs of kettledrums, two bass drums, and a gong in addition to the usual resources of an orchestra! Certainly it had never occurred to any other composer to cover drumsticks with sponges or have horns played in bags! In spite of these obvious blemishes which have provoked the criticism of "more style than substance," there is something splendid, a sort of bare grandeur about Berlioz's music which marks it as the work of a genius. And of that purely musical beauty worshiped by the classicists, there is more than enough to admit Berlioz to the company of great composers.

His rhythms know no metrical fences. They move with the freedom of life itself carrying his fresh and expressive melodies. "Some phrases taken separately," says Schumann, "have such an intensity that they will not bear harmonizing — as in many ancient folk songs — and often even an accompaniment spoils them."

Even greater than his rhythmic sense is Berlioz's genius in the treatment of the orchestra. He had an unerring instinct for tone color. He seemed to know just the right instrument for a theme and just the right combination of instruments for the effect he sought. Berlioz has been called "the first virtuoso" of that most complex of instruments, the orchestra, and the "father of modern orchestration" with its startling effects. His "Treatise on Instrumentation" has had far-reaching influence.

No characterization of Berlioz's work is more exact than his own: "The dominant qualities of my music," he says, "are passionate expression, intense feeling, rhythmic animation, and unexpected changes."

Berlioz may have been sensational, but he was never cheap. Beneath all his extravagance of expression lay the sincerity of an idealist who could proudly say, "The love of money has never allied itself in a single instance with my love of art. I have always been ready to make all sorts of sacrifices to go in search of the beautiful and to insure myself against contact with those paltry platitudes which are crowned by popularity."

What did Berlioz set out to do? Why, to express through music the varied emotions of a dramatic story. Having discovered his purpose, "fair-minded appreciation" rests upon the question, "Did he do it well?" The answer to that question can only be found in his music.

"ROMEO AND JULIET" SYMPHONY

Scherzo, "Queen Mab," or "The Fairy of Dreams"

Shortly after Berlioz's return from Rome he gave a concert of his own compositions. When the program was over, "a man with long hair, piercing eyes, and a strange, haggard face" came up to him and praised his music warmly. It was Paganini, the man whose incredible fiddling had dazed musical Europe. Five years later the great violinist happened again to be in Paris and attended the "massacre" of Berlioz's opera *Benvenuto Cellini*. The next day as Berlioz sat in his room alone, sick at heart over the failure of his opera, Paganini's little son entered bearing a letter from his father:

> My dear Friend: Beethoven is dead, and Berlioz alone can revive him. I have heard your divine composition, so worthy of your genius, and I beg you to accept, in token of my homage, twenty thousand *francs*, which will be handed to you by the Baron de Rothschild on presentation of the enclosed.
>
> Your most affectionate friend,
Nicolò Paganini
>
> Paris, December 18, 1838

Berlioz was overcome by the gift and eager to prove his gratitude. "I must," he writes, "leave off all other work and write a masterpiece on a grand new plan, a splendid work, full of passion and imagination, and worthy to be dedicated to the illustrious artist to whom I owe so much."

After much indecision, he decided to write a symphony with a chorus, vocal solos, and recitative on the "sublime and ever-novel theme of Shakespeare's *Romeo and Juliet*." For years he had dreamed of an opera based on this drama, which, he declared, was "actually created for music." When a student in Rome he had gone eagerly to see Bellini's *Romeo* and came away disgusted with its commonplace music. And once, while riding with Mendelssohn, he says, "I told him how surprised I was that no one had written a *scherzo* on Shakespeare's glittering little poem, 'Queen Mab.' He was equally surprised, and I instantly regretted having put the idea into his head. For several years afterward I dreaded hearing that he had carried it out. Had he done so he would have made my double attempt (a vocal *scherzetto* and instrumental *scherzo*) in the 'Romeo and Juliet' Symphony impossible or, at any rate, highly undesirable. Fortunately he never thought of it."

This "glittering" poem which was, happily, spared for Berlioz's inspiration, occurs in the fourth scene of the first act of *Romeo and Juliet*. Mercutio is talking of the Fairy of Dreams, mischievous Queen Mab, who comes:

> In shape no bigger than an agate-stone
> On the forefinger of an alderman;
> Drawn with a team of little atomies
> Over men's noses as they lie asleep;
> Her waggon-spokes made of long spinners' legs;
> The cover, of the wings of grass hoppers;
> The traces, of the smallest spider's web;
> The collars, of the moonshine's watery beams;
> Her whip, of cricket's bone; the lash, of film;
> Her waggoner, a small grey-coated gnat.

> * * *

> Her chariot is an empty hazel nut
> Made by the joiner squirrel, or old Grub,
> Time out of mind the fairies' coach makers.
> And in this state she gallops night by night
> Through lovers' brains, and then they
> Dream of love.

A hushed, hesitant chord poised for flight, a gnat-wing quivering of rebounding bows, an eager trilling of strings, and the fairy troop is off:

At first their dazzling speed is broken by sudden pauses as if the tiny creatures were frightened or uncertain of their way. Then, reassured, the microscopic hoofs of the team of atomies settle into a steady galloping:

As they race along, the tune, without slackening its speed, makes a surprising harmonic detour:

then slips back into its first key.   But these sprites are wayward travelers and vary their course with all sorts of frolicking and unexpected pranks.

Suddenly the *tempo* changes.   A soft call sounds in flute and English horn:

growing into a quiet songlike theme:

which might suggest a halting of the fairy train to mix the dreams of some unsuspecting mortal.

Then, as suddenly, away they dash again.   Faster and faster fly the gossamer figures, while in the distance we hear "the horns of elfland faintly blowing" and the tinkling harps and cymbals of a fairy world.   Once again come the mysterious chords, now long drawn out, and the frightening pauses.   A fairy bell rings — one — two — three — and obeying its signal the hazel nut coach with Queen Mab and all her elfin courtiers goes galloping out of sight and sound.

Not even Mendelssohn, whom Berlioz called "the own brother of fairies," has achieved such a miracle of lightness as this.   It is almost impossible for clumsy mortal eye and ear to follow the music in its flight.   It even runs away from Shakespeare's words and eludes the swiftest picture-making imagination.   For all its apparent reality of ink and paper, of wood, string, and brass, the "Queen Mab" *Scherzo* is as unreal as transparent as dreams, which, says Mercutio:

> . . . are the children of an idle brain,
> Begot of nothing but vain fantasy;
> Which is as thin of substance as the air.

SYMPHONIE FANTASTIQUE

Rouget de Lisle, composer of the famous "Marseillaise," once wrote to the young Berlioz, "Your head seems to be a volcano in a perpetual state of eruption."   It was a perfect description, particularly of the Berlioz of those early Paris years, the Berlioz whose heart as well as head seethed with fire, smoke, and cinders.   He was working at top speed, eating little, tramping the streets when he should have been sleeping, and in a continual ferment with his many trials for the *Prix de Rome*. The weird "Tales of Hoffman" and Goethe's *Faust*, best-sellers of those days, only added fuel to his emotional fire; and his desperate infatuation for an English actress, whom he had not even met, supplied the match.

When the lady sent word that his attentions were as useless as they were unwelcome, Berlioz's volcanic head erupted in an orchestral work which he called, "Episode in the Life of an Artist — a grand Fantastic Symphony in five parts."

Writing to a friend about its first performance, he said, "I hope that unhappy woman will be present. . . . If she reads the program, she can't help recognizing herself" — and *me*, he might have added.

Berlioz invented and wrote his own program, prefacing it with this significant notice:

> The following program should be distributed among the audience whenever the *Symphonie fantastique* is performed dramatically — that is to say, followed by the mono-drama *Lelio*, which ends and completes the "Episode in the Life of an Artist." In that case the orchestra is invisible and placed upon the stage of the theater with lowered curtain.
>
> But when the symphony is played alone in a concert, this arrangement is unnecessary; indeed, even the distribution of the program is not absolutely essential so long as the titles of the five movements are set forth. For the author hopes that the symphony can provide its own musical interest independent of any dramatic intention.

It would seem almost as if Berlioz had anticipated the controversy as to whether the *Fantastique* is music or merely sound effect for a bad dream!

As to the program itself, it must be admitted that Berlioz did let his pen run away with him. He had a great gift of words, and music seemed to stimulate it. It is more than likely that much of the horror of the *Fantastique* was an afterthought, suggested to him by the music itself after it was written and re-expressed in the wording of his program. Certainly in his letters to his friends we find the horror growing with every mention of the work. What in an April letter was described as "a little violent" became in August "a furious orgy . . . the intoxication of blood, joy, and rage. . . ." This is the program, taken from Berlioz's own version:

> A young musician of morbid, sensitive nature and vivid imagination is in love and has poisoned himself with opium in a fit of desperation. He falls into a deep sleep in which the feelings and memories of his sick brain take the form of musical imagery. Even the girl he loves becomes a melody which he hears wherever he goes.

This melody was a little song which the twelve-year-old Hector Berlioz had written to his first love, Stella of the "bright eyes and pink boots." Incidentally, Stella, too, had spurned him!

The melody, appearing in all five movements of the symphony, symbolizes the hero's idea of his beloved — an *idée fixe*. It differs from the conventional main theme of a symphony in that it is used dramatically, not organically. Other ideas do not spring from it, and, except for a burlesque in the *finale*, it does not change. It is literally an *idée fixe* — an obsession, with all the word implies of mental aberration. It is not much of a tune.   It has the long, winding rhythm characteristic of Berlioz, also the characteristic scant harmony.   But somehow it sounds well in the symphony. Berlioz's music always sounds well.   Sometimes one suspects it of sounding better than it is!

First Movement — Reveries and Passions

Of the first movement, "Reveries and Passions," Berlioz says:

The hero remembers the uneasiness of mind, the aimless passions, the baseless depressions:

and elations:

which he felt before he saw the object of his adoration [and here she is, the *idée fixe*]:

then the volcanic love which she instantly inspires in him:

his delirious agonies, his jealous rages, his recovered love, his consolations of religion.

The changing moods of "Reveries and Passions" are easily followed, and no one can mistake the "consolations of religion" at the end:

To those who expect in a first movement music's most beautiful conventional design, first-movement form, this *Largo-Allegro* is a disappointment. It lacks the very core of first-movement form, a proper Development section. It is said that originally there was a sort of Development section but that Berlioz, afraid of "note-spinning," cut it out in great chunks of thirty-three measures to the cut. This first movement does not expose, develop, or recapitulate its themes, neither does it fall to pieces. "Reveries and Passions" and wild young men aside, it has, as Berlioz hoped, "musical interest independent of any dramatic intention."

Second Movement — A Ball

In the second movement the hero goes to a ball:

but in the midst of all the gaiety he is haunted by the vision of his Beloved:

Third Movement — Scene in the Fields

Of the third movement, a "Scene in the Fields," Berlioz says:

On a summer evening in the country he hears two shepherds playing a *ranz des vaches* in dialogue:

This pastoral duet, the place, the gentle sound of wind in the trees calm his heart and cheer his thoughts:

Solo Flute
and Violin

But she appears again.   Dark forebodings return.   What if she should deceive him?
. . .   One of the shepherds resumes his simple lay.   The other does not answer.   The
sun sets.   Distant thunder.   Solitude.   Silence.

At the close of this movement occurs one of Berlioz's most novel and realistic effects
and surely one of the strangest duets in music literature, a dialogue between an English
horn and four kettledrums tuned in a peculiar way which has ever since been the model
for stage thunder.

There was a personal as well as a musical reason for this drumming.   Berlioz loved
the tympani, and at the first performance of the *Fantastique* he himself played them,
gazing soulfully at Miss Smithson and, whenever his eyes met hers, pounding his kettles
like mad!

Fourth Movement — The March to the Scaffold

The fourth movement, written in one night, is "The March to the Scaffold."

He dreams that he has killed his beloved, that he has been condemned to death, and
is being led to execution.   To the sound of a march that is at times somber and wild, at
times brilliant and solemn, the procession advances.   There is the dull tread of heavy
feet.   At the end the haunting melody returns like a last thought of love, only to be
interrupted by the executioner's fatal stroke.

To the muffled roll of sponge-headed drumsticks and a wailing dirge from the horns:

Horns Muted

the crowd gathers.

Then 'celli and basses strike up the death march:

Allegretto non troppo

Basses
'Celli

a strangely somber, heavy-footed tune.   Its ruthless rhythm marks the tramping of
soldiers, executioners, and the curious rabble;   the melody, in hopeless, downward
line, suggests the despair of the doomed man;   quite suitably, there is no harmony, no
chance of escape, the attention is bound by an unyielding unison.

But the heaviness of the march is relieved, and at the same time accentuated, by a rapid *staccato* obbligato in the bassoons.   Strange chords, like shouts from the crowd, break in.   Then the march itself bursts into a defiant major:

Woodwinds
Brass

a grimly joyous theme which might suggest a last gesture of bravado from the prisoner or the triumph of the crowd, whose blood lust is about to be satisfied.   Wild excitement agitates the strings.

This, however, is but an episode, and incidentally the conventional middle section of the march.   Again we hear the death theme, heavier now and even more relentless with the weight of full orchestra.   Again the wild shouts ring out, and the excitement increases as the procession nears the scaffold.

Then, in the midst of the tumult, the ghost of the love theme appears:

Oboe
pp dolce assai e appassionato

only to be silenced by the blow of the headsman's axe, which cuts through the whole orchestra in a shuddering chord.   With a savage rolling of drums the weird scene ends on a bright major chord!

Fifth Movement — Dream of a Witches' Sabbath

The *Finale* is entitled, "Dream of a Witches' Sabbath," though Berlioz in his more grisly moments liked to call it the "Dream of a Cut-off Head."

The hero now finds himself in a witches' Sabbath in the midst of a frightful crowd of ghosts, sorcerers, and all manner of monsters who are assisting at his burial.   Weird noises, groans, bursts of laughter, distant cries and echoes.   The Beloved melody enters again, but it has lost its noble modesty.   It has become a vulgar tune, trivial and grotesque.   She has come to the witches' Sabbath.

Here we have one of the cleverest touches in the whole symphony.   The *idée fixe*, which has made its calm way through the four preceding movements:

now, bewitched by a broomstick rhythm:

ppp lontano
Clarinet

makes sport of love.

"Roars of joy at her arrival," writes Berlioz. "She joins the devilish orgies." Here there occurs a descending passage for bassoons, 'celli, and contrabass which makes the famous descent to the dungeon in Beethoven's *Leonora No. 3* seem a mere going-down-cellar!

"Funeral bells; the *Dies Irae*" — Day of Wrath — that most solemn of plain chants:

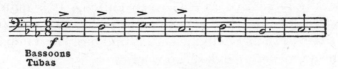

which is later hustled into a sort of jig.

"Then a round dance of witches" — a stunning fugue:

and as a crowning impiety an ensemble of the *Dies Irae* and the *Witches' Dance.*

"For daring imagination, for rhythmic vitality and certainty of orchestral effect," says Walter Spalding, "the *Symphonie fantastique* was and remains a work of genius." [1] It seems almost incredible that this strange music was composed only twenty-one years after the death of Haydn! Yet, shocking as it was to audiences of a century ago, it made a great sensation in Paris. The "March to the Scaffold" and the "Witches' Sabbath" were frequently heard on concert programs — too frequently for Berlioz's good. It won for him a "noisy fame" as composer of bizarre and sensational music which to this day has cheated him of the appreciation due to the creator of the purely musical beauty of his "Romeo and Juliet" Symphony, the nobility of the *Requiem*, the spirituality of his *Childhood of Christ*. To those who know him, Berlioz is far more than a composer *fantastique!*

The Damnation of Faust

Rákóczy March

Berlioz was a great admirer of Goethe's *Faust*. Its fantastic side appealed to him, and when quite a young man he wrote music to eight scenes from it. Seventeen years later he revised this music on a much larger scale, including both vocal and instrumental scenes, and gave it the title, *La Damnation de Faust*. Many musicians consider this Berlioz's masterpiece.

One of the early performances of *The Damnation of Faust* was to be given in Budapest. On his way there Berlioz stopped in Vienna, where a friend, handing him a book of old Magyar airs, said, "If you want to please the Hungarians, write a piece on one of their national themes. Here is a collection from which you have only to choose." Berlioz wanted very much to please his Hungarian audiences, so he followed his friend's suggestion. He chose the stirring "Rákóczy Tune" with which to pay his compliment.

[1] From "Music, an Art and a Language," by Walter R. Spalding. Copyright, by the Arthur P. Schmidt Co.

He could not have chosen better, for this old war march was almost sacred to the Hungarians.   It is said to have been written by a gypsy court musician to celebrate the traditional exploits of the picturesque Rákóczy family, champions of Hungary in the ancient struggles against the Turks.

Now, while the medieval Faust legend may belong to all the world, the Faust of literature is generally recognized as a German citizen.   It is quite characteristic of Berlioz, the "cracker of barriers," that because he wished to use a Hungarian national air he did not hesitate to tamper with the classics and turn Faust into a tourist watching a party of Hungarian soldiers march off to war!

The success of the venture is interestingly recorded by Berlioz in his memoirs:

As the hour [of the first performance] approached, a certain feeling of nervousness kept rising in my throat.   I began the March with a trumpet passage in the rhythm of the melody:

after which the theme itself appears *piano* in the flutes and clarinets, accompanied by the strings *pizzicato:*

This was a treatment to which my audience were quite unaccustomed, and at first they listened merely with respectful attention; but when the *crescendo* arrived, and fragments of the March were heard amidst the thunder of cannon from the big drum, they woke up; and when the final explosion burst upon them in all the fury of the orchestra, the shrieks and cries which rent the hall were positively terrific, and so extraordinary as fairly to frighten me.   In fact, from that moment the rest of the piece was inaudible amid the clamor of the house.

Like the main theme, the subordinate themes are in martial mood and are interesting illustrations of the vigorous effect of repeated ascending phrases.

The popularity of the Rákóczy March soon spread beyond the borders of Hungary, and for almost a hundred years it has been one of the good old "war horses" of bands and orchestras, both amateur and professional.

Dance of the Sylphs

Having shown Faust a vision of Marguerite, Mephisto lulls him to sleep on the bank of the Elbe and, in the composer's words, "calls the spirits of the air and bids them sing and dance before him." Berlioz has set Faust's vision to the music of this ethereal waltz in lullaby mood:

First violins play the melody to softly swaying chords in gentlest syncopation by muted second violins and violas, sustained by harps and basses.

At the end the melody hushes to a mere whisper, with dreamlike *arpeggios* floating up and away from the harps. The score bears this line, "The spirits of the air hover around Faust, who has fallen asleep; then they disappear one by one."

Minuet of the Will-o'-the-Wisps

After the Dance of the Sylphs, Mephisto tries to bewilder Marguerite and make her an easy victim to the wiles of Faust. He summons the will-o'-the-wisps to flit before her eyes and dazzle her with their brilliance. The tiny sparks of light appear and dance a delicate, grotesque minuet:

This is charming woodwind music, with piccolos the brightest of the dancing sparks, accompanied by measured chords in the brasses.

The minuet is interrupted at intervals by a curious questioning of strings, answered briefly and to almost impertinent point by the piccolos:

Violins try to introduce a triolike singing melody:

But no, the dazzling woodwind will-o'-the-wisps claim this music as their own and end the dance with a series of running figures *presto e leggiero*.

GEORGES BIZET

Paris — 1838
Paris — 1875

A packet of old letters, a few impressions and incidents remembered by his friends, and some newspaper criticisms of his works make up the scant source material available to biographers of Georges Bizet.   There was really nothing remarkable about his life beyond the fact that it was busier and briefer than his admirers would have wished, and that it was devoted solely to music.

Alexandre César Léopold was the name given at the christening; but the godfather, disregarding this impressive appellation, called the baby Georges, and Georges he was from that time forth.   Little Georges's childhood was literally set to music.   His father was a teacher of singing and his mother a fair pianist.   By the time the child was four he was showing such intelligent response to music that his mother taught him the notes along with his ABC's.   Georges loved the music game, and, not content with his mother's lessons, did some research outside his father's studio door, picking up the most difficult singing exercises, which he would sing by ear quite correctly.   His progress soon became the astonishment and pride of the family.

Before many years had passed, the parents realized that Georges had outgrown home instruction and that his unusual talents deserved the best possible training.   The Conservatoire was, of course, the goal of their ambition, but unfortunately the Conservatoire did not accept little boys.   However, the father determined to see what he could do, and through a friend succeeded in getting Georges a hearing with one of the Conservatoire officials.   When that bored gentleman began the examination of what he supposed was just another tiresome little would-be prodigy, he could not conceal his surprise.   The boy not only played well and read at sight remarkably, but could name any chord or interval he heard.   A few weeks later, the register of the Conservatoire bore the name of Georges Bizet, aged nine.

Little Bizet was a joy to his teachers.   He was a handsome, wholesome child, bubbling over with friendliness and good nature.   And he had the kind of mind that makes short and happy work of learning.   He simply collected prizes — prizes for piano and organ playing, for *solfège* and fugue and composition.   At the age of eighteen he won the final grand prize, the dream of every French music student — the *Prix de Rome*.

Full of high hopes, young Bizet set out on his great adventure, thrilling to everything he saw along the way.   Indeed, the glimpses of Provence which he snatched from the car window on this memorable journey were his only first-hand material for the *L'Arlésienne* music written fifteen years later.   The letters to his family and friends during those Roman years are full of enthusiasm for Italy.   Bizet loved to wander through the picturesque country, exploring the ancient cities and marveling at the treasures of cathedrals and galleries. And his merry heart rejoiced in the folk festivals and the Carnival. He entered into the student life at the Villa Medici with zest. It is said that shortly after his arrival he scored a social triumph by appearing at a masked ball as a baby, dressed in an amazing infant costume put together for him by the wife of one of the servants. His charming personality and beautiful piano playing made him a favorite not only at the Villa Medici but also in other interesting groups.

But the delights of Roman life did not make Bizet forget his obligations and the reason for his being there. He worked as heartily as he played, and the three compositions which, according to the terms of the *Prix de Rome*, the laureate was to send back to the Institute, were well written and favorably received by the Paris examiners. Encouraged by this, Bizet had visions of himself as a successful composer with publishers competing for his manuscripts. He wrote confidently to his parents that he would soon free them from anxiety about "silver, that terrible metal to which we are all in subjection." He would write such successful operas that the Bizet family fortunes would soar; "a hundred thousand francs, why, it is nothing!"

Poor Bizet was to have a rude awakening from these rosy dreams. The home-coming to which he had looked forward with such joy was desolated by the death of his mother. Then, too, he discovered that a three years' absence was long enough for Paris to forget the bright boy who had won a former *Prix de Rome*. There was nothing to do but begin from the ground up to make a living and a name for Georges Bizet.

Few composers have worked harder. Bizet gave lessons, made transcriptions and arrangements, corrected proof for publishers — in short, did all of the things he had hoped to escape and did them with a cheerful, "*Il faut vivre!*" — "One must live." But just to live was not enough, "*Il faut monter*" — "One must advance." These two oft-repeated phrases were the motif of this brief, busy life.

Bizet was a brilliant pianist and could no doubt have earned his living easily and pleasantly on the concert stage. But he was too ambitious to be known as a composer to risk the doubtful reputation of a pianist-composer. He preferred to do his bread-and-butter hack work out of the public eye and steal time for his composing, even though it meant working fifteen hours a day. "I work enormously," he wrote to a friend, "I am writing, on the run, six songs for Heugel [a publisher]; my opera, my symphony are under way. When shall I finish them? Good Heavens, it takes a long time, but how amusing it is!"

He even tried his hand as music columnist. In one of his articles, speaking of the many fads and factions that agitated the musical world, he says with characteristic good sense: "We have French music, German music, Italian music, to say nothing of Russian music, Hungarian music, Polish music, and so on, and so on. . . . We have the music of the future, the music of the present, and the music of the past; then, too, philosophical and political music, recently discovered. . . . For me there exist but two kinds of music, the good and the bad."

Fortunately, Bizet's *joie de vivre* never failed him. His enthusiasm for music and his buoyant good nature made light of long hours and uncongenial work, and with his charming wife and many friends he was far from unhappy.

Nor was he without recognition as a composer. He was awarded the red ribbon of the Legion of Honor, and in musical circles his works always had an interested hearing. He had numerous opportunities to write for the stage and worked on various librettos. Many of his operatic scores Bizet himself shelved, either because the music did not satisfy him or because another idea or another story had struck him as better. For Bizet was as temperamental as he was exacting in his judgment of his own work.

Of the operas which reached production, all made favorable impressions, yet, curiously enough, not one was a popular success. *The Pearl Fishers* had too tame a book to inspire Bizet's fiery genius to the utmost; *The Fair Maid of Perth* could not sustain its first night interest; *Djamileh* was badly cast, and so on.

Even *Carmen*, which was to make Bizet famous, was, at first, coldly received. Some critics called the music overradical and daring; others objected to a death on the stage of the Opéra-Comique, where tradition demanded that the first soprano and tenor marry at the end of the last act; and still others branded *Carmen* as immoral and unfit to be seen by respectable French family parties. Later, *Carmen* became the pride of the French operatic stage and today is one of the most popular of all operas. But, unfortunately, Bizet died before the reaction set in.

Bizet died at the age of thirty-six, barely three months after the production of *Carmen*. There are various sentimental stories of his having walked the streets of Paris all of that historic first night, mourning the failure of his *Carmen*, then retiring to his home to die of a broken heart.

But while *Carmen* was coolly received and much criticized, some of the criticism was highly favorable. The piece ran thirty-seven performances and was in no sense an ignominious failure. And even if it had been, Bizet was not the man to die of wounded vanity. Naturally he would have enjoyed a popular success with its attendant box-office receipts. But no amount of applause, or the lack of it, could measure *Carmen's* artistic value. Bizet knew that his work was good, and he had long ago accepted music as "a sad trade but a splendid art."

As an artist, Bizet had the gift of brilliance, a gift which almost invariably carries with it the defect of lack of depth. From babyhood, ideas had come flashing through his brain and found expression so easily that he knew neither the struggle nor the triumph of creation. His music, therefore, lacks something of the dignity and grandeur found in the works of the great masters who had to wrestle with their angels. But it lacks nothing in warmth, picturesqueness, and dramatic appropriateness.

Bizet had the true French instinct for drama. His genius for recognizing and reproducing local color was uncanny. He could read a story or a play and with the help of a volume or two of pertinent folk songs write as true a musical setting as if he had visited the country in which the scenes were laid. *L'Arlésienne* is thoroughly Provençal, yet Bizet had only passed through Provence on the train, en route to Rome. *Carmen* is convincingly Spanish, yet Bizet's only contact with Spain was by way of a Paris library!

Along with this instinct for the dramatic and picturesque, Bizet had as fine a feeling for form and balance as any of the classical composers — a rare combination. He had a natural gift for harmony and tone color and a wonderful sense of rhythm that keeps his music alive and arresting.

There is very little languor and moonshine even in his love songs. Bizet's music sparkles with sunlight and the infectious gaiety and vitality of gypsies, bullfighters, brigands, and street urchins. It may not be great music, but it is certainly very good music. Those who would belittle it have only to ask the question which serves as a simple but fairly accurate test of good music — does it linger in the mind? In answer, any good music memory can produce enough Bizet tunes to keep the scoffers busy whistling and humming!

L'ARLÉSIENNE — SUITE NO. 1

Bizet's fame rests upon his *Carmen* and the music for *L'Arlésienne*. *Carmen*, being the more pretentious, may display more of the composer's talents and promise for the future, but *L'Arlésienne*, in the opinion of many scholarly musicians, is Bizet's most finished, most artistic work.

Daudet's play, *L'Arlésienne* — The Woman of Arles — was a true melodrama, that is, a drama in which music is heard during the action of the play as well as between acts. Bizet was commissioned to write the music. It was a difficult and thankless task for a French composer of that period. Incidental music was considered of real importance in Germany, as is shown by the success of Beethoven's *Egmont*, Mendelssohn's *Midsummer Night's Dream*, Schumann's *Manfred* and other theater music. In France, however, it had no standing. The French public cared little about the musical value of anything heard at the theater, and Bizet knew that his *L'Arlésienne* music would probably either be ignored or used as background for entr'acte conversation. Then, too, the composer of incidental music had to score his compositions for the players the theater happened to employ, however inadequate they might be in number and ability. The Vaudeville, at which *L'Arlésienne* was to be produced, boasted an orchestra of twenty-six pieces — seven violins, one viola, five 'celli, two double basses, two flutes, one oboe, one clarinet, two bassoons, one saxophone, two horns, kettledrums, and piano. For this curious collection the composer had to create his masterpiece.

Bizet wrote twenty-seven numbers for *L'Arlésienne*, some of them mere fragments, yet so perfectly in the spirit of the play that they seemed to underline the dramatic action, the characters, and the atmosphere. With the exception of Grieg's music for *Peer Gynt*, there is no more perfect incidental music to be found than that written for *L'Arlésienne*.

But the combined beauties of Daudet's play and Bizet's music made little impression on the Paris audiences of 1872. They were postwar audiences accustomed to the strong fare of shocking tragedy or uproarious and equally shocking comedy. They had no taste for the delicate poetry and tragic simplicity of *L'Arlésienne*, and after a few performances the piece was withdrawn. Bizet, however, transferred the most important of his musical numbers to the concert room, where they won instant and lasting favor. There are two *L'Arlésienne* suites, No. 1, arranged by Bizet himself, and No. 2, by his friend Guiraud.

The scene of *L'Arlésienne* is laid in Provence at the old farmstead of Castelet. Frédéri, the young son of the house, has fallen madly in love with a beautiful, dark-eyed woman of Arles, who, however, never appears in the play. But just as the family are about to celebrate Frédéri's engagement to L'Arlésienne, a stranger arrives with letters that prove, beyond a doubt, that the beautiful woman of Arles is simply a common adventuress who has taken advantage of young Frédéri's love to make herself mistress of the rich estate of Castelet.

This cruel discovery leaves Frédéri brokenhearted. For days he will neither eat nor sleep and goes about as one demented. His mother is wild with anxiety and calls a family counsel. She fears that the boy will become seriously ill or that he may even take his own life, for, she says, "There is death in his eyes." But her brother, a bluff sailor, reassures her, saying, "One dies of pleurisy, a crack on the head, or is swept overboard by a big wave; but, Devil take it, a boy of twenty, solidly moored to his anchor, will not let himself be carried away by a contrary love affair!" He ends his speech with a song having the refrain, "Luckily, one does not die of love."

For a time it seems as if the sailor uncle were right. Frédéri, though saddened, becomes almost his old self, and in a few weeks announces that he will marry Vivette, his childhood playmate and friend. The family is delighted, for Vivette is a village favorite and will make Frédéri a far better wife than any dark, dancing stranger from the city.

The last act of the play shows Castelet in holiday mood. The old courtyard overlooking the Rhône is decked with flowers. Gaily dressed peasants with flutes and tambourines troop in to dance the *farandole* and to make their merriest, for this is not only the fête night of Saint-Éloi, patron of farmers, but also the betrothal celebration of their young master Frédéri and their little friend Vivette.

In the midst of all the singing and dancing the stranger reappears. He has come to get the letters he had left. The sight of him and the memory of those fateful letters are too much for Frédéri. The old love and jealousy for the beautiful woman of Arles sweep over him, and in despair he throws himself from an upper window and dashes his skull to pieces on the stones below.

The terrified revelers burst into the house, and as they stand stricken at the tragedy, an old shepherd who had heard the sailor singing, "Luckily, one does not die of love," goes to the window and points down at the broken body, lying in the courtyard. The play ends with his lines, "Look from this window and you will know whether or not one dies of love!"

In contrast to this furious passion and tragedy of young love, Daudet pictures two old lovers, Mère Renaud, a peasant woman, and Balthazar the shepherd. They, too, had been youthful sweethearts, separated by some whim of Fate. All their lives they have loved one another, and all their lives they have lived in the same community, yet, purposely, they have never met. Now, meeting by chance in the courtyard of Castelet on the night of the tragic betrothal feast, they talk together, happy in the security of a love that is faithful, unselfish, and "without shame."

Prelude

The *Prelude*, which serves as the introduction to the play, begins with the stirring March of the Three Kings, an ancient Provençal Christmas song said to have been written by King René:

Sur un char
Doré de toutes parts
On voit trois rois graves comme des anges.
Sur un char
Doré de toutes parts
Trois rois debout parmi les étendards.

It is a well-chosen theme, for not only is it characteristic and vital, but it is a theme which suggests interesting possibilities to a musical mind. Bizet treats it as a theme and four variations. First he presents the naked melody, daringly scored for all the instruments that can play it in unison, and since the tune has a limited range, that means practically the whole orchestra excepting the trumpets and double basses. After this "brimming sonority" comes a quaintly harmonized version for solo clarinet and woodwinds; then a second variation for all the woodwinds and brasses, accompanied by a queer climbing figure in the strings; a third variation follows in major mood for horns and 'celli accompanied by curious dancing triplets in the bassoons; and finally, a triumphal processional for full orchestra.

Having set his stage for a tale of old Provence, Bizet now introduces two of the characters. First, Frédéri's brother, called *l'Innocent* because of his clouded mind. This wistful one wanders unimportantly through the story until the last scene, when the shock of Frédéri's death clears his brain, and, according to an old prophecy, a great catastrophe restores a son to Castelet.

The theme of *l'Innocent*:

is sung by the saxophone, a comparatively new instrument in Bizet's time. He was one of the first composers to use the saxophone in orchestral music, and surely no one has ever used it more beautifully.

An appealing, childlike quality is given to the theme of *l'Innocent* by the persistent little figure:

heard in every other measure, always the same, yet with each repetition forming a new harmony with the theme itself. Bizet's music is full of just such clever little harmonic devices.

The gentle Innocent wanders out, and the strings enter with the theme of the despairing Frédéri, expressed in sighing, downward chromatics:

There is something strangely Tristan-and-Isolde-ish about this theme, so bittersweet with hopeless love. It is indeed a theme of love and death, for it is played as old Balthazar, pointing to the body of Frédéri, utters the closing lines of the play, "Look from this window and you will know whether or not one dies of love!"

Minuetto

The *Minuetto* which is used as an entr'acte in Act II has little of the stateliness and candlelit delicacy of its drawing-room successor. This is the original peasant minuet — the dance with the little steps — joyous, vigorous, and full of fresh air.

The violins lead off with the first figure of the dance:

The second figure is broken into two-measure phrases, first:

then the answering:

This suggestion of two, the maid and the man, is often found in the music of the minuet. The familiar Boccherini minuet gives it very plainly.

The dance is followed by several measures of scraping fifths:

unmistakably peasant bagpipes with their drone bass, introducing the middle or *trio* section of the minuet. Here the clarinets, modern substitutes for the pipe and tabor of old Provence, play a lovely singing theme:

while a second melody for strings:

weaves in and out, above and below in fragile, fairy counterpoint. Later the singing theme is heard in the violins with harp and flutes wreathing the dainty garlands of countermelody. The *trio* ends with a charming reminiscence for solo oboe and strings:

The harmonies of this *codetta* were as daring in 1872 as they are delightful today.

The *Minuetto* ends with the return of the dance theme, this time in thirds, with strings and flutes chirruping energetically and reminding us, as has been cleverly said, of an orchestra of ambitious crickets.

Adagietto

It fills but a single page of score paper, this tiny *Adagio*, yet nothing save "a worship of sheer bulk" could prevent its recognition as one of the most masterly pages in all music literature. Like "The Death of Ase," with which it may well be compared, the *Adagietto* is pure gold, without alloy. It contains not one unnecessary measure, not a single meaningless note. It is perfect in musical form and rhythmic symmetry and scored with that fine instinct for harmonic and instrumental color which was one of Bizet's great gifts.

In the concert room the *Adagietto* is simply a beautiful piece of music for muted strings. But in the play, heard at the chance meeting of Mère Renaud and the shepherd Balthazar, who, after a lifetime's separation, find each other again in the courtyard of Castelet, it becomes a masterpiece. The music, telling so quietly of humble heroism, sounds softly while the two old lovers talk together:

Balthazar
God keep you, Renaud!

Mère Renaud
Ah! — O my poor Balthazar!

Balthazar (speaking softly)
It is all my fault.   I knew you were coming tonight.   I should not have stayed.

Mère Renaud

But why not?   Because of your vow not to see me again?   Bah!   It is not worth the trouble.   God himself cannot wish that we should die without seeing each other again. That is why He has put love in the hearts of these two young people.   And after all, He owes us this as a reward for our steadfastness.

Balthazar

And there was need of steadfastness!   Often when I was minding my sheep I saw the smoke of your cottage, and it seemed to call to me: "Come!   She is here!"

Mère Renaud

And often when I heard your dogs bark and recognized your big cloak off there on the hillside, it took all my courage to keep me from running out to you!   But now our sorrow is over and we can look at each other without shame.   Balthazar —

Balthazar
Renaud!

Mère Renaud
Would you be ashamed to kiss me now, all old as I am, and wrinkled by the years?

Balthazar
O Renaud!

Mère Renaud

Then hold me close to your heart.   For fifty years I have owed you this kiss of friendship.

There is but a single theme in this music, as there had been in the lives of the two old people, a simple theme of steadfast devotion:

In the *Adagietto*, as in all the *L'Arlésienne* music, there is a haunting pathos but no poignant sorrow or bitter anguish.   Unerringly Bizet has followed his poet, sensing and intensifying the tragedy and at the same time softening its sharp edges, thus giving each of Daudet's scenes the quality of a luminous picture.

Carillon

The *Carillon*, or bell music, introduces the fourth scene of *L'Arlésienne*.   It is the fête of Saint-Éloi, patron of farm folk.   The courtyard of Castelet is gay with garlands of poppies and cornflowers and beribboned Maypoles. Peasants in holiday dress, carrying flutes and tambourines, troop in to sing and dance the *farandole* and drink the health of their young master, whose betrothal is to be celebrated.

The village bells begin to ring for the saint's day, and as their sweet notes float out upon the evening air, they give happy promise of the wedding bells which soon will be ringing for Frédéri and Vivette:

This chimelike figure for harp, horns, and second violins rings continually through fifty-six measures. Above it is heard a gay little dance which suggests the merrymaking:

Then Mère Renaud enters, and, as she crosses the courtyard, the memory of her pathetic romance falls like a wisp of cloud shadowing the music. Softly the wood-winds, led by two flutes, introduce the lovely *Andantino*:

But presently the horns, having had enough of wistful reminiscence, insinuate their little motif. At first it seems merely a part of the *Andantino's* accompaniment:

It soon changes, however, to the familiar chime figure:

and leads back to the merry mood of the bell music, which comes to an end with a joyous ringing and clanging throughout the whole orchestra.

CAMILLE SAINT-SAËNS

Paris — 1835
Algiers — 1921

Charles Camille Saint-Saëns, who was to have one of the longest and most active musical careers on record, began life precariously. When he was less than three months old, his father, a minor government official, died of tuberculosis. The doctors held out little hope for the child of such sad inheritance and environment, but advised taking him to the country. So the frail baby was left with a nurse at Corbeil, where two years of fresh air and sunshine transformed him into a happy, fairly sturdy little boy.

Meanwhile, young Madame Saint-Saëns had gone to live with an aunt, Mme. Masson, who had been her foster mother. Mme. Masson was a woman of unusual culture, education, and common sense. Mme. Saint-Saëns, says her famous son, made up for any lack of training by "an imagination and an eager power of assimilation which bordered on the miraculous." Such were the "two mothers" who welcomed Camille on his return to Paris and set to work on his mental, moral, and physical development with zealous devotion. They were delighted with his alert little mind and with his interest in sounds, which seemed to promise musical talent.

In his "Musical Memories," Saint-Saëns pictures his small self most beguilingly.

> When I came home from the nurse . . . I began to listen to every noise and to every sound; I made the doors creak, and would plant myself in front of the clocks to hear them strike. My special delight was the music of the tea kettle — a large one which hung before the fire in the drawing room every morning. Seated nearby on a small stool, I used to wait with a lively curiosity for the first murmur of its gentle and variegated *crescendo* and the appearance of a microscopic oboe which gradually increased its song until it was silenced by the kettle boiling. . . .
>
> At the same time, I was learning to read. When I was two years and a half old, they placed me in front of a small piano which had not been opened for several years. Instead of drumming at random as most children of that age would have done, I struck the notes one after another, going on only when the sound of the previous note had died away. My great-aunt taught me the names of the notes and got a tuner to put the piano in order. While the tuning was going on, I was playing in the next room, and they were utterly astonished when I named the notes as they were sounded. I was not told all these details — I remember them perfectly.

Soon Mme. Masson, who had been well trained in music, began to give the child regular lessons, using a popular instruction book by Le Carpentier. Camille romped through the entire "method" in a month's time, alarming the ladies who feared that such activity might be bad for so young a child.

> They couldn't let a little monkey like that work away at the piano, and I cried like a lost soul when they closed the instrument. So they left it open and put a small stool in front of it. From time to time, I would leave my playthings and climb up and drum whatever came into my head.
>
> [The lessons were continued but a new difficulty arose.]

⟦ 372 ⟧

They did not know what sort of music to give me. That written especially for children is, as a rule, entirely melody and the part for the left hand is uninteresting. I refused to learn it. "The bass doesn't sing," I said in disgust.

Then they searched the old masters, Haydn and Mozart, for things sufficiently easy for me to handle. At five, I was playing small sonatas correctly, with good interpretation and excellent precision. But I consented to play them only before listeners capable of appreciating them. . . . It was necessary to tell me that there was a lady in the audience who was an excellent musician and had fastidious tastes. I would not play for those who did not know.

About this time, the small Camille seems to have been making his first attempts at composition, writing down precise little tunes with chords and intervals too wide for his own tiny hands to play. Looking through these childish pieces, some half a century later, he says, "Among these scribblings, I have found some notes written in pencil when I was four. The date on them leaves no doubt about the time of their production."

When Camille was seven, his aunt turned him over for instruction to a professional pianist, Stamaty. Three years later, at the age of ten, he gave his first public concert with orchestra at the Salle Pleyel, playing concertos by Beethoven and Mozart, a prelude and fugue by Bach, and a number of smaller pieces. The concert was a tremendous success, the Paris papers announced the discovery of a second Mozart (how many second Mozarts there have been!), and Stamaty was eager to exploit his precocious pupil in a series of concerts. "But," says Saint-Saëns, "my mother did not wish me to have a career as an infant prodigy. She had higher ambitions and was unwilling for me to continue in concert work for fear of injuring my health. The result was that a coolness sprang up between my teacher and me which ended our relations. At that same time my mother made a remark which was worthy of Cornelia. One day some one remonstrated with her for letting me play Beethoven's sonatas. 'What music will he play when he is twenty?' she was asked. 'He will play his own,' was her reply."

For the next half dozen years, Camille Saint-Saëns was merely a schoolboy, laying the foundations of an excellent general education. At the age of fourteen he was allowed to enter the Conservatoire as a listening pupil in the organ class of Benoist. But he listened so intelligently and worked so well at home that he was soon accepted as a regular pupil in spite of the fact that he was under age. Later he joined Halévy's class in composition. It must have been a curious class, for Halévy is said to have come only "when he had time," which was seldom. The pupils, however, met regularly and taught each other. On the days when the teacher was absent, Saint-Saëns says, "I used to go to the library and there, as a matter of fact, I completed my education. The amount of music, ancient and modern, I devoured is beyond belief."

When he was seventeen, Saint-Saëns received his first professional appointment, that of organist at the Church of Saint-Méry. The following year, he won his first laurels as a composer and in rather an amusing way. Up to this time it had been almost impossible for a young or unknown composer to gain a hearing in Paris. The only orchestral concerts worthy of the name were those given under the auspices of the *Société des Concerts* connected with the Conservatoire, and only members could attend. The repertory of the orchestra was as limited as its public and was almost exclusively confined to the symphonies of Haydn, Mozart, and Beethoven. At last a Belgian violinist named Seghers, himself a member of the *Société des Concerts*, rebelled at this restricted musical diet, withdrew, and formed the *Société Sainte-Cécile*. Assembling a sizable orchestra which he himself conducted, he rented a square hall (at a time when curved walls were considered the only proper reflectors of music) and determined to prove that all concert literature was not divided into three parts — Haydn, Mozart, and Beethoven. It was at Seghers' that Paris audiences first heard many of the works of contemporary composers such as Schumann's *Manfred*, Mendelssohn's Symphony in A Minor, the overture to *Tannhäuser*. And it was there that French composers, particularly beginners like Bizet and Saint-Saëns, had their first recognition. In his "Musical Memories," Saint-Saëns tells how his own Symphony in E-Flat was presented as the work of an unknown German composer, Seghers fearing that the committee would reject it if they knew it was the work of an eighteen-year-old French boy. "I can still see myself at a rehearsal, listening to a conversation between Berlioz and Gounod. Both of them were greatly interested in me, so that they spoke freely and discussed the excellences and faults of this anonymous symphony. They took the work seriously, and it can be imagined how I drank in their words. When the veil of mystery was lifted [neither Berlioz nor Gounod knew that they were discussing the new symphony before its composer], the interest of the two great musicians changed to friendship."

Saint-Saëns's boyhood and youth were peculiarly rich in heroes. Besides Berlioz and Gounod, there was Victor Hugo, whose poetry he so admired and who received him cordially at his literary evenings; there was old Rossini, who had the young composer's duet for flute and clarinet played at one of his musical evenings, and then, in the midst of the admiring murmurs of "Ah, Master, what a masterpiece!" replied, "I agree with you. But the duet wasn't mine, it was written by this gentleman," and introduced Saint-Saëns to his guests. There was Liszt, whom he met at Seghers' house and whose music he studied with much enthusiasm. And, for further inspiration, there were Wagner, Meyerbeer, Anton Rubinstein, Schumann, Mendelssohn, Chopin, all at the height of their careers and most of them appearing in Paris. It was an exhilarating atmosphere for an ambitious young artist. Saint-Saëns seemed to live in a pleasant and encouraging world. The *curé* of the Church of Saint-Méry, in appreciation of a mass which his young organist had dedicated to him, took him to Rome. There Saint-Saëns heard the Sistine choir sing the Allegri *Miserere*, that famous, jealously guarded piece which the boy Mozart had written down from memory.

But absorbed as he was in his music, Saint-Saëns was by no means a recluse or a drudge. Paris was as gay as it was stimulating, and at his mother's Monday evening *salons* and those of her friends the young man had a chance to exercise his many social gifts. On these occasions there was always music, often played or sung by celebrated artists. But sometimes the younger set would arrange a frivolous evening, perhaps a burlesque of some popular opera. Then Saint-Saëns shone, for he was a born mimic, and his high-pitched voice was perfect for the role of heroine. There is an amusing story of an evening at Mme. Viardot's where Saint-Saëns, in long blond braids, appeared as Marguerite in *Faust* and warbled the famous, florid "Jewel Song" with sidesplitting success!

In the year 1858 a piece of great good fortune came to Saint-Saëns in his appointment as organist of the Church of the Madeleine, the most fashionable church in Paris. The position carried not only professional honor, but also a salary which meant financial security for the twenty years Saint-Saëns was to fill it. Shortly afterward he was made professor in the École Niedermeyer. Although his position as a composer and a brilliant performer on both organ and piano was now unquestioned, he had failed in two attempts to win the *Prix de Rome*. However, in 1867, he won a unanimous first among more than a hundred musicians in a competition instituted by the government at the time of the International Exhibition. And in 1858 he received the seal of official approval, the decoration of the Legion of Honor.

At thirty-three, Saint-Saëns's position seemed all that any man could wish. One thing only was lacking — that dearest dream of every French composer of the time — a successful opera. In his article, *Histoire d'un Opéra Comique*, he tells of the struggles, not only his own, but also those of Bizet, Delibes, and Massenet to win a hearing for their operas. Instead of a hearing, they were "invited to be seated," to stop talking about their own poor little works and show proper gratitude for the models from the older masters which a benevolent opera management continued to place before them. He also tells of a certain princess who, when asked to speak a good word for his [Saint-Saëns's] opera, replied, "What! Isn't he satisfied with his position? He plays the organ at the Madeleine and the piano at my house. Isn't that enough for him?" It was far from enough for the future composer of *Samson et Dalila!*

But operatic dreams faded, along with many others, before the tragic realities of 1870. The Franco-Prussian War, followed by the fall of the Second Empire and the terrible Red Days of the Commune, silenced the music of France. During the Siege of Paris, Saint-Saëns served as a soldier of the National Guard, and the memory of that time was a permanent scar on his sensitive nature. Three of his dearest friends were killed — one, the painter Regnault, to whom he dedicated his *Marche héroïque;* another, the *Abbé* Deguerry, *curé* of the Church of the Madeleine. The priest was one of the hostages shot down by the Communists. Finally, the horrors of the Commune forced Saint-Saëns and a number of other exiles to seek refuge in London. Thus began his long and pleasant association with England.

After the fighting was over and comparative quiet restored, Saint-Saëns returned to Paris to take his part in the renaissance of French music which was to begin in the seventies. One glimpse at the names — Gounod, Ambroise Thomas, César Franck, Reyer, Lalo, Bizet, Delibes, Massenet, Guiraud, Widor, Fauré, and, during the later years, Vincent d'Indy, Bruneau, Debussy, Charpentier, and many others — gives an idea of the brilliance of this period. And most brilliant, perhaps, of them all, surely most indefatigable, was Saint-Saëns, playing his triple rôle of solo pianist, conductor, and composer. His pen was never idle. The famous symphonic poems, the Concerto in C Minor, the oratorio, *Le Déluge*, several operas, including *Samson et Dalila* — one work followed another with amazing rapidity.

Then came the terrible year of his life, 1878, in which he lost both of his little sons within a few months. The eldest, a two-year-old, fell from a fourth floor window and was killed, and, shortly afterward, the baby of seven months died. Work and still more work was the narcotic with which Saint-Saëns deadened the pain of this double tragedy. Only a man of tremendous will and power of concentration could have created acceptable music, even gay music, under such circumstances.

During the last quarter of the century Saint-Saëns made a number of successful concert tours in England, a country for which he always felt great affection and admiration. The admiration was mutual for, in 1893, he received the honorary degree of Doctor of Music from Cambridge. He has written an interesting account of the whole affair, ending with the assertion that he has "returned confirmed once more in the idea that the English love and understand music, and that a contrary opinion is a prejudice. They love it in their own way, which is their right; but that way is not such a bad one, considering that art owes to it the oratorios of Handel, the great symphonies of Haydn, Weber's opera, *Oberon*, the *Elijah* and 'Scotch' Symphony of Mendelssohn, the *Redemption* and *Mors et Vita* of Gounod, all written for England, and which without her would probably never have been born." The same might be said of his own opera, *Henry VIII*, with its English hero and background. Saint-Saëns spent many hours as an honored and fascinated guest in the Royal Library at Buckingham Palace, looking through its treasured manuscripts. There, in a bundle of sixteenth-century harpsichord music, he found the theme upon which he built his opera.

Soon after the first performance of *Henry VIII* in the spring of 1883, Saint-Saëns's overtaxed strength reached the snapping point, and he was ordered off for rest and change. He went to Algiers, which became a haven of warmth and sunshine for the rest of his life. He visited it at intervals for the next thirty-eight years and died there. Unlike the typical home-loving Frenchman, Saint-Saëns became an enthusiastic traveler. He loved to explore faraway places and to observe strange patterns of life. The variety of these experiences added color and picturesqueness to his music. The Canary Islands, Ceylon, Cairo, Argentina, even distant Saïgon, capital of Cochin China, saw this alert, bustling little Frenchman taking the keenest interest in everything he saw and heard.

In the autumn of 1906 Saint-Saëns came to the United States. Unfortunately, he became ill on the way over, and the whole of his stay was a physical struggle. In spite of it, he managed to play in a number of cities. I remember, as a schoolgirl in Cincinnati, the fire of his playing and the square little figure in long coat, bowing and smiling in acknowledgment of applause and of a wreath of bronze leaves almost as tall as he. He carried away agreeable impressions of America and the Americans, from which we quote:[1] "A great many things had been said to me in disfavor of the New World. 'America will not please you,' they told me, 'everything you see will shock your artistic temperament.' Pictures had been given me of excited and busy crowds, something like an exasperated England." Then he goes on to tell how pleasantly surprised he was with New York, how he admired the beauty of the Hudson, marveled at the tall buildings, and thrilled at the vitality of the city. He did not approve of "twenty-floor" skyscrapers but he admits:

[1] This quotation and others on pages 377–380 taken from "Outspoken Essays on Music," by Camille Saint-Saëns, translated by Fred Rothwell, published by E. P. Dutton & Co., Inc., New York.

After all, these high buildings are quite pleasing to dwell in. From such heights, a man feels as though he were floating in a balloon, he becomes intoxicated with light and space. In an electric lift, the top is reached in a few seconds. In Europe we can form no idea of such comfort. Every hotel bedroom has a bathroom adjoining, and wardrobe large enough to contain trunks and boxes.

As regards the inhabitants, I did not find them as they had been depicted to me. Going about at their leisure in spacious streets everywhere, I judged them to be rather quiet compared with the bustling inhabitants of certain towns in the North of France. I found them both courteous and sympathetic. Besides, how could one help being satisfied with a country in which all the women are charming? And they really are, for those who chance not to be beautiful find it possible to pass themselves off as beautiful. I was afraid I might meet some bachelor women with short hair and harsh expression of face, and was agreeably surprised to find that it was not so.

Another agreeable surprise awaited him in the way of American nurses. "At the beginning of my stay in New York," he writes, "I was so ill that my doctor insisted on procuring a nurse for me. I protested, dreading to be handed over to the tender mercies of some ugly, frowsy old person. What was my amazement to find myself confronted with a delightful young lady, slender as a reed and fresh as the spring, highly educated, discreet and graceful, neither a prude nor a coquette. The mere sight of her was a comfort and consolation."

What pleased him most, he said, was "not so much the present America [1906], as the idea of what America will eventually be." One wonders what he would think of us now! "Yes, America pleased me well," wrote Saint-Saëns, "and I would be willing to revisit it, but as for living there . . . that is another matter. Born in the early part of the nineteenth century, I belong to the past, whether I like it or not. I shall always prefer our old cities, the sacred relics of Europe, before all the comfort of a young nation. On returning from New York, Paris seemed to me like some pretty *bibelot* [trinket], but how glad I was to see it again!"

Globe-trotting seemed to interfere little, if any, with Saint-Saëns's work. No place was too outlandish for his composing, so perfect was his power of concentration. From his journeys he usually brought back several new compositions, as well as the ordinary traveler's souvenirs. Upon his return to Paris he would plunge into concert work and his many other activities with renewed vigor.

Honors were heaped upon him at home and abroad. In 1907, he was present at the unveiling of a statue of himself at Dieppe, where there is also the Musée de Saint-Saëns. In 1912, at the invitation of the General Association of German Musicians, he went to Heidelberg to take part in the Liszt Centenary. And in 1913, he went to London for a Jubilee Festival in his own honor, celebrating the seventy-fifth anniversary of his musical career, from the time when, as a baby of two and a half years, he had first experimented at the keyboard. Saint-Saëns's charm of manner made him a great favorite with the many royal personages with whom he came in contact, particularly with the aging Queen Victoria and the gracious Alexandra. Indeed, says one biographer, "To mention the Royalties of the eighties and nineties whom Saint-Saëns did *not* meet would be simpler than to refer to all those whom he did know."

But even dearer to Saint-Saëns than these professional honors were his personal friendships. He had hosts of friends everywhere, and no wonder, for with all his cleverness and fame, he was kind and generous, with a delightful sense of humor and an almost childishly affectionate nature. An English woman who knew him well treasures this memory: "The first thing that struck me was his devotion to his mother, which was very beautiful. When I went to his house in Paris as a child (having won a scholarship at the Paris Conservatoire), he would not let me leave, after playing him one of his piano works, until he had taken me into another room to see his dear mother, to whom he told all the details of my visit."

Another appealing trait of Saint-Saëns was his love of animals. He was ever their champion, and his admiration for their intelligence is shown in his essay, "Observations of a Friend of Animals." There are anecdotes of spiders in Cochin China, of ants in the forest of Fontainebleau, of squirrels in Central Park. One of his pleasantest memories of New York was of the "large and admirable park in which grey squirrels will come right up to your side and beg for nuts." And there were many dog friends, his own pets and other people's. Dalila, a little black griffon with dark blue eyes, "for ten years," he says, "has been the delightful companion of my solitary old age." Unfortunately, Dalila was no music lover and set up a fearful howl at the sound of the piano. "On the other hand," says Saint-Saëns, "I once knew a dog which adored the piano; as soon as the music began, he would come up and crouch beneath the pedals, a matter troublesome enough for the player. To rid oneself of him, all that was necessary was to play Chopin's music. Before eight bars had been played, he had left the room, with dejected ears and his tail between his legs." Only a man with Saint-Saëns's sympathy and appreciation of animal personalities could have written the inimitable *Carnaval des animaux*, one of the rare examples of real humor in music.

In 1914, Saint-Saëns, then in his seventy-ninth year, but still active and full of *joie de vivre*, looked forward to peaceful closing years. Instead, he was to live through World War I in the midst of death and horror, compared with which the Franco-Prussian War, the Siege of Paris, even the Commune seemed insignificant. The old patriot could no longer shoulder a gun, as in the days of 1870, but he took up his pen, wrote a forcible booklet, and a number of pieces of music, including the *Marche interalliée* and several patriotic songs. He appeared in benefit concerts and did "his bit" in every possible way.

In October, 1920, Saint-Saëns celebrated his eighty-fifth birthday, and in that same month appeared at the Trocadéro in Paris as soloist in a concert of his own music. Paris went wild over him. The following autumn (1921) found this wonderful old man again in Paris superintending a gala performance of his opera *Ascanio*. He was still practicing at the piano for two hours a day! A few weeks later, he went to Algiers, as was his custom in the winter months. There in early December, the life which had begun so hopelessly, yet achieved eighty-six effective years, came to its gallant ending.

THE ARTIST

In the make-up of an artist, it goes without saying that inherent genius is the first and essential element. Next in importance are those traits of character of the man and artist which cast that genius into its particular mold. In Saint-Saëns the dominating characteristics are versatility and balance. These qualities, operating from the base of an excellent musical education and wide outlook upon life, and with that Gallic clearness of expression which was his birthright, give us Saint-Saëns the artist.

There is a so-called versatility, a literal turning from one thing to another, which produces merely the Jack-of-all-trades, good at none. In the world of art, Jack is apt to be a restless, superficial fellow, inconsistent to the point of insincerity. Saint-Saëns's versatility, however, was not of this type. It was the result of an inquiring mind. Its turning was not from one *thing* but from one *thought* to another, and, having turned, it followed that thought as far as possible. From the time when the two-year-old Camille had conducted his research in creaking door hinges and, seated on his little stool, had tried to solve the mystery of that "microscopic oboe" that sang in the teakettle, to the time, more than half a century later, when he began to explore the physical world, Saint-Saëns's insatiable intellectual curiosity gave him no peace.

Evidence of the extent and seriousness of his interests is to be found in his writings. One marvels at the amount of his literary work, hardly more than half of it being directly concerned with music. The two volumes, *Harmonie et melodie* and *Portraits et souvenirs*, deal with music and musicians; *Problèmes et mystères* records the philosophical conclusions of a long and active life; *Rimes familières* and the comedy, *La Crampe des écrivains* (Writers' Cramp) show Saint-Saëns as poet and dramatist; while *Au Courant de la vie* (In the Course of a Life) and *École buissonnière* (The Runaway from School) are collections of delightful essays and observations on many subjects from animals to America. Besides these volumes, there are the letters which, for many years, Saint-Saëns contributed to the leading musical journals of Paris.

But it is in his music that Saint-Saëns best displays his amazing versatility. Symphonies, chamber music, piano pieces, program music, opera — he was equally successful with them all. And he was not only a master of form, but also of style, by which we mean the individuality of expression which distinguishes one artist from another. When Gounod said of Saint-Saëns that "he could write at will in the style of Rossini, Verdi, Schumann, or Wagner," he paid him a doubtful compliment, for it might imply that Saint-Saëns was merely a clever imitator. What Gounod meant, however, was that Saint-Saëns had such perfect sense of style that, if he set out to write a work in a manner which had become associated with a certain man or period, he followed it consistently and made it serve his own purpose. Saint-Saëns was no hodgepodger, topping a Greek façade with a Gothic spire, nor was he a rehasher of other men's ideas. He was an absolutely independent thinker, and it is only further proof of his artistry that, while keeping so consistently within the bounds of the various traditional forms, he could achieve a style so distinctively his own.

Although Saint-Saëns is perhaps best known for his picturesque and program music, the symphonic poems and colorful suites, his finest work was done in the realm of pure music, that is, music without words or definite poetic ideas. This does not seem strange when we remember that Saint-Saëns was an intellectual rather than an emotional composer. In spite of the fact that he lived in the Romantic Period and shared its love of color and poetry, he was, perhaps unconsciously, a Classicist, devoted to clear outline, logical design, and precise workmanship. And he stands next to Brahms in his scholarly use of rhythm.

Yet when Saint-Saëns chose to tell a story in tone, he did it with a wit and finesse which is typically French and as typically Saint-Saëns. He had the flair for color, harmonic and instrumental, which is indispensable to program music. And, what is even more important, he could create an atmosphere and draw a character — or a caricature — to perfection. He was never at a loss for a subject, mythology, the Bible, classical literature, the zoological gardens, his own travels, all provided him with stories and pictures to turn into music.

Saint-Saëns was an able, often illuminating critic. His own love of exploration and freedom made him lenient in his attitude toward even the most extreme experimenters of his day. But he gave no quarter to the "prophets of noise as an art," the man who "abandons all keys and piles up dissonances which he neither introduces nor concludes and who, as a result, grunts his way through music as a pig through a flower garden." Nor had he any patience with the theory that in time people would become accustomed to such dissonance and accept it as music. "One can become accustomed to uncleanliness, to vice, even to crime. . . . Why cannot we understand that in art, as in everything else, there are some things to which we must not accustom ourselves!" He felt that the incoherence and sensationalism of many of the younger composers was but a mistaken idea of originality. "Above all," he wrote, "let the young avoid all straining after originality. Allow your personal contribution to music to express itself naturally. By eagerly desiring to be original, the result is very likely to be a blend of folly and *bizarrerie*. An instance of such madness is seen in the Italian architects of the twelfth century, who, in their eagerness to break away from the banality of the vertical, constructed those leaning towers which disfigure the city of Bologna.

"At this very moment, the entire world of music is suffering from a like disease: a craving for novelty at any cost. There are people now living who proclaim aloud their right to become a law unto themselves. Persons knowing nothing either of grammar or of orthography, a law unto themselves! We know what the result will be."

Whether in tones or words, Saint-Saëns always expresses his thought with precision and admirable clearness, and his opinions, however violent, are always interesting, often entertaining, as for example such a remark as, "From the *Opéra-Comique* was born a daughter, Operetta, who turned out badly, so to speak." Saint-Saëns contributed neither new forms nor techniques to his art. Nor is his music remarkable for its depth of thought or feeling. But it has one characteristic which is too often overlooked by those who, comparing him with Bach or Beethoven, place him rather far down the list of composers. Saint-Saëns's music is unique in its range of appeal. It is equally suitable for a "Pop" concert or a formal symphony program. Even the musical highbrow has lighter moments in which he can well afford to listen to the Symphony in C Minor, the Piano Concerto in G Minor, the *Suite Algérienne*, the delicious *Carnaval des animaux*, or even to one of the slightly worn symphonic poems. It is all clever music and in faultless taste. And it offers a breathing space of order and control, a welcome landing, so to speak, in the ascent to emotional heights, or the descent to depths of confusion of supposedly greater music.

As for the artless listener who goes to a concert in the hope of enjoyment, he is rarely disappointed by the pleasantly rhythmic, optimistic music of Saint-Saëns. After all, music should be heartening, should afford comfort and refreshment to jaded nerves at least once in a while! And it is difficult to understand why the composers who accent grief and deal almost exclusively in melancholy and frustration are so apt to be considered more significant than those who have captured some of the sparkle of life. Saint-Saëns did not intentionally brew tonic music; he merely reflected his own outlook upon life, and if his music sent his audiences away with lighter hearts, why, that was just another reason for giving thanks to *le bon Dieu*. But he did feel that with music holding so important a place in the modern world, a better type should be heard by the masses, even in the cafés and places of amusement. In his essay, "Popular Science and Music," he says, "There is plenty of gay music, easy to understand, which is in harmony with the laws of art, and the people ought to hear it instead of the horrors which they cram into our ears (at the cafés) under pretence of satisfying our tastes. What pleases most is sentimental music, but it need not be silly sentimentality. Instead, they ought to give the people the charming airs which grow, as naturally as daisies on a lawn, in the vast field of *opéra-comique*. That is not high art, it is true, but it is pretty music, and it is high art compared with what is heard too often in the cafés." Saint-Saëns's own music is far more than "pretty music," but its life and color and, above all, its clearness make it instantly appealing and enjoyable.

We have spoken of Saint-Saëns's versatility; now a word about the balance which is so notable in his life and work. Too often, genius is sadly lacking in balance and, cometlike, goes shooting off in one direction with startling effect, but to its own undoing. Saint-Saëns's star may have been less bright than some others, but it shone steadily and for a long, long time. His life was balanced. As a child he had been loved and petted, but expected to live up to his mother's high ambitions; as a youth he had had a rigorous Classical training in the midst of thrillingly Romantic surroundings. His spiritual life was molded by long hours in the organ loft of the Madeleine, where he became part of the service of that wonderful old church. And his love of gaiety was satisfied in the bright salons of Paris and at the Opéra-Comique, where he laughed at his own and other people's nonsense. As the years passed, work and play, war and peace, sorrow and joy seem to have woven for Saint-Saëns, the man, an unusually even pattern of life. As for the artist, Arthur Hervey sums it up in the following words:

> Saint-Saëns is indeed absolutely unique and has no counterpart. He has found it possible to be learned without being pedantic, to be tuneful without becoming banal, to employ all musical forms with ease and absolute mastery of resource, to remain clear and concise in his musical utterances, and to avoid all exaggeration. His wide outlook on life has prevented him from ever falling into extremes one way or another, and has contributed to preserve that perfect equilibrium which exists in all his works. He has always remained absolutely master of himself, and the sound common sense engrafted in his nature has stood him in good stead in his life and work.

The versatility which made Saint-Saëns an equally successful composer of symphonic, program, and stage music did not desert him when it came to the ballet. Here his French love of the dance, his precision of writing, and his feeling for color proved a perfect equipment. Moreover, he was always quick to sense the exact spot where dancing would fit into the action and atmosphere of the story, and to use it effectively. Saint-Saëns's ballet music is not only excellent, but also of many and varied types — cleverly simulated Tudor music for *Henry VIII*, Oriental music for *Samson et Dalila*, French music for *Étienne Marcel* — and so on down the list.

A characteristic and familiar example of Saint-Saëns's ballet music is the *Bacchanale* which precedes the final catastrophe in the opera *Samson et Dalila*. The last tableau shows the interior of the temple of Dagon; the sacred fire burns blue on the altar; priests and priestesses chant deliriously, while a crowd of men and women, drunk with wine and excitement, mills in and out on the floor below. The Philistines are about to offer a sacrifice of thanksgiving for the downfall of the Israelites and their leader Samson.

Shorn of his locks and his strength by the treacherous Dalila, and blinded by his enemies, Samson has been turning a grinding mill in the prison of Gaza. But now, as a last touch of vengeance, the Philistines have brought him to the temple that they may taunt him in his misery. Samson is led in by a little boy and stands between two of the great pillars that support the temple roof. In his blindness he hears the mocking voice of Dalila, the shouting of the drunken crowd, the music of the mad dance, and, clearer than by physical sight, the whole revolting picture comes before him. It is more than he can endure and, in a loud voice, he calls upon the God of Israel to restore his lost strength for but a moment. His prayer is granted, and, clasping the great pillars, he brings the roof crashing down and buries himself, his beautiful betrayer, and thousands of the Philistines in the ruins. This orgy in the temple gave Saint-Saëns opportunity for a vivid splash of the Oriental color which he always found so fascinating.

The *Bacchanale* opens with a cadenza:

a call that might have come straight from some eastern piper in the bazaars of Bagdad.

After a moment's silence, it is answered by the Oriental drumming of plucked strings, and flutes and clarinet lead off:

in a wild, swirling dance.

A second figure in the dance is indicated by a little, close-knit theme:

Violins
Violas

that seems to edge its way up to a climax, accompanied by the tinkle of triangles, the click of castanets, and shrill cries in the woodwinds.

Then, through this breathless motion, comes an insistent, plaintive wail:

Oboe
English Horn
Harp

which certainly never originated in the brain of a Frenchman! Saint-Saëns is said to have used a genuine Oriental theme given him by General Yusuf.

Such is the thematic material of the *Bacchanale*. But the effect — the whirling confusion of sound, motion, and color, the blinding flashes of brass, the throbbing, syncopated tympani, the whole mad frenzy of it — can only be felt in the music itself. And, as it comes to an end, one almost feels a physical relief and surprise to find the walls still standing, the roof intact!

THE SYMPHONIC POEMS OF SAINT-SAËNS

In this "century of the symphonic poem" it is a bit difficult to realize that only fifty or sixty years ago the musical world was rather violently divided on the relative merits of "program" *versus* "absolute" music. Even today there are formalists who feel that contact with the outside world, even the touch of poetry, is a violation to the art of music. In one of his clever essays, Saint-Saëns sums up the situation, then and now, when he says, "For many people, program music is a necessarily inferior *genre*. Many things have been written on this subject which I find it impossible to understand. Is the music in itself good or bad? Everything lies there. Whether it has a program or not, it will neither be better nor worse." He acknowledges music's indebtedness to Liszt for this new type of music: "Not so very long ago, orchestral music had only two forms at its disposal: the symphony and the overture. Haydn, Mozart, and Beethoven had not written anything else; who would have dared to do otherwise? Neither Weber, nor Mendelssohn, nor Schubert, nor Schumann had ventured to do so. Liszt had the courage to do it." And he describes the symphonic poem of Liszt's creation as generally consisting of "an ensemble of different movements depending on each other and proceeding from a fundamental idea, these being connected together in the form of one piece. The plan of the musical poem thus understood can be varied indefinitely."

It is natural that Saint-Saëns, a composer whose lively imagination was balanced by a love of order and clearness of expression, should have been attracted by this form which offered opportunity for both. While following the Liszt idea, in his own four symphonic poems, *Le Rouet d'Omphale*, *Phaëton*, *Danse macabre*, and *La Jeunesse d'Hercule*

(1871–77), Saint-Saëns made highly individual use of the form. And he widened its scope more than any other composer until, a dozen years later, Richard Strauss began his contribution of nine magnificent symphonic poems.

One could scarcely find a more discriminating estimate of the symphonic poems of Saint-Saëns than is made by the scholarly critic, Philip Goepp.

> Aside from the general charm of his art, Saint-Saëns found in the symphonic poem his one special form, so that it seemed that Liszt had created it less for himself than for his French successor. A fine reserve of poetic temper saved him from hysterical excess. He never lost the music in the story, disdaining the mere rude graphic stroke; in his dramatic symbols, a musical charm is ever commingled. And a like poise helped him to a right plot and point in his descriptions. So his symphonic poems must ever be enjoyed mainly for the music, with perhaps a revery upon the poetic story. With a less brilliant vein of melody, though they are not so Promethean in reach as those of Liszt, they are more complete in the musical and in the narrative effect.

LE ROUET D'OMPHALE

Saint-Saëns prefaced the score of his *Le Rouet d'Omphale* (The Spinning Wheel of Omphale) with this enlightening *Notice:*

> The subject of this symphonic poem is feminine allurement — the triumphant struggle of weakness against strength. The spinning wheel is a mere pretext chosen solely for its rhythmic interest and for atmospheric background to the piece.
>
> Those who may be interested in following the details of the story will find (at letter J in the score) Hercules groaning in the bonds which he cannot break, and (at letter L) Omphale mocking at the vain efforts of the hero.

Le Rouet d'Omphale was the first of Saint-Saëns's four famous symphonic poems. When it was written, in 1871, program music was new and violently disputed, hence, no doubt, the somewhat apologetic, "Those who may be interested in following the details of the story. . . ." Today, with the symphonic poem an accepted and favorite form, it goes without saying that everyone who wishes to fully enjoy Saint-Saëns's charming music will be interested in the story which gives it meaning.

As poetic background for *Le Rouet d'Omphale*, the composer chose an episode from the story of Hercules. Hercules seems to have been a favorite hero, for he figures not only in two of the symphonic poems but also in the opera *Déjanire*. (Indeed, Saint-Saëns must have been unusually attracted by strong men, for he chose Samson, the strong man of the Bible, as hero of his greatest stage work.)

The son of Jupiter and a mortal princess, Hercules was born to trouble. He was inordinately proud of his mighty father, from whom he had inherited his great strength, and boasted of him so shamelessly that ordinary mortals would have nothing to do with him. On the other hand, the gods despised him because he was only a demigod. There seemed to be no place for him and, as a result, his life was a series of entanglements ending in amazing adventures. Juno, the jealous queen of Olympus, particularly hated Hercules. She sent two great serpents to destroy him in his cradle, but the lusty baby strangled the serpents and grew to powerful manhood. Then Juno sent a destroyer far more fatal than serpents — fits of terrible temper and madness, in which Hercules often disgraced himself by most shocking deeds. As punishment for his behavior during one of these brain storms, he was given twelve supposedly impossible tasks — the famous labors of Hercules. But the mighty hero slew all the wild beasts and many-headed monsters, filched the golden apples of the Hesperides, in short, labored so valiantly that both gods and men had to acknowledge him world champion for strength and courage. And then this invincible hero met defeat in the laughter of a pretty woman.

Hercules, in one of his fits of frenzy, had killed a friend. For this, the assembled gods sentenced him to three years' slavery in Lydia, land of the warrior queen, Omphale. Now Omphale knew that bars and chains meant nothing to Hercules. Nor could he be punished by force or hard labor. But, clever woman and shrewd psychologist that she was, she also knew that nothing was so devastating to manly pride as ridicule, particularly the ridicule of a loved woman. So she proceeded first to captivate Hercules with her charms, which were many, and then, when he was hopelessly in love with her, to lay him waste with laughter. It is this last stage of his punishment which is pictured in *Le Rouet d'Omphale*.

The scene is laid in Omphale's spinning room, where, among the maidens, sits a miserable, burly figure — none other than Hercules, in woman's dress. Queen Omphale has taken away the famous club and lion's skin which were the insignia of the hero — it is said that she added insult to injury by swaggering around in them herself! The air is charged with suppressed laughter. The maidens nudge each other, and now and then a giggle escapes as they see those great hands that had so deftly torn the Nemean lion apart, tangling and breaking the thread. Omphale enters and, watching the young giant struggle with the hateful spinning wheel and still more hateful petticoats, bursts into peals of merry laughter. What was the nine-headed Hydra, the giant, Antaeus, or even the disgusting Augean stables compared with this? Hercules groans aloud in anguish! So abject is his misery that at last the gods take pity and send him off to recover on the battlefields of the Trojan Wars.

The music begins with the spinning-wheel figure, which, as Saint-Saëns states, is to serve as background and which, with little interruption, persists throughout the piece:[1]

There is something elusive about these first muted measures with their alternating flute and violin color and abrupt key changes — something as elusive and intangible as the unseen power which is to frustrate the blustering Hercules. At first, the wheels turn brokenly, but soon the humming of the strings suggests a steady motion.

[1] Permission to reprint excerpts granted by Durand & Cie., Paris, France, and Elkan-Vogel Co., Inc., Philadelphia, Pa. Copyright Owners.

Then, below the whirring strings, the clarinets and bassoons give out a curious, beckoning rhythm:

the truly "come-hitherish" rhythm of the first and main theme (the second theme is subordinate). Unlike many symphonic poems which have two or more themes of equal importance, *Le Rouet d'Omphale* has but one — "feminine allurement," here personified by Omphale. This theme appears in three rhythmic variations, which is consistent enough, since Omphale's wiles certainly took various forms! Saint-Saëns takes his time (18 measures) preparing the entrance of his queen, but at last here she is, symbolized by a graceful, apparently harmless, but slightly impertinent theme:

This melody plays lightly among the strings and woodwinds until suddenly the oboes let out a soft giggle:

and instantly all the woodwinds are shaking with suppressed laughter.

Saint-Saëns treats the Omphale theme as if it were a song with several stanzas. At the end of the first, he uses the rhythmic introduction as an interlude, then begins the second — the Omphale theme again, but rhythmically altered:

This time the laughter is much more hearty and more open.

Again we hear the rhythmic interlude and expect the third variation of the main theme. But no, it is Hercules this time, a mournful, complaining fellow:

It seems an added bit of irony, although perhaps unconscious on the composer's part, that the Hercules theme should be accompanied by the beckoning rhythmic figure of Omphale's!

There is no mistaking the groans of the suffering hero:

That his misery increases by the moment is loudly testified by many mounting voices. And then, oh, final touch of humiliation, an impudent oboe takes off the doleful Hercules theme:

and mocks him shamelessly:

This really has gone quite far enough!   Saint-Saëns quickly changes the subject (very good musical procedure it is, too) to the third and last variation of the Omphale theme:

last but for a reluctant syncopated fragment near the end:

Is she sorry that the fun is over or, perhaps, just the least bit sorry for her victim?

The human figures fade from the picture.   *Zum, zum* — softer grows the humming, more slowly turn the whirring wheels until, on the final D-sharps, they seem to reach a sticking point and come to rest.   The thread is spun — the story's done.

Danse macabre

In his comments on the symphonic poems of Saint-Saëns, Mr. Goepp says that, in his opinion, "the most original, profound, and essentially beautiful" of the works of this versatile composer is none other than the familiar *Danse macabre*. (This may surprise certain lesser critics who have hoped to show their superior taste by making fun of this popular piece.)   *Danse macabre* was the third of Saint-Saëns's symphonic poems.   It was suggested by some verse of Henri Cazalis which, in English, runs something like this:

> Zig-a-zig, zig-a-zig-a-zig,
> Death sits on the tombstone and drums with his heel.
> Zig-a-zig, zig-a-zig-a-zig,
> Death tunes up his fiddle and plays a weird reel.
>
> 'Tis midnight and sadly the winter wind moans;
> From shadowy lindens, with loud sighs and groans,
> The skeleton dancers in white, whirling crowds,
> Come leaping and skipping and waving their shrouds.
> Zig-a-zig-a-zig, what a horrible sound,
> The rattle of bones as they dance 'round and 'round!
>
> *   *   *
>
> But hark!   Bold young chanticleer heralds the day,
> And Death and his dancers have vanished away!
>
> — L. L. B.

The stroke of midnight sounds from the harp, supported by a horn and muted violin chords.   A soft stirring in the darkness, then a weird sound of tuning:[1]

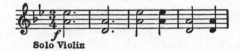

as Death, the fiddler, summons the ghostly dancers.

A single flute gives out the dancing tune:

which is at once taken up by the violins.

Then the sweet, half sobbing voice of a solo violin begins to sing the second theme, a plaintive, descending melody:

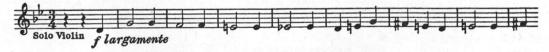

These two main themes, upon which the piece is built, lend themselves equally well to musical development and to the poetic suggestion of the verses.   As they play back and forth in ever varied form, they keep us constantly aware of the two contrasting moods of the poem, the ghastly gaiety and the wailing helplessness of these dancers of death.

The main violin, Death, the fiddler, seems always to be leading, urging the dancers

---

[1] Permission to reprint excerpts granted by Durand & Cie., Paris, France, and Elkan-Vogel Co., Inc., Philadelphia, Pa.   Copyright Owners.

on. Often he plays the first phrase of the tune, to which the others respond with wild energy. But for all its suggestion of a crowd of dancers, the music is cleverly thin. The *staccato* melody, supported mainly by *pizzicato* chords, lightly tapping triangle, and cymbals, with now and then a bony clatter from the xylophone, has a curiously fleshless feeling.

Having sketched the picture in the introduction of the two main themes, Saint-Saëns proceeds to make the most of them musically. For a moment, the expressive second theme seems to be caught up in the jigging rhythm of the dance:

One after another, the strings take it up, entering in fugal fashion, and then passing on to a bustling *arpeggio* figure.

Then follows a strange little episode. How gay the tune:

until one suddenly realizes that it is unmistakably related to that most somber funeral chant, the *Dies Irae* (Day of Wrath):

a bit of sly Saint-Saëns humor!

As if in protest against such levity, several voices repeat the second theme in a most plaintive form. This is followed by little shivering gusts of wind, winter wind moaning in graveyard trees.

The music then begins to gather a sort of demonic momentum. The brasses assert themselves; flutes and clarinets break into peals of mirthless laughter:

Death tunes up again as if for still wilder fiddling. The wailing voice sounds ever more hopeless:

and the strings, in a great upward surge, seem to lift the music to mad heights. Plainly, one can see

> . . . skeleton dancers in white, whirling crowds,
> Come leaping and skipping and waving their shrouds.

Then, through the chaos of this ghostly bacchanale, pierces a sharp, clear call:

Chanticleer, herald of dawn and a world of returning reality.

The music falters, trembles. The mournful voice of the solo violin droops in a weeping-willow theme:

hauntingly reminiscent of Brahms's "In the Churchyard" song. Then, with a few last capers:

the specter revelers vanish and the *Danse macabre* ends.

Great music? Perhaps not. There is certainly nothing profound in the eccentric poem which inspired it. But original and delightfully clever Saint-Saëns's music unquestionably is, and a perfect re-expression of the verses. Moreover, much of it is essentially beautiful.

PAUL DUKAS

Paris — 1865
Paris — 1935

Paul Dukas was a true Parisian. Paris born and trained, he lived there throughout the entire seventy years of his busy life and died there in the spring of 1935. Not much about his boyhood is known to the outside world. He seems to have been just a normal little French boy who loved to sing at his play and pick out tunes on the family piano. Not until he was fourteen did he show any special gift or interest in music. Then he began to teach himself *solfège* and to experiment with composition. He must have been a good teacher even then, for soon we hear of his entering the Paris Conservatoire, an institution by no means hospitable to dullards.

In 1888, Paul Dukas won his second *Prix de Rome* for his cantata *Velléda*, and felt himself well on the way toward becoming a professional musician. But about that same time his years of compulsory military service fell due, and reluctantly he left the Paris studios and teachers, the concerts and the operas for the routine of soldiering. Not to be completely cut off from his beloved music, he took along scores of Bach, Beethoven, and Wagner to keep him company in his free hours. The result of this companionship was that he came out of service convinced that, up to that time, he had learned very little. This was not exactly flattering either to his teachers or the Conservatoire! And although he was a *Prix de Rome* scholar, Dukas had the courage to back his estimate of his own musical education by completely reconstructing it. This time he based it upon a deep study of the works of the master musicians of all periods.

Dukas won his first real recognition as a composer in 1897 with his Symphony in C Major, and later in the same year he won fame with his brilliant *The Sorcerer's Apprentice*. He had many interests and activities besides his study and composition. He did a great deal of arranging and revising works of earlier composers, such as Couperin and Scarlatti, making their quaint harpsichord scores available for modern use. For the publishing house of Durand he edited, among other things, a complete edition of Rameau. And like so many of the French musicians — Berlioz, Saint-Saëns, Debussy — Dukas could compose words as well as tones. He was a master critic and wrote regularly on musical subjects for the leading French journals.

In 1928, Widor's resignation left vacant the post of Director of the Paris Conservatoire. It is an important post and one which it has always been considered an honor to hold. Dukas was immediately chosen as Widor's successor, but he modestly declined, saying that he preferred his quiet life to one of such publicity and that he felt that there were several French musicians who would fill the position better than he. The directorship was then offered to one after another of these able musicians, and to a man they refused it. They were determined that Paul Dukas should accept the recognition he so richly deserved as the leading *musicien français*. And so with double honor, from the institution and from his admiring colleagues, Dukas became Director of the famous old school.

Everything in Dukas' personality and experience seemed to contribute toward making him a wonderful teacher. To begin with, he was an honest man and an unselfish artist, always more interested in what he could do for music than in what music could do for him. And he was an eclectic — a chooser rather than a blind follower. In his boyhood he, too, had taken sides, insisting that Wagner had seen the one true light. Then, during those years of studying and exploring the works of many masters, Dukas realized how foolish it was to think that any one man or time or trend of thought could be all-important. And as for fencing off musical techniques and ideals and marking this little plot *Classical*, that one *Romantic*, or *Impressionistic*, and expecting a composer to choose one plot and stay within it, why that was nonsense. The field of music is too big and free for such fencing. A composer should be able to wander at will over the whole range, taking whatever seems good to him. The important thing, as Dukas often told his pupils, is that music should always express *something* and *somebody*. By *something* he meant some idea — in other words, a composer should have something to say or else keep still. And by *somebody* he meant the composer's own sincere self. Since only Wagner could express Wagner, only Mendelssohn express Mendelssohn, why should Paul Dukas make a fool of himself by trying to climb into another artist's skin? Paul Dukas should express himself, and so should every honest nobody of a pupil at the Conservatoire. Incidentally, every one of them should first see to it that he was worth expressing!

Dukas was always abreast, even in advance, of the times. Not a single so-called "modern" trick escaped him. But he was too good a musician, too much of an artist to mistake novelty for originality. "The young," he says, "believe that to write in accordance with extreme tendencies is to be in advance, but they are not in advance. Originality and personality are things that you cannot give yourself when you have not got them."[1] And again, "Today everybody specializes, and there are too many artisans and not enough artists. Everybody has technique and there is also abundance of idea — what is terribly lacking is not composing but the *motive* to compose."

Dukas has written a comparatively small number of compositions, yet all of them are finished, the product of reflection and meticulous workmanship. And most of them seem to have won a permanent place in musical repertory. From the day of its first performance *The Sorcerer's Apprentice* has been a prime favorite. The opera *Ariane et Barbe-Bleue* (Ariane and Bluebeard) shares first place on the French operatic stage with Debussy's *Pelléas et Mélisande*, and the dance poem *La Péri* is a most interesting modern work. Yet this composer, who with daring rhythms and unusual harmonic and orchestral colorings can give us the shivers of Bluebeard's chamber, this very "modern" composer, was ever the champion of "musical music." "What music needs," said he, "is to rediscover the musical phrase and to renew melody. Nothing more completely reveals the musician than the musical phrase he creates."

The whole world of music mourned the death of Paul Dukas, knowing that it had lost a musician of fine techniques, finer motives, and rarely balanced judgment.

THE SORCERER'S APPRENTICE

From an ancient book of startling title, *The Lover of Lies*, written by Lucian, a famous Roman satirist and dialogist of the year 150 A.D., comes the story of *The Sorcerer's Apprentice*. Lucian's exposition of the universal theme of the meddler who, with little knowledge and great conceit, starts something he cannot stop, so intrigued the poet Goethe that he turned it into a ballad. Goethe's ballad, *Der Zauberlehrling*, apparently did not have the desired moral effect on German youth, but it undoubtedly served a brilliant purpose as the inspiration of Dukas' tone poem. It is evident that the composer wished his listeners to know the story of *The Sorcerer's Apprentice* in detail, for after the title page of the score is a prose translation of the poem in French. Here is our own free version of Goethe's ballad.

(The scene is laid in the workshop of Pancrates, a famous sorcerer.
His apprentice, young Eucratcs, speaks:)

Ah, at last the old magician's gone away! Gone and left me master over
all the spirits. I have watched him working wonders, listened to his
charms and passwords. Now I, too, will make some magic!

[1] Quotations from "Paul Dukas: A Brief Appreciation" by Irving Schwerke, reprinted by permission from *The Musical Quarterly*, July, 1928. Copyright, 1928, by G. Schirmer, Inc.

Water, Water, set in motion
Little waves that from a distance
Come in streams and flowing, swelling,
Quickly fill the bath and basins!

Now, you old broom in the corner, come and stir your wretched carcass!
Long enough you've been a servant, and today you'll do my bidding.   Now
then, stand up on two legs there.   Head on top and take the pail, Sir,
for today you fetch the water.   And see to it that you hurry!

Water, Water, set in motion
Little waves that from a distance
Come in streams and flowing, swelling,
Quickly fill the bath and basins.

See, he runs down to the river!   He has reached the bank already!
Back again as quick as lightning, then a second time returning!
Hooray, how the water's rising in the master's bath and basins!

Stop now, stop!   Your gifts have served us quite enough.
Oh, gracious heavens, what's the word? I've clean forgotten!

Oh, that word!   That word of magic which alone can stop this deluge!
There, he's running to the river, fetching yet more pails of water!
Oh, a hundred hateful rivers now are pouring in upon me!

No, I cannot, will not bear it!   'Tis a demon, and its glances
drive me almost mad with terror!

Oh, you villain!   Oh, you devil!   Do you really mean to drown me?
See, the water's crossed the threshold!   Oh, mad creature, stop, I pray you,
Be a broom just as you once were!

So you won't leave off?   I'll fix you, Wooden Head, with my sharp hatchet!

See, he's coming, slipping, slopping — Now you goblin, now you'll catch it!
Crash!   There goes my valiant hatchet.   Right in two he's cut!
Thank Heaven!   Once again I can breathe freely!

Can it be that both the pieces now are standing up and moving?
Two slaves now to carry water.   Oh, ye gods above, protect me!

Off they go, and wet and wetter grow the steps and all the workshop now is flooded.
Master, Master, hear my cry, my plight is ghastly!
I have summoned evil spirits and I know not how to stop them!

(The old Sorcerer suddenly appears and speaks:)

In the corner, broom!   Be still, now.
And you, boy, had best remember
That the master summons spirits
Only for some worthy purpose!

As the music begins, one half suspects Dukas of having himself been apprentice to
a sorcerer.   Where else could he have learned the secret of such otherworldly sounds.

High, thin violins, siren voices, tempt the boy — "Why not try a little magic making yourself?"[1]

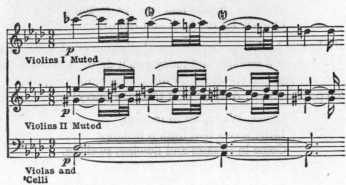

they seem to whisper. Woodwinds answer in a little motif which is soon to be all too familiar:

There is something eerie, something a bit chilling in these harmonies, the curious flageolet quality of the strings and the hollow tones of the woodwinds.

Then a sudden, sharp chord loosens a spraylike stream of chromatics, perhaps it is a fine idea striking the apprentice —to get the Master's bath filled by magic and without a turn of his own lazy hand! A muted trumpet then suggests the means — the old broom which the magician sometimes makes do his bidding. It is all too alluring! The music takes on a feverish activity of rushing woodwinds. In the brass the magic summons is heard, shouted by Eucrates in a loud and confident voice:

There follows a trembling excitement from piccolo to double bass — then, tense silence. Will the magic really work! Will the old broom — didn't something move then?

Wait! There it goes again:

As sure as the world, the broom is standing up — moving — trying its legs:

and there it goes, trotting off to the river, water pail in hand!

For a time little snatches of the magic theme can be heard:

as the apprentice, pleased with his wonder working, watches his slave run to and fro. But soon the hurrying footsteps of the broom drown out all other sounds.   And speaking of drowning, a long stream of chromatics, smooth and liquid compared to the trudging theme, begins to pour down from the strings:

water, to be sure!

Faster and faster trots the hard-working broom.   Then, as if the affair had turned into a sort of demon festival attended by all the mischievous sprites of the underworld, the tune takes a new turn, and with bells and harps becomes a frolicking song:

which rises happily into higher keys.

The water is now pouring in in torrents.   Above the chromatic streams, the voice of the poor apprentice can be heard commanding, beseeching, cursing the broom, but all in vain.   He cannot remember the word, the countercharm which alone can stop the deluge.   His rage rises with the water.   Then the hatchet chord goes splintering through the orchestra.   The broom stops, the water stops, and we join Eucrates in that long breath of relief.

But, half drawn, the breath catches in horror at that familiar fumbling, stirring sound. This time there are twice as many notes stirring (the score is amusingly graphic). Both pieces come to life, two brooms, two water carriers (a bass clarinet and bassoon) begin their devilish trudging to the river! Soon all is in wildest confusion. The violins and woodwinds seem to bob and splash, and there are actually little waves rippling in the 'celli and basses:

Everything is drowned, even the cries of the miserable apprentice shouting, "Master! Master!"

Brief and to the point is the ending of both story and music. Just as the tumult has become unbearable to everybody, the loud voice of the old magician is heard, the master's voice, which sends the broom scurrying into its corner without so much as a sound. Then the weird opening harmonies are heard again:

This time only the ghost, the memory, of the broom theme answers, and at the same time, the loveliest "all's well" phrase in the viola:

We are almost hypnotized with this soothing melody after all the furious commotion. Then, perhaps to add a French touch of lightness to the German moral, and incidentally to remind us that *The Sorcerer's Apprentice* is a *scherzo*, the whole orchestra joins in a surprisingly loud and vigorous tailpiece:

The spell is broken!

CHAPTER VIII

Music and the Ballet

The ballet, like the opera, is a meeting place of three arts — music, the spectacle, and drama — with this difference, that in the ballet the human voice is replaced by bodily movements and the story is told in pantomime. Glancing backward, we find the ballet taking its name from the Italian word *ballata*, meaning a dancing piece, an entertainment of song and dance. It was a pastime of the people, and far apart as the two may seem, the old *ballata* and the highly specialized modern ballet bear the same relationship as the folk tune and the symphony.

In the course of years and of its use by many peoples, the singing part of the *ballata* became detached from the dancing and set up for itself as the *ballad*, the story-song or poem. But it still showed traces of the old alliance in its tune, for, as is interesting to note, most ballad tunes are simple dance tunes. As for the dancing part of the *ballata*, it also took up an independent life, found a royal patron, and became an aristocratic institution known as the *ballet*.

French enthusiasm for dancing is as much of a tradition as Italian love of singing, and it seems quite natural that the ballet, the most scientifically developed form of the dance, should have had its origin in France. In 1661, Louis XIV founded *L'Académie Royale de la Danse*, and the ballet became a definite and favorite part of French opera. The best talent of the Grand Monarch's court was devoted to the ballet. Molière wrote many of the librettos, Lully composed the music, and painters, costumers, and dancing masters vied with each other in producing gorgeous stage effects. Louis grew so enthusiastic over this novel form of entertainment that he himself took to the stage, and a rare spectacle he must have made, marching pompously about among the dancers, dressed in preposterous costumes to represent Apollo, Neptune, Jupiter, and other exalted beings! He even went so far as to invite members of his court to join in the dancing, which was quite possible since the dances were merely the favorite social dances of the period — the *Bourrée, Courante, Chaconne, Gigue, Minuet, Sarabande, Passepied*, and *Passacaglia*. This may be one explanation of the conventionality of the early ballet music, for composers were not only content but also were expected to fashion their tunes after the popular dance patterns. All suggestion of the story or character was the business of the costumer and scene painter, and Neptune danced the minuet not because it was appropriate, but because it was a dance he knew!

In 1708, the Duchesse de Maine, in search of a novelty for an evening party, commissioned a composer to write music illustrating the fourth act of Corneille's play *Horace*, and had two actors mime the story as the music was being played. This glorified charade was the beginning of the dramatic ballet.

In the ballet, as in the arts of music, painting, and sculpture, there has been a constant shifting of emphasis between two ideals — abstract design (beautiful patterns created for their own sake) and the expression of definite ideas and emotions. So significant have been these points of emphasis — design versus expression — that they have given rise to the two important types or schools of art known as *Classical* and *Romantic*. The eighteenth-century ballet was classical in spirit. It was an art of graceful posturing in which the dancers were as decorative as the figures on a Greek vase, and almost as impersonal. Like the eighteenth-century opera, of which it was so often a part, the ballet was elaborate, artificial, and stiffly formal. Gone were Louis XIV's pretty amateurs in their stuffy court finery, and in their places, professionals danced in skirts shortened to give freedom to the feet. The lines of the dance, too, were changing from the easy horizontal to the difficult vertical, as is shown in the ballet terminology, which now included such words as *ballon* (the bounce), *élévation* (dancing off the ground), *entrechat* (a jump during which the feet change position, giving a twinkling effect), and *pirouette* (a complete turn of the body, pivoted on one leg). Definite techniques were being developed, and, as was the case with the Singer's Opera, far more attention was paid to the perfection of a performance than to its meaning.

The inevitable protest against this meaningless dancing found expression in the work of Jean Georges Noverre (1727–1810), one of the first master choreographers (arranger of dances). Developing the Duchesse de Maine's little experiment in pantomime dancing, Noverre created the dramatic ballet and, in his "Lettres sur la danse," laid down principles which are still in use. He insisted that every ballet, whether part of an opera or an independent entertainment, should have a carefully thought-out plot or theme, and that every detail of the stage setting, costuming, pantomime, and foot work should be designed with the one idea of expressing that theme as beautifully and naturally as possible. It was the same back-to-nature idea, the same qualities of truth and simplicity that Gluck was trying to express in the opera. The two men knew each other; in fact, Noverre directed many of the ballets for which Gluck wrote the music.

From this time on, and well into the next century, the ballet made such progress that it rivaled opera in popularity, and famous dancers became the idols of Paris, London, Vienna, and Milan. New steps and techniques were devised, one of the most important being that of dancing *sur les pointes*, "on the points" — the familiar toe-dancing, which gives the illusion of floating through space.

In 1832, an Italian dancer, Marie Taglioni, delighted Paris with a new type of ballet, *La Sylphide* (The Sylph). The lightness of her movements and her faultless technique made her seem a creature of the air, and her dancing gave to the ballet a spiritual quality it had never had before. Taglioni's costume — the tight-fitting bodice, the bell-shaped skirt of white tarlatan, flesh-colored tights, and satin slippers — became the accepted uniform of nineteenth-century ballet dancers.

But more important than a new costume or a new style of dancing was the subsequent beginning of a new relationship between music and the ballet. In any composite art, there is always the danger of over-emphasizing certain elements to the neglect of others.

Up to this time in the history of the ballet, the spectacle and the drama had received most of the attention, and music had played a part of humble service. The composer was expected to provide tunes of obvious rhythms and sentiments and of so little musical importance that they could be stretched out or lopped off at the dancer's convenience without anyone's being the wiser. The music, being mere accompaniment and poor at that, had no life of its own and was never considered worthy of concert use. There are, to be sure, exceptions in the beautiful ballet music of Rameau, Handel, Gluck, and Mozart, but these tunes, written at a time when the ballet itself was little more than a collection of social dances, belong as much to the ballroom as to the stage. And there was Beethoven's ballet music for *Prometheus* and Schubert's lovely *Rosamunde*, but even this music did not come into its own until a much later date.

In the first decade of the twentieth century, *Les Sylphides* (named after Taglioni's earlier success) reversed the whole process of ballet making. Instead of arranging a ballet and then adapting music to it, the choreographer of *Les Sylphides* chose suggestive music (one of Chopin's Preludes, a Nocturne, a Mazurka, and two Waltzes), and interpreted it in dancing. This was the beginning of the long list of so-called Romantic Ballets, in which the music provides the theme and the inspiration, as in Delibes's *Coppélia* and *Sylvia*, Schumann's *Carnaval*, Tchaikovsky's *Swan Lake*, Rimsky-Korsakov's *Scheherazade*, and many another old favorite.

For a time, about the middle of the nineteenth century, the popularity of the ballet began to wane, partly because the golden voice of Jenny Lind had turned public attention to singing, and partly because the ballet makers had become so concerned with showing off the marvelous technique of the star dancers that they neglected the production as a whole. The male dancer, who had once played such an important part, was now reduced to the role of mere *porteur*, the "lifter" who literally supported the leading lady in her delicate balancing acts. In an effort to regain their lost popularity, the dancers now twirled faster and jumped higher than ever. The poetry of the dance was lost in acrobatic contest and "One-two-three — kick!" became the *Leitmotiv* of the ballet.

The revival of the ballet as an art was to come from Russia, where, since the days of the Empress Anne (1693–1740), there had been state schools of dancing. There, under the French master, Petipa, the technique of ballet dancing had been brought to the highest degree of perfection and refinement. And there, in 1905, Petipa's pupil, Michael Fokine, realized an entirely new idea of the ballet in his daring and original arrangement of *The Swan*, to Saint-Saëns's music, for Anna Pavlowa.

In a letter to the *London Times* (1914), Fokine set forth the famous "five points" upon which he based his work. First, the dance should be composed, not of ready-made steps and combinations, but to correspond with the subject in both time, place, and spirit. Heretofore, the conventional toe-dancing had been displayed whether the scene of the ballet was laid in Spain, India, Greece, or the legendary Venusberg of *Tannhäuser!* Second, gesture should be used only when it helped to tell the story, and not because a certain sweep of the arm was becoming to the dancer. Third, gesture should be of the whole body, Fokine insisting that facial expression, the movements of the shoulders and hips, the carriage of the head, the angle of the trunk, even the back, should be expressive. Gone were the old absurd formulae — finger on lips equals secrecy, hand on heart equals love! Fourth, instead of one brilliant star dancer backed by an ornamental group which merely kept time and line, there should be an ensemble of artists, each one engaged in dancing the theme. One mechanical *coryphée* with set and toothy grin can upset the whole balance and destroy the illusion of the dance. Fifth (and here we quote from Fokine's letter), "In the arts associated with ballet, perfect freedom shall be allowed to the composer and decorator. The music need not be a simple accompaniment to the dancer's movements; every kind of music shall be permissible so long as it is good and expressive. Finally, it is not imperative that the dancer be costumed in the traditional ballet skirt."

Noverre, more than a century earlier, had spoken wisely and for all time when he defined the ballet as "Nature embellished with the charms of art," and warned ballet masters not to think of dancing "as if all consists in the action of the legs only." Fokine, too, was a close student of nature and, living in a less rigidly formal time than Noverre, was able to translate nature's moods into bodily movement. And, just as the musician composes and orchestrates his symphony, so Fokine and every great choreographer composes and orchestrates the dance, using each dancer as a note or motif in the complicated score of the ballet.

It is not difficult to recognize in Fokine's five points much that is familiar in the ballet as we know it — the peasant and character dances, the picturesque costumes and scenery, the pantomime, truthful to the point of daring representation of the ugly and grotesque, and the perfect blending of the music and the dance.

We have watched the relationship of music and the ballet change from the early stages, in which the dance was all that mattered and the music mere accompaniment, to a second stage, in which the music led, providing the themes which the dancer illustrated. Now, with the greater freedom and realism of the Russian ballet, comes a third relationship, in which the choreographer and the composer work together. The first important example of this specially commissioned ballet music was *The Fire Bird* (1910) by Stravinsky. In it Stravinsky and Fokine collaborated, the composer writing a musical version of the old legend, and the choreographer suggesting what was needed and effective for the dance. Following *The Fire Bird* came the two other great Stravinsky ballets, *Petrushka* and *The Rite of Spring*, Ravel's *Daphnis and Chloë*, de Falla's *Three-Cornered Hat*, Bartok's *Wooden Prince*, Carpenter's *Krazy Kat* and *Skyscrapers*, and many others in a line of specially composed ballets extending to and through the present. At no time in its long and colorful history has this ancient art form, the ballet, shown greater vitality or aroused greater public interest than it does today. For not only the stage, but also the cinema and radio's promise of tomorrow's television seem peculiarly congenial to picture dancing.

Occasionally, a group of present-day dancers revives one of the old symmetrical ballets with the quaint, patterned tunes of Rameau, Handel, or Gluck, and a pleasing novelty it is. But it would be no more possible for a modern composer to write sincerely in that old-time style than for him to return to the use of quill pens, bagwigs, and sedan chairs. Choreographers still adapt ballets to already-existing music. Since the days of *Les Sylphides* this practice has gone so far as to include the use not only of romantic and picturesque music but also of the classical symphony.   Twentieth-century choreographers, attempting to arrange dances for everything from a Bach chorale to a Brahms symphony, seem to have taken as their slogan, "All music can be danced." It is a dangerous idea, for, despite certain masterly exceptions, there is a whole field of music that lies beyond the sense of seeing, beyond the limits of definite ideas and meanings.   It belongs to the realm of pure feeling, and can no more be objectified than can our conception of God be expressed in a graven image.   Such music *should not* be danced.   As for the specially composed ballet, that happy idea is welcomed by contemporary artists and audiences.   Composers are glad to accept commissions for a ballet, not merely for the immediate rewards of money and publicity, but also because the poetic idea of the ballet is a challenge to the imagination and because they know that if they meet it, they are linking their musical art to the fine art of dancing in a composite form which is as aesthetically satisfying as the union of music and poetry in the art song.

The ballet, a combination of music, the spectacle, and drama in pantomime, depends for its success upon the effective use of all three of these arts.   They are of equal importance, and no one of them can be stressed at the expense of the others or the balance is destroyed.   Yet there is no denying the fact that music has been the vitalizing element in the modern ballet, the inspiration of the dancer, the shared experience which links performer and spectator.   Music *is* the feeling to which the dance gives meaning.   Or, as Théophile Gautier puts it, "The ballet is music that one can see."

LÉO DELIBES

Saint-Germain-du-Val — 1836
Paris   — 1891

Léo Delibes was born, more than a century ago, in the little town of Saint-Germain-du-Val.   The death of his father left the family with scant resources, but Mme. Delibes, ambitious for the little son who showed signs of musical talent, determined to take him to Paris, where even a poor boy might make his way.   Léo was ten years old when they came to the big city and found him a position as choir boy in the Church of the Madeleine.   He was admitted to the junior classes at the Conservatoire, where he soon began to carry off the prizes which are regarded as symbols of achievement in the education of a French child.   Somehow or other, his thrifty mother managed to place him with the best teachers of piano, harmony, and composition, and so, busily and happily, his boyhood passed.

Playing a church organ seems to be a traditional occupation with French composers, and, like Saint-Saëns, César Franck, and many others, Delibes held several positions, ending with that of organist at the church of St.-Jean-St.-François, where he served for ten years.   But a more congenial occupation was that of accompanist at the Théâtre Lyrique, and later at the Opéra.   For Delibes was intensely interested in stage music and, early in his career, had made modest experiments in writing operettas and little one-act operas. When, in 1865, he was promoted from the position of accompanist to that of second chorus master at the Opéra, a new world seemed to open for him. The following year, Delibes and another composer were assigned the task of writing music for the ballet *La Source*. Delibes's music not only stole the show, but also indicated to him and to the musical world where his talent lay.

The course of Delibes's life ran along smoothly, marked neither by sensational success nor failure. At the age of thirty-four, he married the daughter of an actress, with whom he seems to have lived happily enough. He was appointed professor of advanced composition at the Conservatoire, member of the Institute, and, in recognition of his work, was made a Chevalier of the Legion of Honor, of which he later became an officer. Delibes was a hard worker, not only at his composition, which was considerable, but also at teaching, which with him was a real enthusiasm. He lived very simply. His opera *Lakmé*, with the famous "Bell Song," was written in a tiny study of "hall-bedroom" type at the top of a crowded house on the Rue de Rivoli. There was barely room for a little upright piano, two tables loaded with books, and an unpainted trestle table for his writing.

Delibes was a gay fellow, over six feet tall, with thick blond hair and beard, merry eyes, and a famous laugh that shook the rafters. He never had much money, but that did not seem to matter, for he had what money cannot buy — friends, a sense of humor, and the sense of beauty which makes the humblest life worth living. Unfortunately, this pleasant, useful life came to an end at the too-early age of fifty-five.

With the exception of a few choruses, a mass or two, and a handful of songs, Delibes wrote exclusively for the stage. His operas, of which *Lakmé* and *Le Roi l'a dit* are the best known, are pleasing examples of the old-fashioned type. Today they seem a trifle too elegant, like the slightly tarnished epergnes and cruet stands of forgotten dinner tables. But his ballet music, the lovely dances from *Coppélia* and *Sylvia*, like old-time crystal fringed with prisms, have never lost their twinkling charm. Like their pictured counterparts, the famous Degas paintings of ballerinas, the Delibes dances are recognized as permanent works of art.

Delibes made an original and important contribution in his ballet music. Before his time, the music written for stage dancing had been, for the most part, either formal social dances or tinkling melodies with marked rhythm and no meaning. Composers had looked upon the ballet as merely a part of the machinery of opera, a *divertissement* put in to satisfy the French love of the dance. But to Delibes, the ballet was a poem come to life in beautiful bodily movement. The ballet was an opportunity. Eagerly he seized it and wrote the first picturesque ballet music, music full of mood and character suggestion to fire the imagination of the dancers. And he was the first to give to ballet music the richness of rhythm, melody, harmony, and instrumentation which characterizes symphonic music. It is these two qualities — poetic content and musical interest — that made Delibes's ballet music so delightful both for dancing and concert use. And the fact that these two qualities, developed and varied, have been the foundation of all subsequent music for stage dancing, has given to Delibes the title "father of modern ballet music." His music is, perhaps, best described in a line from Bruneau, the French critic, who speaks of "the distinguished, spirited, luminous, singing melodies of Delibes."

Delibes was not a great composer in the Bach-Beethoven sense. He rates but a modest paragraph or two in the music histories. But he was, says Olin Downes, one of those "men of true talent . . . not deceived about themselves, but giving their best to their art"; and, we might add, one of the many clever, well-balanced, poetic artists which the nineteenth century seemed to produce as a matter of course.

BALLET SUITE, SYLVIA

Antiquarians trace the ballet back even further than the old *ballata*, back to the ancient Greek festivals in honor of Bacchus, god of wine and revelry. Whether this be true or not, the association is happily apropos in the ballet *Sylvia*, in which a page of Greek mythology comes to life and Bacchus himself roisters across the stage.

Sylvia is less a story than a series of moving pictures, *tableaux vivants*. The curtain rises upon a smooth, grassy place near the seashore. In the background is the temple of Diana, goddess of the moon and of the chase. Near the temple porch is a giant oak, and in its dappled shade Greek peasants are holding a festival. Into the midst of these human revelers comes the god Bacchus with his rollicking train of satyrs and fauns, and Diana, heavenly huntress, with her nymphs, of whom Sylvia is the most charming. They meet, and nymphs and fauns mime their light and heartless love-making. It was a perfect subject for Delibes's happy, heartless music and for the dainty, artificial ballet dancing of Paris in 1876. The fantastic *ballon* and *élévation* of the dancers seemed quite appropriate to airy nymphs and fauns, who might well mock the laws of gravity. And the blue and silver light which transforms the painted back-drop into an antique temple and lends an unreal beauty to the dancing figures is but the moonshine of Diana!

Prelude — The Huntresses

The Ballet Suite *Sylvia*, in which the numbers are arranged with the idea of musical contrast rather than in the order of the dance, begins with a majestic *Prelude:*

A faint horn call:

followed by a little running figure:

and a loud "halloo!"

Horns

announces the entrance of *Les Chasseresses*, The Huntresses, Diana and her nymphs.

They come bounding in on a horn theme:

Horns
Violas

almost as vigorous as that of the winged horses of the Valkyries. But the shimmer of accompanying strings lightens the galloping rhythm, and with the entrance of the second theme, a dainty, tripping melody for violins:

Violins I *p leggierissimo*

all suggestion of horsiness vanishes. These are the fleet-footed Moon Maidens.

Again and again, above the excitement of the chase, the horn call is heard, and, from time to time, a sweeping of strings and woodwinds, suggesting flying draperies. The first theme comes back — as one knows it will — and the huntresses make their exit, escorted by animated trumpets.

Intermezzo — Valse lente

The intermezzo is the music for a little pantomime between two dances. The nymph Sylvia comes down to the bank of a tree-bordered stream. Using the overhanging roots as a swing, she balances herself there, dipping one foot in the water and making a lovely picture in the moonlight.

A graceful phrase, passed from violins:

Violins I *p*

to oboe:

Oboe *mf*

then to flute:

Flute *mf*

through the bright major keys of B, D, and F gives one of those gleams of color that distinguish Delibes's music. It seems as effortless and unself-conscious as the color effects in nature. The three little phrases might be three morning-glories, pink, blue, and lavender, swinging together on a trellis, their very freshness and simplicity the secret of their charm.

Still more striking contrast comes with the expressive theme for solo clarinet:

for now, smooth, singing melody replaces the sprightly *staccato*, and the deeper voice of the clarinet suggests a velvety purple among the clear, bright colors of violins and high woodwinds.

As for the pantomime, it is easy enough to imagine, for the music's suggestion of the laughing coquette and the pleading suitor is unmistakable.

Gently the clarinet leads into the waltz:

For all its swaying, three-four rhythm, this waltz offers little temptation to the amateur, who would certainly be at a loss to know what to do with ordinary arms and legs during the little pause on the sustained high note at the end of each phrase — a pause so obviously meant for pretty posturing!

Beneath the tripping violins, we now hear a solo horn in a more singing version of the melody:

which the clarinet takes up in minor mood:

This is followed by a repetition of the violin and horn duet, to which the flutes add a flock of birdlike trills.

The ending of the *Valse lente* is as leisurely and as colorful as the *Intermezzo* which preceded it. To a light *staccato* accompaniment of woodwinds, the violas and 'celli have this little interlude:

a tender farewell, it might be. Then the opening measures of the waltz float lightly up and away. It is noticeable that Delibes never ends his ballet music abruptly. He always gives the dancers an effective exit. And it is equally acceptable to listeners at a concert to be thus gently let down after the mild excitement of such rhythmic music.

Pizzicati

The *Pizzicati* is a solo dance for Sylvia. After a hesitant entrance of little running steps and shy pauses:

the familiar tune begins:

It is an idealization of dancing *sur les pointes*, the French toe-dancing. Plainly, as if portrayed with brush or pencil, appears the dainty figure in fluffy tarlatan skirts which emphasize the wasp waist and the frailty of arms and legs. Airily she twirls on pointed satin toes, springing lightly off the ground at the end of each phrase. What else could she do to such a tune?

In contrast to the tingling *Pizzicati* (the literal meaning of the word is "to pinch; to sting or tingle") comes a soothing melody for solo flute:

Then the violins bring back the first theme, this time bowing the strings instead of plucking them. It lasts but a moment, and off she flutters, *sur les pointes*, like a great white moth.

Cortège de Bacchus

After the fragile *Pizzicati*, the glaring, blaring *Cortège de Bacchus* comes in striking contrast. This is no procession, marching with dignity, but a *cortège* in the literal sense of the word, "a court or train of attendants." And it is the most bizarre court imaginable — fauns and satyrs clad in goat skins, crowned with vine leaves, and carrying Panpipes — the court of Bacchus, god of wine.

With a brilliant, repeated fanfare:

answered by full orchestra, the processional begins. The strings then give out a rollicking tune:

set to the caperings of little cloven hoofs. And, as if these irrepressible creatures could not keep even their own wayward step, the tune begins to leap and bound:

and clash its cymbals.

A quieter interlude (the conventional trio section of the march) follows:

But it is interrupted by excitement in the strings and woodwinds, presumably caused by a glimpse of the huntresses:

The excitement dies away and the quiet theme plays itself out.

The fanfare sounds again, bringing back the opening section and an animated variation of the first theme:

which increases in speed and volume.   One feels that the music — and the dance — is working itself up to a climax, and here it is, the entrance of Her Heavenly Highness, Diana of the Moon and the Chase:

Full Orchestra

in all the magnificence of full orchestra reinforced by side drum, bass drum, triangle, and cymbals.

Then follows a long Coda, *Allegro vivace*, long enough to see the whole fantastic company well off the stage.

Sylvia old-fashioned music?   Perhaps it is.   But who today is creating melody of lovelier line, or rhythms more compelling?   Who is tone-painting with more gorgeous color?   And what could be more theatrically effective than the contrast, so plainly suggested, of Diana and her airy nymphs, with the roistering Bacchus and his grotesque, earthy train?

A well-known critic calls Delibes's *Sylvia* "a revival of the past in modern manner and an anticipation of the future."   And no less an artist than Tchaikovsky, writing from Paris in 1877, said, "My own *Swan Lake* is poor stuff compared to *Sylvia*."

IGOR STRAVINSKY

Oranienbaum — 1882

Igor Stravinsky was born in a suburb of St. Petersburg where his father was a celebrated singer at the Maryinsky Theater.   Having both an inheritance and environment of music, young Igor's talents were developed as a matter of course, and he became a clever amateur pianist.   Law, however, not music, was to be his chosen profession, and to it he gave his serious study.   In his twenty-first year, having finished college, Stravinsky took a trip abroad.   There he met his famous countryman, Rimsky-Korsakov, and this chance meeting turned the course of his life from law to music. On his return from St. Petersburg, Stravinsky began to study with Rimsky-Korsakov and rapidly mastered the techniques of composition and orchestration.

He first tried his hand at composing a symphony, then a song cycle, after which came *Fireworks* and *Scherzo fantastique*, two rather startling orchestral adventures. Fortunately for Stravinsky, these pieces happened to be heard by Serge de Diagilev, the man who made the Ballet Russe world-famous.   Diagilev, whose genius lay in recognizing and utilizing other men's talents, saw in the picturesque music of this unknown young composer just what he wanted for his combination of "dance, music, and *décor*."   He commissioned him to write the music for a ballet.   *The Fire Bird* was the result and the beginning of a collaboration, lasting almost twenty years, which was to make Stravinsky famous.

Stravinsky has been aptly described as "an agitated little man with the will of a giant, fine formal gestures, and a cyclonic temperament." He is fond of people, and his drawing-room talents are many and varied, including a passion for argument. He is also fond of things, luxurious appointments, fine brandies, and exotic raiment. His desk, at which he works on strictly scheduled time, is the orderly desk of the lawyer he was trained to be, and his beautiful meticulous manuscripts would put Beethoven's smudgy pages to shame. And how Beethoven and many another domestically forlorn musician might have envied the wife, whimsically called the "oldest friend," the four clever children, the delightful shared interests, and the devotion to each other which has made the Stravinsky home a veritable citadel, a shelter in any kind of storm!

As both man and artist, Stravinsky has led a migratory life. During World War I he lived in Switzerland. Later he made his home in Paris, applying for French citizenship. In 1925 came the first of a number of visits to the United States as guest conductor with leading orchestras, and in 1939 he settled in Cambridge, Massachusetts, where he carried on triple activities as composer, conductor, and lecturer at Harvard University until Hollywood, but not moving pictures, lured him to the West Coast. He is now an American citizen.

The frequent sceneshifting in Stravinsky's personal life has been paralleled by radical changes in his musical style. Beginning his career at the time when Russian Ballet, an enchanting novelty, was temporarily eclipsing both the symphony and the opera, Stravinsky believed, with many other young composers, that the day was forever past when an artist could create quietly, expressing what was in his own heart and trusting that someday the world would understand. Moreover, being a practical as well as a musical young man, he had no sympathy with the tradition of the neglected, poverty-stricken composer who lived in the hope of posthumous appreciation. Like Richard Strauss, Stravinsky meant to wear his laurels and collect his royalties in the flesh, and who can blame him! One of his own countrymen, Sabaneiev, makes this harsh but perhaps just appraisal: "Stravinsky is more a genius of musical business than purely of music. . . . His fame rests chiefly on his virtuosity in making full use of musical conditions and taking full account of fashions and fads. . . . He is a deliberate innovator, deliberately glittering, sharp, shrill voiced, flickering and blinding as an electric sign."

We find Stravinsky, then, a man of his own realistic time, winning his first great success with music for ballets in which puppets and fantastic fairy-tale creatures take the place of living men and women. It is brilliant music, full of ingenious rhythms, pungent chords and discords, and little scraps of melody repeated and repeated. It is music admirably suited to its purpose, which was the effect of the moment rather than the carefully planned continuity of the work as a whole. And, regardless of definite memories of Rimksy-Korsakov and Debussy which linger in *The Fire Bird*, it is highly individual music, realistic and as free as possible from emotion, which Stravinsky and his contemporaries condemned as romantic, soft, and intellectually lacking.

The Fire Bird, written in 1910, was followed in 1911 by *Petrushka*, a gorgeous specimen of this colorful, heartless music, and in 1912 by *The Rite of Spring*, to which the composer himself gave the subtitle *Pictures of Pagan Russia*, and which many people feel represents

Stravinsky at the height of his powers.   Since then a long list of compositions have come from this sincere and industrious composer — compositions in which he has experimented with all sorts of unusual types of instrumentation and new dramatic forms and for which he has sought inspiration all the way from Pergolesi to Irving Berlin.   But none of these later works have equaled those of the earlier days before the life line of connection with his native Russia was severed.

Stravinsky himself realizes the difference between then and now, for, in his autobiography, speaking of his public, he says,[1] "Liking the music of *L'Oiseau de feu* [*The Fire Bird*], *Petrushka*, *Le Sacre du printemps* [*Rite of Spring*], *Les Noces* [*The Wedding*] and being accustomed to the language of these works, they are astonished to hear me speaking in another idiom.   They cannot and will not follow me in the progress of my musical thought.   What moves and delights me leaves them indifferent, and what still continues to interest them holds no further attraction for me.   I believe that there was seldom any real communion of spirit between us."   Remembering Beethoven's remark about his own music — "From the heart it came, to the heart it shall go" — an ideal of artistic expression as a close communion between the creator and the receiver, one can but feel that Stravinsky has put his finger on the fatal flaw in his music when he says, "I believe that there was seldom any real communion of spirit between us." The flesh has been so willing, but the spirit, the purely musical imagination, has been too weak to carry out the great conceptions of Stravinsky's clever mind.

The impact of Stravinsky on the younger composers of his day has been great and not always beneficial.   Following him down new paths of experimentation on which even he lost the way, many of them, less gifted, less well trained, and less sincere, came to dead ends of imitation and boredom.

Surely nothing is more tragic than a broken promise of genius.   Those who are most appreciative of the earlier music of Stravinsky are frank in their disappointment over his later work.   Ernest Newman might well have been speaking of Stravinsky when he called Richard Strauss a clever man who was once a genius.   Alfred Swan writes in David Ewen's "Book of Modern Composers":

> Much as Stravinsky would like to be viewed as the typical musical craftsman of the present generation, as the real, unemotional, objective creator of purely musical values, whose ideas are unaffected by any non-musical considerations, he will probably never succeed in being the musician's musician or attain a place with the greatest in his art.   There are two fundamental factors which will forever stand in the way of such recognition: his inability to produce a sustained melody, the one ingredient of music without which it almost ceases to be music, and his incapacity to appreciate the force of simple, strong, concordant harmonies which nature itself has put in man's ear for the spontaneous support of his songs.   No amount of dynamism, of sense of colour and timbre, of stark originality in the planning of his scores, and of meticulous care in their execution, will quite replace the above two paramount prerequisites of the truly musical.

And from the Twentieth Century chapter of McKinney and Anderson's excellent work "Music in History" comes this sad summary of Stravinsky: "Never has there been so great a disappointment in music."

[1] Reprinted from *Chronicle of My Life*, by Igor Stravinsky.   Copyright, 1936, by Simon and Schuster, Inc.

Yet, despite the disappointment, we do have *The Fire Bird*, *Petrushka*, and *The Rite of Spring*, stunning contributions to dramatic music by a born ballet composer.

SUITE FROM THE BALLET, THE FIRE BIRD

The legend of *The Fire Bird*, relating the triumph of the Good Fairy over the Dark Spirit, is said to be an oriental tale which, in some dim and distant past, found its way into Russia. Like most old folk tales, it has varied widely in the telling. This is the Stravinsky-Fokine version as told in music, dancing, and *décor* by the famous Ballet Russe.

The young Prince, Ivan Tsarevitch, hero of many a Russian tale, has wandered in the course of a night's hunting into a deep wood. Suddenly he sees a marvelous bird with flaming feathers flash through the trees and vanish in what seem to be the grounds of a castle, lost in the wilderness. Can it be that mysterious creature, the Fire Bird, dreamed of by Russian children but never seen by mortal eyes? Young Ivan dashes off in pursuit of the beautiful bird, heedless of dangers which may lie beyond the wall of that gloomy garden.

As he runs across the clearing which makes the lawn, he sees a luminous silver tree all hung with golden apples. He is about to examine it when a flash of light warns him that the Fire Bird is near. Hiding in the foliage, Ivan watches the glittering creature alight, and, as she approaches the silver tree, he seizes her in his strong arms. But the Fire Bird begs so piteously for freedom that the kindhearted Ivan lets her go. Before she flies away, the Fire Bird, to show her gratitude, gives him one shining feather, which has power against evil and is a pledge of her help in time of trouble.

Now the darkness which has curtained the forest begins to lift, revealing the tower of an old castle. Through its archway, thirteen lovely maidens in long white gowns, come tripping out, ghostlike in the gray light. Quickly Ivan conceals himself in the shrubbery where he can watch them unobserved. The maidens dance around the silver tree, tossing the golden apples about with such easy grace that the young Prince knows that they must be princesses! So charming is their play that at last Ivan breaks from his hiding place and joins them. The frightened maidens drop the golden apples and start to run away. But Ivan doffs his cap and bows in such a courtly manner that they, in turn, know he must be a Prince and are reassured.

They tell him that he has strayed into the domain of the terrible King Kastchci Live-for-Ever, an ogre who preys upon travelers. Some he bewitches, turning them into fearful monsters; others he keeps shut up in his horrible castle; and still others he turns to stone, as can be proved by the rows and rows of statues in the castle garden. The maidens themselves, Ivan learns, are a luckless princess and her attendants, who fell into the ogre's power. They are prisoners, allowed but one brief hour of freedom, just before dawn. That hour is now over and they must return to the enchanted castle, but before they go, they beg Ivan to flee while there is yet time. Alas, it is already too late. The gallant Prince has fallen captive to the thirteenth princess, the lovely Tsarevna, and as she and her maidens disappear into the dark tower, he runs after them, and grasping the iron gates, shakes them violently.

The gates fly open and, to Ivan's horror, out swarms a motley horde — Turks, Chinamen, slaves, and clowns, two-headed freaks, and bent-legged dwarfs, the Kikimoras and Bolebochki — some with swords and lances, some studded with jewels, and all behaving in a most incredible fashion. Following this bedlam crew comes King Kastchei himself, a hairy, unclean monster with green-taloned fingers. His evil eyes glitter as they light upon the hapless Prince. The Tsarevna and her maidens run forward and plead for Ivan, but are thrust angrily aside. Making strange passes in the air with his awful talons, Kastchei begins to work his spell. Ivan resists with all his might; nevertheless, he feels the magic, feels himself turning into stone! Then, happily, he remembers the flaming feather of the Fire Bird, said to have power over evil. Drawing it from his girdle, he waves it in the face of the ogre, causing him to stagger back.

At the same moment, true to her pledge of help in time of trouble, the Fire Bird appears. With rhythmic gestures, she hypnotizes Kastchei and his monsters and sets them dancing with such frenzy that at last they fall exhausted to the ground. The beautiful Tsarevna she lulls into a magic sleep which will protect her from all evil power. Then the Fire Bird reveals to Ivan the surprisingly simple secret of Kastchei. In a casket, hidden in a hollow tree, lies a monstrous egg which contains the ogre's soul. He is Kastchei Live-for-Ever only so long as the egg remains unbroken. Desperately Kastchei and his court try to protect the precious casket. But Ivan is too quick for them. Flinging up the lid, he seizes the great egg, holds it high, swings it to and fro, swinging the crowd with it, and dashes it to bits on the ground. There is a loud crash, then black darkness.

When, presently, the light returns, Ivan finds himself still standing in the forest clearing, but the ogre, his castle, and all his monstrous court have vanished. Near by stand a group of handsome young men, whom he recognizes as the statues come back to life. Now enter a company of grateful men and women, who, but a moment before, were the horrible creatures of Kastchei's court. And, best of all, there are the white princesses, released from enchantment, and with them the Tsarevna, now wide-awake and lovelier than ever. Joyously the Prince claims her as his bride.

Pages bring a crown and scepter, which Ivan Tsarevitch accepts amid the acclaim of a loyal court. Above them flashes a last gleam of flaming gold as the Fire Bird, the good fairy, leaves them all to live happily ever afterward.

Although written for the stage, the music of *The Fire Bird* is more frequently heard in concert halls. Unlike the later Stravinsky ballet music which, minus the ballet, leaves a sense of something lacking, *The Fire Bird* music is completely satisfying. In it the composer has created a realm of pure fancy, a free fairy world, filled with characters too fantastic to seem absurd, and in which movement itself, having lost all association with everyday life, takes on a strange, abstract beauty.

There are two orchestral suites from *The Fire Bird*, the first containing:

Introduction
The Fire Bird and Her Dance
The Supplication of the Fire Bird
The Princesses Playing with the Golden Apples
The Dance of the Princesses
The Infernal Dance of King Kastchei

The second suite, reorchestrated for smaller orchestra, has the following numbers, which we present:

Introduction
The Fire Bird and Her Dance
The Dance of the Princesses
The Infernal Dance of King Kastchei
Berceuse
Finale

Introduction

Midnight in an enchanted wood!   Low, muttering strings: [1]

weird voices of trombones:

and shivery-sounding woodwinds and horns in a characteristic sequence of thirds — a minor followed by a major —

conjure up the classic fairy-tale forest of lost children and hapless travelers, where every bush and gnarled tree may hide a goblin or itself stretch out a thorny arm or tripping root to terrorize the wanderer.

There is no melody in this *Introduction*, only murky harmonies pricked by will-o'-the-wisp lights in the eerie *arpeggios* of harp and violins.   And there seems to be no time, as we commonly know it, only rhythm, a slow, heavy treading as of unseen monsters passing just a little too close by.

The Fire Bird and Her Dance

The curtain rises upon Kastchei's enchanted garden, and down through the quivering dark, flashes the bright apparition of the Fire Bird.   The music seems to glitter. Unreal and elusive as the wondrous bird, it is not to be caught in any recognizable tune.   Throughout the ballet, there is never a real melody associated with the Fire Bird — only little chromatic figures like:

[1] Copyright, 1920, by J. & W. Chester, Ltd.   Galaxy Music Corporation, New York.   All quotations from score reprinted by permission.

in broken rhythms and, one might also say, broken orchestration, since these tune fragments seem to flit from one instrument to another.

The music pictures the Fire Bird playing about the silver tree and daintily plucking the golden apples. She dances a wayward little *scherzo*:

piped by piccolo, flute, and clarinet to a syncopated bass which gives a curious rhythmic effect described by Stravinsky as "pecking."

The rush and leap of the strings suggests Ivan's attempts to seize the beautiful creature. And always there is the glitter, the showering of light and color:

which accompanies her every movement.

The dance ends abruptly:

The Fire Bird is captured. (The struggle, her piteous pleading, and release are not pictured in the music of this suite.)

The Dance of the Princesses

Ivan Tsarevitch, concealed in the shrubbery, watches the thirteen Princesses tossing the golden apples. So alluring is the play — and the players — that at last he rushes from his hiding place and appears in their midst. The Princesses, startled by the sudden stranger, are about to run away, but Ivan's princely manner reassures them. They invite him to join them in a *Horovod*, an old choral round dance or roundelay, which in the ballet is, of course, wordless.

The dance begins with a dialogue in canonic imitation between two flutes:

an exchange, perhaps, of formal salutations between the dancers.

Then follows the first singable tune of the suite and one of the rare long melodies to be found in Stravinsky's music. It is taken from an old Russian folk song, "In the Garden," which Rimsky-Korsakov had also used in the slow movement of his Sinfonietta and which appears in his collection of Russian folk songs, in this form:

The oboe sings the childlike melody:

but already in the second phrase it begins to stray from the folk tune.

A second theme of folk-song type:

is introduced by the violins and becomes the principal subject of the *ronde*. It is interrupted by a return of the first theme, then resumed with increasing animation. Near the end of the dance, the eerie harmonies of the *Introduction*, those curious thirds of the enchanted garden, cast a faint shadow across the simple roundelay, as if to remind us that the Princesses are Kastchei's prisoners and may dance but one brief hour.

It is charming music, grave and gently dignified as befits young princesses. And the picture — wreaths of morning mist, the gray sky of dawn faintly tinged with rose, maidens with rosy lips and hair of silver-gilt, dressed in long white gowns, and circling a silver tree. How delicate and calm it is compared with the glowing color and fantastic movement of the Fire Bird!

The Infernal Dance of King Kastchei

Ivan Tsarevitch, made bold by his love for the Tsarevna, follows her to the ogre's castle and recklessly flings himself against the magic gates which hold her captive. The gates fly open and out pours the whole revolting horde of Kastchei's court, the dreadful Kikimoras and Bolebochki, Turks, Chinamen, slaves, clowns, hideous freaks, and last and most loathsome, the ogre himself. Waving his green talons in the air, Kastchei begins the incantation which is to turn Ivan to stone. Twice he utters it, but before the fatal third time, Ivan remembers the magic golden feather. He waves it before Kastchei's face, the ogre falls back, and at the same moment the Fire Bird flies to the rescue. She sets Kastchei's court whirling in a mad dance, which, on the stage, was considered the finest of all Fokine's amazing ensembles.

With a fierce *fortissimo* chord for full orchestra, the clang of the tubular bell, and a pummeling of kettledrums, the dance begins. The music is cast in rondo form with this principal theme:

There are various episodes, the most important being this plaintive wail:

an elaborate version of the theme of *The Princess Playing with the Golden Apples:*

and a suggestion of the Fire Bird:

But one is scarcely aware of them or even of the recurring main theme in the unholy confusion of the dance. *Infernal* is the word for this dance and its music. The orchestra seems indeed possessed of devils; the woodwinds which so sweetly sang the roundelay of the Princesses now snarl like angry cats; the strings shriek; the brasses sneer and shout themselves hoarse, until, at the final chord, it would seem not too surprising if players as well as Kastchei's retinue fell exhausted to the ground!

These frenzied voices, these clashing dissonances and wild, uncivilized rhythms were the beginning of those vivid portrayals of the savage and bizarre which were to make Stravinsky the most conspicuous and controversial figure in the music of two decades.

Berceuse

The *Berceuse* is the sleep-charm which protects the Tsarevna from Kastchei's evil power. It begins with a monotonous little figure:

which continues throughout the piece with almost hypnotic effect. (The use of a persistent rhythmic figure to provide an emotional undercurrent to the music is characteristic of Stravinsky.)

A drowsy bassoon, like a voice from an enchanted forest, gives out the simple melody:

an oboe speaks:

then a 'cello:

and subdued as they seem, these little phrases are unmistakable and ingenious reminders of the Fire Bird.

There is but one theme, repeated over and over like a magic incantation. At the end, it vanishes in a shimmering of strings which make one think of the dancing star-points seen by a sleepy child as he rubs his eyes in a vain effort to keep awake.

The *Berceuse* is one of the rare instances of Stravinsky in a tender mood. Its spell is irresistible. And those rash persons who insist that enchantment is a thing of a fairy-tale past have only to watch an audience, howsoever sophisticated, to discover that the Fire Bird's sleep-charm is still potent!

Finale

When Ivan Tsarevitch broke the monstrous egg containing King Kastchei's soul, a sudden awful darkness fell upon the earth. Out of this ominous darkness emerges the serene and radiant *Finale*, the music to which the stone figures return to life and the hideous creatures of Kastchei's retinue become normal men and women.

In the *Finale*, as in the *Dance of the Princesses*, the theme:

is taken from a Russian folk song, "By the Gate."

It is interesting to notice that while Stravinsky uses broken rhythms and bright chromatic bits in picturing the Fire Bird, and weird harmonies for Kastchei and his enchanted garden, he chooses simple diatonic melodies, folk tunes, for the human beings in the story. And it is also noticeable that these folk tunes are almost the only long melodies in the suite.

As in the *Berceuse*, there is only one theme, but there is nothing monotonous about its repetition. Beginning softly as a horn solo, it gathers volume and dignity as it proceeds. And as the strings and woodwinds sing it in unison:

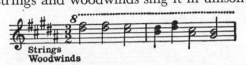

above an upward surging scale in the brass, it becomes a hymn of thanksgiving for all the happy people released from the wicked Kastchei's spell. There is the suggestion of chiming bells, foretelling the wedding of Ivan Tsarevitch and the beautiful Tsarevna.

A last glimpse of the Fire Bird, the Good Fairy who has brought about all this happiness, comes at the end, in a series of strange chords — "escaped chords" — in which the tones of the twelve-tone scale are harmonized in parallel motion:

Startling as they seemed when first heard in 1910, they sound mild enough to ears accustomed to the abandoned chords of Stravinsky's later music!

There is much that is surprising in the *Fire Bird* music, but most people learn to like it. It is so fine and free, so exactly like a colorful page from an old fairy tale. After several hearings, one can appreciate the remark of Rimsky-Korsakov, Stravinsky's teacher, who, when he first heard the *Fire Bird*, said, "Look here! Stop playing that horrid thing or I might begin to enjoy it!"

CHAPTER IX

Music Made in England

Music has always been happily at home in England.   The ancient Saxon Chronicles tell of a land ringing with that lusty melody which gave it the name *Merrie England*. One of the oldest pieces of secular music in existence, "Sumer is icumen in" (circa 1250) is an early English greeting to spring.   Chaucer's squire, in the "Canterbury Tales," "went singing and fluting all the day," and in the "Prioress's Tale," another pilgrim "cannot stinte of singing by the weye."   No wonder an early historian called England "a nest of singing birds"!

The writings of the Elizabethans, Shakespeare especially, and of the later diarists and essayists are as full of musical allusions as a pound cake of raisins.   Thomas Turner in his "A Hundredthe Good Points of Husbandrie lately married unto a Hundredthe Good Points of Huswifry" (1570) recommends that mistresses choose servants who are fond of music, for, says he:

> Such servants are oftenest painful [painstaking] and good,
> That sing in their labour as birds in the wood.

Thomas Morley whispers a bit of society scandal of 1597 — a dinner guest unable to read his part when the music books were passed at table — "How can he have been brought up!"   Peacham, in his *Compleat Gentleman*, declares that "Music is a gift of Heaven, granted to man that he may praise and extol his Creator and console himself for the cares and griefs with which life is assailed at every hour."   He adds what sounds strangely like some supposedly recent therapeutic discoveries, that, according to sixteenth-century physicians, music "prolongs life, cures certain diseases, is an antidote to the bite of the tarantula, corrects defects of pronunciation, and is a remedy for stammering in children."

Vendors cried their wares through the streets of old London to real tunes, some of them as charming as the well-known "Cherry Ripe" and "Lavender's Cry."   Cobblers, tinsmiths, tinkers, and coal heavers amused themselves by singing *catches*, short canons or rounds in which the words were ingeniously arranged to catch a double meaning — and the singers!   Tunes of all sorts could be heard in shops, coffeehouses, and on the Thames barges.   Lutes hung in every hall, and virginal, cittern, and viols for the amusement of waiting customers were as commonly found in barbershops as are newspapers today.   Incidentally, "barber-shop harmony" seems already to have established its reputation, for a contemporary critic says:

> In former time 't hath been upbrayded thus
> That barber's musick is most barbarous.

And so from the time of "Piers Plowman" down to the present day, English literature gives full and fascinating proof that music has always been a source of acute pleasure to English people of all classes.

Why is it then, that on any list of great composers, one finds few — if any — English names? A satisfactory answer to this question would involve a study of the racial, intellectual, and spiritual make-up of that amazing island nation, an analysis of all that is implied by the term *British*. We cannot be quite so casual in our explanation as was that early Italian scholar who accounted for the English singing voice by saying that it was doubtless so cold up there in the North that singers dared not open their mouths wide enough for a warm *bel canto;* nor even so casual as Purcell who apologized for the state of English music, "Being farther from the sun, we are of later Growth than our Neighbor Countries and must be content to shake off our Barbarity by degrees."

But the comparatively small amount of art music composed in a country having such fine folk music and such excellent musical taste and knowledge is at least partly explained by two words, always ominous for England, *foreign invasion.*

Italian and French musicians were in attendance at the courts of the Tudor rulers, and it was the importation of the Italian madrigal that helped to create the glorious English madrigals of the Elizabethans. So popular did the Italian songs become that native musicians began to protest. Henry Lawes in the preface to his "Court Ayres and Dialogues" (1653) says, "I acknowledge the Italians the greatest Masters of Musick, but not all." Then he tells of the joke he played on the *dilettanti* who would listen to none but Italian music. Taking a list of Italian song titles, he strung them together and, setting the ridiculous result to music, gave out that it came from Italy, "whereby it passed for a rare Italian song." Tom d'Urfey prefaced his "The English Stage Italianized" with this satirical note, "For the benefit of the English Quality and others who have forgot their Mother-Tongue, this play is translated into Italian by an Able Hand; and will be sold by the Orange-women and Door-keepers at sixpence each, during the time of its performance."

The Commonwealth interrupted the importation of foreign court musicians but not of foreign music. French dance tunes continued to be popular, and it was during this time that Playford published his "Court Ayres, or Pavins, Almaines, Corants, and Sarabands" (1655).

With the return of the monarchy under Charles II (1660) came a Restoration of music as well as of matters of state. The Musicians Company, a guild of church musicians which had been dissolved at the Revolution, was reorganized as was the Chapel Royal, and Captain Cooke went scouting far and wide for likely lads to press into the king's musical service. New theaters were built and, as the pages of Pepys diary testify, amateur music making flourished as never before.

Still more important was the growing interest in setting up professional standards of musicianship, even to the licensing of teachers and the regulation of the "Waites" and "common minstrells." In January, 1662, it was ordered that "Edward Sadler, for his insufficiency in the art of musique, be from henceforward *silenced* and disabled from the exercise of any kinds in publique houses or meetings." One result of this new professionalism was to encourage the practice of listening to music. Up to this time the privilege of hearing good music had been largely confined to court and aristocratic circles. But about 1664 simple music meetings began at a house near St. Paul's Cathedral where there were organ recitals "and some shopkeepers and foremen came weekly to sing in consort, and to hear and enjoy ale and tobacco." In 1672 John Banister opened a concert room in Whitefriars, "rounded with seats and small tables, alehouse fashion. One shilling was the price, and call for what you pleased." Six years later Thomas Britton, the "small-coal man," set up a series of concerts in a room over his shop. This ambitious coal dealer introduced many of the latest masterpieces of the continent to English music lovers and lived to welcome Handel at his meetings.

But the Restoration enthusiasm for music only meant a more complete foreign invasion. Charles II, that "brisk and airy prince," was determined to be just as Continental as he could be and still keep his seat on an English throne. He sent to France for a band of twenty-four stringed instruments, similar to the *Grande Bande* of the French court. Conservatives like "Old Mace" protested at the "new Corants and Jigs by Foreigners" and hated the "scoulding violins" which King Charles preferred to the "noble lute" and "generous viols" of former days! In addition to the French instrumentalists, Italian singers dominated Restoration court music, both in the theater and palace concerts. And a further cosmopolitan touch was given to London musical life by Charles II's queen, Catherine of Braganza, who had brought with her a company of Portuguese musicians.

Not content with bringing continental music and musicians to London, Charles proceeded to send young Pelham Humfrey, most promising of the Chapel Royal choristers, to study with Lully in Paris. It is rather amusing to think that Humfrey was sent to the most famous Italian operatic composer of the day to learn how to write English church music and that later, Humfrey's pupil Purcell should have become the greatest writer of English stage music by following in Humfrey's footsteps in the matter of church composition!

So strong was Italian and French influence that in the preface to a collection of his sonatas, Purcell states that he has "faithfully endeavored a just imitation of the most famed Italian masters," and calls attention to his use of technical terms unfamiliar to English musicians, such as *Adagio*, *Presto*, *Largo*, *Vivace*, and *Piano*. But Purcell was far from a mere imitator. He was a serious student of Italian and French music, upon which his original genius was building a far finer type of English music than that of the lyrical Elizabethans. "But," says Roger North, "unhappily Mr. H. Purcell, the Orpheus Britannicus, while he was warm in the pursuit of it, Dyed."

The untimely death of Purcell was a terrible blow to British music, which soon became submerged by the rising tide of Italian music. John Gay tried to stem that tide with his *Beggar's Opera* in which he presented the British public with a bouquet of old ballads, hoping to turn their attention to the beauties of their national folk music. But the foreign invasion continued, and for two centuries English music almost lost consciousness of itself.

Fifteen years after the death of Purcell young Mr. Handel came to London, where he reigned supreme for fifty years. And there was Haydn, setting the fashion with his "London" Symphonies in spite of "Rule, Britannia"; and in the nineteenth century it was Spohr, Mendelssohn, Gounod, Brahms — foreigners all, providing musical fare for a taste which the modest English masters of the period could not satisfy.

It is only within the last fifty years that England has been recovering her musical independence. There has been a regular renaissance, drawing its inspiration from the early Tudor music and from the folk songs which have fascinated collectors, composers, and consumers. English folk music is a rich heritage from which to create great art music. The tunes have simplicity and economy; they have the rhythmic freedom and naturalness which comes only when words and music have grown up together; and they have that combination of emotional beauty and impersonal restraint — that nice balance of head and heart which is so truly English.

Twentieth-century English music has developed along two lines — nationalism and impressionism. In the work of certain composers one or the other of these traits predominates — with Vaughan Williams it is nationalism, the folk-song flavor, with Delius it is impressionism, the atmospheric quality. But it is a noticeable and healthy sign that the two trends mingle and lose their sharp lines in the work of the stronger men, Elgar and Holst.

Whether future music historians will record an "English school" in the twentieth century, no one knows or cares. Since individuality is the keynote of British character it also becomes the keynote of British music. For this reason it is doubtful if there will ever again be as definite a style, or school, as that of the English Madrigal group. But when the fog of tonal experiments, novel ideas, and pseudo-this-and-thats which have obscured much of the work of our time shall have lifted, there will unquestionably remain a proud contribution of music made in England.

HENRY PURCELL

City of Westminster — 1659
City of Westminster — 1695

Sometimes a Hero in an age appears,
But once a Purcell in a Thousand Years!

Henry Purcell was the most famous English musician of his age, "the delight of the nation and the wonder of the world." His death was the occasion of many funeral odes and lamentations in which the writers called upon the Muses, the Graces, Venus, Cupid, and all Nature to share the common grief. He was buried in Westminster Abbey, "without charge being made upon the widow" and "in a magnificent manner." (*Post Boy*, November 28, 1695.) He was also buried in extravagant adjectives and expressions of awed astonishment, for both his contemporaries and successors seem to have accepted him uncritically and with little comment.

The garrulous Pepys who surely could have given us a few tidbits of current gossip, unfortunately stopped keeping his diary in 1669 when Purcell was a child of ten. In the *Memoirs of Musick* of Roger North, who must have known him, he is merely "the divine Purcell." He himself left no letters, only the formal dedications and prefaces to his few published works and a brief will, written the day he died. Not even the exact date of his birth is known, though it was supposedly in the summer of 1659. His life story is hidden in the rate-books of St. Margaret's Parish, Westminster, and in the official records of the appointments he held and the commissions he undertook as church and court composer. It is the story of a short life of astonishing industry.

Young Henry Purcell first appears, stepping out of the pages of the account book of the *King's Musick* in the year 1673, as a "late child of his Majesty's Chappell Royall, whose voice is changed and gone from the Chappell." The record of the fourteen years preceding this entry is somewhat hazy. However it is known that Henry Purcell's father, whose Christian name was also Henry, was one of the gentlemen of the Chapel Royal. He seems to have been an undistinguished but versatile musician, for he was a member of the Royal Band and of the choir of Westminster Abbey, also Master of the Children connected with the Abbey and one of its staff of music copyists. The father died when little Henry was five years old, and the child was given to an uncle, Thomas, also a musician and like his brother a gentleman of the Chapel Royal. Thomas Purcell loved the small nephew and spoke of him as "my son."

When Henry was old enough, his uncle succeeded in having him appointed as one of the Children of the Royal Chapel, definitely an honor, since His Majesty's singing boys must have the best voices obtainable. There were only twelve boys, the very cream skimmed from cathedral choirs all over England. These children were under the direction of a master, who not only taught them to sing and play on lute, violin, and organ, but was also responsible for seeing that they were properly housed, fed, clothed, and educated — principally in writing and Latin. As servants of His Majesty, the choirboys had their uniforms, and we can picture young Henry Purcell from this record of the Lord Chamberlain in the *King's Musick:*

> For each of them, one cloak of bastard [imitation] scarlett cloth lyned with velvett, one suit and coat of the same cloth made up and trimmed with silver and silk lace after the manner of our footman's liveries, and also to the said suit three shirts, three half shirts, three pairs of shoes, three pairs of thigh stockings, whereof one pair of silk and two pair of worsted, two hats with bands, six bands and six pairs of cuffs, whereof two laced and four plain, three handkerchers, three pairs of gloves and two pieces and a half of rebon for trimming garters and shoestrings.

The boys were sent to bed at eight o'clock. When they were ill with smallpox or spotted fever, a doctor and nurse were provided, and in very cold weather they had a fire in their music room. And when the time came for them to leave the choir, they were cared for until they found employment.

Purcell left the choir in 1673 but not the Chapel Royal. He was appointed assistant to John Hingston as keeper and repairer of the king's wind instruments, for which service he was paid thirty pounds a year plus his linen and a fine felt hat. And when Hingston died, Purcell took over the position of Organ Maker and Keeper and kept it all the rest of his life. In the seventeenth century there was no distinction between the workman and the performer on an instrument.

In addition to this work, young Purcell also served as one of the official copyists at the Abbey. In these days of many music publishers it is difficult to realize what it once meant to keep up the music library of a choir or orchestra. Printed music was so expensive and so scarce that musicians expected to transcribe most of the works they wished to play or study. In Purcell's youth the churches of England had not yet recovered from the Puritan regime when statues, stained-glass windows, musical instruments, and service books, all that had to do with the beauty and splendor of worship, had been destroyed. Westminster Abbey had been one of the worst sufferers. Cromwell's soldiers had taken their battle axes to the organ, bartered its pipes for pots of beer in London taverns, and scattered the precious music books far and wide. Purcell must have had to write out the parts of many a work by such older masters as Gibbon and Byrd, as well as newer anthems, all of which had to be borrowed from whatever church or person had been lucky enough to keep a copy. It was excellent training for a young musician, and explains the fine technique in polyphonic — many voiced — writing which Purcell was to show in his own later works for both church and theater.

The list of Purcell's appointments is a remarkable one, even for a time when a musician had to be a pluralist, a veritable Jack-of-all-trades, to live. To the positions already mentioned, Organ Maker and Keeper and Abbey Copyist, was added Composer for the King's Violins (1677 — no small responsibility for a boy of eighteen!), Organist of Westminster Abbey (1680, succeeding his teacher John Blow), Organist at the Chapel Royal (1682), Composer in Ordinary to the King's Musick (1683), and Harpsicall-player to King James II (1684). In addition to this he seems to have been in demand as composer of occasional pieces for various feasts and festivals and even to have taught some of the young ladies at Mr. Josias Priest's academy for whom he wrote *Dido and Aeneas*.

Purcell had begun his career as a composer when he was a choirboy. At the age of twelve he wrote for the King's birthday an ode which has the imposing title of *The address of the Children of the Chapel Royal to the King, and their master, Captain Cooke, on his Majesties Birthday, A.D. 1670, Composed by Master Purcell, one of the children of the said Chapel.* As composer for the king's violins he must have written some of the light airs and dances which are found in collections of his music. Later he shared with Blow the task of writing those extravagant Birthday Odes and Welcome Songs which flattered royal ears with absurd praises. He wrote Odes for St. Cecilia's Day from the time of its first public observance, pieces for special gatherings in London, Coronation Anthems, Funeral Anthems, and even an anthem to welcome a royal baby.

Once he quite unintentionally provided music for a fierce political fight. James II had appointed as Lord-Lieutenant of Ireland the Roman Catholic General Talbot, who had made himself hated by the Protestants because of his oppressive government. A piece of disrespectful doggerel was written, beginning:

> Dere was an old prophecy found in a bog:
> "Ireland shall be ruled by an ass and a dog."
>
> And now dis prophecy is come to pass
> For Talbot's de dog, and King James is de ass.

Then came a rollicking refrain — *Lero, lero, lilli burlero*, which gave it the name "Lilli-burlero." Someone set the words to Purcell's *Quickstep* music, and soon the whole army, as well as the people, took it up, and, as the Puritan Lord Wharton boasted, "sung a deluded king out of three kingdoms." To this day, Purcell's "Lilliburlero" is a party tune in the North of Ireland.

From his childhood Henry Purcell was a court musician. His anthems and services impressed the congregations at Westminster Abbey and in the Chapel Royal. His operas and "Ayres for the Theatre" delighted fashionable London. Yet with all his professional prestige, Purcell was one of the few composers ever to write music for amateurs. For the tavern and coffeehouse singers he wrote some fifty catches — short canons or rounds with tricky words — which were printed in "Catch that catch can, The Pleasant Musical Companion." For the polite singers of the day, he wrote what he called "single songs" — that is, songs that do not depend upon any dramatic or sacred context — and chamber cantatas, most of them pastoral pieces for two voices. And for the ambitious instrumentalists, there were the suites and pieces for harpsichord and the sonatas for groups of strings — true part-music made for musical companion-ship rather than to give individual players a chance to shine.

These "composures" for amateurs reflect a genial and delightful man behind the music — a man one would like to know. But in spite of diligent searching of the records and of a few unfounded anecdotes offered by hopeful biographers, little is known of the private life of Purcell beyond the facts that he was successful, financially and professionally, that he had a wife and six children, three of whom died in infancy — there was consumption in the family — and that he himself died in his thirty-seventh year, probably from the same cause. He was and is simply "the famous Mr. Henry Purcell."

THE ARTIST

A first impression of Purcell's music is apt to be one of quaintness. We are conscious of the old-fashioned cut of his melodies and of the thinness of his harmony and instrumen-tation. If Purcell himself were to step out of the frame of the Clostermann portrait and speak to us, we would, no doubt, be so diverted by the oddity of his clothes and manners and of his quaint seventeenth-century speech that we could scarcely attend to what he was saying. But after a little the strangeness would wear off, we would forget the curled wig, the satin coat, and lace frills, forget *how* he spoke in our enjoyment of his conversation.

So it is in listening to Purcell's music, the strangeness wears off, if we are sensible enough not to try to analyze him — which is as unprofitable as trying to judge his billowing coat and knee breeches by the fashions of the well-dressed young man of today. Only students of the music of the Restoration period and all that led up to it have any business with the "juxtaposition of adjacent semitones" and the like in Purcell's works.

Having accepted his quaintness, we are free to enjoy his melodies, for Purcell was one of the world's sweetest singers. He belonged to a singing age, and even when he wrote for instruments it was in what might be called a vocal style. In the seventeenth century, instrumental music was still young. To many English music lovers the violin was "the upstart instrument that put the viols out," and little had been done about it in the way either of techniques or literature. The orchestral material at Purcell's disposal consisted of the violins, the flute, oboe, bassoon, and the trumpet and kettle-drums — scant resources compared with those of our modern orchestra. And although he succeeded in getting many novel and happy instrumental effects, the best of Purcell is found in his vocal music. The most noticeable thing about Purcell's music is its singing quality. Sometimes the melody is thrown into relief by the harmonic background, sometimes by a closely woven counterpoint, sometimes it is blended with one or the other; but from beginning to end of the piece it pours out as easily and naturally as a bird's song.

On paper Purcell's music often seems overladen with dotted notes, grace notes, trills — what Dr. Burney called "furbelows and flounces which require to be removed in the interests of good taste." But much of what looks like overdecoration is merely Purcell's habit of writing out what the voice really does, and in his day, singers were full of turns and trills. Purcell's music sounds much simpler than it looks. And those melting *appoggiaturas* of which he was so fond help to give the feeling of tenderness which is so characteristic of Purcell.

But the tender quality of Purcell's music is not a sign of weakness. There is certainly nothing lifeless in his favorite syncopated rhythms, or in the resolute march of his melodic line, both so essentially English. English, too, are his cadences and a certain touch of sternness sometimes felt in his music. As a harmonist Purcell had, in his own day, a reputation for discords. He was a daring modulator, and did not hesitate to repeat a harsh note until he was good and ready to resolve it in a succeeding chord. He loved the minor mode — G minor being his favorite — and many of his most cheerful dance tunes are written in the "melancholy flat key." But it was more than a mere fondness for the minor tonality, which was fashionable in the seventeenth century. One of his contemporaries writes, "Mr. Purcell has been heard to declare more than once, that the variety which the minor key is capable of affording by the change of sounds in the ascending and descending scales, induced him so frequently to give it preference."

Variety was certainly the spice of Purcell's genius — variety of subject, of treatment, and of mood. He was as many-sided, as contradictory in his sentiments as Shakespeare. It is a supposedly English characteristic. He wrote all kinds of music, and whether it was the swinging quickstep known as "Lilliburlero" or the devotional *Thou knowest, Lord, the secrets of our hearts* for his Queen's funeral, whether it was the merry catch "My wife hath a tongue," or Dido's exquisite death song, his music was always, in the words of old Dr. Tudway, "rightly fitted and adapted."

It was, indeed, this very fitness, linking Purcell's music inseparably with the particular play or occasion for which it was written, that is responsible for its not being heard again after those occasions had passed. Purcell lived in an age when music was written for immediate use rather than for publication, which was an expensive and difficult business. It is not surprising then that the manuscripts of his church music, so much of it composed for special services and for a cathedral choir, should have gathered dust in the Abbey cupboards; or that the dramatic music, fitted to plays which had only a passing popular appeal and written for the elaborate Restoration stage, should have been thrown aside with the rest of the scenery when the play had had its run. Only the chamber music was complete and self-contained. The chamber music and some of the incidental songs and dances were published, and this was all that was heard of Purcell for nearly two centuries.

Purcell's most important contribution, however, was in working out the connection between word and tone, a connection upon which, a hundred and fifty years later, Wagner insisted so strongly that many people think he discovered it! In his preface to *Dioclesian* Purcell calls music "the exaltation of poetry," and adds, "Both of them may excell apart, but surely they are most excellent when they are joyn'd, because nothing is then wanting to either of their proportions; for thus they appear like Wit and Beauty in the same person." Weighing every accent, making every important word musically conspicuous, Purcell set his verse so smoothly, so expressively that no one hearing it could say that English is not a singing language or that the only hope of opera in English lies in the misfit and make-over of translations.

Musical history has known many revivals of forgotten composers. Such a composer was Bach, whose music, neglected for more than a century, later became so important a part of the musician's creed that every note of it, good and bad, had to be performed! Some day there may be a rediscovery of Purcell and his theater-music, the finest ever written for the English stage. Meanwhile, whatever may be our personal taste in the matter, the fact remains that in Purcell England came nearest to producing a complete composer on the scale and of the scope of the half-dozen greatest composers in the world. Echoing the *Post Boy* of November, 1695, he was indeed "a very great Master of Musick."

Suite for Strings

I (From The Gordian Knot Untied)

From the rich treasure of Purcell's dramatic music, John Barbirolli has chosen six pieces, and, arranging them as a suite for strings with optional woodwinds, has given a beautiful sampling of Purcell's style.

The first movement of the suite is a souvenir of that mysterious play, *The Gordian Knot Untied*, of which only Purcell's incidental music survives. A vague reference in *The Gentlemen's Journal*, January, 1692, speaks of it as a comedy, though there is no promise of laughter in the opening *Andante maestoso*, which is a rather dolorous dialogue between soprano and bass with the other voices supplying the harmony:[1]

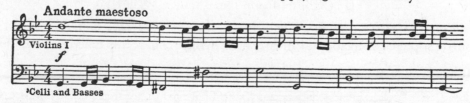

[1] Quotations from the Suite for Strings used by permission of the Oxford University Press and Carl Fischer, Inc., sole agents in this country.

It is characteristic of Purcell's basses that they were seldom mere time-markers. They usually had something to say. He advised composers to reinforce the soprano part with a bass as "airy" — meaning as supple and tuneful — as the soprano will allow. He himself often used a whole air as a bass part; for example, the *Quickstep* known as "Lilliburlero" which serves as the bass part of the jig in *The Gordian Knot Untied.*

This movement, which was probably the overture to the play, follows the form of the overtures of Purcell's church anthems, a stately prelude after which comes a livelier section in triple time and in more or less fugal style. After the *Andante maestoso*, the strings engage in a vigorous contrapuntal discussion of this subject:

in which they are later joined by the four horns.

The movement ends with one of Purcell's brief *Adagios:*

II (Minuet from The Virtuous Wife)

For Tom D'Urfey's comedy, *The Virtuous Wife or Good Luck at Last*, Purcell wrote some fourteen pages of incidental music, from which comes this delightful minuet:

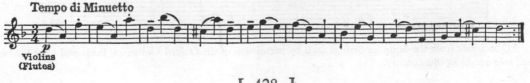

Although daintily scored for strings and two flutes and marked "elegant and languid," the wide skips and the rather driving accents give this minuet more motion than is found in many examples of the "dance of the little steps" so fashionable at court in Purcell's day.

III (Air, "Fairest Isle" from King Arthur)

If there was a moment in English musical history when the union of poetry and music seemed destined to produce something in the nature of a national music-drama, it was when Dryden invited Purcell to collaborate with him in his operatic play, *King Arthur*. The foremost English poet and the leading English composer of the day — it was a promising combination.

— A. K. Holland, "Henry Purcell"

The story of the play is a quaint mixture of historical legend and pure fantasy, a typical Restoration piece.   It tells how Arthur, king of the Britons, fought with Oswald, heathen king of the Saxons, for the hand of Emmeline, blind daughter of the Duke of Cornwall.   Each king was attended by his court magician and a train of sprites and fairies.   It was an amazing spectacle, with bold realistic touches as when, in the last act, the armies of Britons and Saxons come together and "fight with Spunges in their Hands, dipt in blood!"   Arthur meets and disarms Oswald in hand-to-hand combat, Emmeline and her royal lover are reunited, and the magician, Merlin, announces Arthur to be the first of "three Christian worthies."   Then, by magic, the winds are laid, Britain's island rises from the sea,

> Fairest isle, all isles excelling,
> Seat of pleasures and of loves.

and the play ends in a patriotic celebration, with banners and bugles and everybody dancing and singing praises of St. George.

Dryden had written this play some years earlier.   But he seems to have revised it with the composer in mind, for in his preface he says, "There is nothing better than what I intended but the music: which has since arrived to a greater perfection in England than ever formerly, especially passing through the artful hands of Mr. Purcell, who has composed it with so great a genius that he has nothing to fear but an ignorant, ill-judging audience."

The audience must have judged *King Arthur* a success, for it survived on the English stage for more than a century, though no present day producer would be likely to consider it worth the outlay.   Our interest is in the music which, in spite of several very tedious moments, contains some of Purcell's best work.

The air "Fairest Isle" is sung in the final masque of *King Arthur*, in which even the sea-creatures join in praising the "Queen of Islands."   Venus herself sings it:

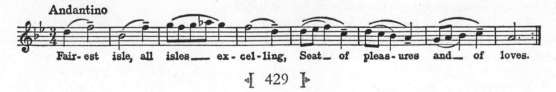

It is a spacious tune, one of Purcell's finest. Even Dr. Burney, a rather grudging critic of Purcell, said, "This is one of the few airs time hath not the power to injure. It is of all ages and countries." And yet it is a peculiarly English tune. Sung in the wordless beauty of quiet strings it voices something of that spiritual patriotism, that touch of holiness which the actual earth of England has always held for her island-born.

VI ("Second Musick" from King Arthur)

Following the Elizabethan custom of having a concert before the play began, Purcell provided two instrumental pieces — the "First Musick" and the "Second Musick" — to precede the real overture to *King Arthur*. From this "Second Musick" comes the closing movement of the Purcell-Barbirolli Suite. It is a bold fugue on the theme:

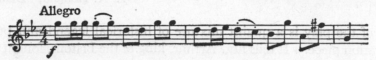

with horns playing an important part. Brasses would certainly seem indicated in this curtain music preluding the clash of arms between the Britons and the Saxons, which is the main motif of *King Arthur*. In Purcell's time C and D were the only normal trumpet keys, which is no doubt the reason why this music was originally written in the key of D minor, rather than in the favorite Purcell G minor of Mr. Barbirolli's arrangement.

Clear-cut and daring as any page of Bach, this music surely refutes the erroneous idea of Purcell as merely a composer of quaint, fragile airs and touching laments!

IV (From Abdelazer)

In addition to his operas, Purcell wrote incidental music for more than forty plays. The plays, like most things created for popular amusement, are long since forgotten. Fortunately, however, most of Purcell's incidental music has been preserved in manuscript, in song collections, and in the volumes of "Ayres for the Theatre," published soon after his death.

From Volume XVI of the Purcell Society Edition (not Volume XV as given on both score and record) comes the fourth movement of the suite, the *Allegretto giocoso*:

It is written in the composer's favorite key, G minor, and illustrates Purcell's practice of writing many of his gayest tunes in minor modes.

This little piece, so obviously instrumental, was probably one of the interludes or dances which Purcell supplied for an absurd play by Mrs. Aphra Behn, *Abdelazer or the Moor's Revenge*.

V (Lament from Dido and Aeneas)

In his thirtieth year, Henry Purcell, court and church composer, was commissioned to write a piece to be performed by the young gentlewomen of Josias Priest's boarding-school at Chelsea. Besides being completely outside his official routine, it was a work in which his stock in trade as a composer of popular theater music was of little use. There would be none of the elaborate pageantry, the flying cupids, devils, witches, and other fantastic trappings of the Restoration stage. There would, supposedly, be no professional singers, only young ladies mildly trained in singing, deportment, and dancing — particularly dancing, since Josias Priest was a dancing master. And, for this bevy of innocents, there could, of course, be no typical Restoration drama of illicit love and vulgar wit. The occasion called for something short and unaffected, something with music fairly simple in range and style and a story which might be expected to appeal to schoolgirls.

Tragic love was the chosen motif, in a libretto made from Vergil's story. Aeneas, fleeing from ruined Troy, is driven by storm to Carthage, where he is royally welcomed by the widowed queen, Dido. They fall in love, but the jealous gods forbid their marriage. Aeneas sails away to fulfill his destiny in Latium, and the lovely queen ends her sorrow by her own hand. (Purcell's poet, considering suicide unsuitable for a girl's school, has the heroine die of a ladylike broken heart.)

Except for an occasional line, such as "Peace and I are strangers grown," the "words made by Mr. Nahum Tate" are pretty poor. But it is a mark of Purcell's genius that however feeble the poetry, and whether writing a "Yorkshire Feast Song," an Ode on the happy return of His Majesty from Newmarket, or an anthem for a royal funeral, his music is always "rightly fitted and adapted." And never did Purcell compose more spontaneously or more humanly than in this little chamber opera for amateurs. He had no idea that he was making an important contribution to future English opera and, busy as he was with the fashionable English compromise of semi-opera, he never tried the like again. Yet *Dido and Aeneas*, created by happy accident, is not only the first English opera worthy of the name, but also for most discriminating critics, the greatest.

For the fifth movement of the Purcell suite, Mr. Barbirolli has chosen the air of the death song from the closing scene of *Dido and Aeneas*. In the opera this air is preceded by four lines sung in recitative. This was a daring stroke on Purcell's part, for the English public did not favor this Italian style of singing declamation. Says *The Gentlemen's Journal*, 1692, "Other nations bestow the name of opera only on such plays whereof every word is sung. But experience hath taught us that our English genius will not rellish that perpetual singing." Yet no one ever questioned the pathetic voice of the dying queen, murmuring to her confidante,

> Thy hand, Belinda, darkness shades me,
> On thy bosom let me rest;
> More I would, but death invades me,
> Death is now a welcome guest.

Then, to one of the most touching airs ever written, the final lines:

> When I am laid in earth, may my wrongs create
> No trouble in thy breast;
> Remember me, but ah! forget my fate.

The air is composed on what is known as a "ground bass" — meaning a set formula or figure in the bass part, repeated again and again throughout the piece. It is a dangerous device in the hands of an unskillful composer. It was, as one writer says, "a mine that Purcell in particular was apt to overwork; but here he struck a vein of purest gold."

The five-measure phrase:

is reiterated nine times — once as introduction, twice after the voice has ceased — there is no other bass. But that softly persistent downward melodic line suggests the very feeling of sinking and finally of rest.

Upon this monotonous bass Purcell builds an ever-changing melody and harmony. The rhythm is that of the stately *passacaglia* which, in the opera, follows the death song.

In exquisite contrast to the drooping bass, the voice rises in the repeated, "Remember me."

Never has the universal longing for immortality through remembrance been more poignantly expressed or more simply. Maeterlinck does much the same thing in his *Bluebird* when the old grandfather tells the children that one cannot die as long as he is remembered by those who love him. But how many words it takes, how much translating into emotion! Purcell's few tones speak directly!

The postlude is very effective. Instead of stopping rather tamely on a tonic chord in the sixth measure from the end, it lingers a moment in the key of D minor before coming to the cadence, giving a parting touch of reluctance.

Purcell's air is so simple, so sincerely beautiful — truly it is music in which "technique and passion are miraculously fused in one." And the perfect fitness of the words and music, even in this fragment of his work, bears out the statement of his seventeenth-century publisher that Purcell, while "His extraordinary talent in all sorts of Musick is sufficiently known, was especially admired for the vocal, having a peculiar genius to express the Energy of English words whereby he moved the Passions in all his Auditors."

In the orchestral version the voice part is given to the English horn, of all instruments most suited to the role of lamentation. For reasons of his own — timing perhaps — Mr. Barbirolli omits the repeat of the first two lines of the air, making it some nine measures shorter than was Purcell's intention.

FREDERICK DELIUS

Bradford — 1862
Grez-sur-Loing — 1934

On first hearing Delius, one is struck by the strangeness of the music. Elusive as the scent of wild grape, it wafts across the consciousness with no apparent form or purpose. Modern music — yet who in this disillusioned, fact-ridden modern world could have written anything quite so detached, so idyllic? And this Delius, this Arcadian, so happily free from pedantry, propaganda, and the itch for publicity, who was he?

Frederick Delius was just an old-fashioned child. No one encouraged him to create free verse while dressing or to express himself over his porridge. He was one of the ten children of a prosperous wool merchant of Bradford, England. It was a typical provincial family, ruled by an autocratic Victorian father from whom the small boy shrank in frightened awe. Frederick was a sturdy fellow, fond of all sorts of outdoor sports. He also had a taste for thrillers and read so many exciting tales that he finally had to take his turn at playing hero. He ran away "to seek his fortune," but was discovered, some fifteen miles from home, and brought back, an empty, dirty, dead-tired child. Another time he was inspired to become a circus performer and practiced such daring stunts on his pony that he was badly hurt and had to lie abed for a long time.

This venturesome boy showed but one sign of the man Delius, and that was his unusual love and talent for music. Even as a young child he had played the piano by ear, and often surprised the family with imaginative little pieces of his own. Later he was given lessons on the violin, and delighted his teachers with his accomplishment. But Father Delius had no intention of allowing Frederick to become a musician. He was to enter the family firm, and at nineteen, when he had completed his preparatory schooling, he was sent to Germany to study the wool business.

No one seems to have reckoned with the effect of Germany's music upon this impressionable, musically gifted boy. Young Delius had, probably, heard very little good music in provincial England. But in Germany, on hearing Wagner's *Meistersinger* and Karl Goldmark's *Queen of Sheba*, his wits went woolgathering in a direction not included in his father's plans for him. He was now fired with an ambition to become a composer. One can easily imagine the tempest stirred up by Frederick's timid letter asking permission to give up the wool business for music! The permission was not granted, and after the storm had died down, young Delius went to Manchester to serve his apprenticeship under an uncle who was also a wool merchant.

Two years was all that he could stand of pelts and fleeces. At the end of that time he went to his father with a compromise. If he must go in for business, could it not be something besides wool? What he preferred was to plant oranges in Florida. From his boyhood Delius had been interested in Florida, and the more he read about those river plantations, the more he wanted to try life there. He must have argued well, for his father not only consented to the plan but also purchased an orange plantation, Solano, on the St. John's river, then a three days' journey from Jacksonville, the nearest city.

In the spring of 1884, the twenty-two-year-old Delius reached Florida. It was indeed a New World to him, but also a very old world. So primitive was the life at Solano among the easy-going Negroes, and so completely detached from nineteenth-century civilization, that Delius, the only white man there, might as well have been living in the heart of the African jungle. He soon yielded to its drowsy spell. The business of the plantation was left to an overseer while the young master spent his time reading, daydreaming in a canoe on the river, walking alone in the woods at twilight, and listening to the music of the Negroes. Speaking of this music in after years, Delius said: "I loved it, and began to write music seriously myself. Night falls quickly there, and the native voices, always in harmony, sounded very lovely. It was mostly religious or gay music, by no means like the Negro spirituals often sung or broadcast from London today. . . . This mad jazz has nothing to do with the Negro. Jazz is an invention of so-called Americans who have taken rag-time and pretend that it is Negro music."

After a few months at Solano, Delius had gathered so many impressions that he began to feel the need of expression. Fortunately he had brought his violin with him, and as he played upon it the old enthusiasm for music came back. He decided that he must have a piano at Solano and made the long trip to Jacksonville to buy one. As he sat trying out different instruments in the warehouse, a prominent Jacksonville musician, Thomas Ward, was attracted by the unusual beauty of his little improvisations, and stopped to talk with him. The two became so interested in each other's musical views that the chance meeting ended in Ward's returning with Delius to Solano. The visit lasted for six months, during which Ward repaid his debt of hospitality by giving Delius lessons in harmony and counterpoint. This introduction to composition resulted in Delius's first significant work, *Appalachia*, for chorus and orchestra, a series of musical impressions of America.

Another six months of experimenting with composition convinced Delius of the folly of his pretending to be a businessman. Once more he wrote to his father, begging to be allowed to give up the plantation and take up the serious study of music. But the senior Delius would not even consider it. This time the junior Delius would not give in. He simply abandoned Solano and started out to make his own way. He went first to Jacksonville, where for a time he sang in a Jewish synagogue. Then, with a letter of recommendation and one dollar in his pocket, he proceeded to Danville, Virginia, where for a little while he taught in the Old Roanoke Female School. He next tried playing an organ in New York City. But about this time something — it may have been Frederick's pluck — seemed to soften the father's heart. He agreed to finance the music study. Delius left America, and a few months later was happily at work in the Conservatory at Leipzig.

In the summer of 1887, Delius went for a walking trip through Norway and there had the good fortune to meet Edward Grieg. The Norwegian composer became interested in the young Englishman, and when, in the following winter, Grieg visited Leipzig and heard a performance of one of Delius's early compositions, *Florida*, his interest grew. That same year Grieg came to England, hunted up Father Delius, and told him what he thought of his son's talent. Grieg was then one of the most important figures in European music, and his praise won the skeptical wool merchant's consent to his son's musical career and even the promise of a small allowance.

On leaving Leipzig Delius went to Paris, where a generous uncle gave him an income which meant complete freedom from money worries. Paris in 1890 was a stimulating place for any young artist, and Delius was quick to respond to it. He studied music intensively, poring over scores, going to concerts and operas, and talking over every phase of the art with other musicians. He met and exchanged views with many interesting people, notably Gaugin the painter and Strindberg the dramatist. Meanwhile, he was devoting himself to composition, and in 1892 his first published work, *Legende* for viola and orchestra, came from a Paris press.

It was during these Paris days that Delius met Jelka Rosen, a girl of unusual artistic gifts and a delightful companion. Delius was a frequent guest in the Rosen home, where he became a great favorite. But there was no romance between him and Jelka, and for a reason — the memory of a young Negro girl in far-away Solano. With his characteristic, almost childlike honesty, Delius made up his mind to return to Florida after a twelve years' absence and either marry his first love or forever lay its ghost. But he could find no trace of the Negro girl, and returning to France, went straight to the Rosens' and shortly afterward married Jelka. Despite its strange prelude, this marriage proved an ideally happy one for the thirty-six years until Delius's death.

In 1899, soon after their marriage, Madame Rosen presented the young people with a house, set in spacious grounds, in the small French town of Grez-sur-Loing, not far from Paris. It was in this peaceful place that, during the next fifteen years, Delius wrote the music which has made him famous — *Brigg Fair*, *In a Summer Garden*, *Dance Rhapsody*, *Summer Night on the River* and *On Hearing the First Cuckoo in Spring*.

But recognition came slowly to Delius, and then, strangely enough, neither from England, his own country, nor from France, the country of his adoption. It was in Germany that nearly all of his outstanding works had their first performance. At one of these, Richard Strauss is said to have remarked, "I never dreamt that anybody except myself was writing such good music!" However, Delius's music never has been and probably never will be popular. It is too elusive, too pleasantly blurred to give a clear first impression. Only after repeated hearings does it reveal its true beauty, and even then not to every listener. Its restraint and delicacy will never appeal to those who demand sentimental melodies and thumping rhythms.

To those who must label artists and their works, Delius has been a sore trial. How can one classify music which shows traces of an English background, of Negro warmth and fervor, of Scandinavia's wistful coolness, of the German Romanticism of Leipzig, and of the French Impressionism of Paris in the nineties? Delius is uniquely Delius, a dreamer and a poet-philosopher speaking a language all his own. Those who accept it find it delightful, and perhaps all the more so because it never seems to be forced upon them. Music, to Delius, was a medium of personal expression. He enjoyed what he wrote and frankly confessed it. Whether or not others enjoyed or approved of it was, to him, a matter of slight concern.

Life drifted pleasantly along at Grez-sur-Loing until suddenly, in 1914, the guns of the first World War shattered the quiet of France. Delius, then past fifty and unfit for military service, buried his valuables in his cellar and fled with his wife to London, where he remained until the war ended. But the happiness of his return home was short lived. Symptoms of serious illness were beginning to be apparent, and by 1925 Delius was hopelessly paralyzed and totally blind. During the nine years of physical bondage that followed, Delius could never reconcile himself to his tragic fate. Yet outwardly he bore it with the sweetness and serenity of spirit which distinguishes his music. His last photographs, particularly one made at Fontainebleau, show a spirituality seldom seen except on the faces of saints in the old religious paintings.

With the help of a young musician, Eric Fenby, Delius was able to continue composing, even during these years of illness. Sitting in the garden which he so dearly loved, he held court with his friends. Delius was a keen thinker and expressed his views on many subjects — art, religion, philosophy — fearlessly and well. His opinions on music are particularly interesting, these for example:

> In my opinion the adherents of the "wrong note" school are merely sensationalists. . . . Many young composers nowadays have undeniable cleverness but lack real feeling and inspiration. They are obsessed with the idea of being original at all costs. They do not see that in spite of their "wrong note" harmonies and jazzed rhythms, their work is as commonplace in essentials as that of the most hidebound academies. Originality comes only when you have worked right through your influences and have learned to express your emotions in your own way. Superficial virtuosity will never conceal a lack of inventive power and ultimately results in complete sterility.

Although Delius cared little for public acclaim, it was none the less gratifying to him and to the many who had appreciated his music, when in the winter of 1929, England paid him belated honor. A great Delius Festival was held in Queen's Hall, London, with six concerts of his music. Newspapers headlined his story; critics contributed their choicest adjectives; Oxford University conferred an honorary degree; phonograph records of his music became best sellers, and the radio broadcast it far and wide. And through it all, a frail stranger in an invalid's chair, faced the cheering crowds with unseeing eyes but with a smile on his fine face.

Frederick Delius died at Grez-sur-Loing in the early summer of 1934. One of his last wishes was to lie near some little church "where the winds are warm and the sun friendly." A year after his death his body was brought to Limpsfield, in the south of England. There, in the churchyard under a great tree, centuries old, they had made a grave, lighted by two hurricane lamps and lined with laurel leaves. And there England paid last tribute to one of her greatest composers, while an orchestra led by his friend and admirer Sir Thomas Beecham played the beautiful *Summer Night on the River* and *On Hearing the First Cuckoo in Spring*.

ON HEARING THE FIRST CUCKOO IN SPRING

Delius was one of music's most delightful daydreamers. Unlike Debussy, whose daydreaming was inspired by sense impressions which are caught and passed on in his music, Delius seemed to have drifted up and away from this visible, audible world into a realm of pure emotion. In his music he is not in the least concerned with suggesting definite things or ideas. He does give the starting point of his dream in a poetic title, but that is all. Once the music begins, the listener must depend upon his own imagination for what he sees, hears, and smells! Delius seeks to express neither the thing nor his own sensory response to it, but the feelings aroused by his contemplation of it. A most charming example of this rare contemplative music is the fragile masterpiece, *On Hearing the First Cuckoo in Spring*.

No bird has been more celebrated in song and story than the cuckoo. Since the time of Aristotle, and perhaps long before, the cuckoo has been the hero of all sorts of legends shocking to ornithologists. In the old days the first cuckoo was both loved and feared. He was loved because he was the harbinger of spring. His lonesome little song sounding from bare April woods meant the end of winter's sadness. But the cuckoo could also cause great consternation, for he was supposed to have the gift of prophecy. Young girls ran out into the fields in the early morning and called:

> Cuckoo, cherry tree,
> Good bird, tell me,
> How many years shall be
> Until I marry?

Anxious old folk whispered:

> Cuckoo, cherry tree,
> Good bird, tell me,
> How many years have I to live
> One—two—three?

And of course the children never left off their questioning! Indeed, the poor bird was kept so busy answering questions that he had no time for his own affairs, and they say (though there are those who doubt it) that is why the cuckoo never builds a nest!

Of all God's creatures, surely the cuckoo has been most serviceable to poets and music makers. He appears in the earliest English secular song on record:

> Summer is icumen in,
> Lhude sing cuccu!
> (circa 1250)

in the plays of Shakespeare, and in reams of spring poems everywhere. His little two-note song strummed on Daquin's *clavecin* added greatly to the popularity of the first experiments in program music. It has been heard even within the austere precincts of the classical symphony.

But not for Delius these naïve cuckooings of Haydn and Beethoven or the picturesque effects of such tone poets as Saint-Saëns in his lovely *Cuckoo in the Depths of the Wood.* Knowing Delius, one is not surprised that he should write a cuckoo piece in which the familiar call is heard but once, near the end, and so faintly that it might be merely the ghost of the little feathered prophet. To Delius the cuckoo call was not a convenient formula suggesting nature and the out-of-doors, but a symbol of all the hopes and fears, the mingled joys and longing which fill the human heart in springtime.

On Hearing the First Cuckoo in Spring has two themes, one original with the composer, the other taken from a Norwegian folk song, "In Old Valley." Delius loved Norway, where he is said to have spent eighteen summers, and doubtless the song of the first cuckoo turned his thoughts to that beautiful North Land with its brief, bright spring.

Divided strings topped with a persistent high B, make a delicately dissonant background for clarinet and oboe as they forecast the two themes:[1]

(Quotations from a Delius score are as unsatisfactory as snapshots of a garden in bloom. They cannot give the color or the fragrance.)

There are only three measures of introduction but enough to recall the mood of a northern spring.

> Spring with that nameless longing in the air
> Which dwells with all things fair.

Then "with easy flowing movement" the strings give out the first theme:

a sequence of phrases which echo each other, suggesting distant cuckoo calls.

[1] Quotations used by permission of the Oxford University Press, and Carl Fischer, Inc., sole agents in this country.

Flutes and violins follow with the second theme, a lovely folk song:

with a last phrase:

which sings like a refrain throughout the piece.

But it is not with themes or thematic contrast and development that Delius works his magic. Rhythm and melody might give us the exuberant spring of "Pippa Passes," the lovely May of Mozart, the laughing brooks of Schubert, or the passionate spring of Schumann's love songs, but only harmony — the delicate blending of many tones — could give the feeling of misted April which Delius has caught in this spring rhapsody.

There is a certain mistiness about the music, too. The folk tune, heard in fragments and veiled by the changing harmonies, never has a clear-cut line. In both harmony and instrumentation Delius has used pale pastel tints and used them sparingly. Yet the texture of the music is never thin, the sound never merely sweet. The score is rather clumsy-looking with its vertical blocks of chords, but it is surprisingly delicate when heard. In Delius's music, feeling, not seeing, is believing. It makes no eye appeal by suggested pictures or even by intricate, beautiful design, but aims straight at the heart through the emotional appeal of tone and tone combination. Because of this singleness of purpose, because it needs no program beyond the title's suggestion and no technical knowledge or analysis, *On Hearing the First Cuckoo in Spring* stands out as a charming example of pure music in the modern manner.

Brigg Fair

"An English Rhapsody," Delius called his *Brigg Fair*, and in that sub-title hands us the key to his music. *Brigg Fair* is, in the truest sense of the word, a rhapsody — a direct presentation of emotion rather than a representation of the sights and sounds that cause it. The thoughts and the musical theme came from an old Lincolnshire folk song, but the rhapsody, the expression of the feelings they aroused, is Delius's own.

Percy Grainger, a tireless searcher among British folk tunes, unearthed the old song and gave it to his friend Delius, who later returned the compliment by dedicating his *Brigg Fair* to Grainger. Nothing could be more characteristically different than the ways in which these two composers use folk themes. Remembering *Shepherd's Hey*, *Molly on the Shore*, and a host of others, it is safe to say that, if Grainger had written *Brigg Fair*, he would have suggested an old English country fair with all its hearty color and action. Grainger is always the spectator, not only on the spot but also quite ready to take his turn at the fiddle or in the dance should opportunity offer. But Delius never mingles with the noisy flesh-and-blood crowd. For him *Brigg Fair* recalls no festive confusion of men and animals, of voices bartering and bantering, of vagrant fiddles and wheezy roundabout organs; no happy rustic lovers keeping tryst. The quaint tune and imperfect lines of the old song set him thinking of the pathos of young love with its solemn promises and high hopes, sure to be bludgeoned by circumstance and, as surely, remembered with a sigh.

Prefacing the score of *Brigg Fair* are the verses of the folk song:

It was on the fifth of August,
    The weather fine and fair,
Unto Brigg Fair I did repair,
    For Love I was inclined.

I rose up with the lark in the morning
    With my heart so full of glee,
Of thinking there to meet my dear,
    Long time I wished to see.

I looked over my left shoulder
    To see whom I could see,
And there I spied my own true love
    Come tripping down to me.

I took hold of her lily-white hand
    And merrily was her heart,
And now we're met together
    I hope we ne'er shall part.

For it's meeting is a pleasure
    And parting is a grief,
But an unconstant lover
    Is worse than a thief.

The green leaves they shall wither
    And the branches they shall die
If ever I prove false to her,
    To the girl that loves me.

The music begins with a slow pastoral introduction with the flute in a birdlike melody:[1]

lightly accompanied by harp and divided strings.

[1] Excerpts printed by permission of Associated Music Publishers, Inc., New York, owners of the copyright.

Then the oboe pipes the old Lincolnshire air:

To Elizabethan ears this no doubt seemed a gay little tune, but to us its Doric mode gives it a wistful cast.

Having given out the simple folk tune, Delius now makes it the subject of a series of seventeen variations. Variation is the life of Delius's compositions. Instead of making his music grow by the contrast and development of several themes, he usually chooses but one main theme and then enlarges upon it by subtle alterations of melody and harmony. There are few of those abrupt changes of rhythm that mark the clear-cut variations of the older classical composers. Delius's variations are largely harmonic and play across the music as quietly as the changing lights in a sunset sky. There are no sharp edges, no startling dynamics to break the serene contemplation of the theme.

After the sixth variation the folk theme disappears for a moment, and in a lovely middle section the composer speaks:

The folk theme keeps its triple meter throughout with the interesting exception of variations eleven and twelve, where it changes to a slow and solemn four beat:

accompanied by the clang of bells and gravely syncopated strings. It is an effective bit of contrast, and suggests to the imaginative listener the lover's vow:

> The green leaves they shall wither
> And the branches they shall die
> If ever I prove false to her,
> To the girl that loves me.

The flutes, in a brief transition passage, lead out of this solemn mood into the gay variation thirteen.

As it nears the end the music seems to unfold until it reaches the impressive, full-blown *maestoso* of the last variation; then, growing gradually softer and slower, it fades away in a plaintive coda.

> For it's meeting is a pleasure
> And parting is a grief —

GUSTAV HOLST

Cheltenham — 1874
London   — 1934

Gustavus Theodore von Holst, eldest son of Clara and Adolph von Holst, was born September 21, 1874, not in Germany, as the name might suggest, but in the English town of Cheltenham. The Holsts were a Swedish family, and a family of musicians. The composer's great-grandfather, Matthias von Holst, had lived in Russia, where he had taught and played the harp at the Imperial Court at St. Petersburg. He had come to England with his Russian wife early in the nineteenth century. His son Gustavus, also a harpist, had settled in Cheltenham, where in turn his own sons Gustavus and Adolph, father of the composer, had followed the family profession of music making.

Gustav Holst gradually shortened his name, dropping the *von* in 1914 when such prepositions went out of the names of many other English people. "I am glad it went out," said one who knew him, "first for the reason that this Gustav Holst always seemed to me a beautiful type of Englishman; and secondly because the simpler name of 'Gustav Holst,' plain, energetic, yet spacious, denotes the character of the man and the character of his music."

The little house in Pittville Terrace, Cheltenham, became a scene of sad confusion when Clara Holst died, leaving her sons Gustav, aged eight, and Emil, aged six, to a kindly but bewildered father. Adolph led a very busy life, giving concerts, playing a church organ, and teaching a large number of piano pupils. For him, home was a place to practice, and two small boys, however dear, were decidedly a wrong note. His sister, Aunt Nina, came to the rescue, but she, being also a musician, knew more about Chopin than children. She could help Gustav with his practicing, but with little else. And Gustav needed help. He was an over-sensitive child with weak eyes and a weak chest, neither of which was improved by long hours at the piano. But Gustav enjoyed his piano playing, and the way he could twirl off the Turkish March from *The Ruins of Athens* was the wonder of all the small boys in the neighborhood!

One day when he was about twelve he was given the poem "Horatius" to learn by heart. He was so impressed by it that he decided to set it to music for chorus and orchestra. He had never had a harmony lesson in his life, but he couldn't let a little thing like that hinder him. Finding a copy of Berlioz's "Orchestration," scarcely a child's primer, he set to work in secret. When, after several weeks, he had a chance to try his great composition on the piano, he was so shocked at the mess of sound that he never added another note — Horatius died then and there!

But the boy did not give up the idea of composing, although it was frowned upon by his father, who was determined to make a concert pianist of him. Again and again Gustav tried for a composition scholarship, but always just missed it — perhaps because he was just a little too original. At last, when he was nineteen, some music he composed for a local operetta was performed. People liked it, and even Adolph von Holst was so impressed that he borrowed a hundred pounds and sent his gifted son up to the Royal College of Music to study.

That was a wonderful year in London. Gustav Holst learned the young artist's most important lesson — that originality does not mean ignorance or defiance of accepted rules and techniques, but rather, so complete a knowledge and assimilation that techniques can be forgotten in the real freedom of sincere expression. He heard his first great music — was deeply moved by a festival performance of Bach's *B Minor Mass* and quite intoxicated by Wagner.

But there was misfortune, too. The neuritis which was to be his lifelong enemy began to cramp his right hand so that he could no longer practice hours at a time. Even holding a pen was so painful that for writing music he had a special nib that he could fasten on his first finger, leaving the rest of his hand free. The idea of becoming a concert pianist had to be given up, and for a time it seemed that the end of his world had come. Then he decided to take up the trombone — at least the blowing might be good for his weak chest, and the experience of playing in an orchestra would be useful if ever he were to realize his dream of becoming a composer. There was also a chance of earning a living as a trombone player.

Money matters were becoming serious for young Holst about this time. He lived on as little as possible, seldom had a satisfying meal, partly because he could not afford it and partly because of a wild idea that an artist should not indulge in the good things — the old "garret" tradition. He had no piano in his room, and it is a wonder that his experiments in unresolved discords and cross-rhythms in 7/4 were not buried in the envelope marked "Early Horrors" along with "Horatius." Perhaps it is just as well that he could not hear what he was doing! But with all his frugality, the borrowed hundred pounds came to an end and it looked as if he would have to leave college. Then, at the last moment he managed to win the open scholarship for composition. This meant a grant of thirty pounds a year which, with what he earned as trombone player at seaside resorts during the holidays, kept him going.

At one time Holst played in the White Viennese Band, famous for its Strauss waltzes. Most of the men were English, but they got more pay if they wore white uniforms with brass buttons and called themselves foreigners! Later he was appointed first trombone with the Carl Rosa Opera Company and he also played with several first-class orchestras. He was not a brilliant trombonist, but he played well, and the experience was invaluable since it gave him the feeling of "an orchestra from the inside." It also gave him knowledge of what he called the *impersonality* of orchestral playing — a broader horizon than that of the musician who has known only the very personal, self-centered experience of the soloist or composer.

In 1901, Gustav Holst married Isobel Harrison, whom he met when he was directing the Socialist Choir in Hammersmith. Theirs had been a long engagement, full of good works on the part of Isobel. She had taken her lover in hand, made him give up his diet of dried nuts and cocoa, his ridiculous beard, grown to make him look older when applying for jobs, and with her beauty and kindness had illuminated his drab life. In return he had written her a new love song each week and worked harder than ever at his composition. With a tiny legacy from Adolph von Holst, the young couple took a holiday in Germany — they called it their honeymoon though it was two years late.

Returning to England without a penny, they decided that Gustav should now give up his trombone — the one visible means of support — and dedicate his life to composition. Hard times followed. Gustav wrote diligently, but publishers refused his compositions. Isobel made clothes for her friends, did music copying, and used all her practical skills to keep things going. Just as it seemed as if they could not make it, Gustav was asked to substitute for one of the teachers at the James Allen Girls' School at Dulwich. He did so well that at the end of the term he was asked to stay on in charge of the music.

This was the beginning of the teaching which, for the rest of his life, was to be one of his greatest contributions to English music. Later he became professor of music at the University College, Reading, and at the Royal College of Music, where he had studied as a boy. But the teaching Holst loved best was done at St. Paul's Girls' School, Hammersmith, where as a tribute to him they built a spacious, soundproof music room for his composing, and at the Morley College for Working Men and Women, where he had the joy of associating with real amateurs — people who sang, played, and studied for the pure love of music.

Imogen Holst, in her delightful biography of her father, tells of his relationship to his "Morleyites" and of how he once said to them, "Morley exists for the training of amateurs. A little knowledge is not dangerous as long as you remember that it is only a little. And the test of success is the amount of artistic enjoyment you can get from performing, writing, or listening to music." And again, "We all begin our education by being amateurs, and, in the real sense of the word, we must remain amateurs, like the famous Japanese artist who wrote his own epitaph, 'Here lies an old man who was fond of painting.'"

"And there was no weeding out at Morley," says Miss Holst. "The people who could hardly hold their violins were surrounded by more competent players so that the damage they did was negligible. Among the singers there were several whose voices would not have passed an audition in a more orthodox choir. But Holst would tell them of a Bishop who had been heard to say, 'Now, gentlemen, we will sing a hymn. Those of you who can sing will sing; those who can't, make a cheerful noise to God.' And by the time Holst had finished with them the cheerful noise had invariably turned to singing." But while he encouraged everyone to share in the music making, with his whimsical theory that "if a thing is worth doing at all, it is worth doing badly," there was never any letting down of musical standards. The Morleyites struggled with Purcell, Bach, Haydn, and Wagner until their performance became something more than merely an ambitious undertaking. Holst had given them a taste of and for music's best. No wonder they flocked to his classes, sick or well, rain or shine. As one of them remarked, "it's a sort of heaven we go to on Mondays and Wednesdays."

His own scattered comments and the memories of those who knew him well picture Gustav Holst as a master teacher, one who taught people, not a subject. His letters from Salonika, where he was sent during the first World War by the British Y.M.C.A. as Musical Organizer of their educational work among the troops, give these revealing glimpses:

> . . . . After many years of education with a small e, I have now got to play about with Education with a big one. Mercifully I get in a lot of the other as well . . . throughout the world we are in danger of forgetting that *life* should be organized, and seem to be trying to vitalize (and worship) organization.

In a letter to his wife there is this note of homesickness for his old work:

> . . . There was a fearful lot of it, but it was the real thing: — real people to teach, and real music to give them, and no palaver,

as compared with this supposedly more important job having to do with

> Committees, education schemes, and co-ordination. In other words, talking about a thing instead of doing it. It may be necessary — I fear it is — but I don't feel it's my job, whereas teaching a kindergarten or the Thaxted choir is. . . . My only consolation is a dear man here who has been a slum school headmaster for thirty years and who therefore knows that the moment one ceases to think of human beings and dwells mentally amid schemes and systems, one is just damned as a teacher. This is a bit mixed, but all I mean is that I'm not so keen on a big education job. . . .

Holst had little patience with the mere accumulation of knowledge in art, which, says his daughter, "reminded him of the White Knight in 'Through the Looking Glass,' who set off on horseback with a mousetrap and a beehive in case they might be useful." His idea of education was the unfolding of the pupil's mind, a delicate and natural process, with the teacher standing by ready to do — or not to do — whatever might be helpful.

To him teaching was never mere potboiling business, as, unfortunately, it has been for so many artists. It was the very essence of creation, with life itself for a medium. Indeed, he was convinced that all really great artists were also great teachers, and he scorned "the other type of artist who tries to live in a world by himself; one who despises the vulgar herd and only condescends to allow it to share the beauty of his art in the spirit of a despot of the Middle Ages, throwing largesse to the mob."

Gustav Holst was an artist-teacher because he could lose his little self in the greater wonder and beauty of the music he was sharing. From the common ground of his own devotion to music and that which he inspired in his pupils, grew up what he called, "that beautiful comradeship which is the great reward of teaching." His friend Vaughan Williams ("Music and Letters," 1920) says, "As the years go on, his ideals of thoroughness, of beauty, and above all, of comradeship have remained and grown stronger," and from this ideal has come the "almost mystical sense of unity which is the secret of Holst's power as a teacher." But the acid test of his or any teaching is the carry-over in the out-of-school hours and years. Holst was never so happy as when he discovered his schoolgirls singing madrigals "unofficially" before the morning bell rang, and even in forbidden times; or when on one of his famous walking trips he stopped at the house of a former pupil and found that the music of the old St. Paul or Morley days had been transplanted into a new home. Then he knew that he had done what he often said was "the last and hardest duty of a teacher — to make himself unnecessary."

Teaching, composing, and an occasional round of lectures or conducting filled the years for Gustav Holst. Walking was always one of his chief delights, and a tramp through the Cotswold hills, "especially," he said, "with a rain-sodden S.W. wind in your face," or a walk to Corfe Castle, Dorset, on a wild wintry day was for him the best of holidays. There were also excursions abroad and three trips to the United States, the last in 1932 when he came as lecturer in composition at Harvard University.

Many professional honors were offered him, but his dread of publicity made him refuse most of them. In America he could have been in the spotlight day and night, lecturing and "stick-wagging" in his "crêpe-de-Chine," as he always called his dress suit. He actually had to employ an agent to take care of the many requests for his time. Otherwise, as he wrote to his wife, he would have had to resort to printed forms saying, " 'Dear Sir or Madam, I'll see you damned before I'll conduct, lecture, dine, be interviewed, be photographed' — I forget the others but there are a few left." But he thoroughly enjoyed American hospitality and American audiences, and made many warm American friendships.

Gustav Holst was a reader in many fields besides his own. At twenty-five he became interested in Sanskrit literature, particularly in the philosophy of the *Bhagavad-Gita* from which he took his ideal of the wise man as one who is "fearless and free from vanity, egoism, impatience, and the dread of failure. He is indifferent to worldly ambition; he is just, impartial, and ready to do whatever work is given him, without complaint and without hope of reward." Translated into Holst's everyday life and speech it became "Get on with the job, whatever it is, and don't bother about what's going to happen" — his motto.

He was so impressed by the hymns of the *Rig-Veda* and other poems that he learned Sanskrit in order to translate them and set them to music. He also studied astrology, not with any faith in the fortune-telling part of it, but because he was interested in the character of the different planets which had intrigued the wise men of ancient times. And, like most people who come under the spell of folk tunes, Holst became a student of the early modes and all the fascinating background of English music.

Holst was a slight man physically, and never strong. Indeed, it was said that his laughter was the only robust thing about him. During the last ten years of his life, his delicate nervous system was upset by a fall in which he struck the back of his head. There had to be frequent long periods of rest, alone in the country or in a nursing home. But to the end, he was a busy, merry invalid, writing and listening to music — some of it his own — on the radio. And when his friends visited him, he talked and joked so uproariously that they feared he might literally die a-laughing!

In May, 1934, Holst underwent the operation which they hoped would make him well again, but his tired heart could not stand the strain. They buried his ashes in the north transept of Chichester Cathedral, near the memorial to Thomas Weelkes, who had been organist there more than three hundred years before and whose music Holst had always loved. The Whitsun Singers, a group Holst had organized in the church at Thaxted, came down that midsummer afternoon to sing a last time for their leader. They sang Weelkes's "Let Thy merciful ears" and afterward Holst's own joyous setting of an old secular carol, "This have I done for my true love." They sang it because it was his favorite and theirs and perhaps his finest unaccompanied chorus. But for Gustav Holst, who, having reached professional heights was still at heart an amateur, working out of love for music, there could scarcely be a more fitting last line than, "This have I done for my true love."

THE ARTIST

Gilbert Murray's statement — "Every man who possesses real vitality is first the child of a tradition. He is secondly a rebel against that tradition. And the best traditions make the best rebels" — really sums up Gustav Holst the artist. He was a child of tradition — first it was Wagner, then Bach, Haydn, and the absorbing interest in early English composers and in old folk tunes. *Rebel* seems too strong a word for one so calm and otherworldly, yet Gustav Holst certainly made his way from convention to individuality. In a space of twenty-five years, there was not a phase of so-called modernism through which he did not pass.

The best appraisal of Holst the artist comes from his lifelong friend and critic, Vaughan Williams, in a preface to Imogen Holst's life of her father. In it he says:

Beethoven and Holst have this in common, that they are both uncompromisingly direct in their utterance. Holst never fumbles; he says what he means without circumlocution; he is not afraid of a downright tune like both the tunes in *Jupiter*. On the other hand, where the depth of the thought requires obscure harmony he does not flinch. The strange chords in *Neptune* make our "moderns" sound like milk and water. Yet those chords never seem wrong, nor are they incongruous; the same mind is evident in the remote aloofness of *Egdon Heath* and the homely tunes of the *St. Paul's Suite*.

This downrightness produces a certain pungency of effect which is, I believe, an offence to some pusillanimous aesthetes. His music probably does not appeal to the aesthetes, nor would he wish it so, but it does appeal to the storekeeper on the lonely Yorkshire coast.

Holst's art has been called cold and inhuman; the truth is that it is suprahuman: it glows with the white radiancy in which burning heat and freezing cold become the same thing. But though his music lives in mystical regions, yet it is never indefinite or shadowy; indeed, it may be a fault that it is occasionally too clear-cut — a sharp outline where perhaps a vague impression would have sufficed. Those who knew him see him in his music. He was a visionary but never an idle dreamer. He seemed sometimes to be living away from the world of the senses, but as he himself said, "Only second-rate artists are unbusinesslike." He would lose himself hopelessly on a holiday, but he never missed an appointment. Though he seemed sometimes to be living in a world of his own, yet if a friend or even a stranger wanted help, advice, or even a rebuke, he was there to give it. His music reaches into the unknown, but it never loses touch with humanity.

In artistic matters clarity was his watchword. He simply could not understand slovenly workmanship, half-hearted endeavor, or artistic dishonesty. Holst was a leader in the revolt against the riot of luxurious sentiment which marked the decadence of the Romantic period, but his early love of the true Romanticists, Bach and Wagner, prevented his ever succumbing to the poverty-stricken aridity of modern pseudoclassicism. Much as he loved Wagner, he is never "Wagnerian." Much as he loved Bach, he was never tempted to write those dreadful exercises in "Bach up to date" which have lately become the fashion.

Holst inherited the English tradition of adventurous comradeship in the arts; that spirit which made Weelkes and Byrd and Wilbye throw off the shackles of Italian academicism and experiment in strange rhythms and harmonies. . . .

Whatever his hand found to do he did it with his might.

Some of Holst's music is frankly experimental, interesting to students but not beautiful. The critics were always ready to pounce upon him with their choicest expressions of disapproval. But he never minded what they said "except when they began to treat him with respect, which he considered to be a sign of old age."

Like his wise man of the *Bhagavad-Gita*, he was indifferent to worldly ambition. In fact, he once wrote to Clifford Bax, "Someday I expect you will agree with me that it is a great thing to be a failure. If nobody likes your work, you have to go on just for the sake of the work. And you're in no danger of letting the public make you repeat yourself. Every artist ought to pray that he may not be a 'success.' If he's a failure, he stands a good chance of concentrating upon the best work of which he is capable." Surely the history of art and artists bears out Holst's theory!

As a composer Gustav Holst has style but not *a* style. He was too much of an adventurer ever to settle down to anything resembling a formula. Every one of his compositions has to be judged separately and for itself alone. But critical analysis is the last thing Holst would have wished from his listeners. He asks only a hearing. If we do not like what we hear — well, it would not have mattered much to him. But if we can respond to his music, then somewhere a shy but friendly ghost will be pleased, perhaps even feel successful, for as Holst himself said, a composer is "one who records what all men feel."

THE PLANETS

Mars, the Bringer of War

The Planets, a suite for large orchestra, is perhaps the best known of Holst's works, as well as one of the most important compositions by a contemporary English composer. There are seven movements, *Mars, the Bringer of War; Venus, the Bringer of Peace; Mercury, the Winged Messenger; Jupiter, the Bringer of Jollity; Saturn, the Bringer of Old Age; Uranus, the Magician;* and *Neptune, the Mystic.* The titles are intriguing, but the appeal of this suite lies in its abstract musical beauty and power rather than in any program idea.   Indeed, the composer himself warns us that it is not the mythological significance of these gods and goddesses that matters, but the astrological powers connected with the planets named after them.   Yet who can listen to this music, to *Mars*, for example, without picturing the old Roman God of War — brute force in the body of a man and topped by the grim and terrible mask of a hate-scarred human face.

Gustav Holst was three years writing *The Planets*.   *Mars, the Bringer of War* came first and might supposedly have been inspired by the first World War.   But *Mars* was written *before* August, 1914.   It is not the first time an artist has seemed to sense a world mood, the shadow cast by coming events!   And again prophetically, the war which this music suggests is not the hand-to-hand combat of Roman legions.   This is machine-made war, the ruthless war of the twentieth century.   There is little that is picturesque about it.

The dominant feature of this music is the rhythm — a relentless 5/4: [1]

which from the first measure to the last goes smashing through every attempt at melody or harmony, smashing tanklike through everything in its path.

After a few bars of this rhythm, marked by tympani, harps, and strings — the latter insured against sweetness by the mark, *col legno* (played with the wood of the bow) — the bassoons and horns are heard in this curious, growling figure:

over the constantly repeated G of the rhythm-marking instruments.

All this is in preparation for the main theme, if such a writhing blur of brasses can be called a theme:

Later, woodwinds and strings join in, working it up to a wailing climax.

Suddenly, in welcome contrast, the insistent rhythm gives way to a straight five beats to the measure, and the tenor tuba introduces a second theme:

which, with its trumpet fanfare, recalls the romance and pageantry of ancient warfare.

[1] Copyright, 1921, by Goodwin and Tabb, Ltd., J. Curwen & Sons, Ltd.   Excerpts printed by permission.

Then comes something in the nature of a short development of the two themes. The bassoons and bass strings give out the first theme:

softly at first, then working up to a *crescendo* for full orchestra which ends in a loud crashing of the dominant rhythmic figure. The romantic second theme also returns, only to be growled out by brasses and woodwinds, now more ferocious than ever.

Near the end there is a bombardment of harsh detached chords, then a sinister whistling of strings and woodwinds, and a final battering by the relentless rhythm — a fitting conclusion to what, says one commentator, is "probably the most forceful piece of music ever written."

Mercury, the Winged Messenger

In 1917, Holst completed his suite, *The Planets*, with the *scherzo* movement, *Mercury*. The composer chose the winged messenger as a symbol of Thought flashing through time and space. As one watches any winged thing, bird, airplane, or even the picture or statue of Mercury with his beautiful body poised for flight, one is conscious of speed and movement, rather than of any particular moment of its passing. So it is with Holst's music. Stop it long enough to see what makes it move, and the lovely flight is broken.

However, a study of this remarkable score reveals two unusual features which seem to be the secret of its effectiveness. Quite appropriately, they have to do with time and space. The time signature of the piece is 6/8 which, as a rule, is considered a *duple* rhythm, meaning that the measure is divided into two groups — in this case groups of three eighth notes each — and the two accents give a duple or "two" feeling. But it is also possible to divide the measure into *three* groups of two eighth notes each, which gives the feeling of three beats or triple rhythm. Now Holst has used both divisions, playing the duple and triple against each other so cleverly that the effect is not the usual feeling of strictly measured rhythm, but of free motion — a feeling of wings. The listener is not tempted to beat time — he can't, for this is not foot music, it is flight!

An even more noticeable feature is the wide compass range of the notes, which gives a feeling of space. The music begins with a bounding figure which springs from bass to high treble and cannot be shown in the few measures of a quotation. Then the celesta, harps, woodwinds, and violins give out a little chiming melody which, since it is heard throughout the piece, might be called a main motif:

A solo violin introduces another theme, one which illustrates the play of duple against triple:

Solo Violin

This theme is taken up by the different instruments in turn, rising, expanding, then gently sinking until the main melody is heard only in the English horn.

The opening figure flies by, again followed by the other themes, but all so swiftly and with such whimsical variation that they are only vaguely recognized. A final, fascinating leap from the depths of the contrabassoon, shooting up through the woodwinds to the top tones of the piccolos, and the winged messenger, like some wild bird, passes from sight and hearing, leaving only a bright feather — a chord drifting down through the celesta and harps — to remind us of its passing.

This little *scherzo* is another of those rare miracles whereby ordinary mortals may glimpse Mercury, Ariel, Puck, creatures

> Begot of nothing but vain fantasy;
> Which is as thin of substance as the air.

With this music Gustav Holst joined Berlioz of the glittering "Queen Mab" *Scherzo* and Mendelssohn, "own brother to fairies," in proof that even in our age of science and cold reason, magic is still at work!

The Planets was a success. After the first complete performance (1920), Ernest Newman wrote: "Holst has one of the subtlest and most original minds of our time; it begins working at a musical problem where most other minds would leave off." An amusing incident occurred when New York and Chicago began to argue as to who should have the honor of the first American performance of *The Planets*. Finally, it was decided that both orchestras should present it the same night, but the difference between Eastern Time and Central Time gave Mr. Albert Coates in New York an hour's advantage over Mr. Frederick Stock in Chicago, which was perhaps fair enough since it was a case of one Englishman introducing another!

EDWARD ELGAR

Worcester — 1857
Worcester — 1934

In 1904, just two hundred and nine years after the death of Purcell, London held a three-day festival of the works of one man, a Worcester musician named Edward Elgar. In the same year, this same Mr. Elgar was knighted by King Edward VII for "his services to English music." And what were those services? Why, the first English composition strong enough to find a place in the repertory of continental orchestras: the *Enigma Variations* (1899); *The Dream of Gerontius* (1900), one of the greatest oratorios since Mendelssohn's *Elijah; Pomp and Circumstance* (1901), a set of military marches which have become as suggestive of Great Britain as "God Save the King"; *Coronation Ode* (1902); *The Apostles*, featured at the Birmingham Festival in 1903. After so long a time, it seemed that England had again produced a composer who was "the delight of the nation and the wonder of the world!"

Like Purcell, Edward Elgar was largely a self-taught musician, a boy with a keen interest and a driving curiosity who learned by persistent doing. He was one of the seven children of the organist at the Roman Catholic Church of St. George in Worcester. His father also played the violin in the local orchestra and was a partner in the town's music shop. In the busy Elgar household young Edward's development received no special attention. But he was fortunate in having an unusually challenging environment for a thoughtful child and in being allowed to explore it alone. He would spend hours in the organ loft and wandering about the empty church while his father practiced the music of Johann Sebastian Bach. He was interested in the medieval carvings in the church, and so interested in the music he heard that he wanted to see the pages on which it was written. There were also other intriguing music books at home — a piano arrangement of Beethoven's First Symphony, which was really exciting — good as any puzzle to figure out. He began writing out the exercises in the harmony books, and when he was twelve he made up the music for a play the neighborhood children had concocted. He wrote these pieces down in a notebook, and, some forty years later, transplanted them from their "domestic orchestra" setting to the real orchestra as the charming *Wand of Youth Suites*, I and II. And there were other books, Sir Philip Sydney's "Arcadia," Shakespeare's plays, dusty volumes which he devoured in his own special stable-loft library.

They tell an amusing incident of Edward's first day at boarding school. The headmaster asked his name.

"Edward Elgar," replied the boy.

"Add the word *Sir*," said the master sharply.

Obediently — and prophetically — came the answer, "Sir Edward Elgar."

When Edward was sixteen, he was sent up to London to study law. Three years in a solicitor's office were more than enough for a boy homesick for Worcester and its music. He begged, and was given permission, to come home, help in the shop, and earn what he could with his music.

Then began such a laboratory experience as few musicians have known. With all the instruments, as well as the theory books right there in the shop, he began to master them. He had picked up enough organ facility to substitute occasionally for his father at St. George's. He joined an amateur wind ensemble as bassoon player and took some part, even that of conductor, in every local orchestra within miles of Worcester. He even became parish bell ringer, but was dismissed because his absorption in the musical sounds prolonged the curfew beyond public endurance! And, when the Elgar music shop got a commission for a march or a song for some special occasion, who but Edward turned out the composition.

But his dearest dream was to become a concert violinist. He appeared on every possible occasion and really made quite a reputation as a fiddler. He went up to

London again to study with a well-known teacher of violin. But after five lessons he decided that the career of a virtuoso was not for him, after all. So he returned to Worcester, where in the next few years he held a number of positions, among them, pianist and conductor of the Worcester Glee Club, bandmaster at the Worcester County Lunatic Asylum, and later, organist at St. George's, succeeding his father. Perhaps the most that can be said for these activities is that they stimulated his composition. He poured out a flood of music of all sorts, choruses, sacred and secular, for his glee club; military marches and dance tunes for his band; and organ pieces.

At the age of thirty-two, Elgar married Caroline Alice Roberts, who became his greatest inspiration and his most constructive critic. Shortly after their marriage, they decided that Edward should give up organ playing and musical odd-jobbing and devote himself to serious composition in larger forms. It was a brave decision, for Elgar knew only too well how little money a composer earned. His original quadrilles for the Worcester County Lunatic Asylum had brought him one dollar and twenty-five cents a set, minstrel songs, thirty-six cents apiece! But the Elgars moved up to London, where Edward gave music lessons to pay the rent and worked away at his composition. He soon found, however, that a large city was not the best place for creative work, and for a third time turned his back on London and went to Malvern, which was to be his permanent home.

Elgar's genius was of slow growth. He was a man of complex nature and of an astonishing variety of knowledge. He had studied law; he read history and poetry with a scholar's thoroughness; he was interested in architecture and woodcraft; and, as an avocation, set up a chemical laboratory where he spent many hours. He was the sort of person who had to think his own way through to the reality of things. He had to believe before he could sincerely express what to him were the spiritual truths, the meanings of life. He himself realized that the pleasant music he had written in his youth, the *Salut d'amour* type, was not enough to justify a life spent in composition. But slight and even commonplace as much of that early music was, it was sincere and really the best he could do at the time.

The great Elgar appears at the age of forty-two with the *Enigma Variations*. These variations are a series of musical portraits, each labeled with initials — the first is of the composer's wife, the last, a self-portrait, the others, of various friends. Once begun, Elgar's career as musician laureate was a long, triumphal progress, the way marked by two symphonies, a concerto for violin and one for 'cello, sonatas, part songs, and chamber music.

During the first World War he served in the Hampstead Volunteer Reserve and also with his music on patriotic themes. In 1920, the source of so much of his inspiration and enthusiasm suddenly failed — Lady Elgar died. For nine years nothing could induce him to compose a bar of music. His friends begged him to complete the trilogy of oratorios, of which *The Apostles* and *The Kingdom* were finished. They begged for a third symphony, but in vain. Then, in the winter of 1929, when King George was so desperately ill, Elgar, from the depths of his heart, composed a Christmas carol as a hymn of prayer for the recovery of His Majesty.

From that time he began slowly to return to his creative work. The third symphony was sketched and begun, only to be interrupted by the illness which, on the twenty-third of February, 1934, caused his death.

In his music, as in his life, Edward Elgar was a thorough gentleman, always correct in dress, speech, and manners, conventional but kindly. He was a master craftsman. His harmony and counterpoint are almost flawless, and in the use of the modern orchestra he is second to none. An English critic, after hearing his E-Flat Symphony, makes this interesting observation: "Elgar's orchestration does the work for the players. When the music requires a *sforzato* in the melody, his placing of the instruments gives it. If the band has the size and balance Elgar stipulates, the players could perform one of his works without rehearsal. In the case of most other orchestral music the players have to be told what to do." Elgar's music contains many lovely melodies, and it has a sturdy vigor which is very satisfying.

But Elgar's style is as difficult to describe as that of Gustav Holst, though for an exactly opposite reason. Holst was so much the experimenter that his style seemed to be constantly changing. Elgar, on the other hand, was so little the adventurer, so little the pioneer, that in all the forty years of his music making he failed to produce a style distinctly his own. Even his greatest works are haunted by the idioms of other men, most often by Schumann and Wagner, whom he all but out-Wagnered in the use of the *Leitmotiv!* Elgar was everything but an original composer. If, as the years pass, his beautiful, ingenious music wears thin, it will be because neither sincere feeling nor ingenuity can ever be a lasting substitute for originality.

But whatever may be his rank in the musical world, Edward Elgar is unquestionably "first in the hearts of his countrymen." In 1928, one of them left him a legacy of $35,000 with this tribute: "He saved my country from the reproach of having produced no composer worthy to rank with the great masters." Grove sums it up when he says in his article on Elgar: "No English festival is complete without him; every choral society and orchestra gives his music a large place in its repertory."

All this praise might have gone to the head of a man less well-balanced than Elgar. But he knew and confessed his own strength and weakness as a composer. He frankly liked most of what he composed, but he was charmingly modest about it. "When I see one of my own works by the side of, say, the Fifth Symphony of Beethoven," he once said, "I feel as a tinker might when he looks at the great Forth Bridge!" And while we are quoting Elgar, these lines seem a peculiarly appropriate ending to the sketch of this man and artist, "To make good music and also good listeners, instead of tinkerers on the keyboard" is the duty of musicians and teachers. "The new education should include music in its widest sense and tend to create listeners, not merely performers." And this, a splendid *Leitmotiv* for us all, "We ought to bring the best music to the people who are least able to pay for it."

POMP AND CIRCUMSTANCE, NO. 1

The famous *Pomp and Circumstance Marches* portray Elgar both as patriot and artist. From his boyhood he was always responsive to the excitement of patriotic feeling, and, as he developed musically, always a little ashamed of the poor quality of English military marches. He felt that in music, as in many other things, the practical and the artistic could and should be blended.

Choosing a motto from a poem, "The March of Glory," by Lord de Tabley:

> Like a proud music that draws men to die
> Madly upon the spears in martial ecstasy,
> A measure that sets heaven in all their veins
> And iron in their hands.

he proceeded to write that "proud music."

The most familiar of the *Pomp and Circumstance Marches* is the Number 1, in D. After a short and rousing introduction, the strings in unison give out the stirring tune:[1]

The introduction is used again, and not too satisfactorily, as a connecting passage leading into the middle or Trio section with its beautiful air:

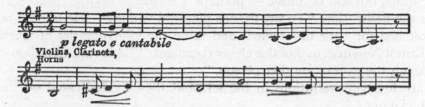

A year after the march appeared, this air passed into the *Coronation Ode* as "Land of Hope and Glory," with the majestic refrain:

> Land of Hope and Glory, Mother of the Free,
> How shall we extol thee who are born of thee?
> Wider still and wider shall thy bounds be set;
> God, who made thee mighty, make thee mightier yet![2]

Pomp and Circumstance is an expression of both the militant and the devotional spirit which, combined, make the perfect patriotism. Grieg has caught the same two emotions in his beautiful March of Allegiance, from *Sigurd Jorsalfar*. As studies in nationalism, these two marches are very interesting — both expressing the same thing, but the one so typically English, the other so unmistakably Scandinavian!

Pomp and Circumstance is a parade march, you feel the prancing, the flying pennants, the color of uniforms, and, in the trio, the love of country that surges up in the hearts of the crowd as the soldiers and the flag pass by. Yet it is, as it was meant to be, a

---

[1] Excerpts reprinted by permission of the copyright owner, Boosey & Co., Ltd.
[2] Copyrighted, Boosey & Hawkes, Inc., New York. Reprinted by permission.

practical military march. Elgar had a definite military instinct. Tall, erect, with his rather imperial dignity of bearing, his friends used to say that he looked more like a cavalry officer than a composer. Surely he must also have felt like one when he wrote this brilliant, commanding music!

When King Edward VII first heard *Pomp and Circumstance*, he exclaimed, "That tune will go round the world!" And so it has, in times of peace and times of war, a messenger of the hope and glory of England.

Enigma Variations

With the first performance of the *Enigma Variations* in the summer of 1899, Edward Elgar ceased to be merely a writer of good English music and became a composer of world music. This set of variations was his first important work for orchestra and, in many opinions, his best. When questioned as to the meaning of the word *enigma* in the title, the composer would only say that "another and larger theme," which is never heard, "goes with" the real theme and with each variation of it. But the enigma remains an enigma! Many have been the theories about it, one of them being that the enigmatic theme was some well-known tune, such as "Auld Lang Syne" which, if we only "knew which," might be played in counterpoint along with Elgar's melodies. But knowing Elgar's sly and twinkling wit and how he enjoyed tweaking the tail of curiosity about the meaning of music, this "larger theme" might just as likely have been some idea quite outside of music — perhaps the theme of friendship. For Elgar's score bears the dedication, "To my friends pictured within." He himself tells us that "I have sketched for their amusement and mine the idiosyncrasies of fourteen of my friends." Ernest Newman makes this clever comment: "Each variation shows the theme as seen through the eyes of another person."

There are fourteen variations in the set, and they are indicated on the score by initials or nicknames.

1.	C.A.E.	*Andante*	8.	W.N.	*Allegretto*
2.	H.D.S.P.	*Allegro*	9.	Nimrod	*Moderato*
3.	R.B.T.	*Allegretto*	10.	Dorabella	*Allegretto*
4.	W.M.B.	*Allegro di molto*	11.	G.R.S.	*Allegro di molto*
5.	R.P.A.	*Moderato*	12.	B.C.N.	*Andante*
6.	Ysobel	*Andantino*	13.	*** Romanza	*Moderato*
7.	Troyte	*Presto*	14.	E.D.U.	*Allegro*

There is no mystery as to the identity of the people, and a recent biographer of Elgar has listed them all, from "C.A.E.," Lady Elgar, to whom the composer was married in the year the *Variations* appeared, to the final "E.D.U.," Elgar himself under a nickname and expressing a John Bull determination at a time when, he says, "friends were dubious and generally discouraging" about his musical future. But, as the composer states, the friends pictured in this music were a "personal matter and need not have been mentioned publicly." The formal *tempo* headings given to the variations promise what the music itself fulfills, namely, enjoyment of musical beauty, which is every great composer's purpose, regardless of poetic inspiration or any other of the enigmas which become the pastime of commentators.

The work begins, without introduction, with a quiet statement of the theme: [1]

This theme, a simple tune, rather serious, reserved but promising, might indeed be a character sketch of the composer. It is typically Elgarian, from what Mason calls "the serrated profile of the melody" to the steady moving bass.

The variations are as interesting as they are different. Elgar shows himself master of the formal and often deadly musical device — a number of variants of a single theme. Not since the Brahms Variations on a Theme by Haydn has there been such rich contrast in musical detail — rhythms, dynamics, key relationships, and instrumentation — as well as in moods.

Number 10, "Dorabella," is a variation only by courtesy, for it has little trace of the original theme. Elgar has cleverly used it as a moment of relaxation of the listener's attention. Muted strings and *staccato* woodwinds in a delicate, fluttering theme:

suggest a charming miniature of "Dora."

Number 13, with its quotation from Mendelssohn's *Calm Sea and Prosperous Voyage*, was inspired by a friend who was then crossing the ocean. It is a lovely sea picture with a feeling of the roll and throb of waves and, at the end, a wonderful sense of the ship vanishing over the horizon.

Elgar is at his best in Variation 9, "Nimrod," who being translated into German becomes the composer's dear friend and musical adviser, Jaeger. Elgar tells us that this variation "is a record of a long summer evening talk when my friend grew nobly eloquent (as only he could) on the grandeur of Beethoven and especially of his slow movements." There is a touch of grandeur and "noble eloquence" in this short, slow movement of Elgar's, and a sincerely affectionate tribute to a friend.

The delightful fancy and warm beauty of the *Enigma Variations*, their honest workmanship, and glowing orchestral color make them not only a monument to Elgar's genius but also a lasting joy to listeners.

[1] Excerpts reprinted by permission of Novello & Co., London; Agents for the U. S. A., The H. W. Gray Company, Inc., New York, New York.

RALPH VAUGHAN WILLIAMS

Down Ampney, Gloucestershire — 1872

Most English of them all is Ralph Vaughan Williams, born in a Gloucestershire rectory and brought up to the best of everything in English tradition. His father, a clergyman of independent fortune, wisely decided to give the boy a liberal education unshadowed by a sense of haste or the necessity of preparing for earning a living. After his early schooldays, young Vaughan Williams went to Charterhouse, to the Royal College of Music, and to Trinity College, Cambridge. Then he went to Germany, where he studied with Max Bruch and made a pilgrimage to Bayreuth to hear Wagner's music. Returning to England he continued his studies at Cambridge, where, in 1901, he received his doctorate in music.

It was during this time of graduate work that he became interested, then immersed, in the study of English folk music. He joined the Folk-Song Society, and would wander through the English countryside using all his tact and charm to get the old villagers to sing for him the all-but-forgotten songs of their locality. For Vaughan Williams folk music became a living reality, a thing having life in the present, not merely an antiquarian fad or an artificial revival. As he set down on paper these treasured folk-song finds, he could not resist a touch of reconstruction here and there or a modern harmonization. He gave many of these neglected songs a new lease on life, and the famous English Singers carried them out into the world.

As a student Vaughan Williams did not attract attention by his compositions, partly because he was a quiet fellow and slow in his development, and partly because the music which most appealed to him, and in which he later excelled, was not the type the other boys or the teachers considered worth while. It was natural that his keen interest in folk music should influence his original composition. At first he used folk tunes as themes, and even after he invented his own melodies, the folk song flavor was still there. As with Grieg and Sibelius, the music of his own country was so much a part of him, its spirit so sincerely his own, that even its idiom became his mother tongue. He could write just as "folksy" tunes as those of the early unknown singers.

But Vaughan Williams was a severe self-critic. He suffered the "divine discontent." Soon after the completion of his three *Norfolk Rhapsodies* and the enthusiastic reception of his *Toward an Unknown Region* at the Leeds Festival, 1907, he grew so dissatisfied with his technique that he went to Paris to study. For his teacher he chose, of all people, Maurice Ravel! They were an oddly assorted pair, the sensitive, clever, almost overrefined little Frenchman and the strong, slow, serious Englishman. They had little in common except that both were artists. Ravel gave to his pupil a surer, clearer sense of form and encouragement to go ahead with his own original ideas, even though the critics laughed! What Ravel learned no one knows, but he could scarcely have failed to sense the largeness and the calm of this man from Gloucestershire.

After eight months in Paris, Vaughan Williams came back convinced that he had allowed the folk songs to smother his own creative ability. He determined to use folk material more sparingly, and from this time on he did his best and most original work.

In 1914, although he was then forty-two years old, Vaughan Williams went to war and saw the thick of the fighting. On his return he extended his musical life by becoming conductor of the Bach Choir and also one of the faculty of the Royal College of Music. Reading the biographies and writings of twentieth-century composers, one is constantly meeting Vaughan Williams, the teacher — counselor might be the better word. This man whose wisdom was so firmly rooted in the past, who yet was so ready to welcome anything good in the present or hopeful for the future, this calm, friendly man was a tower of strength to young musicians trying to find their way through a fog of new and extreme musical ideas.

Purcell's remark about English music, "Being farther from the sun, we are of later Growth than our Neighbor Countries," seems also to be true of English composers. Remembering the youthful genius of Mozart, Schubert, Mendelssohn, and other musicians of the "Neighbor Countries," the Englishmen seem late in arriving — both Delius and Elgar were past forty. Vaughan Williams was forty-nine when his "Pastoral" Symphony, one of his most famous works, declared his independence and maturity as a composer. He had proceeded to his symphonies — four, up to date — by logical steps. Beginning with orchestral impressions, rhapsodies, and fantasies based on folk songs, he worked from the tranquil tone painting of the country toward a less suggestive type of music.

Vaughan Williams is unique in having aimed at composition from the very beginning of his studies — the piano and organ were merely useful tools. Unique, too, was the economic freedom which made it possible for him to grow mentally, spiritually, and musically in the contented, unhurried way that nature grows. He was always happily indifferent to things that did not interest him, such as the ridicule of critics or the details of dress. To him a hat is a head covering, nothing more, and why think twice of a coat buttoned wrong or trousers that bag if said garments are made of good, stout cloth and are decently clean!

His is the brooding mind which absorbs the quiet, patient life of the country or the rapidly shifting scenes of the city, making them a part of his own inner life. He is famous for the "local color" in his music, the suggestion of a popular song, a Salvation Army hymn, a street cry, or a bird call gone almost before it is recognized and always before it has cheapened the music. This same brooding, receptive mind allows him to relive the music of earlier times, not only the folk songs but also the music of the Middle Ages with its entire lack of individual emotionalism.

Vaughan Williams has been likened to Wordsworth — another English poet of nature and philosophy. But Vaughan Williams is warmer than Wordsworth, more rugged and more human, more like Thomas Hardy. His music involves the listener in no problems. Whatever its mood, whether austere or genial, it has the impersonal quality of storm or sunshine.

Greensleeves — Fantasia

The word *Fantasie* (German for imagination) from which we also have the musical terms *fantasy* — and *fantasia* — has nothing to do with our word *fantastic*, which suggests imagination run wild! A fantasia is a piece in which the composer has not held himself strictly to any musical form. Bach wrote fantasias for clavichord and organ. Mozart,

Beethoven, Schumann, Chopin — in fact, most of the composers — have used the term for music less formal than the dance types and sonatas.

Vaughan Williams wrote many fantasias, taking a theme from early English music or a folk song and letting his imagination play with it. Among the most beautiful of these is the *Greensleeves Fantasia.*

"Greensleeves" is one of the oldest, as well as most popular, of English ballads. Its very title suggests the days of chivalry when both a fair lady and her knight were distinguished by the color of a silken sleeve. The earliest record of "Greensleeves" is in 1580 when one Richard Jones was licensed to print "a new Northerne Dittye of the Ladye Greene Sleeves," but it was probably sung and danced long before that time. It must have been popular in the days of Queen Elizabeth, for Shakespeare mentions it in *The Merry Wives of Windsor:* "Let the sky rain potatoes; let it thunder to the tune of 'Greensleeves' "; and again, where one of the Wives complains of Falstaff's habit of saying one thing and doing another — of the two sides of his disposition she says, "They do no more . . . keep place together than the Hundredth Psalm to the tune of 'Greensleeves'!"

In Cromwell's time the old ballad tune was used by the Cavaliers for a political song. Today we know it as the lovely Christmas carol, "What Child Is This?" But originally, "Greensleeves" was a ballad which was also danced — a singing game:

After an introduction by flute and harp, the low strings play the old song through. Then, by way of contrast, comes another modal melody, probably another old English folk tune, or it might be one of the composer's own — so closely do they resemble the real thing. Again as at the beginning, the flute is heard in the downward — one might almost say backward — phrase, for it seems to carry us back through several musical centuries. And again comes the "Greensleeves" tune, beautiful in its own gracious rhythm and melody but even more so in the harmonies and instrumental colorings of Vaughan Williams's fantasia. His imagination has re-created the atmosphere and the background of this charming old song. One can almost hear the voices of long ago and see the dancers in their quaint costumes stepping their paces on an Elizabethan village green.

ERIC COATES

Hucknall — 1886

Eric Coates is a native of Nottinghamshire, England. In his youth he won a scholarship at the Royal Academy of Music which took him up to London, where he has spent most of his life. Young Coates studied the viola and made a name for himself as an artist in chamber music. In 1907 he made an African tour with the Hamburg String Quartet, and in 1912 became first viola player in the London Queen's Hall Orchestra. Today Eric Coates is best known as conductor of the Queen's Hall Promenade Concerts and as a composer.

He has written a number of delightful songs and pieces for instruments. His musical material is slight but always gracefully handled. The titles of his pieces — *A Countryside Suite for Orchestra, The Merrymakers Overture, Miniature Suite, Joyous Youth Suite, Summer Days, From Meadow to Mayfair, The Jester at the Wedding, London Suite* (and *London Again*), *The Selfish Giant, Cinderella, Wood Nymphs, The Three Bears*, etc. — and the music itself with its snatches of familiar tunes are pleasantly suggestive of those lighter moments which, fortunately, are just as much a part of life as the problems and philosophies expressed in the great works of Beethoven and Brahms.

LONDON SUITE

Covent Garden

In the three little pieces for orchestra called *London Suite*, the composer has sketched three characteristic scenes of his city. First, Covent Garden, which is often said to have more literary and human interest than any other spot in London. It was originally part of the grounds — perhaps of the gardens — of the ancient Convent of Westminster. But with the forfeiture of church property to the crown, this little plot, losing the *n* from its name, became *Covent* Garden, the historic fruit and vegetable market of old London. Two hundred years ago Covent Garden was a grand square, with the Bedford Coffee Tavern, the Piazzi Hotel frequented by Garrick, Sheridan, Goldsmith, and other famous theater folk from the near-by opera house, and with many fine old residences. There are also gentler memories of Old St. Paul's burial ground. But for most Englishmen, and for travelers, too, Covent Garden is a spot of gay color, heaps of brilliant fruits and vegetables, and millions of flowers. It is a place where town and country meet — London ladies, children happy in a marketing adventure, businesslike buyers for hotels and shops, country men and women behind the stalls, and the picturesque fruit and flower sellers, some of them crying their wares to century-old words and tunes.

In a lively pattern of the *tarantella*, but without its tarantula-bitten frenzy, Eric Coates has written his gay little *Covent Garden*. Quite appropriately, the piece is dominated by the old song, "Cherry Ripe." The words written by Robert Herrick (1591–1674) and the music by an eighteenth-century composer, Horn, are artists' versions of the old cries of London cherry sellers:

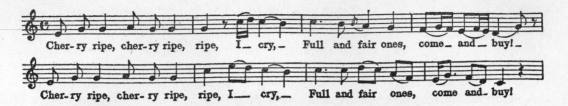

The opening motif of "Cherry Ripe" is heard in the first theme of *Covent Garden*. The second theme is one of those chameleon tunes which by constantly changing its key color brings back the old song in an interesting variety of tonalities and instruments. One could easily imagine several cherry sellers, calling here and there until their cry is lost in the market medley of *Covent Garden*.

Westminster

Westminster is the second scene of the *London Suite*. The composer has given it the suggestive subtitle, *Meditation*. And surely even the most indifferent tourist, wandering through the great Abbey, could scarcely fail to think, or wonder, about England's past of which it is such an eloquent reminder. Westminster is a place for meditations, both sacred and secular. It is the very heart of England's history.

The great church began as a little Saxon chapel built in the year 616 on part of the left bank of the Thames known as Thorney Island. After the Norman Conquest it became the chapel of the monks of Westminster, but since Tudor times it has been the royal chapel of the kings of England. It has survived the destruction of Cromwell's soldiers and, in our time, the Nazi bombings. In spite of the rather haphazard additions and remodelings of many centuries, it remains one of the purest examples of Gothic architecture in England.

What tales of vanished pomp and circumstance those ancient walls could tell — of royal weddings, christenings, funerals, and all the pageantry of state! Every English king since Harold, last of the Saxons, has been crowned at Westminster, and there most of them lie buried. There, too, lie England's great men of all times and classes, heroes, statesmen, poets, artists, and the Unknown Soldier in a tomb inscribed, "They buried him among the kings because he had done good toward God and toward His House."

To an accompaniment of bells the quiet theme of *Westminster* is given out. Its pensive downward line and unhurried wandering movement are well suited to meditation.

There is a short contrasting episode; then the original melody returns and goes singing on its way until it is interrupted by the sound of Big Ben chiming from the tower of the Houses of Parliament next door.

The hour has struck — the Present calls — and with parting chords for woodwinds and muted brass, a sweep of the harp, and a last high sound of strings the meditation ends.

Knightsbridge

Once upon a time two English knights were riding up to London town to receive a blessing from the Bishop of London. Alas, they began to quarrel, and by the time they had reached the bridge over the Westbourne they were fighting. They killed each other on the spot, which ever after was called the Knyghtsbrigge.

But all this was long ago. The great city of London, reaching out on all sides, has gathered in the little hamlet, and today Knightsbridge is part of the fashionable West End, skirting Hyde Park.

In 1933, when Eric Coates was writing the *London Suite*, Knightsbridge suggested a pleasant and prosperous scene — shoppers coming and going, "horsey" people on their way to the weekly auctions at Tattersall's famous racing stables, and after dark, Londoners in evening clothes, gay young officers and pretty girls, off to the theater, a dinner party, or dance. No wonder he called the piece *Knightsbridge — In Town Tonight!*

The piece is a march in quick time, with a "snappy" introduction and an arresting rhythm. An interlude of fanfares and flourishes precedes the quieter middle section. Then, abruptly, "right about," and we have it all over again with a very grandiose ending.

Knightsbridge is definitely a parade march, like the Schubert *Marche militaire*. There is little suggestion of the sterner martial music. In fact, only ballet soldiers could step to it and be fit for service at the end! But it is a refreshing little piece and must have sounded very well indeed at the Promenade Concerts for which it was written and conducted by the composer.

CHAPTER X

Americana

Looking backward over more than three centuries, one can distinguish three fairly definite periods in American musical life. The first, beginning with the Plymouth settlement, extends through the days of New England Psalmody and the varied musical activities of the Colonies to the opening of the nineteenth century. Those were the days of borrowed tunes brought from old homelands to comfort and refresh people struggling for "life, liberty, and the pursuit of happiness" in a wild new world.

In the first half of the new century (1800–1860) American freedom and independence began to show itself in music. Concerts and operas and ambitious musical societies became important in the American scene, even in the West. Music found its way into the schools. Lowell Mason and his contemporaries gave us hymn tunes of our own. American life was reflected in popular ballads, and the songs of Stephen Foster and native humor sparkled in the early minstrel shows. But the shadow of an older culture was still heavy. The revolutions in Central Europe brought a musical invasion from Germany to our shores, and this brief middle period ended with foreigners in the foreground and Americans self-conscious and apologetic for their homespun tunes compared with the silks and velvets imported from abroad.

The third period begins about 1860 and continues to our own times. During these years America has been finding her own voice and making her own music. In the last half of the nineteenth century the whole musical world seemed to be under the spell of German Romanticism. American musicians went abroad — mostly to Germany — to study with the great teachers. Their own country could then give them neither music education nor listening opportunities adequate for a rich musical experience. The music of our best American composers of that time, Chadwick, Foote, Parker, and the rest of the "New England Group," of Nevin, MacDowell, the later Griffes, and many others shows foreign labels. But it is no sign of mediocrity or un-Americanism to gratefully acknowledge the European influence in our music. After all, our Declaration of Independence did not cut us loose from the roots of Old World culture and fine craftsmanship. Too much of the radical talk about scrapping musical traditions and conventions has been but an excuse for dodging the hard work and years of apprenticeship which have made European music great. The true artist is always sensitive to outside influence. His own originality protects him. How far would Bach have gone had he been afraid to study the music of other men? How far would Beethoven have gone had he ignored Haydn and Mozart? How far does anyone get who thinks that wisdom began on the day that he was born? The American composer, to the point of his own detour, need not fear the great artists who have blazed the trail he must follow. And as for our boasted independence, if such a thing were possible in art, it would leave us all but naked or clad in what Carl Sandburg whimsically calls the "rag bag of strips, stripes, and streaks of color" of our few folk tunes.

Up to the beginning of the twentieth century there had been little national feeling in American music. Then, with a suddenly awakening national consciousness, came the idea that since Norway, Russia, and Spain had achieved nationalism in music by using their folk tunes, all we had to do was to turn to the Negro and Indian melodies, and, presto, American music! Dvořák had led the way with his beautiful symphony, "From the New World," which popular enthusiasm failed to recognize as a Bohemian impression of America, stunningly expressed with synthetic Indian and Negro themes. Oddly enough, the appropriation of folk themes by American composers was unconvincing except in the few instances where the folk tunes had been part of the composer's childhood.

The subject of nationalism in music always brings up discussion of whether it is the idiom — the picturesque folk costume — or the spirit of the man inside it that best represents a nation's art. We know that much fine music has come from European folk tunes and folklore put to artistic use. America, too, has, if not a true folk music, at least what serves the purpose of good local color. American composers do well to make the most of Indian and Negro themes, of mountain melodies and songs of the Western plains. But we believe that American music is too large-hearted for the narrow nationalism of folk idiom, too broad-browed for the war bonnet, the bandanna head 'kerchief, or the ten-gallon hat.

In the midst of the enthusiasm for folk music came jazz, which has been cleverly described as "good for the feet but poor for the head." After jazz came "swing," "jive," and "what have you!" It was all very intriguing, and some of our most accomplished musicians began experimenting with it. Once more arose the hope that here, at last, was the real American music. Here at least was a smart formula, if not an art form! Whether we blush to admit it or not, this type of popular tune has, so far, been America's unique contribution to twentieth-century music. Unquestionably, the result of a number of complex and powerful emotional ingredients thrown together in this great international melting pot, stirred with American energy and flavored with American freedom, has created something new in music. It is often crude, needlessly ugly, and blighted by publicity, but it is alive and revealing in its expression of the spirit of the times.

From "Music in History," by McKinney and Anderson, comes this significant comment:

> One reason why up to this time America has remained so sterile in musical creation is that those who have been born or reared in one of her traditions seem to have remained so largely ignorant of the others. We have shown that whatever real vitality American music has possessed has been in the line of the folk and popular idioms; and anyone familiar with the situation will admit that there is more vitality to sustain life, more characteristic personality, more distinct individuality of content in one of Stephen Foster's or Sousa's or Gershwin's works than in most of the symphonies so far composed in the country. There is no question that the works of all these men are simple and unpretentious; but they do say something that has not been said in just that way before.

This is a good deal more than can be said of the works of most of their ostentatious compatriots.

The same book, "Music in History," quotes this newspaper criticism of a recent American composition, a criticism which applies only too well to many contemporary works:

> Mr. X's concerto, which enjoyed admirable interpretation by the orchestra, is a work of uneven worth. It reveals certain originalities of idiom and rhythmic pattern, set down by a musician thoroughly cognizant of the orchestral means at his command. The influence of certain contemporary modes is apparent, even persistent. The first and last movements begin promisingly, but inspiration lags, and platitude and contrivance lead to a disappointing end. The slow movement has a decided harmonic strength and an almost Brahmsian weight and solidity, but little of tenderness and tranquillity. At times, it seemed as though Mr. X had tried frantically to be "different."
>
> — J. S., *New York Herald Tribune*

Could it be that the American composer has gone too far in his search for novelty, in his substitution of clever contrivance for inspiration? Could it be that he needs to turn back to Gluck's "Beauty in simplicity" and bring down from his attic those quaint old-fashioned emotions, "tenderness and tranquillity"?

What is American music? There is yet no satisfactory answer to this vexed question, there may never be one, and perhaps it will be just as well. But many of us believe that if and when an "American School" does emerge, it will not be characterized by folk songs, by Tin Pan Alley tunes, or yet by an exclusive adherence to academic traditions, but by a blending of all three of these phases of American musical life. The true American composer will think less of the way he says it and more of what he has to say. His ambition will be to achieve the distinction of individuality in the expression of musical beauty.

Edward MacDowell, the first great American composer, once said, "Before a people can find a musical writer to echo its genius it must first possess men who truly represent it — that is to say, men who, being part of the people, love the country for itself; men who put into their music what the nation has put into its life. . . . What we must arrive at is the youthful, optimistic vitality and the undaunted tenacity of spirit that characterizes the American man. That is what I hope to see echoed in American music."

All of us hope to see it — indeed we are already seeing it. We no longer need to apologize for American music. Nor do we need to keep repeating the platitude that America has produced no Beethoven — neither has Europe since that winter day in 1770! America is definitely music-minded. Her people have learned in the bitter school of two World Wars that the material side of life is not all-important. Social scientists have discovered that the arts offer one of the best solutions to the problem of machine-made leisure. Even "big business" agrees that the practical, which absorbed men's attention in pioneer days, must be tempered with the imaginative if our nation is to survive. Only as Americans become artists in everyday living, enjoying and expressing the beauty about them, can the American spirit be fitly set to music.

The list of our music makers is impressive. Claire Reis in her "Composers in America" names nearly two hundred men worthy of the title. John Tasker Howard presents an equally proud array in his two valuable volumes, "Our American Music" and "Our Contemporary Composers." It is obviously neither easy nor satisfactory to select the few Americans and their works which may be included in one brief chapter. However, since the pattern of this listener's book has been to choose music which may be enjoyed whenever and wherever one wants it through the obliging phonograph, the responsibility for inclusions and exclusions must be laid at the door of the recording companies, who have their own reasons for the disks they make. We earnestly hope that these same gentlemen who have done so much for consumer music in the past will realize the importance of their service to the American composer and to the future of American music, which, in the end, lies with the listening public. None of us should forget that "music exists only as it is heard."

EDWARD MacDOWELL

New York — 1861
New York — 1908

1861, one of the darkest years in the history of the United States, shines brightly in the history of music as the birth year of America's first internationally recognized composer, Edward MacDowell. With his birthright of mysticism, inherited from Celtic and Quaker ancestors, and his own wonderful gift of music, this creator of beauty seems to have been sent as compensation to an ugly, war-torn land. And although the pet tune of his baby days is said to have been, "Tramp, tramp, tramp, the boys are marching," to which his little feet stepped proudly, none of the war spirit lingered with him. Never could Edward MacDowell think of killing and destroying as either heroism or sport.

Little Edward MacDowell spent a happy childhood in the pleasant old house in Clinton Street. New York in the sixties was not today's roaring, traffic-mad monster, ready to eat up venturesome small boys. There were still peaceful buggy rides up Fifth Avenue and family picnics in Central Park. A father, out for a Sunday afternoon walk with his two little sons, would stroll over to the river or down to the harbor to watch the big boats come and go. For the MacDowell children there were also excursions up to Grandfather's farm where the boys could explore the real woods — woods where Indians had once lived and left strange musical names for mountains and rivers. Edward loved these days out of doors, and stated what was to be one of his principal life motives when, after a visit at Grandfather's, he protested, "I want to stay where the green fields and the trees are and where the birds sing."

Once back in town, however, he found much to interest him. There were his precious books — fairy tales, poems, legends of knights and heroes, books about plants and animals, books of travel and adventure, of which he never tired. He loved pictures equally as well. Because he was a born creator, whatever he loved, he tried to make — stories, verses, pictures, tunes. He made them all as a matter of course and with remarkable cleverness.

Soon after his eighth birthday, the boy began to have piano lessons with a Colombian musician, a Mr. Buitrago, who was a friend of the family. Edward proved such an unusual pupil that after several years this friend advised sending him to a professional teacher. It was at this time that another famous South American, the Venezuelan Teresa Carreño, also became interested in the boy and gave him occasional lessons and much encouragement.

But while he lived in a world of books and music, Edward MacDowell was anything but a sissy. He was a normal, often naughty boy. He loved games, and he was the best dancer in the crowd. His keen eye, alert mind, and steady hand made him good at all sorts of sports, and he is even said to have won the prize at a shooting match. Someone who knew him well said, "He loved a fast and furious boxing match. The call of his soul won him for music and poetry. Otherwise he might have been a sea captain, a soldier, or an explorer in faraway countries, for he had the physique and he had the big manly spirit."

In his fifteenth year it was decided that he should go abroad to study, there being at that time no great opportunity for serious music study in America. So in the spring of 1876, Edward and his mother left for Paris, where he was entered at the Conservatoire. Another brilliant youngster, the fourteen-year-old Claude Debussy, was also there that year, already puzzling his teachers with his strange ideas. Edward MacDowell passed the entrance examinations in piano and theory and went enthusiastically to work. He soon found, however, that his limited knowledge of French made it hard for him to understand the lectures, and he added language lessons to his program. It was during a monotonous French lesson that Edward, yielding to an old habit of illustrating his books, drew a portrait of the teacher, a man with an extravagant nose. Much to the young artist's confusion, he was caught and asked to exhibit his drawing. The teacher, instead of raging at the unmistakable likeness, was struck by its cleverness and showed it to one of the instructors at the École des Beaux-Arts. The painter was even more impressed, and went to Mrs. MacDowell with the proposal that Edward be given to him for a period of three years, during which he would not only give the boy free instruction in drawing and painting, but also support him as well. It was a flattering and tempting offer, but after talking it all over, the mother wisely left the decision to the boy himself. No one will ever know what the art of painting lost by that decision, but music certainly gained when Edward made up his mind to stick to his piano.

But young MacDowell was not altogether happy at the Conservatoire. Much of the teaching there seemed to him to be rather in a rut. In the midst of his doubt and dissatisfaction, he happened to hear Nikolai Rubinstein play Tchaikovsky's B-Flat Minor Concerto for piano. It was a revelation. "I can never learn to play like that if I stay here," said the boy to his mother as they left the concert hall. Again they were plunged into a whirl of indecision. They considered many teachers and many cities, even Rubinstein's remote Moscow. Finally they chose Stuttgart, and went there only to find the rut of routine instruction even deeper than in Paris. It was in Frankfort that MacDowell at last found the free, inspirational teaching he wanted, and there his mother left him. He had piano lessons with Heymann, who, as he said, "dared to play the classics as if they had been written by men with blood in their veins," and he had composition with Raff.

Joachim Raff played a most important part in the direction of MacDowell's career. From MacDowell's boyhood, the family, the friends, and Edward himself had thought only of his becoming a concert pianist. His constant "scribbling" had been but a pastime for which he even felt guilty, since it was often done when he might have been practicing. Raff, however, saw real promise in this "scribbling." There were plenty of people who could play the piano, but so few who could write for it, thought Raff, and he determined to turn this young man's attention toward composition. MacDowell tells an amusing story of the composition of his first piano concerto. One day Raff paid his pupil a surprise call, and as he was leaving, asked what Edward had been writing. MacDowell, always a hopelessly shy fellow, had been so upset by his master's visit that he stammered something about working at a concerto. "Good," said Raff, "bring it to me next Sunday," and went away leaving consternation in his wake. MacDowell did have some ideas which he had thought of trying to work up into a concerto, but he certainly had nothing in the way of a finished product ready to present to the critical Raff on the next Sunday and before the group of students which the master usually entertained at that time! Cursing himself for his idiotic reply, he dashed at the promised concerto, but when the fatal Sunday came, only the first movement was finished. He wrote Raff a note making some flimsy excuse and putting off his visit until the following Sunday. By good luck something happened then to give him two more days of grace, by which time the concerto was ready. It seems to have turned out surprisingly well for so hasty a concoction. Raff was pleased, and later suggested that MacDowell take it to Liszt in Weimar. Liszt, with his characteristic generosity to young artists, received MacDowell kindly and praised his work. Shortly afterward he invited MacDowell to play his first *Modern Suite* for piano, which is dedicated to Liszt, at the meeting of the *Allgemeiner deutscher Musikverein*. With such encouragement and such remarks as Raff's, "Your music will be played when mine is forgotten," it is not surprising that Edward MacDowell began to think of himself as a composer.

During the Frankfort years, MacDowell began his teaching. It was dull business with such pupils as the fat and sleepy little counts and countesses at Castle Erbach-Fürstenau. But any boredom or weariness, even the long journey over to Darmstadt where he had a class, was more than made up to him by one pupil, young Marian Nevins, an American girl. In the early summer of 1884, MacDowell, after eight years' absence from his own country, followed Marian Nevins back to America and married her. A few days later the two again started off for Germany.

Returning to Frankfort, MacDowell found his pupils scattered, but that was of scant importance, since he had decided to devote himself to composition. The next four years might be called the prelude to a rare companionship. It was a season of deep contentment; long happy hours of work, walks in the beautiful woods from which comes the mood of his *From a German Forest*, coffee and *Kuchen* at little wayside inns, and quiet evenings of reading aloud. MacDowell's love of books had grown with the years, and now English and German poetry, medieval romance, memoirs, Victor

Hugo, Mark Twain, and a host of others had joined the old loved fairly tales and legends of his youth. It was at this time that the MacDowells found the tiny house in the edge of a wood near Wiesbaden. It was not a proper house at all, just an elaborate summer house, but nothing would do but that they must buy it and move in!

Songs, piano pieces, tone poems for orchestra flowed from MacDowell's pen and found places on both European and American concert programs. It was all very gratifying but not very remunerative, and since the butcher, the baker, the candlestick maker must be reckoned with, even by those who live in a fairy-tale house in the woods, the young artists had to consider other plans. Friends in America were already urging them to return and take part in the musical development of their own country. It seemed good counsel, and in the autumn of 1888 the MacDowells said a reluctant good-by to Germany and sailed for home.

Boston was the city of their choice, and there began what was to prove the most fruitful period of MacDowell's career. He was an immediate success as a concert pianist. American audiences were enthusiastic over the way he played his own and other men's music. In 1889 he was honored by an invitation to play his Second Piano Concerto on an American program at the Paris Exposition. Meanwhile, he was turning out a steady stream of compositions and teaching a large group of private pupils. There was no longer any question of the name and fame of Edward MacDowell, composer, pianist, and teacher.

Unfortunately his fame attracted Columbia University, then in search of a head for its newly endowed department of music. In the spring of 1896, this precious professorship was offered to MacDowell as "the greatest musical genius America has produced," and, after much hesitation on his part, accepted. The $100,000 which established Columbia's music department had been given with the express purpose of "elevating the standards of musical instruction in America." Edward MacDowell took this purpose literally and seriously, as is shown in his statement of his aims: "First, to teach music scientifically and technically, with a view to training musicians who shall be competent to teach and to compose. Second, to treat music historically and aesthetically as an element of liberal culture." Five courses were offered:

    I. A general course in the history and aesthetics of music.
   II. A course in the development of musical forms and types.
  III. A course in general theory and harmony.
  IV. A course in counterpoint, analysis, and the beginning of composition.
   V. Free composition, instrumentation, and symphonic form.

For two years he carried these five courses unaided, with all the drudgery of correcting daily exercise and examination books, a task which his conscience and thoroughness would never let him slight. And, following the delightful European custom of musical companionship, he held open house on Sunday mornings for students who wanted to bring their special problems and compositions to discuss with him. MacDowell made teaching an art. He brought his students the inspiration as well as the facts of music. Many of his classes and lectures were really delightful informal concerts. Even the examinations, which were oral and private, became helpful talks between teacher and student, so greatly did MacDowell value the personal and human element in education. No student fortunate enough to have had contact with this great teacher ever forgot the experience.

At the end of eight years, into which he had crammed the brain stuff and the energy of eighteen, MacDowell decided that his results at the university did not warrant the sacrifice of his health and all his other work, and gave up the Columbia professorship. His resignation was accepted ungraciously and misrepresented unpardonably.

In the same year in which he had gone to Columbia, MacDowell had bought an old farm in Peterboro, New Hampshire. Here he had spent his summers and here, in a little log cabin in the woods, he had written his finest and most mature music. Had he only gone to his beloved "Hillside" after those heavy years at Columbia and lived the calendar 'round in the quiet of the woods and mountains, the MacDowell tragedy might have been averted. Instead, he continued to teach his piano classes and to work away at his composition with the same unsparing energy. But he had spent himself too prodigally. A strange nervous exhaustion overcame him, and, in spite of all that love and science could do, Edward MacDowell, that "handsome American" with the scholar's brain and the poet's heart, gradually found the tragic way back to childhood. The picture of him sitting day after day by the window, turning the pages of a book of fairy tales, his brave blue eyes vacant but still smiling, is almost unbearably pathetic.

When the end mercifully came in January, 1908, they took him up to Peterboro, and his friends and neighbors carried him through the snow to an open hilltop and left him there where he had always loved to be. On a bronze tablet marking his grave are these lines which he had written as a motto for *From a Log Cabin*, his last music:

> A house of dreams untold,
> It looks out over the whispering treetops
> And faces the setting sun.

lovely lines for the ending of a biographical sketch. But the story of Edward Mac-Dowell does not end with that grave on a New Hampshire hilltop. It goes bravely on in the living memorial which Marian MacDowell, his wife and perfect comrade, built in his woods at Peterboro. Other little cabins have sprung up, as if from precious seed, around that "house of dreams untold" — shelters for the creative spirit which Edward MacDowell embodied so worthily — so tragically. Here in the leafy quiet where the gentle presence of a great man seems to linger and inspire, other American artists may dream their dreams and, perhaps, work them out.

THE ARTIST

From Lawrence Gilman's study of Edward MacDowell comes this quotation — Philip Hale's estimation of MacDowell the artist: "No doubt, as a composer, he has studied and mastered form and knows its value; but he prefers suggestions and hints and dream pictures and sleep-chasings to all attempts to be original in an approved and conventional fashion. . . . His compositions are interesting, and more than that: they are extremely characteristic in harmonic coloring. Their size has nothing to do with their merit."

The last sentence seems particularly worthy of consideration in an age obsessed by size. MacDowell chose to write short pieces largely because the smaller musical forms best fitted his vivid, passing impressions. His little sketches which unfailingly give us a nature mood or a picturesque personality are far more convincing and unforgettable than most of the musical murals. Indeed they are remembered often to the exclusion of his larger works, the concertos and sonatas. Who of us, hearing MacDowell's name, does not think first of *To a Water Lily*, *Starlight*, *To a Wild Rose*, and *Of Br'er Rabbit?*

But while he worked best in short forms, MacDowell was no miniaturist. His material was grand enough for any long symphony, and the very fact that in the little space of *To the Sea*, *In Mid-Ocean*, *From a Wandering Iceberg* he could condense the majesty, the sinister beauty, and the power of the sea is but further proof of his artistry.

MacDowell was truly a tone poet in that his music is always the expression of some poetic idea. He was too keenly aware of the world of nature, too sensitive to the currents of human life, too imaginative, to be content with abstract beauty. With a world so full of a number of things seeking expression through tone, he could not be satisfied with mere conventional design in music. In his mind, as he wrote, there was always a definite picture. Usually he suggests the picture or idea in the title or in some fragment of verse inscribed at the beginning of the piece. But he never binds his music with a rigid program. Even in a work like *Lancelot and Elaine*, which deals with a definite sequence of events, he allows leeway for individual interpretation. "I would never have insisted," he wrote, "that this symphonic poem need mean Lancelot and Elaine to everyone. It did to me, however, and in the hope that my artistic enjoyment might be shared by others, I added the title to my music."

Next to his poetic imagination, MacDowell's greatest gift was that of melody, fresh, frank melody, instantly appealing yet never commonplace. The songs, which make up a third of all his work, are an almost perfect fusion of verse and music. Like the piano pieces, they are brief in length but broad in scope and deep in their intensity of feeling. "The Sea," a song covering but two octavo pages, holds more of tragedy than any long Wagnerian aria, perhaps because it is all so simple. One feels the pain of parting as the white-winged ship sails away, and one shares the desolation of that hopeless waiting. It is grief distilled into a single shining poison drop. And no one, not even Brahms, has so perfectly caught and held the haunting beauty of the forest, beauty that, like the song of a thrush, is lilting yet wistful. MacDowell was one of the few great song writers.

Words fail when one attempts to characterize MacDowell's style. There is nothing strikingly novel about it, no little tagging tricks of rhythm or harmony, no idiosyncrasies. Yet it is as unmistakable, if as undescribable, as the fragrance of the deep woods. Perhaps its most distinguishing feature is this very elusiveness. And perhaps it would not be extravagant to call it the reflection of MacDowell's personality. His music, sincere, unpretentious, at times shy or even tragically sad, and again twinkling with whimsical humor, mirrors a great man and a great artist.

SUITE NO. II — INDIAN

The *Indian Suite*, MacDowell's second suite for full orchestra, is one of the finest and most mature of his works. It was first performed by the Boston Symphony Orchestra, to which it is dedicated. A famous critic, writing of that first performance, says: "Here are no echoes of Raff or Wagner or Brahms, men that have each influenced mightily the musical thought of today. Here is the voice of one composer, a virile, tender voice that does not stammer, does not break, does not wax hysterical, the voice of a composer who not only must pour out that which has accumulated within, but who knows all the resources of musical oratory — in a word, the voice of MacDowell."

In a note prefacing the score, MacDowell says that he has derived most of the themes used in this suite from the tribal melodies of the North American Indians, a people who had fascinated him from his boyhood and whose life, legends, and music he had carefully studied. It is not, however, these borrowed themes, cleverly interwoven with subsidiary themes invented to go with them, that give the suite its charm and power, but the picture of Indian life which the music brings before us. MacDowell, with his uncanny gift of sight into the past, has projected the life of our primeval forests as on a lantern screen, and made those first Americans, fighting, mourning, loving, laughing, take shape before our very eyes.

The music is strong and unadorned as befits the saga of elemental men, but through it all runs a throbbing note of sadness, a lament for a noble, vanquished race. In the same preface in which he gives the origin of his themes, the composer, with amusing reluctance to commit his music to a definite program, says: "If separate titles for the different movements are desired, they should be arranged as follows:

I. *Legend*	III. *In War-Time*
II. *Love Song*	IV. *Dirge*
V. *Village Festival*	

Legend

Legend, a movement "with much dignity and character," gives the emotional keynote to the suite. Thomas Bailey Aldrich's poem "Miantowona," telling the old tale of the Indian maiden who, grieving for her lost lover, threw herself in the lake and was changed into the pond lily, is said to have suggested to MacDowell the idea of creating something like it in music. However, the composer makes no attempt to tell any particular story but merely to evoke the half-solemn wonder which artists, primitive peoples, and children feel for the heroes and happenings of long ago. So successfully has MacDowell caught the legend feeling that he might have prefaced his music with the first lines of "Miantowona":

> Let us revere them —
> These wildwood legends,
> Born of the camp-fire.
> Let them be handed
> Down to our children —
> Richest of heirlooms.
> No land may claim them:
> They are ours only,
> Like our grand rivers,
> Like our vast prairies,
> Like our dead heroes.

The main theme of *Legend* is said to be an old harvest song of the Iroquois. It is one of the call-and-answer themes so characteristic of Indian music. Without introduction the horns sound the call:[1]

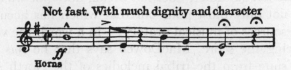

After an expectant pause comes the answer:

soft and distant, a century or more away!

The whole movement is but a play on this theme. It takes on many moods, suggesting the various happenings in the story. We hear it sounding briskly:

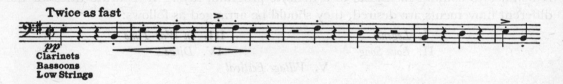

austerely:

and with many little variants of rhythm, melody, and harmony.

Near the end a new theme, a songlike theme in brighter major, appears:

But it soon lapses into the elegiac mood of the legend, and the movement closes with the call and the answer:

thundered from the trumpets, supported by full orchestra.

Love Song

Love Song, the second movement of the suite, begins with a love call of the Iowa Indians, scored, as it should be, for the flute, which among the Indians was the lover's instrument:

Violins answer in a deceptively simple three-measure phrase which, by its fresh harmonic tint and slightly altered figuration, introduces a second personality:

A second theme is given out by flutes and clarinets in imitation:

It has the same tender mood as the first theme, but in contrast to the sharp, clear call, this theme might be a whispered conversation between the lovers. It is followed by a little episode which is one of the loveliest things in the whole suite, a touch of pure MacDowell. Here the essence of the *Love Song* seems to have been gathered into a few precious measures.   Flutes, soft but insistent, whistle the call, stripped now to its original wild-bird simplicity, while oboes remind us of that whispered second theme:

Then the strings, like sympathetic, unseen watchers, murmur to themselves the age-old, "Bless you, my children!"

And now the familiar themes are heard again with little passionate outbursts of feeling.   The call comes once more, and then with a yielding two-note phrase:

the *Love Song* reaches a happy ending.

In War-Time

A war tune of the Iroquois in all its savage nakedness opens this movement:

It is followed by another stark tribal melody, one which Cadman also uses as the theme of his song, "The White Dawn Is Stealing":

Like a waiting council, the orchestra, until now silent, receives these two lone messengers and dismisses them with chords, muted but ominously final.   Then, with an upward rushing scale passage, the strings take up the war song and the other instruments join in.   Steadily it grows, working itself up to a fury which seems, for a moment, to exhaust it. Gradually the music sinks to a mere series of thudding accents, broken by lengthening periods of silence. It is almost as if the warriors had galloped away.

Then comes a mournful cry:

the same cry which is later heard in the *Dirge*, and with it the whole atmosphere changes. Ghostly drums begin to throb with that same little accented figure with which the warriors had disappeared:

A solo clarinet sings the war song. The braves now seem to be returning; the music grows in volume. Wilder and wilder it surges and screams, faster and faster the hideous painted figures whirl in the frenzy of the war dance, and then, with a series of sharp repeated chords and a pair of sixteenth notes like a savage snarl, *In War-Time* ends.

Dirge

A Kiowa woman's song of mourning for her lost son becomes the *Dirge* of the *Indian Suite*. Accompanied by a monotonously repeated G in the flutes and by two muted horns, one on the stage, the other behind the scenes, the muted violins wail the desolate little tune:

As the music progresses there are moments when a slightly fuller harmony, an upward line, or a more vigorous rhythm seems to promise a change. But it never comes. The single simple theme of mourning dominates the short movement.

Hopeless as it is, there is a quiet dignity and restraint in this grief, and in this music. It ends with a sigh from the trumpet:

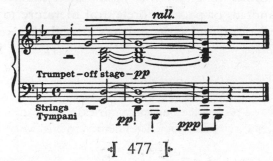

Suggestively it comes from offstage.   Not even sympathy intrudes.   This is one alone with sorrow.

Village Festival

The *Village Festival* is a medley of lively tunes, beginning with a little hopping dance:

which soon gives place to another:

In the increasing noise and activity there is a suggestion of festivity.

A slightly quieter, broader theme is heard:

but beneath it runs the lively rhythm which finally leads back to the original mood and *tempo* in a bassoon and clarinet dance theme:

The several themes are so closely related and so varied, after the extempore fashion of savages, that their outlines mingle even as do the merrymakers at the festival.   One might turn through hundreds of pages of orchestral literature to find music as vividly imaginative, as truly American, and as deserving of an orchestra's skill and a conductor's insight as this *Indian Suite*.

> . . . ours only,
> Like our grand rivers,
> Like our vast prairies,
> Like our dead heroes.

GEORGE W. CHADWICK

Lowell, Massachusetts — 1854
Boston, Massachusetts — 1931

Outstanding in the "New England Group" of American musicians is George White-field Chadwick.   Born in Lowell, Massachusetts, in 1854, he grew up in the neighboring town of Lawrence, son of a typical better-class musical amateur, and for many years leader of a singing class.   An older brother who was studying music gave young George his first lessons at the piano, and together they played four-hand arrangements of the Beethoven symphonies.   George also sang in the church choir and took a turn at playing the organ.   Later he was allowed to go into Boston for lessons at the New England Conservatory of Music, though it was understood that he was to enter his father's office.

But, by the time he was twenty-one, George Chadwick had enough of insurance and announced his choice of music as a life work.   Then followed one of those family disagreements so familiar in the life stories of most musicians.   The father opposed a musical career, in fact refused to finance it.   Whereupon young George declared his inde-pendence, got a position as music teacher at Olivet College, and set out for Michigan.

As soon as he had saved money enough, he went to Germany, first to Leipzig, then on to Munich.   He studied with Reinecke, Jadassohn, and Rheinberger, three men who have had much to do with the development of American music.   From them he gained what he described as "an orderly idea of strict composition."   Before going to Munich, Chadwick seriously considered studying with César Franck, and as one writer says, it is interesting to speculate as to what might have resulted from the influence of the great French mystic upon this matter-of-fact New Englander!

Chadwick returned to America in 1880 and began his long career of teaching and composing.   It was spent in Boston, where he served first as instructor, then as director of the New England Conservatory, which post he held until his death at the age of seventy-seven.   Chadwick's influence upon American music is no doubt as great as it is immeasurable.   Sympathetic, clear-minded, keenly analytical, he was one of the great teachers of his time, and the long list of his pupils shows such bright names as Horatio Parker, Arthur Whiting, Sidney Homer, Henry Hadley, and many others.

As a composer, Chadwick explored all musical forms, and his published works include many songs and choral compositions, much chamber music, and twenty-four major works for orchestra.   But he was perhaps most successful with music in ballad style, as is shown by such songs as "He Loves Me" and "Lullaby" and the symphonic ballad, *Tam O'Shanter*.   Chadwick's music shows a curious blending of the academic — that "orderly idea of strict composition" — learned in Germany, and an irrepressible Yankee humor.   It is characteristic that this man who had so reverently mastered the craft of Bach, Beethoven, and Brahms and who preached tradition to his pupils should have written a comic opera called *Tabasco*, and been intrigued by Lewis Carroll into the orchestral "whifflings" and "galumphings" of his *Jabberwocky!*

In the progress of serious American music, Chadwick carried on where the pioneer, John Knowles Paine, left off, but he carried on with what Philip Hale called "a certain jaunty irreverence" all his own. George W. Chadwick was not a great composer, but he was a good one. His music is well made. There is a warmth and a steadiness about it that satisfies, and above all, a freshness of spirit which caused someone to remark, "The man is far older than his music."

JUBILEE — FROM SYMPHONIC SKETCHES

In the year 1895 Chadwick wrote the four symphonic sketches, *Jubilee*, *Noel*, *Hobgoblin*, and *A Vagrom Ballad*. There were many manuscript performances of the work before it was finally published in 1907, with a dedication to Frederick S. Converse and this notation from the author: "Although these pieces are intended to be played in succession, they may be performed separately if more expedient."

Prefacing each sketch is a bit of verse, a key to the composer's mood. This, for *Jubilee*:

> No cool gray tones for me!
> Give me the warmest red and green,
> A cornet and a tambourine,
> To paint MY jubilee!
>
> For when pale flutes and oboes play,
> To sadness I become a prey;
> Give me the violets and the May
> But no gray skies for me!
>
> D. R.

There is certainly nothing cool or gray in the exultant opening theme for full orchestra: [1]

After twenty-seven measures well peppered with *sforzandos*, the low strings and woodwinds introduce a new idea, a patting juba:

which gives the music a touch of Deep South flavor. For *juba* is the stamping of the foot on the strong beats, followed by two *staccato* pats of the hands on the weak beats in duple meter:

[1] Copyright, 1907, by G. Schirmer, Inc. Excerpts reprinted by permission of the publisher.

with which the Negroes often mark the rhythm for their dancing. A third of the dancers will keep time in this way while the others dance, or sometimes the whole crowd will juba for a solo dancer, urging him on to the most fantastic performances.

After the juba theme, a horn call in C major announces a melody of simple folk-song type:

with a haunting refrain:

Both skill and ingenuity are shown in the use of this thematic material. The first theme comes back in *scherzo* mood with interesting new touches. Near the end, the singing melody, *lento espressivo* in the woodwinds, suggests:

> . . . when pale flutes and oboes play,
> To sadness I become a prey;

but suddenly the whole orchestra, in *presto* coda, seems to shout:

> No cool gray tones for me!
> Give me the warmest red and green,
> A cornet and a tambourine,
> To paint MY jubilee!

ARTHUR FOOTE

Salem, Massachusetts — 1853
Boston, Massachusetts — 1937

Arthur Foote, born in Salem, Massachusetts in the year 1853, had no special musical inheritance or surroundings. When he was about twelve, the boy had lessons on the family "square" piano and made fairly rapid progress. "But 'progress,'" as he later said, "meant merely playing notes faster; no idea of phrasing, pedaling, or expression." The real beginning of his education in music came when he entered Harvard College, where, by happy chance, he enrolled in the classes of John Knowles Paine, the pioneer of organized music study in American colleges. There young Foote must have progressed far beyond fast finger work, for he was chosen conductor of the Harvard Glee Club. In the summer vacation following his graduation, Foote decided to have some organ lessons with Benjamin Lang, probably as a last, leisurely musical adventure before going into business. Under Lang's encouragement his interest in music mushroomed until, by the end of the summer, the plans for going into business were cast aside. Arthur Foote had chosen music as his profession.

Unlike his colleagues of the New England Group, Chadwick, Parker, Whiting, and Mrs. Beach, Foote did not go abroad to study. He continued the organ and piano lessons with Lang for two more years, then started on his own as a piano teacher. For more than half a century Arthur Foote was a prominent figure in musical life around Boston. In addition to his extensive teaching, he was for many years organist of the First Unitarian Church in Boston and one of the founders and for a time president of the American Guild of Organists. He appeared in many piano recitals and in concerts of chamber music with the Kneisels and other quartets.

But the permanent contribution of this long and busy life is the considerable list of Arthur Foote's compositions: eight major works for orchestra, including the lovely *Night Piece* for flute and orchestra; the symphonic prologue, *Francesca da Rimini; Four Character Pieces after Omar Khayyám;* eight compositions of chamber music; over thirty organ works; choral settings of "The Wreck of the Hesperus," "The Farewell of Hiawatha," and "The Skeleton in Armor"; and many delightful songs and piano pieces.

Foote's music shows his "fondness for chords in close formation, in the richness of lower registers," which may be a memory of his Harvard Glee Club days. John Tasker Howard characterizes Foote's music as "distinguished by clarity and directness, good taste and craftsmanship," while yet another critic writes, "His music is the pure and perfectly formed expression of a nature at once refined and imaginative." But perhaps the nicest of all the adjectives used to describe this American composer and his music is the modest but meaningful word *agreeable*. The world being what it is, why should we not appreciate and welcome the agreeable as well as the great!

Arthur Foote saw the passing show of many musical fashions in his eighty-four years, and through it all he was consistently open-minded and blest with the rare faculty of being kindly toward persons and ideas he clearly disliked. In his later years when the innovations of Stravinsky, Schönberg, and others were causing much discussion and taking of sides, Foote called himself a conservative. But it must be remembered that his devotion to Brahms during the late-Victorian flurry over that "impossible" German composer was anything but conservative!

In his delightful article,[1] "A Bostonian Remembers," written for the *Musical Quarterly*, January, 1937, just a few months before his death, Foote says:

> As one of the older generation, I should hardly be expected to feel the same way about the happenings in the past twenty-five years — about polytonality, linear counterpoint, etc.

[1] Excerpts reprinted by permission from *The Musical Quarterly*, January, 1937. Copyright, 1937, by G. Schirmer, Inc.

Dissonance and consonance seem to me to be complementary: while music entirely consonant soon becomes monotonous, that which is entirely dissonant is not only tiresome but, worse than that, unpleasant. Dissonance is not undesirable in itself, but often becomes so because of the unskillful way in which it is used. It is rather "old hat" to bring logic into the question, but after all, this does exist in music from Bach to Sibelius.

He sums up those years which saw the flowering of music in New England with this significant remark:

All in all, ours has been a great time in which to be living and to watch the development of music.

SUITE FOR STRINGS IN E MAJOR

For the first performance of the Suite for Strings in E Major, in 1909, at a Boston Symphony concert, the composer himself wrote the following program notes:

The Prelude — E major, 2/2, is brief and is based throughout on the first phrase of eight notes:[1]

It is of flowing, melodic character with much imitation among the several voices.

The Pizzicato — A minor, 6/8, is continuously so:

It is interrupted by an Adagietto in F major, 3/4:

which is played with the bow, the instruments being muted.

The Fugue is in E minor, 4/4, and is pretty thoroughly planned out with a long pedal point just at the last return of the theme; there are no inversions or augmentations, etc. The first four notes of the theme:

are heard often by themselves, and if those notes are observed by the listener at their entrance, the fugue will be very clear at the first hearing.

[1] Excerpts from Suite in E, Opus 63. Copyright by The Arthur P. Schmidt Company.

There is a refinement about this music which distinguishes the composer, who, in an era of lavish scoring and lush Wagnerian harmonies, cultivated a dignified simplicity of style.

JOHN ALDEN CARPENTER

Park Ridge, Illinois — 1876

The story of John Alden Carpenter seems to be refreshingly free from the prodigious anecdotes and from the acute situations which we accept as the conventional design of an artist's life. He was just a normal little boy brought up in a comfortable American home. Today he is a normal American business man, carrying on the family firm of George B. Carpenter and Company, dealers in mill, railway, and shipping supplies. His mother was a singer who kept up her music after her marriage, and took special interest in the musical development of her children. Small John had lessons, first with his mother and later with Chicago teachers, but there was no child-wonder business, none of the forcing or forbidding that has gone into the making of so many musicians.

When preparatory school days were over, young Carpenter was sent to Harvard. Here his interest led him into the music classes where he was fortunate in having as his teacher John Knowles Paine, the founder of Harvard's music department and pioneer of music education in American colleges. After his graduation Carpenter returned to Chicago and entered his father's firm. Here again he was fortunate, for the family finances and sympathy with his music made it possible for him to continue his study. Most of Mr. Carpenter's "graduate" work has been done in Chicago, although at one time, while traveling abroad, he had a few lessons with the English composer Edward Elgar.

John Alden Carpenter has had the advantage of the amateur in that he has never had to write music for the market. His market deals in steel rails and sailcloth, and when he leaves that humming office and enters his music room, he can write when, what, and as he pleases. But thanks to a rare taste and talent and to excellent training, what he writes is as far from amateurish as music could be.

His music is distinguished by a delicacy and an exquisite coloring which shows the influence of the French Impressionists. This is particularly noticeable in the songs for which Mr. Carpenter is widely known. In such songs as "The Green River," "When I bring you colored toys," "The sleep that flits on baby's eyes," the mood of the poem seems to gleam through the music as through a translucent case which lends an added lovely tint. There is something about the music that makes one think of rose quartz, jade, or palest amber — something precious.

But there is a surprising other side to this fastidious composer. He is a humorist whose gifts range from the sheer whimsy of a baby's impressions of life to the broad clowning of his comic-strip ballet, *Krazy Kat*. And he is also a bold adventurer, trying jazz tricks on respectable symphony orchestras and even daring to translate the din of our city streets into music, as in his *Skyscrapers*. Perhaps it is this mingling of fragile beauty, particularly the beauty of nature, with an urchin type of humor and a frontier ruggedness and vitality that caused Walter Damrosch to name John Alden Carpenter "one of the most American of our composers."

ADVENTURES IN A PERAMBULATOR

Adventures in a Perambulator was John Alden Carpenter's first important orchestral work. It was written in 1914 and published the following year, a harsh time for so tender a traveler to venture forth. This may explain why, in spite of the fact that it has been played by many orchestras both at home and abroad, there are still too many people who have missed *Adventures in a Perambulator*.

There is nothing grand about these adventures — the grand manner being unbecoming to babies— but there is much that is dear and delightfully droll. Humor in music is as rare as the white blackbird, and few outside of France have been light-witted enough to catch it. John Alden Carpenter is one of the few. His humor seems to be an unmistakably American blend of the ridiculous and the romantic.

In *Adventures in a Perambulator* Mr. Carpenter meant to record a baby's impression of life in the big world of several city blocks. He has accomplished exactly what he intended — more cannot be asked of any artist. His *Skyscrapers* may go higher, his *Sea Drift* farther, yet it is doubtful if he will ever come closer to the hearts of his listeners than in this naïve saga of infancy.

Almost as delightful as the music is the composer's own program for it, supposedly written by the young adventurer. Through the courtesy of Mr. Carpenter and his publishers we are permitted to quote these amusing prefaces to the various adventures.

En Voiture!

Every morning — after my second breakfast — if the wind and the sun are favorable, I go out. I should like to go alone, but my will is overborne. My Nurse is appointed to take me. She is older than I, and very powerful. While I wait for her, resigned, I hear her cheerful steps, always the same. I am wrapped in a vacuum of wool, where there are no drafts. A door opens and shuts. I am placed in my perambulator, a strap is buckled over my stomach, my Nurse stands firmly behind — and we are off!

En Voiture — "In the Carriage" — serves as introduction to the suite, presenting the hero, Myself, the heroine, Nurse, and the instrument of destiny, the pram. On duty in the very first measure is the Nurse: [1]

Although the 'celli are bidden to play *giocoso*, joyfully, one cannot help feeling that Nurse is, as the baby has said, "very powerful." She is indeed one who would "stand firmly behind" and stand no nonsense in such matters as bonnet strings and mittens.

[1] Quotations from *Adventures in a Perambulator*, by John Alden Carpenter, used by permission of the publisher, G. Schirmer, Inc., and of the composer.

Soon the Perambulator is heard in the celesta and strings:

an ambling figure which intimates that this homely vehicle was not built for speed. A pleasant chiming of bells adds a festive touch to the departure.

After barely two measures of the perambulator motif, Myself appears:

Myself's theme is very childish, no doubt purposely suggestive of the classic "London Bridge Is Falling Down."

But "London Bridge" is stepped off by active little feet, while Myself, as the cleverly tied notes indicate, is firmly buckled in — a rider of the leisure class!

The violins are moved to endearing comment:

and aren't we all at sight of such a traveler?

These themes, slightly varied, are heard several times. It seems to take some moments to get well under way, but at last, "We are off!"

The Policeman

Out is wonderful! It is always different, though one seems to have been there before. I cannot fathom it all. Some sounds seem like smells. Some sights have echoes. It is confusing, but it is Life! For instance, the Policeman — an Unprecedented Man! Round like a ball — taller than my Father. Blue — fearful — fascinating! I feel him before he comes. I see him after he goes. I try to analyze his appeal. It is not buttons alone, nor belt, nor baton. I suspect it is his eye and the way he walks. He walks like Doom. My Nurse feels it, too. She becomes less firm, less powerful. My perambulator hurries, hesitates, and stops. They converse. They ask each other questions — some with answers, some without. I listen, with discretion. When I feel that they have gone far enough, I signal to my Nurse, a private signal, and the Policeman resumes his enormous Blue March. He is gone, but I feel him after he goes.

A little fluttering introduction suggests that something disquieting has been sighted. Ah, there it is, "Blue — fearful — fascinating" — the Policeman:

He does indeed "walk like doom."

Nurse becomes much less firm. Her theme loses that fierce **downward swoop**:

and is now all on the up and up!

The perambulator, too, does curious things, perhaps even more apparent to the eye than to the ear, for this score is graphic as a picture book. The pram hurries, hesitates, then stops with a *glissando* scraping of brakes. As Nurse and the Policeman talk, the pram seems to be trying to get on. One can almost see the rider pushing forward in his seat — that familiar rowing motion:

Then, getting nowhere, he tries the springs, up and down:

and gets a sharp admonishing from nurse:

There is no mistaking the downward swoop here!

Mr. Carpenter may have had no such things in mind, or he may have been more clever than he was aware, but if we overinterpret him, he has only himself to blame for putting temptation in our way!

Nurse and the Policeman talk on and ON. She is coy:

He tells a heavy joke:

which she repeats in a high violin voice. Merry *staccato* laughter runs up and down in the strings.

Myself has had quite enough. They are talking nonsense, and anyway, this is *his* adventure. He wants to roll on. He reminds Nurse of his presence in a loud brassy voice:

which causes a guilty scurry of harp, celesta, and piano:

Away goes the perambulator while the Policeman "resumes his enormous Blue March" in the opposite direction, and the adventure ends with the chuckle of a piccolo:

perhaps, an amused bystander!

The Hurdy-Gurdy

Then suddenly there is something else. I think it is a sound. We approach it. My ear is tickled to excess. I find that the absorbing noise comes from a box — something like my music box, only much larger, and on wheels. A dark man is turning the music out of the box with a handle, just as I do with mine. A dark lady, richly dressed, turns when the man gets tired. They both smile. I smile, too, with restraint, for music is the most insidious form of noise. And such music! So gay! I tug at the strap over my stomach. I have a wild thought of dancing with my Nurse and my perambulator — all three of us together. Suddenly, at the climax of our excitement, I feel the approach of a phenomenon that I remember. It is the Policeman. He has stopped the music. He has frightened away the dark man and the lady with their music box. He seeks the admiration of my Nurse for his act. He walks away, his buttons shine, but far off I hear again the forbidden music. Delightful forbidden music!

Myself, happy again, rolls gaily along. Then, suddenly — there it is, that ear-tickling sound, the hurdy-gurdy:

Attached to it are two smiling dark people in most beautiful colored clothes! This is finer than the little nursery music box. It has more tunes and louder:

Surely this must be grand opera!

But here is something even grander — "Alexander's Ragtime Band," that witching, twitching tune people whistle in the street:

And yet another that sets one's whole person swinging:

It is too much:

> I tug at the strap over my stomach [here there is agitation in the perambulator theme, which is now playing along with the waltz tune]. I have a wild thought of dancing with my Nurse and my perambulator — all three of us together.

That happy thought is promptly extinguished. The waltz sways on. Then suddenly come footsteps, heavy footsteps, and a familiar blue figure heaves in sight:

the Policeman!

The smiling dark people fold up the magic box.   There are no more nice tunes.
What a pity:

O "delightful forbidden music!"

The Lake

Sated with adventure, my Nurse firmly pushes me on, and before I recover my
balance I am face to face with new excitement.   The land comes to an end, and there
at my feet is the Lake.   All my other sensations are joined in one.   I see, I hear, I feel
the quiver of the little waves as they escape from the big ones and come rushing up over
the sand.   Their fear is pretended.   They know the big waves are amiable, for they can
see a thousand sunbeams dancing with impunity on their very backs.   Waves and sunbeams!   Waves and sunbeams!   Blue water — white clouds — dancing, swinging!   A
white sea gull floating in the air.   That is *My Lake!*

So this is the lake!   Big waves that roll in on long, heavy swells:

little waves that scamper and break into sudsy scallops of foam:

and underneath, a drowsy, drumming sound as if some monster growled amiably in its
sleep.

How beautifully the music gives the feeling of restless sparkling water.   And how
refreshingly free it is from the persistent rippling motifs commonly used to moisten
the pages of descriptive music.   This is no naïve babbling brook tune.   It is big water
music like Debussy's *La Mer*, with its personality, its many moods.

One is conscious of mysterious life, of endless exquisite detail below that smooth blue
water.   One also knows that beneath the soothing surface of this music lie bits of fine
writing that would well repay investigation.   But why think when sense impressions
are so satisfying!   With the baby, who says that all his sensations are joined in one,
the listener yields to pleasant daydreams.   "Blue water — white clouds — dancing,
swinging!"

Dogs

We pass on.   Probably there is nothing more in the world.   If there is, it is superfluous.   *There IS.*   It is Dogs!   We come upon them without warning.   Not *one* of

them — all of them.   First, one by one; then in pairs; then in societies.   Little dogs, with sisters; big dogs, with aged parents.   Kind dogs, brigand dogs, sad dogs, and gay. They laugh, they fight, they run.   And at last, in order to hold my interest, the very littlest brigand starts a game of "Follow the Leader," followed by all the others.   It is tremendous!

There is a very tuneful introduction to *Dogs*.   The adventurer is leaving the lake content with the pretty world and convinced that there is nothing more to be seen in it.   And then, all of a sudden, "*There IS*.   It is Dogs!"   Quite a shock, the dogs and the doggy music, after so much calm beauty.

From the woofing in the woodwinds we can well believe that they are all there, the whole dog tribe.   They leap and caper in merry confusion.   A nice little tune starts:

but they begin to worry it out of key before it has a chance to go two measures.

Another tune tries its luck.   In spite of a few missing sharps, it is recognizable as "Where, O Where Has My Little Dog Gone?"

Surely no one could say where, for an instrument gets no further than the first phrase before another snatches the tune and runs with it, dog fashion.   By the time the flutes and piccolo drag it to one side for as much as five measures, this is what has happened to it:

"*Ach, du lieber Augustin*," another vagabond tune, now tries to join the fray, but it can scarcely be heard for the shrill "ki-yi's" in the woodwinds.

As a final stunt the dogs snatch up the "Where, O Where" theme:

and begin to play something suspiciously like what humans call a fugue. However, it turns out to be only a little harmless tail-chase.

Can such things be! Myself beams with joy:

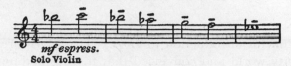

But the dogs run away, you can hear them scampering across the piano keys and barking faintly from a distance. "It is tremendous."

Dreams

Those dogs have gone! It is confusing, but it is Life! My mind grows numb. My cup is too full. I have a sudden conviction that it is well that I am not alone. That firm step behind reassures me. The wheels of my perambulator make a sound that quiets my nerves. I lie very still. I am quite content. In order to think more clearly, I close my eyes. My thoughts are absorbing. I deliberate upon my Mother. Most of the time my Mother and my Nurse have but one identity in my mind, but at night or when I close my eyes, I can easily tell them apart, for my Mother has the greater charm. I hear her voice quite plainly now, and feel the touch of her hand. It is pleasant to live over again the adventures of the day — the long blue waves curling in the sun, the Policeman who is bigger than my Father, the music box, and my friends, the Dogs. It is pleasant to lie quite still and close my eyes and listen to the wheels of my perambulator. How very large the world is! How many things there are!

Overcome with the complexity of life in so big a world, the baby sinks back into the security of pillows. The Myself theme, in smooth duple meter, becomes a lullaby for muted violins, with trusty perambulator accompanying. Everything is beginning to grow pleasantly hazy. The day's adventures — waves, Policeman, organ-grinders, dogs — pass in fragmentary review before drowsy eyes.

A new thought steals in — a nice thought — Mother:

As her gentle theme ends, the sleepiest of horns is heard, yawning the Myself theme.

Then the lullaby again, Myself and the perambulator:

growing softer and slower until Myself drops out and only a faintly tinkling celesta is left — a dream perambulator.

CHARLES GRIFFES

Elmira   — 1884
New York — 1920

Like Edward MacDowell, Charles Tomlinson Griffes was a boy of many talents. He made clever pen-and-ink drawings, water-color sketches, and, in later life, etchings on copper. However, music attracted him most, and in his high school days he decided to become a concert pianist. To this end he went to Berlin to study. There, in addition to his piano study, he had theory lessons with Humperdinck. Those hours with the genial creator of *Hänsel und Gretel* turned his aspirations in another direction, to composition.

At first he followed along the pathway of his teacher, the pathway of German Romanticism, and his early songs are in the Schumann and Brahms tradition. Then one day in his *pension* he heard some one next door playing the most curiously appealing music. He went at once to ask what it was, and found that it was a piece called *Jeux d'eau* by a young Frenchman named Ravel. It was one of those unimportant happen-sos with important results, for it quite definitely led Griffes into musical impressionism. Like so many of the young composers of that period, he was strongly influenced by the sensuous, colorful dream music of Debussy and Ravel, but he was too independent an artist to become a mere follower. He took from the French Impressionists, and later from the Russians, only what he needed for a free expression of his own personality. Griffes's poetic and musical ideas were always his own, and they so completely dominate his music that a borrowed idiom, a little Debussy trick of expression here or there, is of small consequence.

Coming back to America after four years abroad, Griffes took the position of music teacher at a boys' school on the Hudson. A boys' school would seem almost the last place in the world for the spinning of such delicate dream webs as Griffes's music. Yet from that fastidiously bare school studio came all of Griffes's finest compositions. One is reminded of another, the *Komponierstube* at St. Thomas's School, Leipzig, where, thinly partitioned from pillow-fighting choir boys, Master Bach wrote the greatest church music in the world.

Quietly and unassumingly for twelve years Griffes worked away at his teaching and composition. Then, in the autumn of 1919, came the good news that his *Pleasure Dome of Kubla Khan* had been accepted for performance by the Boston Symphony Orchestra. The work was still in manuscript, and since he could not afford a copyist, he set himself to copying out the parts. It was too heavy a task for one already worn with a burden of school work, and when it was finished, Griffes fell ill with a fatal attack of pneumonia. The orchestra played *Kubla Khan* to an enthusiastic audience. It was Griffes's dream at last come true, his first real triumph, but it meant little to the dying man.   Thirty-six years Charles Griffes had lived, to die just as the reason for his living dawned upon an indifferent world.

In his less than forty compositions — songs, piano sketches, and orchestral works — Griffes left to American music a legacy which has proved a treasure.   His artistic ideals were high, his techniques sound, and his music full of poetry and a rare imagination.

Aptly does Mr. Hale, in the Boston Symphony Orchestra's program notes, apply the quotation from Marlowe's *Dr. Faustus:*

> Cut is the branch that might have grown full straight,
> And burnèd is Apollo's laurel bough.

THE WHITE PEACOCK

From *Roman Sketches*, a group of tone poems for piano, comes the exquisite *White Peacock*, inspired by the verse of Fiona Macleod, the pseudonym of William Sharp, a too-little-known Scotch poet.   "The White Peacock" is a feast of delicate sense impressions — frail hues, fragrances that vanish at the moment of awareness, motion which is but the silent ghost of sound.   It is a study in whites.   White magnolias, white poppies, white surf, white cloud, white violets, shadowed in palest blue and lit by flashes of sun-yellow and the gleam of amber fir cones.   Free from the restraint of rhyme, the lovely lines move to a rhythm as lithe as the southern wind.

Rarely has a composer translated from word to tone with such perfection as Griffes. He too has achieved a piece of pure impressionism, cunningly contrived to lure the listener to a lotus-land of day dreams.   His music brings not only the picture, white and azure flecked with gold, but the feeling, an almost physical yielding to the warmth and fragrance of noon in an old Roman garden.

> Here where the sunlight
> Floodeth the garden,
> Where the pomegranate
> Reareth its glory
> Of gorgeous blossom;
> Where the oleanders
> Dream through the noontides;
> And, like surf o' the sea
> Round cliffs of basalt,
> The thick magnolias
> In billowy masses
> Front the sombre green of the ilexes:
> Here where the heat lies
> Pale blue in the hollows,
> Where blue are the shadows
> On the fronds of the cactus,
> Where pale blue the gleaming
> Of fir and cypress,

With the cones upon them
Amber or glowing
With virgin gold:
Here where the honey-flower
Makes the heat fragrant,
As though from the gardens
Of Gulistan,
Where the bulbul singeth
Through a mist of roses,
A breath were borne:
Here where the dream-flowers,
The cream-white poppies
Silently waver,
And where the Scirocco,
Faint in the hollows,
Foldeth his soft wings in the sunlight,
And lieth sleeping
Deep in the heart of
A sea of white violets:
Here, as the breath, as the soul of this beauty,
Moveth in silence, and dreamlike, and slowly,
White as a snow-drift in mountain valleys
When softly upon it the gold light lingers:
White as the foam o' the sea that is driven
O'er billows of azure agleam with sun-yellow:
Cream-white and soft as the breasts of a girl,
Moves the White Peacock, as though through the noontide
A dream of the moonlight were real for a moment.
Dim on the beautiful fan that he spreadeth,
Foldeth and spreadeth abroad in the sunlight,
Dim on the cream-white are blue adumbrations,
Shadows so pale in their delicate blueness
That visions they seem as of vanishing violets,
The fragrant white violets veinèd with azure,
Pale, pale as the breath of blue smoke in far woodlands.
Here, as the breath, as the soul of this beauty,
White as a cloud through the heats of the noontide
Moves the White Peacock.

Mysteriously the music begins, with a questioning call: [1]

[1] Quotations from *The White Peacock*, by Charles Tomlinson Griffes, used by permission of the publisher, G. Schirmer, Inc.

and answer:

as if evoking the spirits of the garden, the antique gods of the earth.

Instantly the spell is cast.   The real world fades, and

> Here, as the breath, as the soul of this beauty,
> Moveth in silence, and dreamlike, and slowly,

the White Peacock:

Delicately suggestive is the spread chord with which the theme sweeps in, the slight thrusting movement of the dotted eighth followed by sixteenth notes, and the unhurried 5/4 meter picturing the stately, strutting bird of Juno.   And definitely reminiscent of the pavane, that ancient ceremonial dance said to have been named for the peacock, is this main motif.

On a chiming fall of chords in odd progressions, a languorous song is wafted by:

perhaps from the gardens

> Of Gulistan,
> Where the bulbul singeth.

The music begins to glow and gleam, but always with subdued colors.   As a frost-white landscape lit by sudden sun can surpass even summer's miracle of green and gold, so the white peacock seems even more gorgeous than his brother in bronze and blue. In the ebb and flow of the music the imaginative listener can see:

> . . . the beautiful fan that he spreadeth,
> Foldeth and spreadeth abroad in the sunlight.

can even see those "pale adumbrations" etched in minor tonalities as shadowy as "vanishing violets."

Then, quite simply, the first theme returns, and on a gentle, almost hesitant rise of tones, the white peacock disappears.   Again the little questioning call sounds:

There is no answer this time. Without so much as the reality of a closing cadence the music dies away. Ah, well, it was but a dream,

> . . . as though through the noontide
> A dream of the moonlight were real for a moment.

The White Peacock was originally scored for piano. Later Griffes himself arranged it for orchestra, and a masterly arrangement it is. The woodwinds with their translucent tones are given the melody. Cleverly the composer has used the "white tone" of the oboe, the silver of the flute, and the wood-thrush note of the clarinet, with here and there an amber gleam from the brass. Harps and celesta suggest the shimmering warmth and light of noon, while the strings, often in unison and always *legato*, seem to bear the music up as if on strong, free wings.

It has been the writer's privilege to make these notes from Griffes's original manu-script for orchestra. The erasures, the blue pencilings that transfer a phrase from harp to clarinet or lengthen the span of a tone gave a strangely personal touch to this impersonal, unreal music, and perhaps intensified the poignant regret which every music lover feels for what might have been had Charles Griffes lived even a few years longer.

The Pleasure Dome of Kubla Khan

For the first performance of *The Pleasure Dome of Kubla Khan*, by the Boston Symphony Orchestra, in the fall of 1919, Griffes sent the following explanation to Mr. Philip Hale for the program notes:

I have taken as a basis for my work those lines of Coleridge's poem describing the "stately pleasure dome," the "sunny pleasure dome with caves of ice," the "miracle of rare device." Therefore I call the work *The Pleasure Dome of Kubla Khan* rather than *Kubla Khan*. These lines include 1 to 11 and 32 to 38. It might be well to quote in the program book some of these lines, at least the last six.

> In Xanadu did Kubla Khan
> > A stately pleasure-dome decree:
> Where Alph, the sacred river, ran
> Through caverns measureless to man
> > Down to a sunless sea.
> So twice five miles of fertile ground
> With walls and towers were girdled round:
> > And there were gardens bright with sinuous rills . . .
> Enfolding sunny spots of greenery.
>
> * * *
>
> The shadow of the dome of pleasure
> > Floated midway on the waves;
> Where was heard the mingled measure
> > From the fountain and the caves.
> It was a miracle of rare device,
> A sunny pleasure-dome with caves of ice!

It might also be well to know something of the curious story of the poem which so inspired Griffes. In the summer of 1797, Coleridge, in the hope of regaining his health, retired to a lonely farmhouse on the Exmoor. One day the sick man, who had been given an anodyne, fell asleep in his chair as he was reading an old travel tale, "Purchas's Pilgrimage." The soothing effect of the medicine, mingling with the last sentence he had read — "Here Kubla Khan commanded a palace to be built, and a stately garden thereunto. And thus ten miles of fertile ground were inclosed within a wall" — spun a lovely dream of the East which subconsciously sang itself into verse.

The poet wakened with such a vivid recollection of it that he seized his pen and eagerly began to write it down. He had reached the fifty-fourth line when, unfortunately, he was interrupted by a man from the neighboring town, calling on business. Returning later to his desk, Coleridge found to his dismay that the dream poem had vanished. He could remember only a scattered line or image here and there! Although he always hoped to recapture the vision or, at least, complete the poem by conscious creation, he never did. "Kubla Khan" remains a fragment, merely those first fifty-four lines snatched from a poet's dream.

Returning to the composer's comments on his music, Griffes wrote:

> As to the argument, I have given my imagination free rein in the description of this strange palace as well as of purely imaginary revelry which might have taken place there. The vague, foggy beginning suggests the sacred river, running "through caverns measureless to man down to a sunless sea."

A long succession of mysterious, "sunless" chords for piano above vibrating strings and softly murmuring brasses:[1]

suggests the sacred river.

Then gradually rise the outlines of the palace:

[1] Quotations from *The Pleasure Dome of Kubla Khan*, by Charles Tomlinson Griffes, used by permission of the publisher, G. Schirmer, Inc.

"with walls and towers girdled round." The gardens and fountains and "sunny spots of greenery" are next suggested:

From inside come sounds of dancing and revelry:

[Here Griffes shows the influence of Oriental music, of which he was an enthusiastic student.]

which increase to a wild climax and then suddenly break off. There is a return to the original mood suggesting the sacred river and the "caves of ice."

But neither Griffes's comments (into which we have inserted quotations from score) or the suggested lines from Coleridge's poem give the least idea of the sensuous charm of the music. It takes a whole orchestra to create the color, the perfume, the spell of this Oriental fantasy.

JOHN POWELL

Richmond, Virginia — 1882

An interesting contributor to musical Americana is John Powell of Virginia. His father was the head of a well-known girls' school in Richmond, and there, in an atmosphere of culture and intellectual activity, the boy grew up. Music was always an important part of both the school and family life, and from an older sister young John had his first lessons. So marked was his talent and interest that when his school days were over he was sent to Vienna to study with the famous piano master, Leschetizky.

John Powell won a reputation as a brilliant young pianist. For a number of years he toured Europe and America giving piano recitals and playing with the leading orchestras. Meanwhile he had developed a serious interest in composition and began to give more and more of his time to it. Nor was music his only interest. John Powell is a graduate of the University of Virginia, and as an astronomer he is recognized by scientific societies. Today he makes his home near Richmond and divides his time between concert work and composition.

His compositions include both the large and smaller forms. Although he has written several attractive sonatas for violin and piano and string quartets, Powell is perhaps most successful in the works for his own instrument, the piano, and for orchestra. Some of the best known of these are the piano suite, *In the South;* the *Sonata Noble* and the famous *Negro Rhapsody*, both for piano and orchestra; *In Old Virginia* and *Natchez-on-the-Hill* for orchestra.

"One might write on indefinitely," says Daniel Gregory Mason, "about the many-sidedness of Powell, about the expression of his vigorous mind in social, political, and even in scientific fields; about his fearlessness as a critic of certain decadent modern tendencies; about his versatility as the composer of the popular *Banjo Picker* and of the epic *Negro Rhapsody*, which he has played all over Europe with orchestras."

But for all this many-sidedness, John Powell has one consuming interest and that is American music. His ideas on the subject are original and very valuable. Because of his effective use of Negro melodies in such a work as the *Negro Rhapsody*, it is easy to mistake his purpose and jump at the conclusion that he considers this typical American music. When he uses a Negro theme he seeks to interpret the Negro, not America. John Powell believes that the way to nationalism in American music lies in an entirely different direction. He would find it in the Anglo-Saxon music, the old Tudor songs and dances that came with the first settlers to the New World and for hundreds of years have been locked away in the southern mountains. He expresses his enthusiasm for these old tunes in his notes written for *Natchez-on-the-Hill*, which we quote elsewhere.

Much as he loves the frontier tunes, he heartily dislikes many other forms of so-called American popular music. "As for jazz," he says, "it is already a worn-out and limited style. It is a weak, elementary way of saying things, and, as I see it, things which need a far richer and more adaptable speech than it is able to give."

Socially and intellectually, John Powell himself is a valuable piece of Americana, a representative of that old Virginia which was so truly and proudly American in its dignity and culture. Because both in his music and his ideas about music he seeks to keep alive an appreciation of "the quality" which lent a certain gallantry and graciousness to early America, John Powell is sometimes called "the prophet of the White South."

In Old Virginia

"To 'The University' on her hundredth birthday" is the dedication of John Powell's overture for orchestra, *In Old Virginia*, and a handsome birthday present it is! Powell has taken as his two main themes two old folk tunes, the first, a "party song" of which we give a common variant:

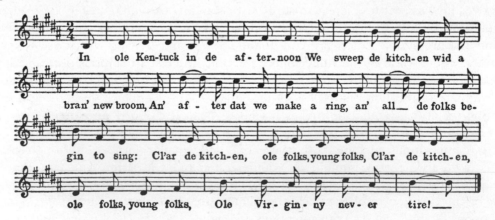

In ole Ken-tuck in de af-ter-noon We sweep de kitch-en wid a bran' new broom, An' af-ter dat we make a ring, an' all— de folks be-gin to sing: Cl'ar de kitch-en, ole folks, young folks, Cl'ar de kitch-en, ole folks, young folks, Ole Vir-gin-ny nev-er tire!—

the second, a nameless tune which a Negro nurse girl sang to little John Powell.

The overture begins with a rather slow and formal introduction in which the main theme, given out softly in triple meter and away from the key:[1]

seems but a subdued shadow of its boisterous self. Perhaps the composer meant to suggest the long and shadowy way over which the fancy must travel back to Old Virginia.

But at last we arrive. The *tempo* and the mood change to *Allegro commodo ma grazioso ed amabile* (Lightly moving but graciously and amiably) which characterizes the Old South as John Powell would have us see it. Merrily the fiddles strike up "Cl'ar de Kitchen, Ole Folks, Young Folks":

and this time it is easily recognized.

Another change of mood comes as the solo clarinet introduces the second theme:

one of those quaint modal tunes whose flatted seventh marks it as very old, probably of English derivation.

These two themes pass through many interesting phases, but nothing new happens until well along in the piece when a little tune of obviously Scottish ancestry appears:

[1] Quotations from *In Old Virginia*, by John Powell, used by permission of the publisher, G. Schirmer, Inc.

And then there blossoms out *fortissimo* and *maestoso* a tune which has been hinted at several times during the piece, the tune of tunes for those who live below the Mason and Dixon line:

And after that — ah, what could follow "Dixie" in Old Virginia, but a triumphant ending!

NATCHEZ-ON-THE-HILL

When *Natchez-on-the-Hill* (Three Virginian Country Dances) was played for the first time at the Worcester (Massachusetts) Festival in the autumn of 1931, Mr. Powell himself wrote the following program notes for it. It is always interesting to hear a composer express his ideas in words as well as tones, and so we quote these program notes in full, not because *Natchez-on-the-Hill* is a particularly important piece of music, but because in talking about it, John Powell reveals the secret of his art — an enthusiasm for the old "White South" of the early nineteenth century and for the quaint tunes that were a part of that picturesque life.

This piece is a setting of three traditional Virginia fiddle tunes: *Natchez-on-the-Hill, The Hog-Eyed Man*, and *The War-Whoop*. All three are authentic old dance tunes in particularly fine versions and unusually well preserved. They came to Mr. Powell from Mrs. John Hunter, just as she used to dance them, when — as Miss Polly Boston — she heard them played by her grandmother in Louisa County, Virginia.

The tunes are remarkable not only for their charm of local color, their ear-taking melodiousness, their foot-compelling lilt, which are irresistibly captivating to all hearers whether musically versed or not, but even more on account of aesthetic qualities which only the trained musician can appreciate. In beauty of melodic line and structure, in sustained length of phrase, with delightful surprise of punctuation by emphasis on unexpected degrees of the scale, the unfailing pointing of climax with cunning preparation therefor, the inexhaustible diversity, freshness, and vigor of rhythmic effects both in measure and phrase-rhythms keep the interest continuously tense and alert. Most remarkable, however, is the organic quality of their structure. These tunes are not the result of accretion, not pieced together in mechanical sequences, but living entities that grow into being like organisms. That is the reason why, with all their saucy nonchalance and their exuberant spontaneity, the ultimate impression is that of a gracious elegance, of a chaste and classic nobility.

The tune *Natchez-on-the-Hill* is one of a large group of variants deriving from the old (probably Tudor) English country dance, *Old Mother Oxford*. It is in every way worthy of its ancient and honorable lineage, although I feel sure it would never deny its close kinship with its more boisterous cousin, *Turkey in the Straw*.

This is the tune, as given out by the fiddles in the beginning of Powell's *Natchez-on-the-Hill:* [1]

The name recalls an interesting and forgotten bit of last century history, when Mississippi was the frontier of this country, and conditions there were similar to those in California somewhat later. A short quotation from "High Stakes and Hair Trigger," by R. W. Winston of Williams College, will vividly present the picture:

> On Mississippi soil, indeed, long before the Civil War, everything converged to a mighty tragedy. Time, place, and circumstance had met. The actors, too, were fitted to play their parts. Thither adventurers had flocked by thousands. Mississippi was the melting pot of America; aristocrats from the worn-out lands of Virginia and Carolina settled near Natchez, Washington, and Woodville; roughnecks from Georgia, Pennsylvania, and Tennessee, and from foreign lands, preempted the rich bottom lands. Today we drink, tomorrow we die! was the Mississippi motto. Duels were of frequent occurrence. Natchez-under-the-Hill typified the times — barrooms, dives, brothels, gambling hells, courtesans, murders, highwaymen — the offscourings of the earth — thugs from the four corners of the world, made up Natchez-under-the-Hill. And yet, just above the bluff was Natchez proper, Natchez-on-the-Hill, a comely city with banks, churches, residences ornate and beautiful, and a theatre where Booth and Barrett filled an engagement of nine nights.[2]

The sordid criminal background so dramatized and threw into vivid relief the refinement and elegance of Natchez-on-the-Hill that it came to personify these qualities, highly prized throughout the South, and gave its name to the widely loved folk tunes which so aptly embodied them. In a way, Natchez-on-the-Hill typified the whole South, led by its "quality," dancing gaily and gallantly on the verge of the abyss. And this condition left its impress on the tunes to which they danced — certainly not to their aesthetic detriment.

The Hog-Eyed Man:

[1] Quotations from *Natchez-on-the-Hill*, by John Powell, used by permission of the publisher, G. Schirmer, Inc.
[2] From "High Stakes and Hair Trigger: The Life of Jefferson Davis," by Robert W. Winston. Copyright, 1930, by permission of Henry Holt and Company, Inc., Publishers.

is of even greater antiquity than the preceding tune, as evinced by the fact that it is in the Aeolian mode. More vigorous in rhythm, its minor third and flatted seventh keep it hovering between plaintiveness and whimsicality with an effect not unlike that of certain Celtic dance tunes.

The War-Whoop, sturdiest and most unrestrained of the three:

is nevertheless of far more complicated anatomy, and more than the others suggests Beethoven in a rollicking mood.

The composer has used the three old tunes with suitable simplicity and directness and with an orchestration in which the fiddles, appropriately, play the leading role. No one, certainly no one of John Powell's musical standards, could call *Natchez-on-the-Hill* great music. But it is an interesting and valuable bit of Americana, and, what is more, it has the charm of a quaint old keepsake.

GEORGE GERSHWIN

Brooklyn — 1898
Hollywood — 1937

George Gershwin came of a typical New York East Side Jewish family — simple, kindly people, but apparently lacking in the artistic gifts so often found among those of their race. Pudgy Papa Gershwin, hero of many a naïve anecdote, had but a single thought — to get ahead in the world. So indefatigably did he pursue his ideal that, after a long and devious business career, he actually became the proud owner of a chain of restaurants and a Turkish bath, and the family moved uptown to a three-story brick house near Riverside Drive.

The scene of George Gershwin's childhood, however, was laid mostly on the sidewalks of that teeming neighborhood just off Grand Street. Sidewalk tunes — from vagabond fiddles and hand organs, from pianos banged near open windows, parade tunes with a tail of whistling urchins tagging behind the band — these made up the early musical experience of the little black-eyed Jewish boy. The child loved music so dearly that when he was ten years old it was decided that he should have piano lessons. Twenty-five cents a week it cost Papa. The teacher was a half-deaf fellow, the pupil neither apt nor diligent, the result — nothing to boast of!

But the love of music lasted, and George at fourteen made up a song. It was not much of a song, but it was a first taste of the heady wine of artistic creation. From that time on George, like Papa Gershwin, was the slave of a ruling passion. He would be a professional musician, perhaps even a composer. He began to study again, this time with true Gershwin attention to business. He soon acquired a surprising facility in piano playing, perhaps an unfortunate facility, since it no doubt tempted him later to substitute finger fireworks for musical content in his own compositions. He also took up the study of harmony with Rubin Goldmark and began to familiarize himself with the works of great composers. To the end, his favorites were Mozart, Debussy, and Stravinsky — a strangely assorted trio.

At sixteen young George got his first job as pianist with a publishing house which specialized in popular music. Here for three years Gershwin's nimble fingers served the jazz tunes of the day. His impressionable young mind soaked up the intriguing rhythms, the sentimental moods, the catchy tricks of harmony and orchestration which are the makings of jazz. He experimented with some tunes of his own and found that the formulae worked. Thus it chanced that regardless of Rubin Goldmark, Mozart, or any other influence, Student Gershwin took his Master's degree in Tin-Pan Alley.

In his twentieth year Gershwin was commissioned to write the music for George White's *Scandals* and shortly afterward produced a "smash hit" for Al Jolson. He had arrived in the song business.

In 1923, Gershwin met Paul Whiteman, and soon the two were sharing the dream of a symphonic future for jazz. A year later Whiteman hired a well-known New York concert hall and announced a concert of all-American music for which his friend Gershwin was to write a long symphonic-jazz composition. The story of those anxious weeks before the concert, with Whiteman imploring Gershwin to hand over the manuscript and Gershwin always insisting upon more time for revision, is well known. The composition was finished in the nick of time, with the help of Ferde Grofé, who scored it for orchestra. Such was the genesis of the famous *Rhapsody in Blue*.

The *Rhapsody in Blue* was a success, and Gershwin enjoyed an almost hysterical popularity. It was a very well-paying popularity, for the piece, printed in various arrangements, recorded for phonograph, radioed, and filmed, brought in a small fortune. The former lower East Side boy now lived luxuriously in a spacious upper East Side duplex apartment. He cultivated a rich man's hobby — the collection of valuable paintings. When he died, at the age of thirty-nine, press and radio outdid themselves in extravagant eulogies. Remembering Bach's simple, hard-working life, the poverty of cheery Schubert, the nameless grave of Mozart in contrast to the princely ease and loud acclaim of Gershwin, one cannot resist certain long thoughts on changing times, changing values. It could only have happened in these United States!

In the thirteen years after the creation of the *Rhapsody in Blue*, Gershwin divided his time between the composition of musical comedies for Broadway — among them, *Lady Be Good*, *Oh Kay!*, *Strike up the Band*, and *Of Thee I Sing*, and symphonic jazz pieces such as a Concerto for Piano and Orchestra, a symphonic poem, *An American in Paris*, a *Cuban Overture*, and his opera, *Porgy and Bess*. But whether in serious or popular vein, whether an early work or a late one, all of Gershwin's compositions show the same weakness as well as the same touch of genius.

The touch of genius is found in his tuneful main themes. George Gershwin had the heaven-born gift of melody. It was so much a part of him that it responded to his every mood. Humor or pathos was reflected in a melody as spontaneous as a smile or a frown. Gershwin, like Schubert, was a "melodic millionaire." But, unlike Schubert, he did not, in his short span of life, develop the power of enriching all forms of music — the symphony, chamber music, the art song, church music — with his melodic gift.

His weakness lies in the fact that he simply could not compose, in the literal sense of the word *compose* — "to put together." With the elementary A-B-A song form he was successful enough. But in a larger work, try as he might, he could not put his bright bits of inspiration together so that they made a meaningful whole. As a result, the *Rhapsody*, the *Concerto*, *An American in Paris* are scarcely more than musical patchwork, and, after all, patchwork is patchwork whether the patches be of gorgeous silks or faded calico! Speaking of this weakness, David Ewen says: "One confronts, in these works, endless padding of empty chords and vacuous scales to bridge one idea with another; developments of an almost schoolboyish ingenuousness — in which the original themes, far from gaining in effectiveness from the added decoration and enlargement, lose much of their original spontaneity; a feeble attempt at variation in which a theme is changed by an all-too-obvious transformation of rhythm or instrumentation." It should be added that Mr. Ewen, in his admirable sketch of Gershwin, has given an equally just and generous appraisal of the composer's strong points.

In his book, "Our Contemporary Composers," John Tasker Howard writes of George Gershwin under the subtitle, "Jazz in the Concert Hall," which aptly places Gershwin and his unique contribution to American music. Attempting to appraise Gershwin's work at this still-too-close range, some of his admirers predict that he will go down in music history as a writer of popular songs which, like those of Stephen Foster, characterize an era. Others feel that Gershwin's fame rests with his larger works. Whatever time's verdict may be, Gershwin's tunes show that peculiar quality of inevitability that marks all true folk songs. Given the time and the place, one feels that they could not have been otherwise!

One of the shrewdest comments on Gershwin's music comes from Arnold Schönberg, who says: "It seems to me beyond doubt that Gershwin was an innovator. What he has done with rhythm, harmony, and melody is not merely style. . . . His melodies are not the product of a combination, nor of a mechanical union, but they are units, and could, therefore, not be taken to pieces. Melody, harmony, and rhythm are not welded together, but cast."

Whether we like jazz or not, there is no question but that Gershwin's jazz is the real thing. He is speaking in his mother tongue, not imitating or borrowing an interesting musical idiom as did several clever European composers. Gershwin himself says:

When jazz is played in another nation it sounds false. Jazz is the result of the energy stored up in America. It is a very energetic kind of music, noisy, boisterous, and even vulgar. One thing is certain, jazz has contributed an enduring value to America in the sense that it has expressed ourselves. It is an original American achievement which will endure, not as jazz, perhaps, but which will leave its mark on future music in one form or another. . . . Jazz, to be sure, is only an element, it is not the whole. An entire composition written in jazz could not live.

The analyst in any field is primarily interested in form and content. Since Mr. Gershwin in the famous *Rhapsody in Blue* seems to have been concerned with effects, the musical analyst faces a poser, even when Ferde Grofé's comparatively conventional score of the work lies before him, because effects are as impossible to analyze as is the odor or flavor which eludes even the most meticulous chemist.

The *Rhapsody in Blue* begins with several measures that feel like an introduction. Then the trumpet gives out one of the main themes. But it doesn't sound as it looks, for on the score, beneath these seemingly conventional notes, is the direction "Wha-Wha effect" — and there you are!

Almost at once the piano bursts into a display of virtuosity. Mr. Gershwin himself used to play the piano part both at concerts and on the phonograph record made by Paul Whiteman's orchestra. This piano padding, which is heard at intervals throughout the piece, is attractive, in its way, but as unrelated and irresponsible as a shower of sparks from a Roman candle. It lasts for quite a while with an occasional comment from the strings and a grotesque bit of "lip" from the contrabassoon.

Every now and then one hears that first theme in some form or other. There are also snatches of foot-tickling jazz rhythms. Every instrument seems to be doing pretty much what and when it pleases — *con licenza*. This gay free-for-all comes to an end with the entrance of the famous melody for saxophones and 'celli — a perfectly charming tune! Once introduced, there seems nothing to do but play with it — play it here, there, and everywhere; play it *agitato e misterioso*, *pomposo*, *molto stentando*, and then bring the *Rhapsody* to a close — *grandioso*, *molto allargando*, and *fortissimo sforzando!*

With every desire to be just to a sincere effort in a new idiom, one accustomed to the thoughtful compositions of Bach, Beethoven, and Brahms, cannot call the *Rhapsody in Blue* great music, even if great of its kind. It is, rather, a clever bag of musical tricks — not all of them Gershwin's — played upon several charming bits of melody. It has moments of irresistible rhythm of the sort that calls for bodily response, which is, after all, the *raison d'être* of all jazz. As a concert piece, to be heard in decorous quiet, it is both amusing and satisfying.

PORGY AND BESS

The last and, perhaps, most enduring of Gershwin's larger works is his folk opera *Porgy and Bess*, based on the book and play, *Porgy*, by Dorothy and DuBose Heyward. In this simple story of life in Charleston's Catfish Row, of the crippled Porgy and his tragic love for Bess, the sensitive artist heard and felt the living themes of a sensitive race. Here, sharply etched in light and shadow, were the Negro's good humor and pathos, his love of singing and dancing, his instinctive turning to God as a tired, troubled child runs to a comforting father. For two years Gershwin worked at this music, worked alone and for the first time without collaborators on the instrumentation. He lived with Porgy and Bess until all the wildness, the fear, and the pain of their love found sincere and valid expression in his music.

Like most long works, *Porgy and Bess* is not all of a piece. There are bright pages and dull ones, and, as one reviewer remarks, "shadows of great names stalk across the pages," for Gershwin has "heard everything and forgotten nothing." There are those who hear Brahms in the duet of Porgy and Bess, Act II, Scene I, a theme which characterizes their love throughout the opera. But, for that matter, shadows of other men fell upon Brahms's own pages at times, and as for Handel and Wagner — one could scarcely call their transplanted tunes shadows! The subtle question of originality reminds us of the old saying, "there is nothing new under the sun." The great artistic principle of assimilation and fusion works subconsciously, whether we will or no, and even in what we honestly believe to be our most original, creative moments, none of us can be quite sure that we are free of the shadows of our background and inheritance.

There are those who feel that the "song hits" and choruses, those moving spirituals, are the best parts of *Porgy and Bess*, while others, including no less an authority than Lawrence Gilman, feel that they are a blemish — "musical-comedy treacle." Nevertheless, it is these haunting, hummable tunes that are remembered and will doubtless give a Schubert-Tchaikovsky immortality to George Gershwin. A greater blemish than the "popular" tunes occurs in the last act, which is much less effective than in the book or play because Gershwin, trying to build up the big final chorus of the conventional opera, overplays the tragically simple last scene when the heartbroken Porgy starts off for New York in his poor little goat cart.

What really matters is that, despite its weaknesses, *Porgy and Bess* has a freshness and a vitality that mark it as not only a good native work, musically rooted in the American soil, but also a permanent contribution to folk opera along with Russia's *Boris Godunov* and Bohemia's *The Bartered Bride*.

The American composer Robert Russell Bennett, an intimate friend of Gershwin, was commissioned by Conductor Fritz Reiner to prepare an orchestral version of *Porgy and Bess*. Commenting on his work, which he calls *Porgy and Bess — A Symphonic Picture*, Mr. Bennett says:

Dr. Reiner selected the portions of the opera he wanted included and set the sequence. He also expressed his ideas as to instrumentation, wishing to make generous use of the saxophone and banjo, and to dispense with Gershwin's pet instrument, the piano. I proceeded not only to follow his ideas faithfully, but also to remain completely loyal to George's harmonic and orchestral intention. I have been careful to do what I knew, after many years of association with Gershwin, the composer would like as a symphonic version of his music.

This is the sequence of the opera tunes chosen for the *Symphonic Picture* of *Porgy and Bess*.

Opening of Act III.
Opening of Act I.
"Summertime" — "an' the livin' is easy" — a haunting lullaby.
"I Got Plenty o' Nuttin' " — a bit of lazy, good-natured philosophy.
"Bess, You Is My Woman Now" — one of the loveliest and most expressive of Gershwin's tunes.
"Picnic Party" — a bubbling tune with "Happy feelin' in my bones a-stealin'."
"There's a Boat Dat's Leavin' Soon for New York" — Sportin' Life's "hot-time number."

"It Ain't Necessarily So" — "de t'ings dat yo' li'ble to read in de Bible" — in happy humor.

Finale — "Oh, Lawd, I'm on my way . . . to a Heav'nly Lan',
It's a long, long way, but you'll be there to take my han'."

Porgy's last song expresses his touching acceptance of a promised Heaven as compensation for Earth which has denied him happiness.

As has been so often proved by concert versions of stage music, Russell Bennett's fine *Symphonic Picture — Porgy and Bess* will spread the enjoyment and appreciation of the work of his friend George Gershwin.

FERDE GROFÉ

New York — 1892

Ferde Grofé came of four generations of musicians. His grandfather was 'cello soloist in the Metropolitan Opera Orchestra in the eighties, sharing the first desk with Victor Herbert. His father was a Boston singer; his mother was a 'cellist well known in the West where Ferde spent his childhood, and his uncle was concertmaster of the Los Angeles Orchestra. This musical family hoisted the child to the piano stool before he was five years old. At nine he was composing boyish pieces for string quartet. But knowing only too well the uncertainty of a musician's financial position, the family decided that the boy should go into business.

At the age of fourteen, however, young Ferde took his career in his own hands and ran away. He tried his luck as elevator boy, truck driver, milkman, iron worker in a foundry, and pressman in a bookbindery. But the call of the blood was too strong. He could not let music alone, and before he was twenty Ferde Grofé was earning his living by banging the piano in the crowded cabarets of the West. So successful was he in his cabaret course in music and so conspicuous, that the family, in worried consultation, decided to finance him in more conventional music study if he would take it. Ferde did take it, forsaking the light-footed ragtime tunes for Bach and Beethoven. Under the tyrannical eye of his grandfather Bierlich, who had now become a member of the Los Angeles Orchestra, he had to read through most of that orchestra's repertory, and it was a painful session when he read it wrong! A few years later Ferde, too, was playing first viola in that orchestra, along with his grandfather and uncle.

But in summer when the orchestral viola and the orchestral paycheck were on vacation, Grofé, for love and for money, went back to the dance halls. There he stored up a curious lot of musical knowledge and, of necessity, learned to pinch-hit on every instrument from piccolo to bass drum.

First World War times played havoc with concerts in Los Angeles; the orchestral paycheck took an indefinite leave of absence. Then came jazz, that unseemly mixture of the old ragtime and a new-old barbaric rhythm. This queer stuff which kept going by chance effects and novel tricks, rather than by any serious musical intent, was at once shocking and intriguing to this descendant of four generations of musicians.

Ferde Grofé had to live, and since jazz was then the top of the musical market, he began to study it. One of the things that bothered him about it was that it was so extemporaneous. No one in a jazz band seemed to know in advance just what he or any other player was going to do. And if they did strike a clever effect, as was often the case, they couldn't repeat it because it was not written down. This seemed to Grofé a great waste, so between numbers in the San Francisco café where he played the piano, he used to try to jot down on menu cards effective bits he wanted to remember. Little by little he evolved a system of scoring this unconventional music, and is said to have been the first to really pin jazz down to paper.

It was in San Francisco that Paul Whiteman, another stray from the symphony orchestra fold, heard Ferde Grofé play. He lost no time in engaging him as pianist in his own jazz band. It was a fortunate move on Whiteman's part, for Grofé not only scored every note Whiteman's orchestra played for the next ten years, but by his clever ideas of instrumental contrast, took the worst of the noise out of jazz and made it bearable to listen to. Speaking of the Whiteman-Grofé combination in an article in *Scribner's Magazine*, Earl Sparling says, "If Whiteman has been the king of jazz, Grofé, beyond question, has been the prime minister."

The two came East to New York with the daring scheme of launching jazz concerts. Feeling the need of a *pièce de résistance* for their opening performance, something just a little more like concert music than their cabaret tunes, they called in George Gershwin to help. He brought an unfinished piano solo which Grofé proceeded to turn into a full-blown jazz orchestra piece — it was the famous *Rhapsody in Blue*.

From that time on, Grofé ceased to sit at the piano in Whiteman's orchestra and became a jazz arranger, *the* jazz arranger, and composer. A list of curious original compositions followed: *Metropolis*, caricaturing New York City and including, of all things, a jazz fugue; *Three Shades of Blue*, celebrating Tin-Pan Alley; *Free Air*, the concert début of garage noises; *Tabloid*, a tone picture of newspaper life which may or may not include in its scoring the alleged unoiled lawn mower to suggest the thinking processes of a headline writer; and later, *The Grand Canyon Suite*.

The jazz decade is over. In the North and certainly in Europe, jazz was just a queer musical stunt, a half-learned trick. It had no meaning away from the deep South where it originated, and down there, where jazz *is* jazz, the bewildering racket, the groaning saxophones, the fake excitement of commercial jazz have never been accepted. Even such successful jazzists as Whiteman and Grofé, being fundamentally good musicians, must have realized that they had missed the point. Whiteman is said to have hated the word "jazz," and he and Grofé, intentionally or otherwise, helped to kill the music. But from their jazz experience came certain clever tricks in counter-rhythms, certain ingenious harmonies and appealing orchestral colorings which are unquestionably a contribution to American music.

THE GRAND CANYON SUITE

The Grand Canyon Suite, one of Ferde Grofé's most original works, presents five pictures of that amazing spectacle of nature so familiar and dear to the heart of every Westerner. This is frankly descriptive music, a type which, from an aesthetic point of

510

view, has the flaw of imitation — of trying to make the abstract art of music express concrete things.   But *The Grand Canyon Suite* is not cheap descriptive music which gets out of bounds and uses unmusical ways and means.   It is a very agreeable, if for some people a too literal, musical translation of nature, made by a man who knew his orchestra and how to use it effectively.   Unfortunately, virtuoso conductors are not always faithful to Mr. Grofé's score, and their innovations have sometimes made it more descriptive than the composer intended it to be.   The suite might have been called *A Day in the Grand Canyon*, since it follows the sun from rising to setting.

Sunrise

Sunrise, the opening number, is as effective a picture of the thrilling *crescendo* of dawn as is Mussorgsky's "Dawn over Moscow" in the introduction to the opera *Khovanshchina*. It begins in the dark with a distant roll of kettledrums and a series of soft, mounting woodwind chords which are to be heard throughout the piece.   There is the stirring of birds, sleepily calling the opening notes of the main theme:[1]

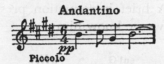

Then the English horn, the first instrument fully awake, gives out the sunrise theme:

which is repeated by solo flute in higher register.

With a brighter second melody for strings:

the light, which at first tipped only the peaks, seems to increase until it outlines the canyon in all its awesome immensity.   Then, with a triumphant fanfare, the full orchestra proclaims the daybreak.

The Painted Desert

In a musical kaleidoscope of strange harmonies and curious instrumentation, we see the unreal color effects and the shifting light and shadow of the Painted Desert. The mysterious voice of the bass clarinet is heard:

[1] Quotations from *The Grand Canyon Suite*, by Ferde Grofé, used by permission of Robbins Music Corporation, owners of the copyright.

but is interrupted by muted trumpets in a strange figure and by the piano in brilliant high chords.

For a moment the unstable theme takes form in a melody for low strings:

but drifts back to the inscrutable mystery and silence of the beginning. The Painted Desert keeps its secret!

On the Trail

The third picture, the familiar *On the Trail*, shows a cowboy with his pony and pack burro trailing down one of the hazardous canyon paths. With a loud discordant whoop — one of those derisive scoots down the uncouth interval of the seventh, beloved of jazz — the piece begins. A brief introduction presents the principal characters, first the burro — by his hee-haws we know him:

Then the cowboy with his cheery "Hi-lee, hi-lo":

After some apparent reluctance on the part of the burro, they are off, hoofs clicking merrily as they trot along:

The cowboy sings and the burro asserts his personality by an occasional shying *accelerando*.
Then the mood of the music changes. A rippling figure:

almost too reminiscent of the water motif in Respighi's *The Fountains of Rome*, suggests that the trail now winds along a stream. The cowboy rides more slowly, and, as if under the spell of the canyon's majestic beauty, his song takes on a new dignity:

But they must get along, and soon the lively trotting begins again. Toward the end the tinkling tune of a music box tells the lone traveler that he is nearing the road house, that bright spot in frontier life, with its promise of food, shelter, and human companionship. No more singing now! Thoughts of hay and hash inspire a last spurt of speed, and with a final whoop they draw up at the end of the trail.

Sunset

Man and animals have disappeared down the trail. A horn call:

and its echo playing back and forth in the empty canyon introduce *Sunset*.

Then, to a murmuring accompaniment, the solitary theme is heard:

tinkling faintly and far away in the orchestra bells, then coming closer in the oboe (where most phonograph recordings begin). It glows for a moment in rich string colors, then fades to a curious indeterminate ending on the second scale step instead of the usual home tone. This little jazz trick is surprisingly effective. The echo idea persists throughout the piece, and the composer depends upon orchestral color, always his strong point, for the mood of sunset.

Cloudburst

Cloudburst is the most descriptive of all the Grand Canyon pictures. Grofé has labeled the sections of the music, beginning with "Lull before the Storm" (a peaceful prelude filled with memories of the day), a snatch of the cowboy's "Hi-lee, hi-lo," and many happy returns of the quiet sunrise theme. Then, after a few sultry measures, we hear the "Approach of the Storm." The labels "Lightning," "Thunder in the Distance," "Rain" are scarcely necessary. One could not miss the ominous thundering of the tympani, the wind whistling in slow violin *glissandos*, the lightning flashing up and down the white keys of the piano. There is a pelting of tones marked "as fast as possible and irregular," and we have "The Cloudburst at Its Height." Quotations from the music are impossible, as only a full page of Grofé's score could do justice to this downpour.

Finally, as is characteristic of storms in the mountains and in music, "The Storm Disappears Rapidly," "The Moon Comes from behind the Clouds," and "Nature Rejoices in All Its Grandeur." Incidentally, the cowboy rejoices, too, for his song dominates the final moments of the music.

Cloudburst is descriptive music, comparing rather well with the storms in Rossini's *William Tell*, Beethoven's "Pastoral" Symphony, and even with some of the inclement weather of Mr. Wagner!

One recognizes the jazz touches in *The Grand Canyon Suite*, particularly in the unconventional scoring and in the many solo passages, for the jazz band has a very democratic policy of giving every instrument a chance to show what it can do. This is not great music, there are no breathless moments, but it is pleasantly diverting, and it bears the mark of a very definite period in American life. Also, it does what most of the so-called popular music does not even attempt to do and that is, to induce a mood and to suggest a picture, something for the listener to think about, something for the head as well as the foot.

Since its *première* in Chicago, 1931, under the baton of Paul Whiteman and with Ferde Grofé an auditor in a packed, enthusiastic house, *The Grand Canyon Suite* has been enjoyed by thousands of people.

HARL McDONALD

Near Boulder, Colorado — 1899

From The Journal of the Philadelphia Orchestra, Season 1934, on the occasion of the performance of Mr. McDonald's Symphony No. 1, "The Santa Fé Trail," comes this brief autobiography:

I was born on my father's cattle ranch in the high Rockies above Boulder, Colorado. I grew up in Southern California, but having no particular talent for the life of a rancher, I decided to become a musician. Every member of my large family played at least one instrument, and my mother, who was an excellent musician, gave me my first training. Piano practice began at the age of four; dictation, harmony, etc., came a year or two later; and I started composition at the age of seven.

I have played a number of instruments at various times — the horn in several orchestras, the violin, a little. I have been organist and choirmaster in any number of churches; have toured as accompanist with several vocalists and violinists, and have had quite a lot of experience as a piano-recitalist in various sections of the country.

In addition to study with many American teachers, I had a period of study in Germany. There, in 1922, I heard my first Symphonic Fantasy, *Mojave*, played by the Berlin Orchestra. Before that time I had done a Mass, a String Quartet, a Piano Concerto, a Ballet Suite, and many small works for instruments and voices. The above works have all had several performances from which I learned a good deal.

Since that time I have been teaching composition and sometimes piano in several schools. I am now occupied with my work in the University of Pennsylvania, where I teach composition and conduct the choral organizations.

During the past six years my compositions included two string trios, another string quartet, a set of variations for orchestra, a Rhapsody for orchestra, a suite for dramatic soprano and strings, St. Luke's version of the Crucifixion, for double chorus, a *Te Deum* for chorus and wind instruments, a suite for orchestra, *Festival of the Workers,* and the usual assortment of small works.

Between 1930 and 1933, I did some research work in collaboration with two electrical engineers and a physicist. This work in the field of measurement of instrumental and vocal tone, new scale divisions and resultant harmonies, in recording and transmission of tone, etc., was done under a Rockefeller grant and will, I hope, result in a book on music theory.

To Mr. McDonald's autobiography we add the interesting note that in 1939 he became manager of the Philadelphia Orchestra.

Harl McDonald is a Nationalist and a Modernist to the extent of believing that an artist should be fully alive to the spirit and idioms of his time and place. In his music there are flashes of local color, largely due to his boyhood associations with the vivid Spanish-Indian-Anglo-Saxon tunes of the Mexican border country. But there is no conscious straining for effect, no attempt to pass off overdressed folk tunes for original compositions.

"I do not believe," says Mr. McDonald, writing on "The Problems of the American Composer" in *The Magazine of Art*, "that Nationalism in music has any purpose as an aim in itself. The use of native source material is valuable to the composer in that it tends to discourage artificiality and helps him to maintain emotional poise in harmony with humanity." This desire of the man and artist to be "in harmony with humanity" has found expression in Mr. McDonald's most interesting and significant music.

DANCE OF THE WORKERS, FROM THE FESTIVAL OF THE WORKERS

For enlightening comments on this interesting work, we turn to the composer himself. "Naturally," he writes, "our troubled times have led to more and more speculation and discussion along these lines, and several years ago I began to think of a large-scale composition which would be based on my reactions to the reflections on the current turbulent scene. At about this time [1933] I wrote my *Festival of the Workers*."

Prefacing the score of this work in three movements is the following program:

I. Procession of the Workers

Faintly, approaching from a distance, is heard the ponderous tread of a great company of toilers. A bleak melody indicates the dullness and monotony of their lives.

As they come near, one is conscious of a spirit of gaiety which the festival occasion has created in them and which combines with the thunderous pulse of their step as they pass by. As they move into the distance one hears again the bleak melody.

II. Dance

A few of the multitude are dancing. There is an occasional flash of a cheerful, merry humor in them, but one hears in the midst of their pleasure the melody which indicates the melancholy cast of their lives.

III. Exultation of the Workers

The melody of monotony and bleakness is heard again in sharp contrast with a fanfare which is the call to a spirit of unity among the toilers. The tragic futility of the individual is lost in a hopeful and exultant pulse as their forces are combined. The ponderous movement of heavy, rough boots becomes the symbol of power and virility in the unified mass.

The *Festival of the Workers*, introduced in Philadelphia by Stokowski, was misunderstood by many as a bitter social preachment. This was not at all the composer's purpose. He meant, as he says, merely "to give the mood and spirit of workers living in a great industrial civilization."

The Dance of the Workers begins with a grotesque little jigging theme for solo bassoon: [1]

given out by a solo bassoon and taken up in turn by a clarinet and a flute. Just as it seems to be getting merrily underway, the dance is interrupted by what seems to be a bit of good-natured mockery in the upper woodwinds:

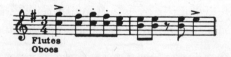

But the bassoon keeps right on with the dance, its little tune emerging every now and then from the increasing babel of voices.

Then, above a series of soft chords on the harp and a syncopated figure in muted strings, rises the plaintive melody which "indicates the melancholy cast of their lives."

As the theme passes from one solo woodwind to another, the harmonies grow bleaker and bleaker.

But with the return of the dance the mood changes, and the piece ends with the intrepid bassoon treading his measure until brought up sharply by a soft but peremptory cymbal.

[1] Permission to reprint excerpts granted by Elkan-Vogel Co., Inc., Philadelphia, Pa.

Shortly after the *Festival of the Workers*, and in much the same vein, came the Second or "Rhumba" Symphony, cast in the conventional four movements, *Grave-allegro*, *Andante moderato*, *Rhumba*, and *Grave-allegro brioso*. The emotional key to this music is found in the subtitle, *Reflections on an Era of Turmoil*, and in the sentence in which the composer speaks of having written it, thinking of "the bitterness [I], the satisfactions [II], the gaiety [III], and the insanity [IV] of the most amazing period in history." Mr. McDonald makes it quite clear that "this symphony is in no sense a program composition, and the title 'Rhumba' Symphony has to do only with the fact that I have used rhumba rhythms in the third movement."

Speaking of the third movement of his "Rhumba" Symphony, Mr. McDonald says: "With all the tumult of accomplishment and frustration, I am always conscious of the fact that I am living in an age that has an almost insatiable appetite for gaiety and entertainment. In this part of my score I have used a rhumba for the reason that I like rhumba rhythms and also because they seem to be a part of the pulse of our time."

The rhumba is a dance of Cuban origin. It is a primitive dance, accompanied by primitive instruments such as the pebble-filled gourd which rattles out the dominant rhythm. The dancers seem to extemporize a pattern of quick and slow steps within a loose framework of 4/4 time. In the rhumba, as in most primitive dances, the figuration is as wayward as the rhythm is compelling. So compelling is this rhumba rhythm, which Mr. McDonald likes, that even in this highly organized piece of symphonic music it steals the listener bodily. Nice little themes are apt to go unnoticed, and as for the clever orchestration — why, in many places the score might just as well have called for eighty gourds full of pebbles, a tom-tom, and occasional cries from the side lines!

After a few bold introductory measures, the strings and percussion instruments set the basic rhythm: [1]

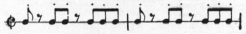

above which bassoons and tenor saxophone give out the main theme:

Tenor Saxophone
Bassoons

which is carried on by solo clarinet and alto saxophone.

The smooth-running main theme is interrupted by a savage declaration of the rhythm:

Full Orchestra

[1] Permission to reprint excerpts granted by Elkan-Vogel Co., Inc., Philadelphia, Pa.

This bit of contrast, so characteristic of the rhumba, is to be heard frequently throughout the piece.

After the interruption the music grows more tuneful. A little song theme is passed about among the woodwinds:

Clarinet
Tenor Saxophone

until it too is drowned out by the savage rhythmic theme.

From this point on there is nothing new in the way of thematic material but much that is clever and effective in orchestration and harmonization. The dance gathers momentum and abandon; the brasses grow bolder; the horns blare:

Horns
Saxophones

the whole percussion battery is let loose — bass drum, snare drum, kettles, tom-tom, tambourines, cymbals, castanets, and rattles — and on a reminiscent motif:

the rhumba comes to a sudden, stunning end.

WILLIAM GRANT STILL

Woodville, Mississippi — 1895

Fifteen years ago the name of William Grant Still was unknown outside of a small circle of friends to whom he was a hard-working young man with serious musical interests. Today William Grant Still is recognized on two continents as not only a significant contemporary musician, but also the leading Negro composer of his time. He was born in a little town in Mississippi and spent his boyhood in Arkansas and Ohio. His father died while the boy was quite young, and it is to an ambitious mother and grandmother that he owes his early training, although these good women did not set out to raise a composer.

Still was a student at Wilberforce, then at Oberlin, later at the New England Conservatory in Boston, where he studied with Chadwick, and in New York, with Varèse. It was a long apprenticeship, during which the boy did everything from waiting on table to musical chores such as arranging tunes for Paul Whiteman's band. In recent years he has been active in writing and directing programs for the radio. In 1934 and again in 1938 he received the Guggenheim fellowship for the excellence of his work, and in 1939 was honored with a commission to write the music for one of the special features at the New York World's Fair. In that same year Still was awarded the Rosenwald fellowship.

As a composer Still has devoted himself to the expression of the life and aspirations of his own people. He considers the Negro spirituals the most important native American contribution to music, and uses them reverently and proudly. But while the color and feeling of Still's music is racial, the workmanship is that of the trained musician. The melody lines are skillfully drawn, the harmonic and orchestral colorings nicely blended, and the forms well molded. The list of his compositions shows a wide variety of works — an opera, *Blue Steel;* a stagework, *Sahdji;* a ballet, *La Guiablesse;* chamber music, *From the Black Belt* and *Log Cabin Ballads; Lenox Avenue*, for radio; *From the Land of Dreams* and *Levee Land*, for orchestra and voices; and the orchestral works, *Darker America, From the Journal of a Wanderer, Puritan Epic*, and the famous "Afro-American" Symphony, which has been played both in Europe and the United States.

More significant than the devotion to his art and its mastery is William Grant Still's devotion to an underlying purpose which he states as "the study of life itself with a view to learning that which will enable me to make my life more serviceable to mankind." Not many young artists struggling for recognition in a world where popular appeal spells success would work with such a purpose, much less confess it openly. The score of the "Afro-American" Symphony, dedicated "With humble thanks to God, the source of inspiration" and ending with "He who develops his God-given gifts with a view to aiding humanity, manifests truth," makes one think of the manuscripts of a great master of long ago, one Johann Sebastian Bach, who headed his cantatas with the little prayer, "Jesus help me!" and wrote as finis, "To God be the glory."

"Afro-American" Symphony

Writing of his "Afro-American" Symphony in 1930, the composer says:

The "Afro-American" Symphony is based upon an original theme in the "blues" idiom, employed first as the principal theme of the first movement and reappearing in different forms in the course of the composition.

It is possible that some may regard the use of this theme as an undignified and insincere step on my part. But I have no delusions as to the triviality of the "blues," the secular folk songs of the American Negro, despite their lowly origin and the homely sentiment of their texts. For the pathos of their melodic content belies the banality associated with them due to their origin and their texts.

A study of the composition will prove the utter absence of insincerity and that the use of the "blues" idiom was advisable. I seek in the "Afro-American" Symphony to portray, not the higher type of colored American, but the sons of the soil who still retain so many of the traits peculiar to their African forebears, who have not yet responded completely to the transforming effect of progress. Therefore the use of a decidedly characteristic idiom is not only logical but also necessary, and the student is certain to discover that it is sincerity which has purged the idiom of its vulgar characteristics.

In a general sense, one may apply to the movements the following titles:

I — *Longing*   II — *Sorrow*   III — *Humor*   IV — *Aspiration*

Printed on the score at the beginning of each movement is a bit of verse by the Negro poet, Paul Laurence Dunbar, setting the mood.[1]

I — *Moderato assai*

All my life long twell de night has pas'
Let de wo'k come ez it will,
So dat I fin' you, my honey, at las',
Somewhaih des ovah de hill.

II — *Adagio*

It's moughty tiahsome layin' 'roun'
Dis sorrer-laden earfly groun',
An' oftentimes I thinks, thinks I,
'Twould be a sweet t'ing des to die,
An' go 'long home.

III — *Animato*

An' we'll shout ouah halleluyahs
On dat mighty reck'nin' day.

IV — *Lento con risoluzione*

Be proud, my Race, in mind and soul;
Thy name is writ on Glory's scroll
    In characters of fire.
High 'mid the clouds of Fame's bright sky
Thy banner's blazoned folds now fly,
    And truth shall lift them higher.

Scherzo

William Grant Still's purpose in the "Afro-American" Symphony, "to portray, not the higher type of colored American, but the sons of the soil who still retain so many of the traits peculiar to their African forebears," seems admirably fulfilled in the *scherzo* movement.   For if there is one trait peculiar to the Negro, it is that *moll-dur*, major-minor temperament which shadows his brightest moments with wistfulness and edges the dark clouds of his despair with golden glints of humor.

The *Scherzo* opens with the sound of the gong, then the brasses announcing the motto: [2]

---

[1] Reprinted by permission of Dodd, Mead & Company, Inc.   From *The Complete Poems of Paul Laurence Dunbar*.

[2] Excerpts reprinted by permission of the copyright owner, J. Fischer & Bro.

somber, challenging, and as fateful as another famous two-measure **motto:**

The answer comes immediately in the carefree main theme, flung out by the strings:

Then comes a second melody, almost a tonal translation of Dunbar's lines which head the movement:

> An' we'll shout ouah halleluyahs
> On dat mighty reck'nin' day.

The composer does not follow the conventional design, *scherzo-trio-scherzo*. He does something more cleverly consistent with his idea of expressing Negro humor. He literally plays with his thematic material, making a jest of it! Delicate woodwinds, now wistful, now impudent, strings singing and swinging the main melody, brasses sternly suggesting the motto, and all carried along by the irresistible "blues" rhythm.

But perhaps the most fascinating thing about this music is its harmonic variation, if a textbook term may be used to describe the irresponsible flickering of its major-minor mood. A comparison of the first appearance of the main theme:

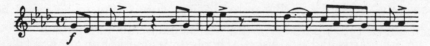

with its last:

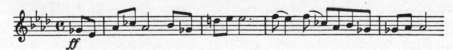

and the bright major ending are significant. Here we have those "sons of the soil," abandoned, a bit bewildered in both their joy and sorrow, feeling so much for which they ask no explanation, and so ready with a laughing response to sunshine or a smile from Lady Luck.

Call it "jazzy," "bluezy," or what you will, surely no one who gives the "Afro-American" Symphony the serious consideration it deserves could call it either undignified or cheap. As the composer says, its "sincerity . . . has purged the idiom of its vulgar characteristics."

LATIN AMERICANA

Latin American music, which to most North Americans means *tango*, *carioca*, and the sultry, repetitious love song, has recently become a subject of eager interest and surprising revelation.   Two World Wars, cutting the last psychological ties of "colonial" dependence upon Europe, have brought the two Americas together in every way. Music, presenting no language barrier, is already proving one of the strongest links connecting the two great continents of the Western Hemisphere, for music, happily free from all social and political differences, creates a community of heart and spirit.

The two Americas share many of the same musical problems.   Both are engaged in developing American music, music which will express life in the Americas rather than a mere pastiche concocted from the works of European masters and tagged with an occasional American folk tune.   Both are concerned with establishing a musical environment for all Americans, opportunity and background for what we are pleased to call the creative listening, so vital to both composers and performers.   In music education, we of the United States have pioneered with the idea of musical opportunity for everybody — children and adults — and so successfully that the other American Republics pay us the compliment of studying and borrowing many of our plans for use in their own musical life.   We have also shared the common fault of applauding Old World music at the expense of our own, thus forcing the native composer to be as European as possible if he hopes to succeed.   And while American compositions must be judged by their intrinsic musical value, a supercilious attitude toward them is childish, to say the least, and must be outgrown if we are to reach artistic maturity.   But the most important and certainly the most aesthetic bond between the two Americas is the mutual appeal of their music.   Our neighbors "south of the border" are intrigued with the energy and, shall we say, sophistication of our northern music, while we find theirs strangely beautiful and satisfying.

Although the national school of Latin American music is young and sometimes crude, it already shows the patina of an ancient culture not to be found here in the North.   One hundred years before the founding of the first permanent colony in New England, the Spaniards had established schools for teaching European music in Mexico. There they taught the natives to make neat copies of the music of the Church and to make and play on European instruments.   Seven music books, the first of them an Ordinary of the Mass, were printed in Mexico before 1600.   Our first music book, the Bay Psalm Book, was printed in 1640, and no music was added until the edition of 1698.

In what is known as the Colonial Period — the sixteenth, seventeenth, and eighteenth centuries — Spain and Portugal brought to the New World the music of the medieval church, the polished and romantic music of contemporary European courts, and, via sturdy colonists and soldiers, the gay songs and dances of the people.   From Mexico City in the north to Lima, the brilliant Peruvian capital, in the south, all the arts of Spain were transplanted and took root awaiting the slow process of cross-fertilization with the aboriginal arts of the native Indians.

The folk music of Latin America is the most varied in the world.   A recent study reveals no fewer than one hundred and thirty-one different folk music forms, among which are found not only traces of Spain and Portugal but also of the African Negro, added in the seventeenth century when Spain introduced slavery into South America. The result of all this intermingling was a mestizo music, Spanish in form, tonality, and harmonic structure, but Indian in nuance, rhythmic complexities, and ornamentation.

In the nineteenth century came political independence and the relinquishing of church leadership, which at first left Latin American music all but stranded. In the New World as in the Old, Spanish national music, in spite of its widespread popularity, was slow to find its place in the larger forms of the symphony and opera. This was largely due to the lack of orchestral techniques of Spanish and Latin American composers. And so it happened that for a time the best Spanish music was written by foreigners, for example, Bizet's *Carmen*, Lalo's *Symphonie Espagnole*, Chabrier's *España*, and Rimsky-Korsakov's *Capriccio Espagnol*. Debussy was, perhaps, the first to fully appreciate the beauty of Andalusian popular music and make artistic use of its modal tints, its shifting, conflicting rhythms, and sharply contrasted moods. Ravel, born only a few miles from the Spanish border of parents who had lived for many years in Spain, quite naturally reflects Spanish idioms and a deep affection for Spanish life in his music. The kinship between these two Latin peoples, the French and the Spanish, is very close, and the trail of France is plainly marked across the music of nineteenth-century Latin America. North Americans of the same period went to Germany to study, and their music is strongly influenced by German Romanticism. Latin Americans, for the most part, studied in France along with their Spanish cousins. Their Romanticism was of the Chopin-Liszt brand, later colored with French Impressionism. Latin America, too, had its season of salon and parlor music, its whirl of Viennese waltzes, its devotion to Italian opera, and its concert and operatic life mostly dependent upon touring European artists.

Today the scene has changed. A generation of well-trained Latin American composers, Mexico's Ponce and Chavez, Cuba's Roldan, Argentina's Paz and Castro, Chile's Santa Cruz, and Brazil's Villa-Lobos, who is rated as one of the half-dozen musicians of creative originality of the Western Hemisphere — these and many others are working with great energy and sincerity to crystallize their native idiom into a serious art music.

Three interesting trends define three distinct types among contemporary Latin American composers: first are those who try to express national feeling in the musical style of the late nineteenth-century Romanticists or early twentieth-century Impressionists; second, those who seek to assimilate folklore and idiom and at the same time express their own individuality; and last a widely varied group of contemporary composers — some who profess little sympathy with either folklore or the national movement and work along the radical lines of atonality, new scales, and new instruments with fractional tones; others, too broadly and deeply concerned with music as a fine art to be listed in any particular category, musicians who might well say with Tchaikovsky, "My ideal is to become a *good composer*."

We in the north have heard all too little Latin American music, save for the catchy songs and dance tunes purveyed by radio and the folk songs shorn of their original texts. But the present impetus toward publication and phonographic recording of Latin

American scores should, within the next decade, make us as familiar with the music of our southern neighbors as they seem to be with ours.

"Latin American music" is a very loose term. Since each of the twenty republics is a cultural as well as a political unit, there are wide differences in both their folk and art music. But beneath the surface differences runs the continuity of the old Spanish and Portuguese music superimposed upon the ancient cultures of the aborigines. It is a heritage which modern Latin American composers can no more afford to overlook than the followers of the Spanish nationalist Pedrell (1841–1922) could ignore the music of the great Spanish masters of the sixteenth century.

Latin American music promises much for the future, not only because of the skill and artistry of present-day composers, but because music has always meant so much to Latin American people. What Waldo Frank, in his "America Hispana," says of the Mexicans is equally true of all Latin Americans, for whom:

> Music is the freedom of the slave, the health of the brokenhearted. In a world of unwieldy earth like Mexico, whose history for many hundreds of years has been bondage and body-betrayal, the breath of music is the release of the spirit. This most unsubstantial form makes the soul substantial; and its rhythm makes real the flight of the soul's burden.

INDEX

>>|<<

48